OLYMPIC CITIES

The first edition of Olympic Cities, published in 2007, provided a pioneering overview of the changing relationship between cities and the modern Olympic Games. This substantially revised and enlarged third edition builds on the success of its predecessors. The first of its three parts provides overviews of the urban legacy of the four component Olympic festivals: the Summer Games; Winter Games; Cultural Olympiads; and the Paralympics. The second part comprises systematic surveys of seven key aspects of activity involved in staging the Olympics: finance; place promotion; the creation of Olympic Villages; security; urban regeneration; tourism; and transport. The final part consists of nine chronologically arranged portraits of host cities, from 1936 to 2020, with particular emphasis on the six Summer Olympic and Paralympic Games of the twenty-first century.

As controversy over the growing size and expense of the Olympics, with associated issues of accountability and legacy, continues unabated, this book's incisive and timely assessment of the Games' development and the complex agendas that host cities attach to the event will be essential reading for a wide audience. This will include not just urban and sports historians, urban geographers, event managers and planners, but also anyone with an interest in the staging of mega-events and concerned with building a better understanding of the relationship between cities, sport and culture.

John R. Gold is Professor of Urban Historical Geography at Oxford Brookes University.
Margaret M. Gold is Senior Lecturer in Creative Industries at London Metropolitan University.

Planning, History and Environment Series

Editor:

Ann Rudkin, Alexandrine Press, Marcham, UK

Editorial Board:

Professor Arturo Almandoz, Universidad Simón Bolivar, Caracas, Venezuela and Pontificia Universidad Católica de Chile, Santiago, Chile

Professor Nezar AlSayyad, University of California, Berkeley, USA

Professor Scott A. Bollens, University of California, Irvine, USA

Professor Robert Bruegmann, University of Illinois at Chicago, USA

Professor Meredith Clausen, University of Washington, Seattle, USA

Professor Yasser Elsheshtawy, UAE University, Al Ain, UAE

Professor Robert Freestone, University of New South Wales, Sydney, Australia

Professor John R. Gold, Oxford Brookes University, Oxford, UK

Professor Michael Hebbert, University College London, UK

Selection of published titles

OLYMPIC CITIES

City Agendas, Planning and the
World's Games, 1896–2020

Third Edition

edited by

John R. Gold

and

Margaret M. Gold

Routledge
Taylor & Francis Group

LONDON AND NEW YORK

Third edition published 2017
by Routledge
2 Park Square, Milton Park, Abingdon, Oxfordshire OX14 4RN

and by Routledge
711 Third Avenue, New York, NY 10017

Routledge is an imprint of the Taylor & Francis Group, an informa business

© 2017 Selection and editorial matter: John R. Gold and Margaret M. Gold; individual
chapters: the contributors

This book was commissioned and edited by Alexandrine Press, Marcham, Oxfordshire

The right of the author has been asserted in accordance with sections 77 and 78 of the
Copyright, Designs and Patents Act 1988.

First edition published by Routledge 2007
Third edition published by Routledge 2017

British Library Cataloguing in Publication Data
A catalogue record of this book is available from the British Library

Library of Congress Cataloging in Publication Data
A catalog record for this book has been requested

ISBN: 978–1–138–83267–1 (hbk)
ISBN: 978–1–138–83269–5 (pbk)
ISBN: 978–1–315–73588–7 (ebk)

Typeset in Aldine and Swiss by PNR Design, Didcot

For David Pepper

Contents

Part III City Portraits

Preface

Much has happened with regard to Olympic Cities since the first edition of this book. Games have come and gone, with the relentless onward movement of the calendar meaning that there are now further Olympics and Paralympics that need attention. Beijing, in 2007 at the point of running test events for the following year's Summer Games, is now, somewhat remarkably, looking forward to reusing some of the same facilities for the 2022 Winter Olympics. London 2012 – still a distant prospect in 2007 – has become a magnet for those interested in long-term post-Games legacy. Games that had not yet been allocated to host cities when the previous editions went to press are now part of the roll call of Olympic Cities, with Sochi 2014, Rio de Janeiro 2016, Pyeongchang 2018, Tokyo 2020 and Beijing 2022 joining the list. Each nomination starts chains of new experiences that, beyond their implications for the sports and cultural communities, have consequences for funding, stakeholder partnerships, architecture and planning, construction history, spectacle, ticketing, volunteering and legacy. Each event also creates new knowledge that needs to be chronicled, analysed, categorised and, hopefully, made available to successors through processes of knowledge transfer.

To some extent, this accretion of knowledge is reflected in the slight change in the book's subtitle with its purview now extending to 2020 rather than 2012, but that is only a quiet indicator of considerable change. More importantly, the Olympics have shown a remarkable tendency to become the focal point of new debates and controversies. In this respect, concerns about funding priorities, corruption, public accountability, environmental sustainability, security and, in particular, legacy have impacted upon thinking about the Games and have prompted the staging of innumerable specialist seminars and conferences to discuss emerging problems and shared challenges. Often involving a mixture of academics and practitioners and sponsored by publishers or funding agencies, these events have stimulated a new wave of publications about the Olympics that, at their best, have helped to move scholarship decisively forward. Understandably, therefore, an essential part of the purpose of this edition has been to take stock of the new literature and give adequate recognition to its findings.

Having emphasized the need for change, however, we also stress that the core aim of this book remains precisely the same as its predecessors. In broad outline, it seeks to draw on the expertise of an international group of authors to examine comparatively the experience of cities that have hosted the Olympics in the years from the creation of the modern Games in 1896 through to the present day and beyond to 2020. As such, it remains a book framed around historical analysis, seeking not just to account for past Games but also to study recent and future Olympics in the light of established and emerging narratives. For a festival as deeply immersed in precedent and invented tradition as the Olympics, we believe that this comprises an eminently appropriate approach to set alongside much of the instant punditry about the subject that is now on offer in conventional and social media.

Further similarities concern structure. We have retained the same multilayered approach to our subject matter as in the previous editions, with the chapters arranged into three main parts. The book opens with chronologically-arranged surveys of the component festivals; followed by chapters that scrutinize significant planning and managerial themes arising from cities acting as hosts; and then by a representative selection of portraits of cities staging the Summer Games – understandably concentrating on the period from the 1960s onwards when host cities became more interested in using the Olympics as a catalyst for development. The continuity of structure also allows us to bring in new chapters that reflect recent developments and debates within the original terms of reference. As a result, previous editions can be seen as resources that stand in their own right. Rather than being superseded and redundant, each edition testifies to ideas and debate current at the time of writing. Moreover, the various editions essentially supply a series of snapshots of progress on the Games of the twenty-first century. They chart sequentially the various positions that cities such as Beijing, London and Rio had reached in the decade or more between bidding for the Olympics to the works necessary for post-event site conversion and potential legacy. Chronological coverage inevitably means revisiting the same festivals at several points in the text from different angles and perspectives. Naturally, the correct balance between allowing authors scope for initial context and removing unnecessary repetition by employing cross-references is difficult to achieve, but we hope that the results are acceptable. Certainly, we have not regarded it as part of our task to remove differences of interpretation or even fundamental disagreements that may emerge from the ensuing chapters of this book. As befits a subject as complex and as controversial as the modern Olympics and Paralympics, there is no party line to which authors have had to adhere.

Certain elements of standardization and conventions deserve some clarification. Statements of expenditure frequently occur in local currencies and exchange rates at points in the past are not always easy to obtain, especially when sources are unclear about precise dates. Although Euros and various local currencies are occasionally used, wherever possible we have attempted to use pound sterling or US dollar equivalents, and all sums where dollars are shown without qualification relate to the US currency. In addition, anyone familiar with using Olympic documentation, especially Official Reports, will realize that there are often different language versions available. We have retained the linguistic version used by our contributors in cited references, even though this means that different language versions of the same publication might be listed separately in the consolidated bibliography. Finally, Olympic sport is a realm in which institutional acronyms abound. Our policy is to present acronyms in their most common form regardless of the language from which they are derived. Thus, for example, the abbreviation COJO (standing for Comité d'Organisation des Jeux Olympiques) is used in relation to Games held in Francophone nations, whereas the equivalent Anglophone body is normally referred to as an OCOG (Organizing Committee for the Olympic Games) elsewhere. To avoid confusion, a listing of such acronyms occurs at the start of this text, with our practice being to provide names of bodies in full wherever they first occur in a chapter.

As ever, we have incurred a variety of debts in the lengthy process of preparing this book. First and foremost, we would like to express our sincere gratitude to our contributors for their patience with the editorial process and for their willingness to redraft material to benefit the book as a whole. Dennis Hardy and Ann Rudkin suggested the original idea and Graeme Evans provided valuable contacts when bringing the first edition together. The International Planning History Society's Barcelona conference supplied an invaluable opportunity to gather an initial group of contributors together. We would particularly like to acknowledge the assistance of the British Olympic Association for allowing us access to source materials and Martin McElhatton, Chief Executive of Wheel Power, for sparing generous amounts of time to show us round the Stoke Mandeville Stadium. Next, it is a pleasure to record our thanks to Brian Chalkley, Ruth Craggs, Jo Foord, Vassil Girginov, Willy Guneriussen, Elsa-Minni Heimgard, Paul Kitchin, Lorraine Johnson, James Kennell, Peter Larkham, Daniel Latouche, Chuck Little, Sarah Loy, Kat Martindale, Javier Monclús, Verity Postlethwaite, Jill Pearlman, George Revill and Matthew Taylor for various and sundry kindnesses. Oxford Brookes University and London Metropolitan University have provided finance and other assistance to facilitate our work. Iain, Josie, Thomas, Jenny, David and Mathilda tolerated the things that did not happen in order to allow us time and space to complete this text. The late and much missed Mark Fisher, architect of Olympic spectacle, contributed nothing directly but everything indirectly to the writing of this book. Finally, we have great pleasure in dedicating this book to David Pepper, a man for whom sport occupies its proper place in life.

West Ealing
April 2016

Acknowledgements

We are grateful to the following for permission to reproduce the illustrations as recorded below:

Acervo AGCRJ: figure 20.1

Yasushi Aoyama: figures 21.1, 21.4, 21.5

Christopher Balch: figure 3.5

Ian Cook: figures 18.1, 18.2, 18.3

Graeme Evans: figure 19.3

Lucas Faulhaber: figure 20.7

Robert Freestone: figure 16.2

Beatriz García: figures 4.3, 4.4

Gerkan, Marg and Partner: figure 13.5

Greater London Authority: figure 19.1

International Olympic Committee: figures 3.2, 3.7, 4.1, 4.2, 4.5, 4.6, 4.7, 15.1, 19.2, 21.2

London Legacy Development Corporation figure 19.5

Monika Meyer: figures 13.3, 15.2, 15.3, 15.5, 15.5

Nelma Gusmão de Oliveira: figure 20.6

Mike O'Dwyer/Lendlease: figure 8.5

Rio de Janeiro City Council: figures 20.2, 20.3, 20.4, 20.5

Tony Sainsbury: figures 8.1, 8.2, 8.3, 8.4

Andrew Smith: figures 10.1, 10.2

State Library of New South Wales, Government Printing Office: figure 16.1

Sydney Olympic Park Authority: figure 16.7

Tim Throsby & Associates: figure 16.3

The following illustrations are from historic postcards, from now defunct publishing houses for which no successor can be found or from other sources from which no publisher has been traceable: figures 2.2, 2.3, 2.4, 2.5, 2.6, 2.7, 13.1, 13.2, 13.4, 14.1, 14.2.

All remaining photographs were taken by the editors.

The Contributors

Yasushi Aoyama is a Professor at the Graduate School of Governance Studies at Meiji University in Tokyo and also a Lecturer in the Faculty of Engineering at Tokyo University. His courses focus on international policy, crisis management and disaster relief, and policy development at the local government level. He was a member of the Bid Committee that won the nomination for the 2020 Summer Olympic and Paralympic Games to be held in Tokyo.

Michael Barke lectured in Geography at Northumbria University, Newcastle upon Tyne for most of his career. He has written extensively on socio-economic change in southern Spain, on urban morphology and the historical geography of North East England and Newcastle upon Tyne. He retired as Reader in Human Geography at Northumbria University in July 2015.

Jon Coaffee is Professor in Urban Geography at the Centre for Interdisciplinary Methodologies at the University of Warwick and an Exchange Professor at New York University's Centre for Urban Science and Progress. His research interests revolve around the interplay of planning, regeneration, urban management and security policy. He is the author of *The Everyday Resilience of the City* (2008) and *Terrorism, Risk and the Global City* (2003, 2009).

Ian G. Cook is Professor Emeritus of Human Geography at Liverpool John Moores University and formerly Head of the Centre for Pacific Rim Studies. He is the joint editor or author of eight books of which the most recent are *The Greening of China* (2004), *New Perspectives on Aging in China* (2007) and *Aging in Asia* (2009).

Jiska de Groot is a researcher in the Energy Research Centre at the University of Cape Town. She holds a PhD in human geography and her research focuses on development and energy, particularly around place and change.

Özlem Edizel is Senior Lecturer in Tourism and Events at the University of Westminster and Research Fellow at the School of Art and Design at the Middlesex University. Her research interests centre on sustainable urban governance, event-led regeneration and mega-events.

Stephen J. Essex is a Reader in Human Geography at the School of Geography, Earth and Environmental Science, University of Plymouth. His teaching and research focuses on urban and rural planning, especially the infrastructural implications of the Olympic Games and post-war reconstruction planning. He has co-authored a number of journal articles and book chapters on the urban impacts and planning of both the Summer and Winter Olympic Games with Professor Brian Chalkley (also at the University of Plymouth).

Graeme Evans is Professor of Art and Design Cultures in the School of Art and Design at Middlesex University. His book *Cultural Planning: An Urban Renaissance?* (2001) was the first to consider culture and city planning from both historic and contemporary perspectives.

Robert Freestone is Professor of Planning in the Faculty of the Built Environment at UNSW Australia in Sydney. His research interests are in urban planning history, metropolitan change, heritage conservation, and planning education. He is a former President of the International Planning History Society and Chair of the Editorial Board of *Planning Perspectives*. His books include *Urban Nation* (2010), *Florence Taylor's Hats: Designing, Building and Editing Sydney* (2007), *Designing Australia's Cities: Culture, Commerce and the City Beautiful 1900–1930* (2007), and *Model Communities* (1989).

Pete Fussey is a Professor of Sociology at the University of Essex. His main research interests concern the dissemination and application of technological surveillance to tackle crime and terrorism. He is also researching the form and impact of London's 2012 security operation and conducting ethnographic research into organized criminality in East London's Olympic market place. Recent work includes *Securing and Sustaining the Olympic City* (2010 co-authored with Jon Coaffee, Gary Armstrong and Dick Hobbs) and *Terrorism and the Olympics* (2010 co-edited with Andrew Silke and Anthony Richards).

Beatriz García is Head of Research in the Institute of Cultural Capital, University of Liverpool. She acted as academic collaborator to the Palmer/Rae team evaluating the impact of 1995–2004 European Capitals of Culture for the European Commission, has been academic advisor to the London 2012 Culture and Education team since the bid stage, and is a member of the IOC Postgraduate Research Grant Selection Committee. In 2009, she was appointed as a member of the DCMS Science and Research Advisory Committee. Her monograph *The Olympic Games and Cultural Policy* was published in 2012.

John R. Gold, Professor of Urban Historical Geography in the Department of Social Sciences at Oxford Brookes University, is the author or editor of nineteen previous books on urban and cultural subjects. He is currently working on the third of his trilogy on architectural modernism in Great Britain, entitled *The Legacy of Modernism: Modern Architects, the City and the Collapse of Orthodoxy, 1973–1990*. In addition, he and Margaret Gold are working on *Festival Cities: Culture, Planning and Urban Life since 1918* (forthcoming).

Margaret M. Gold is Senior Lecturer in Creative Industries at London Metropolitan University. She is the joint author of *Imagining Scotland* (1995) and *Cities of Culture* (2005) and joint editor of *The Making of Olympic Cities* (2012). She is currently working with John Gold on *Festival Cities: Culture, Planning and Urban Life since 1918* (to be published in the Planning, History and Environment series).

Simon Gunasekara is an experienced planning consultant with a background in statutory and strategic planning for both local government and the private sector. He is a graduate of the Bachelor of Planning at the University of New South Wales receiving first class honours, as well as a corporate member of the Planning Institute of Australia.

Eva Kassens-Noor is an Assistant Professor of Urban and Transport Planning in the School of Planning, Design, and Construction at Michigan State University. She holds a joint appointment with the Global Urban Studies Program and is an Adjunct Assistant Professor in the Department of Geography. Her research work centres on resilience, sustainability and large-scale urban planning projects that are triggered by global forces. Her latest book is *Planning Olympic Legacies: Transport Dreams and Urban Realities* (2012).

Monika Meyer is Managing Director of the Institute for Housing and Environment, a joint research institution of the State of Hessen and the City of Darmstadt. She was formerly Head of Research on 'Urban and Regional Development in Europe' at the Leibniz-Institute of Ecological and Regional Development Dresden. Her main fields of work are urban development and mega-events.

Steven Miles is Professor of Urban Culture at the University of Brighton. He is interested in the impact of consumption on city life and in particular the role of consumer culture in the context of social change in China. His publications include *Consuming Cities* (2004, with Malcolm Miles) and *Spaces for Consumption* (2010).

Holger Preuss is Professor of Sport Economics and Sport Sociology at the Johannes Gutenberg-University in Mainz, Germany and also at the Molde University College, Norway in the field of Event Management. He is also adjunct professor at the University of Ottawa, Canada and international scholar at the State University of New York (SUNY, Cortland). He is currently Editor of the journal *European Sport Management Quarterly* and has published eighteen books and more than seventy articles in international journals and books.

Tony Sainsbury was London 2012's Villages' General Manager, prior to which he was Head of Villages and Paralympic Integration during the bid phase. His previous professional 20-year career was initially as a teacher and then local government sport and leisure services director, which concluded as Director of Sport at the University of Manchester. He has been extensively involved in the development, use and management of Olympic and other Games Villages for more than 30 years. He was awarded the OBE for his contribution to Paralympic sport in 1995.

Gabriel Silvestre is a visiting lecturer in Tourism Management at the University of Westminster and a PhD candidate in Urban Planning at UCL Bartlett School of Planning, where his study has been funded by grants from the Olympic Studies Centre of the International Olympic Committee (IOC). Over the past 6 years he has been involved with research on the implications of mega-event hosting for cities in the Global South with a particular attention to the city of Rio de Janeiro and its Olympic project.

Andrew Smith is Reader in Tourism and Events at the University of Westminster. His research centres on sports events (in particular their role as tools for urban regeneration), destination imagery, and city tourism. He is author of *Events and Urban Regeneration*, published in 2012.

Stephen V. Ward is Professor of Planning History at Oxford Brookes University. He was President of the International Planning History Society (2000–2006) and was formerly Editor of the journal *Planning Perspectives*. His books include *Selling Places* (1998), *Planning the Twentieth-Century City* (2002) and *Planning and Urban Change*, second edition (2004).

Mike Weed is Professor of Sport in Society and Director of the Centre for Sport, Physical Education and Activity Research (SPEAR) in the Faculty of Social and Applied Sciences at Canterbury Christ Church University. He is author of *Olympic Tourism* (2008) and *Sports Tourism: Participants, Policy and Providers* (2009), as well as editor of *Sport and Tourism: a Reader* (2008). He is Editor of the *Journal of Sport and Tourism*, has acted as Guest Editor for issues of *European Sport Management Quarterly*, *European Journal of Sport Science* and *Psychology of Sport and Exercise*.

List of Acronyms

The list below contains an alphabetical listing of acronyms used substantively in the text rather than simply for bibliographic purposes:

ACOG	Atlanta Committee for the Olympic Games
AOBC	Athens 2004 Olympic Bid Committee
ATHOC	Athens Organising Committee for the Olympic Games
BBC	British Broadcasting Corporation
BOCOG	Beijing Organizing Committee for the Games of the XXIX Olympiad
COJO	Comité d'Organisation des Jeux Olympiques
CONI	Comitato Olimpico Nazionale Italiano
COOB	Barcelona Olympic Organising Committee
DCMS	Department of Culture, Media and Sport (UK)
FIFA	Fédération Internationale de Football Association
GLA	Greater London Authority
IBC	International Broadcast Centre
ICC	International Coordinating Committee of the World Sports Organizations
IOC	International Olympic Committee
ISMGF	International Stoke Mandeville Games Foundation
IPC	International Paralympic Committee
LDA	London Development Agency
LLDC	London Legacy Development Corporation
LOCOG	London Organising Committee of the Olympic and Paralympic Games
OCOG	Organising Committee for the Olympic Games
ODA	Olympic Delivery Authority
SOCOG	Sydney Organising Committee for the Olympic Games
TOK	Transfer of Olympic Knowledge
TOP	Olympic Partner Programme
TOROC	Organising Committee of the XX Turin 2006 Olympic Winter Games
WWF	World Wildlife Fund

For David Pepper

Chapter 1

Introduction

John R. Gold and Margaret M. Gold

July 2015 was not an auspicious month for the International Olympic Committee (IOC). On the 17th, the Japanese Prime Minister Shinzō Abe announced the scrapping of the chosen design for the new National Stadium, which would have been the $2 billion centrepiece for the Tokyo 2020 Games. The design in question had been selected in November 2012 from entries submitted to a competition organized by Japan's Sport Council. The brief was for a new 80,000-seater stadium to replace the one previously constructed for the 1964 Olympics, with the proviso that it would be ready in time to host the 2019 Rugby World Cup (Fulcher, 2012). The winning submission from the eleven shortlisted entries supplied by international architectural practices was a sinuous design by the London-based Zaha Hadid Architects that resembled a giant cycling helmet.

Justifying their selection, Tadao Ando, the chairman of the adjudication panel, stated: 'The entry's dynamic and futuristic design embodies the messages Japan would like to convey to the rest of the world… I believe this stadium will become a shrine for world sport for the next 100 years' (Ryall, 2013). For more local consumption, the addition of a retractable roof was hailed as supplying a flexible arena that could be easily transformed from a sport to a concert venue. In September the following year, Hadid's striking design was undoubtedly a selling point when Tokyo won the nomination for the 2020 Games, with IOC President Jacques Rogge praising 'the excellent quality of a very well-constructed bid' (Gibson, 2013a).

Yet by 2015 thoughts of symbolism, spectacle, multifunctionality and long-term cultural kudos seemed secondary to considerations of price and value-for-money. Announcing cancellation of the original scheme and the decision to seek a re-design from scratch, Abe alluded to 'criticisms from the public which made me believe that we will not be able to host a Games that everyone in this country would celebrate' (Wingfield-Hayes, 2015). The strategy of blaming the architects for 'greatly inflated construction costs' was added to assuage any concerns over possible loss of face[1] amongst the international community. This populist move, however, would have its downside. Deciding to 'start it over from zero' meant, among other things, that the stadium would not now be ready for the Rugby World Cup (*Ibid.*).

Abe's declaration and his recognition of the need to address sustained disquiet resonated with wholly separate developments in the USA that came to a head shortly afterwards. On 27 July, the United States Olympic Committee (USOC) announced that Boston (Massachusetts), the city chosen to bid for the 2024 Olympics, had withdrawn its candidacy. Once again, this was the culmination of a lengthy chain of events. In February 2013, Boston had been one of the thirty-five US cities to which USOC had sent invitations to prepare a bid. After a protracted selection process and the emergence of a shortlist that pitted it against Los Angeles, San Francisco, and Washington DC, USOC gave the nod to Boston on 8 January 2015. At first, the major local stakeholders had provided strong support, with Mayor Marty Walsh issuing a statement that resounded with the rhetoric of place promotion. He duly recorded the city's acceptance of this 'exceptional honour', which recognized 'our city's talent, diversity and global leadership', and how 'Boston hopes to welcome the world's greatest athletes to one of the world's great cities' (Nessif, 2015). Of particular note, too, was the way that the bidders emphasized 'marketing Boston as a site of innovation, contending that the city [was] … not only capable of hosting a Games but also well placed to develop new planning models for the Olympics in general' (Lauermann, 2015, p. 3).

Other potential stakeholders saw things differently. There was concern about lack of public consultation and a growing sense that no proper economic case had been made. Organizations such as 'No Boston Olympics' and 'No Boston 2024' challenged the legitimacy and the rationale of the bid, using Freedom of Information provisions to document 'municipal risk-taking and other indirect subsidies' that had been deliberately downplayed (*Ibid.*, p. 6). As the summer progressed, USOC pressed Boston to sign a host city contract that would leave it responsible for any cost overruns (Moore, 2015). On 27 July Mayor Walsh called a press conference at which he delivered the *coup de grâce* to the project that he had so recently supported. Walsh announced: 'I cannot commit to putting the taxpayers at risk … if committing to sign a guarantee today is what's required to move forward, then Boston is no longer pursuing the 2024 Olympic and Paralympic Games' (Arsenault and Ryan, 2015). Faced with that rebuff, USOC were ignominiously forced to seek a substitute.

Finally, on 31 July came what seemed rather better news for the IOC. Amidst the conventional Oscar Awards-style razzmatazz, the 128th IOC Session in Kuala Lumpur chose Beijing over Almaty (Kazakhstan) as the host city for the 2022 Winter Olympic Games. The world's television networks that chose to cover the event were treated to the usual pictures of a smiling IOC President announcing the winner followed by images of backslapping victors in the conference hall and scenes of jubilant crowds back home at the Olympic Green in Beijing. In some respects, it could be presented as a triumph. The 2008 Summer Games in Beijing had been the most lavish in Olympic history, giving rise to memorable spectacle while still supporting the IOC's core values. There was no reason to suggest that a Winter Games there would not produce the same desirable outcome and certainly the Chinese were regarded as offering a safer pair of hands than their Kazakh rivals for staging this festival.

Nevertheless, the surprising closeness of the voting – 44 votes to 40 for Beijing over untried competitors who were bidding for the first time – reflected an underlying sense of unease. Questions were asked about the credibility of Beijing's bid. Almaty had pointedly campaigned under the slogan 'Keeping It Real' and had featured many images of ice and snow in its bid videos. It also emphasized the possibility of staging a compact Games (Borden, 2015). This contrasted with Beijing, which had no history as a winter sports venue and where neither of the two distant mountain sites for the snow events – Yanqing and Zhangjiakou – could stage their events without copious quantities of artificial snow. In such circumstances, an unusually large number of IOC members seemed willing to take a chance on what normally would have been a rank outsider.

A related and perhaps more disconcerting consideration was the proven difficulty in assembling and retaining the usual roster of four to six cities to provide a convincing choice for the final vote. Back in November 2013, the IOC had announced a shortlist of six applicant cities, with Oslo (Norway), Kraków (Poland), Lviv (Ukraine) and Stockholm (Sweden) bidding in addition to Almaty and Beijing.[2] Informal ideas about continental equity – never an official part of IOC policy but never far from thinking about the political realities of host city selection – suggested that a Northern European bid would be favoured. After all, the three previous Games had been allotted to Vancouver (2010), Sochi (2014) and PyeongChang (2018). In quick succession, however, 'every potential host city with a democratically elected government dropped out … mostly over economic concerns and lack of public support' (Manfred, 2015). The bid from Stockholm was quickly withdrawn due to inability to produce effective costings around which to seek public support (Abend, 2014). The Kraków bid was terminated after it failed to win support in a local referendum. The Lviv bid also partly foundered on lack of public support as well as from the instability stemming from the political crisis caused by Ukraine's territorial conflicts with Russian-backed separatists (AP, 2014; see also Chapter 3).

Most damagingly, though, the Oslo bid – judged as comfortably the best of the three in the preliminary bid assessment – was cancelled as late as 1 October 2014. At that point the Conservative Party, the main Norwegian political party that favoured the bid, withdrew its support meaning that it was no longer possible to achieve a necessary Parliamentary majority to provide cost guarantees. Although made primarily on economic grounds, the decision was also made more palatable to the Norwegian public by the decision to publish what were termed 'the hopeless pampering requirements' of the IOC (Crouch and Blitz, 2014). These included: a drinks reception with Norway's King Harald to be paid for by the royal family or the local Organizing Committee (OCOG); instructions as to appropriate ways in which IOC members should be greeted; chauffeur-driven transport to be provided along lanes reserved for their use, with traffic lights adjusted to give them priority; supplying each delegate with a Samsung mobile phone with a paid Norwegian subscription; ensuring that all furniture should be Olympic-shaped and have Olympic appearance; demands over ambient room temperature, quality of food and late-night opening on bars; and exclusive control over all advertising space throughout Oslo during the Games, which would then be used exclusively by official Olympic sponsors (*Ibid.*; also Matthis-Lilley, 2014).

For their part, the IOC hierarchy was both incensed by the Norwegian withdrawal and genuinely surprised by the ferocity of response to demands that had been freely granted by predecessors (albeit sometimes modified or partly withdrawn in due course). Christophe Dubi, the IOC's Executive Director of the Olympic Games, issued a press statement that was curtly dismissive of the arguments about the likely costs of the Games, blaming the Norwegian bid team for failing to discuss the terms properly with the IOC and allowing decision-making to be made on 'the basis of half-truths and factual inaccuracies'. Above all, he asserted: 'This is a missed opportunity for the City of Oslo and for all the people of Norway who are known world-wide for being huge fans of winter sports … [and] a missed opportunity for the outstanding Norwegian athletes who will not be able to reach new Olympic heights in their home country' (Dubi, 2014). After various retaliatory salvoes from the Norwegians who, among other things, accused the IOC of behaving like capricious rock stars, the matter was laid to rest (Crouch and Blitz, 2014).

The IOC-Host City Relationship

Taken together, these separate developments represented setbacks for the IOC in various ways, but also have to be seen in their broader context. In the first place, previous experience suggests that none will prove critical to the staging of future Olympiads. Problems with main Olympic stadia have been experienced before and it is quite likely that the events of July 2015 will later seem only a blip in the development of Tokyo 2020. The withdrawal of Boston from being US Applicant City for 2024 paved the way for the selection of Los Angeles, the host on two previous occasions (1932 and 1984) and probably always a stronger candidate than Boston. Finally, for all the problems in retaining a convincing shortlist of applicants, there were few doubts about the outcome in terms of the Chinese being able to stage the Winter Games successfully. Certainly, by any comparison, whatever anxieties might currently exist over attracting candidate cities are minor compared with the situation that pertained in the mid-to-late 1970s, when the supply virtually dried up (Payne, 2006; see also Chapter 2).

That finding in itself underlines a second key point, namely, that a proper understanding of the staging of Olympic Games rests substantially on an appreciation of the relationship between the IOC and its host cities (Gold and Gold, 2012). At once complex, richly textured and continually evolving, it is a relationship that has given each Games a unique character while still being part of a recurrent series. Moreover, its flexibility has also been a vital factor in ensuring the extraordinary longevity of the Olympics despite the challenges presented by changing times.

To elaborate, the IOC's decision in the 1890s to re-establish the modern Games as an ambulatory event that moved to a new destination every 4 years immediately placed the relationship between the IOC and its host cities at the centre of the Olympic project. Like any contract entered into by two parties with different starting positions, it was always likely to be a fluid and occasionally uneasy partnership. This was particularly so because that partnership often rested on changing and sometimes contrasting views about the ways in which the increasing size of the Games should be accommodated and about the extent to which the hosts could use the Games as vehicles for achieving positive outcomes for their cities.

In the early days, the Olympic movement sought to use the Games' ambulatory path to encourage longer-term sporting outcomes in host nations around the globe. Members of the IOC tended to nominate cities in their own countries as potential hosts, believing that the value of the event came from the prestige that accrued to centres that held the Games. Naturally, the organizers of earlier Olympiads were aware of the economic potential that the Games might have, particularly with regard to tourism but, given the attachment to amateurism and antipathy to profit on the part of the IOC, it was considered inappropriate to glory in what the Games would do for the city rather than for sport and the pleasure of its citizens (McIntosh, 2003, pp. 450, 452).

This arrangement was feasible when the burden on the host city was small, with the local organizers staging the early Games in adapted stadia or temporary arenas, but the rapid growth in the scale and complexity of the Olympics quickly created new circumstances. Increasingly, host cities were expected to act as risk-takers. Special venues were needed, with London's White City Stadium, purpose-built for the 1908 Olympics, setting the trend. Five years later, the Swedish organizers of the 1912 Games wistfully concluded that: 'to carry out the Olympic Games of the present day ... required not only personal effort on the part of the organizers, but also the most ample financial resources' (SOC, 1913, p. 51).

In the fullness of time, the Games' organizers saw that much more could be achieved as by-products of being nominated to stage the Olympics. Los Angeles's bid for the 1932 Games, for example, was crafted by aggressive local entrepreneurs and political leaders who wished to boost the city's credentials on the national and international stage. The organizers of Berlin 1936 saw the Summer Games used as a medium for the Third Reich's spectacular representations of the New Germany, albeit with a surprisingly small impact upon the host city apart from the completion of an enormous sports complex on the city's outskirts. Rome 1960, the first Games held after the end of the Austerity that followed the Second World War, saw the first thoroughgoing attempt by a host city to attach a general exercise in urban development to the festival. Over time, a tacit bargain effectively developed between the IOC and the host city, particularly as mediated by the OCOG. In broad terms, this allowed the Games to be used to address the needs of the home city in return for the extraordinary investment of time, effort and resources needed to stage the modern Games. By the time of Barcelona 1992, the balance had altered so dramatically that only 17 per cent of total expenditure actually went on the sports element of the Games compared with 83 per cent on urban improvement.

In the 1990s, the issue of sustainability entered the frame. In 1994, the IOC adopted the principle that the candidate cities for the Summer and Winter Games should also be evaluated on the environmental consequences of their plans (Gold and Gold, 2013). This was matched by the decision to construe 'environment' as a 'third pillar' of the Olympic movement's core philosophy of Olympism, alongside 'sport' and 'culture'. In 1996, the Olympic Charter was itself amended to assert that one of the IOC's roles is 'to encourage and support a responsible concern for environmental issues, to promote sustainable development in sport and require that the Olympic Games are held accordingly' (quoted in Pitts and Liao, 2009, p. 67). In October 1999, the Olympic Movement published its own Agenda 21 document as a response to the recommendations of the 1992 Rio Earth Summit to serve as a 'useful reference tool for the sports community at all levels in the protection of the environment and enhancement of sustainable development' (IOC, 2006, p. 10). To a large extent, the idealistic tenor of environmentalism conveyed by these measures struck a resonant note with the Olympic movement – itself not adverse to idealism. Yet it may also be argued that the sustainability agenda gave the IOC the chance to respond to accusations of 'gigantism', in which it was blamed for requiring host cities to expend vast amounts of resources in constructing and staging one-off events. Direct advocacy of environmental responsibility helped to show that the movement was addressing these issues by seeking to reduce the impact of the Games and to ensure the future generations of the city's residents gained lasting benefits from the expenditure.

If sustainability led the way in renegotiating the core relationship between host cities and the IOC, it would quickly be joined by a new and explicit concern for 'legacy' – a notion that now exerts a powerful sway over the way in which the outcomes of the Games are imagined, conceptualized, negotiated and realized (Gold and Gold, 2014, 2017). The word 'legacy' itself had had sporadic and non-specific usage in Olympic parlance, largely lacking the conceptual impedimenta now attached to it. The first significant mention of the word *per se* occurred in the city of Melbourne's bid document for the 1956 Games (McIntosh, 2003, p. 450), but that was an isolated occurrence – particularly as there was no further use of the term in the Official Reports either prepared for the Melbourne Games or for successors for several decades thereafter. This did not mean, of course, that organizers were indifferent to achieving beneficial outcomes for their host cities. At Melbourne, for example, the OCOG's Official Report talked of putting resources to good use and creating 'a continuing asset' (Organizing Committee, 1958). For Rome 1960, the Official Report comments on 'meeting ever-increasing needs' (CONI, 1963) and the Montreal Summer Games in 1976 were intended to leave an 'inheritance of benefit' (Organizing Committee, 1976).

Legacy, in the contemporary sense, started to be used in a concerted manner in the Official Reports for Los Angeles with eleven mentions (LAOOC, 1985) and the Winter Games in Calgary 1988 with forty-two mentions (COWCOG, 1988). As measured by the Official Reports, the notion of legacy became increasingly entrenched in thinking over the last 20 years, with Atlanta 1996 recording seventy-one mentions, forty-three for Sydney 2000, fifty-five for Salt Lake City 2002 and twenty-three for Athens 2004 (see respectively ACOG, 1990; SOCOG, 2000; SLOC, 2002; and ATHOC, 2005). The informal and *ad hoc* usages of the term, however, were in many ways racing ahead of substantive definition. It could clearly consist of a melange of sporting, urban regenerative and environmental elements. Equally, the term could encompass a disparate range of intangible ingredients that include skills, sports and cultural participation, volunteering, national pride and city status.

In attempting to come to terms with the growing diversity, therefore, a symposium met under IOC auspices in 2002 to consider the relevant theory and practice. After extensive deliberations, it concluded (IOC, 2003b, p. 2) that:

> the effects of the legacy have many aspects and dimensions, ranging from the more commonly recognised aspects – architecture, urban planning, city marketing, sports infrastructures, economic and tourist development – to others … that are less well recognised … the so called intangible legacies, such as production of ideas and cultural values, intercultural and non-exclusionary experiences (based on gender, ethnicity or physical abilities), popular memory, education, archives, collective effort and voluntarism, new sport practitioners, notoriety on a global scale, experience and know-how…

This all-encompassing definition delimited a broad category, within which further differentiation has been made by establishing dichotomies. The one recognized by the symposium was tangible (measurable) versus intangible legacy (non-measurable), but other dichotomies, often sharing common ground, have subsequently been added. They include direct (arising from investment in the Olympics) versus indirect (associated) legacy; short term versus long term; and hard (physical structures and infrastructure) versus soft (other tangible and intangible outcomes). In addition, other terms like 'pregacy' have become a jocular way of identifying impacts occurring before the event. The term pre-legacy has been employed more formally by the Rio Organizing Committee for infrastructure completed before the Games; a phase considered to have begun when Olympic venues were opened to underprivileged communities (Anon, 2015c).

The Ascendance of Legacy

Considerations of the hydra-headed beast known as legacy arise at many points in this text and now act as an ascendant shared frame within which policy-makers and scholars alike have started to think about the trajectory of the development of the Olympic project over time in the host city.[3] Viewed analytically, the workings of legacy rest on a 'narrative', understood here as a structured account of a sequence of events that connect actions (actual or putative) with specific outcomes. The nature of that narrative, however, has changed over time and varies with the values of the observer. For most policy-makers, the underlying narrative is one that links positive outcomes back to decisive actions. By contrast, for Olympic critics the corresponding narrative might well portray connections that lead from ideologically-motivated actions to outcomes that are variously conceived as being unintended, dysfunctional or even undemocratic (Gold and Gold, 2011).

With these thoughts in mind, it is worth making five points that help to contextualize the subject of legacy. The first is that the concept remains in its infancy. Despite now ostensibly being central to the *raison d'être* of the Games, no city to date has yet undergone a full and rigorous longitudinal evaluation of the legacy from an Olympic Games: a process that might easily take several decades to run its course. In attempting to gain better data, for example, the IOC established the Olympic Games Global Impact project in 2003, retitled the Olympic Games Impact Study (OGI) in 2006 (Dubi and Felli, 2006). Under OGI arrangements, candidate and then host cities are committed to look at the economic, environmental and social impact of the Games over a period of 11 years, namely when the city applies (baseline report); in the preparation phase; a report on staging the Games completed a year after the Games have ended; and a closing report supplied 3 years after the end. Although Athens 2004, Turin 2006 and Beijing 2008 cooperated in limited ways with this project, Vancouver 2010 and London 2012 were the first hosts to go through the full cycle. What has emerged from the reports to date, however, has been meagre and often more concerned with the problems of methodology than with supplying concrete evidence about legacy. The first of London 2012's OGI reports, for example, had reported:

> No negative impacts were found as a result of preparing for the 2012 Games, some positive impacts were found but many indicators were inconclusive. Such inconclusiveness is not a criticism; it may stem from data issues, but also from the diverse policy landscape of the UK, London and East London. (UEL/TGIS, 2010, p. 125)

The next report – published in December 2015 and the most recent available at the time of writing – concluded by repeating the above finding (UEL, 2015, p. 183), before understandably underlining the complexity of the task; justifying the broad absence of more substantive findings by adding:

> As with any long term project that is intended to be a catalyst for long term change and transformation, the analysis of three years into legacy that this report presents is only the beginning. The urban transformation of the Olympic Park is not expected to be complete before 2030. As we have noted, cultural changes towards, say, more healthy and active

lifestyles can take a long time, may even be generational. That London 2012 has been a catalyst for positive change is not in doubt, but when and where the process ends and what will be the full magnitude of the effect is not yet known. The story of London 2012 will continue to unfold for a long time to come.

The second contextual point about legacy concerns the role of values. Although many researchers would choose to see the term 'legacy' as representing a balance of negative as well as positive elements, IOC practice has accented the latter. Tomlinson (2014, p. 152), for example, noted that a bibliography from the IOC's Library and Study Centre contrasted 'legacy' with 'impact'. Legacy' was used in 'presenting positive effects … also … in association with those effects that are of longer duration', whereas 'impacts' were regarded 'as implying an adverse effect or a damaging or destructive result' (IOC, 2013, p. 3; quoted in Tomlinson, 2014, p. 152). Games organizers and local growth coalitions[4] have adopted similar policies. Elsewhere (Gold and Gold, 2011, 2016), we have written about the prevalence of Whig interpretations of history (Butterfield, 1931) that have long dominated writings about the Olympics; an interpretative approach that stands for historical narratives that selectively view the past in terms of the march towards ever greater achievement and enlightenment. Equally many academic observers have tended towards suspicion or hostility towards the assumptions linked to Olympic legacy, especially in light of instances of inadequate or overambitious planning, poor stadia design, financial corruption, heavy cost overruns, environmental damage and lack of accountability (e.g. see Cohen, 2013; Raco, 2014; Pavoni, 2015).

It is neither part of the function of this book to lionize or debunk the Games nor to argue that their impact on host cities is positive or adverse on *a priori* grounds. However, what is apparent from the standpoint of Olympic cities is that staging the Games is now divorced from the economic rationale that surrounds almost all other festivals. The Olympics are commonly hailed as mega-events – cultural and sporting festivals that achieve sufficient size and scope to affect whole economies and to receive sustained global media attention (Gold and Gold, 2005, p. 4: see also Roche, 2000; Preuss, 2015; Gruneau and Horne, 2016).[5] Such events, through their size and prestige, are held to bring a highly desirable package of benefits to the host city. These include, *inter alia*, boosting a city's economy, improving its international standing, repositioning it in the global tourist market, promoting urban regeneration, revamping transport and service infrastructures, creating vibrant cultural quarters, establishing a network of high-grade facilities that could serve as the basis for future bids, and gaining a competitive advantage over rivals. Some of these benefits are visible and readily measurable; others are confidently proclaimed but intangible; yet others are a mixture of the two. Shortfalls in one area might be offset by reference to another, with disagreements largely unresolvable due to incompatibilities in the evidence cited and the conflicting values of the parties to the argument.

Moreover, the Olympic festivals are also prime candidates for classification as 'megaprojects'. Defined as prestige schemes involving large-scale and high-risk investment over a lengthy period, megaprojects notoriously suffer heavy cost overruns, often failing to deliver the supposed benefits and regularly provoking financial crises (Flyvbjerg *et al.*, 2003; Flyvbjerg and Stewart, 2012; see also Hall, 1980). Indeed, as Flyvbjerg and Stewart (2012, p. 3) have noted from their analyses of the costs and cost overruns for the Olympic Games from 1960 to 2012:

> We discovered that the Games stand out in two distinct ways compared to other megaprojects: (1) The Games overrun with 100 per cent consistency. No other type of megaproject is this consistent regarding cost overrun. Other project types are typically on budget from time to time, but not the Olympics. (2) With an average cost overrun in real terms of 179 per cent – and 324 per cent in nominal terms – overruns in the Games have historically been significantly larger than for other types of megaprojects, including infrastructure, construction, ICT, and dams.

The Olympics may suffer more in this respect than other megaprojects by virtue of having an immutable deadline for completion. Compromises with the need to keep public spending within bounds are inevitable. The swift cooperation of the private sector is required but often at the cost of providing incentives for investment in the form of grants of land, loans on favourable terms, and adjustments to building regulations.[6] The eventual appearance of gentrification in the housing market by private developers eager to generate income on their investment is a natural concomitant of such policies. In addition, works running behind timetable can add further cost pressures by forcing organizers to instigate high-cost emergency building programmes, with round-the-clock working and additional contractors, in order to get laggard projects back on schedule.

Acknowledgment of these unwelcome characteristics and the degree of risk attached is rarely countenanced before winning the bid and almost never once the Games have been awarded. The right to host the Olympics represents the ultimate accolade that a city can earn on the world stage. Expenditures might be disputed and lower priority events, such as the Cultural Olympiad or associated youth programmes, might have their budgets slashed, but the prestige element of the expenditure will go ahead. Ways will be found to finance the Games regardless of the logic of the balance sheet, probably with the nation as a whole rather than the Olympic city picking up the bulk of the bill. Without cost as an effective constraint, debate inevitably centres on the seductive promise of legacy to sustain popular enthusiasm and drive the project ahead.

The third initial contextual point concerns the balance of sports to non-sports legacy. It goes without saying that sports-related elements are a key dimension in the equation, particularly for the IOC which is not altogether happy about the over-identification of notions of legacy with the housing and infrastructural interests of the host city and the approach that this appears to embody. Certainly bid documents by candidate cities pay close attention to sports legacy, which routinely incorporates four interrelated and overlapping themes. The first is sports infrastructure. With the Summer Games requiring new, renovated or temporary facilities for twenty-six to twenty-eight sports, there is always likely to be a stock of new facilities available for elite or local use. The second, sports development, comprises encouraging sports participation for its own sake or for instrumental reasons (for example, promotion of public health or for tackling unequal access to sports opportunities). The third, sports performance, relates to raising standards and promoting excellence. The final element, sports tourism, involves travel to participate in or watch sporting events. Taken collectively, though, these various aspects of sports legacy are often easier to propose conceptually than to achieve, especially in terms of sports participation and inculcation of public health.

The fourth contextual point involves inclusion and exclusion. Anything that involves major long-term investment for an Olympic Games immediately invokes questions of equity. Although detailed discussion of these matters lies beyond the scope of this chapter,[7] it is possible to recognize, in outline, at least five dimensions of equity connected with Olympic legacy.[8] These are: *intergenerational* equity or the passing of resources from one generation to the next; *social* equity, whereby people within society have equal rights and opportunities with respect to the gains to be realized from legacy, regardless of their class or status; *economic* equity, in which wealth created as part of the legacy of the Games is distributed fairly throughout the community; *environmental* equity, which offers a safe, healthy, productive, and sustainable environment for all; and *spatial* equity or fairness of distribution of legacy outcomes regardless of location. These five loosely-defined dimensions, of course, represent ideal states that are difficult to implement, and pursuit of one may create tensions with others. Nevertheless, there is little doubt that these problems of definition and tensions need to be resolved if host cities are to make full sense of the indeterminate notion of legacy.

Finally, although the point is wider than purely a matter concerning legacy, the emergence of Agenda 2020 is shaping the Olympic project for the years ahead. Initiated by the incoming IOC President Thomas Bach in December 2013 and approved by the IOC in December 2014, the first host city selection procedure to fall fully within the new framework is that for the Summer Games of 2024 (IOC, 2014*a*; see also IOC, 2014*b*). In strategic terms, legacy has been recognized by the IOC as a persuasive notion for gaining public support for and demonstrating public benefit from staging the Games. It is also a way of tailoring the Olympic project to the needs and characteristics of aspirant host cities. Under Agenda 2020, legacy is now to be embedded more emphatically from the outset: '[it] should be at the heart of informing the decision whether or not to bid for the Games' before the city has even entered the bidding procedure formally (IOC, 2015*c*, p. 167). Moreover it is a key element of the evaluation of the candidature as cities proceed through the bidding process.

Under Agenda 2020, the bidding procedure can take up to 30 months with an initial six month 'invitation phase' in which interested cities enter a dialogue with the IOC prior to joining the bidding process formally. The bidding phase is divided into three periods with each requiring a formal document to be submitted; these documents together constitute the full bid. Phase 1 of the bidding process focuses on 'vision, Games concept, and strategy' and demands an articulation of the legacy. Phase 2 covers 'governance, legal and venue funding'. The final phase 'Games delivery, experience and venue legacy' requires the strategy for legacy planning. Applications can be 'deferred' by the IOC at the end of phase 1 and 2. The final IOC decision is made between those candidates continuing to the end of phase 3 (IOC 2015b). This new procedure is intended to be supportive of potential host cities, more sensitive to their needs, reduce the cost of preparing for and staging the Games, and encourages a wider variety of cities to consider applying to stage the Games. At the time of writing, however, it remains to be seen how these provisions will work out in practice.

Aims

Selection by the IOC as an 'Olympic city', then, invites the host to contribute to a process that remains in continual evolution despite the passage of more than a century. The Olympic city gains the right to stage a festival carefully wrapped in the trappings of historical precedent, but which, as we have seen above, also possesses a remarkable malleability that allowed the event to survive repeated crises and emerge, by the start of the twenty-first century, as unquestionably the 'World's Games'.[9] Olympic cities are risk-taking partners in the staging of the Olympics rather than nominees that run a festival crafted by its sponsoring body. The IOC guards the continuing traditions of its festival but each recipient city shapes the Games to greater or lesser extent and contributes to the body of customs and practices associated with the Olympics. In a process of continual adaptation and change, the Olympics and host cities enjoy a flexible and symbiotic relationship.

This book explores that relationship, examining the experience of Olympic cities and the balance sheet of success and failure from the revival of the Games in 1896 to the plans for the Summer Games in Tokyo in 2020.[10] As such, it has three main aims. First, it examines the city's role in *staging* the modern Games, a word that covers the full spectrum of activity from initial selection of sites to final modification of these sites to their post-festival condition. Secondly, it explores the underlying *agendas* that host cities have brought to bear on staging the Games, recognizing the different blends of social, political, cultural and economic aspirations that have emerged over time. Finally, it recognizes that, despite being an exceptional event in the life of a specific city, the business of staging the Games is now commonly related to the wider *planning* process. In this respect, we focus particularly on issues concerned with legacy, including infrastructural development and urban regeneration projects, which are now regarded as central to the process of planning for the Olympics.

Having said this, two points are important in understanding the scope of this book. First, while rightly giving prominence to the Summer Games as by far the largest, most prestigious and visible of the Olympic events, we seek a more comprehensive approach. The Olympics are not a single event. The advent of the Winter Olympics in 1924 and the gradual convergence of the Paralympics with both the Summer and Winter Games have added further strands to the Olympic sporting competitions. In addition, the revival of the modern Games predicated a cultural festival, now usually formulated as a 4-year Cultural Olympiad, to exist alongside the sports events. Each of these strands merits coverage as intrinsic parts of the experience of being an Olympic city.[11]

Secondly, the prevailing focus is historical. This does not mean that we have confined the scope of this book purely to dealing with the past since later chapters deal with Olympics that, at the time of writing, are yet-to-come. What this volume does stress, however, is the value of seeing even these forthcoming Games as the product of a chain of events that reaches back into the late nineteenth century and has been steadily developing since that time. The staging of the Olympics positively invites historical analysis. Continuity between Games arises from each new Organizing Committee scrutinizing the experience of previous OCOGs, with transfer of knowledge from one to another facilitated both by the IOC's own procedures and a small army of freelance consultants and specialists who offer their services to Games organizers. In addition, each new host city prepares its Olympic festivals in the sure and certain knowledge that its efforts will be compared to those of predecessors and will, in turn, provide a new point of comparison.

Structure

As befits the multi-stranded nature of the narratives that surround the Games, the ensuing chapters divide into three main sections, each of which offers different perspectives on the Olympics. Part 1 contains four parallel but complementary essays that look chronologically at the progress of the individual Olympic festivals from inception to the early twenty-first century. Chapter 2 provides an overview of the relationship between the Summer Olympics and their host cities, acting as a general framework for the case studies of selected cities found in Part 3 as well as adding coverage of Summer Games, particularly from the early years, which are not tackled there. After examining the circumstances behind the revival of the Olympics, it traces eight phases in the history of staging the festival from the opening Games in Athens 1896 to the most recent manifestation in 2012. In a similar vein, Chapter 3 provides a historic overview that identifies a five-phase framework for analysing the role of the Winter Olympics in changing and modernizing the built environment of its host cities. In looking to the future, it briefly touches on potential developments given the new thinking emerging in the context of the IOC's Agenda 2020. Chapter 4 examines the cultural dimension of the Games and its attachment to both the Summer and Winter Games. It provides an overview of the programme's evolution, from initial art competitions through to more recent 4-year Olympiads, examining the problems and challenges encountered. After emphasizing how recent developments have seen the cultural festivals growing in scale, particularly in response to the economic interests of host cities, it also notes the potential role of Agenda 2020 as an emerging framework for the future. Chapter 5 examines the Paralympic Games. It charts their development from small beginnings as a competition for disabled ex-servicemen and women in England in the late 1940s to the present day ambulatory international festivals for athletes with disabilities, which now take place in the Olympic city immediately after both the Summer and Winter Games.

Part 2 provides surveys of seven key aspects of activity involved in planning and managing the Olympics. Chapter 6 examines the finance of the Olympics. It provides an economic overview of the development of the Games and identifies the broad group of stakeholders who benefit from staging them; a group that goes well beyond the main shareholders (the Olympic family). Chapter 7 deals with city marketing, recognizing the importance of the Olympics in global place promotion and particularly the importance of marketing in securing the bid in the first place. Chapter 8 draws on the experience of a practitioner with 30 years' experience to consider the provision and role of Olympic and Paralympic Villages. It reflects on the historical development of Villages as an integral part of staging the Games, identifying six strands that materially influenced the approach that was manifested at London 2012. Chapter 9 switches attention to the question of security, which has rapidly become one of the key parameters for site organization. It discusses the gradual but inexorable increase in the securitization of Olympic sites, offering a perspective on London 2012 responding to international terrorism and on Rio de Janeiro as responding to tensions arising from the pacification of the city's *favelas* and drug-related violence.

Turning to issues involving event spaces, their surrounding areas and subsequent use, Chapter 10 reviews how and why the Olympic Games is used as a vehicle for regeneration, conclusions drawn from the Olympics are also applied to regeneration processes in general. Critical comment is directed against commonly-expressed rhetoric such as that staging the Olympic Games provides 'flagship' urban projects and 'catalysts' for regeneration. The discussion of particular Games then focuses particularly on those which were staged on brownfield sites. Chapter 11 addresses Olympic tourism. It outlines a range of Olympic tourism products, before outlining how the Summer and Winter Games can be leveraged to generate tourism. The two substantive parts of this chapter then examine how cities staging the Winter Games can act as tourism gateways to their wider regions and how Summer Games can contribute to the development of their host cities' tourism product and image. The final chapter in this section (Chapter 12) addresses the important dimension of transport, widely considered to be one of the key parameters that need to be addressed when staging the Olympics. It opens by briefly analysing the experience of transport strategies adopted by cities staging Summer and Winter Games in the twenty-first century before discussing the three main stages in preparing transport for an Olympic Games: the planning of Olympic transport, managing Olympic transport, and the leveraging of legacies. Examples of best practice are identified.

Part 3 offers nine portraits of Olympic Cities, arranged in chronological order. The opening segment examines three selected Olympiads from the twentieth century. Chapter 13 discusses the various phases in development of the Olympic sports complex in Berlin and its subsequent problematic history in light of the postwar division and eventual reunification of the city. Chapter 14 recalls the first occasion that the Games were held in a developing nation, analysing the way that the bid was won and the economic and political consequences of the 1968 Olympics for Mexico City. Chapter 15 deals with Munich 1972, an event inseparable from the history of mid-twentieth century Germany, both in the sense of wanting to create an event to counter the abiding image of Berlin 1936 and seeking to address the reconstruction of a city still bearing the scars of wartime destruction. After considering the general redevelopment of the city after 1945, this chapter examines the vision offered in the bid documents and the ensuing planning and construction of the Olympic venues and infrastructure. The ensuing sections examine the post-Games legacy of Munich 1972 from the perspectives of its consequences for the urban environment and as a focus for further bids for sporting and cultural mega-events.

The next chapters deal with the first four Summer Games held during the twenty-first century. Chapter 16 focuses attention on Sydney 2000, examining in particular the physical planning and transformation of the main site at Homebush Bay. The authors consider the process of development through the lens of legacy, briefly considering the nature of that concept before identifying a chronology of thinking that frames their narrative. They characterize the Sydney experience in four main stages before reflecting on the broader implications of this episode in both Olympic and planning history. The ensuing Chapter 17 analyses the Games' return to Athens in 2004, discussing the serious delays incurred by belatedly switching from a nucleated to a dispersed locational policy for Olympic facilities. It also highlights the lip-service paid to the much heralded goal of environmental sustainability before the event and the continuing desolation of the Olympic sites in their transfer to post-Games usage. Chapter 18 examines the astonishing expenditure and associated spectacle that was part and parcel of Beijing 2008. In doing so, it recognizes not only the urban dimension of this Games but their significance within wider processes of development taking place within the city of Beijing, in its region and in the People's Republic of China as a whole. London 2012 was a Games in which the prospect for regeneration of a deprived and environmentally blighted area of East London was as much part of the bidding process as the image of an inclusive and spectacular Olympic festival. Using data that include perspectives from resident surveys, Chapter 19 provides an opportunity to take stock of the event process, its legacy and the future planning of the Olympic park and its environs. From their critical review of the emerging legacy experience, the authors argue for the importance of continuing longitudinal analysis of the Olympic project.

The two remaining chapters look ahead to Games that are yet to be held. Rio de Janeiro, the latest addition to the family of Olympic Cities and the first city in South America to have received an Olympics, remains in the late stages of site and infrastructural preparation. Chapter 20 charts the history of urban change in Rio, examines the different Olympic bids the city has prepared in the last two decades, and analyses the preparations and their impacts 6 years after the Olympic nomination. It ends by attempting to answer recurrent questions that still hang over the event. The final chapter looks even further ahead to Tokyo 2020. Drawing on the insights available from an academic observer and former politician who was part of the bid team, Chapter 21 surveys Tokyo's history as an Olympic city. It notes the importance of the 1964 Games in the city's development, especially in acting as a catalyst for the reshaping of transport networks. After outlining the plans for the 2020 Games and the progress to date, the author ends in a manner that provides the perfect finale for this book; namely, what are the larger purposes of Olympic-inspired improvements, what visions are they are serving, and how they might act in transforming Tokyo and Japanese society as a whole.

Notes

1. See Matsumoto (1996, p. 20) on the significance of losing face for Japanese society. In passing, it is worth noting that Zaha Hadid strenuously denied the accusations that her design was not within the budget that had been set.

2. Munich, like Beijing wishing to be the first city to host both the Summer and Winter Games, had already withdrawn after the proposal failed to win public support in a referendum. For more information, see Coates and Wicker (2015).

3. For a selection of a large and rapidly-growing literature, see Thornley (2012), Graham et al. (2013), Thompson et al. (2013), Davis (2014), Gold and Gold (2015), and Nichols and Ralston (2015).

4. For more on the nature of 'growth coalitions' and their influence, see Andranovich et al. (2001), Kearins and Pavlovich (2002), Zhang and Wu (2008), and Boykoff (2014).

5. The term 'mega-event' was first used in 1987 at the 37th Congress of the Association Internationale d'Experts Scientifiques du Tourisme in Calgary in 1987 (Müller, 2015b, p. 2).

6. Practices clearly identified at many points in this book: inter alia, see Chapters 6, 10, 19 and 20.

7. For further information and contrasting perspectives, see Swart and Bob (2004), Vigor et al. (2004), Shipway (2007), O'Bonsawin (2010), Minnaert (2012), and Noland and Stahler (2015).

8. Originally based on http://gladstone.uoregon.edu/~caer/ej_definitions.html.

9. It is important to distinguish this commonly applied aphorism for the Olympics from the 'World Games', a multi-sport event staged at four-yearly intervals since 1981 by the International World Games Association and covering sports not represented in the Olympics, such as billiards, netball, surfing and body-building. These aspire, as yet unconvincingly, to equal or even exceed the importance of the world championships that are organized individually by each individual participant federation.

10. Source papers relating to the contents of this book can be found in the four-volume set, The Making of Olympic Cities (Gold and Gold, 2012).

11. While recognizing the recent creation of youth editions of both the Summer and Winter Games – the former in 2010 (Singapore); the latter in 2012 (Innsbruck) – these much smaller events are not yet considered within the scope of this book. For more information, see Judge *et al.* (2009), Parry (2012) and Parent *et al.* (2015).

Part I

The Olympic Festivals

Chapter 2

The Enduring Enterprise: The Summer Olympics, 1896–2012

John R. Gold and *Margaret M. Gold*

Yet let us all together to our troops,
And give them leave to fly that will not stay;
And call them pillars that will stand to us;
And, if we thrive, promise them such rewards
As victors wear at the Olympian games.

William Shakespeare[1]

Knowledge about the Olympics and its significance for ancient Greek society had never fully faded from European consciousness despite the centuries that had elapsed since the Roman Emperor Theodosius I prohibited the festival in 393 AD. Shakespeare's matter-of-fact reference to the Games shows that the Olympic idea 'was a shared, not isolated reference' in the arts throughout Western Europe (Segrave, 2005, p. 22); indeed, the Olympics were 'probably the one' among the 'incalculable influences of the Greeks in the modern world … of which the general public [were] the most aware' (Littlewood, 2000, p. 1179). Much the same applied to Olympia, the place with which the Games were associated. As the English theologian and antiquarian Richard Chandler (1766, p. 308) remarked, its name would 'ever be respected as venerable for its precious era by the chronologer and historian', for whom:

> [it] had been rendered excessively illustrious by the power and reputation of its ancient princes, among whom were Œnomaus and Pelops; by the Oracle and temple of the Olympian Jupiter; by the celebrity of the grand *Panegyris* or general assembly held at it; and by the renown of the *Agon* or Games, in which to be victorious was deemed the very summit of human felicity. (*Ibid.*, p. 303)

Yet despite its lasting reputation, no one was certain as to Olympia's exact whereabouts. Despite being indicated on maps since 1516, when the Venetian cartographer Battista Palnese referred to it as 'Andilalo',[2] the passage of time meant that 'Olympia has since been forgotten in its vicinity' (*Ibid.*, p. 308).

Matters changed in the 1770s when travellers ventured to the Peloponnesus on the west coast of Greece, then an obscure corner of the Ottoman Empire, in search of this important place. For example, towards the end of a trip in 1776 sponsored by the Society of Dilettanti, Richard Chandler and his companions took local advice as to where Olympia might have been. There was little immediately apparent on arriving at the spot that had been indicated. Two earthquakes had levelled the buildings, already in ruins, in the sixth century AD (Fellmann, 1973, p. 109). Periodic flooding by the two rivers (Cladeos and Alpheios) that meet there had subsequently deposited a layer of alluvium several metres thick. Yet despite the site appearing 'almost naked', closer inspection revealed some wall footings and a massive capital from a Doric column that had recently emerged from the river mud. The latter, Chandler correctly inferred, was a fragment of the Temple of Jupiter (Zeus). He made further deductions about a depression occupied by a pestilential pool: 'At a distance before it was a deep hollow, with stagnant water and brickwork, where, it is imagined, was the Stadium' (Chandler, 1766, p. 308). From these fragments, Chandler provided a mind's eye account of classical Olympia, drawing on ancient descriptions to outline the grandeur of buildings, temples and stadium that had made this 'no inconsiderable place'.

Chandler attached no special significance to these observations within his travelogue, but the rediscovery of the site brought new waves of visitors. Surveys carried out for Lord Spencer Stanhope in 1807 revealed an imposing complex replete with temples, gymnasia, stadium, hippodrome and accommodation (Stanhope, 1824). Noticeably, Stanhope's account extended to the ruined city of Elis, the prime settlement of the *polis* in which the festival site was located, and recognized the links between the two. Adopting a similar approach to his subject matter, William Leake (1830, I, pp. 23–44) described Elis as the 'place of ordination and preparation for the *athletæ* of the Olympic Games' (*Ibid.*, II, p. 220) and the point from which participants set out in procession to traverse the 22 miles (36 kilometres) to Olympia. The journey, complete with ceremonies of ritual purification *en route*, took place before the start of each Games (see also S.G. Miller, 2003, p. 9). The complex of permanent structures at Olympia also contained buildings that served the Elis-based civil government's need for political administration rather than having religious or sports functions (Crowther, 2003; see also Drees, 1968). These were early and intriguing recognitions of the close relationship between host city and Games.

Understandably, discovery of the ruins prompted campaigns for archaeological work since, as Leake (1830, I, p. 44) observed, 'there is every reason to believe that the most interesting discoveries in illustration of the arts, language, customs and history of Greece, may yet be made by excavations at Olympia'. The first fruits of those campaigns were small-scale digs by English and then French archaeologists in the early nineteenth century, but these aroused Greek sensitivities about removal of artefacts. The third set of excavations, however, proved decisive. Licensed by the Greek Parliament after negotiations between the Greek and German governments to ensure that artefacts did not leave the country, excavations between 1875 and 1881 by a team from the Imperial German Archaeological Institute provided systematic analysis of the core of the site and vital insights as to its usage (Kyrieleis, 2003). Progressively, a picture emerged of a venue sufficiently intact to evoke not just the layout of a complex with a 210-yard (192-metre) running track and designated buildings but also to allow free rein to the imagination as to the activities associated with this place (Perrottet, 2004).

The reports coming from the excavations aroused excitement beyond archaeological circles. Historians and other scholars eagerly devoured news emerging from Olympia and reflected on the mystique of the Games and the place of sport in classical Greek society. Their interest was not simply antiquarian, since many saw the achievements of the past as offering parallels for the modern age. For example, in a public lecture Sidney Colvin, the Director of Cambridge University's Fitzwilliam Museum, enthused over the new archaeological findings, but wistfully remarked that:

> It has been said that Englishmen and ancient Greeks are much like one another in two respects. One is their ignorance of all languages except their own, and the other is their love of physical sports. We have our Epsom and our Grand National, our games of cricket and football, our rowing and our running matches, and we despise Frenchmen and foreigners, generally, with the most impartial disdain; but somehow we don't make of our athletic sports so much as these ancient Greeks did. (Colvin, 1878, p. 7)

Colvin primarily had in mind the link between sport and art, seeing the Games as bridging the sacred and secular and creating a vital exemplar for contemporary cultural life. Others also felt that the ancient Games *per se* had an important ethos that might be revived and recaptured. Their model was that of a peaceful yet competitive sporting festival which brought nations together notwithstanding the pressures of a turbulent external environment.

This chapter provides a review of the principal phases in the development of that festival, as expressed in the evolution of the Summer Games. It opens by discussing the revival of the modern Olympics, before providing an overview of the intricate history of cities staging the Summer Games from Athens 1896 through to the most recent Games in London in 2012 (see table 2.1). We then identify six phases in the development of the relationship between the city and the Games. The first (1896–1906) traces the way that the nascent Olympics narrowly survived negative associations with the fairground, with two sets of Games held in Athens a decade apart offering a more positive path forward that intimately involved city and stadium. The next phase (1908–1936) saw local Organizing Committees

Table 2.1. Cities bidding for the Summer Olympic Games, 1896–2020.

Games	Year awarded	Host city	Other candidates
1896	1894	Athens	London
1900	1894	Paris	
1904	1901	St Louis★	Chicago
1908	1904	London★★	Berlin, Milan, Rome
1912	1909	Stockholm	
1916	1912		Berlin, Alexandria (Egypt), Budapest, Cleveland, Brussels
1920	1914	Antwerp	Amsterdam, Atlanta, Brussels, Budapest, Cleveland, Lyon, Havana, Philadelphia
1924	1921	Paris	Los Angeles, Atlantic City, Chicago, Pasadena, Rome, Barcelona, Amsterdam, Lyon
1928	1921	Amsterdam	Los Angeles
1932	1923	Los Angeles	
1936	1931	Berlin	Barcelona, Buenos Aires, Rome
1940	1936		Tokyo, Helsinki, Rome
1944	1939		London, Athens, Budapest, Lausanne, Helsinki, Rome, Detroit
1948	1946	London	Baltimore, Lausanne, Los Angeles, Minneapolis, Philadelphia
1952	1947	Helsinki	Amsterdam, Chicago, Detroit, Los Angeles, Minneapolis, Philadelphia
1956	1949	Melbourne	Buenos Aires, Chicago, Detroit, Los Angeles, Mexico City, Minneapolis, Montreal, Philadelphia
1960	1955	Rome	Budapest, Brussels, Detroit, Lausanne, Mexico City, Tokyo
1964	1959	Tokyo	Brussels, Detroit, Vienna
1968	1963	Mexico City	Buenos Aires, Lyon, Detroit
1972	1966	Munich	Detroit, Madrid, Montreal
1976	1970	Montreal	Los Angeles, Moscow
1980	1974	Moscow	Los Angeles
1984	1978	Los Angeles	Tehran
1988	1981	Seoul	Nagoya (Japan)
1992	1986	Barcelona	Amsterdam, Belgrade, Birmingham, Brisbane, Paris
1996	1990	Atlanta	Athens, Belgrade, Manchester, Melbourne, Toronto
2000	1993	Sydney	Brasilia, Beijing, Berlin, Istanbul, Manchester, Milan, Tashkent
2004	1997	Athens	Buenos Aires, Cape Town, Istanbul, Lille, Rio de Janeiro, Rome, San Juan, St. Petersburg, Seville, Stockholm
2008	2001	Beijing	Bangkok, Cairo, Havana, Istanbul[SL], Kuala Lumpur, Osaka[SL], Paris[SL], Seville, Toronto[SL]
2012	2005	London	Istanbul, Havana, Leipzig, Paris[SL], Madrid[SL], Moscow[SL], New York[SL], Rio de Janeiro
2016	2009	Rio de Janeiro	Baku, Chicago[SL], Doha, Madrid[SL], Prague, Tokyo
2020	2013	Tokyo	Baku, Doha, Istanbul[SL], Madrid[SL]

Notes

★ The nomination was originally to Chicago.

★★ The nomination was originally to Rome.

[SL] Short listed.

Source: Partly based on Buchanan and Mallon (2001).

(OCOGs) devote ever-increasing resources to preparing stadia and associated facilities. By the time of the 1936 Berlin Games, the Olympics had started to gain a consensual content with ingredients broadly replicated by each succeeding festival, although remaining an event that gave the home nation scope to mould the associated spectacle according to its own needs. After the Second World War and a brief series of lower-key events framed by Austerity (1948–1956), the Olympics witnessed, and benefitted from, growing acceptance of the economic importance and general promotional significance of the event for the host cities. The years from 1960–1976 saw host cities view the Olympics as catalyst for initiating major infrastructural and related works; a period that ended with the misfortunes of Montreal 1976. After an interlude when the Games became dominated by late-Cold War ideological issues with rather less attention to regeneration (1980–1984), the success of the strategies introduced at Los Angeles 1984 and Barcelona 1992 heralded a new phase of commercialism and regeneration programmes (1988–1996). The final section deals with the four Summer Games of the twenty-first century (2000–2012). These found cities actively competing to host a festival justified in terms of sustainability and then legacy, starting with Sydney 2000's attempts to stage a 'Green Games' and ending with London 2012's clear emphasis on post-Olympic legacy.

Revival

The idea of appropriating the title 'Olympic' had long appealed to organizers of sporting events (Redmond, 1988; Buchanan and Mallon, 2001). Robert Dover, described as an 'English captain and attorney' (Anon, 1910, p. 453), established a 'Cotswold Games' on his estate in 1604, largely as a protest against Puritan proscriptions of sporting pastimes and other apparent frivolities (Mandell, 1976, p. 29). The festival that contemporary writers described as 'Mr Robert Dover's Olimpick Games upon the Cotswold Hills' included 'cudgel-playing, wrestling, running at the quintain, casting the ball and hammer, hand-ball, gymnastics, rural dances and games, and horse-racing, the winners in which received valuable prizes' (Anon, 1910, p. 453). The Cotswold Games lasted until 1644, although were briefly revived during the reign of Charles II, with a separate 'Olympics', largely devoted to dog racing, occurring at Hampton Court Palace in 1679.[3]

During the first half of the nineteenth century, a series of separate initiatives consciously sought to use Olympic sport to cement nationalist or pan-national aspirations. The Scandinavian Olympic Games of 1834 and 1836, founded at Ramlösa (Sweden) by the sports educator Gustav Johan Schartau, were designed as national festivals for the 'strong sons of Scandinavia' (Øresundstid, 2003). The Anglophone community in Montreal staged an Olympics in 1844 to assert their identity against the Francophone majority. The influential Much Wenlock Games, founded by Dr William Penny Brookes, grew from an initially limited affair to subsequent grander aims. Founded in October 1850 and still held annually, they aimed 'to promote the moral, physical and intellectual improvement of the inhabitants of the Town and neighbourhood of Wenlock' (WOS, 2006). Gradually, Brookes's vision expanded, most notably assisting the establishment of a National Olympian Association (NOA) in the 1860s. This eventually foundered, particularly due to opposition from the Amateur Athletic Club – an aristocratic and elitist group founded in 1866 to counter the NOA. Nevertheless, during its brief lifespan the NOA stimulated a brief flowering of athletics events in British cities, including the London Olympics – which attracted 10,000 spectators to Crystal Palace between 31 July and 2 August 1866 (Jefferys, 2014).

Understandably, there was considerable interest in reviving the Olympics in Greece. Having achieved political independence in 1830, groups within the country campaigned to restore the Games as a symbol of their re-emerging nationhood (see Chapter 17). In 1859, an Olympic sports festival took place in Athens, assisted by sponsorship from Evangelis Zappas, a wealthy expatriate Greek landowner living in Romania (figure 2.1). The so-called 'Zappas Games', held again in 1870 and 1875, constituted a different scale of competition and spectacle than other events previously styled as 'Olympian'. The 1870 meeting, for example, attracted 30,000 spectators to watch Greek athletes compete in the partially restored Panathenian stadium.

Historians, however, show considerable selectivity in relation to these events.

Figure 2.1. Statue of Evangelis Zappas, situated outside the Zappeion, the building named in his honour and used for the fencing competitions at the Athens 1896 Games.

Official versions of Olympic history typically styled them as 'pseudo-Olympics' (Redmond, 1988): interesting as expressions of the desire to create prestige sporting competitions, but not representing progenitors of the revived Games as developed by the IOC under Baron Pierre de Coubertin's leadership.[4] This selectivity had an ideological purpose since, by emphasizing the originality of Coubertin's vision and downplaying the contribution of others, it privileged the IOC's claims for ownership of the Games. The traditional treatment of the personal relationship between Pierre de Coubertin and William Penny Brookes is a case in point.[5] Historical accounts recognize that the two men actively corresponded and that Brookes had staged a special Autumn version of the Wenlock Games in Coubertin's honour when he visited England in October 1890, which featured award ceremonies and pageantry that greatly impressed Coubertin (Young, 1996, p. 78). The 1866 London Olympics, by contrast, received no mention in official Olympic histories; nor do Brookes's speeches in which he proposed an international basis for the Games and advocated that they should have a permanent home in Athens (Young, 1998, p. 31; Toohey and Veal, 2000, p. 29). Brookes, therefore, emerged as the organizer of a small rural sporting festival rather than one of the lynchpins of the Games' revival.

The ideological dimension was even stronger in the disparagement of Greece's attempts to reinstate the Games. Downgrading the significance of the Zappas Games denied approval to any proprietorial claims by Greece to the revived Olympics, even though they were clearly based on a classical festival held on Greek soil for almost 1,200 years. In one sense, this ran counter to the mood of the times which favoured folk revival and saw collectors scouring the margins of Western nations in a nationalistic search for the 'authentic' roots of folk culture (Gold and Revill, 2006). Instead, the founders of the Olympics perceived their task as resuscitating an event that represented the quintessence of ancient cultural achievement to which Western civilization in general, rather than the late nineteenth-century Greek state, was heir (Christensen and Kyle, 2014). That outlook, in turn, imbued the modern Olympics with an internationalist stance, able continually to move to new host cities without loss of purpose, rather than needing to return permanently to Greece as a geographic hearth that would give the revived Games authenticity. Ceding control to the Greeks would have interfered with the freedom of action to pursue that policy.

Yet recognition of alternative precursors scarcely detracts from the importance of Coubertin's role in campaigning for the revival of the Olympics and subsequently for his influence on the Games' early development. Commentators (e.g. Mandell, 1976; MacAloon, 1981) rightly identify Coubertin's contribution as a reformer who gradually moved beyond specific concern with promoting sports education within France as a medium for fostering national regeneration to addressing the 'democratic and international' dimension of sport. On 25 November 1892, his speech at the Sorbonne in Paris exhorted a somewhat sceptical audience to aid 'this grandiose and salutary task, the restoration of the Olympic Games' (quoted in Müller, 2000, p. 297).[6] Coubertin repeated his exhortation, with greater success, at an international Sports Congress that he organized in 1894, which supported the re-establishment of the Games and laid down key principles for organizing them.

To summarize its recommendations, the revived Olympics would reintroduce the ancient Games' 4-yearly cycle, but would be ambulatory rather than based at a permanent site. They would be open to amateur sportsmen and should comprise modern rather than classical sports, although there was no definitive list of which sports to include or exclude. The Games would also have a cultural dimension that was intended to be co-equal with sport. For Coubertin in particular, the modern Games would take on the ethos of the *panegyris* from the classical festival – a festive assembly in which the entire people came together to participate in religious rites, sporting competitions and artistic performance. To recreate this characteristic in a modern idiom represented a considerable challenge, but Coubertin felt that much could be done, first, by adding ceremonies to dignify the Games and so provide some continuity with the past, secondly, by creating festivities to accompany the Games and, thirdly, by introducing artistic competitions as part of the Olympic programme. To help codify these ideas, the Congress initiated the process of constructing a Charter of 'fundamental principles, rules and by-laws' to run the Games, normally known as the Olympic Charter. Central to its outlook was 'Olympism', a humanistic philosophy that mediated the cultural construction of the revived Games and guided the development of the supporting ceremonial content that subsequently accumulated (see Chapter 4). Finally, it founded the IOC to control the movement and to select the host cities, although local Organizing Committees would plan the Olympics.[7]

The first two Games were scheduled for Athens in 1896 and Paris in 1900. Both locations were pragmatic choices (Young, 1987, p. 271). The Congress accepted the inevitable by recognizing that Athens's symbolic associations made it the only city that could effectively launch the modern Olympics, in spite of wanting to resist Greek claims to ownership of the Games and having given serious consideration to London in view of its advantages regarding access and venues. The choice of Paris for 1900 reflected Coubertin's hope to capitalize on the International Exposition (World's Fair) taking place that year and to draw spectators to the newly established Games.

Surviving the Fairground (1896–1906)

The first distinct phase of development saw a sequence of four Summer Games, in which the fortunes of the Olympics fluctuated profoundly. Athens 1896 proceeded against a difficult political and economic background that made preparations problematic and led to the first airing of a perennial question: should money be spent on the Olympics as a prestige project in light of competing needs? In this instance, one side, led by Prime Minister Charilaos Tricoupis, argued against the Games for economic reasons; the other, led by Opposition leader Theodorus Delyannis and supported by the monarchy, sympathized with the Games as a prestigious project that might reflect well on Greek identity and international standing (MacAloon, 1981, p. 182). The latter camp won the day, with the necessary finance raised through a mixture of public funds, appeals for subscriptions, private sponsors and the first special issue of Olympic postage stamps (*Ibid*., p. 196; see also Chapter 6).

Athens 1896 set an early pattern of low expenditure, pressing into service the existing Zappeion Building and the restored Panathenian stadium, with new construction restricted to a velodrome, shooting gallery and seating for the swimming events (Davenport, 1996, pp. 4–5; Gordon, 1983). This policy posed some problems. The Panathenian stadium, for instance, successfully held crowds of more than 50,000 and accommodated a modern running surface, but its traditional elongated horseshoe shape with accentuated curves at each end, hindered athletic performance (figure 2.2). Nevertheless, the revived festival worked well. The

Figure 2.2. The Panathenian stadium, Athens during the 1896 Olympic Games.

Games, symbolically opening on Greek Independence Day (6 April), attracted 245 athletes from fourteen countries to compete in forty-five events. The Opening Ceremony filled the stadium, with the spectators that occupied the surrounding hillsides and streets swelling the audience to an estimated 80,000–120,000.

The city beyond the stadium readily embraced the Games. The Athenian authorities decorated the streets, illuminated the Acropolis and arranged an entertainments programme that included torchlight processions, parades, fireworks, a concert by the Athens Philharmonic Orchestra and a performance of Sophocles's *Antigone* (Mallon and Widland, 1998). The marathon, introduced for the first time, added spectacle, provided a link with tradition[8] and supplied an important, if invented, symbol. Spectators lined the route through the Greater Athens region and filled the stadium to see the finish. Its popularity, enhanced by the victory of a local man, Spiridon Louis, not only brought a new fixture to the athletics calendar,[9] but also served to provide a focus that stressed the unity of city and Olympics.

Although small by contemporary standards, the 1896 Games showed that the modern Olympics had considerable potential as a coherent framework for a new international festival. By contrast, the two succeeding Games came perilously close both to derailing the Olympic movement and to downgrading the relationship between host city and Games to inconsequentiality. In both cases, the reason lay in the conflict between the nascent Games and larger, more important International Expositions. At Paris 1900, the connection between the events was the conscious, if misguided policy of associating the second Games with the 1900 Paris Exposition Universelle. Coubertin believed that the Olympics could capitalize on the Fair's many visitors and festive backdrop and, in particular, wanted to build a replica of Olympia, with temples, stadia, gymnasia and statues and an archaeological display.[10] The organizers, however, remained unmoved by this idea. Disputes over the control of the sporting element resulted in the Olympic movement effectively withdrawing, with a new committee appointed to plan the Exposition's Games (Mallon, 1998, p. 6). The Olympics became an International Games rather than a true Olympics. They were of indeterminate length given that they lacked Opening or Closing Ceremonies and that the organizers haphazardly added events to the programme, some of which, like fishing in the River Seine (Harlan, 1931, p. 88), did not conform to Olympic standards. Indeed some competitors in tournaments connected with the Exposition never realized that they had actually entered Olympic competitions. For example, Michel Theato, the marathon winner, only learned in 1912 that he was the 'gold medallist' at the 1900 Olympics (Mallon, 1998, p. 9).

Compared with the considerable impact that the Exposition had on Paris – with a 543-acre (219-hectare) fairground located in the heart of the city in the Avenue Alexandre III and the Bois de Vincennes – the Olympics scarcely registered a presence. Only thirteen nations competed and few bothered to send representative teams. The Games received no publicity as they were regarded as a sideshow to the Exposition and, not surprisingly, competitors often outnumbered spectators (Rogan and Rogan, 2010, p. 27). There was no stadium or running track. The track and field events were held at the Racing Club of France's grounds in the Bois de Bologne, but the owners refused permission to remove any trees. As a result, discus and javelin throws often landed in wooded areas. The 500 metre (546 yard) grass running track sloped and undulated. Rigid former telegraph poles served as hurdles. The organizers hastily constructed a grandstand, but a row of trees obscured the track from spectators (Howell and Howell, 1996). Wholly overshadowed by the Exposition, the movement that had shown 'so much promise in 1896 seemed to have collapsed by 1900' (*Ibid*., p. 17).

The next Summer Games at St Louis proved equally inimical to the revival of the Olympics. The IOC had strongly backed selection of a North American city and chose Chicago in May 1901 to stage the 1904 Games. Spoiling tactics by the organizers of St Louis's Louisiana Purchase International Exposition, however, led the IOC reluctantly to revise that decision even if it was inevitable that the Olympics 'would only be a sideshow attraction to the much larger international exposition' (Barnett, 1996, p. 19). Their fears had justification. The Exposition itself brought considerable kudos to St Louis, created an extensive fairground from the wooded Forest Park, and allowed much needed improvement works to the erstwhile heavily polluted and flood-prone Des Peres River. By contrast, the Olympics left little trace. There was at least a stadium, capable of seating 10,000 spectators, although with a one-third mile (536 metres) track instead of the standard quarter-mile circuit of the time, and 'something approaching' an Opening Ceremony on 14 May 1904 (Mallon, 1999a, p. 11). The programme, however, supplied little sense of continuity, with sporting competitions held at irregular intervals through to November, with scarcely any distinction between 'Olympic' sports and other competitions. The organizers added sports of their own choosing such as college football (gridiron), local cross-country championships, professional events, the national championships of the American Athletic Union of the United States, and 'automobiling' (Anon, 1904, pp. 3, 48). In addition, the festival was tarnished by the infamous 'Anthropology Days' (12–13 August 1904) when African, Asian and Native American competitors competed in racially motivated athletic contests that denigrated their performances and gave succour to theories of white supremacy (Brownell, 2008). Following hard on the heels of the 1900 debacle, St Louis 1904 threatened the continuance of the modern Olympics (Barnett, 1996, p. 23).

In the event, it took a sporting festival not usually reckoned as part of Olympic history – the 1906 Intercalated Games held in Athens – to secure the future (Young, 1996, p. 166; Mallon, 1999b, p. 5). This was the first, and only, product of a tactical compromise made in 1897, when a Coubertin-inspired initiative offered Greece the opportunity to hold a series of Intercalated Games at 4-yearly intervals in non-Olympic years. Greece's defeat in the first Greco-Turkish War (1897) had left the country bankrupt and unable to initiate the series (Daven-port, 1996, p. 10), but improved economic circumstances allowed the staging of an Intercalated Games in 1906. This returned to the Panathenian stadium, with more extensive and eye-catching rituals and accompanying festivities than those staged in 1896. The sporting festival once more spilled over into the city, in a manner that contrasted with the experience of Paris and St Louis. The streets and buildings of Athens were again decorated, the city's squares staged evening concerts and there was a sustained programme of entertainments. The international press was more in evidence than at previous Games, although the eruption of Mount Vesuvius (4 April) and the San Francisco earthquake (18 April) detracted from the coverage that the Games received (Mallon, 1999b, p. 6). Nevertheless, the Intercalated Games effectively rescued the Olympics from its disastrous flirtation with the fairground and initiated a period in which host cities actively welcomed the Olympic Games as a premier and prestigious sporting event that merited purpose-built facilities.

Olympics by Design (1908–1936)

Just as the Vesuvius's eruption detracted from the coverage of the Athens Intercalated Games so, arguably, did it put pay to its successor as the severe strains that recovery from the devastation placed on the Italian economy led to Rome abandoning its attempt to hold the 1908 Games.[11] In November 1906, the IOC formally confirmed its transfer to London (Mallon and Buchanan, 2000, p. 3). With just 20 months in which to prepare the Games, the OCOG decided to use existing venues in the London region wherever adequate facilities were available. Hence, *inter alia*, the tennis competitions were held at Wimbledon, polo at Hurlingham and shooting at Uxendon School Shooting Club and Bisley Rifle Range. Nevertheless, the organizers also decided to seek a purpose-built stadium where most of the Olympic competitions and ceremonies could take place; a strategy that broke with the practice of the previous Games.

Its construction was facilitated by developing a partnership with the Franco-British Exhibition of Science, Arts, and Industry, held to celebrate the recent Entente Cordiale between the two nations, which was due to open in the summer of 1908. This arrangement seemed at first glance to pose precisely the same threat of eclipsing the Games as at Paris 1900 and St. Louis 1904. That this did not happen was due largely to the 1908 Games being both organizationally and spatially separate from the International Exhibition. Organizationally, they were firmly under the control of sports interests, in the shape of the newly-formed British Olympic Association. Spatially, they gained distinctiveness from having a separate stadium. The Franco-British Exhibition, then under construction on a 140-acre (56-hectare) plot of former agricultural land and brickfields at Shepherd's Bush (West London), had included plans for entertainments to be staged at a small stadium with spectators standing on a surrounding mound. Under the new agreement, the Exhibition Organizing Committee agreed to develop this prototype into a full-blown stadium in return for 75 per cent of the Olympics' proceeds.[12]

The largest stadium of its day, its enormous concrete bowl enclosed athletics and cycle tracks, a 100 metre swimming pool, platforms for wrestling and gymnastics and even archery. Dressing rooms, restaurants and emergency services were located under the stands (figure 2.3). The foundation stone of the White City stadium, so-called because the Exhibition Buildings were finished in gleaming white stucco, was laid on 2 August 1907 and the stadium was inaugurated on the opening day of the adjoining Exhibition (14 May 1908). It held 93,000 spectators, with 63,000 seated. A newly opened station at Wood Lane, on an extension of the Central London Railway from its terminus at Shepherd's Bush, supplied both the Exhibition and Olympics with direct connections to central London.

London 1908 left a considerable positive legacy for the Olympic movement by developing the spectacle of the festival and supplying the basis for 'a compact and independent Olympic festival' (Wimmer, 1976, p. 22). Yet while it allowed the Games to prosper as an event in its own right, London 1908 also provided the less

Figure 2.3. The White City stadium, Shepherd's Bush, London, 1908.

desirable physical legacy of a huge and largely unwanted stadium. Although the initial intention was to demolish the stadium and provide 'no permanent addition to the athletic grounds of London' (Anon., 1907), its continued existence after 1908 made it arguably the first instance of the 'limping white elephants' associated with the Olympics (Mangan, 2008).[13] It remained scarcely used for two decades before passing to the Greyhound Racing Association in 1926. The stadium was then renovated, with its capacity reduced from 93,000 to 80,000, installation of a greyhound track over the existing running track, and removal of the cycling circuit and the defunct swimming tank (Hawthorne and Price, 2001, p. 7; Jenkins, 2008). In 1932, the reconfiguration of the running track to a new 440-yard (402-metre) circuit allowed the stadium's use for national and international athletics events. On occasions, the White City staged large-scale sporting festivals, such as the 1934 British Empire Games and the 1935 International Games for the Deaf, and provided a base for British athletics from 1933 onwards. However, when the athletics events moved to their new home at Crystal Palace in 1971, the stadium languished before eventual demolition in 1985 to make way for offices for the British Broadcasting Corporation and housing.

The 1912 Games in Stockholm saw the Olympics move to a far smaller city.[14] Partly as a result, the Stockholm OCOG found it easier to create a festival that integrated city and stadium. The design of the latter, built in the grounds of Royal Djurgården (Zoological Gardens), assisted that aim. More modest than the White City, it seated 22,000 people, with stands arranged around a 400-metre running track (figure 2.4). From the outset, it was intended to be multipurpose, a decision that Coubertin applauded:

The Gothic Stadium … seemed to be a model of its kind. You could see it turned into a banquet hall, a concert hall, or a dance hall, and yet on the following morning always

Figure 2.4. The American team entering the stadium during the Opening Ceremony of the Olympic Games, Stockholm, 1912.

ready once again for carrying on with the contests. You could see how in a single night it got covered with ready-made squares of lawn, how hurdles were being put up, and how it decked itself with blossoming brushwood for the riding tournaments. All this was achieved without any ado, any delay, any blunder. While in London it had proved impossible for the life of the great city to be in any way affected by the proximity of the Olympic Games, Stockholm turned out to be thoroughly imbued with them. The entire city participated in its efforts to honour its foreign guests, and one had something like a vision of what the atmosphere must have been like in Olympia in the ancient days ... (quoted in Wimmer, 1976, p. 27)

The stadium's evening entertainments included military concerts, displays of Scandinavian sports, gymnastic displays, fireworks and illuminations. The city provided street decorations, opera, theatre, a two-day aquatic festival, the usual round of receptions and banquets, and played reluctant host to the artistic competitions that were a cherished part of Coubertin's vision of linking sport and the arts. For the first time, too, the organizers took steps to publicize the Games internationally, through the Olympic movement, the Swedish diplomatic service and advertisements in national newspapers of other countries. The makings of the promotional activity that typified later Olympics Games had started to emerge.

The next Games took place 8 years later. Hidebound by its observance of the 4-year cycle of Olympiads despite the inconvenient reality of the First World War, the IOC retained the fiction of a sixth Olympiad in 1916. In the still non-belligerent USA, six cities (Chicago, Cleveland, Newark, New York, Philadelphia and San Francisco) had offered to act as hosts to avoid disrupting the series, but the IOC maintained that it had awarded Berlin the right to stage the 1916 Olympics and could not withdraw a nomination without that city's agreement. As the German Olympic Committee remained adamant that Berlin held the nomination, the sixth Olympiad was never held and the Games resumed their 4-year cycle with the seventh Olympiad in Antwerp in 1920.

Awarded at an IOC meeting in Lausanne in April 1919 as much as a political act of moral support for Belgium than as a sporting event, Antwerp 1920 utilized the quickly renovated Beerschot stadium. Shortage of resources and materials meant that the standard of facilities was much poorer than at Stockholm, with constant rain leaving the running track pitted and rutted. A canal at Willebroek near Brussels, used for the rowing events, provided an industrial setting so ugly that Coubertin called it 'anti-Olympic' (Renson, 1996, p. 57). There were few associated festivities in the city. Yet despite the austerity, Antwerp 1920 recorded a deficit of 626 million Belgian francs, prompting accusations of acute financial mismanagement and leaving the organizers accused of treating the event as 'a symbol of conspicuous consumption' (*Ibid.*, p. 59).

The responsibility of consolidating the progress made at London and Stockholm therefore passed to the OCOGs of the two ensuing Games. Paris 1924 represented the first occasion on which the growing prestige of the Olympics led to serious international competition among cities to act as hosts. Four American cities (Los Angeles, Atlantic City, Chicago and Pasadena) and five European (Rome, Barcelona, Amsterdam, Lyons and Paris) expressed interest in staging the Olympics (Welch, 1996, p. 61). The return to Paris proceeded with assurances that, unlike 1900, the organizers would treat the Olympics as an important international event. Rather than employ the Pershing stadium, which staged the 1919 Inter-Allied Games,[15] the Organization Committee decided in June 1922 to construct a purpose-built stadium at Colombes. The Stade Olympique Yves-du-Manoir had seating for 20,000 spectators, standing room for an additional 40,000 (*Ibid.*, p. 64) and would remain the main venue for national soccer and rugby matches until the opening of the Parc des Princes in 1972. Paris 1924 saw the birth of the concept of the Olympic Village at Rocquencourt (see Chapter 8), although the barrack-like accommodation with few services had 'very little to do with what was to be the first Olympic village' at Los Angeles 1932 (Muñoz, 1997, p. 30). Paris also witnessed the first significant dissatisfactions about the growing size of the Games, given that the scatter of the Olympic venues around the Paris region necessitated long bus journeys for most competitors.

Amsterdam 1928 favoured the now familiar idea of clustered Olympic sites. Although the athletes were housed on ships in the harbour rather than in a specially constructed Village (Goldstein, 1996), the Dutch employed Pierre de Coubertin's cherished ideal of a 'Cité Olympique' to bring the stadium and associated facilities together in a sporting complex. The new athletics stadium, built on reclaimed marshland, had seats for 40,000, with the other venues having a capacity of a further 30,000. The open-air swimming pool was located next to the main stadium

Figure 2.5. Water polo competition in progress, the Olympic Pool, Amsterdam, 1928.

(figure 2.5), with adjacent gymnasia for boxing, wrestling and fencing. Concerns were again expressed about the growing size of the Games, although the target was now the 'excessive festivities', with proposals that there should be reforms to allow only those that 'the reception of authorities and officials demanded' (Organizing Committee, 1928, p. 957).

The two final interwar Games completed the Summer Olympics' evolution into a high-status international festival that would play an important part in the lives of host cities. Los Angeles 1932 was an Olympiad conceived in the American boosterist tradition, resolutely advancing the city's economic and cultural interests against rivals. The city gained the right to stage the 1932 Olympics in 1923, but faced severe funding problems in the wake of the 1929 Wall Street Crash, with the federal government refusing to contribute. The Games' survival rested on the city issuing bonds and capitalizing on connections with the private sector, most notably the film industry which actively promoted the Olympics. Yet perhaps the key to encouraging participation lay in making the Games affordable to competitors by assisting travel and in constructing the first true Olympic Village, an innovation that combined economy with the spirit of Olympism.[16] The Official Report of the Games (TOC, 1933, pp. 235, 237) waxed lyrical about the symbolism of the Village and intermixing of peoples, to the extent that the observers recommended the Organizing Committee for the Nobel Peace Prize for their work in promoting the fellowship of the Games through the nations' athletes living peacefully side-by-side (Stump, 1988, p. 199; see also Chapter 8).

With the assistance of substantial subsidies for food and accommodation, 1,500 athletes from thirty-four nations competed at Los Angeles 1932 despite the vicissitudes of the international economy. Apart from the auditorium for the indoor competitions, most of the stadia were at Olympic Park (the former Exposition Park). The Memorial Stadium, the last Olympic arena to use the old-fashioned modified U-shape (Wimmer, 1976, p. 39), was created by refurbishing and enlarging the Coliseum into a venue with a seated capacity of 105,000. The swimming stadium and the State Armoury, which staged the fencing competitions, were built nearby. The Olympic Park also housed the Los Angeles Museum of History, Science and Art, which held more than 1,100 exhibits from the thirty-two countries that supplied entries for the Olympic Art Competition. The organizers added another important innovation by coordinating the decoration of the Olympic venues and the city using streamers and bunting in the official colours of blue, yellow, black, green and red. Flags of the competing nations, Olympic banners and large insignia hung across the main streets. The organizers also encouraged the owners of buildings and businesses to buy specially manufactured materials to embellish their buildings.

Despite the economic environment, the Games achieved an enviable operating surplus, with 1.25 million people paying $1.5 million to watch events over the 16 days of the Games. Tourist agencies put together packages featuring the Olympics and the scenic attractions of southern California. Sixty-two conventions were attracted to Los Angeles, enabling their delegates to enjoy the Games and further boosting the local economy (TOC, 1933, p. 215). A visiting journalists' programme catered for several hundred reporters from around the world in the 3 years leading up to the Games (*Ibid.*, p. 211); a strategy that maximized the possibility of favourable coverage. Not surprisingly, the 1932 Games left the city eager to repeat the exercise, with repeated candidacy before the Olympics finally returned in 1984 (see below).

Berlin 1936, the final Summer Games before the Second World War, was a landmark in political as well as sports history. The background to the Berlin Games, as Chapter 13 shows, resonated with German history in the interwar period. Berlin, the host city, bid unsuccessfully for both the 1908 and 1912 Games, had seen the cancellation of the 1916 Games for which it held the nomination, and saw its further ambitions placed in abeyance until Germany was readmitted to the Olympic movement in time for the 1928 Games in Amsterdam. In May 1931, the IOC awarded the 1936 Games to Berlin as an act of reconciliation, but the choice proved problematic with Hitler's rise to power. The Nazis' initial hostility to the financial burden and avowed internationalism of the Games seemed likely to bring rapid cancellation, but subsequent reappraisal of the classical origins of the Games to align them with National Socialist ideas of German origins[17] quickly brought enthusiastic support. This led to concern within the Olympic movement that the Games would be hijacked by the Nazi leadership for propaganda purposes (Hart Davis, 1986).

Certainly the creation of the stadium, the surrounding complex and other Olympic venues proceeded with wider ideological and propaganda goals in mind. As Chapter 13 shows, the regime vetoed Werner March's original plans for

Figure 2.6. Aerial view of the Reichssportfeld, Berlin, 1936.

expansion of the 1913 stadium, already approved by the IOC, favouring instead a proposal for a 110,000-seater stadium with a steel- and stone-clad structure. The stadium would lie at the heart of the Reichssportsfeld, soon to become the world's largest sports complex, complete with swimming and diving pools (with seating for 18,000), facilities for lawn tennis, hockey, equestrian sports, the House of German Sports (Deutschland Halle) for boxing, fencing, weightlifting, wrestling, the Reich Academy of Physical Education, accommodation for female competitors and the Maifeld Parade Ground (figure 2.6). Located in a peripheral area of Berlin but well connected into the city's U-bahn rail system, the site became the focus of attention throughout Germany in the period leading up to and including the Games for a regime that relished and mobilized the opportunity for powerful spectacle. Berlin was specially decorated throughout the Games and codes of behaviour issued to present the best possible impression to visitors, with careful concealment of explicit aspects of racial policies. After the Games, the city and state gained the infrastructural legacy of a sports complex and parade ground that could be used for military purposes and for future National Socialist celebrations.

Austerity (1948–1956)

The bidding process after 1945 revived the pattern set in the interwar period. American cities, with their ingrained city rivalries, featured prominently, with formal bids for the 1948 Games from Baltimore, Los Angeles, Minneapolis and Philadelphia as well as informal interest from several other potential US contenders. There was a feeling, however, that the United States was too far away for affordable travel in these austere years (Voeltz, 1996, p. 103). Therefore, after conducting a postal ballot, in 1946 the IOC officially awarded the Fourteenth Summer Olympics to London.[18]

The next 2 years proved far more difficult economically than the British had anticipated when agreeing to host the Games, with few surplus resources available (Holt and Mason, 2000, pp. 27–29). The organizers quickly abandoned any idea of laying on stunning spectacle and custom-built stadia in favour of employing existing sports facilities. Mild renovation of existing facilities saw the Empire Stadium at Wembley, originally built for the 1924 British Empire Exhibition, become the Olympic Stadium, with the adjacent Empire Pool staging the swimming events. Although both venues needed conversion and repair, along with a new approach road to link the stadium to Wembley Park railway station, the costs were borne by Wembley Stadium Ltd rather than by the state – as with 1908 for a share of the proceeds (Hampton, 2008, p. 29). Royal Air Force accommodation at Uxbridge, a convalescents' camp in Richmond Park, Southlands College in Wimbledon, and convenient school premises provided bargain basement substitutes for an Olympic Village. Other venues pressed into service included the Herne Hill Velodrome (cycling), Bisley (shooting), Henley-on-Thames (rowing) and the more distant Torbay (yachting). The organizers borrowed sports equipment from the Armed Forces or from manufacturers on a lend-and-return basis. The Board of Trade adjusted rationing regulations for participants and new Tourist Voucher Books made it easier for foreign visitors to spend money in British shops.

Despite the difficulties, there were tangible and intangible non-sports legacies from London 1948. The city was not *en fête* as Berlin or Los Angeles had been, but the Games undoubtedly lifted the mood of postwar Britain and recorded a profit of £30,000. The city's hotels enjoyed bumper visitor numbers (Holt and Mason, 2000, p. 31). The nation also received the morale-raising experience of hosting a premier international event and temporary respite from the greyness of Austerity. Yet the main legacy from London 1948 was again for sports. Admittedly, there were few tangible outcomes given the lack of purpose-built facilities or associated infrastructural improvement. By contrast, in intangible terms London 1948 successfully relaunched the Games after the traumas of war, drawing the highest-ever attendance figures for an Olympics. In return, the Games sowed the seeds of important change for British society through sports development. They eroded the long-established notion that participation in such sports was the preserve of gentlemen amateurs (Hampton, 2008, p. 318). In addition, they indirectly played a catalytic role in developing disability sport. As Chapter 5 shows, the archery competition held on the front lawns of Stoke Mandeville Hospital on 28 July 1948 – the same day as the Opening Ceremony of the London Olympics – is widely accepted as the first competitive sporting event for seriously disabled athletes. This symbolic event also marked the start of the process of convergence that would see London 2012, like other aspirant twenty-first century host cities, bidding to stage the Olympic *and* Paralympic Games rather than just the former.

The two succeeding Games followed London's low-key approach. Helsinki

Figure 2.7. Olympic stadium, Helsinki, 1952.

had held the nomination for the Twelfth Summer Olympics in 1940, after the Japanese withdrew, and had built a stadium, swimming and diving arena, and a competitors' village in anticipation of that event. The organizers renovated and expanded the sporting facilities for the 1952 Games (figure 2.7), with the aid of a $1.25 million grant from the Finnish government but, as noted in Chapter 8, the Olympic Village posed greater problems. The one originally constructed at Käpylä, 3.7 miles (6 kilometres) from the city centre, had long since been converted to public housing. The increased size of the Games required new accommodation not just at Käpylä, but also at two new sites, Otaniemi and Töölö. The situation was further complicated by the Soviet Union's demands for a separate village for the socialist bloc's athletes (Hornbuckle, 1996, p. 117). In response, the organizers allocated the Otaniemi site to the USSR and its allies, placing competitors literally as well as figuratively into two ideological camps.

Melbourne 1956 was the last Summer Olympics developed under conditions of postwar financial stringency. The city's bid document for the Games (MIC, 1948) projected an image of a prosperous, developed and well-equipped 'city of culture', with the promise of a new Olympic stadium complex on the banks of the Yarra River east of the Melbourne Cricket Ground (MCG). Once Melbourne won the Games, the organizers decided to reduce costs by modifying the MCG and restricting construction of major new buildings to the swimming pool and velodrome. Available spaces at the local university, museum, art school and public library were employed to display the four associated art exhibitions – on architecture, painting, graphics and literature. The Olympic Village was built as a cheap housing project in the suburb of Heidelberg, using the existing system of government loans. These buildings, however, presented so many subsequent construction and social problems that the Games might well have been 'a force for urban degeneration rather than regeneration' (Essex and Chalkley, 1998, p. 194).

Catalyst (1960–1976)

Although important for their host nations, the financially straited 1948–1956 Games made little lasting impact on the Olympic cities. By contrast, Rome 1960 propelled the Games into the modern era (Telesca, 2014). The city's Olympian aspirations stretched back many years. Rome, as noted above, initially held the nomination for the 1908 Games and, under Mussolini, had lobbied hard for the right to stage the 1940 Olympics. Indeed, Rome 1960 effectively capitalized on two districts developed by the Fascist regime with international festivals in mind. The first, the Foro Italico in the north of the city, already offered two imposing arenas: the Stadio dei Marmi, built in 1932, and the Stadio Olimpico, built in 1936. The second district was EUR, so-called because it was initially designed to supply a spectacular setting for the cancelled 1942 Esposizione Universale di Roma – itself dubbed the *Olimpiadi della Civiltà* (the Olympics of Civilization) (Casciato, 2015, p. 29). Located to the south of the city, it was only partially developed before the Second World War, but its monumental and spacious qualities made it an ideal place for the core of the Olympic facilities. These included the Palazzo dello Sport (Sport Palace), the Velodrome, the Piscana delle Rose (swimming pool) and the Fontane Sports Zone training area. Ten other venues were scattered throughout the city, with several using sites with classical associations to underline the Games' pedigree. The vaults of the Basilica of Maxentius built in 303 AD, for instance, housed the Greco-Roman and free wrestling contests, while the Caracalla Baths (217 AD) staged the gymnastics.

These 'Olympic areas' made a permanent contribution to the city's sporting and cultural life. The Village at Campo Paroli provided private sector housing (Wimmer, 1976, p. 202; see also Muñoz, 1997) and the city also gained from infrastructural improvements undertaken with the Games in mind. These included new roads and bridges built to connect the Village to the main Olympic sites, modernization of the airport, improvement of the telephone, telegraph and radio networks, and initiatives to expand hotel accommodation. The Rome Olympics also had a major impact on financing the Games. Core funding came from the Italian soccer pools, the Totocalcio, but now supplemented for the first time by sales of television rights. Broadcasters had refused to pay for rights at Melbourne, arguing that covering the Games was akin to televising news and should be similarly free to the broadcaster. The organizers of the Rome Olympics, however, managed to convince the major television networks that the Games were a proprietorial commodity for which payment was necessary. The American Columbia Broadcasting System (CBS) paid

$600,000 for US television rights, with Eurovision subscribing another $540,000. It marked another significant step towards realizing the economic potential of the Games and ensured that, when leaving aside wider infrastructural improvements, the Rome Olympics ran at a profit.

Tokyo 1964 followed Rome's example by embarking on major redevelopment projects before the Games, merging the specific proposals for the Olympics into the city's 10-year development plan. Aiming to cater for Tokyo's infrastructural needs up to the year 2000, the combined works cost $2.7 billion. They included road improvements, comprising a remarkable system of grade-separated highways that employed verticality to maximize traffic flow within narrow spaces (c.f. Gold, 2012), the birth of the Shinkansen high-speed 'bullet' trains, housing, hotel developments, harbour improvements, a monorail system, water supply, sewage disposal and a public health programme (Essex and Chalkley, 1998, p. 195; see also Chapter 21). The city had thirty Olympic sites, with thirteen major facilities concentrated in three districts: the Meiji Olympic Park, which contained the Olympic Stadium; the Yoyogi Sports Centre, which housed the swimming competitions; and the Komazawa Sports Park. Accommodating participants in six Olympic Villages ensured, at least in principle, that competitors and officials had no more than a 40-minute journey to reach their venues (Organizing Committee, 1966, p. 114). Hoteliers received grants to remodel their premises for Western tourists, with a further 1,600 visitors lodged on ships in Tokyo harbour. Importantly, Tokyo saw the introduction of an approach concerned with the 'look' of a city during the period of the Olympic festival. This represented more than the old approach of simply decking the city in flags, but instead saw conscious attempts to unify the disparate sporting and Olympic infrastructure into a cohesive whole through design of signage, dressing the venues and decorating the streets. As a result of an open competition, the Japanese designer Yusaku Kamekura won a contract to provide visually consistent designs for all the ephemeral elements of the Games – symbols, signs, pamphlets, posters, tickets, decorations and even the colour scheme used for the city and at Olympic venues (Yew, 1996, p. 176).

The 1968 Games in Mexico City saw Latin America, and more specifically a developing nation, host the Olympics for the first time. Set against a background of political tension and sports boycotts, the Olympics stretched Mexico's resources and contributed to domestic unrest in the months leading up to the Games. The organizers' approach was to use existing sports facilities and blend them with new venues by means of a common 'look', in the manner pioneered by Tokyo, to supply a sense of visual unity (see Chapter 14 for details). Despite troubled beginnings, Mexico City 1968 finished with a favourable balance sheet. Costing $175 million, much of which was expended on facilities with a lifespan that extended well beyond the festival, the Olympics were considered to have covered their costs. For some observers, the 1968 Games represented an important moment of achievement and harmony for the Mexican nation that fully justified the cost (e.g. Arbena, 1996), but others argued that money diverted into the Olympics had exacerbated the divide between Mexico City's rich and poor. Before the Games, for example, the city chose to transfer $200 million from the social services budget to city improvement projects in an elaborate urban and national re-imaging campaign. Not only did this have a detrimental long-term impact on the city's provision for the poor; it also prompted protest demonstrations that left no less than 325 dead (Lenskyj, 2000, pp. 109–110).

The ability of the Olympics to polarize opinion would escalate steadily over the next decade. In their different ways, Munich 1972 and Montreal 1976 created crises for the Olympic movement: the former due to problems over security and the latter finance. Initial planning for both events, however, proceeded unproblematically with an upbeat view that emphasized the Olympics' apparently risk-free character; seemingly guaranteeing host cities advantageous international attention and endless prospects for undertaking urban development. Partly because of this mood, the 1970s Games were lavish affairs, with huge expenditure on iconic facilities and distinctive urban quarters.

The return of the Olympics to Germany in 1972 inevitably raised the spectre of 1936. The powerful militaristic and nationalist images still associated with that Olympics encouraged the Munich organizers to stage a 'Carefree Games' (Organizing Committee, 1972, p. 28). Their bid to the IOC emphasized Munich's claim to embrace international and modern cultures; a rich hearth of 'the arts and Muses' that offered four orchestras, twenty-three museums and seventeen theatres (*Ibid.*, pp. 24, 28). At the same time, Munich in the early 1970s was in the throes of rapid economic and demographic growth, with severe pressures on services and physical infrastructure. Preparation for the Games, therefore, also addressed the host city's broader planning goals, aligning Olympic developments with schemes designed to restore and pedestrianize Munich's historic centre, to improve and extend public transport, construct 145 miles (233 kilometres) of expressways, provide underground parking, and build new retail and hotel accommodation (Essex and Chalkley, 1998, p. 195).

The location for the new Olympic Park in the north of the city was a derelict area long earmarked for redevelopment. Originally flat, its surface was bulldozed into a gently rolling landscape, with a hill created from wartime rubble and a small lake formed by damming the Nymphenburg Canal. The organizers then placed the athletes' warm-up facilities, the swimming pool and many smaller sports venues, a theatre, restaurants, the Olympic Village, press centre and stadium around the lake. The 80,000-seater Olympic stadium was an innovative tent-roofed structure designed by Gunter Behnisch and Frei Otto. The Olympic Village, which housed 10,000 athletes, was designed for legacy conversion into a 'self-sustaining' community for single people and middle- and lower-income families – groups who found it difficult to find accommodation in the city (Essex and Chalkley, 1998, p. 195; Organizing Committee, 1972, p. 125). Trams, an underground rail line and a rapid transit provided physical links between the complex and the city centre. Symbolic links were added by attention to the 'look' of the city.

Coordinated by a German designer Otl Aicher, the city adopted a holistic design policy towards decorations for the city, venues and orientation of visitors. Besides choosing colours felt to resonate with Olympic values, the dominant colour of blue was chosen to symbolize peace with the 'aggressive' colour red deliberately avoided (Organizing Committee, 1972, p. 269; Yew, 1996, p. 213).

Viewed in organizational and financial terms, the Twentieth Summer Games were critically regarded as a success. They generated a working profit, with marketing and television rights producing over $12 million for the IOC and international federations. Munich and Bavaria gained lasting publicity benefit (Brichford, 1996, p. 151). Other aspects of their legacy proved more difficult. Despite the efforts to promote the 'carefree' theme, Munich 1972 brought the Olympics face-to-face with the realities of security. The massacre of Israeli athletes and officials on 5 September effectively destroyed the OCOG's attempts to stage a light-hearted, non-nationalistic Olympics. It also ensured that future host cities faced a bill for security measures of a wholly different order, recognizing the Olympics' new, and unwanted, status as a prime target for international terrorism (see Chapter 9).

The ensuing Games were a landmark for the extent that they were ill-conceived and poorly planned. Although intended as a 'modest Games', Montreal 1976 produced a final shortfall of $1.2 billion, primarily caused by cost overruns on over-ambitious buildings. Admittedly, the times were not propitious. The Games took place against a background of severe world recession and inflation that profoundly affected costings, especially those concerning the surfeit of transport infrastructural projects associated with the Olympics. Nevertheless, a large measure of the blame rested with the counterproductive machinations of the political regime led by Jean Drapeau and the flawed architectural design of the Olympic complex, particularly the stadium. The organizers ditched the notion of providing an orthodox open-air Olympic stadium in favour of a design that might be used all-year round. As the Olympic movement would not countenance a covered stadium for athletics, it was decided to build a new stadium with a retractable roof – understandably at much greater cost (Killanin, 1983, p. 123). The chosen design by the French architect Roger Taillibert, architect of the critically acclaimed Parc des Princes in Paris, exacerbated the problems by embracing an unmistakeable monumentality. Most notably, it featured an innovative system for opening and closing the roof involving a 575 foot (190 metre) tower, inclined at 45 degrees, which supported the roof on twenty-six steel cables (figure 2.8). This radical conception produced problems that plagued construction. In fact, the infamous roof was not completed until 1987 and quickly became unusable. It was an episode that eventually led to a stadium with an impressive observation tower and a non-retractable roof.

Other buildings contributed their share of problems. Difficulties with subsoil meant the velodrome needed new foundations to support its roof (Organizing Committee, 1976, pp. 16–17). The adjacent Olympic Village lodged participants in four architecturally innovative ziggurat structures, around nineteen storeys high at their tallest points, which proved difficult to service. Among the infrastructural

Figure 2.8. Olympic stadium, Montreal 1976 (architect Roger Taillibert).

investment projects was the remote, expensive and unnecessary international airport at Mirabel, which closed three decades later without ever achieving any useful function. In addition, labour problems caused the loss of 155 working days in the 18 months leading up to the Games. Lack of proper operational planning and failure to sequence the construction process led to delays and bottlenecks. Round the clock working was introduced at great expense to meet the Games deadline, but it still proved impossible to complete all the facilities. In May 1976, emergency work began to erect temporary installations for several sports rather than continue with the intended venues. It all contributed to an event that inevitably presented a 'kaleidoscope of contradictory narratives and outcomes' (Kidd, 1996, p. 153).

Ideological Games (1980–1984)

The 1980 and 1984 Summer Games were essentially rival Olympics, staged by two superpowers as indicators of the superiority of their ideological systems, but which left less mark on their host cities than the Games of the previous two decades. Moscow and Los Angeles were the only candidates for the 1980 games and Los Angeles was the sole formal bidder for 1984 after the withdrawal of a half-hearted bid from Teheran. With an eye to the lessons of the Montreal Games, both OCOGs made virtues out of economy and pragmatism. Both would also have to cope with political boycotts orchestrated by their superpower opponents. The USA led a boycott of Moscow 1980, as part of a package of measures taken in response to the Soviet intervention in Afghanistan. This reduced participation to eighty competing nations compared with 121 at Munich and even ninety-two at boycott-hit Montreal, with many other nations sending weakened teams. Not surprisingly, a Soviet-led tit-for-tat boycott of Los Angeles 1984, ostensibly over the security of athletes and officials, saw fourteen socialist countries miss those Games. These Cold War gestures, however, only materialized in the final weeks before these Games and, therefore, did not materially impinge on the plans made by the host cities for staging their respective Olympics.

The OCOG for Moscow 1980 made much of rejecting the recent trend towards gigantism that had left behind expensively maintained and underused sports facilities. Rather they 'sought efficiency', building only 'essential' installations that would 'not remain monuments to vanity' but would be 'in constant use for the benefit of the Soviet People' (Organizing Committee, 1980, p. 43). They therefore planned to use Moscow's existing sports facilities wherever possible, employing temporary grandstands and ensuring that any new structures would be designed as multi-purpose venues. The main ceremonies and the track and field competitions, for example, centred on the renovated Lenin Stadium (built originally in 1956).

Given the nature of the command economy, the authorities subsumed preparations for the Olympics into the city's planning strategy (the General Plan for the Development of Moscow 1971–1990) and the state's tenth Five-Year Plan of Economic and Social Development. The former adopted decentralist principles, dividing Moscow into eight functional zones, each with a population of between 600,000 and 1.2 million and their 'town public centres' and subsidiary centres, to achieve a 'balance between labour resources and employment opportunities' (Lappo *et al.*, 1976, pp. 138–140). The Olympics provided the opportunity to improve access to sporting, cultural and entertainment facilities for those living within these zones by designing new venues for use once the Games were over (Promyslov, 1980, p. 230). The main Olympic facilities were distributed into six main areas, with the Village in a seventh. Located in the south west of the city, the Village comprised eighteen blocks, each sixteen storeys high, arranged in groups of three with associated communal catering facilities, entertainment, shopping and training facilities. After the Games, the Village would become a self-contained neighbourhood complete with cultural and sporting facilities (*Ibid.*, pp. 245–246; see also Chapter 8). This dispersal posed logistic problems, but there was little need for new road construction given the low levels of private car ownership at this time. Infrastructural improvement was primarily confined to building new media centres and renovating the city's three airports, with a new international terminal added to Sheremetyevo Airport. The authorities also renovated historic buildings (especially churches), planted trees, and commissioned new hotels, cafés and restaurants. In a distant echo of Berlin 1936, Moscow was unusually free of banners expressing party slogans, posters and even the legendarily flinty guides working for Intourist desisted from propaganda during the Games (Binyon, 1980).

Notwithstanding the rhetoric of virtuous utilitarianism, the regime could not resist the urge to display Soviet technological expertise in designing large structures. This contributed to the organizers commissioning the world's largest indoor arena in north Moscow for the basketball and boxing competitions. Capable of seating up to 45,000 spectators, it could be used either as a single space or divided into two separate auditoria, allowing it to serve as a multipurpose space for sports, political and cultural events after the Games (Promyslov, 1980, pp. 236–237).

Like Moscow, Los Angeles sought economy in staging the Games, with the organizers' commitment to funding the Games without the public funds available in the USSR resulting in an event that added fine-tuned commercialism to cost-consciousness. This meant using volunteers wherever possible and making maximum use of existing facilities. The Los Angeles Memorial Coliseum was refurbished as the Olympic stadium, with just four new venues required – for rowing, cycling, swimming and shooting. Each attracted high levels of sponsorship. The McDonald's Swim Stadium, for example, was built in Olympic Park for the University of Southern California. The Southland Corporation, parent company of the 7-Eleven chain of convenience stores, funded the velodrome on the California State University site. Fuji Film sponsored the shooting range. The three Olympic Villages used sites on university campuses (University of California, Los Angeles; University of Southern California; and the University of California, Santa Barbara), with the accommodation later available for students (Burbank et al., 2001, pp. 76–77). This emphasis on named sponsorship and private finance introduced a measure of commercialism that the Olympic movement felt powerless to resist at that time. Rather more serious perhaps was the lack of intimacy caused by using existing facilities scattered around the sprawling, car-based Los Angeles city region rather than creating a nucleated Olympic Park. Some effort to create a sense of place came from decking the city in standardized colours to create a 'festive federalism' (Yew, 1996, p. 288), although it was recognized that only so much could be achieved by design.

Where Los Angeles 1984 scored most heavily was its success in changing ideas about Olympic finance. Los Angeles's commercial approach dramatically altered the prospects for other prospective host cities. The Games made a profit of $225 million that was channelled into American sports bodies and programmes. Local universities gained major new facilities. The event injected an estimated $2.4 billion into the Southern Californian economy.[19] After the events of the 1970s, the act of being host to the Olympics was fully restored as the pinnacle of ambition for cities with global aspirations.[20]

Shifting Horizons (1988–1996)

Seoul's decision to seek the 1988 Games was less inspired by that logic – which had yet to re-emerge when the city gained the nomination in 1981 – than by the success of Tokyo 1964, which the Koreans believed had altered perceptions of the Japanese and helped Japan join the ranks of the developed world in the cultural, social, diplomatic and economic fields. The Games would provide a positive context for international scrutiny, show the economic transformation and political progress within Korea, and establish dialogue with Communist and non-aligned nations, even though there was a real risk of terrorism or international conflict from continuing tensions with North Korea. It also provided an opportunity to regenerate Seoul. The South Korean capital faced severe environmental, economic and demographic problems for which staging the Olympics seemed to offer a means to short-circuit the process of replanning and reconstruction.

The organizers concentrated the Olympic facilities in the Seoul Sports Complex, built in the Chamshil area on the south bank of the Han River around 13 kilometres south of central Seoul, with another six venues at the Olympic Park, just over 3.5 kilometres to the east. The South Korean government had originally commissioned the Seoul Sports Complex in 1977, when the country lacked the facilities even to host the Asian Games. The 145-acre (59-hectare) site contained a major stadium, which became the 100,000 capacity Olympic stadium, as well as a 50,000-seater venue for the exhibition sport of baseball. The complex was linked to the Olympic Expressway, which connected the airport with Seoul's downtown. The Olympic Park provided the venues for the cycling, weightlifting, fencing, tennis, gymnastics and swimming events. The Athletes' Village comprised blocks of flats of various heights (6–24 storeys) clustered in groups around common open spaces. In total 5,540 units were built, which were sold after the Games as private housing for upper middle-income families (Kim and Choe, 1997, pp. 197–198). During the construction of the Park, the discovery of the earthen walls of a fortress from the Baekje Kingdom (18 BC–660 AD) led to the designation of a historic park within the master plan (*Ibid.*, p. 208; also see Yoon, 2009).

Beyond the Olympic Park, the authorities conducted a programme of repairing historic monuments, including palaces and shrines, tree planting, and improvements to streets, drainage and power supply. Two new urban motorways linked the airport to the Olympic sites and improved east–west traffic flows in the city. The authorities built new Metro lines and expanded the airport. Seoul's planners instigated the Han River Development Project, which combined anti-flood measures, water treatment for the heavily polluted river, habitat regeneration and the creation of a series of recreational areas. Temporary measures that applied for the duration of the Games included encouraging dust-producing firms along the marathon route and around Olympic venues to switch to shorter working hours or night-time operation, and advising public bath houses to take holidays on days of key events.

The strategies chosen to improve the city's built environment and infrastructure, however, drew international criticism for paying greater attention to urban form than social cost. Ideas of improvement centred on the removal of slums and the creation of modernistic, often high-rise, developments for high-income residential or commercial use. Traditional walking-scale urban forms (*hanoks*), built at high density with narrow streets and passageways, were bulldozed for commercial redevelopment. Laws covering preservation and conservation were not introduced until 1983 and, even then, only the oldest historic buildings with connections to the Yi dynasty benefitted. Clearance continued in areas without that historic cachet (Kim and Choe, 1997, pp. 209, 212).

Barcelona 1992 would take the regeneration theme further and supply a model that is a benchmark for prospective Olympic cities. Although still facing significant domestic security threats from Basque separatists and other groups (see Chapter 9), the Games took place against a political background of brief-lived optimism about the world order, with no boycotts and lowered security problems. In conditions that allowed the potential of the Olympics to act as a vehicle for urban development to shine through, Barcelona launched a challenging package of regenerative measures that countered years of neglect under the Franco regime (Maloney, 1996, p. 192). This was not an entirely new strategy. The city had used earlier international festivals to address urban planning goals, with the 1888 Universal Exhibition in the Parc de la Ciutadella to the east of the old medieval centre and the International Exhibition of 1929 on Montjuic to the west both resulting in urban improvements and enhancements to the city's cultural institutions, open space and transport (Hughes, 1996; see also Chapter 14).

The Olympics were seen in a similar light. Barcelona had previously bid to host the Games for 1924, 1936 and 1972. Selected at the IOC meeting in 1986 over Paris, the only other credible candidate, Barcelona's bid claimed that 88 per cent of the necessary facilities for the Games *per se* were already 'available'.[21] The Olympic Stadium was an updated and renovated version of that used for the 1929 International Exhibition. Ten other venues came from refurbishments to existing facilities, with forty-three other facilities used very much in their existing state (Essex and Chalkley, 1998, p. 198). The promoters emphasized that only fifteen new venues would be required. Altogether, only 17 per cent of the total expenditure for the 1992 Games went on sports facilities (Varley, 1992, p. 21), with the lion's share of the investment devoted instead to urban improvements. Barcelona's planners concentrated the Olympic facilities in four areas located in a ring around the city, roughly where the outer limits of the nineteenth-century city met the less structured developments of the second half of the twentieth century. These were: the Vall d'Hebron in the north (cycling, archery, and accommodation for journalists); the Diagonal (football, polo and tennis); the Montjuic (the major Olympic site including the 60,000-seater stadium, the Sant Jordi Sports Palace, and the swimming and diving pools); and Parc de Mar, which housed the Olympic Village (figure 2.9). Large-scale investment in the city's transport systems,

Figure 2.9. The Olympic Village, Barcelona 1992.

substantially stimulated by the Olympics, served to link sites together. The Metro system was extended, the coastal railway rerouted, the airport redesigned and expanded, and the telecommunications systems modernized (see also Brunet, 2009).

Barcelona 1992 codified the changing nature of the criteria by which to judge whether or not a Summer Games had been a success. The spectacle of the Games delighted the Olympic movement and television audiences were captivated by images from the outdoor pool, showing divers performing against the panoramic backdrop of the city beyond. Economically, the Olympic festival *per se* performed less well. Cost overruns ate into the projected $350 million surplus such that the Games barely broke even (a mere $3.8 million surplus). The innovative Sant Jordi Sports Palace, for example, may have supplied stunning architecture but cost $89 million rather than the estimated $30 million. Construction costs on the ring road were 50 per cent more than the estimated $1 billion. The Cultural Olympiad also spawned heavy losses, despite trading on Barcelona's rich heritage in the arts and architecture (Hargreaves, 2000, p. 106).[22] Inflation and adverse movements in foreign currency rates also severely increased costs. Unemployment rose by 3 per cent in the city immediately after the Olympics, prices soared and business taxes rose 30 per cent (Maloney, 1996, p. 193). Nevertheless, critical opinion remained highly positive with regard to the wider regenerative impact on Barcelona. The city had deployed the Games as part of a conscious long-term development strategy that existed before obtaining the nomination to stage the Olympics and continued afterwards. It represented a major transformation in the fortunes of Olympic cities just 16 years after the debacle of Montreal. Not surprisingly, therefore, Barcelona 1992 has had a lasting fascination for scholars and practitioners alike.[23]

Atlanta 1996, by contrast, would renew questions about staging the Games, particularly regarding commercialism. Unusually for Olympic practice, a private consortium undertook the organization, with heavy representation of and deference to business interests. Funding came from sponsorship, broadcasting rights and merchandizing which, when combined with ticket sales, raised $1.72 billion (Burbank *et al.*, 2001, p. 94). In addition, the federal government expended nearly $1 billion on infrastructure, housing, safety and security, with smaller amounts spent by the State of Georgia and the city (*Ibid.*, p. 116). Most of the spending on the Games and on infrastructure took place in central Atlanta's 'Olympic Ring' – an area around 3 miles (5 kilometres) in radius that contained sixteen of the twenty-five Olympic facilities and most of the urban improvements. The Atlanta Committee for the Olympic Games (ACOG) made use of existing facilities such as the Georgia Dome and Omni Arena, coupled with facilities at Atlanta's universities. The Georgia Institute of Technology, for example, provided sites for the Olympic Village, a new aquatic centre (swimming, diving and water polo) and boxing. ACOG commissioned a new but temporary Olympic Stadium in the Summerhill district in the south of the Olympic Ring. This was tied in with a longer-term plan to develop baseball in the city. The Olympic Stadium was located next to the Atlanta Fulton County Stadium, which was used for the baseball competition. Built to seat 85,000 spectators, the Olympic Stadium was scheduled for partial demolition after the Games to create a new 47,000-seater stadium (Turner Field) for the Atlanta Braves, with the Fulton County Stadium demolished to provide parking space (Larson and Staley, 1998, p. 281). Neighbourhoods near Olympic sites experienced beautification, with projects designed to improve central city streets and upgrade twelve pedestrian corridors that linked the venues. This work included widening pavements, burying power-lines, installing new street furniture, tree planting, history panels, signage, and the redesign of five parks and plazas.

Atlanta disappointed those who looked for more from the Games that marked the centenary of the modern Olympics. The conduct of the Games and the quality of ceremonial content led Tomlinson (1999, p. 69) to describe it as 'an elongated event of tattiness and tawdriness'. Concentrating so many facilities at the centre of the city placed pressure on the transport systems. Traffic congestion, slow journey times, and long queues to use the shuttle buses added to the difficulties for athletes, officials and spectators reaching venues (Larson and Staley, 1998, p. 278). The organizers' claims that Olympic sites were within walking distance of one another proved meaningless given the excessive summer temperatures. The repeated systems failures of the results service, the arrogance of officials, poor relations with the press, the large numbers of unauthorized street vendors, aggressive sponsorship and rampant commercialism undermined Atlanta's desire to stage a modern and efficient event. The city's policy towards regenerating two areas close to the Olympic sites encountered particular condemnation. One, the Techwood and Clark Howell public housing district to the south of the Georgia Institute of Technology, was demolished and replaced by a mixed gated

Figure 2.10. Centennial Park, Atlanta 1996.

community, effectively replacing poorer tenants with more affluent residents. The other, a rundown housing and industrial area near the Georgia World Congress Centre (GWCC), was cleared to create Centennial Park as an area where visitors and spectators could congregate during the Games and where entertainment could be provided (figure 2.10). Clearance here and in nearby Woodruffe Park removed more than 16,500 of Atlanta's poorest inhabitants to make way for the stadium. The additional loss of a hostel and three shelters displaced around 10 per cent of Atlanta's homeless (Burbank *et al.*, 2001, p. 112). Aggressive use of city ordinances that criminalized anti-social behaviour and measures to remove the homeless resulted in the physical eviction of 'undesirables' from the vicinity of the Games (Lenskyj, 2000, pp. 138–139).

The passage of time has eroded the force of some of these criticisms. For example, Atlanta's policy towards the stadium fully acknowledged the realities of post-Games use and spared the city from being saddled with expensive and underused venues, as was subsequently the case with Sydney, Athens, Beijing and, arguably, London. The central area was remodelled and Centennial Park stands as a memorial to the Games. The Olympics raised Atlanta's profile as a sporting and conference venue, even if it failed to enhance its broader image as a cultural centre. Nonetheless, the distaste for commercialism has persisted, with the IOC vowing that the Games would never again be entrusted to an entirely privately-run organization (Whitelegg, 2000, p. 814; see also Poynter and Roberts, 2009). Even a century after the revival of the modern Olympics, the formula for staging a successful event remained downright elusive.

Sustainability and Legacy (2000–2012)

Although chosen as Australian nominee for applicant city in March 1991, Sydney's bid for the Olympics had actually been in gestation since the late 1960s (see Chapter 16). The city drafted feasibility plans for both the 1972 and 1988 Games, with the latter envisaging an Olympic Park at Homebush Bay, approximately 9 miles (14 kilometres) upstream from Sydney's city centre. Originally tidal wetlands and scrub, Homebush Bay at different times had housed Sydney's racecourse, the country's largest abattoir, a saltworks, the state brickworks and a naval munitions store. In the 1930s, the bay had regularly spawned algal blooms through contamination from waste products from the slaughterhouses and from depositing household and industrial waste in landfill sites. Work had begun in the 1980s to clean up the area and some rehabilitation had taken place to create a nucleus for Sydney's suburban expansion (Cashman, 2008, p. 28), but a successful Olympic bid would help regenerate the remainder of the site, tackle its severe environmental problems, supply the city with a replacement for the Royal Agricultural Society's outmoded Showground at Moore Park, and provide a cluster of modern world-class sports facilities. Any bid would involve the state and federal governments as funding agencies and as the owners of the land, as well as the city of Sydney.

Sydney gained the nomination for the 2000 Games in September 1993 against competition from Beijing, Manchester, Berlin and Istanbul, with a key element in its candidacy being the promise to concentrate the Olympic venues in one central park, which would eventually have a built core surrounded by parkland. The main Olympic venue, named Stadium Australia, was built using public funds, sponsorship and sale of corporate packages. Designed to hold 110,000 spectators during the Games, its capacity would be reduced to 80,000 for its subsequent life as a rugby and Australian Rules football stadium. The other major stadia at Homebush were the Hockey Centre, Superdome (basketball and artistic gymnastics), International Athletics Centre (warm-up facilities), Tennis Centre, the Aquatic Centre (swimming and diving) and the Archery Park. The adjacent Olympic Village would accommodate all participants at a single centre for the first time. It comprised a mixed development of apartments and town houses, arranged in three precincts and designed to ecologically sustainable guidelines. Provision of a school and commercial precinct looked ahead to the area's post-Games future as a residential suburb of Sydney. The other Olympic facilities, particularly those associated with rowing and sailing, were located within the Sydney city-region at a maximum distance of 60 miles (100 kilometres) from Homebush Bay.

Planning for the Games embraced different agendas. First, responding to the growing mood of environmentalism, the bid claimed these would be a 'Green Games' expressing environmental responsibility in use of resources and design of facilities. Secondly, the Sydney Games were a national project, celebrating the 'entire continent of Australia' rather than just the host city: a strategy also adopted at Melbourne 1956. Thirdly, capturing the Games would allow the organizers to highlight the profound changes that had taken place in the 44 years since Melbourne, in particular the need for explicit recognition of the multicultural identity of Australia. The organizers of the Sydney Olympics in 2000, for example, were mindful of problems that arose at the Australian Bicentennial in 1988, when the celebration of European conquest had led to severe inter-communal frictions. Part of the adopted solution was to broaden the constituent basis of support for the Olympics, making efforts to gain the involvement of community leaders. Another element lay in seeking to change modes of representation, particularly with regard to tackling prevalent negative and stereotypic representations of Aboriginal peoples. Most notably, the Olympic Opening Ceremony commenced with an enacted encounter between indigenous and white Australians, emphasizing the antiquity of indigenous culture, its diversity, myths, legends and spirituality. The Aborigines emerged as environmentally-wise managers of the land, in contrast to the approach of what the Official Report described as the European period of 'vitality and violence' (SOCOG, 2000). Later in the ceremony, the Aboriginal athlete Cathy Freeman was selected to receive the relay-run Olympic torch and light the cauldron of the Olympic flame in the stadium.

One indication of the IOC's sense of relief at the success of the resulting Games came with the IOC President Juan Antonio Samaranch, resurrecting the statement that 'these have been the best Games ever', a description that he had pointedly omitted at the Closing Ceremony of Atlanta 1996. An early study of impact by the Australian Tourist Commission revealed that 75 per cent of the Americans surveyed had seen pictures and stories concerning Australia as a holiday destination as part of the Olympic coverage and half reported that they were more interested in Australia as a destination (Morse, 2001, p. 102). Locally, the Games passed off well. Potential demonstrations about homelessness, the plight of Aborigines, ticketing, and the claimed misuse of public funds did not occur. An economic analysis (Haynes, 2001) argued that the total cost of the Games at A\$6.5 billion was roughly neutral in that it was covered by an equivalent amount in extra economic activity in Australia between 1994–1995 and 2005–2006, of which A\$5.1 billion would accrue in New South Wales. For this price, Sydney had achieved the regeneration of a severely blighted industrial region, gained significant improvements to infrastructure, improved its tourist standing, and gained world-class sport facilities. For the Olympic movement, it again showed the value of a festival largely held at a nucleated venue rather than the dispersal of Atlanta.

The experience of Sydney 2000 continues to influence subsequent OCOGs, albeit sometimes in complex ways (Cashman, 2009). The Sydney Games retain a positive aura in terms of organization, friendliness and raising the profile of the city, but questions remain about aspects of the Olympic Park. Environmentalists have continued to question whether the decontamination of the toxic waste site had been fully tackled (Berlin, 2003). Critics note the lack of the promised affordable housing. The main stadia have had a chequered history. The Superdome, rebranded first as the Acer Arena (2006–2011) and then as the Allphones Arena, had no pre-agreed legacy use and initially languished before developing into a thriving and internationally recognized entertainments venue on the basis of a successful private–public partnership.[24] By contrast, Stadium Australia, first renamed the Telstra Stadium (2002–2007) and then the ANZ Stadium, has laboured to shake off the 'white elephant' tag, and continues to struggle against competition from the pre-existing modern stadia clustered in the Moore Park area of east Sydney (Searle, 2002, p. 857).

Above all, there were criticisms about the delays in producing a viable legacy plan. The Sydney Olympic Park Authority (SOPA), established in 2001 to plan and manage the Olympic Park, struggled to take stock of the situation, producing a sequence of three master plans between 2002 and 2008. These progressively lengthened the development timeframe of 7 to 10 years to a more realistic 22 years, increased targets for the 'daily population' from 5,000 to 50,500; and raised target levels for employment and visitors. SOPA also started to change its frame of reference. Although still responsible for a delimited area of suburbia, it variously described the embryonic settlement as 'an active, vibrant town within metropolitan Sydney' and, more ambitiously, 'a unique, world-class urban centre' (SOPA, 2014). The new settlement, now known as Newington, would be 'responsive to its context' and further the Olympic Park's 'initiatives in energy and water management [and] green building design' (SOPA, 2009). Mixed land-use and densification policies would seek to create a blend of residential and business activities that would 'activate the precinct on a 24/7 basis' (*Ibid*). The new street networks would be 'pedestrian friendly' and use of public transport would be enhanced by full integration into the Sydney Metropolitan system.

Uncertainties continue to cloud the legacy of Athens 2004, although any Games involving Greece inevitably involves circumstances unique to that country. As Chapter 17 shows, the reconstruction of Athens and the return of the Olympics were parallel themes in the consciousness of the Greek people during the nineteenth century and continued to have resonances in the late twentieth century. The city's successful bid in 1997 for the 2004 Olympics claimed that most of the competition venues and almost all the training venues were already in place, with the makings of an Olympic Stadium and Park in the complex already constructed for the 1982 European Athletics Championships. The subsequent decision to revisit the plans and make drastic alterations, in particular exchanging the nucleated Olympic centres for a more dispersed approach, undermined the timetable to the point where completion on time hung in the balance.

The immediate impact of the Games was a profound psychological boost for the country and agreement that tourism had benefitted from transformation of the city centre, creation of pedestrianized routes interlinking Athens's major archaeological sites, and investment in the city's hotels, cultural sector and, especially, public transport. Yet, as with Sydney, wider questions about sustainability quickly surfaced. In the narrower sense, critics focused on the way in which the environmental guidelines for the Olympics were, at best, perfunctorily observed. In the more

Figure 2.11. The Olympic Stadium and Park for the Athens 2004 Games, June 2009.

general sense of sustainable development, profound doubts surrounded the potential use of the Olympic facilities (see Chapter 17). Despite its architecturally sophisticated buildings being intended as a symbol of the new Athens, the Olympic Sports Complex at Maroussi remains heavily underused (figure 2.11), with the stadium only open to the public when concerts or soccer matches are being staged. The Faliro and Helleniki complexes have also struggled to find alternative uses. All have continued to lose money as borrowing and maintenance costs have still to be met. The evidence suggests that pre-Games plans for post-Games use of Olympic facilities contained a strong dose of wish fulfilment; a product of a lingering wish to have a comprehensive set of facilities available whenever the opportunity arose to stage further sporting mega-events.

Questions of how to turn the lavish and large-scale facilities required for the Summer Olympics into sustainable legacy, however, did not in any way daunt the organizers of Beijing 2008. Rebuffed by just two votes in 1993 in its candidacy for the Millennial Games, largely due to the recent memories of the 1989 Tiananmen Square Massacre and concerns over environmental issues (Poast, 2007, p. 76; also Gartner and Shen, 1992), Beijing decided in November 1998 to launch its candidacy for the 2008 Games. This time, its bid gained overwhelming support, achieving an absolute majority on just the second round of voting against opposition from Istanbul, Osaka, Paris and Toronto. The ease of its victory partly reflected memories of 1993, in which Beijing had led the voting in all rounds apart from the final run-off with Sydney, but the first bid had also served as a valuable learning process. The Chinese team carefully crafted a message that recognized 'the importance of considering what others might think of China and making adjustments to be sure that nothing offended' (Guoqi, 2008, p. 243). The bid team deftly promised an environmentally-friendly but 'high-tech' Games that would promote cultural exchange, act as 'a bridge of harmony' between peoples and embody the 'unique integration of sport and culture' intrinsic to Olympism (*Ibid.*, pp. 243–244). It effectively addressed key areas of dissatisfaction with the first bid and allowed the attractions of the site plan and other elements of the proposal to shine through.

Within days of the city's success in the bidding process, Beijing's municipal government unveiled an ambitious 5-year plan to modernize infrastructure, carry out urban regeneration and improve the environment (Broudehoux, 2004, pp. 200–201). While some of the estimated 180 billion yuan ($22 billion) expenditure would have been incurred anyway as part of the city's development plans, there is no doubt that the Olympics acted as a catalyst for a substantial part of this investment. In addition, a total of $14.25 billion was officially earmarked as funding for developing the sites for the Beijing Games, although as Brunet and Xinwen (2009, pp. 166, 169) note: 'the total investment catalysed by the Games is likely to be much larger – between $20 and $30 billion dollars – especially when the private sector contribution is added'. Modernization and development, however, rested substantially on urban clearance, with estimates in 2007 that at least 1.5 million people had been displaced to make way for Olympic-related developments (COHRE, 2007*a*).

In total, the Games required thirty-seven venues, of which thirty-one were in Beijing and the rest scattered elsewhere within the People's Republic of China (particularly for soccer and sailing) and Hong Kong (equestrianism). Of the venues within Beijing, twelve were newly built, eleven were renovated or extended from pre-existing structures, and eight were temporary sports facilities or related installations (such as the Media Centre). The main examples of architectural spectacle were among the seventeen venues clustered in and around the Olympic Park in the north of the city (He, 2008, pp. x–xiii). The new National Stadium served as the Olympic stadium and the setting for the Opening and Closing Ceremonies. Designed by the Swiss firm of Herzog and de Meuron in association with the Chinese office of Arup Associates, this oval-shaped arena seated 91,000 during the Games, with post-Olympics reduction to 80,000. Its nickname, the 'Bird's Nest', derived from its open lattice structure of interwoven steel trusses, which exposed glimpses of the interior to the outside (*Ibid.*, pp. 2–7). The National Aquatics Centre, situated to the east of the 'Bird's Nest', provided an equal measure of spectacle. Widely known as the 'Water Cube', its exterior covering of 3,000 irregularly-shaped, translucent, blue 'air pillows' provided a highly distinctive panorama when set against the background of the adjacent National Stadium (*Ibid.*, pp. 20–26).

In most respects, Beijing 2008 was a Games for the television audience, without the now customary carnival atmosphere in the streets provided by live entertainments and giant screens. The pre-Games Olympic torch relay proved a public relations disaster when it passed through countries willing to allow protests and occasional disruption by Free Tibet activists and other demonstrators. Once the relay came within the control of the Chinese authorities, however, such incidents disappeared. Viewers around the world joined the spectators in the stadia in witnessing the stunning and intricately choreographed Opening and Closing Ceremonies, albeit with television viewers of the former witnessing effects that were partly enhanced by overlayering of computer graphics.[25] Summarizers and analysts were routinely seen against the backdrop of the Bird's Nest and Water Cube – undoubtedly two of the most iconic structures ever produced for an Olympic Games. After the Games, these facilities have remained very much on the tourist trail, even if the initial signs suggest that their post-Games use is likely to be sparse enough to join the 'white elephant' category.

The legacy agenda in Beijing is overseen in part by the Beijing Olympic City Development Association (BODA) set up in 2009, this was more of an events and sport legacy body than a physical planning agency. While able to advise on 'city development policies and practices' (BOCOG, 2010, p. 300), it is not responsible for planning and directing development in the Olympic Park as in the case of comparable bodies for Sydney and London. Instead, planning is accomplished through the 5-year Beijing plans[26] and the overarching Beijing Master Plan (2005–2020). These plans increasingly envisage the cultural and creative sector as an important pillar of the Beijing economy and seek to promote clusters of activity. As such, they seek to maximize the use of the Olympic venues, boost the construction of new cultural facilities, develop the museum economy and improve the tourism service environment with the aim of creating a centre for international cultural, sporting and business events (NPC, 2011, p. 64).

Projects to realize these objectives began after the Games and still continue. The China National Convention Centre was fashioned out of the Fencing Hall, International Broadcasting Centre and Main Press Centre. The National Aquatics Centre accommodates public use alongside elite sport, along with convention, exhibition and theatrical spaces and retail, food and drink outlets. Investment in new museum and arts facilities include the China Science and Technology Museum and the National Art Museum of China, with plans for a China National Arts and Crafts Museum, and a National Centre of Chinese Traditional Culture. An Olympic Park Observation Tower in the north of the Park opened to the public in 2014.

Official statements that paint a picture of a solid Olympic legacy and vibrant Olympic Park contrast with the Western media's emphasis on 'rotting' and 'abandoned' Olympic venues (BBC, 2012; Engel, 2012). While the current state of some features do support the latter narrative (for example the kayaking, rowing, beach volleyball and baseball venues), the Olympic Green played a central role in Beijing's successful bid for the 2022 Winter Games. The 'Bird's Nest' will stage the opening and closing ceremonies, a National Speed Skating arena will be added along with a new Olympic Village (for sale as high-end housing after the Games). To an extent, the successful bid for 2022 validates the original concept that saw the Olympic Green as a focus that would allow Beijing to compete for international events.

London 2012, the most recent completed Games at the time of writing, was the first Summer Olympics to be awarded once the twin elements of sustainability and legacy were firmly embedded in IOC thinking. That dispensation was clearly articulated in the bid documents and was a powerful factor behind proposing that the prime location for Games would be in the lower Lea Valley at Stratford (East London) rather than in the west of the city (as for 1908 and 1948). In many ways, the reasons this area was available resembled those that applied at Homebush Bay. Long histories of accommodating noxious industries and acting as a dumping ground for toxic waste products had left substantial areas of dereliction and heavily contaminated brownfield land. Development would be expensive but, if completed successfully, would allow the lower Lea Valley's positive attributes to emerge, namely, its proximity to central London, its excellent transport links and the possibility of meeting the IOC's preference for a compact Olympic Park that was integrated into the life of the city. The lower Lea Valley was also situated in the midst of predominantly multicultural districts that were ranked among the poorest urban areas in England (see Chapter 19). The development of an Olympic Park there might then be presented not just as a way of fast-tracking decontamination and urban regeneration, but also for using sports-driven change as a vehicle to overcome multiple deprivation and social inequality (Gold and Gold, 2008).

These ideas resonated with IOC members. Selecting London for 2012 would allow the Olympic movement to show that staging its premier sporting and cultural festival could truly make a difference. Along with effective lobbying and bid presentation, it was a package that helped London to emerge victorious from the selection meeting in Singapore in July by the narrow margin of 54 votes to 50 over Paris, the long-term favourite. Once the bid was accepted in 2005, the Olympic Delivery Authority took charge of creating the venues. The Olympic Park occupied a 607-acre (246-hectare) space and housed the main Stadium and Village, together with the Aquatic Centre, Hockey Centre, Velodrome, multipurpose arena (used for handball) and Media Centres. All were later destined to be permanent fixtures. Two other zones (River and Central) housed activities in existing venues, in temporary structures or in spaces occupied on a temporary basis.

London was the first Olympic city to create a legacy body before the staging of the Games. Set up in 2009, the Olympic Park Legacy Company (OPLC) had responsibility bounded by the limits of what would now be known as the Queen Elizabeth Olympic Park (QEOP). This was replaced in February 2012 by the London Legacy Development Corporation (LLDC), a body under the control of London's Mayor and with a remit to plan the redevelopment of the QEOP and the surrounding area in partnership with the private sector (see Chapter 19).

As originally formulated, the Legacy Master Plan laid down a framework for a new inner-city district (postcode E20). The Athletes' Village, redesignated as the East Village, would offer 2,818 homes with planning permission for a further 2500. The QEOP would gain a further five neighbourhoods constructed after the Games providing over 6,000 new homes. Beyond housing, eleven schools and nurseries and three health centres would be supplied for what, it was envisaged, would be a young population. Employment comprising 7,000–8,000 new jobs would be supplied at three hubs: the Press and Broadcast Centre in the west (now known as Hear East); Stratford Waterfront in the east; and Pudding Mill in the south (OPLC, 2010). Provision of parkland was regarded as vital given the shortage of open space in adjacent boroughs. The northern part of the Park would be characterized by waterways and landscaped parklands with the emphasis on outdoor recreation and biodiversity; the southern area would be leisure- and events-oriented – intended to become an animated space along the lines of the Tivoli Gardens in Copenhagen or the South Bank in London.

After the Games, changes that arose directly from the Olympics took precedence. These included the removal of temporary arenas, carrying out landscaping and related works to restore access to the waterways, and the conversion of the Athletes' Village to market-rented, affordable and social housing (figure 2.12). However, the process of delivering the urban legacy perforce takes place in an environment where little or nothing is available from the public purse. Regardless of the grand plan-making, the need for investment from the private sector can require compromises that challenge the integrity of the original master plan. In addition, by 2013, new ideas had crystallized that were not part of the initial mix. In particular, it was now proposed to create a Cultural and Educational Quarter on three pieces of land wrapping around the Aquatics Centre. This area was originally earmarked as part of Marshgate Wharf neighbourhood: the largest of the five new neighbourhoods planned for the Park. Revisiting this idea Mayor Boris Johnson argued that more ambitious plans were needed to capitalize on the success of the Games and the dynamism of the London economy particularly in the cultural and creative industries. He maintained that the Park needed to:

> move beyond the old preconceptions about the future of the park – essentially that we would build infill housing around the venues. It is now clear that this would be to miss a historic opportunity to accelerate the transformation of east London and to deliver a significant economic boost to the UK. (Anon., 2013)

Dubbed 'Olympicopolis' in tributary allusion to its predecessor 'Albertopolis' in South Kensington created from the proceeds of the 1851 Great Exhibition (Hobhouse, 2002), this new quarter would exploit the 'natural movement of the city' as the 'artists, and the designers and the techies' spread east from Hoxton, Shoreditch, to Hackney, Newham and Tower Hamlets. Olympicopolis would provide jobs and growth to match the housing already created thus contributing to the convergence goals for East London (V&A, 2015).

Figure 2.12. Social housing area in the East Village (formerly Athletes' Village), Queen Elizabeth Olympic Park, Stratford, London, May 2015.

The creation of Olympicopolis would, in effect, represent an approach to leveraging development that looks Janus-like to the past and future. The new Cultural and Education Quarter makes reference to the same marriage of science, education and the arts that underpinned its South Kensington predecessor. The city and nation as a whole would benefit from creating a critical mass of cultural attractions that would complement the area's retail and sporting offer. Yet, at the same time the project is also framed in terms of culture-led urban regeneration that will create connections between Olympicopolis institutions and local communities and businesses. Interestingly, the rhetoric surrounding Olympicopolis revalorizes the East End by emphasizing its traditions in fashion, art, design and craft industries along with the dynamism of its artists. For promotional purposes, this model of development effectively replaces the trope of decline and deprivation for the purposes of justifying the concentration on cultural and creative industries. The vision is that of a development that will stimulate a positive legacy at several levels: encouraging innovation and entrepreneurship; raising aspirations and engaging local people through training and education; enhancing audiences for the arts; and boosting local participation in cultural projects. The fact that these putative benefits will be bought at the expense of the provision of housing is not made readily apparent.

Notes

1. Spoken by Prince George, later Duke of Clarence, in William Shakespeare (1593) *Henry VI*, part 3, ii, iii, 53.

2. Although there was a nearby village called Andilalo – the name means 'village of the echo' – it is just as possible that the name simply relates to the spot where the remarkable reverberating echo found at Olympia occurs (see Leake, 1830, vol. 1, p. 31).

3. The event was mentioned in a letter dated 30 April 1679, written by Colonel Edward Cooke in London and addressed to the Duke of Ormond, Viceroy of Ireland, in Dublin (*Source: Notes and Queries*, Tenth Series, X, 22 August 1908, p. 147).

4. Baron Pierre de Coubertin (1863–1937), a French educational reformer, was the key figure behind the movement that founded the IOC (see note 7).

5. The word 'traditional' needs to be emphasized here, since it can be argued that more recently the IOC's version of Olympic history has started to offer a more rounded picture of Brookes' contribution (e.g. see Heck, 2014).

6. This came at the end of a speech made at a Jubilee event to celebrate the fifth anniversary of the founding of the Union of French Sports Associations.

7. At the outset, the IOC was a small, conservative and entirely male-dominated body, heavily under the sway of Coubertin, comprising prominent sportsmen and titled individuals whose social status might lend weight to the embryonic organization. The first committee comprised fifteen members from twelve countries. By 1904, this had increased to thirty-two members, of whom seventeen had aristocratic or civil titles (eight counts, three barons, two princes, a knight, a professor, a general and a bishop). To Coubertin, that social background seemed to suggest people whose impeccable pedigree and private means would insure their impartiality. To later commentators, it would provide the recipe for cronyism and an unrepresentative self-perpetuating oligarchy (e.g. Simson and Jennings, 1992; Sheil, 1998; Lenskyj, 2000).

8. The marathon made connection with ancient legend, with the story of the runner who brought news of the Greek victory over the Persians from Marathon to Athens in 490 BC. In reality, however, the race had no parallel in ancient Greek practice, where races rarely exceeded 5 kilometres. For other suggestions as to the martial connotations of the original Games, see Rustin (2009. p. 11).

9. Athletes returning from the Athens Games established the Boston Marathon the following year (Lovett, 1997, p. xii).

10. Mallon (1998, p. 5) points out that Coubertin had previously suggested a recreation of Olympia for the 1889 Universal Exposition in Paris, with some sporting events.

11. There may well have been an element of pretext here: it is now suggested that the Italians were preparing to withdraw from the Games before the eruption occurred (Mallon and Buchanan, 2000, p. xxxvii).

12. British Olympic Association, Minutes of Council Meeting, A7/3, 18 February 1907.

13. Martin Polley (2011, pp. 100–127), for instance, argued that the amount of use that the stadium had over the next 70 years was sufficient to absolve it from the accusation of being a 'white elephant'.

14. With a population in 1900 of 300,624 compared with Greater London's 1901 figure of 6.5 million.

15. Named after General John Pershing, the Commander-in-Chief of the American Expeditionary Force, the Pershing stadium was built by the Americans on land donated by the French.

16. This prefabricated encampment was for male athletes and was demolished after the Games. Female athletes were housed in the Chapman Park Hotel as it was thought they required a rather more permanent type of residence (TOC, 1933, p. 292).

17. It was suggested, for example, that ancient Greece was partly settled by early Germanic migrants during the Neolithic period (Arnold, 1992, p. 32).

18. The Games of the Twelfth and Thirteenth Olympiads were not celebrated because of the war.

19. Although accusations of commercial excesses galvanized the IOC into taking control of sponsorship through TOP (The Olympic Programme). For all the disdain of commercialism, the IOC now found itself in the position of inviting corporations to pay tens of millions of dollars to become worldwide Olympic sponsors.

20. Discussion of the televisual portrayals of the Games and their implications is found in MacAloon (1989).

21. *Financial Times*, 15 October 1986.

22. This was partly through facing the competing attractions of Expo 92 in Seville and having Madrid as 1992 European City of Culture.

23. The following comprise a selection from a large literature: Buchanan (1992), Borja (1995), Esteban (1999), Calavita and Ferrer (2000), Monclús, (2000, 2003), Marshall (2004), Capel (2005), Degen and Garcia (2012) and González and González (2015).

24. In this respect, its history resembled that of London's O2 Arena.

25. Notably for a sequence that involved a set of 29 footprints in the sky (Spencer, 2008).

26. The tenth Plan covered 2001–2005, the eleventh 2006–2010, the twelfth 2011–2015, and the thirteenth 2016–2020.

Chapter 3

The Winter Olympics: Driving Urban Change, 1924–2022

Stephen J. Essex and Jiska de Groot

The delay in establishing a separate Winter Olympic Games until 1924, almost 30 years after the revival of the Summer Games, reflected the exclusion of winter sports in the original conception of the Olympics. Pierre de Coubertin objected to their inclusion partly because of Scandinavian fears that to do so would have possible detrimental effects on their traditional sports festivals, such as the Nordic Games and Holmenkollen Week.[1] However, as the popularity of winter sports spread, the movement to include them in the Olympic programme gathered pace. Some of the early Summer Games included figure skating (London 1908, Antwerp 1920) and ice hockey (Antwerp 1920) in their programmes. In 1924, a separate winter sports week was held at Chamonix six months before the Summer Games in Paris. Following the success of this event, the International Olympic Committee (IOC) amended its Charter in 1925 to establish the Winter Olympics, with Chamonix retrospectively designated as the first Winter Games. Until 1948, the country hosting the Summer Games also had the opportunity to stage the Winter Games. Thereafter, the selection of the host for the Winter Games was subject to a separate competition decided by a vote of IOC members, but the event was staged in the same year as the Summer Games. From 1992, further change occurred, with the Summer and Winter Games being staged alternately every 2 years in order to maximize the profile of the Olympics and its television revenue (Borja, 1992).

This chapter documents and reviews the role of the Winter Olympics in changing and modernizing the built environment of its hosts, together with considering the changing organization and funding of the event over time. Certain features, of course, remain relatively fixed. The construction or refurbishment of sports facilities has been a constant requirement of hosts throughout the history of the Winter Games, albeit with different outcomes based on local circumstances. In addition, although the detailed specifications may change, the range of sports facilities required for the event is normally standard. The main sports venues for the Winter Olympics include a stadium, slopes for slalom and down-hill ski runs, cross-country ski-trails, bob-sled and luge runs, and an indoor ice arena. The scale of provision of the associated infrastructure, such as the Olympic Village, Media Centre, hotels and transport, reflect the increasing popularity and interest in the event. However, the impact on host cities involves greater degrees of variability. In this respect, there are inevitable comparisons to draw with the Summer Games, which have witnessed a progression from the minor impact of the early Games to a more substantial, entrepreneurial and business-led approach to urban planning through Olympic-led development (see also Essex and Chalkley, 1998, 2002; Chalkley and Essex, 1999). The Winter Olympics are clearly different from the Summer Olympics in that they are staged on a smaller scale and in fragile landscapes, with less coherence in the types of venues required for the various competitions (mountains to urban ice rinks) and logistical challenges of transporting athletes and spectators to remote venues. The key questions addressed here are whether the Winter Olympics have had the same trajectory of development impacts on host centres, and whether the role of the public sector in the planning and management of the event has contracted in deference to the emergence of more entrepreneurial approaches (Cook and Ward, 2011).

To answer these questions, this chapter draws on the Official Reports of the Organizing Committees and identifies five sequential phases in the development of the event to offer a framework for organizing and understanding the experiences of the past twenty-two hosts of the Winter Olympic Games from 1924 up to the cities scheduled to stage the next two events in 2018 and 2022. These phases are characterized as: (1) minimal infrastructural investment (1924–1932); (2) emerging infrastructural demands (1936–1960); (3) tool of regional development (1964–1980); (4) large-scale transformations (1984–1998); and (5) sustainable development and legacy planning (2002-present). While business interests have consistently been instrumental in galvanizing a desire to stage the Games, the public sector has traditionally organized and funded much of the infrastructural investment for the Winter Olympics, as well as accumulating the main debts. Moreover, although private sources of capital, such as television rights and sponsorship, have emerged since 1984, the public sector remains pivotal for the organization of the event (Essex and Chalkley, 2004).

Phase 1: Minimal Infrastructural Investment (1924–1932)

The first three Winter Olympics (see table 3.1 and figure 3.1) were characterized by relatively low levels of interest and participation. The events were staged in settlements with populations of about 3,000, with less than 500 athletes competing in any of the Games. Nevertheless, the motivations of the hosts in staging the Games allude to some interest in the development prospects, especially given the emerging interest in winter sports tourism. Chamonix, in the Haute-Savoie department of eastern France, appears to have been volunteered as the host by the French Olympic Committee, which was no doubt cognisant of the need to have world-class facilities to develop winter sports. Similarly, the local Chamber of Commerce was not slow to recognize the economic advantages for the town created by the popular interest in the Games (see figure 3.2). Funding of the first Winter Olympics appears to have been shared equally between the public and private sectors. In 1928, the Games in St Moritz were led by the local authority and assisted the consolidation of the resort as an international winter sports destination.

Although the initial idea to stage the Winter Olympics in Lake Placid (USA) in

Table 3.1. Host cities and candidate cities for the Winter Olympic Games, 1924–2006.

Games	Host city	Host nation	Other candidates
1924	Chamonix	France	–
1928	St. Moritz	Switerland	Davos, Engelberg (Switzerland)
1932	Lake Placid	USA	Montreal (Canada), Bear Mountain, Yosemite Valley, Lake Tahoe, Duluth, Minneapolis, Denver (USA)
1936	Garmisch-Partenkirchen	Germany	St Moritz (Switzerland)
1948	St Moritz	Switzerland	Lake Placid (USA)
1952	Oslo	Norway	Cortina (Italy), Lake Placid (USA)
1956	Cortina	Italy	Colorado Springs, Lake Placid (USA), Montreal (Canada)
1960	Squaw Valley	USA	Innsbruck (Austria), St Moritz (Switzerland), Garmish-Partenkirchen (Germany)
1964	Innsbruck	Austria	Calgary (Canada), Lahti/Are, (Sweden)
1968	Grenoble	France	Calgary (Canada), Lahti/Are (Sweden), Sapporo (Japan), Oslo (Norway), Lake Placid (USA)
1972	Sapporo	Japan	Banff (Canada), Lahti/Are (Sweden), Salt Lake City (USA)
1976	Innsbruck	Austria	Denver (USA), Sion (Switzerland), Tampere/Are (Finland), Vancouver (Canada)
1980	Lake Placid	USA	Vancouver-Garibaldi (Canada): withdrew before final vote
1984	Sarajevo	Yugoslavia	Sapporo (Japan), Falun/Göteborg (Sweden)
1988	Calgary	Canada	Falun (Sweden), Cortina (Italy)
1992	Albertville	France	Anchorage (USA), Berchtesgaden (Germany), Cortina (Italy), Lillehammer (Norway), Falun (Sweden), Sofia (Bulgaria)
1994	Lillehammer	Norway	Anchorage (USA), Öestersund/Are (Sweden), Sofia (Bulgaria)
1998	Nagano	Japan	Aoste (Italy), Jaca (Spain), Öestersund (Sweden), Salt Lake City (USA)
2002	Salt Lake City	USA	Öestersund (Sweden), Quebec City (Canada), Sion (Switzerland)
2006	Turin	Italy	Helsinki (Finland), Klagenfurt (Austria), Poprad-Tatry (Slovakia), Sion (Switzerland), Zakopane (Poland)
2010	Vancouver	Canada	PyeongChang (South Korea), Salzburg (Austria)
2014	Sochi	Russia	PyeongChang (South Korea), Salzburg (Austria)
2018	Pyeongchang	South Korea	Annecy (France), Munich (Germany)
2022	Beijing	China	Almaty (Kazakhstan)

Source: Compiled by the author from IOC (2015*e*).

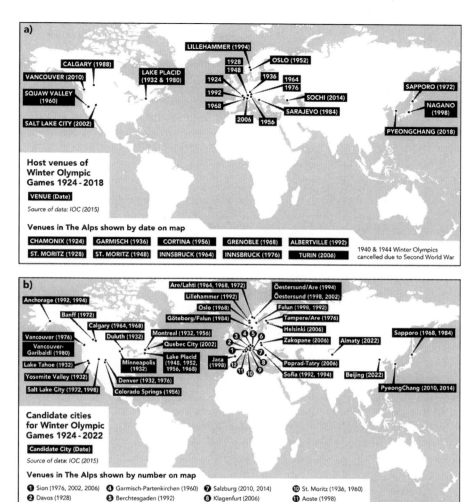

a)

LILLEHAMMER (1994)

CALGARY (1988)

VANCOUVER (2010)

SQUAW VALLEY (1960)

LAKE PLACID (1932 & 1980)

SALT LAKE CITY (2002)

1928
1948

OSLO (1952)

1924

1936

1964
1976

1992

SOCHI (2014)

1968

SARAJEVO (1984)

2006   1956

SAPPORO (1972)

NAGANO (1998)

PYEONGCHANG (2018)

**Host venues of
Winter Olympic
Games 1924 - 2018**

VENUE (Date)

Source of data: IOC (2015)

Venues in The Alps shown by date on map

| CHAMONIX (1924) | GARMISCH (1936) | CORTINA (1956) | GRENOBLE (1968) | ALBERTVILLE (1992) |
| ST. MORITZ (1928) | ST. MORITZ (1948) | INNSBRUCK (1964) | INNSBRUCK (1976) | TURIN (2006) |

1940 & 1944 Winter Olympics
cancelled due to Second World War

b)

Are/Lahti (1964, 1968, 1972)

Lillehammer (1992)

Öestersund/Are (1994)
Öestersund (1998, 2002)

Anchorage (1992, 1994)

Oslo (1968)

Falun (1998, 1992)

Banff (1972)

Göteborg/Falun (1984)

Tampere/Are (1976)

Calgary (1964, 1968)

Helsinki (2006)

Sapporo (1968, 1984)

Vancouver (1976)

Duluth (1932)

Montreal (1932, 1956)

Zakopane (2006)

Almaty (2022)

Vancouver-
Garibaldi (1980)

Quebec City (2002)

❸❹❺❻

Lake Tahoe (1932)

Yosemite Valley (1932)

Salt Lake City (1972, 1998)

Minneapolis
(1932)

Lake Placid
(1948, 1952,
1956, 1968)

Jaca
(1998)

❷

❶

❼

❽

Poprad-Tatry (2006)

❿

❾

Sofia (1992, 1994)

Beijing (2022)

Denver (1932, 1976)

Colorado Springs (1956)

⓬

⓫

PyeongChang (2010, 2014)

**Candidate cities
for Winter Olympic
Games 1924 - 2022**

Candidate City (Date)

Source of data: IOC (2015)

Venues in The Alps shown by number on map

❶ Sion (1976, 2002, 2006) ❹ Garmisch-Partenkirchen (1960) ❼ Salzburg (2010, 2014) ❿ St. Moritz (1936, 1960)
❷ Davos (1928) ❺ Berchtesgaden (1992) ❽ Klagenfurt (2006) ⓫ Aoste (1998)
❸ Innsbruck (1960) ❻ Munich (2018) ❾ Cortina (1952, 1988, 1992) ⓬ Annecy (2018)

Figure 3.1. (*a*) Host venues for the Winter Olympic Games, 1924–2018. (*b*) Candidate venues for the Winter Olympic Games, 1924–2022. (*Source*: IOC, 2015a)

Figure 3.2. The stadium for the Winter Olympics in Chamonix in 1924. (*Source*: IOC/Olympic Museum Collections. Photograph by Auguste Couttet, used in Comité Olympique Français (1924) *Rapport Officiel, Les Jeux de la VIII Olympiade Paris*, COF, Paris, p. 648)

1932 came from the American Olympic Committee in 1927, it was the Lake Placid Club, which owned existing sports facilities in the area, which had investigated the feasibility of the event. The decision to bid for the Games was made only after a representative of the Lake Placid Club had visited a number of European resorts and the St Moritz Olympics of 1928 to convince himself, on behalf of the community, that Lake Placid could match the highest standards abroad and secure longer-term benefits from the investment required. To support the bid,

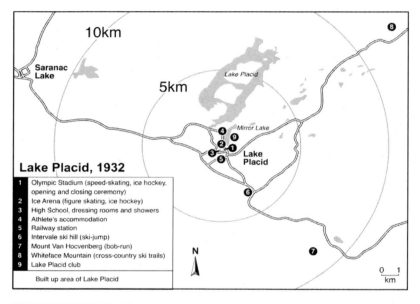

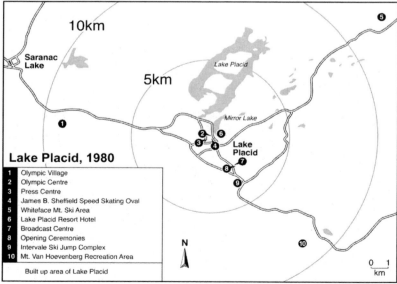

Figure 3.3. Comparison of the Olympic facilities provided for the Winter Olympic Games of 1932 and 1980 in Lake Placid, USA. (*Sources*: LPOOC, 1932 and LPOOC, 1980)

in July 1928, the Lake Placid Chamber of Commerce set up a guarantee fund of $50,000, but it was in fact the State of New York that provided the main funding for infrastructural requirements for the event (see figure 3.3). The involvement of the State eased the concerns of some local residents about the magnitude and responsibility of the task (LPOOC, 1932, p. 43). The organization of the event was a partnership between the State of New York, Essex County Park Commission, North Elba Town Board, North Elba Park Committee and Lake Placid Village Board (*Ibid.*, p. 74). In 1932, substantial funding from New York State led to the establishment of the New York State Olympic Winter Games Commission to ensure that the money was spent wisely (*Ibid.*, p. 60), which is a model that has been followed in subsequent Games.

Many of the hosts of the early Winter Olympics were especially aware of the long-term viability of facilities when deciding whether to stage the event, mainly because of their settlements' small size and limited capacity to sustain expensive, high-order facilities. For example, the skeleton[2] run constructed at the eastern Swiss resort of St Moritz for the 1928 Games proved to be an expensive and unviable legacy. Fewer than thirty people used the facility after the Games. As a result, the organizers of the subsequent Games at Lake Placid 1932 questioned whether the projected cost ($25,000) of a similar facility could be justified.[3] In light of the expected high costs and low post-use,[4] the event was eliminated from the programme at Lake Placid and was not re-introduced until Salt Lake City (Utah) in 2002.

In contrast to this prudence, the Lake Placid organizers were criticized for the extravagance of building an indoor ice rink very late in the preparations. The plan was not supported by the State of New York because of the proposed costs ($375,000). The organizers were responding to a suggestion by the IOC President that such a facility would provide an alternative venue for events in the case of bad weather (which had so badly disrupted St Moritz 1928) and would also be a tangible and physical memorial to the event. The site for the rink was cleared and, with the prospect of a derelict site in the middle of town, the authorities were forced to fund the construction via a bond issue (Ortloff and Ortloff, 1976, p. 77). According to the organizers, the indoor ice rink proved its worth by providing an alternative venue for skating events affected by the unseasonably warm weather and so prevented the programme from being disrupted (LPOOC, 1932, p. 154).

The construction of Olympic Villages or new hotels was certainly not justified in this first phase because of fears of over-provision. Instead, existing accommodation within a wide geographical catchment area was adapted and, if necessary, upgraded for winter occupation. Hotel and cottage owners in the vicinity of Lake Placid were urged to 'winterise' their summer accommodations by the organizers of the Games of 1932 in an effort to house the expected 10,000 visitors. As no additional accommodation capacity was developed near the venue, accommodation in Montreal, which was three and a half hours from Lake Placid, had to be used to cater for the demand (*Ibid.*, p. 112).

Despite the small-scale nature of the event in Phase 1, some Olympic-related developments proposed for early Winter Games raised environmental protests, marking an issue which was to become much more of a prominent concern in later phases. In March 1930, a local action group (the Association for the Protection of the Adirondacks) brought a successful legal action against a proposed Olympic bob-sled run for the Lake Placid Games on environmental grounds and because building on state land was unconstitutional. As a result, a less sensitive site was found at South Meadows Mountain, later renamed Mount Van Hoevenberg (*Ibid.*).

Phase 2: Emerging Infrastructural Demands (1936–1960)

The second phase bears many of the hallmarks of the first phase: host centres were generally small (normally less than 13,000 residents), and had been offered as hosts by a combination of National Olympic Committees, Sports Federations and local authorities, with infrastructural investment funded predominantly by the public sector. The key difference was that, by 1936, there was substantial growth in the number of participating countries and athletes. Investment in Olympic-related infrastructure continued to be constrained by the same factors of long-term viability as in the first phase, but with the added pressures created by the temporary influx of larger numbers of competitors and spectators. Initial plans for an Olympic Village at Cortina d'Ampezzo in northern Italy for the Winter Games of 1956 were abandoned after opposition from local hoteliers who feared the effect of an increase in the town's accommodation capacity on their businesses (CONI, 1956, p. 267). The award of the 1960 Games to Squaw Valley, according to the organizers, had transformed a remote mountain valley into a 'throbbing city' (California Olympic Commission, 1960, p. 27). Although the development of the Olympic Village for Squaw Valley 1960 was out of scale with the small local community, it was considered necessary because of the number of athletes now requiring accommodation and because local hotel capacity was required for officials and journalists (Chappelet, 1997, p. 83). Yet, it was only a temporary construction as the town's small population (*c.* 4,000) meant there was no viable post-Olympic use.

The main exception in this phase was the Norwegian capital Oslo, which hosted the Winter Olympics of 1952. With a resident population of 447,100, the city was by far the largest centre to have hosted the Games by that date. The larger population created new opportunities for the type of facilities provided, as the post-Olympic viability and future use was more assured. In the period before 1960, Oslo was also the only host to have built an Olympic Village, albeit it was dispersed in various locations around the city with planned post-Olympic uses such as university halls of residence, a hospital and an old people's home (Organisasjonskomiteen, 1952, pp. 23, 42). However, new infrastructural requirements were also created by the increased size of the host settlements. For example, larger urban centres were often at some distance from competition sites. Substantial numbers of athletes and spectators required transport to cover considerable distances to isolated locations in difficult terrains and within limited timeframes, sometimes compounded by adverse weather conditions. Investment in transport infrastructure, such as new roads, bridges and ski-lifts, therefore became essential to the operation of the Oslo Games of 1952 and subsequent events.

Phase 3: Tool of Regional Development (1964–1980)

The third phase (1964–1980) was characterized by a number of definite shifts: an expansion of the number of athletes, appreciably larger host centres, and the emergence of regional development and modernization as a key motivation for staging the Games. Four of the five hosts during this period had populations of more than 100,000, with the other having more than one million. Only Lake Placid 1980 had a level of population similar to those of previous phases. Both private development companies and local authorities recognized the potential of the Winter Olympics for justifying major infrastructural investment as part of broader modernization programmes. Television revenue was also emerging and grew substantially as a source of income during this phase, which began to shift the onus of the funding from the public sector to the private sector, although the local public sector remained central to the organization of the event. Innsbruck 1964 received $597,000 from television rights, while Lake Placid 1980 received $15.5 million.

Partly because of their increased size, the Winter Olympics were recognized as a tool of regional development from the 1960s. Innsbruck 1964 was used as a showcase for Austrian businesses, especially those related to ski equipment (Espy, 1979, p. 90). The modernization of the Isère Department was accelerated by Grenoble 1968 (Borja, 1992) and as a means of remodelling its planning system after a period of rapid growth (1946–1968) (COJO, 1968, p. 46). Sapporo 1972 was viewed by the Japanese government as a unique economic opportunity to invigorate the northern island of Hokkaido (Borja, 1992). Most of the spending was on investment in the urban infrastructure, with less than 5 per cent of capital improvements for these Games being expended on sports facilities (Hall, 1992, p. 69).

With the choice of host centres with larger populations after 1960, the post-Games viability of a purpose-built Olympic Village became more assured, usually as a residential area of the host settlement or a student hall of residence for a local university or college. For example, the Olympic Village at Grenoble was built in a Priority Urbanization Zone and subsequently was used as an 800-room university hall, a 300-room hostel for young workers and a tower block with fifty-two apartments (COJO, 1968, p. 71). In Innsbruck, which staged the Games of both 1964 and 1976, the organizers were forced to build an Olympic Village for each event. The four apartment blocks built for the Winter Games of 1964 were not available for the Games of 1976 as they had become a residential suburb of the town in the interim. The second Olympic Village, consisting of nineteen apartment blocks, was therefore built on an adjacent site. The 1976 organizers later reported that having to build another Village was, perhaps, rather extravagant, as not all the athletes wished to stay there, some preferring to be closer to event sites. In retrospect, they felt that accommodating athletes in hotels might have been preferable from cost, security and transport perspectives (HOOWI, 1967, p. 400). Nevertheless, the two Olympic Villages had created a new residential area at Neu-Arzl in East Innsbruck (Chappelet, 1997).

Olympic-related investment in transport infrastructure was often central to the regional development objectives. Road construction accounted for 20 per cent of the total investment for Grenoble 1968 in the French Alps (COJO, 1968, p. 46), and was designed to decentralize the region and facilitate economic growth. The investment included a motorway link from Grenoble to Geneva, which acted as a catalyst for the regional economy and transformed the host town into a major conference and university centre (Chappelet, 2002a, p. 11). The city's old airport at Grenoble-Eybens was closed to make way for the Olympic Village and was replaced by two new airports at Saint-Etienne-de-Saint-Geoirs and Versoud (COJO, 1968, p. 290). For Sapporo 1972, transport investments included extensions to two airports, improvements to the main railway station, forty-one new or improved roads (213 kilometres) and the construction of a rapid transit system (45 kilometres). This last project had already been started by the City of Sapporo, but was completed for the Winter Games using government funding.

With the increasing scale of the Winter Olympics, the risks associated with staging the Games became greater. First, warnings about the long-term limitations of the event as a tool of regional development began with the debt accumulated by the organizers of the Grenoble Games, which was eventually paid off by 1995 (Terret, 2008, p. 1904), together with the abandonment or demolition of some of its venues. It was also during this third phase that the award of the Winter Olympics of 1976 to Denver had to be reassigned, which is the only time in Olympic history that this has happened (Olson, 1974). The reason was local concern about the rising cost of the event and about how the organizers, led by business interests, were ignoring environmental considerations. An action group, Citizens for Colorado's Future, was successful in placing the issue on the State and City ballots in November 1972. The citizens then had a vote on whether the Games should be staged using state funding. The turnout was high (93.8 per cent) and 60 per cent voted against the Olympics, which meant that both state and federal funding for the event would not be forthcoming. Denver was therefore forced to withdraw its candidacy for the Winter Games of 1976, which were then staged in Innsbruck at short notice. Secondly, the changing scale of the event affected the character and operation of the Games. One of the consequences of the Winter Olympics being staged in larger cities and across whole regions was that the focus and impact of the event became dissipated. Critics claimed that the size and dispersed geography of the Games had detracted from the camaraderie of the event and increased transport problems.

In other hosts, efforts were made to mitigate the environmental impacts, though in different ways. For Sapporo 1972, the only mountain close to the host city and suitable for downhill ski events was Mount Eniwa, within the Shikotsu-Toya National Park. The National Park Council gave permission on condition that all related facilities were removed and the terrain in the affected area restored to its original state. A comparable instance concerned Lake Placid 1980, where the town itself lay within Adirondack Park, designated in 1971 and regulated by Adirondack Park Agency. The park's public lands were directly administered by the State Department of Environmental Conservation, which also operated bob-sled and luge runs, the biathlon and cross-country trails and the Whiteface Mountain Ski area (LPOOC, 1980, p. 18). The extensions of the ski jumps, originally built for the 1932 Games, had to comply with standards set by the Adirondack Park Agency and the Federal Environment Agency (*Ibid.*, p. 38).

Phase 4: Large-Scale Transformations (1984–1998)

The fourth phase (1984–1998) is characterized by the most significant increase in participation in the Winter Games. By 1994, the ratio of support staff to athletes was 6.5 times bigger than in 1956. Numbers of athletes were also growing, with over 2,000 athletes at Nagano in 1998 (Chappelet, 2002b). The accommodation of athletes, media and spectators became a substantial infrastructural challenge in itself. After 1988, two or more Olympic Villages became necessary to accommodate athletes closer to their event venues. Separate Villages for the media were also necessary. These demands have favoured centres with larger populations. Perhaps more significantly, television revenue rose from $91.5 million in 1984 to $513 million in 1998, with the additional revenue partly funding ever larger and more ambitious urban redevelopment.

These various changes intensified the advantages of placing the Games in host centres with larger populations. In this phase, the Games were staged in centres with an average population of about 298,000, although three of the five hosts have been substantially larger and two smaller. The role of the Winter Games as a means to secure major urban infrastructural change and modernization has intensified. Sarajevo 1984, therefore, was taken as an opportunity to modernize the city by the government. The motivations for Calgary 1988 and Lillehammer 1994 were to act as stimuli to revive the local economies (e.g. COWGOC, 1988, p. 5). At Calgary, the OCOG moved some venues originally selected by the Calgary Olympic Development Association to make them more viable after the Games (*Ibid.*) and the Games also caused some facilities to be provided much earlier than would otherwise have occurred. For example, the construction of the Olympic Saddledome (20,000 seats, C$7 million), home for a professional ice hockey team established in 1980, was fast-tracked to show the city's commitment to its bid

(Hiller, 1990, p. 124). Large investments required to stage the 1992 Albertville Games appear, however, to have made more difficulties for other northern French Alpine resorts seeking finance for restructuring (Tuppen, 2000, p. 330). This case shows that Olympic investment has 'opportunity costs' which may postpone or eliminate other forms of investment.

Given the changing circumstances, smaller hosts in this phase faced problems in justifying investment in permanent purpose-built Olympic Villages. Albertville 1992, which had a population of only 20,000 at the time, renovated a small spa at Brides-les-Bains as the Olympic Village rather than constructing a purpose-built facility. However, the Village proved to be too far from the sports facilities, so seven smaller Olympic Villages were established in existing hotel accommodation closer to the event sites. After this experience, the IOC stated that it favoured the use of a single Olympic Village in future Games in order to promote contact between athletes from different countries (Charmetant, 1997, p. 115), although this aspiration has not proved possible in more recent events. At Lillehammer 1994, which had a population of 23,000, a temporary Olympic Village consisting of 200 wooden chalets, was constructed. These examples were significant departures from the trajectory of large-scale infrastructural investment.

The increasing scale of the event has also necessitated more formal recognition of environmental issues in the planning and development of related infrastructure (May, 1995). The intrusion of built structures into fragile environments, as well as the use of chemicals to create the appropriate snow conditions, became a major issue in the preparations for the Winter Olympics. Most notably, the preparations for Lillehammer 1994 incorporated, for the first time, principles of sustainable development. The proposed location of one of the main indoor arenas was moved to protect a bird sanctuary, while its heat circulation was generated from excess heat from its refrigeration unit. Contracts with suppliers and contractors included environmental clauses. The approach influenced the IOC to add an environmental commitment to its Charter in 1996 (Cantelon and Letters, 2000), with the candidates for the Winter Games of 2002 being the first to be required to describe their environmental plans in their bid documents (IOC, 1999a, p. 5; Lesjø, 2000: see also Chapter 1).

Phase 5: Sustainable Development and Legacy Planning (2002 Onwards)

During the fifth phase (2002 onwards), the trend for the Winter Games to require large-scale infrastructural investment continued, but with a greater emphasis on the protection of the environment, sustainable development and legacy planning. Consequently, the Games began to be staged by large metropolitan cities together with their surrounding mountain communities, essentially making them multiple-centre events (Chappelet, 2008, p. 1897). There have also been other significant pressures which have altered the character of the Winter Olympics, such as the threat from international terrorism and reforms to the host city selection process following corruption over the award of the 2002 event.

As noted earlier, Salt Lake City was the first host city to have been elected after being required to outline their environmental plans in the bid process. However, the Winter Olympics of 2002 are likely to be better remembered for the corruption scandal that tainted the city's election as host and for the heightened security threat following the terrorist attacks in New York on 11 September 2001 (five months before the Opening Ceremony). In December 1998, allegations emerged that the Salt Lake Bid Committee had made payments to IOC members in return for support in the selection process (Booth, 1999; Lenskyj, 2000; Toohey and Veal, 2000, p. 232). The official inquiries concluded that the IOC's lack of accountability had contributed directly to the gift-giving culture (Kettle, 1999; Sandomir, 1999), although six IOC members were excluded and a further ten were given warnings (IOC, 1999b). The controversy led to reforms in the host city selection process, including the elimination of member visits to candidate cities, the creation of a permanent Ethics Commission, and amendments to the composition of the IOC itself. These changes were relevant to the future selection and conduct of both the Summer and Winter Olympics.

Similarly, the 9/11 terrorist attacks on New York in 2001 made the security risk associated with the Winter Olympics much greater. Salt Lake City was staging the Games only five months after the attacks, so the security measures were enhanced and placed centre stage. Strict constraints were introduced for local air space as well as access to zones within the city (Warren, 2002, p. 617). The organizers spent $200 million on security and public safety measures and deployed 9,750 security-related personnel during the Games (SLOC, 2002, pp. 114, 490). Although security had been a major concern and expenditure since Munich 1972, the Salt Lake City Games set a new benchmark for the implementation of security plans and measures at the Olympic Games in an era of global terrorism.

The development of infrastructure and facilities for the Salt Lake City Games was based on three master plans: for Downtown, the University of Utah, and Park City. A total of seven permanent venues were constructed, with only three requiring investment by the OCOG itself. The other four venues were built by public–private partnerships, with a further twenty temporary venues or overlays[5] (Ibid., p. 187). There was significant investment in transport infrastructure, involving ten Olympic-related roads and highway projects and four non-Olympic related regional projects, including the reconstruction of two interstate routes and two light rail transit lines (Ibid., p. 179).

All Salt Lake City developments were subject to environmental management systems to minimize adverse environmental impacts. The Environmental Plan contained four 'aggressive objectives', which were all achieved. First, 95.6 per cent of all waste was recycled or composted to achieve the objective of 'zero waste' (Ibid., p. 26). Second, the Games succeeded in its goal of 'net zero emissions' by offsetting its carbon footprint of 122,936 metric tons of hazardous and greenhouse gas emissions as well as 243,840 metric tons of pollutants in Utah, the US and Canada (*Ibid.*, p. 196). The event was certified as climate neutral by the Climate Neutral Network. Third, the event's advocacy programme for urban forestry resulted in 100,000 trees being planted in Utah and 15 million trees planted worldwide (*Ibid.*, p. 26). Fourth, zero tolerance for environmental and safety compliance errors was successful (*Ibid.*, pp. 195–198). The environmental and sustainable development agenda had been clearly cemented as part of the organization of the Winter Olympic Games following those in Salt Lake City.

The award of the Winter Olympics of 2006 to Turin, with a population of 1.4 million, represented the use of the event as part of a strategy to transform an old industrial metropolis into a modern post-industrial city, a scenario which is normally associated with the Summer Games. As an industrial centre, Turin had been almost totally dependent on the motor manufacturer Fiat for a century, and had become known as the 'Italian Detroit' (Rosso, 2004, p. 5). With the contraction of Fiat in the city in the 1980s, involving the loss of 110,000 jobs by 2001 (Winkler, 2007, p. 16), there was a need to forge a new urban identity to attract tertiary businesses and improve its tourism potential.

In order to modernize the city's infrastructure, innovations were first required in the city's governance structures. When Fiat had been dominant in the city, a tradition of industrial conflicts and strong economic interests inside the Municipal Council had prevented the creation of an overall vision or strategy for the city (Pinson, 2002, p. 483). Instead, town-planning interventions had only been allowed to act in a pragmatic and opportunistic way. Following the corruption scandals that led to the collapse of both national and local government in Italy in 1992, national political reforms were introduced involving directly elected mayors with increased executive powers and resources (Winkler, 2007, pp. 18–19). In 1993, Valentino Castellani, Turin's first elected Mayor, emphasized the importance of the internationalization agenda to the city's revitalization and long-term future. This focus, assisted by over 15 years of political continuity, created space for dialogue and an opportunity for organizational and entrepreneurial capacity to develop. It placed the municipality at the centre of collective governance as facilitator with an emphasis on open regional partnership, collaboration and networks rather than centralized secretive confrontation and conflict dominated by Fiat (Pinson, 2002, p. 489; Winkler, 2007, p. 23).

An Urban Master Plan had been prepared in 1995 to alter the city's urban structure and create opportunities for regeneration. The Plan focused on the improvement of transport access and private-led investment on brownfield sites within clear land-use zoning and regulation. The organizing principle of the plan was the *Spina Centrale*, which was a north–south avenue along the railway line, which had fractured the city into two parts. The railway line was taken underground, which enabled an increase in service capacity, the physical reconnection of the two halves of the city on the surface and a new urban centrality and image along the central backbone (see figure 3.4). A new cross-rail system, the *Passante Ferroviao*,

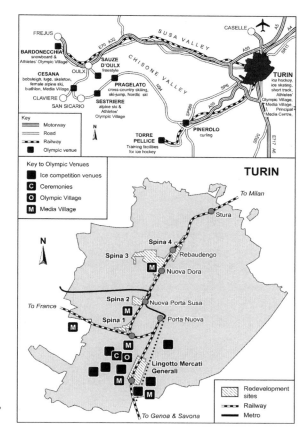

Figure 3.4. The regional setting of the 2006 Winter Olympics in Turin and the Urban Master Plan for the city's redevelopment devised in 1995. (*Source*: Winkler, 2007)

Figure 3.5. Redevelopment along the Spina Centrale in Turin, which reconnected the two halves of the city previously separated by a railway line, and became part of the urban transformations associated with the Winter Olympics in 2006. The restored older buildings on the left were originally a prison (1870–1986), which now operates as a museum (Museo del Carcere Le Nuove). The tower (Il Nuovo Centro Direzionale di Torino) is the headquarters of the banking group Intesa, which accommodates 2,000 employees together with a 364-seater public hall at ground level and a restaurant on the roof. This building was opened in December, 2014. (*Source*: Professor Christopher Balch)

was introduced, and new mixed-use developments, including libraries, theatres, banks and regional government offices, were developed on brownfield sites adjacent to the railway stations, often in iconic landmark buildings (see figure 3.5). A programme to improve the quality of neighbourhoods, public spaces and cultural and leisure attractions throughout the city was implemented (Falk, 2003).

The award of the Winter Olympics to Turin on 19 June 1999 therefore enabled the scope and importance of the new vision for the city to be integrated (Rosso, 2004, p. 17), prioritized (Pinson, 2002, p. 485) and, above all, to be implemented. The Strategic Plan for Turin was formulated through a highly participatory process and signed by all relevant agencies in February 2000. It outlined six overall strategies focused around: the creation of a metropolitan government; integration into the international system; the development of training and research; the advancement of enterprise and employment; the promotion of Turin as a city of culture, tourism, commerce and sport; and the improvement of the overall quality of the city. Implementation of the corresponding twenty objectives was overseen by the Torino Internazionale Association, the 'Invest in Turin and Piedmont' inward investment agency, and Turismo Torino (Pinson, 2002, p. 485; Rosso, 2004, p. 18; Winkler, 2007, p. 28). The Olympics were perceived as an opportunity to modernize the city's infrastructures (Pinson, 2002, p. 485) and galvanize the longer-term vision for the city.

The staging of the Winter Olympics was also organized as a means of regional integration between the three urban centres (Turin, Grugliasco and Pinerolo), which provided venues for the ice competitions, an Olympic Village, Media Village, Press Centre and International Broadcasting Centre; and the surrounding mountain communities, which provided venues for the snow competitions and two Olympic Villages (Torre Pellice, Pragelato, Bardonecchia, Sauze d'Oulx, Claviere, Cesana-San Sicario, Sestriere). The purpose of this strategy was to extend the benefits of Olympic investment beyond the city to the whole region through opportunities to upgrade ski facilities and structures and to extend the tourism season (Dansero et al., 2003). Substantial improvements were made to the local road networks to increase the area's tourism potential, as well as to benefit daily life for its citizens. The transformation of Turin as a European metropolis was also signalled with plans to connect to the high-speed rail lines to Milan (2009) and Lyon (2011), thus positioning the city in the dynamic Mediterranean arc of technopoles in southern France (Sophia-Antipolis and Montpellier) through to Barcelona (Falk, 2003, p. 213).

As with the other recent Winter Olympics, the Turin Games was notable for its emphasis on environmental protection and sustainable development. A strategic evaluation assessment (the so-called 'Green Card') was adopted by the Environment Department of the Turin Organizing Committee (TOROC) to assess the environmental consequences of proposed developments and to monitor environmental impacts. This environmental management system was awarded ISO14001 status.[6] All plans and projects were assessed by the Consulta Ambientale

(Environmental Council) before implementation so that recommendations for environmental sustainability could be implemented. An 'Ambiente 2006' logo was awarded to companies who manufactured goods for the Olympics in compliance with predetermined environmentally sustainable criteria (TOROC, 2005, p. 122), and local hotel accommodation was awarded an 'Ecolabel' for adopting sustainable practices (TOROC, 2005, p. 124; Bottero *et al.*, 2012; Bondonio and Guala, 2011). The Games themselves offset 100,000 metric tons of greenhouse gases through the HECTOR programme (Heritage Climate TORino) (TOROC, 2005, p. 122). Indeed, Turin secured advances in the minimization of the environmental impact of the event for future Games to emulate. The Turin Winter Olympics was noteworthy for its achievements in transforming the city's structures for governance and in mobilizing the city's long-term redevelopment plan. In this respect, Turin is the closest that the Winter Olympics have come to matching the transformational effects of the Summer Olympics in Barcelona, although there are some questions about the long-term trajectory of the Olympic legacies following the 2008 recession (Vanolo, 2015).

The Winter Olympics in 2010 were held in Vancouver, Canada, which also emphasized its credentials in sustainable development (Holden *et al.*, 2008). The centre of Vancouver acted as the venue for the ice competitions and the winter resort of Whistler, 75 miles (120 kilometres) distant, provided the venues for the snow competitions. New and upgraded facilities were constructed, together with a rapid transit link between the airport and central Vancouver and an upgrade of the 'Sea-to-Sky' highway between Vancouver and Whistler. The performance goals of the organizers focused on accountability, environmental stewardship and impact reduction, social inclusion and responsibility, aboriginal participation and collaboration, economic benefits from sustainable practices, and sport for sustainable living (Chappelet, 2008, p. 1896). The provincial government established an independent not-for-profit company called 2010 Legacies Now to ensure that each region in British Columbia benefitted from the Games, through maximizing social and economic opportunities, building community capacity and expanding volunteer resources (2010 Legacies Now, 2009). The agency was funded by grants from various levels of government, contributions by the private sector and investment income, and undertook various programmes in schools education, sport and recreation, the arts, volunteerism and literacy to achieve its goals (2010 Legacies Now, 2008). It created a new model for securing softer Olympic legacies related to people, skills and employability rather than simply the harder legacies related to the built environment.

Despite the apparent concern for securing a positive post-Olympic legacy, the organizers in Vancouver faced criticisms. The onset of a worsening global recession in 2008 threatened to jeopardize the financial viability of many developments, including the Olympic Village where the city government had to subsidize the project in order to ensure its timely completion (O'Connor, 2009). Social impacts resulting from the effects of land speculation and reversals on promises of affordable housing produced substantial concerns about increasing homelessness in the city. During the pre-Olympic development boom, 1,400 low-income housing units were lost from the Downtown Eastside neighbourhood in order to create more space for tourists and corporate investors (Esparza and Price, 2015, p. 32). Rent increases or conversions into high-cost condominiums or boutique hotels resulted in increased evictions and homelessness. Indeed, the concern of the authorities to present the best possible image of the city to the world led to legislation such as the Assistance to Shelter Act (2009), which gave powers to local authorities to place the homeless in temporary shelters, and initiatives such as the Project Civil City (2006–2008) to remove evidence of social inequality from the streets (Boyle and Haggerty, 2011). The latter initiative involved increased CCTV surveillance; public realm improvements to beautify areas, encourage active use and design out crime; and deployment of 'downtown ambassadors' to act as street concièrges for visitors and the 'eyes and ears' of the police on the ground (*Ibid.*, 2011). Between 2008 and 2010, anti-poverty activists staged an annual 'Poverty Olympics' to draw ironic attention to the 'world class poverty' in Vancouver's Downtown Eastside, including events such as 'the poverty-line high jump', 'the welfare hurdles' and the 'broad jump over bedbug infested mattresses' (Esparza and Price, 2015, p. 32; Perry and Kang, 2012, p. 591).

Indigenous peoples objected to their political groups being co-opted on to the local Olympic organization as a means for their artists, cultural performance groups and symbols to be appropriated in Olympic events, while continuing to live in disadvantaged conditions and the Olympics being staged in unceded and non-surrendered indigenous lands (O'Bonsawin, 2010, p. 148). Indeed, some groups considered the use of an Inuksuk as the symbol of the 2010 Olympics as disrespectful as it reduced, objectified and dehumanized over 630 First Nation Aboriginal communities into a singular 'culture', which reflected the dominant colonial view of Canadian nationhood (Perry and Kang, 2012, p. 584). Environmental protests against the construction of the 'Sea-to-Sky' highway through Eagleridge Bluffs resulted in twenty arrests and two jail sentences. The cost of Vancouver 2010 rose to over $6 billion (O'Connor, 2009) at a time of severe cutbacks to health care, the arts, education and social assistance (Perry and Kang, 2012, p. 579). Public displays of opposition against the Olympics were the first to utilize so-called convergence tactics, whereby activists are called to a particular location to protest using social media communications facilitated by the internet (Esparza and Price, 2015, p. 24). The staging of the Winter Olympics had become as contested as their summer equivalents.

The award of the Winter Olympics of 2014 to Sochi in Russia may represent the start of a new phase or even a step backwards in the trajectory of the event (Chappelet, 2008, p. 1897). The decision by the IOC in 2007 to award the Winter Olympics to Russia appears to have been both a political gesture and a commercial opportunity to extend Olympism into the former communist world, along the lines of the Summer Olympics of 2008 in Beijing. For Russia and President Vladimir

Putin in particular, the Olympics was to be a national project and symbolic of a resurgent Russia (Orttung and Zhemukhov, 2014). The bid proposed to develop the small mountain village of Krasnaya Polyana in the Caucasus Mountains from almost nothing into a new 'world class' winter sports resort to be used for the venues of the snow competitions together with the existing seaside resort of Sochi as the venue for the ice competitions (see figures 3.6 and 3.7). Sochi is located in a sub-tropical coastal region, while Krasnaya Polyana, 30 miles (49 kilometres) away, is part of an alpine mountain range. Besides eleven new Olympic sports facilities and over 19,000 new hotel rooms (IOC, 2007, pp. 18, 24), substantial investment was made in power and gas lines, telecommunications, water supplies and transport. No less than seven power stations (some thermoelectric and hydro-electric) were constructed or refurbished to increase the capacity of the region's energy network by 2.5 times and secure a stable power supply for the event and beyond (SOOC, 2009). A new terminal was built at Sochi airport, together with a new offshore terminal at the seaport. A light railway was constructed from the airport to the Olympic Park. Transport between Sochi and Krasnaya Polyana was enhanced by the reconstruction of the railway to a double track line and a new motorway (IOC, 2007, pp. 25–26). The total costs associated with these developments have been estimated at more than $50 billion (Trubina, 2015, p. 2) and so appeared to be

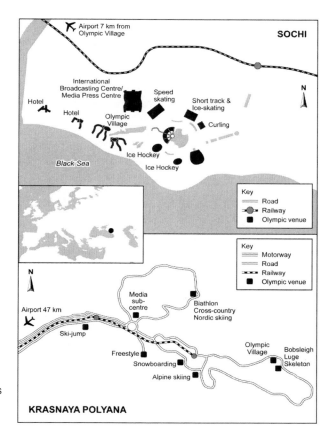

Figure 3.6. The geography of the Winter Olympic Games staged in Sochi, Russia in 2014. (*Source*: SOOC, 2009)

Figure 3.7. The Bolshoy Ice Dome, which was one of the main pieces of sports infrastructure built for the Sochi Winter Olympics in 2014. It was emblematic of the government's use of the Olympics as a 'national' project and symbolic of a resurgent Russia. (*Source*: IOC/Olympic Museum Collections. © 2013/Comité International Olympique (CIO)/MORATAL, Christophe)

at odds with the IOC's concern to reduce the cost and scale of Olympic events. One estimate equated the cost of this government investment to be about €60,000 (roughly $88,000) per inhabitant of the region (Müller, 2012, p. 697).

Serious environmental concerns also existed over the preparations as some the venues were located in the Sochi National Park and the Caucasus State Biosphere Reserve (a UNESCO World Heritage Area). Initially, the National Park was to be re-zoned to allow the construction of an Olympic Village in Krasnaya Polyana, with the bobsleigh and luge runs in a buffer zone of the Reserve. In July 2008, Vladimir Putin, then the Russian Prime Minister, ordered the Olympic facilities noted above to be relocated. Putin is reported as having stated that 'in setting our priorities and choosing between money and the environment, we're choosing the environment' (Finn, 2008). It later emerged that the boundaries of the reserve were changed to accommodate the development (Alekseyeva, 2014, p. 165). An appeal by Greenpeace Russia to the Russian Supreme Court about these environmental concerns was rejected (IOC, 2007, p. 14; GamesBids.com, 2009). Müller (2013, p. 28) argued that the sustainability agenda for Sochi was framed by and for an international audience and so was out of tune with the realities of environmental politics in Russia and national conceptions of sustainable development and nature–society relationships.

The Sochi Games were controversial in other ways, too, not least related to violations of human rights. During the land assembly for the Olympic infrastructure, concerns were raised about the expropriation of property and resettlement of residents with no right of appeal, together with the treatment of migrant construction workers who had to endure poor working and living conditions (Müller, 2014). Other issues raised the threat of international boycotts of the event, such as the discriminatory legislation against lesbian, gay, bisexual and transgender groups and a campaign by a diaspora of an indigenous group (Circassian) who had been defeated by Tsarist forces in 1864 on the site of the Olympic facilities (Arnold and Foxall, 2014).

Security concerns were also voiced over the 2014 Games because Sochi is located close to the disputed region of Abkhazia (Georgia). A website (RevoketheGames. com) was founded to draw attention to Russia's attack on Georgia in 2008 and to campaign for the 2014 event to be moved from Sochi to another host. In November 2008, the Georgian National Olympic Committee requested that the IOC reconsider its decision to award an Olympics which would be staged close to a conflict zone. The IOC rejected the request because security was the responsibility of the Russian organizers and, of course, the 2014 Games were staged as planned. Nevertheless, it is clear that the Sochi Olympics presented a number of challenges to the IOC's concerns about the scale, cost and environmental implications of staging the games.

The Future

The host city of the Winter Olympics in 2018 is PyeongChang in the Kangwon province of South Korea, which shares a border with North Korea (Merkel, 2008). The potential of the event to act as an opportunity for reunification and contribute to world peace had formed an important part of the city's previous bids for the Games in 2010 and 2014. Indeed, the two Korean teams had marched together at a number of Olympic Games between 2000 and 2006, but had failed to agree a joint team for the Beijing Olympics in 2008 (Merkel and Kim, 2011, p. 2369). Its third and successful bid for the 2018 Games (in 2011) ironically did not feature the idea of improving relations between the two Koreas prominently and was a government-led project rather being led by local institutions (Merkel and Kim, 2011, p. 2376; see POPWGBC, 2011). By this time, however, PyeongChang already had a number of venues completed or planned within a 30-minute radius with substantial financial support from the national government and strong public support (93 per cent approval) (see figure 3.8). It won the IOC vote outright in the first round. To avoid any boycott of the 2018 Games by North Korea, possible courses of action might include South Korea offering some competitions to be staged in the North, two countries fielding a joint team, and arranging high-profile events around reconciliation and reunification (Merkel and Kim, 2011, p. 2378). This case represents a very real example of where the Olympic spirit may be able to contribute to reunification where other political means have failed.

The staging of the 2022 Winter Olympics was more problematic for the IOC (see also Chapter 1). Having started with a good field of potential candidate cities (Krakow, Lviv, Munich, Oslo, St Moritz-Davos, Stockholm), only Almaty (Kazakhstan) and Beijing (China) remained as willing hosts by the time of the IOC

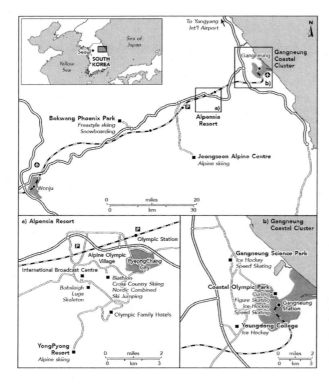

Figure 3.8. The geography of the Winter Olympic Games to be staged in PyeongChang, South Korea in 2018. (*Source*: POPWGBC, 2011)

selection vote (July, 2015). Krakow, Munich and St. Moritz-Davos all withdrew their bids because local residents had voted against staging the event in referenda. The city government in Stockholm declined to offer financial support and Lviv withdrew its bid because of political unrest in the Ukraine (AP, 2014). Beijing was awarded the event and became the first city to have the opportunity to stage both the Summer and Winter Games. While its bid relied on venues built for the Summer Olympics in 2008, there were concerns about the lack of a natural source of snow and protests from human rights groups (BBC News, 2015; IOC, 2015*b*).

The apparent increasing reluctance of cities willing to be hosts of the Olympic Games relates to the scale, cost and demands of both the event and the Olympic movement on these places. Reforms suggested by the Olympic Games Study Commission to control and limit the scale of investment in Olympic preparations at the start of Jacques Rogge's period of presidency of the IOC (IOC, 2003*b*) have resurfaced at the start of Thomas Bach's term of office as IOC President (2013–). The Olympic Agenda 2020, agreed by the IOC in December 2014, has revised the bid process to become an invitation and open dialogue between potential hosts and the IOC rather than as a tender bid, so that the Olympic-related infrastructure can be negotiated to suit the city's long-term development needs rather than being imposed. The IOC appears to be moving away from the concept of a 'compact games' by allowing greater flexibility in venue locations, which can be outside the host city or even host country (IOC, 2014*b*; 2015*a*). The extent to which these reforms will increase the enthusiasm of host cities to stage the Olympic Games will become apparent over the next few years. Certainly, there might be the beginning of a trend away from cities in neoliberal economies which, while seeking investment from the private sector, are unable to raise substantial government subsidy. In contrast, countries with a strong state, substantial government funding, and a more top-down planning culture, combined with less concern for environmental issues and a greater push for modernization and urban transformation, are emerging as the major players as hosts of mega-events in the early twenty-first century (Müller, 2011, 2012; Trubina, 2015).

Discussion and Conclusions

In parallel with the evolving experience of staging the Summer Olympics, a marked growth in the scale, complexity, sophistication, and attendant controversy is discernible in the history of the Winter Games since the 1920s. The chronological sequence of phases adopted as the organizing framework of this chapter offers a means to understand both the broad changes in the scope and character of the Winter Olympics, and the specific circumstances that have affected twenty-two past and two forthcoming hosts of the event. The key characteristics of these urban transformations are summarized in table 3.2. Planning for the Winter Olympics (like the Summer Games) has built incrementally on the experience of past events, the gradual accumulation of knowledge and the desire constantly to raise the spectacle of the event. What emerges from this historical review are a number of clear trends and research themes.

First, the Winter Olympics has shifted from an event that has promoted winter sports tourism in single mountain resorts to one that has begun to emulate the Summer Olympics in its ability to modernize and stimulate urban regeneration. It is now usual for the host of the Winter Olympics to comprise both a large urban centre and surrounding mountain communities. Nevertheless, the scale of investment can still represent a challenge to the hosts in ensuring that the post-Olympic legacy is positive and facilities are sustainable for what are specialized facilities dispersed around remote and mountainous rural regions. Indeed, the increasing scale of the event has introduced new infrastructural demands, such as major improvements to transport systems, enhanced security measures and projects integrating sustainable development. In some cases, the athletes' demand to be closer to competition venues has required the Winter Olympic Villages to be fragmented into smaller units. Given such investments have associated opportunity costs, the extent to which the Winter Olympic Games therefore represents a cost-effective and positive force for sustainable legacies and urban revitalization policies is much contested.

Secondly, in economic terms, legacies appear mixed, with the impacts often experienced as an 'intermezzo', that is a short dramatic interlude yielding a poor long-term return on investment (Spilling, 1998). In Spilling's research into the effects of Lillehammer 1994, there were substantial numbers of new business start-

Table 3.2. Summary of key urban transformations of the Winter Olympic Games (Phases I–V).

Phase	Time	Broad description	Characteristics of urban transformations
Phase I	1924–1932	Minimal infrastructural transformation, apart from sports facilities	Development prospects for winter sport tourism
		Small host populations (around 3,000)	'Winterisation' of existing accommodation rather than over-provision of accommodation
			Event initiated by private interests, but funded jointly with public sector
			Environmental concerns raised
Phase II	1936–1960	Emerging infrastructural demands, especially transportation	Growing volumes of participants and spectators requiring investment in transportation
		Small host populations (around 13,000)	Limited basis for other permanent infrastructure
Phase III	1964–1980	Tool of regional development, especially transportation, Olympic Villages and economic development opportunities	Infrastructure investment as part of regional modernization and development
			Substantial public sector funding, but emerging television revenues
		Medium host populations (around 100,000 or more)	Concern emerges about the increasing size of the event with regard to camaraderie, transport problems, debt and environmental damage
Phase IV	1984–1998	Large-scale urban transformations, including multiple Olympic Villages	Role of Winter Olympics as a means to secure major urban infrastructural change
			Higher television revenues
		Large host populations (c. 300,000)	More formal recognition of environmental issues in planning and development
Phase V	2002–2014	Sustainable development and legacy planning	Large-scale infrastructural investment and re-development reflecting global and political ambitions of host cities
		Large populations/ metropolitan areas (c. 1 million)	High television revenues
			Greater emphasis on environmental protection and sustainable development through environmental management systems

Table 3.2 continued on page 87

Table 3.2 continued from page 86

Phase	Time	Broad description	Characteristics of urban transformations
			Emergence of 'soft' legacies (social inclusion, human rights, integration of indigenous cultures), but also more international debate and controversy over adoption of international norms
The 'Future'	2018–onwards	Reluctance to host Olympic Games in developed economies related to scale, cost and demands of the event	More interest from emerging economies with centralised governments wishing to achieve political acceptance on a global stage
			Reform of IOC expectations for the event: hard and soft legacies determined by dialogue rather than pre-defined; relaxation of 'compact games' concept

Source: Authors.

ups immediately after the Games were awarded, but many did not survive. The impact of the event can also be uneven across different sectors. During Salt Lake City 2002, hotels and restaurants prospered, experiencing a combined estimated $70.6 million net increase in taxable sales respectively, while retailers suffered with a larger net loss of $167.4 million (Baade *et al.*, 2008). The tangible economic impacts might be short-lived but intangible impacts, such as the creation of new networks, skills and images, can have longer-term importance. Research into the effects of the 1988 Games on Calgary's image in twenty-two centres in America and Europe between 1986 and 1989 showed an increased awareness immediately before and after the event but tended to dissipate after a few years (Brent Ritchie and Smith, 1991).

Thirdly, in social terms, it has proved extremely difficult to reconcile the demands of the Games with the kinds of built environment that might be suitable for residents of the locality after the Olympics have finished. Indeed, the host city's concern to use the Winter Olympics as a development and revitalization tool, in order to create new spaces for inward investment and tourism as well as the best possible place marketing and branding, has often led to insufficient public consultation over redevelopment plans, the displacement of former inhabitants (usually disadvantaged groups) and increased street security and surveillance. In the post-Olympic period, redeveloped areas become gentrified and obvious representations of social equality and exclusion. In some cases, such as Victoria Park following Calgary 1988, a process of residential obsolescence was triggered, whereby uncertainty about future mega-events in a residential zone around a stadium impeded investment (Hiller and Moylan, 1999). Intertwined with these issues are those human rights violations (related to land claims, treatment of migrant construction workers and discrimination against minority groups) and the commodification of the symbols of indigenous people for Olympic marketing and external image. The emergence of local action groups opposing bids for Winter Games in several potential hosts has been indicative of some local perceptions of the negative impacts (for example, Helsinki 2006 Anti-Olympic Committee; Nolympics!, Turin, 2006; No 2010 Network and Native Anti-2010 Resistance, Vancouver, 2010).

Fourthly, given that the Winter Olympics are staged in more fragile landscapes than their summer counterparts, the environmental implications of staging the event have been more prominent and evident, even in the earliest hosts. Habitat destruction, heat generation from refrigeration units, chemical pollution and unsuccessful restoration schemes have been common concerns in host settlements. Arguably, the sustainability agenda adopted by the IOC in 1996, and now ingrained in all Olympic events, albeit arguably a 'light green' form of corporate environmentalism (Lenskyj, 1998), was a direct outcome of the criticism of Albertville 1992 and the example set at Lillehammer 1994. Each successive Olympic Games has subsequently claimed to be the most sustainable ever, although practices now appear to be relatively established in terms of recycling measures, low carbon emissions and offsetting, environmental procurement and compliance standards, and environmental management and monitoring. The extent to which Sochi 2014 ran counter to the IOC's expectations in some of these areas raised questions about the institution's ability to hold host cities accountable to their bid promises and accepted international norms.

Fifthly, despite more entrepreneurial approaches to the urban management of the Olympics, the public sector's role appears to remain central to the organization and, to a certain extent, the funding of the event. The initial motivation to stage the Winter Olympics might emanate from business coalitions and the generation of income through corporate sponsorship and television revenue, but it is public-sector expenditure that is usually pivotal to the success of the event. The French government treated Grenoble 1968 as an *affaire nationale*, met 80 per cent of the basic sports installation costs and provided a subsidy of 20 million francs for operational expenses (COJO, 1968, p. 39). While the Albertville Games of 1992 were originally conceived as a means of regional modernization by local businessmen, it was the French government that funded the project. Similarly, the Norwegian government covered the costs and debts of Lillehammer 1994. The staging of the Winter Olympics in Turin in 2006 was central to the city's transformation from an industrial to a post-industrial centre and the Sochi event in 2014 represented a 'national project' to create a new ski and winter sports resort in Russia.

Finally, the debate about the increasing size of the Winter Olympics has been a long-running affair. Preparations for Oslo 1952 included consideration of a proposal to reduce the number of events. It was feared that the increasing size of each Winter Games would detrimentally affect their character and make it impossible for any town to undertake the necessary arrangements.[7] There is no record of the response to this proposal but, in practice, the Games continued to grow. Avery Brundage, the IOC President from 1952 to 1972, criticized the huge expenditures at Grenoble 1968. He wrote: 'the French spent $240m … and when you consider that this was for ten days of amateur sport, it seems to be somewhat out of proportion. With that kind of money involved there is bound to be commercialization of one kind or another' (quoted in Espy, 1979, p. 136). As a result of related controversies, Brundage hoped that the whole Winter Olympics would receive a 'decent burial' at Denver, the original host of the Games of 1976 (Espy, 1979, p. 135). Nevertheless, the Winter Games has survived and, in terms of its scope and size, it has continued its upward trajectory. The risks of staging a Winter Olympics are now immeasurably greater as issues of financial debt, uncertainty over legacy, security and terrorism, political reputation and corruption can potentially taint the best-prepared of hosts. The limited field of finalist cities for the 2022 event is the clearest manifestation of these concerns and, depending on the outcomes from the IOC's Olympic Agenda 2020, a potential theme for the next phase in the trajectory of the Winter Olympics.

Notes

1. The Nordic Games, founded in 1901, were organized by the Swedish Central Association for the Promotion of Sports. The Holmenkollen Week is a leading Norwegian winter sports event.

2. 'Skeleton' refers to a one-person sled which is driven by a competitor in a prone, head-first position down an ice track. The availability of the run at St Moritz meant that the event was held there as part of the 1948 Winter Olympics, although it was generally referred to as 'toboganning'.

3. Olympic Museum Archive, Lake Placid General file 1928–1991. Letter, G. Dewey, Chairman of Lake Placid, to M. Le Comte, President of the International Federation of Bobsleigh and Tobogganing, Paris, 9 November 1929.

4. Olympic Museum Archive, Lake Placid General file 1928–1991. Letter from IOC, 29 March 1930.

5. Overlays are temporary structures such as walkways, which are required for the Games, but might be removed after the event itself.

6. A quality benchmark 'first published as a standard in 1996 and it specifies the requirements for an organization's environmental management system. It applies to those environmental aspects over which an organization has control and where it can be expected to have an influence' (BAB, 2010).

7. Olympic Museum Archive, Oslo Correspondence COJO, 1947–1953. Undated draft of suggestion of the Special Committee regarding the reduction of the sports' programme of the Olympic Games, Jeux Olympiques de 1952 Oslo Correspondence COJO, 1947–1953.

Acknowledgements

The authors wish to acknowledge use of the IOC Archives, Olympic Studies Centre, Lausanne for some of the material presented in this paper. Thanks also to Professor Brian Chalkley for his collaboration in previous Olympic-related papers and to Professor Mark Brayshay for his comments and advice on an earlier draft of this chapter. Credit also to Tim Absalom and Jamie Quinn for the cartography.

Chapter 4

The Cultural Olympiads

Beatriz García

In its eventually unsuccessful candidature file to host the 2012 Olympic Summer Games, New York made a point of commemorating the long, but largely unknown, history of the Cultural Olympiad as a key component of the Games celebration. By 2012, the official Olympic Games cultural programme was turning 100 years old and had been a compulsory part of the Olympics hosting process at every Summer Games since Stockholm 1912. This, argued the New York bid, was a motif for reflection and celebration about the contribution of the arts and culture to the modern Olympic Games (NYOBL, 2008, pp. 180–181).

The notion that the Games should complement its elite sport competitions with a programme of arts and cultural activity was central to the vision of Pierre de Coubertin, founder of the Modern Olympic Movement. It was a notion inspired by Coubertin's interpretation of the Ancient Greek Games tradition, which involved the showcase of human excellence in a variety of forms, from athletics to music and poetry. Despite Coubertin's original vision, the Olympic cultural programme or 'Cultural Olympiad' has a mixed history and is one of the least visible and appreciated components within the process of hosting the Games. This chapter offers an overview of the programme's evolution, from its original presentation in the form of Olympic Art Competitions to its latest incarnation as a 4-year Olympiad. It discusses key trends and challenges and briefly touches on potential future developments given the new thinking emerging in the context of the International Olympic Committee's (IOC) Agenda 2020.

From Art Competitions to Cultural Olympiads

Origins: The Conference on Art, Letters and Sport, 1906

The principle of holding an arts festival in parallel with the celebration of sporting competitions is embedded in the foundations of the Olympic Movement. The Movement was founded in 1894 by Baron Pierre de Coubertin, a French pedagogue who sought to revive the ancient Greek tradition of quadrennial celebrations of athletics and the arts that had been held in Olympia from 776 BC to 393 AD. In the Ancient Games, athletes were called to display their talents in parallel with philosophers, scholars, poets, musicians, sculptors and high-profile leaders. Coubertin defined such gathering of talents as the 'spirit of Olympism', and Olympism was in turn defined as the simultaneous training of the human body and the cultivation of the intellect and spirit, together viewed as manifestations of the harmoniously educated man. On this basis, Coubertin's ambition was to create an environment in modern society where artists and athletes could, again, be mutually inspired. In support of this ambition, the Olympic Charter establishes that 'blending sport with culture and education' is a fundamental principle of Olympism (IOC, 2015d, p. 13).

As discussed in Chapter 2, Coubertin's ability to attract and coordinate the attention of critical decision-makers around the world led to the re-birth of the Games. The first three Games at Athens 1896, Paris 1900 and St Louis 1904, however, lacked any activities alongside the sporting events. To change this, Coubertin convened a 'Consultative Conference on Art, Letters and Sport' at the Comedie Française in Paris in 1906. He invited artists, writers and sports experts to discuss how the arts could be integrated into the Modern Olympic Games. The invitation stated that the purpose of the meeting was to study 'to what extent and in what form the arts and letters could take part in the celebration of modern Olympic Games and become associated, in general, with the practice of sports, in order to profit from them and ennoble them' (Carl Diem Institute, 1966, p. 16).

The original proposal tabled at this first meeting established the following as a possible cultural programme to develop at each succeeding Games (see table 4.1). As a result of the conference and in order to ensure a clear association of the arts with the modern Olympics sport programme, Coubertin proposed the creation of an arts competition and requested it to be a compulsory part of every Olympic Games celebration from then on (cited in IOC, 1997a, p. 92). This competition was called the 'Pentathlon of Muses' and involved the awarding of medals in five classic art categories: sculpture, painting, music, literature and architecture.

Table 4.1. Programme for the 1906 Conference, circulated by Pierre de Coubertin. The material in italics records the first indications of a possibility for 'competitions' to emerge.

Dramatic art	Outdoor productions; essential principles; recent writings; sports on stage
Choreography	Processions; parades; group and coordinated movements; dances
Decoration	Stands and enclosures; mats, badges, garlands, draperies, clusters; night festivals; torchlight sports
Literature	*Possibility of setting up Olympic literary competitions*; conditions for these competitions; sporting emotion, source of inspiration for the man of letters
Painting	Individual silhouettes and general views; *possibility of and conditions for an Olympic painting competition*; photography as aid to the artist
Sculpture	Athletic poses and movements and their relationship with art; interpretation of effort; objects given as prizes; statuettes and medals

Source: Müller, 2000, pp. 609–610; author's emphasis.

Figure. 4.1. Original emblem for the Pentathlon of Muses (Stockholm, 1912). (*Source*: Müller, 2000, p. 628)

The organization of the first 'Pentathlon of Muses' was designated to a special commission in the context of the London 1908 Olympic Games, the first Games after the 1906 Consultative Conference. Nevertheless, time constraints and disagreement over the programme contents led to its cancellation at the last minute (see Burnosky, 1994, pp. 21–22). Consequently, the first official Olympic arts competition did not take place until Stockholm 1912 (see figure 4.1).

From Stockholm until London 1948, arts competitions were organized in parallel with the sporting competitions, and artists, like athletes, competed and won gold, silver and bronze medals (Stanton, 2000). However, regulations and contest parameters changed considerably due to difficulties in defining the different competition sections and disagreement in defining the most appropriate subject for the works presented. Over the years, the competition's sections changed from the five areas composing the 'Pentathlon of Muses' to a long list of sub-categories that tried to account for an ever-increasing range of art-form variations. The appropriate theme for Olympic artworks was also controversial, as there was disagreement over whether or not to restrict the entries to works inspired by or portraying sports activities exclusively. Initially, it was compulsory to present a sporting theme but, with the growth in abstraction as an international artistic trend, this proved difficult and limiting in areas other than architecture or design for sports buildings (Burnosky, 1994, p. 23).

Further problems stemmed from the dominant Western bias in the definition of cultural value and aesthetics, as most judges and competitors were European and, in consequence, it was rare that non-Western artists were awarded a medal. Other problems were of a logistical nature, in particular transport difficulties for large sculptural works, which were accentuated due to the inconsistent funding and operational support received from respective Games Organizing committees.

Another and, eventually, determining factor limiting the appeal and success of the cultural programme was due to the regulation of amateurism in the Olympic

Movement.[1] The 'amateur' regulation implied that, as in the case of athletes at the time, the participation of professional artists capable of making a living out of their art could not be accepted as part of the official Olympic programme. In the arts context of the 1930s and 1940s this became even more problematic than in the sporting context. This was because most artists were considered professional in their devotion to their vocation and high-quality artistic expression was equated with professionalism (IOC, 1949, cited by Burnosky, 1994, p. 34).

Most disappointing for Coubertin and his closest supporters was the poor audience participation attracted by the arts competitions. As noted by Hanna (1999, p. 108): '[c]ultural celebrations based on sport were increasingly irrelevant; while people … watch[ed] competitive sport, their interest did not extend to sport in art'. This was a profound set-back to the promotion of Coubertin's ideals, as a major reason for holding cultural events alongside the sports competitions was to inspire discussion and the promotion of ideas among all Olympic participants and spectators.

In this context, the Berlin 1936 Games stands out. In contrast to other host cities where Olympic arts manifestations had played a minor role, the so-called 'Nazi Games' presented a cultural festival of unprecedented dimensions for which a large-scale national and international publicity campaign was created to ensure maximum recognition and participation. The Official Games report stated:

> Because of the slight interest which the general public had hitherto evidenced in the Olympic Art Competition and Exhibition, it was necessary to emphasise their cultural significance to the Olympic Games through numerous articles in the professional and daily publications as well as radio lectures. (Organizing Committee 1937, vol. 2)

The most ambitious example of Olympic art programming that Berlin 1936 offered has been seen by many as evidence of culture and the arts being used for propaganda purposes; a view that is hard to deny given that the Berlin Arts Committee programme was actually chaired by a representative of the Reich Ministry of Propaganda (*Ibid.*). The Games had been identified by the local host as an opportunity to promote the ideals of Nazi Germany and cultural activity was seen as a good vehicle to represent the supremacy of the Aryan race and Western civilization. This, in turn, meant, that the cultural programme was taken as seriously as the sporting competition programme and it thus secured high levels of investment and public visibility.

Cultural innovations introduced at the Berlin Games included the first Olympic torch relay, travelling from Ancient Olympia in Greece (symbolic cradle of the Olympic Games) to the Berlin stadium; and the first artist-led Olympic film, Leni Riefenstahl's *Olympia*. These cultural manifestations became as central to the Olympic experience as the sport competitions, both during Games time and in subsequent visual and broader narrative representations of the 1936 Olympic Games. Notably, the torch relay and the principle of producing an official Games film have become a key part of the Games staging process and its symbolic representation to this day.

The 1940 and 1944 Olympic Games and related arts programmes were not held because of the Second World War, but by the time of London 1948, the appointed Organizing Committee succeeded in paralleling the sports with arts competitions. After the cultural programme ended, the British Fine Arts Committee that had been set up on occasion of the Games compiled a 'report of jurors' suggestions for future arts contests' (Good, 1998, p. 33). This was intended as a guide to subsequent Organizing Committees since, until then, there had been no operational framework about how to produce an Olympic arts programme. Good (*Ibid.*, p. 20) explained that 'the recommendations included reducing the number of arts categories' and concluded that the 'interest in the exhibitions would be greater if they were more closely linked up with the Games themselves and if a more intensive press campaign had been organised'. By 1950, however, the problems and difficulties that had been common to most Games were perceived to be far greater than the benefits and achievements brought by hosting Olympic art competitions. To review the situation, an extended discussion took place within the IOC from 1949 in Rome to 1952 in Helsinki. As a result of this process, which involved a detailed assessment of the 'amateur' nature of Olympic contributions, it was decided that from 1952, the presence of the arts in the Olympics would take the form of cultural exhibitions and festivals instead of competitions.

Olympic Art Exhibitions and Festivals: Helsinki 1952 to Seoul 1988

The first official (and non-competitive) Olympic arts festival was held at Melbourne 1956, after several rushed changes in focus for the cultural programme in Helsinki 1952. The Melbourne festival was coordinated first by a Fine Arts Subcommittee, elected in 1953 and then by a Festival Sub-Committee created in 1955. The festival had two major components: one of visual arts and literature, and another of music and drama. Exhibitions and festivals were staged simultaneously in the weeks leading up to and during the Games and featured local, national and international artists and performers. A special book on Australian arts was published after the Games, entitled *The Arts Festival: a Guide to the Exhibition with Introductory Commentaries on the Arts in Australia*. The Official Report of the Melbourne Games concluded that 'the change from a competition to a Festival was widely welcomed, since the Festival provided a significant commentary on Australia's contribution to the Arts' (cited in Good, 1998, p. 29).

This new stage in the Olympic cultural programme tradition brought opportunities as well as challenges for the integration of the arts and culture as a core dimension of the Olympic staging process. On the one hand, Games organizers had greater freedoms to define the purpose of such programmes and determine who should be presenting what type of work. On the other, the effect of eliminating the competitive element was to divorce the programme from the patriotic rivalries and nationalistic edge that typically accompany the sporting events. This situation accelerated the trend towards diminishing the numbers of Games participants (particularly, athletes, but also sport fans) that were involved or interested in the cultural programme, and also during the next few Games to a loss in international focus. As highlighted by the Australian report, the programme was now mainly a platform for local cultural representation and was directed by the specific interests of the host authorities (mainly, Ministries of Culture or related bodies), with much less direct involvement and regulation from the top Olympic structures or other sporting bodies.

In this new context, some Olympic host countries saw the programme as an important opportunity to make a statement about their history, and as an opportunity to profile the host nation, far and beyond what was possible within the sporting arenas or the highly regulated Olympic ceremonies and protocol. Despite their disconnection from the sporting world, host cities became increasingly ambitious in their treatment of the arts festivals, progressively aligning them with the 'growing arts agenda' that developed after the Second World War including an aspiration to address 'audience development, access, and inclusion' in the arts (Gold and Revill, 2007, p. 73).

From Melbourne 1956 to Tokyo 1964, the focus was almost exclusively on the presentation of national heritage, however the late 1960s and 1970s saw an upsurge in contemporary cultural initiatives and some radical re-thinking about the role and relevance of the arts as a component of the Games staging process and a key vehicle to project the Olympic city. Mexico City 1968 presented what remains to this day one of the most ambitious and innovative Olympic festivals. It spanned an entire year and featured the best of both Mexican contemporary arts and heritage and folklore. These were showcased alongside the works of leading international artists and art companies. The ambition and quality of the programme proved that while Mexico may have been considered a country that was part of a 'developing world' from an economic point of view, it was at the avant-garde and represented a 'first world' in terms of art and culture. Crucially, Mexico City viewed the Olympic cultural programme in a more holistic fashion than other Games hosts and, beyond the arts, incorporated discussions about education and science as well as advertising, design and communications that were, in turn, used to promote and explain the value of the Games (Organizing Committee, 1969).

Montreal 1976 also presented an innovative cultural programme, exploring the national identity of Quebec and Canada, but also attempting to recover the original Coubertin aspiration to explore the connections between art and sport, a topic that had become secondary since the end of the art competitions. The linkages between art and sport were presented not just as a theme, but as a staging process involving the introduction of arts activity within sporting venues, in particular, the main Olympic Park avenue and the areas surrounding the stadium.

Throughout the 1960s and 1970s, other areas where artists and related creative practitioners made major contributions were the design of banners and logos to

Figure. 4.2. Cultural Olympiad pictograms complementing the sport pictograms, Mexico City 1968. (*Source*: Organizing Committe, 1969)

dress the city and signpost Games venues – what is now termed 'the look of the Games'. The imagery for Mexico City 1968, Tokyo 1964 and Munich 1972 are all exemplars of *avant-garde* visual design rather than simple marketing and branding exercises, and they can be viewed as leading examples of urban cultural policy innovations emerging out of the Games. These elements of the Games were, however, rarely treated as part of the official cultural programme (Mexico City 1968 being a notable exception), and subsequent Games (excepting Barcelona 1992 and Torino 2006, see below) have failed to use 'the look of the Games' as an expression of advanced and place-sensitive creative practice. Table 4.2 summarizes the key format variations and characteristics of Olympic cultural festivals in this period. As this makes abundantly clear, each Olympic host approached their cultural programming with different priorities and the length of activities varied significantly, from four weeks in Helsinki and Melbourne, to one year in Mexico 1968.

Cultural Olympiads: Barcelona 1992 to London 2012

Another stage in Olympic cultural programming was initiated with the Barcelona 1992 Olympic bid, which proposed that implementation of a Cultural Olympiad during the four years of the Olympiad – from the end of one Games to the start

Table 4.2. Olympic Arts Festivals, Summer Games 1952–1988.

Olympiad	Length of Cultural Festival	Content and Themes	Highlights
Helsinki 1952	4 weeks	International exhibitions of architecture, painting, graphic arts, sculpture, literature, music	Submitted musical compositions performed in a concert
Melbourne 1956	4 weeks	National (Australian) culture	Exhibition: Showcase of Australian Art
Rome 1960	6 months★ 3 weeks	National (Italian) culture with an emphasis on history; sporting references in exhibition programme	Exhibition: Sport in History and Art; Medieval historical pageants
Tokyo 1964	7 weeks	National (Japanese) high art and traditional culture	Exhibition: Ancient Japanese Art Treasures
Mexico City 1968	1 year	International; high art and indigenous culture; nation-wide celebration of culture Overall title: Cultural Olympiad	World Folklore Festival Ballet of the 5 Continents; International Exhibition of Folk Art Exhibition of selected works of world art; New Fire ritual at Teotihuacán
Munich 1972	3 months★ 6 weeks	International; high art and folk culture Overall title: *Olympic Summer*	Exhibition: *World Cultures and Modern Art* International folklore festival Avenue of Entertainment: live performance in the Olympic Park
Montreal 1976	4 weeks	National – showcase for Canadian provincial culture	Exhibition: *Mosaicart* – Canadian visual arts *Artisanage* – craft demonstration Canadian festival of popular arts The Celebration – live outdoor performance
Moscow 1980	1 year★ 5 weeks	National, mass participation, high art and folk culture: national art of the peoples of the USSR	Exhibition: *One hundred masterpieces from the Hermitage Collection* Exhibition: *Moscow in Russian and contemporary art* Exhibition: *Sport – Ambassador of Peace* Opera and classical music
Los Angeles 1984	10 weeks	7 weeks: international festival for domestic consumption 3 weeks LA and US culture for international Olympic audience	Exhibition: *A day in the country: impressionists in the French landscape* Performing arts programme Art commissioning programme
Seoul 1988	7 weeks	Korean high culture and traditional culture for an international audience; international artists and companies; contemporary culture for domestic audience	International festivals in folk culture, dance, theatre, music, song The Olympiad of art – contemporary sculpture park International modern art competition Street festivals and Han River Festival

★ Length of cultural festival including exhibition runs and pre-Games programme from official reports of Organizing Committees.
Source: Based on compilations by Gold and Revill, 2007, p. 74.

of the next. Barcelona's Cultural Olympiad thus started in 1988, at the end of the Seoul Games, and evolved up to 1992 with a different thematic emphasis for each year. García (2000) noted how this decision stemmed from the organizers' vision for the Games as a platform to improve the city's urban landscape and assist in Barcelona's international projection far beyond the Olympic staging period. Indeed, Barcelona 1992 has come to be remembered and portrayed by the international media as the Games that placed the city at the heart of the Olympic experience (figure 4.3).

Figure. 4.3. 'Art in the Street' programme, connecting the city and its waterfront. (Barcelona 1992). (*Photos*: Beatriz García)

The festive use of public space during Games was central to Barcelona's perceived success. However, beyond its contemporary public art programme, it is less clear whether the official Cultural Olympiad programme (largely restricted as it was to traditional arts venues such as the opera house and museums), played much of a role within the Olympic city's narrative (*Ibid.*).

Regardless of the actual effectiveness of specific activities within the 1992 Cultural Olympiad, the 4-year format was maintained in subsequent Summer Games up to 2012. This was on the initiative of respective host cities rather than an IOC directive, as there has never been a formal requirement to create a 4-year cultural programme as a build-up to the Games competition fortnight. This stage in Olympic cultural programme development was characterized by two additional phenomena, resulting in large part from the commitment to multi-annual cultural programming. On the one hand, there has been a clearer alignment of the Cultural Olympiad with local and national cultural policy ambitions than ever before; on the other, the programme has faced growing operational tensions.

The first phenomenon means that priority objectives for the Games have become more clearly aligned with established cultural, social and economic agendas. From a cultural point of view, the Games period has been used not only to expand sport audiences but also cultural and arts audiences. Furthermore the Games have been used not only to expand sporting facilities, but to advance broader local creative development aspirations (García, 2012). From a social perspective, it is now common for the Games and its Cultural Olympiad to aspire to improving community inclusion, expanding access to marginal or deprived communities, and strengthening local or national identity. Finally, from an economic perspective, it is increasingly common to present a Cultural Olympiad as a catalyst to advance urban regeneration, reposition the host city, and develop cultural tourism (García, 2004).

In parallel with the above, new tensions have also emerged, mainly due to the high professionalization and global mediatization of the Games (García, 2012). Most notably, the branding tension between 'official' Olympic arts events, sporting competitions and related Games activity has become increasingly apparent and has led on to varied attempts at establishing separate Cultural Olympiad or Olympic Arts Festival brands (García, 2001, 2012). The Cultural Olympiad of Athens 2004 provides an example of the extremes to which organizers have been ready to go in order to establish a strong Olympic cultural programme identity and brand. The programme was given a prime position within the event hosting process, as the city celebrated the contribution of Greece and Greek heritage as the cradle of European civilization and the birthplace of the Olympic Games. The Cultural Olympiad was thus used as a platform to convey ancient Olympic values and claim ownership of the Games in ways not accessible to other Olympic hosts. This involved the establishment of a Cultural Olympiad Foundation in 1998. The Foundation had backing from UNESCO and it aimed to become a permanent institution to coordinate Olympic cultural programming in the same way that the IOC coordinates the sporting programme. However, at the time of writing, more than a decade on from the establishment of this institution, its role remains unclear, providing yet another indication of the persistent challenges embedded within the Olympic cultural programme tradition.[2]

Returning to the most unifying trend within this period a common feature in most Games between 1992 and 2012 was the design of annual thematic festivals, one for each year of the Olympiad. In Barcelona, the themes evolved from a 'Cultural Gateway' in 1988, to the 'Year of Culture and Sport' in 1989, the 'Year of the Arts' in 1990, the 'Year of the Future' in 1991 and the 'Olympic Art Festival' in 1992. Atlanta also covered a wide range of subjects during the 4 years of festivals, arranged into two main themes: 'Southern Connections' within the United States, and 'International Connections'. Sydney (see García, 2012) offered a taste of the many and diverse Australian cultural communities through presenting an indigenous festival in 1997 ('Festival of the Dreaming'), a festival dedicated to multicultural groups and the waves of immigration in 1998 ('A Sea Change'), and international festivals in 1999 ('Reaching the World') and year 2000 ('Olympic Arts Festival'). Finally, Athens reflected on major philosophical and humanistic principles by exploring the notions of 'Man and Space', 'Man and the Earth', 'Man and the Spirit' and 'Man and Man'.

By the time of Beijing 2008 and London 2012, however, this trend was changing yet again. Instead of annual thematic festivals, both sets of organizers opted for generic mass participation countdown events without any specific thematic emphasis other than the aspiration to generate excitement around the Games build-up (e.g. the 'Open Weekend' initiative for London). It was not until their respective Games years that both Beijing and London presented a more ambitious 'Olympic Arts Festival' with a clearly curated and strong international focus (such as 'London 2012 Festival'; see García, 2013a). In addition to this, London went further than other previous Games by also presenting the most extensive national cultural programme to date, with themed programming organized, not per year, but per UK region and thus resulting in twelve distinct Olympic regional cultural programmes (*Ibid.*).

Rio de Janeiro 2016 is the first Summer Olympic Games since Seoul 1988 not to organize a 4-year Cultural Olympiad. This opens what could become a new stage in Olympic cultural programming, as the focus becomes less about the overall duration and more about the ways in which the cultural programme can shape or project the host city and be part of the 'Olympic experience'. The implications of such change are briefly discussed in the concluding section of this chapter.

Culture at the Winter Olympic and Paralympic Games

While this chapter emphasizes the experience of the Summer Games hosting process, it is worth mentioning some of the crucial differences in cultural programming that arise within the Olympic Winter Games and the Paralympic Games. While these events share similar operational frameworks, the Paralympics are delivered at a smaller scale and their approach to organizing the Cultural Olympiad provides a rich counterpoint that, from the viewpoint of Olympic cities, has at times proved to be more effective than that delivered by Summer Games.

Winter Games (1956 Onwards)

The artistic programme of the Winter Games was not formally established until Cortina d'Ampezzo in 1956 and started in a modest fashion. More ambitious cultural programmes comparable to the Summer Games began with Grenoble 1968, the same year that Mexico hosted its year-long international Cultural Olympiad. In the four most recent Winter Games – Salt Lake City 2002, Torino 2006, Vancouver 2010 and Sochi 2014 – it is apparent that the ambition of Olympic host cities to attract attention building on a cultural discourse has kept growing and is aligning with broader urban cultural policy agendas (see also García, 2012).

Along with the more diminutive scale have come interesting nuances that allow for different kinds of cultural programming that have resulted in a growing

Figure. 4.4. Medals Plaza, a way to connect sport with its city and cultural context (Torino 2006). (*Photo*: Beatriz García)

differentiation from Summer Games protocols. This differentiation has evolved since Salt Lake City in 2002. One of the most noticeable is the establishment of a 'medals plaza' (figure 4.4) as a distinct mixed-venue within the host city centre. This is a space where medals are awarded to athletes, thus extending and changing the ceremony that would normally take place exclusively within sport venues. The justification for this extension has been that winter sports take place mainly within mountain resorts away from any urban centre and have thus a low capacity to generate a festival atmosphere. The creation of a medals plaza as an additional Olympic venue has allowed organizers to intensify the experience of the winter Olympic city.

Integral to the medal plaza ceremonies is the programming of cultural activities in addition to the presentation of medals to the winning athletes. For instance, in Turin and Salt Lake City, it was typical for medal ceremonies to be followed by feature performances by international singers and musicians. This is one clear example in which the Winter Games has affected the Olympic protocol in a way that is conducive to more effective and better integrated city programming. Another relevant development has been in the approach to dressing the city during the Games. At Turin 2006, the traditional *Look of the Games* programme, dedicated to highlight sporting venues, was complemented by a comprehensive *Look of the City* programme, dedicated to promoting the city's cultural assets in a manner reminiscent of Mexico City 1968 (García and Miah, 2007).

Innovation continues to occur at the Winter Games. For instance, the Cultural Olympiad of Vancouver 2010 lasted 4 years, a first for any Olympic Winter Games, and it became a visible element within the city's dressing strategy, with dedicated 'culture' flagpoles in the years leading to the Games and during the Games fortnight in 2010. Further, also in Vancouver, the launch of a Cultural Olympiad Digital Edition (CODE) allowed the profiling of new technologies that resulted in creative art-form interventions as well as ways to engage disparate communities throughout Canada. These communities were invited to reflect on their sense of identity via social media environments and share them within a dedicated online platform, Canada CODE, which became one of the most effective mechanisms to generate nationwide involvement in the Games (Klassen, 2012).

Following on Vancouver, Sochi 2014 also presented a 4-year Olympiad and adopted the annual thematic focus approach that had been common to previous Summer Games. At Sochi, the themes evolved from a year of cinema in 2010, to theatre in 2011, music in 2012, museums in 2013 and a combined international arts festival in 2014.

Paralympic Games (2000 Onwards)

With regard to the Paralympic Games, cultural programming remained a low priority until the turn of the twenty-first century. Sydney 2000 was the first Games to work towards a high profile Paralympic Cultural Olympiad and proposed a single team to manage both the official Olympic and Paralympic cultural programme. In the wake of Sydney 2000, a series of agreements between the IOC and the International Paralympic Committee (IPC) resulted in closer synergies between the two Games, including the decision to establish a single Organizing Committee which effectively means that all key programmes are organized under the same operational framework.

In the context of London 2012, the team responsible for the cultural programme was committed to expanding such organizational synergies into an all-encompassing Games cultural policy narrative, where there was no distinction between Olympic and Paralympic cultural activity. Indeed, the London 2012 Cultural Olympiad incorporated a celebration of long established UK disability arts organizations as part of its 4-year national programme and a range of regional cultural programmes placed an emphasis on presenting activity that questioned the notion of 'normality' as a way of bridging the gap between perceptions of 'abled' or 'disabled' bodies, be it in the realm of sports or arts. Furthermore, the Games-time 'London 2012 Festival' spanned both Olympic and Paralympic fortnights without interruption, thus acting as a symbolic bridge between both events. To maximize visibility, London also created a distinct label and brand for its disability arts programme: 'Unlimited' (see Garcia et al., 2013).

The sharing of a common team and a single programme of activity places the Cultural Olympiad in a significant position to promote greater synergies between

Olympic and Paralympic Games in years to come. This is because all other Games programmes, from the sport competitions to symbolic events such as the torch relay or the ceremonies, follow a different planning and delivery cycle. This could help assert the added value brought by a flexible approach to Games cultural programming.

Main Trends, Challenges and Opportunities for Culture at the Games

The dynamic nature of the Cultural Olympiad is manifest in the diversity of formats, objectives and management structures put in place to implement it over more than a century. While the sports competitions and infrastructural dimensions of the Olympic sports programme have become extensively rationalized and standardized, the cultural programme has remained an area open to free-interpretation by respective hosts up to the present. This section offers a brief summary of key programming trends, highlighting the way they have evolved over time.

Thematic Focus: From Sporting Heritage to Contemporary Fusions

The Olympic cultural programme has explored a wide range of art forms and varied approaches to its thematic emphasis. It started with a clear and exclusive focus on classic art forms (fine arts) under a mainly Western (European) canon. Interestingly, during the time it operated as an art competition, rather than just focusing on the display of old masters and well known works of art, it effectively encouraged the production of 'new' artworks that can be considered a major contribution to the development of Olympic cultural heritage. This is because the art on show had to be inspired by Olympic Games ideals as well as sporting achievement. Ultimately, despite the controversies regarding the status of contributing artists as professional or amateur, the founding focus of the Olympic cultural programme resulted in the production of a series of distinct artworks, many of which form the permanent art collection at the Olympic Museum in the IOC Headquarters in Lausanne.

As already suggested, the move away from competitions into art exhibitions and festivals led initially to abandoning production of new 'Olympic' artworks and instead prioritizing the showcase of the host's best-known and longest established national artists and cultural expressions. The focus continued to be on classic art forms but the remit broadened into national folklore displays. A majority of hosts during this time opted to concentrate almost entirely on their national artistic heritage (notably Melbourne 1956, Rome 1960 and Tokyo 1964).

From the 1960s through to the 1980s, however, a majority of hosts placed an unprecedented emphasis on contemporary and often international art. The most outstanding examples within this period were Mexico City 1968, Munich 1972 and Los Angeles 1984, all of which featured world-class artists and invested in new contemporary art commissions to be presented during Games time. Munich and Los Angeles went a step further in their attempts at linking contemporary art trends with the Olympic narrative by introducing the notion of an 'Olympic art poster' series. While the production of Olympic posters was a tradition that had started with the first Modern Games in 1896, renowned artists had never been involved in their production. The point of distinction in Munich, Los Angeles and, subsequently, Sarajevo 1984 and Barcelona 1992, was that world leading artists of the time were commissioned to produce a visual statement representing Olympic achievement without the need to produce a literal representation of sport.

From 2000 onwards, in line with global cultural policy trends, many Western country hosts expanded into what is commonly termed cultural fusion and innovation as part of their Cultural Olympiad programming. This has involved pioneering cross-sectoral collaborations between the arts, health and technology fields, amongst others. This approach has often been articulated as an attempt to use the Games to showcase local aspirations for greater cultural integration and social change rather than just focusing on the presentation of well known cultural icons, as had been the dominant trend up to the 1950s. Vancouver 2010 and London 2012 are two key exemplars in this area. Nevertheless, the 'cultural fusion' narrative is mainly a Western construct that contrasts with the approach taken by most Eastern Games hosts. The latter have continued to prioritize the display of traditional arts and their most valued cultural heritage over cross-sectoral collaborations (for instance, Beijing 2008 and Sochi 2014), but this is expected to change with Tokyo 2020, where organizers intend to highlight youth and technology as top priorities within its cultural narrative.

Despite the broadening of topics and format interests, the one area that has remained secondary since the demise of the art competitions has been the exploration of links between art and sport. While at every Games there are art communities that, on learning about the existence of an Olympic cultural programme, argue in favour of exploring such connections, examples of truly innovative and meaningful collaborations in this domain remain scarce. Indeed, most attempts at an art and sport fusion have been unsuccessful from an audience or media-attention point of view. The only exceptions to this have been the few examples of series of Olympic art posters; a tradition briefly recovered by London 2012 (see figure 4.5), but only previously undertaken by four out of sixteen Art Exhibition and Cultural Olympiads, plus one winter Cultural Olympiad.

Vision and Priority Objectives

The progressive expansion in Cultural Olympiad thematic and format focus is reflected in the expansion of programme objectives and priorities. From a chronological point of view, it is possible to detect a move from traditional cultural objectives (such as emphasizing cultural icons and traditions) into broader political, economic and social objectives (see table 4.3). Furthermore, based on an analysis of programming choices and priority objectives as revealed by documentation

Figure. 4.5. Art and sport links, as represented via the rare tradition of Olympic art posters (London 2012).

Table 4.3. Evolution of dominant Cultural Olympiad objectives.

Key objectives	Dominant Characteristics	Key Exemplars
Cultural (dominant up to the 1950s)	(*i*) Celebrating classic cultural icons (*ii*) Showcasing and promoting *host traditions and folklore* (dominant in the 1950s but also common in the majority of subsequent Games editions, complementing other objectives)	Tokyo 1964, Mexico City 1968, Montreal 1976, Moscow 1980, Seoul 1988; the most recent edition with a strong 'folklore' component has been Sochi 2014
Political (1960s–1980s)	(*i*) overcoming negative international associations and stereotypes about the host nation (e.g. violence, authoritarianism)	Tokyo 1964, Munich 1972, Moscow 1980, Beijing 2008, Sochi 2014
	(*ii*) encouraging or reigniting local/ national pride	Tokyo 1964, Moscow 1980, Barcelona 1992, Sochi 2014
	(*iii*) presenting a distinct local (small nation) story / narrative	Montreal 1976 (on Quebec) Barcelona 1992 (on Catalonia)
Economic (1990s onwards)	(*i*) repositioning a city (or country) from a low (or outdated) profile into a more desirable and globally competitive image in order to attract tourism & inward investment (*ii*) entertaining crowds, assisting with city navigation during Games time	e.g. Barcelona, Sydney and Torino sought to differentiate their cultural tourism from more traditional tourist images of Spain, Australia or Italy and from long-term city rivals Madrid, Melbourne and Milan
Social (2000s onwards)	(*i*) reconciliation with indigenous cultures	Sydney 2000: e.g. *Festival of the Dreaming*
	(*ii*) representation of marginal communities (low income groups, religious minorities etc)	Vancouver 2010: e.g. showcasing artwork from homeless groups
	(*iii*) empowering youth and disabled communities	London 2012: e.g. *Unlimited,* disability arts programme

Source: Author's elaboration, building on official Cultural Olympiad reports (1992 onwards).

available from the Olympic Studies Centre in Lausanne (1952–1996) and from Olympic Organizing Committees since Sydney 2000,[3] it suggests that the vision behind most Cultural Olympiads fall within one or several of four broadly defined typologies: politics and identity; economic regeneration; entertainment, look and feel; and cultural and social change. These, in turn, supply a valuable framework for a commentary on the ways in which such typologies have materialized, supported by specific examples that prioritize the most recent Games.

1. *Politics and Identity: Growing or Reigniting National Pride.* This first typology includes Cultural Olympiad programmes that prioritize a local or national target audience and focus on direct, live participation opportunities rather than media coverage. The two most dominant approaches within this typology are a focus on folklore and popular traditions, or a focus on celebrating classic national cultural icons:

◆ *Folklore and/or popular traditions*: Cultural Olympiads with this kind of focus tend to be embraced by host communities and perceived as meaningful at grassroots levels; however, such programming is often invisible to – or not much appreciated by – visitors and the international media, particularly when it involves local references considered obscure by external audiences. Recent examples include the nationwide choral singing and folklore dances presented (nationally) in the lead to Beijing 2008 and Sochi 2010. In both cases, these were celebrated as a first attempt at a nationwide cultural programme open to exploring the diversity of Chinese and Russian cultures respectively.

◆ *Celebration of classic national icons*: this approach can be a source of pride for local communities but, if not carefully assessed and cognisant of community sensitivities, it can be perceived as tokenistic or aimed at international tourists rather than host citizens. Recent examples include Athens 2004 with its extensive programming of classic Greek theatre in iconic ancient venues, London 2012's programming of an International Shakespeare Festival or the many world-class Russian ballet galas presented during Sochi 2014.

2. *Economic Regeneration: City Reimaging and Tourism Projection.* Securing an economic return has become a common priority for Olympic cultural programming since the 1990s, particularly for cities that view the Games as a key platform to join the league of global cities. The main approaches within this typology are:

◆ *Focus on classic and internationally renowned cultural icons*: as noted above, this tends to be popular with international audiences but it may be viewed as tokenistic or lacking in innovation by local communities if it is not appropriately complemented by traditional or modern cultural expressions. Beyond the examples presented in the previous section, it is worth noting a line of programming in London 2012 which was dedicated to celebrating and pushing forward the tourist appeal of well known British heritage sites such as Stonehenge, Hadrian's Wall and the Tower of London (García and Cox, 2013)

◆ *Projection of modern cultural icons and emerging creative industries*: this is aimed at both local and international audiences and tends to prioritize a 'connoisseur' audience rather than the general public. Cultural programmes with this kind of focus appeal to high-spending cultural tourists and can be very effective in the positioning of host cities as world-class cultural and creative centres. Recent examples include the final Olympic Arts Festival in Sydney 2000, which presented all its performing arts programme at the Opera House; as well as the London 2012 Festival, which presented itself as a distinct component of the London Cultural Olympiad, dedicated to celebrating the most excellent and advanced cultural expressions in the UK (*Ibid.*).

3.   *Entertainment, 'Look & Feel': Crowd Management, City Animation and City Dressing*. This typology tends to be the least ambitious from a cultural policy and long-term urban strategy point of view but is useful as part of the Games hosting process as it helps address short-term needs regarding crowd control and city dressing to create a (manageable) festive atmosphere in the public realm, outside the sporting venues. The two main programming formats within this typology could be labelled as:

◆ *Entertainment*: by which is meant a focus on open-air activity to entertain and divert the crowds. This was championed by Sydney 2000, which launched the now firmly established tradition of 'Live Sites' as hubs for free activity and entertainment throughout the city during Games time.

◆ *Look and feel*: a focus on visual and graphic design interventions to dress the city as well as sporting venues in a recognisable, unifying look.

In the 1960s and 1970s, there were some excellent examples of Cultural Olympiad integration within what we now understand as the 'look and feel' of the Games. As briefly suggested earlier, Mexico City 1968 and Munich 1972 developed cultural iconography components that were simultaneously: innovative from an aesthetic point of view; unique to the local host; and useful as a Games dressing tool and entertainment aid. However, from 1980 through to the first decade of the twenty-first century, the approach to city and Games venue dressing has shown a lowering of cultural ambition in favour of easily replicable, and thus increasingly standardized, formats (García, 2011). This is a trend that may change in the wake of London 2012, where graphic design was once-more aligned with place-specific cultural narratives, in particular, the interest in projecting the UK as a world leading and youth-oriented creative industries centre (see García, 2015; García and Cox, 2013).

4. *Cultural and Social Change: Creative Innovation and Community Empowerment.* This is the most ambitious of all the Cultural Olympiad typologies and the one with greater potential to deliver sustainable and meaningful legacies. It is, however, also the hardest to achieve as it requires long-term planning to enable adequate linkages between widely diverse stakeholders. If associated with Olympic values and understood as a Games-related opportunity and outcome, it can provide a key platform to add credibility to the Games experience amongst often inaccessible communities of interest.

The main approaches and exemplars that fall under this category are as follows:

◆   *A catalyst for cultural advancements*: this occurs when the Cultural Olympiad or specific activities are seen primarily as a catalyst for artistic and creative innovation, an opportunity to push forward a cultural agenda that may have stagnated before the Games were awarded. This has commonly involved dedicated investment in public art during Games time (for instance, Barcelona 1992 'Art in the street', Sydney 2000 'Sculpture by the Sea', Torino 2006 'Luce di Artista'); the use of unusual spaces to present arts activities for the first time (such as London 2012 artistic interventions in distant iconic sites such as Stonehenge; showcase of 'hidden' areas in London); working with new technologies or promoting emerging habits (as with Vancouver 2010 ' Cultural Olympiad Digital Edition' and London 2012 'Pop-up' events, which were reliant on social media).

◆   *Social transformation:* this occurs when the programme is used to advance specific or multiple social agendas in line with Olympic (and Paralympic) Games values such as: empowering youth (such as Beijing and Sochi: country-wide youth singing programmes or London's youth-oriented programme presenting the work of over 6,000 young or emerging artists); expanding opportunities to engage with or show the work of disabled artists (for example, Sydney 2000: *Invincible Summer;* and London 2012: *Unlimited*); working with marginal communities (at Sydney: *Festival of the Dreaming*, led by contemporary Aboriginal artists; at London: collaborations with homeless communities and the unemployed).

Delivery Formats

Despite the ongoing development and expansion of cultural programme objectives and thematic priorities, the underlying challenges in terms of visibility and linkage between artistic programming and other Games activity have remained practically the same since inception. Good (1998, p. 31) argued that the shift from art competitions to exhibitions did not solve the problem of adequate programme integration because it did not address the 'management issues' that had been repeatedly raised in official Games reports up to the 1950s. As argued by Masterton (1973), García (2012) and Miah and García (2012) these problems have been accentuated by the absence of an international cultural organization comparable to the international sports federations in its ability to coordinate and support Olympic arts initiatives. Subsequent attempts to address this gap, such as the proposal to establish a permanent Cultural Olympiad foundation in Greece, have lacked sufficient international backing to become viable models. Instead, as is the case with other cultural event networks, learning and transfer of knowledge regarding operational issues has relied on personal connections and informal word-of-mouth rather than being a thoroughly documented and transparent process.

As a result, there is no established model of delivery for the Cultural Olympiad. As noted in the previous section, up to 1992 the duration of a Cultural Olympiad would vary considerably. Since 1912, the only formal request by the IOC is that 'cultural activities take place during the time the Olympic Village is open' (IOC, 2015d) but few Olympic hosts have limited their cultural programming to that period. As such, we find the variations that were recorded in table 4.2 ranging from 4 weeks in Helsinki 1952 and Melbourne 1956 to 4 years in Barcelona 1992 and London 2012. Other key variations that affect consistency and easy identification of the programme are its geographical spread and the approach to branding and communications.

Geographical Spread

Most Olympic Games have concentrated their cultural programmes in the host city, mainly within central areas or, in some cases, within the Olympic Park

Table 4.4. Geographical locations for the Cultural Olympiad.

City centre – famous cultural venues	This has been the most common approach since 1912 and is the most popular location of Cultural Olympiad events to this day.
City centre – public spaces/ street	This has grown particularly since the late 1960s and is an important area of development as a complement to the so-called Live Sites (i.e. open air entertainment around large screens) so that the street entertainment on offer is not just generic but an opportunity to showcase host cultures or explore innovative creative practices.
Olympic venues/ Olympic Park	There are few good examples in this area. The scarce presence of cultural programming in Games venues has limited its impact and relevance for Olympic fans. Munich 1972 and Montreal 1976 developed artistic programming within the Park, but most tend to offer generic entertainment programmes not related to the distinct aspirations of their Cultural Olympiad. London 2012 has been the first Games to develop a contemporary public art programme within the Olympic Park embodying its vision for innovative, unusual, sustainable and locally representative artistic practices.
Host regions/ nationwide/ internationally	There has been a growing interest in nationwide programming since Barcelona 1992, as the flexibility afforded by multi-annual programming is viewed as a valuable platform to engage communities beyond the host city, welcoming diverse interests and forms of cultural expression. The most accomplished example of nationwide cultural programming is London 2012.

Source: Author's elaboration, building on Cultural Olympiad archives (Official Reports).

and related Olympic venue). However, with the growth in duration of cultural programming, a parallel ambition has been to involve communities beyond the host city to ensure that the Games are owned at a regional and national level – and, sometimes, internationally. This has brought an additional challenge, as the more dispersed the activity, the more difficult it has been to ensure that the programme is widely visible and recognized, particularly from the perspective of media coverage (García, 2001).

Table 4.4 provides a summary of cultural programming locations. The first nationwide cultural programme took place in Mexico City 1968, with various attempts at following this trend taking place in the lead up to Sydney 2000, Athens 2004 and London 2012. London established an Olympic first by supporting the creation of thirteen regional 'Creative Programmer' posts who would coordinate and encourage Olympic cultural activity in their respective regions, without depending directly on the Olympic Organizing Committee for the Olympic Games. This facilitated opportunities for legacy but also made it harder to establish a clear identity and brand.

Promotional Frameworks

From a promotional point of view, little is known about the approach to communicating and attracting interest in the Cultural Olympiad before the advent of global branding techniques and the creation of comprehensive Olympic marketing guidelines (see Chapter 7). However, such techniques have rarely been applied to the cultural programme. With the notable exception of Mexico City in 1968, the visibility and imagery association between the official cultural programme and the sporting competitions has been minimal.

A common approach to identify and promote the cultural programme has been the creation of a dedicated visual icon, often a variation on the main Olympic Games iconography. Los Angeles 1984 offered a variation on the main Games emblem, with no Olympic rings; Barcelona 1992 and Sydney 2000 had two visual identities (pre-Games time, Games time), always including the rings; Athens 2004 received a different identity, unrelated to the Games emblem (no rings); and London 2012 offered a variation on the main logo but with no rings. In the cases of Barcelona 1992 and Athens 2004, where the approach was to create a different brand altogether, it has been argued that there were important communication gaps and a lack of promotional synergy with mainstream Olympic activity (García, 2000; Panagiotopoulou, 2008).

Whether employing a derivative icon or a distinct brand, the most common challenge for promoting and establishing a clear branding association between the cultural programme and the rest of the Games are the commercial restrictions imposed on the use of the Olympic rings. The Olympic rings are the best known symbol of the Games and one of the most recognisable brands worldwide. However, Cultural Olympiad activity has rarely been granted access to this asset due to the fact that the main global Olympic sponsors do not tend to play a part as funders of cultural programming nor agree to be official presenters of artworks during Games time. Instead, most Cultural Olympiad activities are funded by alternative sources which, at times, include competing commercial sponsors.[4]

Given the long established concerns regarding the difficulty for the Cultural Olympiad to be promoted appropriately, the London 2012 culture team engaged in extensive Games branding discussions from the moment they were awarded the event. Their objective was to establish a Cultural Olympiad brand that did not conflict with Olympic sponsor interests but allowed cultural contributors to search alternative sources of funding or acknowledge their own long term sponsors. This resulted in the establishment of an 'Inspired by 2012' mark, a visual icon that was clearly associated with the London 2012 Games but did not include the Olympic rings (figure 4.6). This approach was deemed as successful by many British cultural

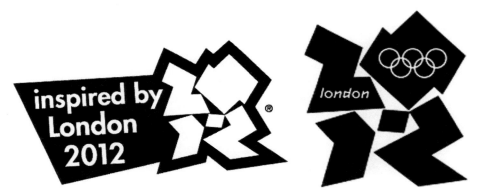

Figure. 4.6. 'Inspired by 2012', a London 2012 brand excluding the Olympic rings. (*Source*: London 2012 Olympic and Paralympic Organising Committee, by courtesy of the IOC)

partners and also benefited other types of Games-related programming, beyond the Cultural Olympiad, such as educational, volunteering and business oriented initiatives (see García, 2013a; García and Cox, 2013).

It is as yet unclear whether the 'Inspired by' initiative can be replicated in other Games contexts and become an avenue for branding cultural activities without conflicting with Olympic sponsor interests. At the heart of this branding debate lies the question of who the Cultural Olympiad is for and what counts as cultural value at the Olympic Games. As long as Cultural Olympiad programming cannot be promoted in association with the Olympic rings, it is unlikely it will be perceived as a core Olympic component and will continue to be excluded from international Games-oriented media coverage. Instead, the trend is to position the Cultural Olympiad as a programme of local and national interest, of merit to host communities as a provider of context and background to the sporting competitions, and as an opportunity for direct engagement and participation, particularly for those not able to access sport competition tickets and attend official Games venues. This divorces the Cultural Olympiad from other aspects of the Games capable of generating global media spectacle, such as the Opening and Closing ceremonies. It also divorces the Cultural Olympiad from the original aspiration by Coubertin, which was to ensure it played a central role in the appreciation of the sport competitions and provide context to the athletic achievement.

The Future

Since 2014, with the nomination of a new IOC president, the IOC has embarked on the comprehensive visioning exercise framed as Agenda 2020 (see IOC, 2014*a*). A commitment within this exercise is to rethink the role of culture in the Olympic Games hosting process and overcome the programme's traditional marginalization. This is in line with the expanding debate over the need for 'legacy', sustainability and a '360 degree' Olympic management experience (IOC, 2009, p. 27), a term that refers to the IOCs ambition to better integrate all Games programming dimensions and ensure that the sporting competitions are rooted within each of the Olympic cities where they take place (figure 4.7).

These aspirations may have important implications for the future of the Cultural Olympiad. First, this new approach has impacted on the Candidate City bidding guidelines, discouraging the traditional relegation of 'cultural programming' to a separate and minor chapter in the bid proposal. Instead, it is made into a core dimension of the Olympic city and of the spectators' experience that is presented within the introductory, framing sections to the bid. While the effects of such change are still to be seen, this suggests a push for organizers to

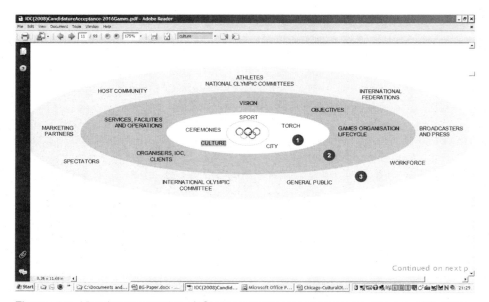

Figure. 4.7. Visual representation of 'Olympic experience' components. (*Source*: IOC, 2008*a*, emphasis added)

think more creatively about ways to embed their cultural proposals within the Olympic Games hosting process rather than treating them as a separate – and easy to isolate or ignore – programme of activity.

Further, for the first time, the IOC has established a 'Culture and Heritage' department, with staff working on a dedicated cultural strategy and policy framework to guide in the delivery of programming that contributes to the development of a distinct Olympic narrative. This team is also looking into options to ensure that Games branding and media relations guidelines are better attuned to the needs of the cultural programme.

Regardless of the possibility for clearer and more strategic regulations from the IOC perspective, host cities have also become more effective and strategic in their profiling of culture around the Games hosting process. Be it as a political, economic, social or broader cultural objective, local organizers have become well aware of the importance of contextualizing the Games as a global mega-event within a distinct and meaningful cultural programme in order to secure a sustainable legacy. This suggests that the role and relevance of future Cultural Olympiads will keep growing, and the demand for greater clarity and effectiveness in their delivery framework will also expand. Olympic cities may come to prominence through the opportunity to host 16 days of international elite sport competitions, but they tend to be best remembered (and differentiated, from one to the next) by their ability to showcase unique skylines, public spaces and approaches to celebration that are sensitive to their specific heritage and diverse community values, as well as engaged with emerging and globally relevant creative practices.

Notes

1. In the original conception of the Olympic Games, a key criterion for inclusion as an Olympic competitor was the need to be an amateur athlete, that is, not to be a full time professional and compete in sport for financial or commercial gain. This rule was also applied to the arts competition, and caused controversy as it became a challenge to attract artworks of the right quality if contributors could not be professional artists. Avery Brundage was elected as IOC president in 1952 and was strongly opposed to any form of professionalism in the Olympic Games. His views prevailed during the lengthy revision of Olympic Arts Competitions formats and priorities that took place between 1949 and 1952 and led to their replacement by Arts Exhibitions.

2. The issue of branding for the Cultural Olympiad in other Games editions is discussed at the end of this chapter.

3. Analysis conducted by the author of documentation stored at the Olympic Museum – Olympic Studies Centre relating to every Olympic official cultural programme between Helsinki 1952 and Atlanta 1996, plus Cultural Olympiad materials and observations collated during fieldwork visits to Olympic summer and winter host cities from Sydney 2000 to Sochi 2014.

4. For a more detailed discussion on Olympic financing and branding regulations, see Chapter 6.

Chapter 5

The Paralympic Games

John R. Gold and Margaret M. Gold

The Paralympics is becoming a truly worldwide event … we want it to be the same as the Olympic Games.

Tanni Grey-Thompson

Speaking to an academic audience, Dame Tanni Grey-Thompson (2006), then the leading medal winner in the history of the Paralympic Games, noted the remarkable convergence of the Paralympic and Olympic movements. From pragmatic beginnings as part of the treatment of spine-injured ex-servicemen towards the end of the Second World War, disability sport has developed so rapidly that it now supports sport-specific national squads of elite athletes participating in international competition. As the summit of disability sport, the Paralympic Games have played a major part in changing social attitudes by emphasizing achievement rather than impairment and by accelerating the agenda of inclusion. They have also forced changes in official attitudes in countries where disability was ideologically problematic, if only to accommodate international opinion when bidding for the Olympics – given that the Paralympics are now closely linked to that process (Gold and Gold, 2007).

This chapter considers the development of the Paralympics from small beginnings as a competition for disabled ex-servicemen and women in the grounds of Stoke Mandeville Hospital (England) to the present day ambulatory international festival held in Olympic cities immediately after the Summer or Winter Games. It traces their origins to the work of Dr (later Sir) Ludwig Guttmann at the National Spinal Injuries Unit at Stoke Mandeville Hospital in Buckinghamshire, who used sport as an integral part of the treatment of paraplegic patients. The sports competition held at the hospital to coincide with the Opening Ceremony of the London Games in July 1948 became an annual event attracting the first international participation in 1952, after which it became the International Stoke Mandeville Games. From 1960 onwards attempts were made to hold every fourth Games in the Olympic host city, although the path towards acceptance by host cities proved difficult. As will be seen, it was only from 1988 onwards that a process of convergence began that brought the Paralympics into the central arena of the Olympics, both literally and figuratively, leading to the host city being required to include a bid for the Paralympics as part of its bid for the Olympics.

The later parts of this chapter discuss the relatively modest ramifications of this requirement for prospective host cities, given that Paralympians make use of many of the same facilities as their Olympian counterparts. Although unlikely ever to drive major infrastructural or regeneration projects, the Paralympics have repercussions for the host city in the need to accommodate a group of athletes and officials with different requirements and in promoting the cause of a barrier-free urban environment. The implications of these provisions are discussed in relation to the Paralympics of the twenty-first century, particularly in relation to the emphasis placed on the disability agenda in the successful bid made by London for the 2012 Games.

Origins

The first stirrings of disability sport emerged in the late nineteenth century, primarily through the work of activists in the deaf community. The first Sports Club for the Deaf was founded in Berlin in 1888 and by 1924 national sports federations for the deaf had emerged in Belgium, Czechoslovakia, France, Great Britain, Holland and Poland. Collectively, these six federations sent 140 athletes to Paris in 1924 to participate in the First International Silent Games – the gathering that marked the birth of a 4-yearly cycle of 'World Games for the Deaf' (Séguillon, 2002, p. 119). Subsequently divided into Summer and Winter festivals after the pattern of the Olympics, these were later recognized by the International Olympic Committee (IOC) as the Deaflympics.

The Deaflympics were important as an indicator of possibilities, but the deaf community retained a separate existence as a disability group rather than participating in the movement that would create the Paralympics. Instead, the latter stemmed from the treatment of severely injured servicemen at the end of the Second World War and particularly the work of Ludwig Guttmann – a figure whose role is comparable to that of Baron Pierre de Coubertin in reviving the modern Olympics (see chapter 2). Guttmann, a prominent Jewish neurosurgeon, had arrived in Britain as a refugee from Nazi Germany in 1939. After appointment to a research post at Oxford University's Department of Neurosurgery and then at the Wingfield-Morris Orthopaedic Hospital, he became director of what would become the National Spinal Injuries Centre at Stoke Mandeville Hospital (Aylesbury, Buckinghamshire). Guttmann later commented that paraplegia was the 'most depressing and neglected subject in all medicine' at this time (quoted in Goodman, 1986, p. 96), characterized by poor patient survival rates, low morale amongst nursing staff, and difficulty in recruiting specialist physiotherapists. His approach instituted a programme of 'total care', having patients turned physically every two hours day and night to prevent pressure sores and improving standards of bladder hygiene to help tackle problems of infection. Physiotherapy assisted limb flexibility and, for some patients, increased mobility. A pre-vocational work regime and various forms of recreation including concerts, visits and *competitive* sports, designed to keep patients busy and create a sense of purpose, complemented the medical regime.

In this context, therefore, sport transcended mere leisure. Not only was it 'the most natural form of remedial exercise', restoring physical fitness, strength, coordination, speed, endurance and overcoming fatigue, but also had the psychological impact of restoring pleasure in life and contributing to social reintegration (Guttmann, 1976, p. 12). Developing these ideas, Guttmann formulated the idea of a sports festival for the disabled that would promote contact with other patients and address attitudes about the capabilities of the disabled. On 28 July 1948, an archery competition took place on the front lawns of the hospital, involving sixteen competitors arranged into two teams: one from Stoke Mandeville and the other from the Star and Garter Home for disabled ex-servicemen in Richmond-on-Thames. The event was consciously chosen as a demonstration of potential, symbolized by being held on the same day as the Opening Ceremony of the London Olympics, with archery seen as second only to swimming in its 'physiotherapeutic value ... for the paralysed' (Special Correspondent, 1948). In 1949, Stoke Mandeville hosted a larger competition, involving sixty competitors from five hospitals participating in what became a steadily widening group of sports (table 5.1). During the meeting, Guttmann gave a speech in which he hoped that the event would become international and achieve 'world fame as the disabled men and women's equivalent of the Olympic Games' (Goodman, 1986, p. 150).

The Stoke Mandeville Games quickly acquired an international dimension, particularly by drawing on institutional connections that the Hospital had developed through training visiting staff, through staff moving to other hospitals and spreading Stoke Mandeville's characteristic approach to sport, and through ex-patients who pioneered paraplegic sport in their own countries. In 1952, another Olympic year, the involvement of a group of Dutch war veterans presaged wider European participation. In 1953, teams from Finland, France, Israel and the Netherlands appeared, along with a Canadian team. The Americans first participated in 1955, followed by the Australians in 1957 – by which time the Stoke Mandeville Games had commonly gained the nickname 'Paralympics' (Carisbroke *et al.*, 1956, Brittain, 2010, pp. 24–25).[1] The word 'Paralympics' at this stage was clearly a pun combining 'paraplegic' and 'Olympic' (IPC, 2006a), effectively confronting Olympian traditions of celebrating excellence and the perfectly formed body with the realities of disability. It was only over time that reinterpretation occurred. In part, this was driven by the Games embracing participants with forms of disability other than paraplegia. Equally, it resulted from a process of convergence that closely allied the Paralympics with the Olympic movement. With an ingenious revision of the etymology, the approved version of the term asserted that the first syllable of 'Paralympics' derived from the Greek preposition 'para', meaning

Table 5.1. Paralympic sports.

Summer Games	Year included in the full Paralympic Programme
Archery	1960
Athletics	1960
Boccia	1984
Bowls	1968–1988, 1996
Cycling	1988
Equestrian	1996
Football 5-a-side	2004
Football 7-a-side	1984
Goalball	1976
Judo	2004
Powerlifting/Weightlifting	1964 men
Powerlifting/Weightlifting	2000 women
Rowing	2008
Sailing	2000
Shooting	1976
Swimming	1960
Table Tennis	1960
Volleyball – standing volleyball	1976–1996
Volleyball – sitting	1980
Wheelchair Basketball	1960
Wheelchair Fencing	1960
Wheelchair Rugby	2000
Wheelchair Tennis	1992
Winter Games	
Alpine Skiing	1976
Ice Sledge Hockey	1994
Nordic Skiing – Cross Country	1976
Nordic Skiing - Biathlon	1994
Wheelchair Curling	2006

Source: IPC (2006a).

'beside' or 'alongside'. Viewed in this way, the Paralympics constitute a festival that exists alongside and operates in parallel with the Olympic Games, while retaining a separate identity (*Ibid.*).

Building Connections

As the Games grew, demands for greater professionalism towards the organization, funding and management of international sport for the disabled saw the establishment in 1959 of the International Stoke Mandeville Games Committee (later Foundation, hence ISMGF). This ran and developed the annual Stoke Mandeville Games and oversaw the organization of a parallel 4-yearly 'Olympic' competition until 1972 (see table 5.2).

The process of building links with the Olympics, however, proved long and torturous despite highly promising beginnings. In 1956, during ceremonies at the Melbourne Olympics, the IOC had awarded the Fearnley Cup to Guttmann for 'outstanding achievement in the service of Olympic ideals' (Goodman, 1986, p.

Table 5.2. Summer Paralympic Games.

Year	Aegis	Location	Number of countries	Number of athletes	Number of sports for which medals awarded	Disability Groups
1952	Stoke Mandeville Hospital	Stoke Mandeville★	2	130	6	SI
1960	ISMGC	Rome	23	400	8	SI
1964	ISMGC	Tokyo	21	357	9	SI
1968	ISMGC	Tel Aviv, Israel★	29	750	10	SI
1972	ISMGF	Heidelberg, West Germany★	43	984	10	SI
1976	ISMGF ISOD	Toronto, Canada★	38	1657	13	SI, A, VI, LA
1980	ISMGF ISOD	Arnhem, Holland★	42	1973	12	SI, A, VI, LA, CP
1984	ISMGF	Stoke Mandeville★	41	1100	10	SI
	ISOD	New York★	45	1800	14	A, VI, LA, CP
1988	ICC	Seoul	61	3013	18	SI, A, VI, LA, CP
1992	ICC	Barcelona Madrid★	82 73	3021 1400	16 5	SI, A, VI, ID
1996	IPC	Atlanta	103	3195	19	SI, A, VI, LA, CP, ID
2000	IPC	Sydney	122	3843	19	SI, A, VI, LA, CP, ID
2004	IPC	Athens	136	3806	19	SI, A, VI, LA, CP
2008	IPC	Beijing	146	3951	20	SI, A, VI, LA, CP
2012	IPC	London	160	4200	20	SI, A, VI, LA, CP, ID
2016	IPC	Rio de Janeiro	176 tbc	4350 tbc	23 tbc	SI, A, VI, LA, CP, ID (tbc)
2020	IPC	Tokyo	tbc	tbc	22 tbc	SI, A, VI, LA, CP, ID (tbc)

★ Years in which the Paralympic Games did not take place in the Olympic location.

Guide to abbreviations: SI Spinal Injury; A Amputee; VI Visually Impaired; LA Les Autres; CP Cerebral Palsy; ID Intellectual Impairment.

Sources: Various and Scruton, 1998.

157), a remarkable degree of recognition less than a decade after the foundation of the Stoke Mandeville Games. The next stage was to take the Stoke Mandeville Games to the Olympic host city itself and, when the Games were held in Rome 1960 and Tokyo 1964, the convergence of the two sets of Games seemed assured. Such arrangements, however, depended on the goodwill of the host city, sponsorship and public funding to cover the cost. The Rome Games, for example, had the cooperation of the Spinal Unit at Ostia, gained sponsorship from INAIL (*Istituto nazionale per l'assicurazione contro gli infortuni sul lavoro* – the Italian National Insurance Institute Against Accidents at Work), and had the support of the Italian Olympic Committee (CONI). The 400 disabled athletes used the Olympic Pool and Village, but last minute changes meant that those parts of the Village equipped with lifts were unavailable. Moreover, withdrawal of an offer to use nearby Olympic facilities meant that competitors were perforce conveyed by a 40-minute bus ride to the Tre Fontane sports ground (Scruton, 1998, p. 308). The Tokyo Games followed on from the Summer Olympics, accommodated competitors in the Athletes' Village, and shared facilities recently used by the Olympic athletes. Its Opening Ceremony, with the Crown Prince and Princess acting as patrons, attracted 5,000 spectators.

From this point, problems with the host city seriously affected further progress. Another 24 years passed before disabled athletes again competed in an Olympic host city (Seoul 1988), with a succession of cities refusing to host the Paralympics. The IOC, in its role of handling the bidding process for the Olympics, was only interested in the candidate cities' ability to meet the costs and needs of elite athletes. There was no stipulation that the Olympic city must host parallel games for athletes with disabilities. Admittedly, the Paralympics became a greater challenge to hosts as they grew in size (see table 5.2), especially with admission of a wider range of disability groups after 1976. The increasing scale of the Games, coupled with prevailing building standards that failed to accommodate the disabled, shortage of available funds and lack of any inclusive philosophy regarding athletes with disability proved obstacles for further collaboration with many Olympic cities.

For example, despite having sent three observers to Tokyo, Mexico City declined the Games in 1968 because of 'technical difficulties'. They were held instead at the sports centre of the Israel Foundation for Handicapped Children in Ramat Gan near Tel Aviv. In 1972, the University of Heidelberg staged the Games rather than Munich, as plans for the post-festival use of the Olympic Village had meant transferring the site to developers for conversion into private apartments immediately after the Olympic Closing Ceremony (Scruton, 1998, p. 320; see also Chapter 15). Lack of suitable accommodation, real or claimed, plagued subsequent events. In 1976, Toronto acted as hosts rather than the Olympic city of Montreal, with the athletes housed at Toronto and York Universities. Their two Paralympic Villages were located some distance from each other as well as from the competition venues. When the Moscow Olympic Organizing Committee failed even to respond to a request to stage the Games, the 1980 festival took place at Arnhem in the Netherlands. Here, too, the available accommodation (an army barracks) was inconveniently located for access to the sports venues. In 1984, the Americans agreed to host the Games for all disabilities, but not in the host Olympic city (Los Angeles). Instead, they were to be split between New York and

Figure 5.1. Stoke Mandeville stadium (Aylesbury, Buckinghamshire).

the University of Illinois (Champaign); an arrangement that foundered when the latter withdrew through funding problems just four months before the Games. As a result, 1,800 amputee, cerebral palsy, visually impaired, and Les Autres[2] athletes competed at the Mitchel Park athletics complex in Uniondale, New York, with 1,200 athletes participating in the wheelchair events that were hurriedly rearranged at Stoke Mandeville (*Ibid.*, pp. 184, 202). Ironically, these were the first Games that the IOC officially recognized as the Paralympics (figure 5.1) although the first full Games to use this title was in 1988 at Seoul.

The early Winter Paralympic Games for the disabled fared little better (table 5.3). Established in 1976, initially they too did not take place at the Olympic venues or even in the same countries. The first Winter Games took place in Örnsköldsvik (Sweden) rather than at Innsbruck (Austria). These were followed in 1980 by Games at Geilo (Norway) rather than Lake Placid, at Innsbruck in 1984 rather than Sarajevo (although an exhibition event was held in the Winter Games there), and Innsbruck again in 1988 rather than Calgary, which declined to hold the Paralympics.

This retreat from the positive pattern seemingly established in the early 1960s greatly disappointed the Paralympic movement. Guttmann (1976, p. 174) denounced the thinking that had prevented Mexico City 1968 or Munich 1972 holding the Games, commenting on 'the lamentable lack of appreciation of the place thousands of disabled sportsmen and women have earned for themselves

Table 5.3. Winter Paralympic Games.

Year	Aegis	Location	Participating countries	Number of athletes	Number of sports	Disability Groups
1976	ISOD	Örnsköldsvik Sweden★	17	250	2	VI, A
1980	ISOD ISMGF	Geilo Norway★	18	350	2	VI, A, SI, CP, LA
1984	ICC	Innsbruck Austria★	21	457	2	VI, A, SI CP, LA
1988	ICC	Innsbruck Austria★	22	397	2	VI, A, SI, CP, LA
1992	ICC	Albertville France	24	475	2	VI, A, SI, CP, LA
1994	IPC	Lillehammer Norway	31	492	3	VI, A, SI, CP, LA
1998	IPC	Nagano Japan	32	571	4	VI, A, SI, CP, LA
2002	IPC	Salt Lake City USA	36	416	3	VI, A, SI, CP, LA
2006	IPC	Turin Italy	39	477	4	VI, A, SI, CP, LA
2010	IPC	Vancouver Canada	44 expected	502 expected	5	VI, A, SI, CP, LA
2014	IPC	Sochi Russian Federation	45	541	5	VI, A, SI, CP, LA, ID (tbc)
2018	IPC	PyeongChang Korea	over 50 tbc	670 tbc	6	VI, A, SI, CP, LA, ID (tbc)
2022	IPC	Beijing China	tbc	tbc	tbc	tbc

★ Years in which the Paralympic Games did not take place in the Olympic location.

Guide to abbreviations: *SI* Spinal Injury; *A* Amputee; *VI* Visually Impaired; *LA* Les Autres; *CP* Cerebral Palsy.

Sources: Various; Scruton, 1998.

in the field of international sport'. Chiefly as a result of this, a new complex of buildings was constructed at Stoke Mandeville (figure 5.2), comprising a Stadium for the Paralysed and Other Disabled (opened in 1969 and later renamed the Ludwig Guttmann Sports Stadium for the Disabled) and an 'Olympic' Village in 1981 (Goodman, 1986, p. 164). Thus the sporting facilities were finally separated from the hospital itself and from the notion of 'illness', reflecting the fact that disabled athletes were now achieving elite status with an emphasis on performance.

Institutional Convergence

The problem, however, was not simply the resistance of Olympic cities and their Organizing Committees, since the definition of disability and competing jurisdictions of relevant organizations also affected progress. The Stoke Mandeville Games originally confined entry to medically controlled paraplegics, but the

Figure 5.2. Cauldron for the Paralympic flame, Paralympic Games, Stoke Mandeville, 1984.

organizers felt impelled to respond when other groups pressed for participation in internationally organized sports festivals. The foundation of the International Sports Organization for the Disabled (ISOD) in 1964 created opportunities for the blind, amputees and individuals with other locomotor disabilities (de Pauw and Gavron, 2005, p. 39). ISOD collaborated with ISMGF in broadening the scope of the 1976 Toronto Games to include amputees, visually impaired and Les Autres. Competitors with cerebral palsy joined the 1980 Games.

The expanding scope of disability sport quickly generated new international disability organizations. The need to coordinate their activities and eliminate duplication of events required further institutional arrangements, leading in particular to the foundation of the ICC (International Coordinating Committee of the World Sports Organizations) in 1982. This brought together nominated senior representatives from the four major International Sports Organizations: ISMWSF (the International Stoke Mandeville Wheelchair Sports Federation, previously the ISMGF), ISOD, IBSA (the International Blind Sports Federation), and the CP-ISRA (Cerebral Palsy International Sport and Recreation Association). These were later joined by CISS (International Committee of Sports for the Deaf) and INAS-FID (International Sports Federation for Persons with Mental Handicap – later changed to Intellectual Disability). Thus constituted, the ICC gave the disabled sports movement a single voice for the first time. It also allowed greater clarity in developing relations with the IOC and Olympic Games Organizing Committees, which found immediate expression in the geographical convergence of the Summer Games at Seoul 1988 and the Winter Games at Albertville 1992.

The ICC oversaw the Games held in Olympic cities in 1988 and 1992, with the exception of the Winter Games in Calgary in 1988. The 1988 Seoul Olympics and Paralympics had separate Organizing Committees, but with sufficient coordination to allow the sharing of venues, equipment and key personnel. With the Olympic Village unavailable after the Games, a specially designed Village was constructed for the Paralympians. They also received the same spectacular Opening and Closing Ceremonies as the summer Games, watched by capacity crowds of 75,000.

Barcelona pioneered the organizational integration of the two sets of Games by giving overall responsibility to the Organizing Committee of the Barcelona Games (COOB), with a separate Division charged with overall responsibility to plan the Paralympics. This ensured explicit attention to the needs of disabled athletes and comparable treatment with Olympians. The Paralympic Games now had their custom-designed Opening and Closing ceremonial spectacles (Rognoni, 1996, p. 264). Free admission to Paralympic events ensured large numbers of spectators and there was substantial television coverage. At the same time, COOB imposed its own decisions, cutting the number of sports to fifteen and refusing to allow the mentally impaired to participate in the Paralympics. Instead INAS-FID held an officially recognized Paralympic Games in Madrid in which 1,400 athletes from seventy-three countries competed. This took place after the Barcelona Paralympic Games. The subsequent inclusion of INAS-FID athletes in the Paralympic Games between 1996 and 2000 was ended abruptly after an investigation showed that ten of the twelve Spanish basketball team were not intellectually disabled. After 2 years of negotiations between INAS-FID and the IPC, the IPC General Council voted in November 2009 to admit athletes for the London 2012 Games in four disciplines: athletics, swimming, rowing and table tennis. The aim was to progress further with inclusion in Sochi 2014 and extend the Rio de Janeiro participation to basketball and futsal (a form of indoor football).[3]

The final stage in the evolution of the institutional basis for the Games came with the establishment of the International Paralympic Committee (IPC) in 1989: an organization similar in structure to the IOC itself. Based in Bonn (Federal Republic of Germany), it serves as the umbrella organization for 176 National Paralympic Committees, five regional bodies, seventeen international disability-specific sports federations, and four International Organisations of Sport for the Disabled (in the areas of cerebral palsy, the blind, intellectual disability and wheelchair and amputees). It also acts as the international federation for ten of the Paralympic sports (IPC 2015a, p. 6; IPC 2016). Its vision is to enable 'Paralympic athletes to achieve sporting excellence and inspire and excite the world' and professes an eleven-point mission which includes sport development 'from initiation to elite level' (IPC, 2006c, p. 3; see also McNamee, 2016). Crucially, since 1992 it is now the sole coordinating body for Paralympic sport recognized by the IOC.

As the IOC and IPC moved closer together, there was identification of areas that had produced conflict, notably, the use of the term 'Olympics' (which the IOC regard as their copyright), and the Paralympic Logo. The IPC Logo, originally introduced at the Seoul Games, comprised five traditional Korean decorative motifs (Tae-Geuks) in the Olympic colours (blue, black, red, yellow and green). Given that the IOC felt this was too close to their five-ring symbol, the IPC reduced the five Tae-Geuks to three in 1994 and replaced them completely as part of a rebranding exercise in 2003. The new logo, comprising three 'agitos' (from the Latin *agito* meaning 'I move'), was first used at Athens 2004, along with the new motto 'Spirit in Motion' (IPC, 2005, p. 6).

Four agreements between the IOC and IPC signed between 2000 and 2006 clarified the relationship between the two organizations, set out the principles for further cooperation and provided financial support for the IPC. An agreement in October 2000 brought the workings of the two organizations closer by co-opting the IPC President to the IOC and including an IPC representative on eleven of the IOC Commissions, including the Evaluation Commission – the body that examines the competing bids from cities seeking to host the Olympic Games. The IOC also undertook to pay an annual subvention towards IPC administration costs ($3 million per annum), annual sums for development projects, and specific assistance to help athletes from developing countries attend the 2002 Salt Lake City Winter Paralympic Games and the 2004 Athens Summer Paralympics (IOC, 2000). An agreement in June 2001 elucidated the organization of the Paralympic Games, confirming that the location would always be the Olympic host city and would take place 'shortly after' the Olympic Games using the same facilities and venues. From the 2008 Summer Games and 2010 Winter Games onwards, there would be full integration of the two Organizing Committees (IOC, 2001). An agreement on revenues for broadcasting and marketing the Paralympics (August 2003) guaranteed IOC payments to the IPC of $9 million for the 2008 Games and $14 million for 2010 and 2012 (IOC, 2003a). The final agreement (June 2006) extended these arrangements through to 2014 and 2016, increased funding for the IPC and set out the respective roles of the IOC and IPC in the planning, organization and staging of the Paralympics, the use of technical manuals, the sports programme, and the number of accredited individuals (IOC, 2006). In 2012 the co-operation agreement signed in 2006 was extended further to 2020 and a new partnership between the IOC and IPC was implemented, identifying areas of IOC activity in which the IPC could participate. These included Olympic Solidarity, Knowledge Transfer, commercial activities and closer cooperation in the planning and delivery of the Games (IPC, 2012).

Accommodating the Disability Agenda

The move towards a 'one city, one bid' approach for selection of Olympic host cities was of vital importance to the IPC. It meant that the two festivals came into line as part of an overall package that prospective host cities would put together. Cities bidding for the Games in 2008, 2010 and beyond had to show complete organizational integration between the Olympic and Paralympic Games, with details of the Paralympic Games fully articulated in the bid documents. Indeed, the speed of integration was more rapid than these agreements stipulated, with both Salt Lake City 2002 and Athens 2004 establishing a single Organizing Committee (IOC, 2003*a*) and information on the Paralympic Games appearing in the official Reports of the Olympic Games since Sydney 2000 (e.g. SOCOG, 2000, pp. 47–49).

This development, of course, needs to be set in proper perspective. On the one hand, it was never likely that this smaller festival, held in the wake of the main events, would assume the same significance as the Olympics or preoccupy the thinking of city planners to the same extent. For many cities, the right to stage the Olympics is a prize aggressively won, whereas 'they inherit the Paralympic Games as an obligation' (Cashman, 2006, p. 247). As such, the Paralympics tend to be fitted into the package offered for the Olympics – a pragmatic strategy given that they produce little demand for additional facilities, other than for a few sports such as boccia and goalball that have special requirements[4] and for modifications to transport and stadia to allow barrier free access for competitors, officials and spectators. It is also scarcely conceivable that the Paralympics *per se* would ever act as a catalyst for major infrastructural investment or urban regeneration.

Yet, on the other hand, their significance for the host city is far from negligible. A city's Olympic bid that features a lukewarm or ill-considered approach to the Paralympics may well suffer regardless of the strength of its proposals for the Olympics. In addition, the act of staging the Paralympics impacts on host cities through the way that they confront questions of disability, most notably with respect to creating a barrier-free environment.[5] Although, as noted, the requirement to integrate the two sets of Games only became binding with the 2008 Beijing Games, hosts with an established record of upholding disability rights and with legislation enshrining rights of access already in place have enjoyed an advantage in the bidding and preparation of the Games. Hence, cities such as Sydney, Turin and London could build on their existing practices which were already recognized in legislation, whereas the Games in Athens and Beijing were the catalysts for initiating the disability agenda. In October 2008, the Russian State Duma passed new legislation embedding IOC and IPC standards in Russian law in anticipation of Sochi's hosting of the 2014 Winter Games (IPC, 2008). Similarly Brazil passed 'The Inclusion of People with Disabilities Act' in 2015 which promised to eliminate accessibility barriers for the disabled across education, transport, housing, services and sport, with the Brazilian Paralympic Committee receiving 37.04 per cent of federal lottery sport revenue – an increase from 15 per cent (IPC, 2015*b*).

In terms of Games planning, Sydney set about addressing problems seen at Atlanta 1996, such as the lack of visibility of the Paralympic Games and poor coordination between them and the Olympics. As host for the Eleventh Paralympic

Games, the city achieved a good working relationship between the bodies responsible for the two Games (SOCOG and the Sydney Paralympic Organizing Committee), which had shared departments, and with other Games-related organizations. The Games themselves took place in the Olympic Park, with the (Paralympic) Village home to 6,943 people, comprising 3,824 athletes, 2,315 team officials and 804 technical officials (BPA, 2007). The design of the Olympic Park also represented a drastic improvement in accessibility over previous Paralympics, with Australia able to capitalize on the country's longstanding active involvement in disability sport. The improved access provided in the Olympic Park, however, was 'only as good as the city and suburban network which fed into it' (Cashman, 2006, p. 254). For example, only 5 per cent of railway stations facilitated easy access for wheelchair disabled, and relatively few buses had low-floor access (*Ibid.*).

The Winter Games in Turin 2006 similarly sought to boost the visibility of the Paralympics. The Italians treated the staging of the Paralympic Games in Italy as a welcome reminder of history, given that Rome in 1960 had been the first Olympic city to welcome the Stoke Mandeville International Festival (BPA, 2007). Continuing the themes adopted by the Winter Olympics (e.g. as in figure 5.3), the Paralympics used the same accommodation and facilities (figure 5.4). The major innovation was worldwide coverage of all sports of the Paralympic Winter Games, with over 100 hours of coverage provided through an internet television channel owned by the IPC, (paralympicsport.tv), narrowcast free-to-air. Seen as a way of overcoming the resistance of the larger broadcasting networks, the service was relaunched in 2007 and provides coverage of all Paralympic sport in addition to

Figure 5.3. Welcoming slogan, Turin Airport, March 2006.

Figure 5.4. Turin Esposizione, venue for the sledge hockey, Paralympic Games, Turin, March 2006.

full coverage of the Games themselves. Over 240 hours of Paralympic coverage was provided during the Beijing Games (IPC 2009, p. 40) and with the use of YouTube and Facebook, the Games are using social networking sites to engage with a broader audience.

By contrast, there was little tradition of disabled sport in Greece. This was addressed in the years leading up to Athens 2004 by developing an accessible sports infrastructure for athletes with disability that could be used in the preparation of Greek athletes and to permit training by other Paralympic teams (ATHOC, 2005, p. 178). Eighty-five per cent of the venues used were the same as for the Olympics, with additional ones for the Paralympic-specific sports. Nevertheless, while it was possible to plan for disabled access in new Olympic investment (including public transport, venues and the public spaces around venues), the wider environment posed challenges. The Official Report of the Games went so far as to call Athens 'unfriendly' to the disabled community and requiring 'drastic measures' to make the city accessible (*Ibid.*, p. 177).

The Organizing Committee (ATHOC) produced design guidelines and accessibility information for the municipalities making up the Greater Athens area, where much of the Olympic infrastructure was located, to encourage them to upgrade their public spaces, particularly along key routes identified by ATHOC (see Chapter 17). Furthermore, it urged private businesses to promote accessibility in their own premises and to raise awareness among their staff. To this end, ATHOC and the Chambers of Commerce of the four cities participating in the Olympics (Athens, Thessaloniki, Heraklio and Volos) developed the Accessible

Choice Programme (ERMIS). Businesses compliant with this programme earned the right to display a symbol indicating that they welcomed customers with disabilities and their details were included in a directory issued to all Paralympic delegations on arrival in Greece. Although attendances were less than at Sydney (850,000 compared with 1.1 million) and some venues were less than half-full, part of the value of the festival was considered to lie in its pedagogic impact. As in Australia, the organizers had developed an educational programme to promote greater understanding of the Paralympics and a large proportion of the audience were children. An accident that killed seven students who were travelling to watch the Paralympics cast a shadow over this strategy, leading to cancellation of the artistic and entertainment sections of the Closing Ceremony out of respect. The ceremony continued, but with only the protocol elements required for the completion of the Games (*Ibid*, p. 511).

Beijing's plans for 2008 also reflected significant shifts in attitude. China's own participation in the Paralympic Movement is relatively recent. When invited to the Rome Games in 1960, the official statement declared there were no disabled in China (Lane, 2006). Relaxation of this ideological stance saw the establishment of the Chinese Sports Association for Disabled Athletes in 1983 (de Pauw and Gavron, 2005, pp. 127–128). Chinese athletes started to compete in international competition, with a small group entering the 1984 Games held in New York. The increasing seriousness with which the Chinese then took sport for the disabled is reflected in the spectacular improvement in the performance of their athletes – rising from ninth in the medal table in 1996, to sixth in 2000, first place in Athens 2004 with 141 medals and 211 medals in 2008 (89 gold, 790 silver, 52 Bronze).

This new priority reflects China's characteristic use of sporting investment as an adjunct of foreign policy (see Chapter 18), as much as any root-and-branch change in prevailing attitudes. Nevertheless, the requirements of provision for 2008 focused attention on the challenge of creating a barrier-free Games in a city where access has only been on the agenda for a short time and where much of the infrastructure was anything but barrier-free. The Beijing Municipal People's Congress adopted the country's first local legislation relating to physical accessibility when passing the 'Beijing Regulation on Construction and Management of the Barrier-free Facilities' in April 2004. The regulations applied to public transport, hospitals, banks, public toilets and parks. As a result, for instance, underground stations had ramps installed, disabled toilets, tactile paths for the visually impaired and public telephones for wheelchair users, with disabled seats provided on trains (CIIC, 2004).

However while reshaping the built environment proved relatively straightforward, the challenge of changing public attitudes towards the disabled was highlighted in May 2008 when the *Manual for being Olympic Volunteers* was published (BOCVWCG, 2008). Chapter 6 dealt with 'Volunteering Skills' and in attempting to provide the volunteer with information on how to engage with visitors from different cultural backgrounds revealed some disturbing attitudes towards people with disabilities. For example, section 2, on the 'physically disabled', stated the following:

> Physically disabled people are often mentally healthy. They show no differences in sensation, reaction, memorization and thinking mechanism from other people, but they might have unusual personalities because of disfigurement and disability. For example, some physically disabled are isolated, unsocial, and introspective; they usually do not volunteer to contact people. They can be stubborn and controlling; they may be sensitive and struggle with trust issues. Sometimes they are overly protective of themselves, especially when they are called 'crippled' or 'paralyzed'. It is not acceptable for others to hurt their dignity, so volunteers should make extra efforts to assist with due respect (*Ibid.*, pp. 6–7).

The guide was hastily withdrawn and 'poor translation' blamed. Dame Tanni Grey-Thompson's reaction to the guide was to observe that the Paralympics themselves would do more to change attitudes and Mike Brace, chair of the British Paralympic Association, called it 'a clumsy attempt to override years of limited awareness' and observed that this was in fact progress given that up to 7 years before, disabled people were often not recognized at all (O'Connor, 2008).

London 2012

In the case of London's bid for the 2012 Games, there was no doubt that, perhaps for the first time, the quality of that portion of the Olympic bid which concerned the Paralympic Games was seen as constituting a major positive factor for the entire candidacy. The location of Stoke Mandeville in London's Home Counties meant that there was a sense of the Paralympics 'coming home'. From the outset, Paralympians were part of the group responsible for organizing and drafting the bid and attended the vital IOC meeting in Singapore in July 2005, when the outcome was decided.

Under the new rules agreed in 2001, the candidate cities for the final phase of the Olympic selection procedure had to complete a questionnaire with seventeen themes. Theme 9 related exclusively to the Paralympic Games and contained nine sets of questions covering the structural integration of the organization of the Paralympics within the Organizing Committee, the dates and the competition schedule, the venues, accommodation, transport operation, travel times, disability awareness (including staff and volunteer training), media facilities, vision for the Games, finance, and the Games' legacy (IOC, 2004a). In its bid, the London Committee capitalized on the heritage of disabled sport in the United Kingdom, a tradition of volunteering for Paralympic events, anti-disability discrimination in service provision dating back to the 1995 Disability Discrimination Act, and a good record in disability awareness training. The London Bid Book promulgated three goals: to strengthen the Paralympic Movement; to deliver accessible and inclusive designs for all facilities; and to maximize media coverage (LOCOG, 2004, p. 173).

The bid contained eight specific commitments for the Paralympics (*Ibid.*, p. 191):

◆ Creating an Olympic Village that is fully accessible to all from the outset;
◆ Maximizing media coverage and exposure, as pioneered by the BBC;
◆ Integrating Olympic Games and Paralympic Games planning;
◆ Training all Games workforce in the principles of inclusion;
◆ Establishing operational policies that encompass Paralympic values;
◆ Recruiting suitably qualified disabled people;
◆ Promoting the Paralympic Games nationwide;
◆ Creating a cultural programme featuring disabled artists.

However much of the subsequent documentation coming out of official agencies as they planned for the Games tended to concentrate on the legacy aims for the Olympics with scant reference to the specifics of the Paralympics. The five legacy promises, for example, were: to make the United Kingdom a world-leading sporting nation; transform the heart of East London; inspire a generation of young people to take a part in local volunteering, cultural and physical activity; make the Olympic Park a blueprint for sustainable living; and demonstrate the United Kingdom is a creative, inclusive and welcoming place to live in, visit and for business (DCMS, 2007*a*, 2007*b*). While projects for the disabled were being developed and were referred to in these documents the main thrust was the Olympics themselves. Even the 'inclusive' goals in the fifth promise were interpreted in the introductions to those documents as being about employment, skills and workforce capacity – getting people into work and long-term employment rather than inclusion of the disabled.

In December 2009, with 1,000 days to the opening of the London Paralympic Games, Tessa Jowell, the Minister with responsibility for London 2012, announced a sixth legacy promise for the London Games: 'to bring about lasting change to the life experiences of disabled people' (Office for Disability, 2009) This finally gave greater visibility to Paralympic outcomes and lent weight to claims that the two games are part of the same project. This was followed in March 2010 with a legacy document *London 2012: A Legacy for Disabled People* which finally set the Paralympic project in the context of the Government's wider disability agenda: 'Our goal is not only to host the most accessible Games ever, but also to ensure that we harness the full power of London 2012 to help realize progress towards achieving equality for disabled people by 2025' (DCMS, 2010, p. 2).[6] The document identified three 'areas of change', within each of which were a further four objectives (see table 5.4).

This legacy document focused on people rather than physical places and spaces. The Olympic venues by this point had already been planned as barrier-free environments and the Olympic Delivery Authority had won a Royal Town Planning Institute Planning Award for their accessibility strategy (*Ibid.*, p. 29). The hard legacy issues identified in this strategy related to 1,000 sports and leisure

THE PARALYMPIC GAMES • 131

Table 5.4. Legacy vision for the Paralympic Games.

Aims	Objectives
1 Influence the attitudes and perceptions of people to change the way they think about disabled people	(a) Ensuring comprehensive media coverage (b) Providing an accessible and inclusive London 2012 Games (c) Connecting the UK with London 2012 (d) Engaging children at home and abroad
2 Increase the participation of disabled people in sport and physical activity	(a) Encouraging disabled people to be more active (b) Widening sports opportunities for disabled adults (c) Widening sports opportunities for disabled children and young people (d) Increasing the supply of accessible facilities
3 Promote and drive improvements in business, transport and employment opportunities for disabled people	(a) Opportunities for business (b) Access to jobs and skills (c) Accessible tourism (d) Improved public transport

Source: DCMS, 2010, pp. 4–7.

facilities to improve access (under objective 2b); to encourage more hotels to adopt improvements in accessibility (under 3c); improve infrastructure of London Transport system (164 stations) and 145 main line stations by 2015 (although Olympic related stations within that group would be upgraded by the Games under 3d).

The real emphasis was on soft legacy. The first aim was about social attitudes (including the role media play in shaping those attitudes), support to participate in the Games and Cultural Olympiad as volunteers, employees, spectators or participants in the ceremonies and torch relay. The second aim concerned participation in sport for all age groups – within and beyond educational institutions covering leisure sport and elite participation. The third aim was about inclusion more generally in the economy for businesses owned by disabled people, access to employment and skills training, and greater customer provision and care in tourism and transport. The document also demonstrated how many of the existing Olympic programmes feed into these goals: Cultural Olympiad-Unlimited; Access to Volunteering Fund; Get Set Programme; Let's Get Moving; Be Active Be Healthy; Playground to Podium, Compete For; Access Now; and Personal Best. These national goals were ambitious targets for a one-off event even on the scale of a Paralympics.

The Games when they came were hailed as a great success. From the Opening Ceremony on 29 August through to 9 September they used the barrier-free, accessible facilities of the Olympic Park, River Zone and Weymouth (for sailing). Public transport was upgraded so that there were sixty-six underground stations and twenty-four overground stations boasting step-free access (although at 24 per cent and 31 per cent of their respective networks there was still some way to go). Nevertheless, LOCOG felt able to claim that 'London now has undoubtedly the most accessible transport system in the world' (LOCOG, 2013b). More importantly, the Games raised the status of Paralympic sport, winning audiences in its own right without recourse to issuing free tickets or bussing in school groups. 2.7 million tickets were sold, most events were full to capacity and a cumulative global television audience of 3.8 billion in 115 countries was achieved. It seemed that disability had become a mainstream topic of news and interest as a result of the Games.

Certainly the President of the International Paralympic Committee felt that the 2012 Games had impacted significantly on the movement. Sir Philip Craven talking at the London School of Economics in 2014 under the title 'The Paralympic Movement Takes Off', pointed to the 'commercial interest' generated by the London Games, leading to IPC success in securing contracts for Paralympic Games television rights and attracting sponsors. In particular he was referring to the two-Games deal signed between the IPC and NBC for significant increases in television coverage for Sochi and Rio de Janeiro. NBC are planning for 66 hours coverage for the Rio Games, compared with only 5.5 hours for London 2012 (IPC, 2014). BP became an international partner of the IPC in 2013, signing an agreement lasting to the end of 2016.

When assessing the impact of the 2012 Paralympic Games on London much of the literature has focused on the impact on public attitudes, disability sport participation, health and mobility issues (e.g. Mahtani *et al.*, 2013; Gilbert and Schantz, 2015; Kerr and Howe, 2015; Li, 2015). For attitudes in the United Kingdom, one of the most significant indicators of possible changes in attitude was the television coverage. Channel 4 was awarded the UK broadcasting rights in 2010. They set about recruiting and training disabled presenters and reporters, building audiences and marketing the Games – increasing public awareness of the Paralympics from 16 per cent at the end of July to 77 per cent by the start of the Games. They provided 16 hours of coverage per day and 500 hours across all platforms during the Games. A peak audience of 11.6 million viewers watched the Opening Ceremony, and 25 per cent of viewers watched the daily live coverage. Post-Games research suggested that the coverage changed perceptions of the disabled, encouraged viewers to see past disability to the excitement of sporting performances and more importantly provided viewers with the vocabulary to talk about disability (Channel 4, 2012).

Further post-Games research suggested a positive effect of the Paralympics on attitudes to disability. An Ipsos MORI survey at the end of the Games indicated that 81 per cent of those surveyed believed that disabled people were now viewed more positively by the British public as a result of the Paralympic Games. Further, in a National Statistics Opinion Survey the following year, 53 per cent agreed that the Paralympics had affected their own perceptions of the disabled positively (HMG/ML 2013, p. 71).

The raising of sport participation rates for the disabled was a key goal and the evidence suggested that rates increased leading up to the Games (from 15.1 per cent of those over 16 in 2004–2005 to 18.3 per cent in 2011–2012) but has since drifted downwards to 17.2 per cent in 2014–2015 (Sport England, 2016). These figures mask complex mechanisms at work upon which a single event can hardly be expected to provide lasting impact. Ongoing and new initiatives that aim to provide this longer term support include Sports Fest, Projectability, Deloitte Parasport, and a National Paralympic Day in early September (initiated in 2013).[7]

For London, there have been both hard and soft legacies accruing from the Games in the Queen Elizabeth Olympic Park. These include the accessible sport facilities themselves and projects to boost participation such as Motivate East set up in 2013. Apart from meeting the targets for creating jobs for the disabled in the run-up to the Games, post-Games there have been positions for the impaired in park facilities. In addition there have been events to showcase disabled sport and the arts. Regular festivals include the Anniversary Games, which includes Paralympians, and the Mayor of London's Liberty Festival for disability arts, which now takes place alongside National Paralympic Day. Together these events attracted 30,000 visitors in 2014 (HMG/ML, 2015, p. 85). The inaugural five-day Invictus Games, an international competition for wounded, injured and sick servicemen and women, was held in the Queen Elizabeth Olympic Park (QEOP) in 2015. This initiative generated new biannual Games, with future Games planned for Orlando (2016) and another for 2018, which is at the bid stage at the time of writing (Invictus Foundation, 2016).

The transformation of the QEOP in the years ahead will create new neighbourhoods for East London replete with housing, hotels, retail, and business (see Chapters 2 and 19). A centrepiece of the development is the new education and cultural quarter dubbed Olympicopolis that will occupy the area around the Olympic Stadium and Aquatics Centre (Gold and Gold, 2017). In parallel with the notion of Olympicopolis, plans are now afoot to embed a significant Paralympic legacy within it – Paralympicopolis. This would involve not only disability sport, but the arts and theatre (linked to the Victoria and Albert Museum and Sadler's Wells) and education, research and development in the universities that are moving to the development: University College London, Loughborough, and University of the Arts. This is intended to consolidate the QEOP as 'the place to come for innovation and research on disability, internationally' (LLDC, 2015a).

Conclusion

The success of the Paralympic Games in Beijing 2008, Vancouver 2010, London 2012 and Sochi 2014 show the progress over the last half-century, with the Games developing from the first competition between 130 British and Dutch athletes in 1952 to the position that they now occupy. Notwithstanding a chequered history and the characteristic dissonance between bid promises and final realities, the Paralympic Games have spread geographically, have moved into new sports, have encompassed a wider range of disabilities, and have helped give credence to the belief that access to sport is available to all. In the early years, the Paralympics went to places best able to accommodate athletes with disability and organizers worked round any shortcomings in the facilities or the wider city. Once the Paralympics started sharing host cities with the Summer Games in 1988 and the Winter Games in 1992, athletes were able to enjoy environments designed principally for the Olympics but adapted for Paralympic use. As the Games came progressively closer to the heart of the Olympic movement, the disabled community have been accommodated, figuratively and literally, within the planning, design, cultural and educational programmes of Olympic cities. However, it does not follow that the two festivals receive equal treatment throughout the planning and consultation stages for it is the Olympics that still drive the desire to host the Games and the legacy agenda. This led Laura Keogh (2009, p. 9) to pose the question as to whether Paralympic legacy is different from Olympic legacy and whether the Paralympics generate 'distinct legacies'. She went on to identify five broad categories of Paralympic legacy: the hard legacy of the Olympic infrastructure; accessibility in the wider environment including buildings, transport, leisure facilities; public awareness of disability issues; the position of the disabled in society as a whole; and providing a legacy for the Paralympic Movement.

As the analysis above shows, considerable progress has been made in recent Games in all these five legacy areas, each trying to build on the evolving Paralympic brand. Rio de Janeiro buoyed by the greater exposure generated by the London Games is planning on increasing ticket sales to 3.3 million; Pyeongchang 2018 has a strategy 'Actualizing the Dream' with an emphasis on developing Paralympic sports and changing public awareness of disability (PyeongChang2018, 2016). Tokyo 2020 is already building on its pioneering Paralympic role in the Games of 1964; indeed, it will be the first city to host two Summer Paralympic Games.

The greater emphases on soft legacies that necessarily dominate Paralympic legacy discourses focus attention on issues of access and discriminatory practices. When considered in relation to an Olympic host city at one point in time, they have the potential to provide a demonstration effect that may well have implications for that city, and the nation beyond, at all other times. However, it can be argued that such considerations perhaps place a disproportionate responsibility on sport to drive disability agendas in wider society. Paralympic legacy, like any other form of legacy, can only materialize if it is nurtured, managed and funded in the longer term.

Notes

1. Nomenclature has varied. Other terms used in the 1940s and 1950s included 'Paraolympics' and 'Paraplegic Games' (Brittain, 2010, p. 15). The first use of the term Paralympic was traced by Brittain to the *Bucks Advertiser and Aylesbury News* in 1953. He also has found a number of newspapers from the *New York Times* to the Dublin *Evening Herald* using the term in 1960 (Brittain, 2008, pp. 21, 247).

2. Les Autres athletes have 'locomotor conditions such as Arthrogryposis, Arthrosis, cerebral palsy (some types), spinal cord conditions (e.g. polio), multiple sclerosis and muscular dystrophy

[and] are allowed to participate in events under the Les Autres classification. Les Autres also incorporates dwarf athletes under its classification. The locomotor conditions may be congenital or as a result of an injury or accident' (BALASA, 2007).

3. For a full discussion of the issues involved, see *inter alia* Howe (2008), Bailey (2008), Cashman and Darcy (2008) and Brittain (2010).

4. 'Boccia' is similar to petanque (French bowls) played individually or as a team game by people with cerebral palsy and other locomotor disabilities. 'Goalball' is a three-a-side gymnasium team game for the blind or visually impaired played on a special court of the same size as that used for volleyball. It involves trying to propel a heavy sound-enhanced ball past the backline of the opponents' half of the court.

5. For more general thinking on planning and disability, see Imrie (1996), Gleeson (2001) and McCann (2005).

6. See the Prime Minister's Strategy Unit's *Improving the Life Chances of Disabled People: Final Report* published January 2005, which sets out the strategy for independent living, support for families of young disabled children, transition to adulthood, support and incentives for getting and staying in employment (PMSU, 2005).

7. For more on these initiatives, see BPA (2015).

Part II

Planning and Management

Chapter 6

Olympic Finance

Holger Preuss

'The best games ever!' was former IOC President J. A. Samaranch's usual remark at the end of each Olympic Games. To host the most successful Games of all time has always been the unwritten aim of each organizer, but how should we measure this success? Should we refer to the financial, social, organizational or sporting success? In addition, from whose point of view shall we measure the success – that of politicians, the construction industry, the medallists, affluent citizens or the IOC? The question of who the real winners are remains open. Various stakeholder groups will benefit differently from hosting the Games and at each new Games the benefits will be apportioned differently.

This chapter provides an overview of the groups who benefit from staging the Olympic Games and identifies those that benefit most noticeably. The information is important because it is the basis on which decisions must be made about who should be involved in the Games, how much should be spent, and who will be held ethically responsible for the Games and their economic outcomes. Many stakeholders, of course, are negatively affected by the Games, but they are not the subject of this chapter.

How stakeholders benefit will depend to some extent on a city's motives for hosting the Games, as table 6.1 shows. The host cities' aims, and consequently the impact on the stakeholders, vary widely. The primary goal of Los Angeles 1984, for example, was to prove that the Games could be organized without deficit. To do this, the event organizers used, wherever possible, the existing infrastructure (Ueberroth *et al.*, 1985). Barcelona 1992, on the other hand, made urban renewal the highest priority (Millet, 1995) and thus invested heavily in new infrastructure. Beijing 2008 had yet another set of priorities – it aimed to demonstrate China's increasing economic potential in a new world order and at the same time to foster patriotism among the Chinese people.

The Olympic Games, as a mega-event, has to be financed by more than one stakeholder group. Its costs and benefits cannot simply be assigned to certain target groups. Hosting this event has numerous positive and negative external effects – almost the entire country is affected by the Games in terms of efficiency and opportunity costs (Preuss, 2009). This chapter discusses 'profit', in the broad sense

Table 6.1. Motives for applying to host the Olympic Games.

Motive for Applying	Examples of Host Cities with This Objective
Image enhancement	Munich 1972, Korea 1988, Sydney 2000, Beijing 2008
Urban development	Munich 1972, Montreal 1976, Seoul 1988, Barcelona 1992, Athens 2004, Turin 2006, Beijing 2008, London 2012, Sochi 2014, Rio 2016
Demonstrating economic power	Berlin 1936, Tokyo 1964, Munich 1972, Seoul 1988, Beijing 2008, Sochi 2014
Demonstrating a political system	Berlin 1936, Moscow 1980, Los Angeles 1984
Increasing tourism	Innsbruck 1976, Barcelona 1992, Sydney 2000, Athens 2004, Sochi 2014, Pyeongchang 2018
Increasing city's importance in host country	Barcelona 1992, Atlanta 1996, Nagano 1998, Beijing 2008, Sochi 2014
Increasing inward investment	Grenoble 1968, Lillehammer 1994, Barcelona 1992, Atlanta 1996, Nagano 1998, Sochi 2014
Increasing domestic political stability and self-confidence	Seoul 1988, Beijing 2008, Sochi 2014
Sport structure development	Sochi 2014, Pyeongchang 2018

Source: Adapted from Preuss, 2015.

of a benefit to society. This profit is determined not only by the stakeholders that contribute directly to the economic benefits of the Olympic Games, but also by the stakeholders who primarily receive the benefits.

The stakeholder approach selected (Freeman and McVea, 2001) explains that the purpose in organizing the Olympic Games is not only that of creating value for the Olympic Family (the International Olympic Committee [IOC], National Olympic Committees [NOCs] and International Sports Federations [IFs]), but also for external groups (such as viewers, entrepreneurs and politicians). This chapter intentionally dissociates itself from the shareholder value approach (Bea, 1997), because observation of the Olympic Family's financial gains reflects only a part of the benefit of such global and, broadly, public events. Although not all stakeholder groups have the same importance for the IOC, the latter prefers to ensure that no significant interest group bears a disproportionate financial burden lest this should undermine support for the Games.

A stakeholder is a body which has certain claims towards an organization (as here the IOC). From a managerial point of view, stakeholders are persons or groups, which initiate certain claims on the organization regardless of whether these are legally sound. Stakeholders, then, are seen as 'pressure groups' which want to persuade an organization to consider their interests. In terms of the Olympic Games these include, among others, environmental or anti-globalization groups (Lenskyj, 1996, 2000, 2002). On this basis, the IOC and the Organizing Committee of the Olympic Games (OCOG) are regarded as coordinating bodies that try to meet the diverse requirements, and sometimes conflicting interests, of various claimants. The Olympic Organization is a social entity that wants, and should want, to satisfy the demands of diverse social groups.

Without claiming to be exhaustive, figure 6.1 shows a selection of Olympic Games stakeholders. Shareholders are distinguished from stakeholders. The main shareholders involved in the Olympic Games are the IOC with its members, who constitute the IOC sessions (the General Assembly). In contrast to the shareholders, the stakeholders consist of wider groups, such as the employees of the IOC, the NOCs and IFs, the athletes, the audience, the TV broadcasters, the sponsors, the suppliers and the 'public' (represented by state institutions). A superficial consideration reveals that the interests of the stakeholders are quite different and often conflicting. In general, the shareholder commits to high profitability and wants to retain the power of his or her organization (here the IOC) by limiting the risk. In contrast, stakeholders as employees claim security of their workplace, pleasant working conditions and high wages. Athletes, another stakeholder group, want to ensure the best training conditions, concentrated support and perfectly organized competitions. The fans and spectators desire a vast, entertaining event

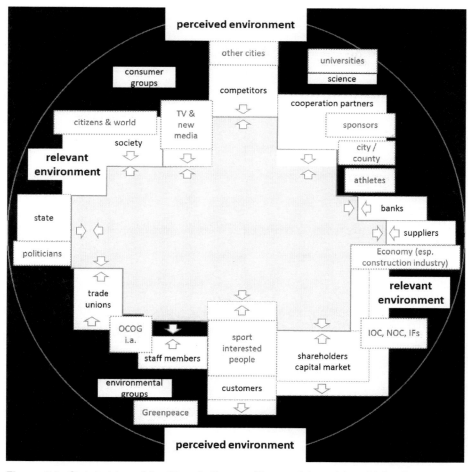

Figure 6.1. Stakeholders of the Olympic Games. (*Source*: Adapted from Müller-Stewens and Lechner, 2005, p. 26)

with decent pricing and great competition; the broadcasters aim for a product with high TV ratings; the sponsors claim the highest output for their advertising campaigns; the suppliers seek good business based on reliable and financially strong customers.

Finally, the public (the state) is interested in secure, entertaining and remarkable events that satisfy the population. These events, especially for the public, should also be inexpensive, and provide economic and social sustainability. Moreover, they should foster the development of the local and regional infrastructure, increase tax revenues and, finally, result in additional jobs. The dispute over alleged conflicts of interest between shareholders and stakeholders in the past often escalated into an emotional debate, although this situation is likely to be much more applicable to Fédération Internationale de Football Association (FIFA) than the IOC. In particular, when the stakeholders accuse the shareholders of unilateral maximization of material values, it is often spoken of as 'over-commercialization' in relation to the Olympic Games, as in the case of Atlanta 1996 or the corruption scandals that arose from the IOC awarding the 2002 Winter Olympics to Salt Lake City. The counter-argument of the shareholders is that their main concern is to offer the best possible organization of the Games to the athletes, fans and spectators. That is also the reason why the IOC initiated the Youth Olympic Games in 2010 to revive the values of the Olympic Movement and to make it more attractive to the younger generation.

The Development of the Games: An Economic Overview

Economic considerations have always been significant in the history of the Modern Olympic Games. Dividing it into five periods, two aspects prevail: the growing importance of new markets and the changing patterns of the groups who profit by hosting the Games.

The first period, 1896–1968 was characterized by financial problems of the OCOG. In 1896, the first Games were held in Athens at a time when Greece had just declared bankruptcy. The staging of the Games was financially secured by the generosity of prosperous Greeks living abroad (Georgiadis, 2000, pp. 208–217). After the first five Olympic Games were hosted – all of them having major financial problems – Baron Pierre de Coubertin drew the conclusion that 'the question is not whether they [the Games] will be held but how they will be held, and at whose expense' (Coubertin, 1913, p. 183). Remarkably, during this first period of the Games, many new funding sources were developed to fulfil the considerable financial responsibilities. Some sources have only been used for one Games while others developed into regular sources of finance, as in the case of postage stamps (Landry and Yerles, 1996, pp. 183–187).

In the second period, 1969–1980, the pressure of developing further financing sources increased due to the ongoing growth of the Olympic Games. Despite the fact that the private financing sources started to develop, such as the sale of TV broadcasting and sponsoring rights, the main source of income for the OCOG remained public subsidies. Munich 1972 was still mainly financed by the public sector. If one excludes the OCOG's own revenue (approximately 19 per cent), the Games were financed by special funding from the government, from surcharges for stamps, mintage and a lottery (50 per cent), and by tax revenues from the government, federal state and city (approximately 31 per cent). The deficit that occurred at the end of the Games was another $893 million (based on a cost estimate in the year 2000), which was covered by the national government (50 per cent), the federal state of Bavaria (25 per cent) and 25 per cent by the cities of Munich and Kiel (Organizing Committee, 1972, pp. 53–54). For the Games in 1976, Canada did not provide financial backing to the City of Montreal. Due to a 'written guarantee that the government would not be called upon to absorb the deficit nor to assume interim financing for organization' (Organizing Committee, 1976, p. 55), the OCOG – supported only by the City of Montreal – had to finance the Games themselves. Ultimately, only 5 per cent of the necessary resources had been generated by sources from the private sector. The remaining 95 per cent was covered by special financing arrangements and by the public sector (*Ibid*, p. 59). The deficit of $2.729 million was exclusively covered by the City of Montreal, the official guarantor. Montreal's taxpayers had to pay the Olympic debt until 2006, ultimately in form of a special tobacco tax. However, it should be stressed that the deficit was not the result of the host's low revenue in the first place but because of huge investments in the infrastructure, mismanagement, strikes on construction sites, and high fluctuations of exchange rates on the market. As a result of Montreal's financial burdens other cities became reluctant to apply to host the next Games (in 1984) that was still to be awarded (Commission of Inquiry, 1977, vol. 1, p. 314). The cost of the hosting the Olympic Games appeared no longer to be acceptable. Figure 6.2 illustrates the declining interest in a bid in this period.

Regarding Moscow 1980, no reliable information is available about finance, though it can be assumed that these Games were mainly financed by the state given the Soviet Union's intention to display the superiority of the communist system (Ueberroth et al., 1985, pp. 55–59). Furthermore, in this period, the state-funded 'amateurs' of the Soviet bloc led the acting IOC President Lord Killanin to connect the status of 'amateurs' in sport with the financing of the Games: 'The word amateur unfortunately no longer refers to a lover of sports but, possibly, a lack of proficiency' (Killanin, 1983, p. 43).

The third period, 1981–1996, started with the new presidency of J.A. Samaranch. At the beginning of this period, the Olympic Games opened to professional athletes in almost all sports. This was possible because at the end of Lord Killanin's presidency the term 'amateur' was removed from the Olympic Charter. This change has contributed to the continuous and stable increase in revenue from the sale of sponsorships and media rights. The development of emerging markets and companies that operate globally opened the Games for sponsoring agreements worth millions of dollars. In addition, the pressure to finance the Games without

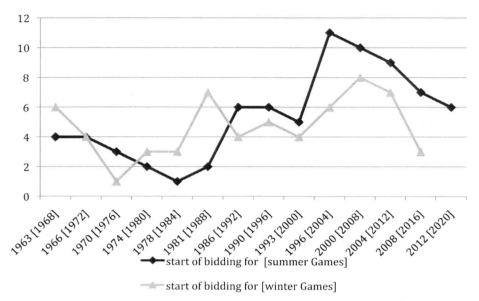

Figure 6.2. Number of Olympic Candidate Cities at the time of bid announcement (Winter Games mentioned in Summer Games year). (*Sources*: IOC, 1997b; Scherer, 1995, p. 375; Schollmeier, 2001, p. 27; www.gamesbids.com)

public resources led to the real beginning of commercialization of the Olympic Games (IOC, 1978). Previously, sponsoring was understood solely as ensuring the visibility of company logos and brands. Henceforth, the IOC expected the sponsors to embrace a stronger partnership with the Olympic Movement, which allowed the sponsors broader advertising opportunities. As of 1984, the prospects of high marketing revenues increased the interest of cities to host Olympic Games (see figure 6.2). This fundamental change contributed to the financial independence of the Olympic Movement. Finally, it ensured the end of political crises and financial shortfalls that had beset the Olympic Games in the 1970s and 1980s (Hoberman, 1986).

The first Games of this period took place in Los Angeles in 1984. After the city's unsuccessful bid to host the 1976 and 1980 Olympic Games, there were no other candidates other than Los Angeles (see figure 6.2) to be elected at the IOC session on 1 July 1978. The OCOG undertook to cover the costs of the city's security, transportation and other services if it could retain a surcharge of 0.5 per cent on hotel tax and 6 per cent on ticket sales (Ueberroth *et al.*, 1985, pp. 121–122). The lack of other candidates and the absence of public subsidies enabled the OCOG to enforce contractual terms and conditions with the IOC, which the latter would not have agreed to had there been alternative candidates (Hall, 1992, pp. 159; Reich, 1986, p. 24; Ueberroth *et al.*, 1985, p. 53). After long negotiations, the Olympic Charter was amended and the City of Los Angeles was allowed to disregard some financial requirements, which were usually associated with the organization of the Olympic Games. These Games were, for example, the first in history that were not associated with public stakeholders in the host city and the first fully financed by the private sector. Therefore, it is not surprising that these Games did not leave any physical Olympic heritage since there was barely any investment in urban infrastructure and sports facilities. The total cost of the Olympic Games was not more than $684 million, an amount that was covered by the revenue of the OCOG. Moreover, there was an official surplus of $381 million that was divided between the Olympic Committee of the United States (USOC), the Amateur Athletic Foundation and the national institutions in order to support Olympic sport (Taylor and Gratton, 1988, p. 34). The Olympic Games in Los Angeles mark the turnaround from publicly-funded to privately-financed Olympic Games.

Nevertheless, funding by the public sector remained important, particularly as nations other than the United States did not have the same potential for commercial financing. The growth of the Olympic Games and, above all, the promotion of national interests became the drivers to organize the Games (see table 6.1). This resulted in an increased involvement of governments. For instance, South Korea was very interested to use the Olympic Games in Seoul 1988 to display the rapid economic growth of the country globally, enhance its status on the international sports stage, and improve diplomatic relations with communist and non-aligned movement states. In addition, the government wanted to open the country for tourism and Korean exports (Park, 1991, pp. 2–5). However, 53 per cent of the costs of the Olympic Games were covered by the public sector (Kim *et al.*, 1989, p. 42), so that the alleged surplus of around $192 million needs to be treated with caution (Hill, 1992, p. 93).

Among others, the authorities in Barcelona took advantage of the Olympic Games to implement political aims. The re-urbanization of the city was intended to allow it to compete with Madrid as an internationally recognized industrial and tourist location. These goals justify the considerable government investments, which compensate for the disregard of long-term investments in socially meaningful areas like leisure, culture, sport, and transport (Millet, 1995, p. 191). Despite the public subsidies of $7 billion, the proportion of private funding increased due to marketing revenues of 38 per cent. The official revenue of the OCOG was low at $3.3 million (Brunet, 1993, p. 113). The increasing costs of the sponsors and TV channels led to a situation in which the Winter Olympics would no longer be organized in the same year as the Summer Games. The goal was to bring stronger attention to the Olympic Movement by spreading the budgets over several years. This was the main reason for shifting the Winter Olympic Games by a 2-yearly alternation with the Summer Olympics starting in 1994.

Similar to the Los Angeles Games, the citizens of Atlanta rejected any financial obligation of the city for the 1996 Olympic Games. The OCOG had to rely mainly on the private sector, which developed the commercialization of the Olympic Games further. To this day, the 1996 Atlanta Olympics count as the most commercialized Games. Shortly after awarding the Games to Atlanta, the

IOC President Samaranch stated that the commercialization of the Games helped to achieve the financial independence of the Olympic Movement. On the other hand, he warned against further commercialization. He proclaimed that the sport should be able to determine its own fate rather than being mainly directed by the interests of the sponsors (Samaranch, 1992). Nevertheless, compared to Seoul and Barcelona, the Olympic Games of 1996 had a very low budget with expenditures of $2.2 billion (ACOG, 1998, p. 222; French and Disher, 1997, p. 384). The city's infrastructure hardly changed, although a few new sport venues were built. After the Olympic Games, the venues were adjusted to fit the needs of the city's population. Many establishments were modified by reducing the seating capacities, dismantling temporary venues, or moving them to different locations, as in the case of the velodrome. With the exception of the publicly funded rowing course in Cumming (Georgia), all sports facilities were financed by the OCOG. The result was that the Games did not generate any surplus revenues. This countered the original intention of the IOC because Atlanta was chosen over Athens to host the 'Centennial Games' in the hope that the profits would have supported the Olympic Movement. Instead, the OCOG used it for financing Olympic facilities in particular the Olympic Stadium. This must be seen as an ambivalent act as it became the ballpark of the Atlanta Braves right after the Olympics.

The fourth period, 1997–2016, began with the Olympics in Nagano 1998 and Sydney 2000. After the negative experiences with Atlanta's OCOG, which was independently managed by the city, this period is characterized by stronger public financing. From this time onwards, the number of state guarantees requested by the IOC has been extended and each country was required to organize the Games in close cooperation with the OCOG. Key responsibilities for both stakeholder groups were defined. For the first time, the OCOG for Sydney 2000 had simply to organize the Olympic Games, while the state-run Olympic Co-ordination Authority was responsible for the development of infrastructure. The investments for the latter were approximately $1 billion (NSW Government, 2001, p. 6.5.). The cost of the Games in Sydney was $4.8 billion (Audit Office, 1999, pp. 59, 161, 156, 157).

Based upon the Sydney model, Athens 2004 separated the organization of the Games from the provision of the necessary infrastructure. Due to massive investments in the transport infrastructure, in security, and in (oversized) sports facilities, these Games were by then the most expensive. The information on the true costs of the Games vary greatly as in some cases non-Olympic projects such as the construction of the new airport have also been included into the 'Olympic costs'. The total cost of the Games amounted to approximately £5.8 billion whereas the budget of the OCOG – just as in the Games before – accounted only for $2.4 billion (ATHOC, 2005, p. 22).

The development of infrastructure and sports venues for the Beijing 2008 Games was also organized by public authorities. The Chinese central government and the Beijing municipality thus covered the expenses. The costs for the construction of sports venues and for the OCOG were in line with the expenses of former Olympics. Nevertheless, the People's Republic of China initiated considerable infrastructure projects including projects to improve air quality and energy supply so that the estimated 'Olympic costs' came up to $45 billion. The city, region and nation had spoken of a total investment of $33.7 billion before the Games whereas only $3.4 billion went on building the Olympic venues (Lin, 2004).

London 2012 intended to gentrify the east side of the city by hosting the Olympic Games. Money for the development of the necessary infrastructure came from public funds. New to this approach was that in the course of preparing for the Games priority was given to the long-term sustainability of investment. By following this strategy, redundant infrastructural projects were to be avoided, in contrast to the case of Athens in 2004.

Rio de Janeiro will mark the end of this period as the current IOC president Dr Thomas Bach launched Agenda 2020, which is an overall reform of the Olympic Games trying to reduce costs and to avoid oversized and unnecessary infrastructure. The Games in Tokyo 2020 will adopt some of the reforms from Agenda 2020 and therefore mark the first Games of a new period.

For more than 30 years, commercialization has had a significant influence on the Olympic Movement. The danger of dependency on sponsors has forced the IOC to re-evaluate these relations. It tries, on the one hand, to avoid over-commercialization and, on the other hand, intensifies the promotion of Olympic Ideals. The IOC is doing this by instructing the sponsors how to make use of the Olympic Ideals in regards to commercialization without causing harm to the moral and ethical values upon which they are based. For this reason, Jacques Rogge, the former IOC President, launched the Youth Olympic Games and, similarly, the IOC intended to sign long-term contracts with sponsors and media corporations aimed at strengthening the sense of responsibility towards the 'Olympic' brand.

The fifth period then starts with financial security. The IOC has taken the lead and control of the negotiations with the sponsors and broadcasters while the marketing of the Olympic Games is run completely in-house. On the one hand, the power of the IOC has increased compared to the hosts. On the other, the financial risk for the bidding cities has been reduced because the IOC provides approximately 40 per cent of their marketing revenues to the organizers of the Games before the selection of the future host city has been made.

Selected Winners through Hosting the Olympic Games

The range of those who benefit from the Olympic Games is large and varies from host city to host city. In this section, we consider stakeholder groups that are involved in the financing and organization of the Games, from which we can identify those stakeholders who expect benefits or profits from the Olympics. Table 6.2 focuses on the interests of these individual stakeholder groups, although

Table 6.2. Stakeholders which profited from the Olympic Games.

Stakeholders	Interest
IOC-members	Culturally / Geographically / Power
Host Country	Improvement of international relations/Positive psychological aspects for the people/Opportunity to show the world the changes in their own country (e.g. modernization)
Host city and its politicians	The expansion of tourism/Become a 'global city'/More attention compared to similar large cities or receiving more attention from the capital/Economic impulse/Accelerated urban development/Career opportunities/New jobs
Construction industry/ Tourism industry	Additional local demand for construction/Better chance in competing for international projects
Sponsors	Improved relations with customers, suppliers, partners, and employees
Media Groups/ Networks	Increased ratings and more lucrative sales of advertising time
NOCs	Funding through the sale of media rights through the 'Olympic Solidarity Program'/Financial resources through the sale of the global sponsorship programme 'The Olympic Partner' (TOP)/Profit shares from OCOG (if the NOC belongs to the host country)
IFs	Funding through the sale of media rights

Source: Adapted and extended according to Preuss, 2005, pp. 421–422.

it does not claim to be exhaustive. In this context, it is necessary also to consider the socio-cultural, political, and economic background of each host nation. The interests listed in table 6.2, however, relate solely to recurring patterns. They do not allow a generalization of the existing socio-cultural, political, historical, and economic characteristics and conditions of the individual host country.

IOC Members

The first stakeholder group consists of the IOC members (shareholders). They have the collective desire to award the Games to cities that are able to develop them in the best way possible and secure their future through excellent organization. Successful Games will strengthen the power of the IOC and its members. This is essential, as one has to be aware that the IOC is the rights holder of just two products, the Olympic Games and the Youth Olympic Games. Neither is organized by the IOC itself but by host cities. So it becomes a matter of fact that the more cities bid to host Olympic Games in the future, the higher will be the commitment of the candidates competing with each other. Thus, a competition among prospective hosts will increase the quality of the Games including the mandatory development of infrastructure and often even more (Preuss, 2004b). Among the IOC members, however, there exist sub-groups with different cultural backgrounds whose interests play an important role in the bidding process. According to Huntington (1996, pp. 315–316), the phenomenon of cultural belonging is the reason that IOC members favour certain candidate cities and vote for them (Persson, 2000, pp. 157–161; Preuss, 2000).

Host Country

Government officials of the host country comprise another stakeholder group. Today, the IOC makes the state's involvement in financing the Olympics a requirement because all the revenues gained from the Games need to be used to finance those Games. To be precise, Olympic earned money cannot be used for infrastructure and general development but needs to be used for the OCOG. This leaves much that has to be covered by the taxpayer.

The public sector is directly and indirectly involved in the organization of the Olympics. Directly, as the economic and infrastructure development of the Olympic city and region generates growth, develops additional employment and increased income, if it is sustainably planned. The stimulated dynamics of the Games and their global presence often allow for developments which, without the upcoming Olympics, would have been politically difficult to implement. Indirectly, the host country can benefit tremendously by improving its worldwide reputation through a perfectly organized Olympics, by maintaining international relations, by implementing domestic goals or by demonstrating the superiority of its political system. Of course, several of these reasons increase the willingness of governments to finance the Olympics with public money. However, the exact effects of the state's contribution to the Olympics in terms of economic growth, job creation, or external effects are difficult to determine (Sterken, 2007; Preuss, 2009; Preuss, 2011). The reasons why governments refuse to support the Games financially are often the lack of confidence in achieving the effects noted above, as well as the risk of possible high levels of public debt. Other explanations would be the possible creation of so-called 'white elephants' which have no post-event benefits for the public and the political concern about any unintentional and socially unjust redistribution of public funds (Preuss and Solberg, 2006).

In general, the Olympic Games offer a city and a country the best opportunity to raise awareness. The sponsors start advertising their partnership with the Olympics several years before the event, promoting the name of the host city in their advertising campaigns. In the months prior to the Opening Ceremony, the press gives preliminary reports about the hosting country and its inhabitants. In the run-up to the Olympics, the Olympic torch relay generates additional media interest. For London 2012, the IOC (2013, p. 1) noted that the combination of 'conventional broadcast media, and online and mobile platforms, made the Games available to a record potential global audience of 4.8 billion people in every corner of the world'.

The nature, the quality and the extent of advertising the Olympics depend on the host and the media representatives. For example, the Australian Tourist Commission (ATC) developed a strategic approach to promote Sydney. In total more than 1,000 individual projects were implemented, with the ATC not only concerned about good working conditions of the media representatives but also providing plenty of additional information about Australia and Sydney (ATC, 2001, p. 3).

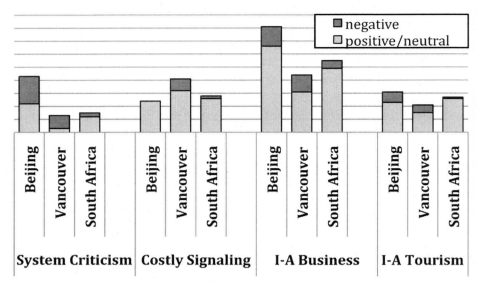

Figure 6.3. Distribution of Internet reports by category, origin and value. (Source: Preuss and Alfs, 2011, p. 65)

Preuss and Alfs (2011, p. 65) analysed internet reports on the 2008 Olympic Games in Beijing. They were interested in examining how the media from China, the USA, Europe, and the 'rest of the world' reported the Olympics. Data were interpreted using common signalling theories, such as principal-agent theory with reference to 'adverse selection' and information asymmetries, as well as signalling by 'demonstrative consumption' to build up symbolic capital (see figure 6.3). Between 1 July and 30 September 2008, 740 messages or reports were collected using Google alerts and searching for the key words 'Olympic Games Beijing 2008'. The data were analysed using quantitative analysis of coding schemes. The findings show that China used the Olympic Games mainly to reduce information asymmetries, which were directly connected to China's active search for potential business partners and investors. Overall, the researchers found out that the four geographical areas studied showed different contents in the communication patterns regarding the Olympic Games. China's success in eliminating the information discrepancies in a positive way was overall an accomplishment although it was also weakened by negative news coverage.

Host City and Its Politicians

The politicians of the host city are another stakeholder group. The economic impulse generated by the Olympics is much bigger for the host city compared to the rest of the host country. The investments in the city increase its attractiveness for tourists and international investors since many location factors improve (Hall, 1992, p. 17; Weirick, 1999, p. 70). It is often observed that Olympic Games are used to solve existing urban problems. For example, Barcelona was able to build a ring road, which significantly reduced the traffic within the city. After many years of ineffective municipal negotiations, this project came to life in the course of preparing for the Games of 1992. Other Olympic hosts like Athens built a new airport outside the city and a high-capacity metro system. Beijing afforested areas and relocated some industrial zones in order to improve the city's climate, and London gentrified the east side of the city. All these examples are initially positive for the host city but they become the opposite for the many residents who are relocated by municipal and governmental authorities from areas of Olympic-related development to the outskirts of the city.

An objective of local politicians is often to obtain prestige in their own country, to achieve more attention and, ultimately, to acquire public subsidies. For instance, Barcelona's desire to host the Olympic Games was also a result of striving for more autonomy from Spain, while Atlanta wanted to demonstrate the power and strength of the South *vis-à-vis* the Northern United States. Beijing also took advantage of the Olympics in its rivalry with Shanghai. Thus, host cities are often interested not only to show the world their productivity and ability as a whole but to signal their success to their rivals.

If a city cannot complete its planned infrastructure projects by the start of the Games it will be exposed to global criticism and the city's image would be severely damaged. This phenomenon happened before the opening of the Olympics in Athens 2004 and in Turin 2006 and may occur in Rio 2016. After a city has been awarded the Olympic Games, time pressures keep urban development on track. It can often be observed that longstanding political stalemates in urban planning will be resolved as the fear of failure leads to accelerated urban development (Cox *et al.*, 1994, p. 35; Daume, 1976, p. 155; Garcia, 1993, p. 263; Geipel *et al.*, 1993, p. 296). In Munich 1972, for example, the urban development supposedly occurred 10 years faster than would have happened without the Olympic Games. With the exceptions of the privately financed Olympic Games in Los Angeles and Atlanta, politicians made use of the Olympics to accelerate urban development and to implement projects that were already planned in the long term. In many cases, the global attention on the host city helped also to overcome internal political differences between planners, politicians and citizens concerning these important urban projects.

However, there is a danger of inefficiency and corruption in construction before hosting the Olympic Games as the IOC demands tight deadlines, high-quality venues, and often overlooks the interests of minority groups. Hall (1992, p. 131) also suggested that pressures of time can result in the suspension of environmental directives or even the suppression of projects of high ecological value. Therefore, it is impossible to generalize by claiming that the best means to stimulate the economy of a region is to host the Olympic Games (Baade and Matheson, 2002, p. 145).

In this context, it seems worthwhile examining the question of whether the necessary investments in the infrastructure for the Olympic Games is the best possible use of the financial resources for the city, as claimed by Szymanski (2002, p. 3). Of course, this depends first and foremost on whether the necessity for infrastructure to organize the Olympics coincides with the future structural needs of the city. In the final analysis, it depends on municipal decision-makers as to exactly what the city aims to 'produce'. Hospitals produce medical care, schools and universities produce education and the Olympic Games produce worldwide attention and entertainment. The primary goal of the organizers of London 2012 was not only focused on productivity but also on the economic, social and environmental sustainability of each newly created or modified facility for the Olympics. For the 2012 Games, LOCOG tried to avoid and reduce the negative environmental impact as best it could. In those cases where this approach was not possible, organizers compensated with an 'appropriate' environmental performance (Levett, 2004, pp. 69–89).

The reconstruction of previous industrial wastelands is often very expensive but the benefits for the environment gained from the rehabilitation of the urban region could compensate for such costs over the long term. The removal of brownfield land indicates a revaluation of the city and, more importantly, it should be judged as a positive impact for the entire urban population.

The structural transformation of the city by hosting the Games also changes the relationship between public and non-public sites. It is not unusual for public land to be transferred into private hands after renovation, for the benefit of

Table 6.3. Use of brownfield land for the Olympic Games.

	Previous Use of Selected Areas (ecological term)	Use of Selected Areas after the Games (benefits to the population)
Munich 1972	Set-aside property, debris, fallow land	Olympic Park, public transport, recreational area, housing space
Montreal 1976	Fallow land	Olympic Park, recreation area
Seoul 1988	Contaminated sites (Chamsil, Han River)	Olympic Park, leisure facilities (sports facilities), water treatment, recreational area
Barcelona 1992	Dilapidated industrial areas, old railway lines, underdeveloped harbours, fallow land	Housing space, docks, parks, complex of service providers, recreation area, sports facilities
Atlanta 1996	Derelict sites, underdeveloped residential area (city centre)	Office building, recreation area
Sydney 2000	Contaminated sites, fallow land, landfill	Olympic Park, residential area, recreation area, 100,000 trees and bushes have been planted
Athens 2004	Airport, military and industrial sites on the coastal region	Recreation area, wetland ecosystem, beach
Beijing 2008	Underdeveloped residential area	Recreation area, 1 million trees have been planted in the city
London 2012	Industrial sites (Lower Lea Valley)	Upgrade and stimulation of economic activity, housing, municipal facilities and infrastructure

Sources: Compiled from Garcia, 1993, pp. 251–270; Geipel *et al.*, 1993, pp. 287–289; Lee, 1988, pp. 60–61); Levett, 2004, p. 82; Meyer-Künzel, 2002; Pyrgiotis, 2001; Preuss, 2005, p. 429.

affluent buyers rather than being built as a habitat for children, elderly people or for the wider public (Siebel, 1994, p. 18). As a result, the city loses a key element of its urbanity and welfare by leaving out important members of society. On the other hand, public decision-makers think they improve the quality of the city by constructing pedestrian zones and public parks. However, pedestrian zones may become dominated by shops for the rich, and events hosted in the parks are often based on entrance fees. The result is that lower income groups are excluded from various leisure activities or are left out by the overpriced market for apartments, as affordable housing no longer exists. The gentrification of housing areas creates exclusive residential areas near the city centre with an attractive and lively city experience (Roaf *et al.*, 1996, p. 9). The middle and upper class, a stakeholder group in their own right, benefit considerably from broader housing offers in the city and from the gentrified areas. Finally, the connection between the Olympics and the host municipality can improve the image of its politicians. The media frequently mention their names in the same breath as the Olympic Games. This allows them to profit from the allure of the Olympics with minimum effort (Snyder *et al.*, 1986).

Construction and Tourism Industry

If cost-benefit analysis is taken into consideration, the main goal of the public sector is the improvement of public welfare. In contrast, the private sector is driven by profit maximization and the growth of individual benefits. Many companies benefit from the investments in the host city during the preparation and while organizing the Olympic Games. This is particularly the case for both the construction and the tourism industries.

The construction industry benefits from the point when a city is awarded the Olympics. In general, investment in infrastructure starts 7 years prior to the Opening of the Games. During a (regional) economic boom, the price for construction work usually increases due to the additional demand. This means that companies gain more profit for the same amount of work than would have been the case without the Games. Moreover, in recession, companies are able to win additional contracts through the Olympics that would not otherwise have been available. It also increases awareness of construction companies, in particular if they are responsible for 'flagship projects' such as building the Olympic Stadium. Figure 6.4 shows the existing infrastructure for hotels and sports facilities that was already in place in Rio de Janeiro before the Olympic award, and the ones that still needed to be built for the Games. Despite having hosted the Pan-American Games in 2007, Rio still had to construct twelve sports facilities as well as numerous hotels for 2016.

Figure 6.5 shows the primary economic impulse caused by the Olympics in the Keynesian model of the consumption and income cycle. The impulse is provided by the autonomous consumption expenditure of tourists, as well as by those of the OCOG. The autonomous money entering the region will increase demand

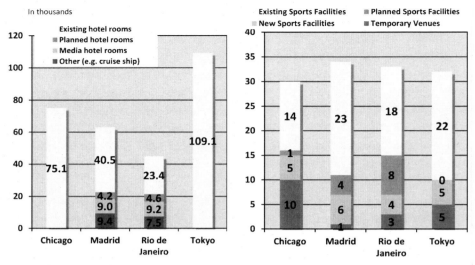

Figure 6.4. Hotel rooms (*left*) and sports facilities (*right*) of the candidate cities for hosting the Olympic Games 2016. (*Sources*: Mini bid books of the candidate cities 2016)

and have positive effects on the regional economy. However, changes in stock, imports and crowding out effects reduce the impulse. The growing demand will directly increase production of goods or services and consequently lead to new jobs and income. After the deduction of taxes and marginal savings rate, the higher income creates additional demand. This increases production further and, in turn, stimulates demand through the operation of the multiplier effect.

The economic benefit of the Olympic Games can also be measured for developing countries when taking into account these relations. The autonomous expenditures (in other words the funds additionally accruing to the city) are limited to the tourists, the Olympic Family and the OCOG. When calculating the primary effect, it is sometimes noticeable that a proportion of the demand caused by the

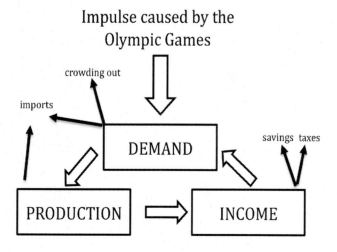

Figure 6.5. Keynesian model of consumption and income cycle. (*Source*: Preuss, 1999, p. 66)

Olympics does not lead to autonomous expenditures in the country or the region of the Olympic city. This happens because many of the products demanded are not domestically produced and therefore have to be imported. This is the reason why the income generated by the primary effect is not significant in many developing countries. Finally, this example demonstrates well that the winners of the Olympic Games may vary from host city to host city.

Sponsors

Many major corporations see the Olympic Games as a unique opportunity to initiate business relations, to make new contacts and to improve their image. The worldwide recognition and the positive association that goes hand in hand with the symbol of the Olympic Rings, brings the Olympic Games up to a higher level of advertising. The companies, the sponsors, the supporters and the suppliers of the Games are therefore another group that benefits from the Olympics. Otherwise, they would not put so much money into being officially associated with the Games.

For its own purposes (administration, Olympic solidarity programmes and Games expenses), the IOC as the shareholder received income from the sponsoring rights of Vancouver 2010. As stipulated in the host city contract: 'The IOC shall receive, from the gross contracted amount, seven and a half percent (7.5 per cent) of the value of the cash consideration of all contracts pertaining to the marketing plan and the joint marketing programs' (IOC, 2003a, p. 24). Figure 6.6 shows the

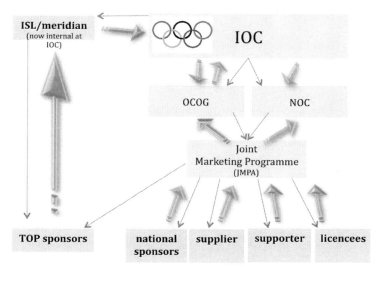

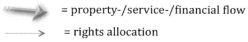

Figure 6.6. Flow and rights allocation of the OCOG supporting marketing programme. (*Source*: Adopted from Preuss, 1999, p. 170)

schematic structure of the cash flow and the assignment of rights between 1996 and 2004. After 2004, the 'Meridian' agency was dissolved and the IOC negotiates now in-house with the sponsors.

The IOC holds all rights to the Olympic symbols. The NOCs have the right to use their own Olympic marketing logos free of charge, but can include the Olympic Rings as well (IOC, 2011, pp. 23–26). The NOCs are allowed to market them exclusively on their territory. In addition, the OCOG holds exclusive rights to their specific emblems and mascots at national level as provided by the 'joint marketing agreement'. In order to protect the exclusivity of the sponsors, the agreement enables the OCOG to control all its relevant Olympic marketing matters for 4 years in the host country.

Broadcast Partners

A further stakeholder group that profits from the Olympic Games is the media corporations. Broadcasting the Olympic Games is the key to the commercial success of the Olympics. The media corporation groups, including the new media, benefit from the Olympic Games by increasing their reputation as the official broadcaster(s). Yet more importantly, based on the high rating TV figures, they can sell high-priced advertising space. The Olympic media rights are sold in a bid contest. This usually consists of a single-sided, auction-like tender process, where various broadcasters, media agencies and, more recently, network operators try to acquire the television and internet rights to attractive sporting events. The tremendous increase in the value of these media packages sold by the IOC to the broadcasters is shown in the development of the cost for TV rights (figure 6.7). NBC recently bought the rights for the combined Winter and Summer Olympics

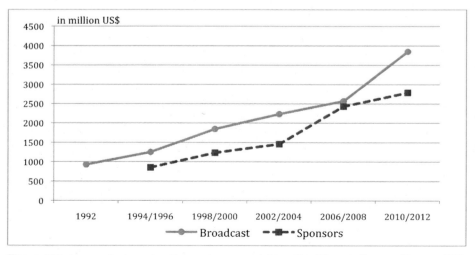

Figure 6.7. Income for broadcasting and sponsor rights of the Olympic Games. (*Source*: IOC, 2014 *a* or *b*, pp. 17, 26)

of Sochi 2014, Rio 2016 and Pyeongchang 2018 at a record breaking $4.38 billion (FAZ, 2011).

The growing importance of media coverage via the electronic media should not be overlooked. In particular, changing leisure behaviour has a large influence on the demand for television because leisure activities compete with the available time to watch TV. Broadcasting attractive sports events can easily result in the daily market leadership of a network. Figure 6.8 shows an example of the TV audience rating during the Opening Ceremony of Athens 2004. Over the whole evening, the demand hardly varied. The small visible 'peaks' are probably caused by the commercials televised by the other mainly private stations; as according to the German broadcasting agreement, the ZDF network is not allowed to include commercial breaks after 8 pm.

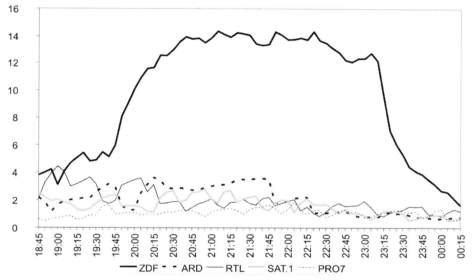

Figure 6.8. Ceremony of the 2004 Olympic Games in Athens on 13 August 2004 on the ZDF network. (*Source*: ZDF Media Research, 2005)

National Olympic Committees and International Professional Associations

The last stakeholder group covered here is the Olympic Family (IOC, NOCs and IFs). While media groups profit from high audience ratings and sponsors benefit from advertising opportunities with the Olympic Rings, the Olympic Organization receives money from both. The distribution of the IOC's revenue generated from the sales of sponsoring and TV broadcasting rights are allocated according to fixed criteria. In the course of recent years, these criteria have been changed moderately but nevertheless continuously.

Figures 6.9 and 6.10 give an overview on how the distribution works. The IOC

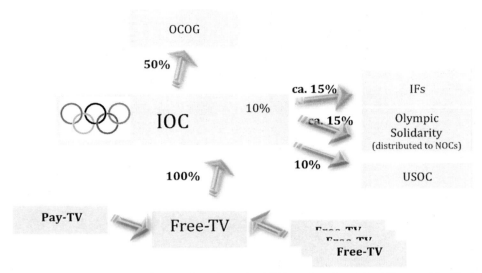

Figure 6.9. Distribution of revenue from the sale of TV broadcasting rights. (*Source*: Modified after Preuss, 2001)

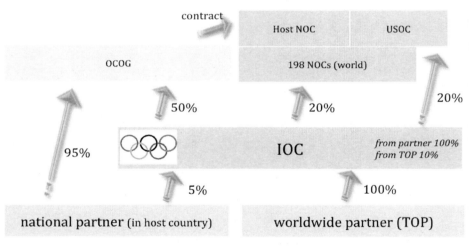

Figure 6.10. Distribution of revenue from the sale of sponsorship rights. (*Source*: Modified after Preuss, 2001)

retains only a single-digit percentage for its own administration and for its security reserves, while the vast majority of the revenue is distributed to the international sports federations (IFs) and the NOCs. Nevertheless, the largest amount of revenue goes to the OCOGs of the hosting countries. With 7 years between the awarding and the hosting of the Olympic Games, an early launch of rights sales is guaranteed. This allows the IOC to provide a financial warranty to the host. While the warranty was linked to a percentage of the revenue in the past, it has recently been decided to provide a fixed amount to cover the organizational costs. This means that the percentages distributed to the OCOG, NOCs and IFs in figures 9 and 10 have to be adapted to the new system from 2010 onwards. Above all, the

Olympic Family is benefiting from the increased commercialization of the Games more than ever before.

The amount of the previous profit sharing is shown in figure 6.11. It is clear that the twenty-six IFs benefit approximately as much as the 205 NOCs. Finally, for London 2012, the balance sheet of the IOC will demonstrate the share of money to the different stakeholders and in particular, the large share for the United States Olympic Committee (USOC) becomes visible. USOC negotiated this share as most of the sponsorship money and the TV broadcast money stem from United States territory (table 6.4).

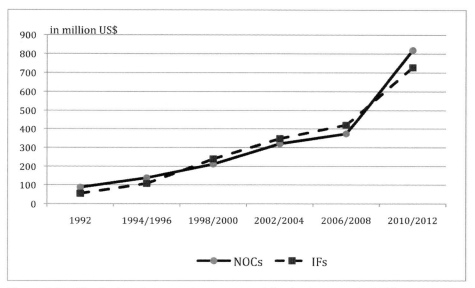

Figure 6.11. Distribution of revenue from commercialization between the NOCs and the IFs. (*Source*: IOC, 2012, pp. 8–9)

Table 6.4. IOC Statement of Activities in 2012 (in thousands of US dollars).

Allocations to:	Revenue (US$ 000)	Programme (US$ 000)	Total (US$ 000)
Organizing Committee of the XXX Games of the Olympiad	713,109	323,141	1,036,250
Organizing Committee of the XX1 Games of the Olympiad	–	9,676	9.676
USOC	150,578	35,363	185,941
International Federations	508,581	–	508,581
National Olympic Committees	376,729	52,417	429,146
IFs and OS share of insurance premium for Games cancellation	2,755	–	2,755
Other costs	–	20,399	20,399
	1,751,752	*440,996*	*2,192,748*
National Olympic Committees' share of revenues reserved in designated funds	(376,729)	–	(376,729)
Distribution of revenues to OCOG, USOG and IFs	1,375,023	440,996	1,816,019

Source: IOC, 2013, p. 92.

Conclusions

This chapter has described the various beneficiaries of the Olympic Games. At each Games more or less the same groups benefit. We can sum them up as those which:

◆   benefit from the increased economic activity in the city (corporations, retail market, hotels, tourism industry, and construction industry);

◆   are capable of consuming the (expensive) products such as entertainment and after the Games to use the gentrified infrastructure such as shopping malls, restaurants, concerts (middle and upper classes);

◆   benefit from the global interest in the Games by the increased media attention. This includes TV broadcasters, sponsors, politicians, and host cities (through location marketing);

◆   share the direct commercial revenue with each other (IOC, NOCs, and IFs);

◆   use the newly created general urban infrastructure, in particular the transport infrastructure (households, companies); and

◆   use the newly created sports infrastructure (professional athletes, recreational sports, entertainment industry).

Chapter 7

Promoting the Olympic City

Stephen V. Ward

City Marketing and the Olympics

We will never know the true significance of French President Jacques Chirac's widely reported casual denigration of Finnish cooking in securing the 2012 Summer Olympic Games for London instead of the longstanding favourite, Paris. According to a secretly recorded restaurant conversation with the German Chancellor and the Russian President in July 2005, he said of the London bid that, '[y]ou can't trust people who cook as badly as that. After Finland, it's the country with the worst food' (Barkham, 2005a). The following day the story appeared in the French newspaper, *Libération* and was widely picked up by international news media. It was variously presented as a huge insult to British and Finnish cookery, a sign of French arrogance or, simply a colossal error of judgement. Two days later the IOC met in Singapore to make its decision (Campbell, 2005). When successive rounds of voting had eliminated all other candidate cities, only Paris and London remained, with London winning by just four votes. Finland had two of these, so its delegates' choices (which remain entirely anonymous, of course) could well have swung the result in London's favour.

It can readily be conceded that other, equally unverifiable, theories about the final reasons for London's 2012 success also have their advocates. The real import-ance of this particular anecdote is, however, the insight it gives on the world's most extraordinary process of competitive city marketing. In one incident it captures the unique mixture of high politics, the expectation of good living, intense media interest and moments of complete farce that descend on the process of trying to win the Olympic prize. Many commentators have noted the rivalry between cities across the world for all kinds of mobile investment and consumption (for example: Hall and Hubbard, 1998; Dinnie, 2011). They have also observed that this competition has intensified in recent years, as traditional city economies have faltered and capital has become more mobile. In turn, this has put growing pressure on city leaders to engage in place marketing and promotion. This serves as a means both to achieve tangible physical and economic change by attracting new investment and activity and, in a deeper sense, to facilitate symbolic reconstruction.

The tangible prizes for city marketers are no longer the manufacturing plants that were once the economic bedrock of cities. Cities now compete to be centres of cultural and leisure consumption. To this end, many have invested heavily in new or extended cultural and other leisure facilities such as museums, galleries, performance venues and sports facilities (Bianchini and Parkinson, 1993). Part of this move into the cultural marketing of cities also embraces major events and spectacles that can animate the new cultural investments and intensify the process of cultural consumption. In a crude sense, all these changes attract more tourists and increase consumption. In the longer term, however, these investments and the activities they contain contribute to raising the quality of urban life which, it is thought, will make cities into magnets for entrepreneurs and the creative people from whom new innovations will flow.

These changes in the physical character and economic activities of cities also play an important part in the process of symbolic reconstruction. New buildings, structures and places, particularly those with iconic potential, play an important part in the rebranding of cities. So too, albeit in a more transitory fashion, do the major events and spectacles staged by cities (Gold and Gold, 2005; Smith, n.d.). New physical icons and spectacles provide images that signal a changing city. As well as being a way of attracting new investment and consumption, city marketing is also a way of manipulating the signs, real and promised, of change and integrating them into a new brand identity for the city. This is self-evidently important in promoting the idea of a changing city to investors and consumers. It is also extremely important as a way of selling the idea of change to those who actually live in the city and have to bear many of the costs of that change, financial and otherwise.

At the pinnacle of this most recent phase of city marketing is that associated with the Olympics. This applies particularly to the Summer Games which are a truly global affair (Miller, 2003); somewhat less so for the Winter Games, although they have the compensatory marketing benefit of reaching the majority of the world's most affluent countries. Given their scale, it is perhaps surprising that these mega-events continue to be awarded to just one city, rather than to a country as, for example, with major soccer events such as the FIFA World Cup. For their part, despite persistent doubts about financial and other benefits, many cities remain willing to compete for the Olympic prize. As of the early twenty-first century, the chosen city gets a large injection of funds from the IOC ($1.1 billion in the case of Sydney in 2000), paid for from world broadcast rights, sponsorship and merchandising deals (Lee, 2005). It also receives a huge temporary boost to tourism and other consumption, substantial new investment (funded from multiple but usually government sources) and, in some cases, an enduring rise in property values (Halifax plc, 2004). Staging these Games signals to outsiders and citizens alike that the host city really is a world city, well placed in other respects to become, or remain, a key hub in the global economy. Even being a serious contender confers real marketing benefits, showing an ambition for international attention.

The result is that no other variant of city boosterism even approaches the extraordinary series of events now associated with the bidding for these events. This begins at the national level as candidate cities are chosen and proceeds through a shortlist as the IOC decides which cities' bids should go forward to the final selection. The city eventually chosen as host is then presented with a colossal media opportunity to show itself to the world, to market its brand to anyone, anywhere. This builds up as the Games approach, culminating with the event itself. In 2012, an official IOC study reported 3.6 billion viewers in 220 territories had watched at least some part of the televised London Summer Olympics (IOC, 2012). This amounted to roughly half the world's total population and three-quarters of the potential audience. Although viewership appears to be stagnating (3.9 billion watched the 2004 Athens Olympics for example), there has been a growth in online and mobile viewing. All this media exposure, provided it is reasonably positive, influences many tourist decisions at the time of the Games. This tourism impact will focus on, but extend beyond the city to the country and the wider global region. More importantly, there is also huge long-term potential for both tourism and investment (Kasimati, 2003).

No other city marketing opportunity achieves this global exposure. At the same time, provided it is carefully managed at the local level, it also gives a tremendous opportunity to heighten and mobilize the commitment of citizens to their own city. The competitive nature of sport and its unrivalled capacity to be enjoyed as a mass cultural activity gives it many advantages from the marketing point of view (S.V. Ward, 1998, pp. 231–232). In a more subtle way it also becomes a metaphor for the notion of cities having to compete in a global marketplace, a way of reconciling citizens and local institutions to the wider economic realities of the world. The notion of competition *in* sport can be elided, fairly smoothly, to embrace competing *for* sporting events, to the idea of cities having to compete with each other more generally.

Who Promotes the Olympic city?

It follows from the foregoing discussion that marketing the Olympic city in the later stages itself becomes a mass activity. Seemingly everyone from heads of government downwards takes part. Particularly important are the media, especially television, radio and newspapers, which play a key part in widening the commitment. They may also play a questioning or critical role but usually, at least for cities whose Olympic bid aspirations progress to the short-list and the final play-off, the net effect will be positive. Yet this mass media involvement normally only becomes critical after the bandwagon has begun to roll, reaching a peak during the Games themselves. More important therefore is the question of who actually starts the more difficult process of getting it moving in the first instance.

The detailed answer has of course varied but one or a small group of individuals have normally been involved (Hill, 1992, pp. 90–238). The national sporting and

Olympic organizations are in evidence, but these are rarely powerful enough on their own to provide the primary leadership for such a complex undertaking that cuts across so many aspects of city and national life. In some cases, the key actors have, not surprisingly, operated mainly within the sphere of government, whether at city or wider level. It is not difficult to appreciate why this has been so in cities with nations within Communist regimes at the time of the Games. Although only two, Moscow and Beijing have actually hosted the Summer Games, in 1980 and 2008, other communist cities – Budapest, Belgrade, Tashkent and Havana – have entered short-listed bids (Gold and Gold, 2005, pp. 179–180).

The government role has also been central in the promotion of Olympic cities under other authoritarian regimes, notably Seoul 1988 – awarded in very controversial circumstances in 1981 (Hill, 1992, pp. 189–217). The best known Games staged by a totalitarian state, Berlin 1936, were not primarily instigated by government (Hart Davis, 1986) although here the special circumstances of interwar Germany need to be taken into account (see Chapter 13). Awarded to the city in 1931, before the Nazi state was created, their initiator had to persuade a suspicious Hitler (who saw them as promoting dangerously internationalist sentiments) that they were worth backing. Once he had been persuaded however, the Führer's Games set new standards in Olympic marketing, albeit with overtly propagandist motives that transcended the city to promote the Nazi regime.

Yet until recently the centrally-planned, totalitarian and authoritarian examples have been the exceptions. The most typical Olympic bidders have been cities within capitalist and more or less democratic countries. Even in these nations however, there are very notable examples of key actors being essentially political figures holding some kind of governmental office. Most typically in such cases, though, the impetus has usually been more genuinely city-based, with Mayors or their nominees often playing a critical part. A notable example was Montreal, which bid for the 1972 Summer Games and staged the 1976 Games, thanks to the drive of its Mayor Jean Drapeau (Organizing Committee, 1976). More recently, successive Mayors of Barcelona, Narcis Serra and Pasqual Maragall, were directly responsible for Barcelona's successful bid for the 1992 Summer Games (COOB, 1992, I). Tokyo's Governor, effectively a very powerful elected Mayor, became Chairman of the city's successful bid for the 2020 Summer Games (Gibson, 2013b). In 2005 the bids of both New York and Moscow for the 2012 Summer Games were led by their cities' Deputy Mayors.

Even where city government leaders have been the driving force, this does not mean that Olympic bidding simply becomes a special municipal department. The most common feature has been what has come to be termed 'regime politics' (Stone, 1989; Painter, 1998). This kind of urban action involves relatively few key figures who might well include city government leaders but would typically also involve local and regional business leaders, national government appointees or relevant Ministers. The resulting partnership thus has an unusual status in which the limits of governmental and private action become difficult to define.

The exact composition of these interests has not been the same in all would-be Olympic cities. However, most differences in the source of promotional effort are ones of degree. The usual pattern of recent years, certainly for successful bids, has been a mix of national, city government and entrepreneurial effort, not necessarily following a consistent pattern even in the same countries. Birmingham's 1986 bid for the 1992 Games and Manchester's first bid (1990 for the 1996 Games) were advanced by city and local entrepreneurial effort without any effective central government backing (Hill, 1992, pp. 90–119). Yet Manchester's second bid (1993 for the 2000 Games) had significant material and symbolic central government backing (Law, 1994). Finally, for London's successful 2005 bid for the 2012 Games central government support of all kinds was very substantial.

In part, these differences reflected the changing political character of national government, under successive Prime Ministers Thatcher, Major and Blair. National governments, whatever their complexion, have little inclination to back bids with little chance of success. All politicians prefer to associate themselves with winners and may lose face if they make the wrong judgement. Barack Obama discovered this when his unprecedented Presidential support for his home city of Chicago did not stop it being quickly eliminated from voting for the 2016 Games (Gibson, 2009b). Sometimes, however, a national leader might prefer simply to abort a bid than allow it, at best, to become a distraction or, at worst to succeed and then be a millstone. Thus the Italian Prime Minister, deeply worried by the country's economic woes, stopped the Rome bid for the 2020 Summer Olympics (Gibson, 2013a).

There have also been cases where the impetus has been predominantly private. This has been especially so in the United States where national government, except in 2009, did not involve itself to any great extent in Olympic bidding (Andranovich et al., 2001). Partly because of this, there have been few of the constraints on city boosterist ambitions that have operated in other countries. Just as they have explored every other conceivable way of promoting themselves, American city business-led coalitions were remarkably quick to see the city marketing potential of the Olympic Games. The result is that an astonishing number and variety of American cities have advanced short-listed bids (for both Summer and Winter Games) (Gold and Gold, 2005, pp. 141, 179–180; Essex and Chalkley, 2004). In part this was possible because until 1955 the United States Olympic Committee allowed multiple American cities to bid against each other for the same Games. Thus four US cities were candidates in 1946 (for the 1948 Games), and five in each of the 1947 and 1949 decisions for the 1952 and 1956 Games. This somewhat farcical process meant that the competition to stage the Olympics became just another means for American cities to assert themselves over their domestic rivals.

Los Angeles, built more completely on promotional puff than any other large American metropolitan city, appropriately holds the record with two hostings (1932 and 1984) and seven other short-listed bids (Andranovich et al. 2001). Had the domestic bidding rules not changed in 1955 it would also have notched up a further seven bids, the latest for the 2024 Games (SCCOG, 2015). Behind all its post-1945 bids has been a private business organization, the Southern California Committee for the Olympic Games. It was formed in 1939 by a group of Los Angeles businessmen intent on of bringing back the Games to the city after its earlier hosting of them. Eventually, in 1978, with Jean Drapeau's financially ruinous Montreal Games fresh in everyone's mind, they regained the 1984 Games against only one other, very half-hearted, contender (Teheran). To the IOC, on one side, and local and state interests, on the other, the promotional language and eventual reality of the Games were the same – frugality and commercialism (Hill, 1992, pp. 156–162). Existing facilities and infrastructure were to be used, commercial sponsorship aggressively sought.

Although the 1984 Games had many perceived weaknesses that reflected this ethos, the approach proved highly profitable (especially so for Los Angeles and the United States) with the result that it both saved and changed the Games. The Los Angeles experience paved the way for the resurgence in competition to stage both Summer and Winter Games during the 1990s and early twenty-first century (until continuing post-2008 economic worries reintroduced greater caution – particularly noticeable in the 2013 bidding for the 2020 Summer Games). However, no subsequent Games have been as completely privatized as the Los Angeles approach.

It was another American city with a long record of boosterism which most closely modelled its own bid on Los Angeles (Andranovich et al. 2001; Whitelegg, 2000). Atlanta's bid for the 1996 Games was led by a local lawyer, Billy Payne, who played the central role in advancing the city's bid. Once again the model was highly privatized though with one key difference: unlike Los Angeles, Atlanta's city government soon sought active involvement after the Games had been secured, seeking regeneration and wider city objectives. Not surprisingly the Games, whose organization remained private throughout, failed to deliver these muddled objectives. Criticisms of Atlanta have subsequently strengthened public initiative, albeit without neglecting the methodologies of private business. These, embracing the full range of marketing and branding arts, remain absolutely central to the Olympic story.

How is the Olympic City Marketed?

In a strictly formal sense the key marketing material produced by would-be Olympic cities is the so-called candidature file. This is the official bid document, in recent years running to several volumes, submitted by short-listed candidate cities to the IOC. It is prepared by the bidding organization to set out the case for their particular city. The file will first be assessed by technical adjudicators (who will weed out unsatisfactory bids) and then forms the basis for the final voting by IOC members. At its core are technical details about the projected budget and how the various sports events and participants are to be accommodated in an effective and secure fashion. Although much of the file is thus very specific, it also has to display the wider city's capacity to host a large international event successfully. Here logistical considerations and hotel capacity assume great importance. There will also be a section that markets the city and its wider setting. This part of the submission tends to showcase the city's attractiveness and openness and will communicate a more general sense of a wide and deep local commitment to sports and to hosting a successful Olympics.

Central it may be, but a city's candidature file is generally reckoned to be less a vote winner than a vote loser if it reveals any significant deficiencies. Thus concerns about technical aspects (albeit masking some deeper worries) saw the elimination of Doha and Baku from the final shortlist for the 2020 Summer Games (Telegraph Sport, 2012). Real doubts about financing, organizational and technical competence have also scuppered most bids by cities from the less affluent world. If its hopes were not to go the same way, it was therefore absolutely vital that Rio de Janeiro did not falter in the bidding for the 2016 Games. In the event, it actually excelled in the technical assessment (Gibson, 2009a) but, like any aspirant Olympic city, Rio's team could not then rely on that endorsement to any major extent.

In all bidding cities, therefore, many marketing approaches and methods have to be deployed around this technical core element, many coming into play well before the IOC even becomes involved (e.g. McGeoch and Korporaal, 1994). Building the wide and deep commitment within the city and beyond is itself a major task. It involves a great deal of public and media relations work by the group initiating the bid to win support first within newspapers, television and radio. Media executives, editors and journalists all need to be briefed and persuaded. Business leaders, politicians and other prominent figures will similarly be schmoozed and convinced of the benefits of making a strong bid (and of contributing to it in money or other material ways to raise awareness). Typical marketing at this stage would involve a local media campaign expressing business, public agency and community backing.

Provided they can be convinced that the candidature will be competently advanced, many companies associated with a bidding city are likely to see benefits in the wider exposure that will result. The experience of Atlanta suggests that bidding for the Olympics (and, once awarded, the preparation period for the Games themselves) can shift business contributions away from more routine city marketing campaigns (S.V. Ward, 1998, p. 207). Overall, however, total business contributions to city marketing tend to increase. If, of course, the bid should eventually prove successful, then the benefits of early support will be even more palpable. This perception of benefits often seems to hold true even if the bid eventually turns out to be unsuccessful. Thus, despite their city's ignominious defeat in consecutive final IOC voting to decide the locations of the 1996 and 2000 Games, much of Manchester's business community would certainly have been happy to see a third bid to host the Summer Olympics. It was this support which also underpinned what became the city's successful bid to host the 2002 Commonwealth Games.

Alongside all this wooing of business, there will be an increasing engagement with the community, locally and more widely, to win the backing of key individuals and gain at least the semblance of widespread popular support. Any local organizations or individuals with sporting links, especially Olympic sporting links, are almost certain to be harnessed in some way to the bid. Typically the bidding organization will sponsor local sports and cultural events that will raise awareness and often involve the distribution of personal marketing items such as tee shirts, flags, balloons, pens and key-rings that bear its logo. Sale of these and the fees to enter mass events are often a way of raising funds for the campaign. Sydney's bidding team, for example, organized a mass community walk across the Harbour Bridge, charging two dollars per participant and thereby raising A$300,000 (SOCOG Sydney, 2001, Vol. 1, pp. 15–17). These approaches have the added benefit of enabling mass voluntary identification with the city's bid. In recent years, bid teams have become more adept at marshalling this, recruiting volunteers at an early stage to help spread the word and provide a tangible sign of the level of popular support. Barcelona, for example, had an army of over 100,000 volunteers to call upon by the time the bid campaign was transformed into the Games Organizing Committee (COOB, 1992, I, pp. 207–208).

The logo itself forms a key identifier for the bidding campaign. This would usually embrace a combination of Olympic imagery and various signifiers of the bidding city. In cases such as Sydney, these would be iconic buildings or structures, in others more symbolic associations (McGeoch and Korporaal, 1994, pp. 67–70). A key requirement, however, is that it has to be capable of being reproduced in many different media. The publicity officers of the bidding organization typically ensure its appearance around the city and beyond, and especially in major media and at airports. Another promotional device occasionally used at this stage has been the Olympic mascot. In most cases mascots have appeared after the award of the Games, the best known being Moscow's 1980 bear cub mascot, Misha. An exception was Barcelona's bid team which launched a competition to design a mascot to build youth involvement (COOB, 1992, I, pp. 299–300).

These and other marketing devices form part of a widening promotional campaign. Business and community commitment provide marketing assets to use in the successive encounters with the National Olympic Committee (especially so if there are other bidding cities from the same country) and the IOC. Governments will be similarly aware that overwhelming local support is fundamental for a credible bid. Tokyo's successful bid for 2020 included detailed polling showing steadily growing popular support for the bid in the city and country. It was categorically stated that there was no major anti-Olympic movement (TOCOPG, 2012, I, 32–34). On the other hand, low and declining public support scuppered both Oslo's bid for the 2022 Winter Olympics and Boston's 2024 Summer Olympic bid (AP, 2015).

For Rio's successful 2016 bid, the highly visible backing of the President of the Central Bank of Brazil was critical, addressing IOC anxieties about the city and country's financial capacity to stage the Games. Commonly, for example, candidature files or accompanying promotional materials will include portraits and brief statements of support from key individuals from business and the community, along with figures from politics and government and those with an international profile. In its bid, Atlanta, for example, secured the endorsement of film star Kim Basinger. Sydney, which borrowed many of Atlanta's marketing tactics, had the support of Nicole Kidman and her then-husband, Tom Cruise (Burroughs, 1999; ACOG, 1990; McGeoch and Korporaal, 1994, pp. 141, 286). Although Cruise was American, there would usually be some local connection between the star and the place. Occasionally though, some bidders make serious mistakes in claiming celebrity endorsement. Berlin's generally rather mishap-prone bid for the 2000 Summer Games suffered when they publicized the endorsement of tennis stars Steffi Graf and Boris Becker without actually having asked them (McGeoch and Korporaal, 1994, p. 108).

From the beginning the bidding organization needs a team well versed in the promotional arts. It is quite common for key individuals to move on to advise subsequently bidding cities. Thus Mike Lee, who worked at the centre of the London 2012 campaign, helped adapt the London template to Rio's successful campaign for 2016 (Gibson, 2009b). All successful campaigners understand that opportunities for personal meetings with people of influence are critical. Any possibility of encountering IOC delegates, such as in meetings of other sports organizations, is seized upon and often planned in great detail (SOCOG, 2000, pp. 17–18). Similarly IOC gatherings ostensibly unrelated to the Games for which bidding is taking place become major opportunities to promote aspiring Olympic cities. Thus meetings to decide the location of Winter Olympics are also significant marketing occasions for later Summer Games. Still more important are the Olympic Games which precede the fateful decision. The festival atmosphere which prevails at these times is particularly helpful to the bidding teams of intending future Olympic cities.

Yet the potential demands on bidding teams' time and effort are huge. Successful bidding cities appear to be those which can field a larger number on such occasions, especially of very senior individuals. London's 2012 bid certainly benefited by having both Lord Sebastian Coe and Keith Mills who were able to share the burden (Campbell, 2005). As well as following the course of the sporting event itself, the bidding teams will be drawing lessons from how the Games are staged. They will need to be attuned to perceived successes and failures to which they can respond in their own bid. Stamina is essential for the many events (including those hosted by opponents) that provide multiple opportunities for persuasion (McGeoch and Korporaal, 1994, pp. 148–168).

The official hotels occupied by delegates usually become the key arenas for this activity. While bidding organizations will have their own hotel suites, the more open meeting places of the hotels are highly significant locations because of their public nature. Here they literally have the opportunity to lobby any passing

IOC delegates. Members of bidding teams will often try to station themselves in strategic positions in lobby areas where they can engineer 'chance' encounters, spy on opponents and generally see who is talking to whom. Some bid teams have tried to use more novel settings for these occasions. At the Barcelona Games of 1992, for example, the Milan team, bidding for the 2000 Games, moored a large yacht in the harbour, until ordered out by a senior IOC official.

Until 2002, a key marketing episode was when IOC delegates exercised their rights to inspect would-be host cities. Not all IOC delegates would visit all places, though those that did would usually come in several waves, creating extraordinarily demanding periods for bidding teams. In preparation, the bidding teams prepared very detailed dossiers on the individual delegates, listing their various interests and personal details. This information was sometimes traded by members of previous bidding teams and cities. Invariably delegates were very well looked after, comparable to official visits by leading heads of state. Sydney, for example, ensured that all traffic lights encountered by visiting IOC groups were changed to green on their approach, to avoid delays or any sense of traffic congestion (McGeoch and Korporaal, 1994, p. 196).

The ostensible purpose of these visits was to show delegates the city, its sporting credentials and its capacity to stage the world's biggest sporting event. In reality, however, they were very much more than this and the technicalities were only a small part of these occasions. Lavish entertainment was usual, along with expensive and carefully selected gifts for all the visiting delegates. In case this luxury might appear too shallow, many bidding cities also tried to introduce a more personal dimension, involving parties in the homes of leading members of the bidding team or other prominent citizens of the host city. Great care would be taken to ensure that language and cultural affinities, so far as possible, matched on these occasions, thereby underlining the openness of the city to visitors from all parts of the world.

Such visits were not without their risks. On occasion, IOC visits gave local opponents to the bid a prime opportunity to market their own viewpoint. Unsuccessful bids by Toronto for the 1996 Summer Games and Berlin for 2000 both suffered in this way (McGeoch and Korporaal, 1994, p. 107; Kasimati, 2003). Their rivals were quick to exploit any such public expressions of opposition in their own marketing efforts. Bidders from more authoritarian countries were naturally at an advantage, though action outside the country by dissidents could have the same effect. It was used, for example, to damage Beijing's first bid (for the 2000 Games), when memories of the crushing of the democracy movement in Tiananmen Square were still fresh (McGeoch and Korporaal, 1994, pp. 225–227).

Corruption also lay not far beneath the surface of this part of the choice process. As competition to host both Summer and Winter Games intensified in the 1990s, it is clear that the proper limits of legitimate marketing and promotional activity during these encounters became very blurred. In part there were genuine cultural differences in expectations about how promotional activity should be conducted

(Booth, 1999). Gifts such as alcohol, tobacco, perfume, luxury products associated with the bidding cities or other personal gifts to delegates were routine (Jennings and Sambrook, 2000, pp. 115–130). There had been growing unease for many years, with allegations of improper favours granted in response to outright or coded demands from delegates in the desire to obtain precious votes. Moreover, since votes in the final selection process remained secret, delegates conceal their voting decisions from their National Committees.

The Olympic movement began to prohibit the most extravagant forms of hospitality by bidding cities in 1991–1992. It was not, however, until 1998 that the practice was comprehensively changed (Jennings and Sambrook, 2000, pp. 115–130; D. Miller, 2003, pp. 321–329). The occasion was the IOC delegate visit prior to the selection of the location for the 2002 Winter Olympics, which were hosted by Salt Lake City. The Utah city's Mormon heritage had scarcely endowed it with a reputation for venality. Yet during the visit several delegates and their families were reportedly bribed with holidays, medical treatment and other favours. When allegations (from a Swiss IOC member) came to light there was an IOC investigation that saw three delegates resign, ten replaced, ten warned and only two exonerated. Following this scandal, the IOC decided to ban delegate visits. Instead it has strengthened the demands for technical and financial information from bidding cities, to provide a stronger and more visible evidence-base for decisions.

Another consequence has been that the final IOC selection meeting has assumed even more importance because this is now the most significant opportunity for bidding organizations to meet rank and file delegates. Despite the new strictures, opinion still differs as to how much lobbying is proper. Bidding teams constantly strive to find new ways to do some last minute promotion. On the eve of the 1990 IOC decision in Tokyo, Atlanta's bid team somehow managed to recruit chambermaids at the hotel where the IOC delegates were staying (McGeoch and Korporaal, 1994, p. 292). The latter thus went to bed to find their pillow cases had been changed to bear a message urging them to sleep 'with Georgia on their minds', a timely linking of Hoagy Carmichael's famous song with Atlanta's home state. Sydney's campaign took a flavour of the city to Monte Carlo where the IOC held its selection session in 1993. Celebrity lunches of the glitterati, sporting and otherwise, were familiar enough fare to Monaco's super rich but the street theatre, koala and kangaroo costumes struck a more exotic note (*Ibid.*, p. 285). Despite meticulous planning and securing of permits, however, some of their efforts were reined in by the city authorities.

Lobbying tactics were also a sore point following the 2005 IOC meeting in Singapore where the 2012 Summer Games venue was determined (Campbell, 2005). In contrast to the Paris bid team, which deployed the already gaffe-prone President Chirac in the main presentation, London used the British Prime Minister and his wife in person only in the pre-presentation lobbying. Over a quarter of the IOC delegates were individually subjected to a full Blairist charm offensive in a two-day series of brief interviews that went on far into the night. These 'unfair'

Anglo-Saxon tactics profoundly annoyed the French, a fact lovingly recorded in the British media.

London's successful deployment of political charisma in 2005 also shaped the tactics adopted by all the candidate cities bidding for the 2016 and 2020 Games. At the 2009 Copenhagen meeting where the IOC made its decision for 2016, Rio and Chicago were supported in person respectively by Presidents Lula and Obama, Madrid by King Juan Carlos and Tokyo by then Prime Minister Hatoyama. Here it was Lula, actively and very visibly involved in the Brazilian city's bid almost from the outset, who held the ace. At Buenos Aires in 2013, Tokyo helped to ensure its handsome victory for the 2020 Games by producing both Prime Minister Shinzo Abe and Princess Takamoto, rarely seen outside Japan (Gibson, 2013b). Madrid produced Crown Prince Felipe (himself an Olympic yachting competitor in 1992) but this did not stop it being eliminated at the first round.

The final selection event itself is the great marketing set piece of the competition. Depending on the number of final bids, each presentation might last thirty or more minutes. In recent years, successful bids have combined charismatic individuals, technical wizardry and pure theatricality. Each candidate city uses individual speeches, not usually of any length, promotional videos, computer-generated simulations of intended Olympic venues, elements of cultural display and political campaigning. In theory, all the work ought to have been done by this stage. Nevertheless the presentation can certainly make a difference. For this reason, they are very carefully constructed and rehearsed, often over a long period. Every word and inflection are carefully judged. Sydney's successful bid, for example, was planned by a TV producer with speeches written by a former Prime Minister's speechwriter (McGeoch and Korporaal, 1994, pp. 277–278). All those making speeches were trained and coached by a communications consultant.

For all this attention to detail, however, there are some common pitfalls. The videos are often a weak point, usually because they try to say too much. Explicit details of a city's infrastructure, cultural assets, love of sport or visual charms, are important to get across but not necessarily very engaging unless done with imagination. There is also a temptation to use video clips to present too many talking heads. As well as subtly reminding delegates of the important people who were not able (could not be bothered?) to come, this can make the presentation disjointed. Nor are there very many people, important or otherwise, who have a sufficiently strong screen presence to engage an audience.

This is not to say that the videos are not made to the highest professional standards and aspire to a celebrity quality of their own (Barkham, 2005b; BBC News 24, 2006). There has been a recent tendency to use well-known film makers to create them. Thus in the 2005 IOC selection meeting for the 2012 Summer Games, Steven Spielberg prepared the New York video and Luc Besson that for Paris. Even so, neither escaped the 'travelogue' and 'talking heads' tendencies already noted. Besson's film, for example, showed an extraordinary technical virtuosity in its opening animated scenes with the Olympic Rings dancing happily through the landmarks of Paris. A truly beautiful city was presented at its most engaging. Within a few minutes, however, Parisian charm and Besson's virtuosity were squandered. There followed an essentially dreary succession of middle-aged men (including, for example, several trades union leaders) expressing their support to camera. It mirrored the style of Paris's overall presentation.

By contrast, London's effort had no celebrity film maker to direct it. Instead two comparative unknowns with almost no feature film experience, Daryl Goodrich and Caroline Rowland, directed and produced its short and, in the circumstances, rather low budget video (Johnston, 2005). It contained no talking heads or touristic scenes. It focused instead on four children from different parts of the world seeing the Olympics and being inspired by a particular moment of sporting achievement. In time, they grew up to become world-class sportsmen and women themselves. Yet the children were from Nigeria, Mexico, Russia, and China, rather than the United Kingdom. Absolutely nothing that was place-specific about London appeared in the film. The idea was instead to associate it with deep-rooted Olympian ideals. Rio's successful use of video in 2009 differed in some significant ways. The well-known director, in this case Fernando Meirelles, was back and the city itself was again the 'star'. Yet, like the London video, Meirelles's video, 'Passion unites us' played on the emotions, with Rio the sparkling embodiment of a diverse world united by a love of sport.

Another source of weakness can sometimes be in the very senior government figures that now normally appear in these presentations, often after only fleeting engagement with the campaign. This perception undoubtedly contributed to the abject failure of Obama, despite an eloquent speech, to rally IOC votes for Chicago in 2009. Turkish Prime Minister, Recep Tayyip Erdoğan, similarly failed to rally support for Istanbul in 2013. Perhaps the most ill-advised was Chirac's 2005 speech supporting Paris at Singapore, delivered shortly after his arrival and generally judged to be unfocused (Campbell, 2005). Nor were the political rivalries between the Gaullist French President and the Socialist Mayor of Paris sufficiently subordinated to the overall objective.

By contrast, Barcelona's 1986 handling of the highly combustible mix of competing Spanish, Catalonian and city affiliations and sensitivities at the Rome IOC meeting showed consummate political dexterity (Hill, 1992, pp. 218–230). Australian city, state and national politics might have been less genuinely explosive but Paul Keating's prime ministerial intervention in 1993 on behalf of Sydney was nonetheless a powerful and meticulously prepared contribution (McGeoch and Korporaal, 1994, pp. 276–278).

Leading sportsmen and women, preferably Olympic medallists, with some charisma or star quality are common in these final set pieces. In a hand that was full of aces, not the least effective in London's final presentation for 2012, was the globally known footballer, David Beckham. The legendary Brazilian footballer, Pelé, performed an even more important role for the Rio 2016 bid. There has also been a growing tendency to exploit the winsome potential of children and young people in the final presentations, either *en masse* in flag-waving or similar roles or as individual speakers. Atlanta had its 'dream team' of fifty-eight youngsters and Sydney used an 11-year old schoolgirl as one of its individual speakers (Organizing Committee, 1996, pp 13–14; SOCOG, 2001, p. 20). The latter is particularly risky, given the greater possibility of a child being either overawed by the occasion or conversely so nauseatingly self-possessed as to irritate the audience.

Yet, alongside such strong presences, the key figure in the final presentation will always be the leader of the bidding team. The necessary qualities of conviction, persuasion and self-confidence, well tested in the earlier stages of the bidding process now have to face their ultimate challenge. Before the world's and, perhaps more searchingly, their country's and city's own media, these figures have to capture in their words and body language the essence of their city's case. They also have to make it look easy, which it certainly is not. However effective and relaxed these people may have been in making off the cuff speeches or in lobbying conversations over the bid's course, the final speech is on a different level. Like the rest of the presentations, these final speeches are normally honed and rehearsed over a long period, every word and nuance carefully judged. Rod McGeoch reckoned to have rehearsed his speech for Sydney at least sixty times so it was deeply imprinted on his memory (McGeoch and Korporaal, 1994, p. 277). It seems unlikely that his was an unusual experience.

The Promotional Message

Marketing methods and presentational style are very important in promoting aspiring Olympic cities. So too are the technical details and the sense of strong backing from business, governments and communities. Yet even taken together, these are not enough. There has to be an overarching marketing proposition around which the bid can cohere in an intellectual sense. To be successful, this will first involve a simple and easily grasped idea of the intended event as it will be delivered at that particular time and in that particular city. In addition, and very importantly, it must also demonstrate that the event will be a historically momentous realization of the internationalism and altruism of the Olympian ideal.

One might reasonably question how far the contemporary Olympic movement itself, with its extraordinary commercialism and luxury hotel lifestyle, may be squared with this lofty ideal (Simson and Jennings, 1992; Barney *et al.*, 2004). The record of IOC delegates in choosing the locations of Summer (and increasingly, Winter) Games certainly suggests a strong preference for highly sophisticated cities. This is a material reality that certainly needs to be addressed in the marketing message. So too do elements that relate very directly to competitive sports and, in a more subtle way, to the higher purposes of the Olympian ideal.

The result is that there are many common features in the marketing messages of Olympic candidate cities. Almost all will have spoken to the internationalism of the movement by portraying themselves in some sense as cities of the world. A good example of this is Barcelona's bid which stressed its international connectedness, the amount and quality of its hotel accommodation and visitor attractions, and its cultural sophistication (COOB, 1992, I, p. 303). Culture has been a theme of increasing importance in the Olympic movement. Barcelona, for example, was able to stress its own high cultural reputation, mentioning legendary figures with strong associations such as Gaudi, Miró and Picasso (*Ibid.*). Living testimony was provided by the Catalonian opera singer, Monserrat Caballé, a powerful ambassador for the city's Olympic hopes.

A further way of signifying culture was to stress the multi-culturalism of the city, a feature especially of Atlanta, Sydney, London and Rio's successful candidatures (ACOG, 1990; SOCOG, 2001, pp. 15–17; LOCOC, 2004). Another important theme was a general openness and welcoming attitude, which was first emphasized by Melbourne's 'friendly Games' in 1956 and which Sydney sought to revive in its 1993 bid (McGeoch and Korporaal, 1994, p. 138). Cities that were less obviously multi-cultural, such as Barcelona (at least in 1986) or Beijing, tended to portray themselves as conduits through which a major cultural group might be claimed for the Olympic movement. Barcelona thus linked itself to its wider linguistic community in Latin America (COOB, 1992, I, p. 312; BOBICO, 2001, I, p. 3). For Beijing, the vastness of the world's Chinese population scarcely needed any labouring of the point.

Alongside these elements of the message that emphasized the city, there were also others that focused more specifically on sports. Candidate cities, certainly those in the most highly developed parts of the world, are virtually obliged to argue that their populations are keen participants in and spectators of all types of sport. They will also try to show that their climate will be particularly conducive to sporting attainment when the Games are held. In keeping with all claims of this type ever made by city promoters, considerable scepticism must be exercised (S.V. Ward, 1998). Atlanta, for example, averaged its night and day temperatures to reach the claimed figure. Similarly Barcelona's claimed mild climate proved stiflingly hot during the actual Games.

In recent years, several campaigns have also sought to claim that theirs will be an 'Athletes' Games', most explicitly by Sydney which used these exact words (SOCOG, 2001, p. 20). By this, cities usually mean that they do not want to allow commercial considerations to swamp sporting ideals. Close proximity of proposed athletes' accommodation and sports venues is often associated with this claim. In part this emphasis has emerged as a reaction to the most highly commercialized Games, notably those of Los Angeles and Atlanta. There may also be a specific need for the marketing message to rebut potential criticisms of the bidding city. For example, the 1963 Mexico City team that successfully bid for the 1968 Summer Games devoted much attention to countering its own, rather serious, weak points, namely, that its altitude and poor air quality would prejudice a successful sports occasion (Organizing Committee, 1969, Vol. 2, pp. 11–13).

Normally this kind of operation would be done in a less overt manner that stresses positives rather than overtly acknowledging negatives, at least in presentational set pieces. Thus all post-Munich Olympic candidates have stressed the safeness of their cities, sometimes against compelling counter-evidence. Even Barcelona's confident campaign experienced a serious wobble when the Basque terror group ETA launched an attack and murdered a policeman in the centre of the city on the eve of the critical IOC meeting in 1986 (COOB, 1992, I, p. 310). In 2005, London's team did not have to face the far more serious atrocities on London's public transport system until the day *after* they had secured the 2012 Olympics. Had these events been transposed that would surely have been a terrible testing of even the most well conceived promotional campaign.

The Olympic movement's fear about terrorism has now morphed into a more general global paranoia, with the result that safety can be represented in odd ways. Rio was able to use Brazil's comparatively low terrorist risk to its advantage in bidding for the 2016 Games. This was plausible enough but it overlooked the city's daily experience of violent criminality which had brought around 6,000 murders in 2008 and made its streets far less safe than any of the other candidate cities. Just two weeks after it won the Games, Rio's drug gangs launched a major assault on the police, bringing twelve deaths and the shooting down of a police helicopter (Phillips, 2009).

Yet safety, however perceived, was one of several widely occurring aspects of all would-be Olympic city's promotional messages. It was prominent in the successful Tokyo bid for the 2020 Games, where fears were running high about radioactive leaks from the Fukushima power plant critically damaged in the 2011 earthquake and tsunami (Gibson, 2013b). The city's presentation tackled this squarely, turning the disaster to its advantage. Prime Minister Abe solemnly promised there was no risk to the city and presented the city's hosting of the Olympics as a way of repaying world generosity for its kindness and help after 2011. Much was made of Japan's Olympic athletes visiting children in the stricken area. Actually, once that worry was laid to rest, Tokyo became the safest option. Madrid lost again but this time because it was feared that the parlous state of the Spanish economy would undermine its plans. Istanbul faced multiple problems including the heavy-handed reaction of the authoritarian Erdoğan government to the 2013 Taksim Square protests and a spate of doping scandals in the Turkish sports community.

Most examples used have come from those cities that won their bids to host the Games. However, it would be equally possible to document broadly similar elements within the marketing messages of those that lost. In 2009, unsuccessful Chicago, Tokyo and Madrid stressed their cultural qualities, accessibility, attractiveness to visitors and safety every bit as much as Rio. Tokyo, Madrid and Istanbul did the same in 2013, when Tokyo won handsomely. So it has been in all recent Olympic contests. This tendency to a generic message begs the question: does the marketing *message* itself really make a difference? Perhaps the role of marketing and promotion is simply to prove commitment, a matter more of method and persistence than of what is actually said?

If the message is important, we can be sure it is not because a city says the same thing as everywhere else. The decisive aspect that arguably sometimes differentiates winners from losers is the presence in the marketing message of a compelling 'big idea'. As Tony Blair later remarked in a reflection on London's success in winning the 2012 Games, it was not simply a case of saying that yours was the sleekest, smartest city.[1] To work, the 'big idea' in the marketing message has to connect to the Olympic ideal in more than a superficial sense. The rhetorical ambition of the ideal itself, based on an altruism and purity of purpose that transcends the ordinary selfishness of humanity, is important here. So too is the associated vanity that lies within the Olympic movement's self-image, that it is a portentous and positive force that anticipates the tides of global history. Candidate cities, if they really want to succeed, do well to flatter this vanity in their promotional rhetoric.

Many successful bids have sought to position themselves and their message, sometimes almost subliminally, as part of a momentous transition or movement. Barcelona's bid, for example, was portrayed by Pasqual Maragall as part both of 'plucky little Catalonia' and the 'great Spain which is awakening' (COOB, 1992, I, p. 312). In this view Spain was finally moving beyond the sterile centralist Madrid-based Franco dictatorship to become a fully democratic and culturally diverse entity, a progressive influence on its neighbours and its linguistic realm. The significance of this proposition was acknowledged when the IOC President, Juan Antonio Samaranch, himself Barcelona-born, pointedly chose to pronounce its winning name not in Castilian Spanish but in the long suppressed but lately reborn regional language of Catalan. A curious echo of this came in the wake of Madrid's ignominious failure in 2013, the third successive time it had tried and failed. Reflecting the recent upsurge in Catalonian nationalism in recent years, much pleasure was taken in portraying the Spanish capital, Barcelona's great historic rival, as a 'loser' (Hamilos, 2013).

The 'big idea' within Beijing's successful bid in 2001 for the 2008 Summer Games was that it represented a China that was now ready to emerge from its own economic and political isolation, '... to speed up its modernisation and integration into the international community' (BOBICO, 2001, I , p. 1). The references were highly coded, so much so as to be almost invisible in the case of moving towards democracy and better standards on human rights. Yet after the city's rebuff largely because of this issue in 1993, helped by some subtle negative campaigning by Sydney and other cities, it definitely had to be addressed if the city's candidature were to succeed (McGeoch and Korporaal, 1994, pp. 226–227). Interestingly though, in 2001, Paris's attempt to use human rights arguments against Beijing rebounded, damaging the French rather than the Chinese bid (D. Miller, 2003, pp. 340–341).

Brazil's economic and political emergence as a new global player with democratic credentials was a powerful theme in Rio's 2009 bid. Brasilia had sought the 2000 Games (though had then withdrawn) and Rio the 2004 Games (Gold and Gold, 2005, pp. 179–180). The difference by 2009 was, however, that the nation's position and status in the world had grown. Rio's grandiose appeal that '[h]istory's first Games in a new continent, in a city with a global image, will open new horizons … [a] compelling new story is ready to be told' now seemed plausible (ROCOG, 2009, I, p. 19). Having been convinced on the technical assessment, the IOC was prepared to give in to the emotions to which Rio's 'big idea' appealed. Far more straightforward was Tokyo's 2013 campaign 'Discover Tomorrow', presenting the city as the place 'where the world comes to discover the future' (TOCOPG, 2012, I, p. xiv).

Other cities have addressed different aspects of the Olympic ideal. The language of Atlanta's black civil rights martyr, Martin Luther King, permeated its message of a brave city that was realizing his integrationist vision and would use the 1996 Olympics to show this to the world (ACOG, 1990). A key word throughout all Atlanta's promotion was 'dream', a direct reference to King's most powerful speech. The prominence in the bid campaign of a black former Atlanta Mayor and Ambassador to the United Nations, Andrew Young, also provided vigorous testimony to the reality, playing a key role in swaying African IOC members. Sydney linked its bid to environmental sustainability, setting a new benchmark for the Olympic movement (SOCOG, 2000, p. 19). It used the Executive Director of Greenpeace International, himself Australian, to substantiate the claim (McGeoch and Korporaal, 1994, pp. 139–141).

We have noted how many cities make use of youth in their message. London was unusual in making youth its big idea. It spoke of the city as 'a beacon for world youth' with a 'voice that talks to young people' (LOCOG, 2004; BBC News 24, 2006). A London Games would inspire the young people of the world to become involved in sport and grasp the opportunities for self-improvement and social betterment that it offered. It was a theme that was consciously echoed throughout its presentation, most obviously in the video mentioned above. The team's leader, the double Olympic gold medallist Lord (Sebastian) Coe, told what was essentially the same story, of how as a boy he too had been inspired by Olympians of an earlier generation (Campbell, 2005). David Beckham brought in the theme of childhood, referring to his boyhood home in the area where London's Olympics were located. His presence, despite then being one of Real Madrid's *galacticos*, also underlined his 'real' loyalty, to his birthplace rather than his adopted city, which in 2005 was London's strongest rival after Paris for the 2012 Games. London also used large numbers of real children on the stage, living testimony to the city's multi-ethnic, multi-cultural character. Most commentators agreed that London's final presentation did make a difference.

Conclusion

Marketing is then a key part of the Olympic selection process. While it is no substitute for a competent bid that is technically and financially convincing, it can make a difference. For those centrally involved in that promotional process, it may well be the pinnacle of their careers. If they win, they are likely to be fêted by an ecstatic city and a grateful nation. They will be the new gods, literally Olympians, of the marketing profession, likely to command, if they so choose, high fees to address business gatherings throughout the world. They may well become advisers to subsequent bidding cities or find lucrative roles in the Olympic movement. The intelligence they collect about IOC delegates and the mechanics of the bidding process will be a tradeable commodity. Even the runners up will be able to cash in on some of the bidding assets they have accumulated.

Yet, paradoxically, winning the right to be an Olympic city is only a prelude to the real marketing event, the actual Games themselves (Barney *et al.*, 2004; Lee, 2005). Once the host city has been selected, the promotional devices invented to advance the bid immediately become commodities that can henceforth be sold to enhance the products of sponsors. The symbols that originated as an image to disseminate a speculative proposition now become the basis for a carefully controlled market brand. Branding is essentially about the ownership of an idea that is then transferred to an actual product, which is quite literally what happens (Gold and Gold, 2008). The big idea of the successful city's vision of its Games is now expressed in an increasingly tangible product. Naturally a burgeoning brand marketing department is needed within the organizing body to police the use of such images and symbols. All this will have been carefully planned and forms a mandatory part of the candidature file. To ensure this plan is properly implemented, cities will find powerful and experienced allies in the IOC, anxious to extract every last scintilla of monetary value from the Games. In the end, therefore, many of the great Olympic ideals resolve themselves into material matters. For all the lofty ambitions of Olympism, it is perhaps appropriate that it falls to the marketers to compete in what has become the greatest Olympic challenge of all.

Note

1.   BBC News 24 Channel, The Olympic Campaign, programme broadcast, 1 January 2006.

Chapter 8

Olympic Villages

Tony Sainsbury

In 1996 the International Olympic Committee supported a major symposium on the subject of Olympic Villages.[1] The programme ranged over many subjects (see de Moragas Spà *et al.*, 1997), but contained a particularly insightful overview by Francesc Manuel Muñoz (1997). He defined and grouped past Villages into specific categories dependent on factors such as location in the host city, the amenities provided, building types and planning issues. What is interesting in retrospect is that, while the location and planning issues and challenges remain similar even today, the nature of the athlete in that intervening period has radically changed.

In 1996 athletes presenting themselves for the Games still primarily held amateur status as far as IOC eligibility was concerned, although the cracks in that much defended characteristic had already appeared. Barcelona 1992 saw the 'Dream Team', the USA's professional basketball team, accepted as participants – a client group that was reluctant either personally or because of their team management to reside in the Olympic Village. The days of the 'youth of the world' living and competing together as an international family for the total period of the Games started to be openly challenged. Furthermore, while Muñoz's categorization of Village types is still applicable to the modern athletes' accommodation, its relevance is less marked as other factors have taken precedence in the preparation of sportsmen and women for Olympic competition. The services and amenities for amateur athletes were based on the understanding that accommodation was needed, and that the host city providing it would save National Olympic Committees (NOCs) the trouble of making necessary separate arrangements in a foreign city. It was also generally felt that, as amateurs who had faced numerous daily challenges to be able to perform at the top level, they would be grateful for what was provided no matter how basic. In this regard, Barcelona 1992 and the succeeding Atlanta 1996 would prove to be watersheds in attitudinal change.

This chapter, which has five major sections, proceeds against this background. It traces the development of Olympic Villages for the Summer Games from the perspective of the athletes and the provision of services. It also considers the role and interplay in that endeavour of the Organizing Committees (OGOGs) of the day, the Olympic host cities, and governments – local, regional and national.

Beginnings

Initially, individuals and teams were left to their own devices when it came to accommodating athletes for the Games. People attending the Games, whether as participants or spectators, simply booked accommodation to suit their pockets as if they were tourists. There was no impetus then to supply a single accommodation space for all the athletes and their support teams. While the national coordination function was served by the respective NOCs, individual accommodation needs were determined by their national sports federations in a parochial way without any thought about multi-sport cohabitation. That would come later as the period over which the Games were staged became compressed and the accommodation became more difficult to secure for the numbers involved. In 1910 Pierre de Coubertin had promulgated the idea of a *Cité Olympique*, wherein sports facilities were concentrated in a particular area of the host city to help create an ambience of Olympism, sportsmanship, friendship and internationalism. As part of that vision, he strongly favoured barracks to house the athletes during the Games (Müller, 2000, pp. 256–268).

Stockholm 1912 created a specific Committee to research and negotiate accommodation within the city, recognizing the ever-increasing numbers of participating athletes and nations and the resulting consequences of such involvement in terms of cost. There was no desire as yet to take up de Coubertin's cry for a barracks to house the athletes during the Games, with the search centred on two categories: schools and other premises offering lodging only (with no food) that would be lower-priced; and higher-price range hotels and pensions. In order to understand the demand, the Accommodation Committee sent a detailed questionnaire to the nations seeking numbers, dates and types of requirement, with a final submission date of 1 October 1911.

The Games' Official Report (SOC, 1913, pp. 226–241) subsequently conveyed the major findings, providing a fascinating insight into the challenges of arranging accommodation for an event of this kind that remains relevant today. *Inter alia*, it pointed to the difficulty for NOCs to be specific about exact numbers before trials were held; their inability to state whether low-cost or high-cost accommodation because of funding uncertainties; and the conviction held by some nations that they could gain a better deal by turning up and negotiating separately from the OCOG. Stockholm was the first Olympic city to realize that, for the good of all concerned, it was essential to try to coordinate these affairs to avoid potential chaos. Three pages of the Official Report deal with where and under what conditions the various delegations used their accommodation. Probably the closest that teams came to the multisport communal living of an Olympic Village was by those teams who travelled by sea and used their cruise ships as accommodation for the Games and those who decided to accommodate their whole team together using school premises. The Stockholm report also reflected one of the concerns of the developers and funders of purpose-built Villages, namely their nervousness about the condition that they would find after the departure of the athletes. However, in this case their worries were unrealized – which is nearly always the situation today:

> On our side it is a pleasant duty to state that the visitors deserve every acknowledgement for the gentlemanly way in which they behaved while in these quarters; with one or two unimportant exceptions there was absolutely no complaint made against our guests. The charges which the Committee had to pay against the damages after the premises had been inspected at the close of the Games ... amounted to no more than a few shillings, a result which must be counted as satisfactory (*Ibid.*, p. 236)

The outbreak of war meant that there were no further Olympic Games until Antwerp 1920 in war-torn Belgium. In some ways, the Village concept did not move on from the lessons of 1912. The Organizing Committee had hoped that the Allies would have made their refugee and other camps available for competitors, but eventually this option was withdrawn. Antwerp therefore established yet another Accommodation Committee tasked with the same research and negotiation undertaken in Stockholm but, just 2 years after the end of hostilities, in a much more challenging environment. Schools, barracks and hospitals were all on the lists for the nations to consider. The results might have been less than ideal, but it is interesting to note that the British Olympic Association would later comment that there was a growing feeling that the team should be together and remark upon the benefits of that togetherness on team morale at Antwerp 1920 even though the team was based in school premises (Renson, 1996, p. 73).

A further interesting aspect of the Antwerp Games and one which inevitably had an impact on later Games and athletes' accommodation was the circumstances surrounding Team USA's use of an alleged cruise-ship for their journey from the USA (as previously mentioned then a common practice). The ship, the USS *Princess Matoika*, was a last minute replacement for the intended vessel the USS *Northern Pacific*. The latter was a modern and fast-moving passenger liner that had been damaged on a voyage to New York, whereas *Princess Matoika* had been used as an Atlantic troop carrier during the War, then as a hospital ship, a vessel for repatriation of the dead and wounded from the Great War to the USA, and finally for transporting prisoners-of-war back to Europe through the port of Rotterdam. It had not been repaired or refurbished during the whole of that period, but was the only available option if the US team was to compete in Antwerp.

The athletes only learned of the change of vessel hours before embarkation and were instructed to make the best of things by their team management. However, before the end of the trip, the majority had assembled a list of fundamental grievances and demands that were sent to the American Olympic Committee and distributed to the press. They castigated the ship for being dirty, vermin-ridden (especially rats), insufficient sanitary arrangements, poor service, inadequate quarters, and incompetent crew. Their action, known today as the 'Mutiny of the *Matoika*', was significant for being perhaps the first time that the voice of the athletes was heard, particularly in regard to the circumstances of their preparations, the accommodation offered and the unacceptability of such a state of affairs for those representing their country after years of dedicated commitment. This collective assertive action presaged important shifts in expectation that needed to be considered when providing accommodation at the Olympics (Phillips, 2015).

Pioneers

For Paris 1924, the organizers were able to develop something of de Coubertin's notion of a *Cité Olympique* through the choice of the Stade de Colombes as the main Stadium. Ironically, this had not been the first choice. After being awarded the Games, the OCOG, supported by de Coubertin, had initially argued for a new stadium in central Paris, clearly seeing how much easier it would be to galvanize the interest of spectators if within the city centre rather than in some remote location on the periphery. Having failed to develop such a stadium, however, they turned to the existing venue at Colombes, at which the Committee concentrated track and field, aquatics, fencing, tennis and training areas. At this point, the idea of 'accommodation' seems to have entered the organizers' thinking, given the large open spaces that surrounded the stadium. Paris, of course, was well endowed with hotels and commercial lodgings, but there was real concern that participants might be deterred if cheaper accommodation was not secured.

It was therefore decided that there would be a *Village Olympique*. Far from lavish, it comprised several hundred three-bedded wooden huts arranged in rows with earthen passage-ways, described by the Official Report of the 1924 Paris Games as: 'la construction à Colombes d'un camp de baraques en bois, aux allées de terre étroites et au confort sommaire' (COJO, 1924, p. 59). Basic washing facilities and temperatures soaring to 45°C on some days would have made life uncomfortable in such a compact community. An estimated 600 bed spaces were provided; clearly only sufficient to accommodate a small percentage of the 3,089 athletes taking part in Paris 1924. There is no record of precisely who took up the French offer to be accommodated in the Colombes Village but the proximity of a number of facilities, including swimming and track and field, suggests that some NOCs used the facility as a base for athletes involved in Colombes-based sports, albeit probably only at the critical periods of their competitions. In addition, the Village was not available for the team sports which preceded the Olympics proper. Diary entries for members of the USA rugby team indicate that they had heard about the provision of a Village prior to their arrival and may have intended to stay, but were unable to do so because 'it will not be ready to receive the team for eight to ten days'. They therefore stayed on at the hotel (Ryan, 2009, p. 32). Similarly, the deliberations of the officials of the Netherlands NOC clearly state that they decided to accommodate only their track and field team in the Village and secured other more centrally-based accommodation for the other members of their team. The Dutch press duly reported their impression of this first Olympic Village:

The organizers, who were scared that they didn't have enough room for all the people to stay, built a village nearby the Colombes Stadium. We have visited this extraordinary place. But it's not that spectacular. It's no more than some wooden barracks without comfort… At this time the area is filled with souvenir shops, potato fries and ice cream shops. We wonder how the athletes would have their rest before the matches. (Translated by author from Vugts, 1992, p. 46)

Whatever is said about the Village for Paris 1924, it was the catalyst for what is known today as the Olympic Village, with a palpable influence on the Games of Los Angeles 1932 and Berlin 1936. The LA Games were staged in the midst of the Great Depression in a location far away from the centres of performance sport in Australasia and Europe. Against the fear that nations might not be able to afford to attend,[2] the OCOG intelligently turned their thoughts to the athletes and their support teams. They set about making deals with steamship companies for reduced fares for teams and with the trans-continental railways from the eastern seaboard. They also recognized that cheap affordable accommodation was required, but Los Angeles faced the same challenge as previous cities (with the exception of Paris). The region was as yet insufficiently developed and hotels were in short supply for the numbers anticipated. From a starting point born out of necessity came thinking about the provision of a Village for athletes and their support teams (Muñoz, 1997).

This could have been done on a shoestring basis rather than providing what was later touted as a 'Village of the Universe' or the 'Village of Dreams'; a development as never before in an imposing location with superb facilities (TOC, 1933). However, William May Garland, the inspiration behind the Los Angeles bid (see Chapter 2), understood that the performance of athletes relied on their needs being met. Mindful of the Mutiny of the *Matoika* and recognizing the pressures on American athletes, who frequently travelled considerable distances to meetings,[3] he realized that supplying them with a comfortable place to rest, good food, a pleasant location, training and entertainment amenities would be important for the success of the Village. It would allow athletes to concentrate on what they did best and not feel the need to embroil themselves in issues outside of their control.

Great care was taken with location. The OCOG, for example, realized that many of the athletes attending the Games came from the temperate regions and might find the potential heat of a Californian summer oppressive and impact negatively on their performance. 'The summer of 1931 (reinforced this concern) was one of the hottest ever experienced in Los Angeles' (TOC, 1933, p. 255). Thermometers were placed in a number of potential locations and eventually Baldwin Hills was chosen because it was 10 degrees cooler on average than any of the other potential sites. Here, a ground plan was prepared at an elevation of 130 metres above sea level to catch the breeze, with a perspective downhill to the centre of the city (25 minutes away) and views of the Stadium (10 minutes away) and of the Pacific Ocean.

Figure 8.1. Today's view of the Baldwin Hills 1932 Village location with Los Angeles in the distance. (*Photo*: Tony Sainsbury)

The resulting Olympic Village (figure 8.1) consisted of around 500 huts, with four beds per hut giving a total of 2,000 bed spaces – enough for the male athletes and team officials reported to have stayed there. The accommodation was uniformly laid out in spacious surroundings with dining facilities and bathhouses at convenient intervals. The residential buildings were made of timber in sections and erected on site. Each building could accommodate its four residents in two rooms with washing facilities. The dining facilities comprised a number of long and wide structures capable of division into various units to accommodate teams of specific size, who had their own kitchen and cooks to prepare meals according to their particular menus and tastes. The rationale to this dining solution was explained in the Official Report (*Ibid.*):

> It was plainly out of the question to attempt to serve special food wanted by the various national groups, in a single dining hall and out of a single kitchen. Not even a Swiss hotel-keeper could achieve that feat.

At this stage, as noted, the Village remained an all-male preserve. The official records state that 1,408 athletes took part, of which 127 were woman from thirty-seven countries. As the idea of a Village for athletes of both sexes was still a thing of the future, the female athletes were accommodated in downtown Los Angeles. The Official Report (*Ibid.*, p. 292) went on to state:

> The Organizing Committee early abandoned any plans it might have had for housing the women contestants in the Olympic Village or in a village similar to the men. It was felt that feminine needs could be more completely met in some permanent type of residence.

Instead, the Chapman Park Hotel on Wilshire Boulevard was chosen and made available at the same price per diem as for the men, two dollars a day, with the additional cost being borne by the OCOG.

The athlete-centred approach, part of the DNA of the OCOG responsible for Los Angeles 1932, had important consequences. The creation of an exemplary Village, endorsed by the participants, would be telegraphed around the world; promoting the image of a city and society that knew how to deliver and giving support to promotional claims about Los Angeles' potential as a global city of the future. Moreover, the details contained in the Official Report together with all the illustrations and coloured photographs made it a handbook for anybody, even today, who wishes to understand what an Olympic Village at its best should deliver.

The resulting worldwide accolades were not lost on the hosts for Berlin 1936. As noted in Chapter 13, Hitler was initially lukewarm to the idea of the Olympic Games and most certainly against spending vast resources on its delivery. However, as with his mind-set generally, once recognizing the opportunity to align the Games with Germany's political goals, he gave the project his full backing. The two architects of the Berlin bid were Theodor Lewald, President of the German NOC during the early preparations for the Games, and Carl Diem who had promoted the bid for Berlin 1916 that never occurred. Both were close to the IOC leadership and had attended previous Games including Paris 1924 and Los Angeles 1932. In particular, they were impressed with the 1932 Olympic Village and were supporters of de Coubertin's idea for a *Cité Olympique*. Much of their planning centred on the Reichssportfeld, a monumental Sport Park which fitted ideally into the regime's ideological sensitivities. In terms of the Village a number of locations were considered and ultimately it was decided to extend a military camp some 15 miles (24 km) from Berlin. It would accommodate nearly 4,000 male athletes and their staff, with the female athletes accommodated in a hostel, the Friesenhaus, close to the Stadium. There were recreation facilities and training grounds, comprising a running track, sports halls and an indoor swimming pool. All this was laid out in 130 acres (52.5 ha) of wooded landscape. Somewhat surprisingly given the fierceness of fighting around Berlin, a significant proportion of the Village estate remains today, albeit largely in a dilapidated state.

Figure 8.2 shows a diagram of how the 140 buildings were laid out in the Village. Each bore the name of a German city, as part of a schema that saw the buildings laid out in the form of a map of Germany. The principal building, which represented the heart of Germany (the city of Berlin), was a huge central structure containing thirty-eight separate dining rooms – one for each nation with their own chefs and kitchen staff. Each house contained thirteen bedrooms with two athletes in twin beds. Showers and toilets were at one end of the building and a sitting room at the other. There was a substantial main entry with facilities such as bank, post office, camera store, travel agency and sports good shop. This was an extension of that provided in Los Angeles but with a variety of provision recognizable in any modern Village. These Games were also the first to have television broadcasts and

Belegungsplan des Olympischen Dorfes

Die Teilnehmer aus Japan, Ungarn, Brasilien, Polen, Dänemark, der Tschechoslowakei, Rumänien und Deutschland wurden in eigens hergerichteten Flakkasernen untergebracht – dem so genannten Nordteil des Dorfes.

Quelle/Foto: Verlag B. Neddermeyer

Figure 8.2. The outline of the Berlin 1936 Village displayed at the site today. (*Photo*: Tony Sainsbury)

the Village was equipped with its own receiver and set. Jesse Owens, for example, remarked how instead of attending the Opening Ceremony he watched it all on a very fuzzy television screen (Schaap, 2008).[4]

The success of the Village, assisted by able management,[5] was born out of a different set of values and perspectives than preceding Games. For Paris, de Coubertin wanted to replicate in Colombes the *Cité Olympique* to which he had often referred, although the Paris organizers also saw this as a cheap solution and an encouragement for NOCs to attend. For Los Angeles, the city's promotional objectives made it important to avoid the poor press that the Paris Village achieved, with the 1932 Village translated into an athlete-centred space. Germany's Third Reich wished to make the Village an exceptional and equally athlete-centred location, but its siting and the security which surrounded it also suited the darker forces in Hitler's entourage: those who worried about too much public exposure to their longer-term ambitions. Since the award of the Games to Berlin there had been concerted efforts, particularly in the USA, to encourage NOCs to boycott the Games because of the regime's anti-Semitism and territorial ambitions (Bachrach, 2001). Notable athletes becoming involved in such matters might undo all the benefits that the Nazi leadership saw coming from staging the event. Hence, it can be argued that confinement and control was a key objective; managing the athletes' movements to and from the venues and making sure there was little reason for them to move away from the comforts of the Village.[6]

The three Villages at Paris 1924, Los Angeles 1932 and Berlin 1936 laid the foundation for all future Olympics, but the outbreak of the Second World War prevented further developments for the time being. Both London 1948 and Helsinki 1952 were marked by 'austerity'. Planning for London 1948 centred on completing the task in the best possible way with the resources available but without any thought of a future model. This was particularly the case with the athlete accommodation. Despite the global circumstances, the Olympic Movement demonstrated its enduring attraction with over 4,000 athletes and fifty-nine nations participating, a record attendance for the Games (Hampton, 2008). Yet, as the Official Report noted, no Village was or could have been planned in such circumstances and there was no single location suitable for all the athletes to be cohabited (Organizing Committee, 1948). In the eventuality, two Royal Air Force camps, a hospital at Richmond and local schools housed the male athletes and their staff, with female athletes accommodated in the halls of residence of three London Colleges. This scattered approach meant significant amounts of time were spent travelling on buses to and from venues. However, the OCOG recognized that athletes' needs were more than bed and food and provided cinema, laundry, bank and small shops wherever possible at each location. Food was the greater challenge because the country as a whole was still facing rationing in many basic commodities. Realizing that this was likely, many delegations either brought with them or acquired extra food supplies, which caused some friction with those who had more limited resources.

Helsinki had been awarded the Summer Games for 1940 when Tokyo withdrew (see Chapter 2) and, with time in short supply, had pressed ahead with its planned Games building programme. This included the first purpose-built piece of permanent residential estate with dual use; hosting the Olympic athletes followed by post-Games community use. By 1940, twenty-three blocks of flats were already constructed for the expected 3,000 athletes, but towards the end of April the organizers accepted that the Games could not proceed given Finland's conflict with the Soviet Union. The IOC cancelled the Twelfth Olympiad some days later.

In 1947 Helsinki won the bid for the 1952 Summer Games against fierce competition from other nations even though, as with London, the country was still in a parlous state. Food was in short supply and rationed. Buildings were being reconstructed and there was a shortage of adequate housing. The previously constructed venues including the Village either needed significant repair or no longer existed for Games use. The Helsinki organizers therefore decided to build the Käpylä Olympic Village. Designed for 7,500 persons, it contained 565 apartments, a hospital, training areas, a cinema, saunas and a huge dining facility. Yet while these numbers suggested that the Village could have accommodated all 5,000 athletes and their staff, this did not happen. A number of sub-Villages were commissioned in educational and war-invalid institutions for sports such as rowing, shooting, equestrian and wrestling. Female athletes were lodged separately in the City's nursing school, which provided beds for more than 500 women from thirty-six countries. For ideological reasons, the Soviet Union and its allies demanded that their teams and staff were billeted separately from the other competitors, with student residences and other facilities at the recently-built University of Technology becoming an Eastern Bloc Village. The entire Finnish team was housed in the Cadet School at Santahimina (Organizing Committee, 1952). Thus, in spite of Helsinki being the first to venture into the realm of building a new residential estate for Games and permanent legacy use, it was impossible to deliver the scope required including the attendant Games overlay. As a consequence there was a mix of the pre-1928 athlete accommodation world and what would essentially become the modern Games mode, a multi-sport, multi-nation Village.

Major Steps Forward

In 1956, the Melbourne organizers first considered using the City's University facilities and municipal state schools before they decided to build a future area of family homes as the basis for the Village in the suburb of Heidelberg, with a canoeing and rowing sub-Village at Ballarat. If Los Angeles 1932 provided the catalyst of the possible and the essence of an athlete-centred service which can be seen today, Melbourne took the model a step further: indeed including many elements that one now finds as IOC obligations.[7]

When deciding to build this new community with post-Games legacy, the OCOG received a government grant to construct a permanent estate of 851 units made up of apartments in two- to three-storey blocks and town houses. The problem was, yet again, that of knowing how many participants would attend. The Main Village had accommodation for 6,500 participants, but in the end only 4,285 athletes and officials resided there due primarily to various politically-inspired boycotts of the Games (see Chapter 2) together with Australia's own decision to decline to host the equestrian events because of its own strict quarantine regulations.[8] Eventually the space not taken up was used to enable, first, the sub-Village team members to return to the main Village after competition; secondly, for all team judges and referees to be accommodated; and, thirdly, to provide beds for the 650-strong workforce who had to be drafted in (chefs and cooks recruited from Europe and Malaysia). Other features included were the first International Plaza[9] comprising a Press Centre and various shops and services, saunas, a cinema, recreation room, kiosks providing free drinks, a main dining area, medical centre and multi-faith centre. For the first time, male and female athletes were housed in the same Village. Attention was given to privacy within the Village and from an inquisitive public by the security arrangements made (Organizing Committee, 1958, p. 129).

If one accepts Melbourne as the link between the old and the new, one can argue that it established in future hosts' minds the need for the Village to be a vibrant centre of communal living that gave primacy to the athletes' needs, even if the boycotts and the equestrian ban meant that these ideals could not be fully realized. By contrast, Rome 1960 ushered in the period of using the Olympic and Paralympic Games (see below) as the catalyst for major urban regeneration on a grand scale. The Rome Olympic Village was located on a piece of flat swampland at a bend in the Tiber. In that location after the Second World War was to be found a shantytown of old railcars, rusting truck chassis and pitiful tin and cardboard shacks of refugees still displaced from the fighting of more than a decade before. It was replaced by a new modernistic estate of 1,348 apartments in thirty-three yellow-brick buildings of two or four storeys that were raised on concrete stilts (*pilotis*), one storey high, to provide shaded areas beneath for cooling breezes from the intense Italian summer sun (Maraniss, 2008). Taken together, these were capable of providing beds for 8,000 participants. The accommodation was supported by amenities including banks, with recreation space and a security fence around the entire complex (CONI, 1963).

Two issues pertaining to the Olympic Village at Rome 1960 deserve further comment. The first concerned housing female participants. Although technically one Village, the women's and men's sections were divided by a fence and a highway that split the two residential areas. This separation certainly helped allay the fears of the anxious parents of young female athletes – there were swimmers who were now just 13 years of age. However one American mother had to write urgently to her 15 year old daughter exhorting her to close the curtains of her apartment at all times because the highway which overlooked the two Villages had become a Village in its own right, with voyeurs armed with binoculars and telephoto lenses. This, at first, was problematic as curtains had not been provided, but was overcome by using bed sheets (Maraniss, 2008, p. 24).

The second issue stemmed from the architecture employed for the Village which, although in keeping with the new era, would also prove to have a negative aspect. As noted in Chapter 5, 1960 was the first occasion when the Stoke Mandeville Games were moved to the Olympic city – a development that would anticipate the eventual convergence of the Olympics and Paralympics. It was an enterprise in which CONI (the Italian Olympic Committee) freely cooperated, making venues and the Village available to the International Stoke Mandeville Games Federation (ISMGF).[10] However, just prior to the arrival of the teams, the ISMGF were informed that the part of the Village with lifts was no longer available for use but that the other stilted parts, which relied on steps and steep ramps, were to be made available instead (Scruton, 1998). Faced with this situation, the parallel Organizing Committee had no choice but to draft in helpers to move the 328 wheelchair athletes between the ground and their accommodation for the period of the Games (Brittain, 2008).

Tokyo 1964, the first occasion that the Games were held in Asia, provided an indication of the increased awareness of the importance of the Village as a key centre for the athletes' final preparations before the sports programme commenced. The Official Report, for example, devoted more than 70 pages to the genesis, planning, operations and delivery of the Olympic Village (Organizing Committee, 1966, p.

281). When the Games were awarded to Tokyo in 1959, war reparations were still in force and, as part of these arrangements the United States military still retained and maintained large areas of land for US army personnel. Initially, therefore, available locations around Tokyo of suitable size and proportions for the Village were not under the control of the Japanese Government. The OCOG was obliged to negotiate with the US military for the use of their preferred location. After months of failed negotiations, a compromise was reached which allowed an area known to the Americans as Washington Heights and as Yoyogi to the Japanese to be handed back permanently to the Japanese government.

Although it was more detached from the Games venues than might have been their first choice, the advantage of this location was that it had been the site of a military housing base containing 249 large two-storey cottages and fourteen concrete apartment blocks. While the OCOG was nervous about the eventual numbers who might attend, they eventually prepared 8,868 bed spaces, of which 1,100 were ultimately given over for delegation support services, offices and medical spaces. In the end some 5,100 athletes attended from ninety-three nations. There were also several sub-Villages for cyclists, canoeists, sailors and the three-day equestrian teams. All the usual services seen in modern Villages existed. The Village had a daily newspaper and to help orientation, it was divided into seven colour- coded areas.[11] Each of these areas now had an Athlete Services Centre, which was broadly similar to the 'front of house' facilities one might see in a hotel, dealing with general information, maintenance reports, special requests from residents, post and other message delivery, and equipment replacement.

For the first time, there was evidence of the growing complexity involved in allotting accommodation to the teams including, then as today: the separation of teams within buildings; the desire of sports within a team to be separate from other sports; and the separation of team support staff from athletes. The one variable not in the mix was that of gender since, as with previous Games, the women had their own quarters. The treatment of the Paralympic athletes also merits comment. These Games were the last for some time where the parallel 'wheelchair Olympics'[12] would be held in the same city using the same facilities. During the transition period between the two Tokyo Games in 1964, the Village was prepared thoroughly in terms of accessibility for its 378 athletes. Few of the traumas of Rome 1960 were repeated in that respect. The presence of the Imperial Family at the events and their visits to the Village during this second phase of its use ensured that the Games were a resounding success and, it can be argued, delivered for Japan and its people an understanding of the abilities and potential of people with impairments rather than a focus on their disabilities.

Regeneration

Mexico City 1968 had its distinctive features. The Village comprised twenty-nine blocks, varying between low- and high-rise, which contained 904 apartments. Of these, twenty-four blocks were used by the men, three by the women and the remaining two were allocated as accommodation for the world's press as their accommodation (albeit separated by fences). There were also two sub-Villages devoted, respectively, to participants in the sailing regatta and three-day eventing. Altogether, some 5,500 athletes from 112 countries attended the Games. The Main Village had six zonal dining facilities, with two dining rooms and kitchens in each zone. The users were themselves split into six groups: Eastern European; Western European; Africa and Asia; Latin; English-speaking; and International. Those, in short, were all the culinary tastes one finds in one place in the monstrous 5,000-seater dining facilities found in today's Villages.

Significantly, a pattern had now been established. Mexico 1968 joined the programme initiated by Rome 1960 of using the Olympic Village as part of a more general programme of areal regeneration. Many of the Villages from Munich 1972 through Montreal 1976, Moscow 1980, Seoul 1988 and even to Beijing 2008 were focused on a model of a densely populated residential footprint, high-rise in many cases, with concrete and glass; a pattern of multi-storey regeneration of mass housing with overlay amenities to supplement whatever legacy provision could be utilized for the Villages' resident services. The challenges then and now are always centred on the dining facility and the transport mall; two enormous pieces of temporary overlay without which the Village would not operate and the participants would not get to the venues. Even in London 2012, where 75 per cent of the athletes could live and compete in the Olympic Park area, a transport mall was needed in excess of 25,000 square metres.

Of all Olympic Villages worldwide, everyone remembers that horrific scene of the balaclava-clad terrorist keeping watch from the concrete balcony of the Munich Village. Post-Games the men's Village became part of a new community and the women's part University student accommodation (Reeve, 2001). For its part, Montreal 1976 was infamous for the cost overruns, in which the Village played its part and where only in recent years the debt has been totally eradicated. Moscow 1980, Seoul 1988 and Beijing 2008 all used the Games to create more housing for their growing populations. Placed side by side in terms of their architecture, the physical outcome could have been any city of this period – major multi-storey modernistic edifices. Even the separate Paralympic Village built in Seoul for the 1988 Paralympic Games followed the same model, coupled with a lack of understanding of the principles of inclusion in spite of all their well intended and much appreciated enthusiasm. At least in the 1980s there was a growing recognition that landscaping and public space were important factors to soften the harsh edges of the residential massing.

In their inception and even now in legacy, these generally austere Villages were unremarkable as sets of buildings or urban environments. In their own ways, they had served the athletes well in a functional sense, but most had aimed to be *outstanding*. That was the mantra of all those planning and designing the Village as that temporary home for the athletes – the principal participants in this quadrennial summer festival. Some Villages, however, did offer important lessons for all future Village planners and developers, with individual characteristics that are worthy of note.

The Campus Model

First in this respect were the Villages for the 1984 and 1996 Games, both held in the USA. Briefly, the broader context was crucial to Los Angeles 1984. Montreal 1976 had overrun in costs leaving a massive debt which took 30 years to clear and suffered from boycotts over South Africa. The subsequent Games in Moscow 1980 suffered boycotts because of the Afghanistan invasion. With the IOC unsure of its future role and struggling financially, the Games and the Olympic Movement looked threatened. That these threats did not materialize is explained by many commentators in terms of three elements coming together to change the downward spiral, namely: the election of Juan Antonio Samaranch to President of the IOC; instigation of the TOP programme; and Peter Ueberroth's role in delivering the 1984 Games in a memorable but frugal manner (Ueberroth *et al.*, 1985).

As noted in Chapter 2, the OCOG for Los Angeles 1984 was essentially a private company receiving little or no capital resources from federal or state funds. The plan therefore was to operate on a revenue-generated basis and use existing facilities and services by begging, renting and borrowing with as minimal outlay as possible. This objective applied equally to the Village and therefore the solution was to use existing University campuses. There could not be a single Olympic Village because there were insufficient bed spaces on a single campus to accommodate the likely numbers. Interestingly perhaps, knowing the significance of the Athletes' Village as an entity and that he could not deliver a single location, Ueberroth always referred to that accommodation as 'Housing of the Olympic Athletes and Team Officials (Villages)'. In doing so, he laid down a principle, grasped by some and less by others, that the project needed to be a partnership of the possible (Baker and Esherick, 2013).

Three university locations were utilized: the University of Southern California (USC); the University of California-Los Angeles (UCLA); and 125 miles (200 km) away at the University of California-Santa Barbara (UCSB), which coined the phrase satellite Village (LAOOC, 1985). In each case, use of the student dormitories (halls of residence), existing dining, recreation and shopping facilities and public space proved a very successful combination. Simple use of scaffolding poles and the application of the Look of the Games transformed what might otherwise have been a visually sterile landscape. Of particular note was the creation at USC of what would now be known as the International Plaza, which compensated for limited space by extending the Plaza area on scaffolding directly over the bleachers of the training track.

The NOCs were given direct responsibility for allocating housing. Of the

139 NOCs that attended, seventy-nine were accommodated at USC and sixty at UCLA. Thirty-four of those same teams had members housed at UCSB for canoeing and rowing. Many elements found in the IOC's Villages' Guide of today stem from recommendations from the 1984 Games report including guest pass quotas, office and medical space quotas, and that athletes should be accommodated two to a room wherever possible since larger, apartment-style 'facilities proved inefficient for team space allocations, despite the space they provided' (LAOOC, 1985, p. 402). This indeed is the reality where the units are family houses offering ten or more bed-person spaces: allocating a small team of four can only be overcome by incorporating its office and medical space in the same unit. In the University model, the ability to subdivide units physically is limited generally by an unwillingness of University authorities to countenance radical alterations to the residences and by the time available for such conversions and retrofit before the beginning of the academic year.

Peter Ueberroth's model was for a private enterprise project driven by a genuine desire to see the Olympic Games maintained and developed in a new way, but the same resolve was not a feature of Atlanta 1996. General consensus on those Games testifies to a dysfunctionally-led project in which athletes' needs and the promotion of Olympism were secondary to delivering an event for the benefit of its instigators with minimal investment. No better example of the paucity of spirit can be provided than ACOG's lack of collaboration and support for the Paralympic Games which followed the Olympics. Apart from the endless battles over marketing and fundraising, in which the IOC had to intervene directly, the Village provided one of the worst examples of a lack of any sport ethos. To elaborate, the transition period between the Games is critical for the Paralympics. The ACOG insisted that removal of Olympic resources would occur before access was given to the APOC to prepare for its Paralympic guests. The ACOG stripped the Village so completely that on the first night no linen, pillows, blankets had been able to be off-loaded into the now Paralympic Village. Many of the new arrivals therefore spent the night solely on mattresses.

Despite those comments, University accommodation can be used successfully where the OCOG recognizes that it needs to start the dialogue as early as possible to convince the University authorities as to the benefits of its use and to establish the key relationships which will give confidence and assurances that all will be well during the Games and that the retrofit and return will not interfere unduly with the academic imperative of the institution. Use, for example, of facilities at Royal Holloway (University of London) for the London 2012 Rowing and Canoe Sprint Village indicated the mutual benefit of collaborative working.

Trend Setters

Barcelona 1992 saw the Village at the heart of the Games. It was built and incorporated into the old city in an area of reclaimed industrial land to the north of Las Ramblas, a 10-minute walk away. While it lacked substantial green public space, it featured a new beach which was a private Village space during the Olympic Games. The Village services were located around a shopping precinct as a central core which, amongst other elements, now features a large supermarket and a multi-screen cinema at its heart (COOB, 1992). Barcelona was the first Games to embrace the inclusion agenda of the Paralympic Games, not only for the venues as in Seoul 1988 but also in terms of the accommodation. The design facilitated easy access for wheelchair users and persons with other disabilities: its flat topography and easy layout greatly enhanced that feeling of inclusion by design. Perhaps the only drawback was the use of the central shopping centre as dining facilities located on a basement level. While the stairs and two small escalators worked for the Olympic Games this was a challenge in the Paralympics which followed. Undaunted, the OCOG created a wide ramp down the central core. With the assistance of military volunteers, everyone could access the dining facilities. The Barcelona Village, in turn, has been the exemplar for many that followed (Muñoz, 2006).

The Sydney 2000 Village developed the 1992 model further in terms of service delivery (Gordon, 2003). The Village topographically had challenges in that it ran north–south on a hillside which sloped down west–east. It was very narrow and stretched in terms of footprint, which meant that principal facilities were based at either end of a 1,500 metres spinal road. Moreover, at the southern end roughly one-third of the Village was given over to beach type wooden bungalows (figure 8.3), which were later sold off. The main permanent residential provision was a combination of apartments and three- or four-bedroom townhouses. In the latter the garages were converted into two twin-bedded bedrooms with the adjacent utility room as a shower area. The gardens had a double metal temporary portacabin, with a twin bedroom at either end and a shared accessible bathroom in the middle of the unit. This configuration on one plot meant that as many as twenty people were accommodated; a nightmare for the allotment team as

Figure 8.3. The beach type bungalows from the Sydney Village. (*Photo*: Tony Sainsbury)

multiple-bedded plots mean potential for wastage when given to small teams (a feature previously observed at Los Angeles 1984).

If Barcelona 1992 and Sydney 2000 provided models of good practice for provision of Villages, sadly the Village for Athens 2004 was equally an exemplar of what not to do. The Village was 110 hectares in area, around double the size of most modern Villages and three times that employed for London 2012. The housing was low-rise apartments in small plots scattered across the whole site. All the main facilities were located at one end and the choice then was to either wait for the in-Village transport system to get around the site or walk in the height of the oppressive Greek summer heat. The NOCs located near the facilities were generally happy with their ability to create their own enclave remote from other NOCs and to service the needs of their own athletes. Those further away had a less positive experience. In addition, despite being an integral part of the Games structure, the Village was remote from the centre of Athens and all the associated events without even any adjacent public transport infrastructure. The Village just about functioned for the Games but it lacked cohesion. In addition, it has not fared well with regard to long-term legacy. Today, it is a wasteland of half empty properties, vandalism and little one can call a community. These conditions and the lack of transport remain a problem for those still living there.

The Village for 2008 has already been mentioned above as exemplifying the model of a densely populated residential footprint, but it would be unfair to suggest that it only had concrete and overlay defunct facilities as its epitaph. The residential element was very well presented and reinforced the hugely positive impact that mature trees, bushes, plants, lawns and sculptures can have on a development (figure 8.4). The appreciation of the athletes was evidenced by their use of these

Figure 8.4. Public art, Athletes' Village, Beijing style. (*Photo*: Tony Sainsbury)

spaces to meet and focus. These attributes also reinforced the sense of maturity of the estate and created goodwill among the residents in those early days that things will work. The old adage of first impression was relevant here.

London 2012

Shortly after the end of the London Games, the President of the IOC declared the Olympic Village as one of the reasons the 2012 Games were outstanding. Carlos Nuzman, President of Rio de Janeiro 2016, declared that the London Village was the best Village ever (figure 8.5). These accolades, of course, were testimony to the thousands of individuals involved in the Olympic Delivery Authority, LOCOG, the contractors and volunteers. At the same time, the essence of the 2012 Village was not an accident but built on what the reader will have gleaned from all the previous narrative. As such, it is possible to identify six elements from the history of Olympic Villages to which tribute is due.

Figure 8.5. A bird's eye view of the London 2012 Village with temporary venue, bottom left. (*Source:* Courtesy of Mike O'Dwyer/Lendlease)

The first tribute (T1) goes to Paris 1924 and de Coubertin for seizing the opportunity to add the Village element to the plan for the event and in doing so creating a *Cité Olympique*, even if in basic form. London recognized this principle. *Cité Olympique Londres* was a bustling sport and globally focused place for weeks with the Olympic Games followed closely by the Paralympic Games. The athletes' accommodation was sufficiently close to the Olympic Park as to be immersed in what was happening there daily and hearing the sounds from the venues reminded everyone of their moment yet to come, in the same way that de Coubertin envisaged the classical athletes' camp in Olympia.

The second tribute (T2) is due to the American athletes and the Mutiny on the *Matoika*, which strengthened Garland's resolve to avoid anything that might provoke a similar mutiny in Baldwin Hills. Garland understood the needs of athletes and that an outstanding Village would also serve his other objectives related to the reputation of Los Angeles. He also wanted the athletes immersed in the excitement of the occasion and arranged for thousands of visitors a day to come to the Village (even though they could not enter). By doing so, he helped to create an atmosphere that made the athletes feel special and not like a valuable commodity locked away in a vault. Based on that principle, the Athletes' Committee at London 2012 made a number of recommendations to reflect the needs of modern participants.

The third tribute (T3) goes to the Village at Melbourne 1956. The organizers developed the 1932 model and created a truly service-driven culture where nothing was too much for the residents, allowing the athletes to prepare themselves for competition and to instil long-term memories of admiration for things Australian. There was genuine appreciation of what high performance athletes of the 1950s cherished most and how essential that understanding would be to supporting those travelling such distances for the first time.

The fourth tribute (T4) is due to Barcelona 1992 where the elements present to make the Village outstanding were developed even further, particularly with regard to the engagement between the Games, the city and the region. London 2012 exploited the proximity of the Olympic Park and the ability for the athletes to walk there if they wished; the Westfield Shopping Centre served as a focus for friends, family meetings and necessary distraction; the ease of access to Central London allowed Village residents to imbibe the atmosphere of the host city; televisions in all apartments enhanced the sense of the moment by images from in and around the Games, the UK and beyond; and the crowds of enthusiastic and excited spectators invigorated both the Olympics and the Paralympics.

The fifth tribute (T5) is due to Sydney 2000 and the Village team led by the indomitable hotelier Maurice Holland. He was passionate about staff being proactive towards 'guests' and being delighted at the opportunity to add to residents' overall experience. This core team was able to convert volunteers and contractors to the same culture even in trying circumstances, which was much appreciated by both athletes and their support staff. Such skills and experience, however necessary to provide outstanding service to the highest level, are developed over years and not just in the few weeks of venue training at Games time. In the case of London 2012, the hospitality-trained professionals of Holiday Inn were critically important at the core of the 8,000 workforce that served the Village.

Finally, a partial tribute (T6) goes to Beijing 2008. Within the residential area, the organizers succeeded in reinforcing the value of a well cultivated, open public green space with features and sculptures that spoke volumes to the athletes about the maturity of the whole estate and the genuine affection of the OCOG towards its guests.

Taken together the lessons of Villages over the previous 88 years, good and bad, were the basis when planning the London 2012 Village. These were summarized by the author in his notes for the section of the Official Report that dealt with the Village (see LOCOG, 2013*b*, pp. 50–52). These are reproduced below, with added cross-reference to the six points of tribute made above:

The Olympic village, and the satellite villages at Eton Dorney for rowing and canoe sprint and Portland for sailing, lay at the heart of London's vision of 'athlete-centred' Games. The goal was to ensure that the villages responded to the needs of athletes, prioritizing optimum performance on the field of play.

The Olympic Village was also an important element of the promise to use the Games to transform East London. Games operations and legacy were planned in tandem from the outset. Both were factors in the selection of the Stratford site, which offered excellent transport links being directly adjacent to the Olympic Park and could therefore help drive the regeneration of the area with a commitment to deliver 2,800 new homes after the Games, 30% of which would be classed as 'affordable housing'.

The Olympic Village site benefited from natural boundaries and was designed with the aim of creating a quiet residential haven in the centre, with the athlete blocks organized around an area of landscaped parkland (*T6*), helping to create the feel of a traditional English village. (*T1*) All of the services were located on the periphery of the site, which had the additional benefit of making life easier for team managers. A bridge connecting the village to the Olympic Park offered many athletes the opportunity to walk to their venues. (*T3*)

London's Village provided direct connectivity, not only with the venues and local communities but also with the wider city. This offered athletes the chance to enjoy the many festivals and activities taking place across London; to connect with their local or national communities in the city; and to visit friends and family staying elsewhere. Providing such access to external attractions helped ensure that the site remained a high performance sport village, and not a party location, throughout the 17 days. (*T4*)

The goal was to ensure that the villages responded to needs of athletes.

Specific improvements were identified by the Athletes' Committee, (*T2*) which played a large role in the development of the Olympic village, informing and validating all key decisions. Their recommendations included introducing:

◆ Soft furnishings in all lounge areas ensuring such comfort was not only the preserve of well-funded teams.

◆ Televisions in every apartment providing live Games feeds for every sport.

◆ 100 % blackout curtains.

◆ Grab-and-go food carts positioned across the site, catering for athletes who did not have time to go to the main dining hall.

◆ Free Wi-Fi internet access in every apartment and in dedicated hot spots and hubs to encourage athletes to come out of their accommodation and mingle.

The focus on individual needs was partly based on an understanding that modern Olympic Villages do not need to serve as 'homes-from-home', accommodating athletes for weeks at a time. Our goal for the Villages was to provide a level of hotel service equivalent to what today's world-class athletes commonly experience when they travel.

We worked with our LOCOG hotel partner IHG to recruit highly experienced hospitality professionals (over 100 multi-lingual senior managers) from around the world. The Village was run effectively as a 17,000-bed hotel with hotel-style staffing structures, operational processes and a service culture that allowed residents the freedom to be themselves. (T5)

Significant emphasis was also placed on the development of the Village Plaza, which was designed to encourage residents to gather and socialize. Attractions included a replica of an athlete's room for showing to friends and family and a time-lapse DVD recording showcasing the development of the Olympic Park.

In the early stages of the project, with venue developers focused on legacy, the Village team faced a challenge in ensuring venue operations were accommodated at every stage. A 'one team' approach was generally adopted towards the project and, in many cases, Games' operational requirements contributed to the post-Games product – for example the accommodation was constructed to a higher sustainability, inclusive and accessible standard than most new-builds in London, bringing amongst other benefits noise reduction and energy efficiency.

Conclusion

It is difficult to highlight what may or may not be the challenges facing Athletes' Village planners of the future. There is no template, ideal model or design manual. While necessarily prescriptive in parts, the IOC's Technical Manual on the Olympic Village (IOC, 2005 *et seq.*) and the comparable publication for the Paralympic Village (IPC, 2013) also seek to encourage host cities to be creative in their delivery to make the Village unique, a truly international community incorporating elements of their own domestic culture. That final report for London Villages omits, as was intended, to clarify the point that, while the OCOG in London's view was not to create an athletes' home-from-home, the host must provide the wherewithal for the NOCs and NPCs to create precisely that feeling and conditions as a key component of an athletes' stress free and familiar environment.

NOCs and NPCs use their housing allotment in different ways for the modern Games, with professional athletes coming and going throughout the event. Team management still needs the flexibility and scope of assignment to help them meet their objectives. However, an estate capable of providing for 17,000 beds is an enormous task for any host city. Options have been tried including providing NOCs with a fixed number of bed spaces which they could assign in conjunction with their known schedules of athletes' attendance at the Games (e.g. see BEGOC, 2015). While this might be suitable for a regional event, it is unlikely to be embraced for the Olympic Games. The challenge remains and not just about 50 or 60 hectares of new development in one moment but also about the entire infrastructure, furniture, fixtures and equipment, and various materials required supporting the Village at Games time.

Throughout the history of the Olympic Games three significant, potential white elephants have stalked proceedings – the costs and after-use of a new Stadium; the need for thousands of spectator seats for an Aquatics Centre for a one off-event; and the Village estate of thousands of housing units. In 2002 the design of the Manchester Stadium demonstrated an ideal model for after-use, whereas the Commonwealth Stadium for Glasgow 2014 showed how using a temporary elevated athletics' facility could be installed in a normal football stadium. In 2002 again and 2012 providing an international Aquatics Centre with removable bleachers to reduce spectator capacity is now a proven model.

What then of the Villages of the future? If the Games are to continue to be truly universal then imaginative ways of providing those 17,000 bed spaces in synergy with its legacy needs will require the attention of the best brains. Perhaps the time has come for a second IOC Symposium on Olympic Villages to make sure that, in any rush to create a sustainable model for Games' residents, future hosts do not destroy the very essence of what makes an Olympic and Paralympic Village unique.

Notes

1.   The event was a collaboration between the Olympic Museum in Lausanne and the Centre d'Estudis Olympics I de l'Esport, Universitat Autònomea de Barcelona.

2.   The fact the number of athletes who attended Los Angeles was only roughly 50 per cent of the numbers competing in Paris and Amsterdam shows their concerns were not unfounded.

3.   The biographies of the likes of Jesse Owens (Schaap, 2008) and Louis Zamperini (Hillenbrand, 2014) indicate that even as students these athletes travelled the length and breadth of their country in pursuit of their athletic ambitions.

4.   Louis Zamperini also acknowledged watching his rivals and fellow track stars in their races back in the Village (Hillenbrand, 2014).

5.   Much of this was due to the German army commandant, Captain Wolfgang Fuerstner: he was in effect the Village General manager responsible for all the planning and delivery of the Village. Tragically just before the arrival of the athletes he was demoted to second-in-command when it was discovered he was a non-Aryan: he committed suicide immediately after the Games (Cohen, 1996).

6.   If evidence is needed, it is found in a seemingly insignificant piece of display in Number 39 Darmstadt, one of the restored houses and now a small museum. On a bedroom wall are two frames – one with a handwritten letter and its envelope addressed to Jesse Owens and a formal letter from the German Secret States Police.

The letter is a plea from an American fan asking Owens not to boycott the races at the Games but simply to refuse to receive the medals he inevitably will win as a protest against Nazism. The second letter accompanied the first and stated that it had been intercepted by the German Post and 'reviewed' by the SS. It had been considered inappropriate for delivery prior to the Games but was now being returned to Owens as he left Germany for the USA (Dost, 2003).

7.   The obligations until recently were laid out in the *Technical Manual on Olympic Village* (IOC, 2005) now renamed as *Olympic Games Guide on Olympic Village*.

8.   They were held instead in Stockholm.

9.   Although not known by that name.

10.   The ISMGF was the equivalent of the IOC and forerunner of the International Paralympic Committee. For more about the organization and management of Paralympic sport, see Chapter 5.

11.   They painted the houses but the paint faded in the sun so the aim was not realized. In modern Villages, this type of orientation tool is used by Look features such a flags and banners (see Chapter 2).

12.   Up until 1976 only spinal cord injured, wheelchair users participated in the Paralympic Games, hence the oft-quoted title, 'wheelchair Olympics' (see also Chapter 5).

Chapter 9

Security

Jon Coaffee and Pete Fussey

The International Olympic Committee (IOC) makes clear in guidance to host cities that it is *their* responsibility to provide a safe environment for the 'Olympic Family' (competitors, officials and dignitaries), while ensuring that such securitization does not get in the way of the sporting activities or spirit of the Games. As Thompson (1999, p. 106) observed, 'the IOC has made clear that the Olympics are an international sporting event, not an international security event, and while Olympic security must be comprehensive it must also be unobtrusive'. However, since 2001, given the escalation and changing nature of the terrorist threat, 'securing' the Olympics is increasingly difficult and costly to achieve (Coaffee and Wood, 2006). As has been well documented, the results of increased fears of international terrorism catalysed by the events of 11 September 2001 have meant that the cost of security operations surrounding the Summer Olympic Games in particular have increased dramatically since the 2004 Games in Athens (Coaffee and Johnston, 2007). A large proportion of this increased cost is attributable to extra security personnel as well as an array of temporary security measures, especially those which are effective at stopping or minimizing the impact of vehicle-borne improvised explosive devices (Coaffee, 2009). For most Olympic organizers, preparations for the Games necessarily include attempts to equate spectacle with safety and to design-out terrorism, often by relying on highly militarized tactics and expensive and detailed contingency planning.

The Olympic Games have become an iconic terrorist target, which imposes a burden of security on host cities well beyond what they would otherwise face. Security planning is now a key requirement of bids submitted to the IOC by prospective host cities, and has become a crucial factor in planning the Games. There is now a broadly accepted security management model for Olympic Games, modified according to local circumstances of place, which comprises elements of governance and organization that seek to forge relationships between the numerous public safety agencies and the local Organizing Committee. This follows the example set over 20 years ago by the successful use of a dedicated Olympic police force at the 1994 Winter Games in Lillehammer, Norway. As well as the planned deployment of police and military personnel and the co-option of private security and safety volunteers, a typical Olympic security regime also deploys the latest technology in an attempt to plan for and deter terrorist attack. For example recent Olympiads, as well as other major sporting and cultural events, have become highly militaristic at certain geographical locations through the construction of large-scale bunkers and barriers, secure fencing around the key sites, as well as almost ubiquitous closed circuit television camera (CCTV) coverage. Pre-Games and Games-time monitoring of key sites also commonly occurs through the use, for example, of scuba divers and helicopters and high-tech devices such as ID badges with computer chips, biometric identifiers and remote detection hardware.

Such exorbitant levels of security also transform the cityscape into a series of temporary 'spaces of exception' (Agamben, 2005) with displacement of the policing by consent as special regulatory regimes are brought to bear to control behaviour and maintain order. As Browning (2000) observed immediately before the 2000 Games: 'Sydney in September will be under siege'. Likewise, for the duration of the 2004 Games, Athens became a 'panoptic fortress' to give assurances to the rest of the world that the city was safe and secure to host the world's greatest sporting spectacle (Samatas, 2004, p. 115).

Securing the Olympic Spectacle

In light of these circumstances, the scrutinizing committees and delegates of the IOC will carefully examine bids to ensure that host cities provide the necessary safety and security for the smooth running of the Games. This is particularly the case with regard to international terrorism which became a crucial factor in planning the Games after the so-called 'Munich Massacre' in 1972. This event, in which members of the Israeli Olympic team were killed after being taken hostage by the Palestinian terrorist organization Black September, is widely considered to have launched a new era of international terrorism (Reeve, 2001). It was also the catalyst for the soaring cost of security at future Games, stimulating a period of reactivity, continuing to this day, whereby organizers have prioritized security to avoid hosting a repeat tragedy.

Sharply contrasting Munich's 'low-key' approach to security (reflecting contemporary German sensitivities over conspicuous public displays of social control), little expense was spared on securing the 1976 Olympiad in Montreal. The fallout from Munich and the global condemnation levelled at the IOC and German authorities also led protection from terrorism to become *the* key security concern for the organizers of Montreal 1976 (Organizing Committee, 1976). This was manifested in the first of many 'total security' approaches alongside the inauguration of several core principles informing the protection of subsequent Olympiads. These incorporated a strong emphasis on preventative strategies, a conspicuous security force presence, enhanced integrative practices (a failure at Munich) and intensive surveillance measures. Within these general principles, specific measures included secure transport corridors between sites, accommodation and transportation hubs; enhanced accreditation requirements for site workers and probably the first widespread and systematic deployment of CCTV to feature at an Olympics (*Ibid.*). Montreal's reaction to the Munich massacre became a blueprint for future Olympic security operations.

These themes were embraced and consolidated at the next Olympic event at the geographically proximate Lake Placid Winter Games in 1980. Augmenting the Olympic site's geographical isolation were a number of strategies aimed at strengthening and surveying its perimeters including 12-foot (3.7 m) touch sensitive fencing, voice analysers, 'bio-sensor' dogs, ground radar, night vision and CCTV (LPOOC, 1980). Together, these measures drew from strategies deployed to secure military sites and airports. Such was the level of securitization, the post-Games legacy of the Olympic village saw its conversion into a correctional facility (*Ibid.*). Another feature of note was the unprecedented scale of private security deployment, a feature that has since become central to almost all subsequent Olympic security operations.

Although seen by some as isolated and distinct from other Olympic operations (Sanan, 1996), the components of Moscow's Olympic security strategy illustrate how these standardized principles may cut across geographical and ideological barriers. For example, the deployment of US-made security apparatus including metal detectors and x-ray scanners used at previous Games, including at Lake Placid during the same year, demonstrates continuity between Moscow and its predecessors. Moreover, the extensive use of zero-tolerance style policing approaches and exclusion orders have also featured at subsequent games, notably Sydney (Lenskyj, 2004) and Beijing (Peng and Yu, 2008), albeit with variations of scale. The form and function of social control in Brezhnev's Russia may have allowed these strategies to be applied with an intensity unacceptable elsewhere, with Sanan (1996) estimating that 120,000 people were displaced by Moscow's security strategy. Nevertheless, many of the underlying principles informed both previous and subsequent Olympic security programmes. According to the *Wall Street Journal*, the average cost of security at the Summer Olympic Games rose from around $80 million to $1.5 billion over the 20 years between Los Angeles 1984 and Athens 2004. When viewed on the basis of cost per athlete, this equates to a rise from $11,627 per capita to $142,857 per capita (see table 9.1).

Table 9.1. Security Costs of Olympic Games 1984–2004.

Games	Total security cost (US$)	Cost per Athlete (US$)
Los Angeles (1984)	79.4 million	11,627
Seoul (1988)	111.7 million	13,312
Barcelona (1992)	66.2 million	7,072
Atlanta (1996)	108.2 million	10,486
Sydney (2000)	179.6 million	16,062
Athens (2004)	1.5 billion	142,857

Source: Adapted from the *Wall Street Journal*, 22 August 2004.

Security for Los Angeles 1984 was organized by the private sector, but successfully launched a relationship between the numerous public safety agencies and the Organizing Committee that has been adopted subsequently. At Los Angeles, the arguments to spend large amounts of finance on security were largely premised on heightened tensions emanating from the Cold War. Notably, less than three months before the Opening Ceremony, the Soviet Union announced that it was boycotting the Games, blaming not only the overt commercialization of the Olympic spectacle, but crucially a lack of adequate security measures. This, they argued, amounted to a violation of the Olympic Charter.

By contrast, Seoul 1988 witnessed the South Koreans engage in a large-scale security operation, with their major concern being North Korea's use of Japanese proxies to bomb Korean aviation in the run-up to 1988 and the spectre of further attacks on the Games. This involved over 100,000 security personnel drawn from the police, military and private security forces – the largest in Games history at the time. The organizers also drafted thousands of volunteers in to help with security. The Korean question became further involved in Games' security when riot police were sent in to break up demonstrations by student protestors seeking unification of the two countries. In addition, North Korean hostility to the Seoul Olympiad led the IOC to adopt a new and unprecedented international diplomatic function. For many, the security operation is what captured the headlines of the news media rather than sporting spectacle.

Barcelona 1992 saw the deployment of over 25,000 security personnel due to fears expressed over reprisal terror attacks linked to the recently finished 1991 Gulf War, coupled with recent action from the Basque separatist movement, ETA, Catalan separatists, Terra Lliure, and left wing extremists, Grupo de Resistencia Antifascista Primo Octobre. Although this operation used fewer security personnel than Seoul, security was highly militaristic at certain sites, for example, with the construction of large-scale bunkers around the perimeter of the main Olympic Village and tanks situated at strategic locations. This complemented secure fencing and numerous closed circuit television cameras within the village, as well as a highly visible police presence at the sporting locations.

Prior to Atlanta 1996, terrorism was not considered the major risk facing the Games despite serious terrorist attacks on American soil at the World Trade Centre (1993) and at Oklahoma City (1995). As the *Wall Street Journal* (2004) emphasized, terrorism ranked behind heat-related illness and the possibility of soccer violence on the official lists of 'potential worries'. That said, law enforcement agencies assigned more than 20,000 military and law enforcement personnel to monitor security measures, supplemented by 5,000 unarmed volunteer security personnel in an operation that, for some, was seen as the most hi-tech and measured in Olympic history. On the eve of the Games, for example, Macko (1996), argued that:

> When it comes to the security of these games, nothing has been left to chance in Atlanta
> and the other venues that will be used by the athletes. An army of law enforcement officers

will outnumber the athletes themselves. The security for the 1996 Games is said to be the tightest ever in history. Security planners for the Olympic Games have tried to cover every angle possible – from cops on patrol to scuba divers and helicopters and high-tech devices such as ID badges with computer chips.

Despite these intensive preparations, the small-scale bomb blast that occurred at an unsecured public space designed for the Olympics, killing one person and injuring over 100, re-ignited fears of further attacks.

Fears of the alternative spectacle of violence led to even tighter measures to protect the official Olympic spectacle at Sydney 2000. The cost and sophistication of security rose steeply from that incurred in Atlanta and involved nearly all Australia's Special Forces plus 30,000 security personnel (drawn from the police, private security and volunteers) who were also called to duty. Even though the National Australian Government considered, in public at least, that the risk of attack was unlikely, the media began highlighting connections between Osama Bin Laden, the most wanted on the CIA's terrorist hit list, and Australia.

Although no major terrorist incident took place during Sydney 2000, the spectre of terrorist violence took on unparalleled concern for Athens 2004, particularly in view of the security situation both in Greece and internationally. The cost of security increased dramatically. As table 9.1 reveals, despite being the smallest nation to host the Games since 1952, the Greek authorities spent well over five times more than the amount spent by the Sydney organizers and deployed over 70,000 specially trained police and soldiers as well as another 35,000 military personnel to patrol the streets. Military hardware used for security was the most expensive used for the Olympics. It included a network of 13,000 surveillance cameras, mobile surveillance vans, chemical detectors, a number of Patriot anti-aircraft missile sites, NATO troops specializing in weapons of mass destruction, AWAC early warning surveillance planes, police helicopters, fighter jets, minesweepers, and monitoring airships (see Smith, 2004). The airships themselves became icons of the Games and attracted much media interest. Indeed the Security Airship patrolling above the Olympic sites was joined by a second Skyship that broadcast images for US television networks and gave spectacular aerial footage of the Games.

The Olympic stadium in Athens, always likely to constitute the most tempting target, received the heaviest fortification. According to Peek (2004, p. 6), Athens was 'supposed to be one of the most secure places on earth, impenetrable to terrorists plotting a possible attack on this summer's Olympics'. Significantly, the Olympics forced the Greek state to speed up the modernization of its state security system. For the duration of the games, Athens became a 'panoptic fortress' to give assurances to the rest of the world that the city was safe and secure to host the world's greatest sporting spectacle (Samatas, 2004, p. 115). However, the retrofitting of such security systems was envisioned as a long-term project that will be maintained after the Olympics, even though critics have argued that it will become a menace to privacy and civil liberties (*Ibid.*, p. 117). Moreover, the technological centrepiece of the strategy, Science Applications International Corporation's 'C4I' ('Command', 'Control', 'Coordination', 'Communications' and 'Integration') system was a colossal failure. Unable to host the large numbers of potential users, the fabled communications system never operated to capacity and, on still failing to establish the system in time for the Beijing Games, its manufacturers were forced by the Greek courts to compensate the Athenian authorities (Samatas, 2007).

As Chapter 18 makes clear, the IOC's award of the XXIX Olympiad to Beijing in July 2001 stimulated large-scale development of the city. Coupled with China's hosting of the 2010 World Expo in Shanghai and the 2010 Asian Games in Guangzhou, the Beijing Games catalysed a monumental security programme across the country both within these epicentres of tourism and beyond. Embedded within this programme has been a central emphasis on technological and surveillance-based approaches, and have included use of Radio Frequency Identification (RFID) tags in tickets to some Olympic events (such as the Opening Ceremonies) to enable their holders' movements to be monitored. Despite such headline-catching technologies, however, the principal emphasis has been on developing and inaugurating CCTV networks. These include the 'Grand Beijing Safeguard Sphere' (developed between 2001 and the start of the Games) which, according to some claims, has cost over $6 billion and invested the city with 300,000 networked and highly capable public CCTV cameras (*Los Angeles Times*, 2007). Nationally, China's hosting of sporting mega-events has also coincided with the 'Safe Cities' programme aimed to establish surveillance cameras in 600 cities (*New York Times*, 2007). As elsewhere, these technological approaches were combined with more traditional low-tech forms of policing. In particular, the state's capacity to mobilize security manifested in the deployment of 100,000 personnel whilst policing strategies adopted 'sand-pile' techniques (Peng and Yu, 2008), vernacular interpretation of zero-tolerance strategies adopted at other Olympiads (notably Seoul 1988 and Sydney 2000). Moreover, security hardware often found itself centre stage in television coverage. As Boyle and Haggerty (2009, p. 64) observed: 'the conspicuous placement of ground-to-air missile launchers near the Bird's Nest stadium formed a striking backdrop for the many televised reports from the Games beamed around the globe'.

Planning for the Worst: The Security Games 2012

Planning for the worst has become a mantra of contemporary urbanism as pre-emptive actions are increasingly mobilized in order to alleviate fears of potential catastrophe. Such pre-emption, developed through the exercising of emergencies in table-top or scenario planning exercises that better allow future security challenges to be addressed, becomes very visible during mega-event hosting where a range of precautionary governance techniques are utilized in order to consider and plan for unpredictable and high consequence 'what if' events. As Boyle and

Haggerty (2012, p. 241) noted in their analysis of Olympic security, the 'expressive dimension of security at the Games provides a window into wider issues of how authorities "show" that they can deliver on the promise of maximum security under conditions of radical uncertainty [and] how officials emphasize that they have contemplated and planned for all possible security threats, especially catastrophic threats and worst-case scenarios'.

In the United Kingdom, the securitizing of sporting spectacles became increasingly prominent as London geared up to hosting the Olympic Games. Not only did security concerns and responses play a critical part in the bidding process; they also dominated media discussion immediately after the host city was announced. On 7 July 2005, the day after the announcement, a series of co-ordinated terrorist bomb attacks took place on the London transport network, prompting even more detailed security plans. The initial security bill quadrupled from £225 million to over £1 billion with the adoption of advanced smart surveillance systems both to monitor crowds and athletes and to track suspects across the city (Fussey *et al.*, 2011). In a global city famed for its policing and surveillance assets, such additions contributed significantly to the overall securitization of the city. Indeed, Olympic security initiatives were grafted over a pre-existing security infrastructure, one of which had evolved over many years due to the threat of Irish Republican and other forms of terrorism. As noted by the Metropolitan Police Authority (2007):

> The 2012 Olympic and Paralympic Games will require the largest security operation ever conducted in the United Kingdom. The success of the Games will be ultimately dependant on the provision of a safe and secure environment free from a major incident resulting in loss of life. The challenge is demanding; the global security situation continues to be characterised by instability with international terrorism and organised crime being a key component.

Olympic Security Planning in Policy and Practice

Demonstrating the domestic influence on mega-event security planning an updated *Olympic and Paralympic Safety and Security Strategy* (Home Office, 2011) was developed in March 2011 which set out the key aims and objectives for the police and government in delivering security for the Games. The strategy's overarching aim was 'to deliver a safe and secure Games, in keeping with the Olympic culture and spirit' (*Ibid.*, p. 7). This strategy was in line with the latest revised UK National Security Strategy: *A Strong Britain in an Age of Uncertainty: The National Security Strategy* (October 2010) and was harmonized with the third iteration of the UK's overarching counter-terrorism strategy, CONTEST (HM Government, 2011). The CONTEST strategy itself specifically focused on the 2012 Games, noting that the UK had guaranteed the International Olympic Committee that it would 'take all financial, planning and operational measures necessary to guarantee the safety and the peaceful celebration of the Games' (*Ibid.*, p. 105). Thus, despite the range of threats and hazards facing Olympic planning, terrorism and its attendant implication of ineffective security became the principal focus of the Games' security planning overshadowing all others.

As the preparations for the 2012 Olympics were finessed a range of diverse agencies became drawn into play. Here, security planning became managed by the UK Security Services, the Olympic Security Directorate, and the multi-stakeholder London Resilience Forum which developed detailed pre-emptive security plans to sit alongside pre-existing resilience strategies, to plan out vulnerabilities in advance. Thus, broader and more disparate security planning became sharply focused on issues of terrorism and on the means of mitigation. In May 2012, three months before the Games were to begin, 'Operation Olympic Guardian' began – a pre-emptive scenario-planning exercise intended to test security and resilience preparedness ahead of the Games. Militarized features in this role-play included the testing of air missile defence systems, the responsiveness of Typhoon jet forces, and the establishment of 'No-fly' Zones over London. As one BBC correspondent noted, such an exercise has the potential both to alarm and reassure in equal measure:

> Exercise Olympic Guardian is an opportunity to fine-tune military plans. But it is also aimed at reassuring the public… The sound of fighter jets and military helicopters, along with the sight of the Royal Navy's largest warship, HMS Ocean, in the Thames may reassure many. But for some, just talk of this military hardware is causing alarm – *most notably the plans to station ground-based air defence systems at six sites* around the capital. (BBC News, 2012*a*)

At this time, campaign groups such as the 'Stop the War' coalition accused the government of causing unnecessary alarm and a 'climate of fear' in the capital (BBC News, 2012*b*). Such claims were exacerbated by related activity which sited anti-aircraft missiles on the top of East London tower blocks. Residents learned through leaflets that a high velocity missile system could be placed on a nearby water tower at Bow Quarter offering a perfect view of the nearby Olympic Park (BBC News, 2012*c*). This again connected with an enduring set of processes by which slowly but surely, we see military-threat-response technologies and procedures being repurposed for use in the civic realm (Graham, 2010).

As the Games drew near and interest in all aspects of 2012 preparation intensified, security-related stories were increasingly common in the print media both in the UK and worldwide. Particularly notable here was the media emphasis on military-carceral features of the overall Olympic security strategy. For example, many reports centred on the use of military hardware to control city spaces, airspace or transport corridors. Headlines included: 'Ministry of Defence to control London airspace during Games for first time since Second World War' (*Daily Telegraph*); 'Anti-terrorism tool at forefront of 2012 London Olympic security' (*Alaska Dispatch*); 'Sonic device deployed in London during Olympics' (BBC News

London); and, 'Armoured cars drafted in as security tightens ahead of the Olympic Games' (*Daily Mirror*). Other reports highlighted a set of issues regarding policing of the Games, often described as an unprecedented UK peacetime operation, with up to 12,000 officers from fifty-two forces deployed at 'peak time', alongside private security staff, and the use of novel security technologies. Headlines here included: 'Metropolitan police plastic bullets stockpile up to 10,000 after UK riots – Scotland Yard confirms August unrest has led to increase in stock of baton rounds as security measures upped before Olympics' (*The Guardian*); 'Metropolitan Police double officers around torch as crowds bigger than predicted' (*Daily Telegraph*); 'Metropolitan Police given 350 mobile fingerprint scanners in Olympics policing boost' (*V3 News*); and 'Former Royal Marines to ferry around super-rich Games spectators' (*London Evening Standard*).

Yet such urban incursions were not universally welcomed. As the Games approached, the uneven impact both on Londoners and visitors to the capital became highlighted: 'Fish photographer caught in Olympics terror alert: a man taking photos of a fish tank was stopped by a security guard who was supposed to be alert for hostile reconnaissance amid pre-Olympics terrorism fears' (*Amateur Photographer*); 'Olympics welcome does not extend to all in London as police flex muscles; Dispersal zone at Olympic Park will target anti-social behaviour, and there are claims sex workers are being cleansed' (*The Guardian*); and, 'Olympic crackdown: UK govt targets protests' (*Russia Today*). 'Brand' exclusion zones around all Olympic venues were also established in the shape of an Advertising and Street Trade Restrictions Venue Restriction Zone, so that the Olympic canvas could belong exclusively to key sponsors. This type of scrutiny also extended to the clothing of spectators which was screened for prominent displays of competing (non-Olympic) brands: 'Brand Police on Patrol to Enforce Sponsors' Exclusive Rights' (*International Business Times*).

As the Games drew near, activist activity intensified and became distinctly focused on the intensive militarized security measures being ushered into East London. One of the highest profile campaigns was the Stop the Olympic Missiles campaign, driven by the Stop the War coalition, architects of the anti-Iraq War demonstrations in 2002–2003. This led to an unsuccessful yet high-profile high court challenge by residents of Fred Wigg Tower in Leytonstone contesting the Army's right to deploy missiles at their place of residence. Anti-Olympic activism reached its zenith the day after the Opening Ceremony with the 'Whose Games? Whose City?' event where hundreds of activists representing more than thirty groups marched through Tower Hamlets in protest at the militarization, territorial enclosure and corporatization of the Games (see Boykoff and Fussey, 2013).

Post-Games Olympic Security as Local Legacy

In the event, the 2012 Olympics passed off without any serious threat of terrorism being reported and with minimum disruption. The visual appearance of security was, in large part, restricted to the entrance to the venues where search procedures were carried out by the British Army. After the Games, missiles were dismantled and troops redeployed.

However, less well documented in the coverage of security planning has been the post-games *legacy* that has been materially inscribed on the East London landscape, and improved organizational ways of working that have been learnt by the agencies involved in security planning. Legacy has become an Olympic watchword in recent years as host cites attempt to extract maximum value from the event as well as seeking a convenient rhetoric for diffusing difficult arguments. As Gold and Gold (2010, pp. 2–3) noted, legacy has now become 'the touchstone' by which politicians and municipal managers judge the cost and benefits of bidding to stage major sporting events. Moreover, as host cities are selected and pre-Games preparation starts in earnest, the rhetoric of 'legacy' promises plays an important function as the justification for a range of disruptions and cost-increases. Legacy, in this context is thus often asserted as 'fact', as what *will* happen, whereas in reality, it is based on a set of loose assumptions about what will *hopefully* occur many years in the future.

Legacy was always a key component of the overall London 2012 security plan and was at the forefront of police strategies. As the Chief Inspector of Metropolitan Police noted in 2006:

> … we want the security legacy to be us leaving a safe and secure environment for the communities of East London after the Games, on issues such as safer neighbourhoods, lighting and crime prevention. We want a Games legacy that will reduce crime and the fear of crime. (Cited in Fussey *et al.*, 2011)

In London, as the post-Games period progresses, there is little sign that much of the hi-tech equipment purchased by police forces has been put away. The security infrastructure is embedded within transformative urban regeneration programmes and is promoted as central to long-term community safety. It is hoped that Olympic-related security will assist in developing safer neighbourhoods, through measures such as improved lighting, and lead to a reduction in crime and the fear of crime. For example the Olympic Village, currently in the process of being repurposed into private housing, was granted a new level of 'Secure by Design' status set to inform the construction of future housing developments, presenting a permanent material security legacy to its residents and users.

The story of securitizing the 2012 Games did not start on 7/7, but evolved over many decades into protection of the Olympic spectacle. Nor did it end once the well-protected Olympic flame was extinguished at the Closing Ceremony. The security legacy in London is the most comprehensive plan seen for urban regeneration *and* security in modern Olympic history. While at previous Olympics these security features have largely been temporary and removed in the post-Games period, in London *permanent* design and architectural features have been embedded within the material landscape. Likewise, a significant repository of knowledge and expertise has been retained in London-based networks regarding civil contingency planning for an array of disruptive challenges, and for securitizing urban areas at home and abroad. In its development of secure regeneration spaces, London's security community has created a 'blueprint' for knowledge transfer across the globe for when mega-events come to town.

In relation to future Summer Olympics, Rio's successful candidacy to host the 2016 Olympic Games also draws on these continuities of mega-event security. Rio's 2016 Candidate file (Rio 2016 Bid Committee, 2009a) argued that the city will be in a position to develop suitable security infrastructure, facilitated by other mega-events it will host in advance of the Games:

> The Games will act as a major catalyst for long-term systemic improvements in safety and security systems in the City of Rio, representing a genuine opportunity for transformation, a process already commenced through the staging of the 2007 Pan American Games and evolving with the preparation for the 2014 FIFA World Cup.

Although security practices are likely to be prioritized towards long-term crime prevention programmes rather than international terrorism (Rio 2016 Bid Committee, 2009a, esp. Vol. 3), security is a major concern for Rio's Organizing Committee. There is, of course, no guarantee that terrorists will not try to exploit the Olympic gaze; thus prevention and preparation towards potential threats to the Games – both criminal and terrorist inspired – are the highest priority, involving active cooperation between different levels of government in Brazil and the transfer of knowledge from the international community of security specialists.

The immediate concerns in Rio were more specifically related to the city's murder rate (that annually stands at triple that of the entire United Kingdom), and fears of theft against tourists. Such issues are likely to elevate the attention afforded to security. Such 'solutions' couple required Olympic security standards with Rio's tradition of delineating 'high-value' spaces from their urban context though crime prevention measures (Coy, 2006; Crowther-Dowey and Fussey, 2010), and reinforce the risk of further splintering of Rio's divided landscape, providing a significant challenge to its regenerative aspirations and legacy. Indeed recent visits to Brazil by the UK Foreign and Commonwealth Office, intended to allow the UK security industry 'to pursue commercial opportunities and become the partner of choice for sport security' has reported that:

> Brazil sees a step change in the security situation in Rio as a legacy of the Olympic Games in 2016 in particular and is making progress on sustainable 'pacification' of favelas. (FCO, 2011)

As in London, security planning in Rio began in the aftermath of the decision to award the Games on 2 October 2009. Two weeks later (17 October), fire fights between rival drug gangs resulted in a police helicopter being shot down and eight buses set on fire. This led public authorities to resolve to enhance security ahead of the Games (and the 2014 FIFA World Cup). As such resources have been poured into programmes to reduce crime and emergency planning organization with authorities prepared to mount an overwhelming security presence at the sporting events to ensure safety. Such operations have widened the security perimeter around Rio's residential and tourist area and notably led to the deployment of specially trained police pacification units (UPPs) in over thirty local areas to deal with communities which for years have been ruled by drug traffickers and paramilitary militias. Notably the extra impetus and funding given to the *favela* 'pacification' programme as a result of the 2016 Games means that the policing units responsible can purchase more advanced surveillance equipment with some local claims that Rocinha, the largest *favela* in Rio, has the most expansive CCTV surveillance in the world, with more cameras per resident than London (BBC News, 2013). Some have also argued in advance of the Games (see, for example, Freeman, 2012) that such pacification is having uneven spatial consequences and forcing the poorest *favela* dwellers out as gentrification takes hold – a type of neo-liberal revanchist strategy which is cleansing and purifying the Olympic city to allow colonization by the rich in areas once considered *terra incognita*.

Rio is also investing in strategic-level technologies to co-ordinate and control its various security and disaster management processes in the build-up to the Olympic Games. Opened in 2010, the IBM-built 'operations centre' now integrates the vast majority of the city's management functions, including security, in what many is hailing as the model for 'smarter city' development (*New York Times*, 2012). Not all are convinced though, and 'some wonder if it is all for show to reassure Olympic officials and foreign investors. Some worry that it will benefit well-off neighbourhoods more than the *favelas*. Others fear that all this surveillance has the potential to curb freedoms or invade privacy' (*Ibid.*).

Rio's overall security plan, however, is explicitly about 'legacy', not for the event organizers who might be able to market Rio as a safe 'event destination', but for citizens of the city and of Brazil more generally. As the Federal Police Chief observed in March 2013, the Rio Olympics seek to create a security legacy following a history of gang-related violence. He noted that crime was falling and the divided city image associated with Rio was diminishing:

> Before now, we have never had a chance to help people in the favelas and they have been very isolated… But now that we have the World Cup coming to Brazil in 2014 and the Olympics coming to Rio in 2016, we have been able to change this… For so long Rio has been divided, but this is our chance to bridge the gap… We are already seeing huge success because crime rates have dropped and we are recovering areas that had never been part of society before. This is a legacy from the Olympic Games that is happening right now and after the Olympics are gone, it will leave legacy of safety and security after so many years of violence… Everything is better and that is the great legacy of the Olympics. (Cited by *Inside the Games*, 2012)

More critically, scholars have also noted how the advanced and fast-paced globalization being experienced in Brazil has impacted upon the likely legacy of the 2016 Olympics. As Gaffney (2010, p. 7) has noted, the uneven geographies caused by mega-events are now a concrete part of the infrastructure planning that 'impose a neo-liberal "shock doctrine", installing temporary regimes of extra-legal governance that [will] permanently transform socio-space in Rio de Janeiro'.

Standardization and the Olympic Security Assemblage

The needs of host cities enable all pervasive but standardized forms of security to prevail. The exceptionality of Olympic security coupled with the transference of its strategies across time and place culminates in standardized approaches that map onto the uneven terrain of diverse host cities. Borrowing from Bauman (2000), such transferable paradigms operate as a form of 'liquid security' where a shared *lingua franca* of defensible motifs coalesces into spaces that become disassociated from their geographical contexts. In turn, these spaces of exception, once constructed, generate a particular vision of order, a dislocated uniformity, owing to, as Bauman (*Ibid.*, p. 103) suggested, 'the lack of overlap between the elegance of structure and the messiness of the world'.

What we can gauge from a study of securitization employed by host Olympic cities is a series of normalized event security features which combine temporary physical features and the officious management of spaces with the aim of projecting an air of safety and security both for visitors and potential investors (Coaffee *et al.*, 2008).

First, there is intense pre-planning involving the development of control zones around the site, procedures to deal with evacuation, contamination and decontamination, and major incident access. Technical information was also scrutinized for all structures and venues so that any weakness and vulnerabilities could be planned-out in advance.

Secondly, there is the development of 'island security' involving the 'locking down' of vulnerable areas of host cities with large expanses of steel fencing and concrete blocks surrounding the sporting venues. This combines with a high visibility police presence, backed up by private security, the security services, and a vast array of permanent and temporary CCTV cameras and airport-style checkpoints to screen spectators. Often events, such as the Olympics, are used to field-test 'new' technologies.

Thirdly, to back up the intense 'island security', peripheral buffer zones are often set up in advance containing a significant visible police presence. This is commonly backed up by the presence of law-enforcement tactics such as police helicopters, a blanket 'no-fly zone', fleets of mobile CCTV vehicles, and road checks and stop and search procedures. The result of these measures is that often access to supposedly 'public' spaces is restricted on roads and footpaths as a result of 'security concerns' (*Ibid.*).

Fourthly, the enhanced resilience that such security planning, in theory, delivers is actively utilized as a future selling point for urban competitiveness in that the ability to host such an event in a safe and secure fashion and without incident is of significant importance in attracting future cultural activities, and in branding a city as a major events venue.

Fifthly, there is increased evidence from major sporting events that a lasting benefit of hosting such events is the opportunity for the retrofitting of permanent security infrastructure linked to longer-term crime reduction strategies. This post-event inheritance of security infrastructures is a common Olympic legacy. Indeed, the legacy of retained private policing following the Tokyo 1964 and Seoul 1988 Olympiads, and the continuation of zero-tolerance style exclusion laws after Sydney 2000 are a case in point. Likewise in Athens, the retrofitting of such security systems was envisioned as a long-term project to be maintained after the Olympics and which was been condemned by civil libertarians (Athens Indymedia, 2005).

In London 2012 the emphasis on a regeneration legacy for the people of East London also extends to the machinery of security. Indeed, in 2009 the tenders for Olympic Park security providers were encouraging companies to supply 'security legacy', thus bequeathing substantial mechanisms and technologies of control to the post-event site (ODA, 2007). Here, questions remain over the security priorities of a high-profile international sporting event attended by millions of people and the degree of infrastructure that will remain to police a large urban parkland (the future incarnation of the Olympic site).

Bidding to host an Olympics is also, in many cases, considered a strong enough stimulus to develop robust security planning procedures. For example the unsuccessful bid by Cape Town for the 2004 Games required the city to be seen as secure enough to host the Olympics. As a result an extensive security infrastructure was introduced into areas posited as likely venues and visitor accommodation centres (Minnaar, 2007). After their bid failed, the CCTV systems were not removed; instead they were justified as part of a general programme to combat crime, which in this case was seen as discouraging foreign tourists, investors and conference delegates (Coaffee and Wood, 2006).

Conclusion

As noted at the outset, IOC regulations and guidance for host cities make the latter responsible for providing a safe environment for the 'Olympic Family' while retaining a sense that the Games take place in a secure environment in which the sporting competitions and the fundamental values of Olympism flourish. This, as we have seen, is a difficult balance to achieve. Certainly if the risk of terrorism remains at its present critical level, there is the possibility of seeing core notions of Olympic spectacle to some extent replaced by dystopian images of cities under siege as organizers, security personnel and the media attempt to deliver an Olympics, in maximum safety and with minimum disruption to the schedule (Coaffee et al., 2011).

Chapter 10

Urban Regeneration

Andrew Smith

Urban regeneration is often cited as one of main justifications for staging the Olympic Games. Regeneration 'legacies' have been principally pursued by the hosts of Summer Games, but recent cases suggest they are increasingly relevant to the Winter Games too. There are even examples where urban regeneration has been influenced by losing Olympic bids (Smith, 2012). The aim of this chapter is to explore how and why the Olympic Games are used as a vehicle for regeneration. Through this analysis, the chapter is able to draw important conclusions not only about the contemporary Games, but also about urban regeneration processes in general. Regeneration can be understood as a discourse as well as a practice and an outcome and, as such, this chapter analyses commonly expressed rhetoric such as the notion that staging the Olympic Games provides 'flagship' urban projects and 'catalysts' for regeneration. The discussion focuses particularly on those Games which were staged on post-industrial sites: Barcelona 1992, Sydney 2000, Vancouver 2010 and London 2012. Rather than discussing these cases in turn, the chapter is organized around themes that help clarify the complex relationship between the Olympic Games and urban regeneration.

Definition and Critique

Urban regeneration means reversing the cycle of decline which afflicts many urban areas. The term is directly linked to the post-industrial era (roughly since 1973), a period when many cities and citizens have struggled to adapt to new economic circumstances. In this context, urban regeneration encompasses policies, programmes and projects designed to help specific parts of cities recover from decline. Regeneration has become a rather generic term, but it can be differentiated from wider urban policy by its geographical focus: it involves targeted interventions in post-industrial, brownfield sites. To provide focus, this spatially focused interpretation is adopted here as opposed to broader initiatives that seek to stimulate economic development at wider scales – the city as a whole, the region and the nation.

Leary and McCarthy (2013, p. 9) define urban regeneration as efforts 'to produce significant, sustainable improvements in the conditions of local people, communities and places suffering from aspects of deprivation'. This focus on long-term, broad-based ambitions reflects the most widely used definition of regeneration: 'to bring about a lasting improvement in the economic, social and environmental conditions of an area that has been subject to change' (Roberts, 2000, p. 17). Definitions such as these highlight that, in the contemporary era, the term refers to social and economic ambitions as well as those linked to physical improvement. This holistic approach represents a welcome reorientation towards the needs of people, although one drawback is that it means regeneration has come to mean almost anything to do with urban change. Regeneration is inherently linked to other processes such as renewal, remediation and renaissance – producing an alliterative lexicon which causes confusion. These three terms are often used interchangeably, but are best understood as more specific phenomena than regeneration: remediation means the reclamation of land; renewal refers to physical change, and renaissance implies the revival of urban culture.

The definitions cited above make regeneration sound like a very laudable, if rather vague and optimistic endeavour. However, there are critics of the concept who point to some of the inherent problems when it is practised rather than merely proposed. Allen and Cochrane (2014, p. 1611) describe regeneration as 'a troubled and troubling concept' because it involves making promises which are incompatible and therefore impossible to achieve. For example, making an area more economically productive may require radical change that does not assist the people who currently live there (*Ibid.*). Too often we see the regeneration *of* communities rather than regeneration *for* communities. There are other reasons to be sceptical about regeneration. Like other normative ideas (such as sustainability), the term has been appropriated by a range of interests for their own ends. For example, it is now part of the language of property developers and used to add value to real estate. Even more worryingly, regeneration is often used as a euphemism for radical urban transformation; something that helps to justify evicting people and businesses out of certain territories.

The Olympic Games and Urban Regeneration

Staging the Olympic Games requires host cities to provide appropriate sports facilities, as well as suitable accommodation and transport provision. Therefore, it is unsurprising that post-industrial cities have decided to use the Games as an opportunity to improve amenities, housing and infrastructure in areas which have suffered decline. The scale of facilities now required, particularly for the Summer Olympiad, means that densely populated cities can only accommodate them within the existing urban fabric by using sites that were formerly occupied by industrial installations, including railway yards, docks, warehouses and factories. Following this logic, regeneration is a practical requirement to stage the Games, rather than a fundamental objective. However, cities have gone beyond what is necessary merely to host the event; instead, they have used the Games as an opportunity to make more radical and more extensive improvements to specific urban areas. This obviously adds to the costs of staging the Games.

During the post-industrial era, two main regeneration strategies have been used by Olympic hosts. The first is to identify a large site that requires regeneration and redevelop it as a new piece of city. For example, in Sydney and London sites respectively of 760 and 250 hectares were assembled, reclaimed and developed as Olympic Parks. In both cases, a large amount of toxic industrial land was decontaminated – something that might not have occurred without the impetus provided by the Games. Post-event these have been redeveloped as multi-functional sites – typical of a new breed of mixed-use mega-projects (Lehrer and Laidley, 2008) – which include sports stadia, but also office space, housing, retail and cultural facilities and parklands. A second approach has been to regenerate smaller sites close to the city centre for individual venues or support facilities. For example, Barcelona used the Games to regenerate a waterfront district as one of four main Olympic sites used to host the Games. In a similar manner, former industrial land in the south-east corner of False Creek was remediated to build the Olympic Village for Vancouver 2010.

The idea of the Olympic Games as an agent that regenerates cities has become widely accepted; but this is an over-simplistic and problematic interpretation. The Olympic Games do not and cannot regenerate urban areas. Regeneration achievements are sometimes attributed to the Games when they are actually the result of parallel urban initiatives or macro-environmental factors. However, staging the Games does offer certain advantages for governments and urban regimes wishing to pursue regeneration ambitions. It may unlock funding that would otherwise be unavailable, help to generate civic support for large-scale public investment in urban districts, and provide a clear narrative and justification for urban change. The high profile nature of the event means that political actors are forced to undertake improvements that might not otherwise be delivered. Finally, and perhaps most importantly, staging the Olympic Games imposes a non-negotiable deadline for urban projects. These characteristics and associated issues are discussed further below.

The Olympic Games as a Flagship

One way that new Olympic venues and associated infrastructure have been linked to regeneration is via their role as 'flagship' projects that kick-start (re)development in ex-industrial sites. Urban flagships are designed as 'marshalling points for further investment' (Smyth, 1994, p. 5) to encourage a 'flotilla' of other developments in their wake (Bianchini et al., 1992). This mode of regeneration involves a top-down, property driven approach that emerged in the 1980s. In such cases, regeneration represents an intervention that helps to address the failure of market forces to instigate post-industrial transformation. Following this logic, staging the Olympic Games provides a good excuse to remediate land and provide new infrastructure and venues, on the basis that this will lead to future commercial investment and jobs. Sydney 2000 was a good example of this type of approach (see Chapter 16). Before the Games organizers had not planned the post-event era: they merely assumed that remediating a well-located site and providing new infrastructure (rail and road connections) and Olympic venues would encourage future growth.

The Olympic Games are seen as a particularly valuable flagship project because investors know that governments have to deliver so, unlike other regeneration projects, there is less chance that development will drift, stall or collapse. The recent global financial crisis helped to demonstrate this. Private consortia were unable to deliver the Athletes' Villages in Vancouver and London, so the government stepped in and funded them. These 'bail outs' would not have happened if these Villages had been conventional housing developments, but Olympic Games were deemed to be 'too big to fail'. Government intervention and public funding reassured any companies that were planning to invest in these regeneration sites. This highlights the way the Games act as a tool that 'de-risks' urban areas for potential investors (Smith, 2014). Improvements to the area's image derived from Olympic symbolism help to achieve this effect, but the scale of public investment is also a major contributing factor.

Using Olympic projects as flagship developments sounds like a practical solution that unlocks the unrealized potential of large derelict areas. However, there are several problems with this type of approach. Olympic regeneration tends to involve using large amounts of public money to lower risks for private investors. So, even if investment is attracted to Olympic sites, commentators have argued that this represents a dubious public subsidy (Scherer, 2011). For example, Van Wynsberghe *et al.* (2013) suggested that public investment in Vancouver's Olympic Village involved a socialization of risk, and a privatization of the benefits (see figure 10.1). The same thing had happened a decade previously in Sydney: large state subsidies were needed to help 'offset the risk' for the consortium tasked with building and converting the Olympic Village (Searle, 2012, p. 198). This links to a wider concern about Olympic regeneration: it tends to serve the interests of the construction and property sectors, rather than the interests of local citizens.

One potential problem with flagship-led regeneration is that further investment does not automatically follow, or that it takes longer than expected to materialize. For example, in Sydney there has been a relative lack of building activity post-2000, with urban densities remaining very low in and around the city's Olympic Park (Yamawaki and Duarte, 2014). The area now competes for investment with other Sydney suburbs, so further development may be at the expense of projects in surrounding districts like Parramatta (Searle, 2012). Even if Olympic facilities do stimulate further development, it is hard to control what types of investment follow. Development which is most commercially viable might not be appropriate for the wider environmental or social objectives for the area. Moreover, aside from

Figure 10.1. Olympic Villages post-Games in Barcelona (top left), Sydney, (top right), Vancouver (bottom right), and London (bottom left).

their symbolic value, it is unclear whether stadia, indoor arenas, swimming pools and the other Olympic facilities are very effective flagship projects that help to attract private sector investment. In some examples of Olympic regeneration, parallel development or infrastructure is deemed to have had a more significant effect. Thornley (2012) argued that the contribution of Olympic venues to urban regeneration in East London is minor compared to the adjacent shopping centre and transport improvements. Here, as in Sydney's Olympic Park, businesses are lured by the availability of infrastructure and parkland, rather than the proximity of sports facilities. However, Olympic structures and associations provide useful visibility for these sites that might otherwise seem rather bleak and anonymous. This symbolic function helps to justify the notion of Olympic projects as flagship developments.

The Olympic Games as a Catalyst

One of the noted advantages of incorporating the Olympic Games into urban regeneration is that it speeds the process up. Regeneration inherently involves long-term objectives, but these might be achieved more quickly in Olympic host cities. Hence Olympic projects are touted not merely as flagship urban developments, but as 'catalysts for urban change' (Essex and Chalkley, 1998). A catalyst increases the rate at which a reaction progresses and, using related metaphors, some accounts suggest the Olympic Games help to achieve 'fast-tracked' or even 'turbo-charged' regeneration. The imposition of an immovable deadline (the date of the Opening Ceremony) means projects have to be finished within a specified timeframe – 7 years under the current system of awarding the rights to stage the Games. This, along with the potential for global exposure of dereliction, provides the necessary impetus to deliver projects more quickly.

The increased 'speed' of regeneration attributed to the Olympic Games varies between cases. It is claimed that the project to regenerate Homebush Bay in Sydney was delivered in half the original timeframe because of the Olympic Games (Wilson, 1996; Cashman, 2006). In Munich, the pre-existing (1963) plan to regenerate the Olympic Park site was scheduled for 15–20 years, but the 1972 Games meant it was delivered in 5 years (Chalkley and Essex, 1999). The gold medal for accelerated regeneration seemingly goes to London. Officials claim that the project to regenerate East London was accelerated by 50 years because of the 2012 Games. At the Emerging Host Cities conference in 2013 Tessa Jowell (formerly the UK government's Olympic Minister) argued that a project that would have normally taken 60 years was delivered in less than 10. This accelerated development explains why a senior official from London's Olympic Delivery Authority referred to the project as 'regeneration on steroids' (Smith, 2014).

It is important to analyse in more detail how the Olympic Games speeds regeneration up. The imposition of a deadline creates an unusual sense of urgency, but complex ambitions still need to be realized. One advantage of the Games is that they have a habit of focusing the minds of politicians, which means decisions are made more quickly. Olympic projects also tend to achieve greater 'buy-in' from key stakeholders than conventional regeneration efforts, and this helps to achieve a faster rate of progress. Regeneration inevitably requires effective partnerships between different government departments, and between the public and private sectors, and staging the Olympics seems to make it easier to get a range of individuals and organizations working together for a common cause. This joint working can persist after the event allowing long-term regeneration objectives to be addressed. In short, the Olympics help to speed up regeneration processes via the 'resources, political will and institutional co-ordination' that are seemingly mobilized when the Games are awarded to a city (Raco and Tunney, 2010, p. 2020).

Any claims made for accelerated development need to be treated with caution – this rhetoric is part of the way Olympic projects are justified. Although the Olympic Games can speed up the initial phases of urban regeneration (such as land assembly and remediation), wider projects often remain incomplete long after the event. In Sydney, work is still being undertaken to redevelop the main site of the 2000 Olympic Games and the latest master plan provides a vision for 2030 (Davidson and McNeill, 2012). Similarly, the 'legacy phase' work for London's 2012 Olympic Park is programmed to 2030. The need for redevelopment in the post-event era to turn sites into functioning areas means that dangers of slow, or stalled, urban development still persist. The Olympic Games may ensure ambitious urban regeneration projects reach a certain stage, but they do not guarantee completion.

Even if acceleration could be proved – which is impossible given the need to quantify a counterfactual rate of development – speeding up the regeneration process is not necessarily that helpful. Often there are good reasons why urban regeneration projects take so long. Shortened timescales restrict opportunities for consultation with the local population, and other planning procedures may also be compromised. The pressure for timely delivery means organizers circumvent normal processes. During Sydney's Olympic preparations, a new Environmental Planning Policy was created which exempted Olympic proposals from proper assessment (Kearins and Pavlovich, 2002). Several years earlier, Montalban (1992, p. 9) described how Barcelona's politicians 'sacrificed the ethical obligations of their office under the pressure of completing preparations on time'. Rushing to finish work may lead to a reduction in quality and extra payments for contractors are usually required to ensure timely completion, pushing budgets higher. As deadlines approach, the requirement for extended shifts can lead to injuries and fatalities amongst construction workers. In short, accelerated regeneration comes with considerable costs.

The need to speed regeneration up is also used as a justification for new governance models. Regeneration is predominantly something that is 'funded, initiated, supported or inspired' by the public sector (Leary and McCarthy, 2013, p. 9), but Olympic projects are used to usher in new 'entrepreneurial' forms of urban governance: public–private partnerships, or new dynamic public organizations that pursue commercial activities. Rather than using existing governance apparatus, Olympic regeneration projects are usually managed and delivered by specialist agencies through which public funds are channelled (Raco, 2014). Local authorities are often under-represented or bypassed, which undermines the democratic legitimacy of Olympic regeneration (Owen, 2002).

Strategic and Integrated Olympic Regeneration

Relying on flagships or catalysts is a rather speculative and spurious approach to urban regeneration, but these approaches can be better justified if Olympic projects are used within an existing strategy. If a stimulus is required to advance established plans for a derelict area, then it may be very helpful to use the Games to kick-start or speed up the development process. This is where Olympic projects can perhaps play the most effective role in urban regeneration. The IOC has recognized this: new bidding procedures encourage consideration of how the Games can be fitted into wider plans for host cities (IOC, 2014a). Barcelona is usually cited as the epitome of this approach. Plans to recover and reorient the waterfront area had existed for many decades (since 1966), but preparations for the Olympics (1986–1992) were used as the opportunity to undertake the work. This strategy was further strengthened because Barcelona's new waterfront district was linked into a wider urban plan. This helped to ensure that Barcelona's regeneration was not led by Olympic projects – instead Olympic projects were used to achieve Barcelona's plans. The Olympic Games provided funding, urgency and civic support for strategic projects that might have otherwise been difficult to achieve.

This strategy of using the Olympic Games to advance pre-existing plans was also deployed in London. The remediation and regeneration of the Olympic Park was originally justified on the basis that it contributed both to the 2004 London Plan (the city's statutory spatial plan), and to the wider regeneration of the Thames Gateway region. Famously, Ken Livingstone (London's Mayor, 2000–2008) expressed his disinterest in hosting a major sport event, but he supported a London Olympics because it would help to achieve his plans for East London. Over time the limitations of this strategy have been exposed. Whereas building the Olympic Park was originally conceived as a way to assist the wider regeneration of East London, regeneration post 2008 refocused on the Olympic Park as a project in and of itself. This was partly an inevitable consequence of the global financial crisis and the more focused ambitions that emerged, but it was also due to the political capital associated with the Olympics. More mundane regeneration ambitions were sidelined in the quest to deliver the Games. Resources were devoted to dealing with the legacy issues that generate most media attention – for example, the future of the stadium – rather than more significant ambitions for East London. This illustrates how Olympic projects can override, disrupt or distort existing regeneration plans. Even in Barcelona, much lauded as the epitome of 'good practice', the Games is thought to have disrupted the city's record of impressive and progressive urban transformation (1976–1992) by ushering in an approach more focused on entrepreneurialism and place marketing (Degen and Garcia, 2012).

Outcomes

Regeneration is often regarded as merely an objective or an intervention. However, it is also an outcome, and various researchers have tried to assess whether regeneration has been achieved. This type of research is notoriously difficult: regeneration involves multiple objectives and appropriate indicators are difficult to ascertain and measure. The timescales involved are usually long which makes it difficult to know when to assess outcomes. The scale at which we measure them is also difficult to pinpoint and it is hard to attribute any changes observed to specific interventions. In the case of Olympic regeneration this is even harder as it is not clear what is and is not part of the intervention. What constitutes regeneration is also highly subjective and contested: it varies according to 'different vocabularies and imaginations' (Raco and Tunney, 2010, p. 2087). This makes establishing the outcomes of Olympic regeneration even more difficult.

Hemphill *et al.* (2004) used a series of weighted indicators to measure 'sustainable urban regeneration performance'. Their research is particularly relevant here as one of the projects analysed was Barcelona's Olympic waterfront complex (Vila Olimpica). Of six developments analysed (in Barcelona, Belfast and Dublin), Vila Olimpica scored highest, with the authors surmising that it was a notable example of good practice. As an example of urban design Vila Olimpica has undoubtedly been successful, with generous provision of open spaces and clever submergence of transport infrastructure. One interpretation of the project is to see it as a democratic one that returned the waterfront to its citizens (Rowe, 2006). But its contribution to the social dimension of regeneration is more controversial. The expropriation and clearance of working-class housing and industrial units to deliver expensive housing and a new yacht marina benefitted some people at the expense of others. It was always unlikely that former residents would be able to remain here as none of the new flats was offered as subsidized or social housing, 'despite promises made to the contrary when the project was first made public in 1986' (Montalban, 1992, p. 6). The wholesale redevelopment of this district had been resisted for many years, but the Olympic Games provided a vehicle with which to placate opposition. When considering the Olympic Games as a *force majeure* that allows development barriers to be overcome (Evans, 2010), we need to acknowledge that this includes its capacity to nullify opposition from incumbent residents and businesses.

Concern about the contribution of Olympic projects to gentrification in Barcelona reflects a wider re-appraisal of the city's transformation, which, according to Arbaci and Tapada-Berteli (2012, p. 307):

> cannot be considered a successful case of regeneration since it has not fully addressed the needs of the long-term (low-income and more vulnerable) residents. Rather than tackle the main sources of deprivation, it has instead increased issues of neighbourhood affordability and housing affordability.

Barcelona's project was one that was successful physically, but not necessarily socially, and this reflects assessments of other Olympic regeneration projects. Their contribution to land remediation and physical regeneration is generally impressive (notwithstanding issues with redundant venues discussed elsewhere in this volume), but it is hard to find regeneration projects that have helped to improve the lives of disadvantaged people. This relates to difficulties in reconciling physical and social regeneration. Olympic regeneration tends to be funded through property sales: the public or private (or public–private) organizations involved hope that Olympic interventions will raise land values allowing them to recoup investment via the sale of assets. This provides an in-built incentive to build the most lucrative housing – which is unlikely to assist disadvantaged citizens. Indeed, it may contribute to their displacement and the 'gentrification' of the area.

Complex issues such as gentrification highlight the contested nature of regeneration objectives and outcomes. For many of the professionals involved, gentrification is not an unfortunate by-product of regeneration projects, it is the specific aim. East London's Olympic transformation provides a useful illustration.

In London there has been much debate about why, given London's shortage of affordable housing, more extensive social housing provision was not prioritized as an Olympic legacy. Of the 2,818 units available in the converted Athletes' Village (now renamed East Village), just under half were made available at subsidized rates (675 for social rent, 356 intermediate rent, 269 shared ownership, 79 shared equity). Cost was one obvious factor which prevented more generous provision, but another consideration was that key stakeholders (including local housing officials) wanted to use the new accommodation to change the composition of households. They wanted more middle-class families to rebalance both the socio-demographic profile of the population and the composition of new development, which was dominated by flats for young professionals (Smith, 2014). In this case gentrification was envisaged as a vehicle for positive change, not a negative outcome. This approach was opposed by citizen groups, who felt that housing existing residents should be the priority, not new ones. The case underlines that regeneration is a political process, not a purely technical one, with any assessment of outcomes also politicized (Raco and Tunney, 2010).

Towards a More People Oriented Approach

The limitations of regeneration projects that rely too heavily on physical transformations are now increasingly acknowledged. These tend to deal with the symptoms of decline – dereliction – rather than more fundamental issues and problems faced by local people. Accordingly, organizers of recent Olympic Games have tried to implement social programmes aimed at disadvantaged citizens in deprived areas. These programmes seek to provide more opportunities for local people, or at least to restrict the negative impacts of Olympic regeneration.

During the build-up to the 2010 Winter Games, Vancouver developed a series of social regeneration initiatives. The Organizing Committee initially committed to an Inner City Inclusivity Commitment Statement (ICICS) to protect the interests of low-income communities (Van Wynsberghe et al., 2013). Employment initiatives were also formulated for those who faced obstacles preventing them from accessing 'traditional employment' (Ibid.). The company awarded the contract to develop the Olympic Village on False Creek signed a Community Benefit Agreement that required it to provide 250 social housing units (Scherer, 2011). However, during the course of the city's Olympic preparations these commitments unravelled (see figure 10.2). This was partly due to economic circumstances but it was also because there was little genuine commitment to these initiatives – they were designed to get community groups on side during the early stages of Olympic regeneration. As this example shows, when Olympic projects go over-budget (as they invariably do), social regeneration ambitions tend to be watered down or abandoned completely. These initiatives are more vulnerable to political and economic shifts because there is less political consensus regarding the social dimension of regeneration. Within the prevailing political philosophy

Figure 10.2. A banner protesting against the changes made to Vancouver's Olympic Village project on False Creek.

(neo-liberalism), regeneration is about providing physical 'platforms' for growth – not about direct assistance for low-income people. In this context, progressive projects which 'leverage' social inclusion and social development remain an underdeveloped aspect of Olympic regeneration.

During the build-up to the 2012 Games, London made more effort than most previous hosts to consider the social dimension of regeneration. In the pre-event period, social regeneration was linked to physical transformation via the implementation of progressive recruitment and training projects. Strong leadership and innovative job brokerage schemes ensured that contractors adhered to targets regarding the composition of the labour force of more than 25,000 people employed to build the Olympic Park and the Athletes' Village from 2008–2011. There were targets relating to the proportion of the workforce who were female, disabled or from minority groups, and there was also a push to recruit people who were from local boroughs, or were previously unemployed. Apart from the proportion of disabled employees, these targets were met, producing a 'soft' regeneration legacy of skills, work experience and training for disadvantaged people (ODA, 2011).

London also adopted the Strategic Regeneration Framework (SRF) which aimed to improve socio-economic opportunities for local residents over a twenty year period (Smith, 2014). The SRF aims to capture the opportunities presented by staging the Games to improve the lives and opportunities of people living in the boroughs that surround the Olympic Park. This meant tackling fundamental education, employment and health issues within these deprived areas. Aspirations revolved around three core themes: creating wealth and reducing poverty; supporting healthier lifestyles; and developing successful neighbourhoods (Host Boroughs, 2011). The SRF aims remain ambitious; the target is that by 2020 disadvantaged Olympic boroughs will be in a median position compared to other London boroughs with respect to key socio-economic indicators. This is an example of a project that uses the Olympics as a flagship, not merely for investment in a remediated site, but for wider social and economic development in the deprived areas that surround it. However, this pioneering strategy is no panacea. Reflecting previous examples of social regeneration, the programme has suffered from a lack of funding, commitment and publicity relative to the (ongoing) physical transformation of the Olympic Park.

Conclusions

This chapter has discussed the various advantages and disadvantages of regeneration associated with the Olympic Games. Staging the Games can help to unlock the potential of areas which have stubbornly resisted regeneration through market forces or more modest interventions. The deadlines and political commitment involved can speed development processes up, especially in the early stages of land assembly, remediation and infrastructure provision. However, the discussion has also introduced a series of problematic aspects of Olympic regeneration. These include an over emphasis on the physical dimension of regeneration (at the expense of the social), the way the Games are used to make wholesale (rather than incremental) urban transformations, and the dubious use of public funds to assist private companies.

It is unfair to suggest the various issues noted here are uniquely Olympic problems, as these tend to feature in large-scale urban regeneration projects generally. For example, in a comprehensive review of European examples, Swyngedouw et al. (2002) suggested that these tend to neglect social issues, create segregated islands of wealth, ignore local democracies, and direct capital from the public to private sectors. This chapter has outlined how Olympic projects neglect incumbent populations and contribute to gentrification, but these are problems with regeneration generally and are linked to the incompatible objectives of many regeneration projects (Allen and Cochrane, 2014). It is unrealistic to expect Olympic projects to surmount these problems or buck the trend for urban development that exacerbates socio-economic polarization in cities. The failings of Olympic regeneration reflect the failings of large-scale urban regeneration projects generally. However, there are some reasons to be optimistic. There is increased recognition of the need to give social aspects more attention within regeneration projects generally and within Olympic regeneration in particular. A new emphasis on the social dimension provides an opportunity to link regeneration to some of the other legacies sought by host cities: sports participation, education and cultural activity. This trend may be assisted by the IOC's recent pronouncement that host cities should use more temporary and existing venues and spend less on expensive new ones (IOC, 2014a). Spending less time and money building venues provides more scope to design and implement programmes that lever the Games for progressive social development (Smith, 2012). Ultimately, the aim should be regeneration *for* disadvantaged communities, rather than the regeneration *of* disadvantaged communities.

Adopting an integrated and strategic approach has helped to achieve more positive outcomes for cities that have staged the Games. In Barcelona, the Olympics were used to advance long-held regeneration ambitions, but this enlightened approach is rarely employed: most cities decide to stage the Games and then think how it might be used to assist regeneration, rather than vice versa. Political, economic and symbolic motivations – not assistance for deprived places – tend to explain why most urban regimes want to stage the Games. In these cases, rather than a strategic objective, regeneration is best understood as part of the way in which Olympic Games are justified. Regeneration rhetoric is particularly valuable in early stages of the process when it is used to get the media and public onside. This highlights that the relationship between the Olympic Games and urban regeneration should not be merely understood as what the Games can do for regeneration, it is also about what regeneration can do for the Games.

Chapter 11

Olympic Tourism

Mike Weed

A regularly cited justification for the hosting of the Olympic and Paralympic Games is that Olympic cities can generate considerable inward tourism, both as tourism destinations in their own right and as gateways to wider regions surrounding the host city. This chapter examines the role of Olympic cities in the generation of tourism. In providing the context for this analysis, the early part of this chapter outlines a range of Olympic tourism products, before briefly outlining the ways in which the Olympic and Paralympic Games might be leveraged to generate tourism. The two substantive parts of the chapter then examine, first, the ways in which Winter Olympic Cities can be tourism gateways to the wider region surrounding the host city and, secondly, the contribution of the Summer Olympic Games to the development of the host city's tourism product and image.

Olympic Tourism Products

Eight years ago Weed (2008) identified six Olympic tourism products, five of which related to sports tourism, and one of which related to more general tourism. The following year, Weed and Bull (2009) further examined the five sports tourism products featured in Weed's (2008) analysis of Olympic tourism and this suggested that Weed's (2008) analysis might be updated as outlined below:

Event Sports Tourism. This refers to the provision of event sports tourism opportunities, both for participants and spectators. Obviously, it will include the Olympic and Paralympic Games themselves, but also the myriad of other events that take place in the years before and after the Games in and around Olympic cities. In this respect, even previously inconsequential competitions can become significant international events as athletes seek to experience and acclimatize to local conditions, providing an increased media and spectator sports tourism draw.

Sports Participation Tourism. The most obvious sports tourism product, this refers to active participation in sports tourism activities, such as skiing, cycling, golf or sailing, or at multi-activity centres such as Center Parcs or various outdoor activity and education centres. For some activities, participating in Olympic venues can be an attraction, or at Olympic winter sports resorts.

Sports Training Tourism. Sports training camps are often talked about as being a generator of Olympic tourism, but the sports training tourism product also incorporates 'learn to play' courses, and also elements of advanced instruction. As such, it can overlap considerably with sports participation tourism in Olympic sports such as sailing and skiing.

Luxury Sports Tourism. Uniquely, this product type is not defined by reference to the sports tourism activity, but to the wider aspects of the experience relating to the luxury nature of the attendant facilities and services. It therefore overlaps with the other product types, and may often use associations with the Olympic and Paralympic Games to add to the feeling of a premium product.

Supplementary Sports Tourism. The broadest of the sport tourism products, supplementary sports tourism refers to the provision of sports tourism activities as a supplement to the providers' main product. Examples include the provision of a range of watersports on beach holidays or the opportunity to hire a cycle for a day. It may also include trips to past or prospective Olympic sites, venues or museums as a supplementary part of a broader city visit.

Generic Tourism. The Olympic Games can be used as part of strategies to generate future non-sports tourism related visits. Such tourism may be generated among those who have visited the Olympic city for sports tourism related products, but who later return for a more general tourism trip, or among those who have been exposed to the city though various Olympic-related written and audio visual media and as a result, believe it may be a nice place to visit.

Drawing on the range of Olympic tourism products outlined above, Weed (2008, p. 22) suggested that Olympic tourism should be defined as, 'tourism behaviour motivated or generated by Olympic-related activities'. This definition covers both pre- and post-Games tourism activity, including *aversion tourism*, in which people leave or avoid Olympic cities as a result of the Olympic Games or Olympic-related activities. It also covers the generation of generic tourism to Olympic cities and their surrounding regions stimulated by exposure to either corporeal (live) or mediated Olympic-related activities.

Strategies for Leveraging the Olympic Games for Tourism Outcomes

The Olympic Games are the resource with which to leverage the six Olympic tourism products outlined above. However, the potential impacts of the Olympic

Games do not just occur during the Games period, but for several years before and after. As such, the Olympic Games as a leverageable resource provide a wide range of potential opportunities to develop Olympic tourism products, potentially over a 15-year period in the run up to and beyond the Games.

Two 'opportunities' are identified in table 11.1 for leveraging the Olympic Games. First, direct Olympic tourism trips may be leveraged by the Olympic Games. Secondly, Olympic media may be leveraged, either by capitalizing on Olympic-related media coverage of the host city, surrounding region or country, or by incorporating Olympic-related material into host city, region or country advertising and promotion. The strategic objective in leveraging Olympic media is to enhance the image of the Olympic host destination, which in turn will help to generate further future tourism business. As the strategic objective of leveraging Olympic tourism is to optimize Olympic-related tourism benefits, the opportunities to leverage Olympic tourism and Olympic media have very similar long-term goals. Perhaps a crude way of looking at the two leveraging opportunities is to view the leveraging of Olympic tourism as referring to immediate strategies to generate tourism business related to the Olympics, whereas the leveraging of Olympic Media is part of a longer term strategy for host destination image enhancement that is aimed at stimulating more generic tourism business in the future.

Table 11.1. Strategies for Leveraging the Olympic Games for Tourism.

Leveraging opportunities to Stimulate Olympic Tourism Trips	Leveraging Olympic-Related Media Coverage to Raise Awareness of the Host City as a Tourism Destination
Entice Olympic Tourism Spending	Benefit from Olympic-Related Reporting and Event Coverage
Retain Local Resident Spending	
Lengthen Olympic-Related Visits	Use of Olympics in Host Destination Advertising and Promotion
Maximize Olympic-Related Visits	

(*Source*: Weed, 2008, adapted from Chalip, 2004)

The Role of the City in Olympic Tourism

Unlike some other sport mega-events, such as the Football, Rugby or Cricket World Cups, the host for an Olympic and Paralympic Games is a city rather than a country. This presents a range of challenges for the country in which the host city is located, one of which is the way in which the Games can be leveraged for tourism, not only to the host city, but also to the surrounding regions and to the country as a whole. In this respect, a useful way to analyse Olympic tourism is to regard Olympic cities as tourism generators. Olympic cities can be divided into those that largely act as a gateway for tourism to the wider region in which they are situated, and those that largely generate Games-related tourism to the Olympic city itself. While these two areas are obviously not mutually exclusive, the respective structures, histories and requirements of the Winter and Summer Olympic and Paralympic Games mean that Winter Olympic cities, although destinations in their own right, can also act as tourism gateways, whereas tourism generated by Summer Olympic cities tends to be largely to the Olympic city itself.

Olympic Cities as Gateways to Tourism Regions: The Winter Games

Unlike the Summer Games that are discussed later in this chapter, Olympic tourism generated by the Winter Games is not dominated by any one Olympic tourism product. Given that the Winter Games focus on skiing and a range of other winter sports, it can be very effective in generating sports participation tourism. However, it can also contribute to the generation of event sports tourism related to winter sports, to luxury sports tourism products associated with the après ski experience, and, of course, to sports training tourism in relation to learning the basic skills for winter sports, to advanced instruction to improve technique, and to the provision of training opportunities for performance athletes.

Given that Winter Olympic tourism opportunities are spread across the spectrum of sports tourism-related Olympic tourism products, it would appear that the greatest leveraging opportunities for tourism in relation to the Winter Games are those that are associated with the direct stimulation of Olympic tourism trips, rather than long-term image enhancements for general tourism. To a certain extent this is because Winter Games host cities are dwarfed by the size of hosts for the Summer Olympics. Despite the trend towards major city hosts, Winter Games hosts still need to be located near to mountainous terrain to provide for the ski events. Therefore, although there has been a continuous growth in the size of Winter Games hosts, the average population size of Winter Olympic cities is still less than one-tenth (236,000) of the average size of Summer Games hosts (2,840,000).

A number of implications emerge from this. While the cost of the Summer Games since 1984 has always been higher than that for the winter event, the Winter Games are far more costly on a per-capita basis (Preuss, 2004b; see table 11.2). Furthermore, because Winter Games host cities, notwithstanding their growth over time, tend to be smaller with less capacity to attract commercial funding for development (Essex and Chalkley, 2002), the burden of investment tends to fall on the public sector (although as noted below, there is a long-standing link with the ski industry). While the Summer Games have increasingly attempted to follow the commercial model adopted by Los Angeles 1984, only the Calgary Winter Games (1988) has had any success in following this approach.

The staging, therefore, of a Winter Olympics can yield varying benefits, with gains often being specific to host cities and to the stage of development of the city

Table 11.2. Respective costs of Summer and Winter Games.

Olympiad	Host cities	Total cost (US$ million)	Cost per capita (US$)
XIV	Winter: Sarajevo, 1984	179	400
	Summer: Los Angeles, 1984	412	121
XV	Winter: Calgary, 1988	628	981
	Summer: Seoul, 1988	3,297	326
XVI	Winter: Albertville, 1992	767	38,350
	Summer: Barcelona, 1992	9,165	5,578
XVII	Winter: Lillehammer, 1994	1,511	65,695
	Summer: Atlanta, 1996	2,021	5,129
XVIII	Winter: Nagano, 1998	3,412	9,451
	Summer: Sydney, 2000	3,438	929
XIX	Winter: Salt Lake City, 2002	1,330	7,628
	Summer: Athens, 2004	–	–

(Source: Preuss, 2004b)

and region at the time. Preuss (2004b) reinforced this, noting that a city's unique characteristics and the economic conditions at the time are largely responsible for relative successes. However, that is not to downplay the potential opportunities of the Winter Games for which, as they are hosted in much smaller cities than the Summer Games, 'effects can be proven much more easily because the economic impact to the host city is comparatively larger' (Ibid.)

Chappelet (2002a) singled out Calgary 1988 as the point where the emphasis shifted from tourism promotion to economic development. The fact that Calgary was able to follow the Los Angeles model can be attributed to the fact that the petrochemical industry in Alberta subsidized the Games in an effort to attract inward investment, and the city had grown to a population of almost 700,000. Notwithstanding the continued presence of tourism promotion as a goal of the Winter Games, not least at Lillehammer 1994 where the coverage of the small Norwegian ski resorts in the region on the world stage as worthy competitors with Alpine countries was significant, such promotion is now but one among a number of goals for Winter Olympic host cities.

1. Salt Lake City 2002

Prior to the XIX Winter Olympic Games in 2002, Salt Lake City and Utah were very much domestic tourism destinations; of the 17.8 million visitors to Utah in 2000, 96 per cent were US residents (IVC, 2002), and Travel Utah's 1,000-day plan reflects this. The plan, seen as long-term at the time, covered the 150 days leading up to the Games and the 850 days after the Games. In doing so, it appears that opportunities to capitalize on the Olympics in the pre-Games period may have been missed as Travel Utah considered that the 'window of opportunity' was only 2 years. One of the main goals of the 1,000-day plan was to capitalize on the 'awareness bonus' of the Winter Olympics and, while trying to improve awareness among Europeans, to focus on the link between Utah's brand values of 'Discovery and Recovery' with Olympic values and memories among the core American market.

Salt Lake City attempted to draw on lessons from Calgary in building a strategy for Olympic-related economic development and tourism. In taking this and the experiences of other past Winter Olympics, Travel Utah (2002) discussed the six key lessons that they had drawn from former Olympic hosts:

◆ *Context*: Each Games is unique and has its own political, social and economic circumstances which, combined with external events, greatly influence future tourism activity in an Olympic region.

◆ *Post-Games Marketing*: Increases in tourism are not a direct function of hosting the Games or of Olympic media – such increases need to be effectively leveraged.

◆ *Economic Returns are Uneven*: Tourism growth is most likely in areas directly involved with the Games – outlying areas should consider ways in which they can associate themselves with an Olympic area.

◆ *Focus Strategies*: Leveraging strategies are most likely to be successful if they are targeted – holistic approaches can dilute resources and messages.

◆ *Sustainable Development*: Normal (i.e. 'without Olympic') growth patterns should guide expectations and development to avoid excess capacity which can destabilize the host region in the post-Games period.

◆ *Preserve Networks*: The people and organizations responsible for the presentation of the Games should also be those involved in leveraging the post-Games environment.

In seeking to examine how useful these lessons had been, Travel Utah (2002) conducted an immediate post-Games analysis of the winners and losers in the Olympic year (see table 11.3).

In relation to the impact of Olympic media, Travel Utah (2002) estimated that the value of print media that focused on tourism related themes during the Games was $22.9 million. In US dollars, this comprised:

$22 million – National and syndicated stories
$89,100 – Features from Sports Illustrated 'Dailies'
$89,800 – USA Today Stories
$420,300 – US Daily Newspapers from major markets
$367,600 – Southern Utah Stories

Table 11.3. Winners and losers from the 2002 Salt Lake City Winter Games.

Winners	Losers
• Hotels	• Business Services
• Restaurants	• Finance, Insurance and Real Estate
• Retailers (particularly Olympic Vendors and 'Made in Utah' products)	• Ski Resorts
	• Transportation
• Olympic travellers	• Construction
	• Business and Ski Travellers

Hotspots: Olympic Venues, Park City and Downtown Olympic District

Empty: Businesses outside Downtown Olympic District

Source: Travel Utah, 2002

Given the Travel Utah strategy of focusing on the USA tourism market, this represents a very useful return. What is not clear, however, from the Travel Utah report, is what leveraging strategies (if any) were employed to generate these stories, and how 'tourism-related themes' are defined. Nevertheless, the generation of $22.9 million worth of print media alone is a significant achievement given the problems of attempting to get tourism/destination themes into media coverage (Chalip and Leyns, 2002).

2. Turin 2006

A clear feature of Olympic host cities in the twenty-first century is a desire to learn from previous hosts. Turin attempted to apply more recent knowledge from both Summer and Winter Olympic cities to its specific modern European city context. Table 11.4 shows the complex range of lessons that Turismo Torino (2004) had attempted to draw from previous Olympic Games, both summer and winter, in the bidding, pre-Games, Games and Post-Games periods.

Table 11.4. Turin 2006 – lessons regarding impact and benefits for tourism.

	Bidding	Pre-Games	Games	Post-Games
Investments	Advertising	Infrastructure Media Interest	Visitor services	Promotion and avoiding the 'intermediate effect'
Effects	Image positioning Increase in popularity	Peak in market interest Creating new "cathedrals" Increase in infrastructures	Customer satisfaction Media publicity Increase in number of tourists	Avoiding drop in occupation Increase in business tourism Long-term image growth
Examples	Sion 2006 Andorra 2010 Salzburg 2010 Beijing 2008	Salt Lake City 2002 Sydney 2000	Sydney 2000	Barcelona 1992 Sydney 2000

Source: Turismo Torino, 2004.

In fact, if there was a 'role model' for Turin, it was the 1992 Summer Games in Barcelona (Bondonio and Campaniello, 2006). Turin, like Barcelona, sought to increase its ranking as a tourist destination on the world stage, but also within its own country:

> [Torino] … envisions a tourist mecca that would finally marry its historic centre – and all of its elegant cafes and museums – with the rustic Alps. 'When people think about northern Italy, they think Milan,' said Cosmo Perrello, a manager of the Amadeus Hotel, a 26-room local fixture just off the grand Piazza Vittorio Veneto'. Torino has been a last stop in Italy. It has always been a town of working people. We hope now that it will become a first stop for Italy. (USA Today, 2006)

Given that Turin, like many other major city Winter Games, was a two-centre Games, with Turin itself only able to host the 'arena' ice events, many venues were located outside the city in the 'Olympic Valleys' at distances of up to 60 miles (97 km) away. This generated high costs for transportation, road construction, communications networks and two Olympic Villages in the valleys (Bondonio and Campaniello, 2006), but it also left an infrastructure that linked the Alpine areas with the city, and thus allowed the city to develop as a gateway for not only winter sports tourism, but also for summer sports such as canoeing, rafting, cycling and hiking, and for general 'lakes and rivers' tourism.

Turismo Torino, unlike Travel Utah (Salt Lake City) which developed only a 1,000-day plan for tourism, considered the tourism impacts of its Winter Olympic Games from bidding to well into the post-Games period. In doing so it noted that, particularly in the pre-Games period, there was potential to displace and crowd out tourism, and that strategies were needed to address this, both in terms of general tourists, who may have felt that the city would be a 'building site' and business tourism organizers, who may have felt that the Olympic Games would have caused price rises for conferences and meetings (Turismo Torino, 2004). This is reflected in the objectives for the Turin Games as laid out in their Olympic tourism strategy, which covered the pre-Games (2002–2005), Games (2006) and post-Games (2006–2008) periods:

◆ Avoiding a decrease in the tourist flow in the years preceding the celebration of the Olympic Games;
◆ Projecting the image of a city and an area under transformation that are evolving thanks to the Olympic Games;
◆ Achieving perfect co-ordination to promote both the Turin 2006 Olympic Games and Turin before, during and after the Games;
◆ Promoting the Olympic Games of Turin 2006 so as to create internal support and awareness, attracting the widest audience and the support of the tourist sector.

Among the strategies that Turin employed was an 'Olympic Turin' promotion programme that focused on generating positive stories about Turin in the non-sports media in the pre-Games period, thus seeking to leverage the image benefits of Olympic media. While the success of this programme does not appear to have been evaluated, it was a clear attempt to move towards the leveraging approach outlined in the early part of this chapter.

In February 2007, Turismo Torino reported on 'Turin 2006: One Year On' in which they noted that Turin's Olympic facilities had already hosted twenty sports events, including the Winter University Games and the World Fencing Championships (showing that Winter Olympic arenas need not exclusively be used for winter sports) as well as over forty non-sporting events (such as rock concerts and exhibitions). Turismo Torino's estimated figures claim an increase of 100,000 to 150,000 tourists per year to the Olympic area following the Games. A special local guidebook for such visitors, *Turin, A Local's Guide to the Olympic City*, was a nice touch in leveraging the post-Games Olympic effect. Organizationally, the Fondazione XX Marzo has been established to run seven of the former Olympic sites and to optimize the legacy of the Games; an indication that Turin recognizes that legacy benefits, like most other Olympic impacts, need to be leveraged.

3. *Vancouver 2010*

A focus on leveraging was a key part of Vancouver's preparations for the 2010 Winter Games from the outset. Eight years before the Games, Inter Vistas Consulting (IVC) were commissioned by British Columbia to report on the economic impacts of hosting the 2010 Winter Olympics in Vancouver, and a central part of this study was a recognition that:

> In order to achieve the higher tourism growth scenarios and capitalise on long-term opportunities, British Columbia's tourism industry will require significant marketing resources and a co-ordinated effort. (IVC, 2002)

Vancouver was fortunate in being able to draw on the recent experiences of Salt Lake City 2002, another North American Winter Games. However, like Turin 2006, Vancouver considered that the potential tourism impact of the Games extended beyond the '2-year window of opportunity' on which Salt Lake City sought to capitalize. The IVC study (*Ibid.*) for Vancouver 2010 drew up four 'visitation scenarios': low, medium, medium/high and high. In all but the high scenario, pre-Games Olympic tourism was assumed to commence in 2008 and the 'tail' of post-Games tourism was assumed to end in 2015. However, in recognizing that the lessons from Salt Lake City did not 'represent the best outcome that British Columbia can achieve', largely because Salt Lake City's marketing efforts did not begin until five months before the Games, the 'high visitation' scenario assumed that pre-Games Olympic tourism would be induced prior to 2008, but noted that this was dependent on pre-Games marketing efforts commencing

7 years in advance of the Games. Similarly, the 'high visitation' scenario for post-Games tourism included post-Games tourism through to 2020, but once again this assumed that tourism marketing organizations used the Olympics as part of a long-term growth strategy and, more importantly, that the funds and the will existed to develop a marketing programme that had a positive impact on international visitors both before and after the Games. IVC's scenarios for incremental (i.e. additional) economic impact of Games visitors and tourists were:

Low	CA$ 920 million	(*c.* US$ 787 million)
Medium	CA$ 1,295 million	(*c.* US$ 1,108 million)
Medium/High	CA$ 2,228 million	(*c.* US$ 1,906 million)
High	CA$ 3,145 million	(*c.* US$ 2,690 million)

In providing a composite estimate of these numbers for the more concentrated 2 years before and 2 years after period, Jane Burns, the Director of British Columbia 2010, claimed that there would be approximately 1.1 million additional international (including US and overseas) visitors to British Columbia across 2008–2012 (Burns, 2005). Burns's estimate was given to a USA Senate sub-committee hearing on the potential impact of Vancouver 2010 on Oregon and the Pacific North West. Submissions to these hearings demonstrated that regions around British Columbia (in this case, those in another country) had been considering the range of Olympic tourism products they could offer and the nature of Olympic tourism flows. Todd Davidson, the Director of the Oregon Tourism Commission identified four opportunities arising from Vancouver 2012 for Oregon:

◆ Acting as a training site for Olympic athletes seeking to acclimatize;
◆ Reaching out to non-accredited media that attend Olympic Games to generate lifestyle stories;
◆ Exploring the potential to develop travel packages to bring athletes and spectators through Oregon and to encourage the extension of visits to include time in Oregon;
◆ Promoting Oregon at Olympic venues to build awareness.

Similarly, Dave Riley, the General Manager of Mount Hood Meadows Ski Resort in Portland (Oregon), only 75 miles (125 km) from Vancouver, noted that a key opportunity for his resort, and for Oregon more generally, was to capitalize on the numbers of skiers and snowboarders that would be avoiding Vancouver and Whistler during and in the run up to the 2010 Games. He identified the key opportunity as 'taking advantage of the displaced visitors who would otherwise have gone to Whistler by developing the amenities on Mount Hood between now and 2010 that are necessary to influence their destination choice' (Riley, 2005).

Planning for Olympic tourism in and around Vancouver was far in advance, in terms of the understanding of the nature of Olympic tourism, of that of the Winter

Games that preceded it. In particular, the explicit recognition that investment and co-ordination in terms of tourism marketing were key to leveraging the tourism potential of the Games was a core part of the planning process even before the Games were awarded to Vancouver. The recognition of this in the IVC study commissioned by British Columbia is a lesson for all future Olympic hosts: '[Tourism] benefits will not materialise automatically. They must be earned by a focussed, adequately funded and skilfully executed marketing programme' (IVC, 2002).

4. Sochi 2014

In contrast to the increasing trend for twenty-first century Winter and Summer Olympic Games to learn from their predecessors and to plan to leverage tourism and image benefits, the Sochi Winter Games showed little sign either of building on experiences of previous Games or of recognizing the need to develop and invest in strategies to leverage the Games for tourism. This was against an explicit and stated aim to develop Sochi, not just for tourism, but to become a major tourism player on the world stage, something that was a key part of the pitch of the Russian President, Vladimir Putin, to the IOC in 2007: 'Sochi is going to become a new world class resort for the new Russia. And the whole world!' (Putin, 2007). This statement also encapsulated the second major goal for the Games. Like the 2008 Summer Games in Beijing (see below), Sochi 2014 was envisaged as presenting the image of a 'new Russia' as an open and modern country, attractive for tourism, investment, and geo-political partnerships. Sochi 2014 posters proclaimed: 'Russia – Great, New Open'.

Unfortunately, the lasting image impacts of the Sochi Games are likely to be those relating to legislation passed 'against the propaganda of non-traditional sexual orientation to minors', which received widespread international coverage and condemnation (Van Rheenen, 2014; Lenskyj, 2014), and Russian intervention, largely seen internationally as aggression, in Ukraine. Economically, Sochi 2014 arguably has the dubious honour of being the most expensive Games in history, be that Summer or Winter. Unusually, particularly for a Winter Games, virtually all facilities and infrastructure had to be constructed from scratch, which led to estimates for the cost of the Games of between $51.4 billion and $55 billion (Müller, 2015a). Local organizers have argued that the vast majority of these costs should not be attributed to the Games as they were part of a wider infrastructure investment in the region that would have taken place anyway. Certainly, there was a 'Federal Target Programme' for the Sochi region that pre-dates the awarding of the Winter Games and this led local organizers to claim that the true cost of the Games was $7.1billion (*Ibid.*).

However, the scale of investment in infrastructure projects undoubtedly increased as a result of the Games. For example, a combined road and rail link, costing over $10 billion between the main coastal resort area and the mountain area was built to serve 20,000 passengers an hour, a capacity that exceeds more than several times the number of rooms available in the Krasnaya Polyana resort (*Ibid*). This is clearly a much larger investment than that required to service even the most optimistic estimates for enhanced tourism. Müller's (*Ibid.*) estimate of the 'sport-related' costs of the Sochi Games is $11.8 billion, which is second only to London 2012's costs of $14.8 billion. However, he argues that costs should be normalized for the size of the Games into a cost per sports event, by which measure Sochi spent an average of $120 million on each of ninety-eight events, which was two and a half times that of the next most expensive Games.

In excluding the wider infrastructure investment from the cost of the Sochi 2014 Games, the organizers claimed an operating profit of $261 million (*Ibid.*), and this became a key part of the IOC's success story of the Games, with IOC President Thomas Bach noting that:

> The extra tens of billions of dollars [are] part of Russia's long-term investment to turn the area from a faded summer resort into a year-round destination and winter sports complex for the whole country… The Games are serving as the catalyst. (Quoted in Wilson, 2014)

In this narrative, the additional capital and infrastructure costs are seen as a positive, with the claim that the Games has catalysed a wider investment in the region's tourism development, which is somewhat contradictory to the organizers' claim that this investment would have happened anyway.

Sochi was formerly the leading spa resort in Soviet Russia (Scharr *et al.*, 2011), but experienced considerable decay in the post-Soviet era, something that the 2014 Games were planned to arrest, re-invigorating Summer tourism, and creating a new Winter tourism market. The key supporting strategy to achieve this was to upgrade accommodation standards from those in 2007, where only about 1,700 of Sochi's 31,000 rooms had international star-rating classifications (Petrova, 2014). Investment to satisfy accommodation requirements for the Games almost doubled the number of rooms to 58,000, with 50 per cent of additional rooms at 3★ standard, 40 per cent at 4★ and 10 per cent at 5★ (SOOC, 2014). As a result, Sochi's room capacity is now roughly equivalent to that of major international established resorts such as Cancun in Mexico (Puls *et al.*, 2013).

Doubling the number of rooms means that to maintain pre-Games occupancy rates, overnight stays would need to double. As such, a post-Games increase of 22 per cent in tourist arrivals in the 2014 summer peak season only delivered an occupancy rate of 40 per cent compared to occupancies of 70–90 per cent before the Games-related rooms expansion (Müller, 2015a). Unfortunately, increased arrivals are also being driven by the domestic market, with a depreciation of the rouble almost doubling the cost of international holidays for Russians. Furthermore, international political tensions have led to a ban on almost five million Russian citizens, mostly government employees, from travelling abroad (Ryzhkov, 2014), and a feeling among many Russians still at liberty to travel that a Europe largely antagonistic to their government is not a comfortable place to visit (Müller, 2015a). While these circumstances have helped tourist arrivals, the preference of domestic tourists remains for the cheaper hotels and bed-and-breakfasts that characterized Sochi's pre-Games room stock (*Ibid.*), with occupancy rates in some of the new hotels being as low as 8 per cent at some times in the year (Weaver, 2014). Longer-term prospects for international arrivals do not appear positive as, despite the Games, Sochi is not an attractive destination for ski-tourists as a result of its ski-trails being relatively small by international standards, the lack of any direct flights, and Russia's demanding visa process.

Unsurprisingly given the lack of any strategy to leverage the Games for tourism, there is virtually no co-ordination of Sochi's post-Games tourism offer. The initial post-Games plan was to use venues for exhibitions, conventions, concerts and shows, but post-Games the Olympic Park does not have an overarching management organization, resulting in venues developing unilateral strategies for use and events, which draw few tourists due to the lack of any major attractions and its remoteness from the city centre and beaches. The Olympic Stadium is being re-constructed as a venue for matches during the 2018 Football World Cup, but Sochi does not have a football club that could take on the tenancy of a stadium of that size post-2018. In the mountain areas, the largest of the four ski resorts has a total trail length of only 77 kilometres, meaning that they cannot individually sustain more than two or three days of skiing, and while linking these areas would create a much more attractive larger resort, this was not considered in pre-games planning. There is no funding available for the *c.* \$25 million investment required (Müller, 2015a), an amount that likely could have been accommodated within the Games budget had it been considered at the planning stage. More broadly, the public and private tourism sectors in Sochi estimate that it would take an investment roughly 10–15 per cent of that made so far, and 2 or 3 years of development, to re-purpose Sochi from an Olympic venue to a tourism resort. However, the local sector lacks the funds for such an investment, and the Russian government has refused all requests for additional funding.

Olympic Cities as Tourism Destinations: The Summer Games

As noted earlier, while the Winter Games generate tourism volumes across Olympic tourism products, sports tourism related to the Summer Games is most significant in relation to events sports tourism. While governments may attempt to claim that sports training tourism (training camps), sports participation tourism and supplementary sports tourism (particularly post-Games) are important products, events sports tourism is undoubtedly the major Olympic sports tourism product. However, the major tourism-related justification for investing in the Summer Olympic and Paralympic Games is the image benefits that hosting the Games bring, and the related future generic tourism numbers that such an enhanced image are likely to generate. As such, the greatest leveraging opportunity to develop tourism from the Summer Games is the leveraging of Olympic media for tourism image benefits. Due to the much more concentrated focus of the Summer Games, such image benefits are often largely reaped by the city itself, rather than by surrounding regions, or by the country in which the host city is situated, although London 2012 showed that country-wide benefits can be achieved. The generation of tourism to Summer Olympic cities is now explored in relation to the first four twenty-first century Summer Games.

1. Sydney 2000[1]

While successive Olympic cities since 2000 have been keen to draw lessons from previous Games, tourism planning for the Olympics in Sydney had to be developed without the benefit of prior experience as at the time there were few examples of how Olympic cities had previously planned for tourism. A review by the Australian Tourism Commission (ATC) concluded that Seoul 1998 had left a legacy of new railways and an upgraded airport but public relations had been oriented internally, to Korea's domestic population, rather than to an audience in the rest of the world. The development of tourism infrastructure and Barcelona's enhanced credibility as an international tourist destination were noted as outcomes of the 2002 Games in the Catalan capital (ATC, 1998). Tourism impacts in Barcelona have been recognized to a greater extent more recently, as certain trends have become more apparent. A review by the Director General of Turisme de Barcelona concluded that the Games 'provided the impulse for Barcelona to become a leader in many respects, but especially in tourism' (Duran, 2005, p. 89). He noted that Barcelona had been named as the best world urban tourism destination in 2001 by *Condé Nast Traveller* magazine and described the dramatic growth in the number of cruise ships that now called at the port and of product launches, particularly for new car models, that had been held in the city. These developments were attributed to the way Barcelona's image had been positively affected by the Games (*Ibid.*).

In contrast to the benefits gained by Barcelona, an assessment of Atlanta's performance judged that 'the city missed out on a golden opportunity for future tourism. Local attractions suffered substantial downturns in visitors, day trips were non-existent, and regional areas suffered. Neighbouring states took out ads telling people to stay away from Atlanta and the city suffered' (ATC, 1998). These findings served to reinforce what needed to be done in Sydney to ensure different outcomes.

Within the city of Sydney, proximity to certain routes and sites that attracted the largest number of Olympic visitors determined the type of impacts that were experienced (Brown, 2001). Some of the impact spread beyond Sydney to other areas of the state of New South Wales (NSW) which were able to host Olympic visitors. However, some areas experienced a decline in tourism demand. The dominance of the Games served to capture the attention and resources of visitors to the detriment of attractions that were effectively competing with the event. This situation was compounded when tour operators were unable to offer their normal services in the absence of buses that had been committed to the Games.

A desire to present the 2000 Olympics as a national event, for the whole of Australia, was contingent upon a sense of engagement by people throughout the country. Thus, strategies to spread tourism benefits were developed. These included attempts to encourage visits by international teams for pre-Games training and to stage events, as celebrations, to coincide with the arrival of the Olympic torch.

Accurate post-Games measures of the impact of the Sydney Olympic Games on tourism are not available as little research specifically examined this issue. As is the case with most major events, considerable effort was spent on gaining support for and justifying the bid and in ensuring that the event could be staged successfully. As such, while considerable research informed the planning stages, post-Games impact analysis received less attention as people with relevant knowledge move on to work on the next event.

Research was conducted by the ATC to track awareness of the Olympics in overseas markets and to monitor community attitudes towards the Games in Australia (ATC, 2000). In 1999, the highest level of awareness about the Games was recorded in New Zealand (92 per cent) followed by China (75 per cent), Korea (71 per cent), Germany (70 per cent) and England (58 per cent). Significant increases in awareness had occurred between 1998 and 1999 in Korea (from 47 per cent to 71 per cent), Malaysia (from 34 per cent to 43 per cent), Taiwan (from 28 per cent to 38 per cent) and England (from 38 per cent to 58 per cent). Nearly half of potential travellers in India (45 per cent) were found to be more likely to consider going to Australia as a result of the Games. The likelihood in China and Malaysia had increased between 1998 and 1999 from 30 per cent to 37 per cent and from 33 per cent to 41 per cent, respectively. Between 1998 and 2000 there was a steady increase in the perception of the host population that the Olympics would boost the image of Australia (1998: 25 per cent, 1999: 27 per cent, 2000: 29 per cent). However, there had also been a fall in the perception that the Games would bring economic benefits to the country (from 25 per cent in 1998 to 19 per cent in 2000).

Data from the Australian Bureau of Statistics reveals that there was a 15 per cent increase in the number of international arrivals in Australia in September 2000, the month of the Games, compared to the previous year with changes from markets closely associated with the Olympics being particularly noticeable. The number of tourists from the USA nearly doubled. Within the city, locations that housed 'Live Sites', such as Darling Harbour, were crowded throughout the Games and retail sales for businesses in the Harbourside complex increased considerably. This contrasted with the situation in regional areas of Australia where a 10–15 per cent decrease in normal visitation levels was recorded (Brown, 2001).

Indications immediately after the Games suggested that Australia would gain the anticipated tourism benefits. There was 9.7 per cent increase in visitor arrivals in October 2000 compared to October 1999 and tour operators throughout Europe and North America were reporting unprecedented interest in and bookings to Australia (*Ibid.*). A record 565,700 international visitors arrived in December 2000, a 23 per cent increase on 1999 – the highest number ever for a single month (ATC, 2001). These increases helped arrivals for the year 2000 to reach a record 4.9 million but everything changed in 2001. The combined impact on demand from the terrorist attacks in New York in September 2001, the outbreak of severe acute respiratory syndrome (SARS) in Asia and the collapse of the airline group Ansett Australia meant that visitor numbers declined for the next 2 years. This was the first time this had happened in Australia. Visitor numbers to Australia have increased since 2003 but it is now impossible to determine the role played by any residual Olympic effect. This is disappointing but it does not minimize the lessons that are offered to other host countries by the strategies developed by the tourism industry in Australia that sought to maximize the benefits offered by Sydney 2000.

2.   *Athens 2004*

Like many other Olympic cities, Athens expressed a desire to follow the Barcelona model to inform its development planning (Poulios, 2006). However, Beriatos and Gospodini (2004) claim that the Athens approach was very different from that used in Barcelona, and that it lacked focus in terms of a coherent urban development strategy. In fact, there were a number of worries among local businesses and policy-makers not only about the escalating costs of the Games (not an unusual thing for Olympic cities), but also about the lack of planning. In 2002, Sports Business carried an interview with the President of the Athens Hotel Owners Association, Sypros Divanis, who claimed that while local hotel owners had invested over €500 million ($437m) in modernizing and expanding hotels, they were being let down by the government which had failed to produce a plan for tourism linked to the Games. Divanis claimed that:

> The Olympics are the most positive event that could happen to the Greek tourism industry, but while there's over-activity on the part of the hotel community, the state ... seeks sloppy solutions which will not offer the infrastructure needed. (Cited in Weed, 2008, p. 164)

One such 'sloppy solution', proposed by Gianna Angelopoulos, the head of the Athens 2004 Organizing Committee, was to accommodate visitors on islands or other tourist hotspots and to watch events on day trips to Athens. The lack of tourism planning for the Games was further highlighted in 2003, when the formal co-operation agreement between the government and private enterprises was launched. At the launch, in August 2003, it was claimed that the focus needed to be on the development of business and tourism after, rather than during or before, the Athens 2004 Games (Yannopoulos, 2003). However, this approach was severely criticized by George Drakopoulos, Managing Director of the Greek Association of Tourism Enterprises (SETE), who stated:

> Tourism is the principal sector where the economic benefits from hosting the Olympics are obvious, even to a child. And yet, neither the government nor EOT [the National Tourism Organization] have done anything all these years to formulate a marketing strategy that would make the Olympics the pole of attraction for millions of foreign visitors to Greece. Let's face it, we have forsaken the chance to make the Olympic theme the linchpin of our tourist publicity drive prior to the Games.

While Athens is by far Greece's most important city, Petrakos and Economou (1999) noted that within the wider European context, Athens represents a large peripheral city with low-level influence in the region. This is a result of a range of spatial disadvantages, including unplanned residential areas on the outskirts, obsolete infrastructure, degraded built fabric, traffic congestion and environmental pollution, caused by unregulated rapid economic and physical growth as a result of rural immigration between 1950 and 1980 (CEC, 1992). Consequently, the 2004 Olympic Games presented a major opportunity to redevelop and re-brand the city. However, despite the city's expressed aim to follow the 'Barcelona Model' (Poulios, 2006), the development of Athens's bore little resemblance to Barcelona's approach, and this might be seen as a planning shortcoming that has failed to leave the city with an infrastructure legacy that best provides for future tourism and inward investment. Specifically, some of the planning failings were:

◆ Lack of integrated planning – partial spatial interventions were not integrated into a strategic plan for Athens as a whole, especially in relation to the post-Games period (Beriatos and Gospodini, 2004).

◆ Failure to redevelop brownfield areas – Barcelona focused on the redevelopment of run-down areas whereas Athens largely developed green spaces on the outskirts or undeveloped sites in the city. Beriatos and Gospodini (*Ibid*, p. 198) express surprise that Eleones, 'a large declined area with light industrial uses centrally located in Athens', was not considered for development.

◆ Architects and urban designers not given a central role – Barcelona incorporated architects and urban designers on the bidding and organizing committees for the 1992 Games, whereas Athens only consulted a few 'big name' architects, and did so much later in the process.

◆ Lack of spatial concentration – perhaps the key failing in creating a long-term legacy for urban tourism was the failure to concentrate spatial interventions and landscape transformations in a limited number of strategic sites. Unlike the approach taken in Barcelona, development and redevelopment projects in Athens were scattered 'all over the plan of the city without a focus' (*Ibid.*, p. 192).

Despite these planning failings, there was a clear intention to create an urban legacy as around 95 per cent of Olympic projects were not temporary, but permanent spatial structures. There were also projects that sought to enhance the city's historic sites, in particular those carried out by the Agency for the Unification of the Archaeological Sites of Athens, which sought to link together a geographically disparate range of historical sites and to enhance the city's 'historic physiognomy' (*Ibid.*, p. 199; see also Chapter 17). The intention, therefore, to link the historic local with the modern global existed, but was poorly implemented in practice.

Business File reported at the end of 2004 that tourism to Athens and Greece was 'lacklustre' during the Games and in Olympic year, and that Olympic ticket sales were much lower than expected. However, there remained hope in the Athens tourism sector that the tourism benefit would occur in the post-Games period, with a gallery owner in Athens's oldest neighbourhood commenting that despite lower than expected tourism in 2004, 'Next year will be better. We don't know, we just hope. It happened in other places and we think it will happen here too' (Business File, 2004).

Evidence in the time since the Games suggests that, despite the *laissez faire* approach to planning for Olympic tourism, the Athens Games have had a positive effect. A study by Alpha Bank, published at the end of 2004 estimated that the Games added €9 billion to Greece's Gross Domestic Product between 2000 and 2004 (against a total GDP of €163 billion in 2003). However, the most optimistic estimates remained predictions: namely that foreign visitors to Greece 'may reach 19–20 million by the end of the decade', from around 13 million in 2004 (Alpha Bank, 2004). It is perhaps worth noting, though, that Alpha Bank was a major sponsor of the Athens Games, and thus had a vested interest in demonstrating a positive outcome from the Games.

3. Beijing 2008

A key goal of both the municipal government of Beijing and the national Chinese government for the 2008 Games (as stated in the Beijing Olympic Action Plan, 2003) was to harness aspects of traditional Chinese culture in presenting the city and the country to the world in the run up to and during the Beijing Olympics. Elsewhere in the plan, the role of traditional Chinese culture in such an 'opening-up' strategy, as part of the humanistic 'people's Olympics' promotional theme, was clearly stated:

> we will take the hosting of the Olympic Games as an opportunity to ... promote the traditional Chinese culture, showcase the history and development of Beijing as well as the friendliness and hospitality of its citizens. We will also take the Games as a bridge for cultural exchanges in order to deepen the understanding and enhance the trust and friendship among the peoples of different countries. (BOCOG, 2003, p. 2)

However, there were no discussions of the strategies by which this was to be achieved, and there was certainly no stated plan to leverage Olympic media, which was a key requirement for Beijing's Olympic tourism strategy. Furthermore, the lack of such a strategy cannot be blamed on the need to concentrate on ensuring that the facilities and infrastructure were ready as, 4 years prior to the Games, Ritchard (2004, p. 2) noted that:

> Beijing will be supported by world-class facilities and logistics planning. The city is well underway in developing its Olympic-related facilities, including a new airport, magnificent stadia, convention centre and a much-improved transport network. Construction is reported to be on time and, in some cases, ahead of schedule.

Such efficiency in construction might be expected in a country that has only relatively recently undergone a transition from a planned 'state socialist' political system to what is still characterized as a 'socialist market economy'. However, as construction and infrastructure projects were well ahead of schedule, the need to turn attention to media concerns might be seen as even more pressing. Ritchard (*Ibid.*, p. 3) claimed that the efficiency of infrastructure development and construction provided Beijing with a world-class tourism product to serve the 2008 Olympics and, as such:

> ... the greatest potential of the Beijing Games will be the marketing opportunity which will instantly create global consumer awareness of 'China – the brand'... Beijing – like no other previous Olympic city – has a fascinating extra dimension: the unveiling of what China really is and what it can achieve, showcased to a global audience which, generally, knows little about the country. Beijing 2008 will be the source of many 'first impressions'. The Games will be the most comprehensive [and nicely packaged] up-close look at China in half a century, and history will judge the event as the vehicle for demystifying the world's image of the country.

The key question, though, was whether the 2008 Games, and the coverage of the city and country in the years before the Games, would be sufficient to 'convert public curiosity into travel bookings for conferences, leisure tours, city breaks, and business' (*Ibid*). In this respect, China did not have such an easy ride, and it was not really the case that an Olympic media leveraging strategy was all that was required. Despite reforms, politically Beijing remains a society strikingly at odds with Western liberalism (Wei and Yu, 2006). Furthermore, one of the key aspects of this difference is the Chinese state's perceived attitude to, and record on, human rights, with organizations such as Amnesty International, Human Rights Watch and the Centre of Housing Rights and Evictions commenting both on the state's previous record and on alleged human rights violations specifically linked to the preparations for the 2008 Games.

The existence and coverage of such issues can increase perceptions of difference and distance from China and Beijing as a desirable tourist destination and, consequently, reduce travel propensities in the key Olympic tourist markets, virtually all of which are liberal democracies with distaste for human rights violations. Specifically, it was alleged that, alongside censorship of the press, the 2008 Games led to the exploitation of construction workers and the use of child labour and the enforced displacement of families and communities from their homes, which have been demolished to make way for Olympic infrastructure developments. Against this background, Ritchard's (2004) comments that 'China is absolutely committed to ensuring the success of the Olympic Games – whatever it takes' (p. 2) and that the Games will be 'nicely packaged' (p. 3) become much more insidious. Of course, the displacement of residents to facilitate Olympic development is not a new phenomenon. Many of the criticisms of the 1992 Barcelona Games, which are often held up as the best example of the positive effects of the Olympics on long-term trade and tourism development (Sanahuja, 2002), highlighted the displacement of 624 families (approximately 2,500 people) to facilitate the redevelopment of the waterfront area (COHRE, 2007a). However, this is a mere drop in the ocean against COHRE's estimations that almost 1.25 million people were displaced in Beijing by 2007, and that this figure was set to rise to 1.5 million by the time the Games commenced in 2008 (*Ibid.*).

With the glare of the global Olympic media spotlight concentrated on Beijing and China in the run up to 2008, these issues continued to feature in Olympic and other media, and could not be addressed by a media strategy without addressing the underlying human rights issues themselves. As the Beijing 2008 torch relay progressed around the globe in the months preceding the Games, there was considerable disruption by protesters seeking to highlight a range of human rights issues in China. This became a major global story in the run up to the Games, although its long-term impact on 'China – the brand', given that Beijing undoubtedly hosted a largely successful and spectacular Games in 2008, appears to have faded in the post-Games period.

4. London 2012

Even before they had begun, the London 2012 Olympic and Paralympic Games were already being touted as the most planned for Games in history. As a result, they invited considerable scrutiny across a range of legacy areas, as it was widely recognized that the London Games had benefitted from a decade of research and knowledge transfer in relation to the opportunities that an Olympic Games can present. In terms of tourism, the UK government, like national hosts before it, tried to buck the general trend of Summer Olympic cities as destinations rather than gateways in order to extend Olympic tourism benefits throughout the UK.

The possibility that a London Games might have an impact on tourism was first recognized even before London was awarded the Games, with the 2004 national tourism strategy, 'Tomorrow's Tourism Today' (DCMS, 2004), recognizing the benefits that London's bid might bring in terms of 'spotlighting the world-class visitor attractions of the capital, and stimulating further improvements in the visitor infrastructure' (*Ibid.*, p. 14). Key issues were identified as: the need to consider the accommodation requirements of the Games; the need to plan for anticipated tourism activities in the years running up to the Games linked to the Cultural Olympiad; the need to plan Olympic-themed marketing activities within VisitBritain's overall 'brand architecture'; and the need to review the tourism opportunities arising from Olympic activities outside London (*Ibid.*).

When London was announced as the winning bidder in July 2005, there were varying predictions for its impact on tourism, including that of a '£2bn tourist boost' and a 'million more international visitors' (BBC, 2005). However, much of the detailed discussion focused on dealing with the issues the Games would bring, with VisitBritain and its industry partners noting that 'there will be a fight for the estimated 200,000 hotel beds available in London in 2012' and that 'July and August are already peak months for tourism' (*Ibid.*). The twelve months following the award of the Games to London were similar to the twelve months preceding it, with much debate focusing on how the tourism implications of the Games would be managed. However, in July 2006, the government's consultation on a tourism strategy for the 2012 Games, 'Welcome>Legacy' (DCMS, 2006), was published, which acknowledged that there were some shortcomings in the British tourism product, and identified the need to 'put the UK's tourism industry in a position to successfully welcome the world in 2012' (*Ibid.*, p. 4). The document also discussed the 'policy and operational levers necessary to deliver outcomes', thus hinting at a change in emphasis towards capitalizing on the tourism opportunities presented by the Games rather than simply managing its consequences.

In terms of improving the quality of the British tourism product, 'Welcome>Legacy' (*Ibid.*) provided the impetus for important changes, with a transition to quality being viewed in terms of value provided and an emphasis on the quality of the welcome, rather than focusing solely on physical infrastructure quality. However, in terms of marketing Britain for tourism through the Olympic Games, it was the publication of the 'Britain Marketing and 2012 Games Global Strategy' (Visit Britain, 2010) 4 years later that marked a step change, with the launch of an holistic 'Britain Brand Proposition', supported by a 'You're Invited' strapline and a 'Britain Now' brand narrative:

> Britain is a stimulating and exciting place to be. A place of constant reinvention where castles host music festivals, museums hold fashion shows, country houses are transformed into spa hotels and where you'll find world renowned historic landmarks right next door to modern art galleries and restaurants. Not just one country but three, each with their own character and traditions, but connected by a common spirit and people who are genuine, down to earth, interesting and quirky. A country that will host the Olympic and Paralympic Games in London in 2012 and also invites you to experience the character and charm of the whole of Britain, right now. (*Ibid.*)

The Britain Brand Proposition, particularly the 'You're Invited' strapline, was utilized within a wider GREAT campaign (using the word 'Great' from Great Britain) to generate exposure for UK business and tourism, which was claimed to be 'one of the most ambitious and far reaching marketing campaigns ever developed by the UK government' (DCMS, 2012, p. 42), expected to generate £1billion in extra business for UK firms (*Ibid.*, p. 39) and '£2 billion additional spend by visitors to the UK in four years after the Games' (*Ibid.*, p. 41). In terms of the tourism spend prediction, three widely available models were developed in the years before the Games that estimate its tourism impact (Blake 2005; Oxford Economics, 2007; Lloyds Banking Group, 2012), two of which were developed before the economic downturn, and even the most optimistic of these (Blake, 2005) falls someway short of the government's £2 billion prediction for post-Games tourism impact.

After London 2012, these three models and their assumptions were consolidated in a meta-analysis (Weed, 2012) which provided an estimate (at 2011 prices) that the Games would generate additional tourism value of £1.6 billion, of which £972 million would be in the five post-Games years. However, Weed (*Ibid.*) also used his meta-analysis to demonstrate that the largest modifiable tourism flows resulting from the Games would be the combined inward flows to London and the UK in the post-Games period. This was because effective marketing campaigns have significant potential to affect these flows and, as Weed *et al.* (2011) noted, a significant legacy of the 2012 Games for tourism was likely to be the way in which the British tourism policy community came together to embed the Games within the broad 'You're Invited' tourism marketing campaign, which itself was part of the wider GREAT campaign. However, it is unlikely that these campaigns will lead to post-Games tourism flows more than twice the size of those estimated by Weed's (2012) meta-analysis.

The lessons from London 2012 for Olympic tourism, therefore, appear to be that long-term planning to leverage the Games for tourism, particularly embedding Olympic themes within a wider general tourism and business investment campaign, can lead to significant tourism impacts. However, London 2012 also showed that, even when there was clear evidence of success, governments still over-claim on the scale of the tourism impacts delivered.

Conclusions

A theme running throughout the discussions of the eight Olympic cities in the first 15 years of the twenty-first century has been their stated desire to learn from the experiences of previous cities. However, the discussions often note planning failings in relation to the way in which the various Olympic cities have attempted to generate tourism. Such failings serve to highlight the very different contexts of the Games hosted by the Olympic cities discussed. The differences between the potential tourism implications of, and the resultant strategies that might be employed in, Winter and Summer Olympic cities have been highlighted. In particular, notwithstanding the ambitions and aspirations of national governments responsible for Summer Olympic cities, Winter Olympic cities appear to have a much greater potential to act as a tourism gateway to the wider regions in which they are situated as a result of the resource needs of the Winter Games (i.e., ski and other winter sports provision). Summer Olympic cities, however, have a much greater potential to capitalize on the image benefits that the Games can bring as they are much larger cities than their Winter counterparts, and therefore have an infrastructure and a range of city resources and icons that can be leveraged for tourism image benefits through Olympic-related media.

However, the latest Games appear to contradict these more general conclusions. London 2012's GREAT campaign was clearly focused on country-wide tourism benefits, which Weed's (2012) meta-analysis suggests will be delivered, whilst Sochi 2014 showed that even the largest infrastructure investment in Olympic history will not deliver expected tourism impacts, either for the city or the wider surrounding region, without clear planning and leveraging strategies. Looking forward, the next Summer Games is in Rio de Janeiro (2016), and the next Winter Games in PyeongChang in 2018. Expectations continue to be raised for the impacts the Games can have on tourism, and the lessons are clear. Tourism impacts can be a significant outcome from hosting the Games, but only if they are the subject of long-term planning and investment in appropriate leveraging strategies.

Note

1. The discussions of Sydney 2000 are drawn from a guest chapter contributed by Graham Brown to *Olympic Tourism* (Weed, 2008).

Chapter 12

Olympic Transport

Eva Kassens-Noor

Over the course of the modern Olympic Games, it has become evident that the management of transport systems is essential to host a successful event. In addition, effectively leveraging the billions of dollars of investments into transport upgrades prior to the Games has become of key concern not only to create a sustainable and viable legacy for the host but also to change the way the local population travels in light of increasing congestion and crowded transport systems in the Olympic cities.

For the first 100 years of the modern Games, transportation was seen as a service requirement that had to connect the main sites of an Olympic Games. To satisfy the ever growing number of visitors and remedy the transport mismanagement of past Games, demands for Olympic transport systems accumulated. Consequently, cities started to see the Games as an opportunity to change the way people travel in congested metropolises. Transport was one of the primary recipients of funding, extremely complex to plan for, expected to bring tremendous benefits to the host, yet little research had been conducted on what exactly transport's benefits were (or could be), and how one could go about leveraging them.

Even though the scale of Olympic transport for the Winter and the Summer Games differs in magnitude and physical environment, the transport tasks and objectives are similar in nature. The main difference between Winter and Summer Games is the substantially higher number of visitors and sports events for the latter. Consequently, transport planning for the Summer Games is more complex and requires more resources. On the upside, Summer Games venues are primarily located within the host city thereby decreasing travel times. The Summer Games also have more reliable travel conditions, longer daylight hours and less event rescheduling. In contrast, the Winter Games have mountain locations, which often require more vehicles, much longer travel times, and have less reliable travel conditions, shorter daylight hours, and adverse weather conditions (IOC, 2013b). This difference increases the likelihood of Winter Games hosts bearing higher costs per spectator.

While Paralympic Games are significantly smaller than Olympic Games in terms of the number of participants (two-thirds less than Olympic Games), they pose much greater challenges. Research on transport for Paralympians, volunteers with disabilities, and spectators with special needs is still in its infancy and focuses on venue accessibility including accessible vehicles, buses and minibuses, and transport stations (Darcy, 2003). Transport planning by organizing committees is seriously lagging behind, despite the suite of significant organizational, environmental, and structural issues identified (Darcy *et al*, 2014).

The key moment when Olympic transport *operations* were rethought was Atlanta 1996. The congestion and consequent bad press (Monroe, 1996) led the International Olympic Committee (IOC) to set new standards on transport to ensure no athlete would ever be late for an event. First, for future Games, athletes were to encounter only free-flow traffic conditions. Secondly, one agency – instead of multiple ones – was to head Olympic transport operations via a sophisticated Olympic transport system (OTS). Thirdly, the media were to be accredited so that they would receive public-exclusive service to broadcast competitions in a timely and reliable manner (Kassens-Noor, 2012).

Through the Winter Olympic Games in Nagano (1998), Japan implemented the Universal Traffic Management System (UTMS) due to fears of traffic congestion (Tanaka, 1997). Assessed as the greatest threat to the successful delivery of the Games by Japan's own media and the international mass media, large-scale Intelligent Transport Systems (ITS) investments were made in order to supply the public and road users with real-time information (Fujimaki, 1997). In addition, the city improved and expanded its local road network and expressways. The greatest investment Japan made was in the expansion of the Shinkansen bullet train from Takasaki to Nagano, itself an invention that was originally introduced for the 1964 Olympic Games in Tokyo (see also Chapter 21).

Sydney 2000 won the Games with their pitch for the Green Olympics. Transport was to play a major role in achieving this goal. Consequently, Sydney's Olympic Organizing Committee (SOCOG) served all visitors via public transport systems to and from the Games. Given 80 per cent of the venues were located in Homebush Bay, SOCOG estimated peak demands on its station of up to 400,000 people per hour. Consequently, a new rail line including station and buses served Sydney's Olympic visitors. Transport performance during the Games was superior, because Sydney was over-prepared. According to Hensher and Brewer (2002) patronage on trains was well below expectations and patronage on buses did not increase significantly due to a number of factors including the shift in behaviour of regular riders, holidays, and commuters on leave.

Organizers of the 2002 Winter Games in Salt Lake City secured close to $90 million in federal funds to improve roads that carried Olympic traffic. In addition, the Utah Department of Transportation (UDOT) developed a travel demand management programme to handle anticipated increases in traffic. While the agency managed to reduce background traffic significantly (Njord, 2002), the city integrated its Olympic transport plan with the long-term goals of the city and region (Endter-Wada *et al*., 2003). Early studies indicated that transportation was predicted to be a benefit the region could expect (Andranovich *et al*., 2001).

Athens 2004 demonstrated the potential of rethinking the approach to leveraging a transport system for the Olympics. The host achieved one of the greatest successes but also suffered one of the greatest failures for transport. The city's greatest success was to leverage the expansion of the metro system and the construction of a new airport, both of which had been planned for decades, but without funds being made available. With the advent of the Games, the plans became feasible. The greatest failures were the construction of facilities and transport modes that had little ridership expectations beyond the Games and were primarily driven by the need to move thousands of spectators from venue to venue. Examples included the tramline from the abandoned airport Hellinikon to Glyfada, or the Express Facility for athletes at Athens International Airport.

In preparation for the Turin Winter Games (2006), state roads and motorways around the city were upgraded, especially those linking Olympic sites. In addition, the Olympic Games acted as a catalyst for new investment in the metro system. Despite this, work on the project was completed well after the Games had left the city. To handle the traffic during the Games, the Organizing Committee (TOROC) relied heavily on public transport, in particular trams, buses, and shuttles. Therefore, 80 kilometres of Olympic lanes within Turin, rail shuttles to and within the mountain areas replaced most car traffic (60 per cent of all spectators reached the mountain venues on public transport, an additional 18 per cent used car/shuttle/bus option) (Bondonio and Campaniello, 2006; Bovy, 2006).

Beijing 2008 and London 2012 overhauled their transport systems in preparation for the Games, aligning their strategic plans with the Olympic project. While Beijing created several new subway lines across the city to improve connectivity for the residents, London established the prime location of Stratford as an international hub, significantly upgraded access to East London, and rejuvenated the Dockland Light Railway to serve Londoners' travel needs for the future. For example, 80 per cent of spectators were expected to arrive by rail (Crawford, 2012). Both cities implemented extensive travel management measures to cope with the demands (Currie and Delbosc, 2011).

Vancouver's 2010 Olympics were held with a focus on sustainability. Therefore, forty-eight new SkyTrain cars, a new SeaBus, and 180 diesel-electric hybrid buses were purchased before the Games. The new Canada Line was inaugurated, connecting Vancouver's airport and downtown (Bracewell, 2009). These investments ultimately doubled the number of trips typically taken on public transit and as well as active modes of travel (walking and cycling) reaching 61 per cent for the sustainable share of transport into and out of the downtown core (Lin and Sayed, 2010). In addition, the highway between Vancouver and Whistler was expanded and upgraded. On that road, as well as within Vancouver, extensive traffic, highway and incident management were provided by the BC Ministry of Transportation and Infrastructure to add traffic capacity and reliability (Kurji and Miska, 2011).

Investment for Sochi 2014 exceeded that of previous Olympic Games with an estimated total expenditure of roughly $52 billion. The need to connect the two Olympic clusters – one on the coast and the other 30 miles (48 km) away in the mountains at Krasnaya Polyana – added substantially to costs. Sochi, a city of 300,000 residents, was already a summer vacation and recreation spot before the Games, but as a result of the significant transport investments planned to develop winter sports tourism. These investments included a new highway linking both clusters, a rail line, and upgraded airport facilities. In addition of course, there were the many investments within the clusters to make the region ready for a world-class event.

Rio de Janeiro 2016 had a grand vision for their transport system, proclaiming in its bid that Rio was to have the greatest transport legacy of the modern Games. The key idea was to connect four areas of the city through four bus rapid transport (BRT) lines, which were to serve its citizens during the Games and 'provide for a growing metropolis'. Even though the original bid only accounted for two new additions, in the planning stages leading up to 2016, ROCOG realized the huge potential the Games could have on their city. Due to rushed decisions resulting in vigorous protests, accelerated construction schedules that ultimately led to poor road structures, and last minute planning changes, ROCOG had to scratch the grand plan in early 2014 and revert to the original bid, which included only two BRTs, one of which was in the matrix for FIFA 2014 and already operational at the time.

Tokyo 2020 promises superior transportation linking two main groups of venues – one a newly created cluster along the coast and the other comprising the historical venues of the 1964 Games. Tokyo will increasingly count on its standing and reputation as the world leader in innovative technology, in particular for transport services during the Olympic Games, using the latest Information and Communication Technologies (TOCOPG, 2012, p. 39). In fact, Intelligent Transportation Systems (ITS) were the key corner stone of Tokyo's bid.

These perforce brief summaries provide the basis on which the following sections of this chapter proceed. It addresses the three main stages in preparing transport for an Olympic Games: planning Olympic transport, managing Olympic transport, and the leveraging of legacies. While the section will identify best practice in Olympic transport, it will also draw on various examples of previous and future hosts to illustrate successes and failures in this area.

Planning Olympic Transport

The gold standard for planning Olympic transport is its integration with strategic development plans for the host's transport system in order to manage passenger demand peaks of millions securely, safely, and reliably (ECMT, 2003; Kassens-Noor, 2010a; Minis and Tsamboulas, 2008). Theoretically, this is a challenge that all cities face as a result of rapid urbanization. The primary difference though is that the IOC sets certain standards on these transportation systems, partly driven by adverse experiences of the past and partly driven by the very specific demands that Olympic Games travellers impose on transportation systems.

Since the poor transport performance during Atlanta's centennial Games, planning Olympic transport has become increasingly challenging for hosts because the IOC has become heavily involved in the process. The Committee sets minimum benchmarks for the performance of Olympic transport systems, demands free-flow traffic conditions, prefers certain venue configurations, and monitors implementation after nomination to ensure a smooth transport experience. The planning should follow the IOC's general recommendation that: 'in developing the Olympic Concept, it is recommended to minimize travel times and distances between venues and principally between Olympic Villages and venues' (IOC, 2013b, pp. 35–471). Since the implementation of the 2020 Reforms, support for bidders is offered even before the initial bid is due (IOC, 2014a).

The IOC evaluates the initial bids through the bid books and in-person visits to applicant cities. For example, for the 2022 Games, Olympic bidders had to report the following (IOC, 2013a): existing transport infrastructure (roads and public transport only); planned transport infrastructure irrespective of hosting the Olympics; and additional infrastructures that are necessary to host an Olympic Games. For each infrastructure, length, current and expected capacity, location, how and by whom work will be financed, and construction timelines had to be reported. Furthermore, travel distances and travel times between venues, the Olympic Village, the airport, main accommodation centres, the Olympic Stadium, as well as media accommodation and their headquarters. The bids are scored ranging from 1 to 10, whereby hosts that score low are usually excluded from advancing to the candidacy stage (IOC, 2001–2013).

The IOC's bid evaluation becomes of critical importance for the submission of the candidacy file (or in case of a rejection for the next bid 4 years later). These documents frequently see significant alterations to the original bid. Even though the final bid documents become the host contract upon winning, alterations thereafter are possible. As we have seen for example, Rio de Janeiro 2016 expanded its proposed bus rapid transport (BRT) system from two lines to four lines connecting the city after they had won the bid in 2009. Ultimately, the city had to back track on this ambitious plan in early 2014 due to the impossibility of completing these vast infrastructural alterations in time for the Olympic Games.

The host city contract has several annexes including the 'Technical Manual on Transport'. This massive document (500 pages for London) is part of the host city contract and had to be fulfilled by the host city. The manual contains best practice solutions and represents the understanding from the IOC and its partners on how transport should function during the Games. The document distinguishes between nine transport planning and operations themes: Infrastructures and Facilities; Client Services; Fleet Operations; Bus Operations; Public Transport; Venue Transport; Traffic Management; Transport Information; and Planning and Support Services. After the signing of the host contract, the IOC implements a monitoring system for the implementation of the transport plans (see table 12.1). The IOC (2013c, p. 34_471) defines the transport task as follows:

Table 12.1. IOC monitoring system for the implementation of transport plans.

Task	Timing months before Games[G]	Description of Task
Candidature Transport Planning	G-90 Candidature transport planning and guarantees	Candidature work is the first global presentation of an Olympic transport scheme as part of a proposed Games concept with guarantees provided on key elements such as additional transport infrastructure projects, fleet and rolling stock capacity improvements, transport operation and traffic management schemes.
Games Foundation Transport Planning	G-70/G-60 Games Foundation Plan – Transport	Formal update of the Candidature File with a much more detailed understanding of the task ahead and an emphasis on how the Organizers intend to organize and stage the Games.
Transport Operation Planning Version 1	G-42 Transport Operation Plan – version 1	This first version integrates six basic transport operational components: Games Client Requirements; Public Transport; Traffic Management; Transport Information; Planning; and Support Services.
Transport Testing	G-16/G-8 Transport tests	Transport tests are an important part of transport planning, risk mitigation and staff training. They are defined by the following elements of the Transport Planning and Operations Themes section • Transport Infrastructure and Facilities Testing • Venue Clusters and Precincts Testing • Client Services Testing • Fleet Operations Testing • Bus Operations Testing • Public Transport Testing • Traffic Management Testing • Transport Information Testing • Workforce Testing
Transport Operation Planning Version 2	G-8 Transport Operation Plan –version 2 – Final	Transport Operation Plan final version is progressively developed from version 1. It integrates the results of testing whenever possible. All basic transport operational components are covered such as: Games Client Requirements, Infrastructure and Facilities, Public Transport, Venue Transport, Fleet Operations, Bus Operations, Traffic Management, Transport Information and Planning and Support Services.
Venue Transport Operating Planning	G-8 Venue Transport Operating Plans	Venue Operating Plans are developed for each venue, both competition and non-competition.
Games-time Transport Management Planning	G-8/G-0 Games-time transport management and delivery planning	Games-time roles and responsibilities of the OCOG Transport function and the various transport entities will be dependent on the Olympic Transport task management approach adopted by the OCOG and the allocation of responsibilities for planning and operations themes.
Legacy and Transport Sustainability Planning	G-90/G+120 Post Games legacy and transport sustainability planning	Transport Legacy and Sustainability planning starts with the Candidature file transport development (about G-90) of the Games concept aligned with the Host City long-term Transport Master planning orientations. Transport Legacy and Sustainability are further developed during the Foundation and Transport Operation planning phases. As indicated by section VII on Sustainability the following aspects are considered as objectives for better transport sustainability: • Maximizing use of public transport and active transportation (walk and cycle) • Public Education regarding urban mobility • Integrating Games transportation with urban and regional plans • Sustainable sourcing for cleaner fuels and vehicles • Showcasing effective sustainable transportation technology and solutions

Source: Created by author based on IOC, 2013c, pp. 55_ 471–457_471.

The OCOG shall provide a safe, reliable and efficient system of transport, free of charge, for the following accredited persons: competitors, team officials and other team personnel, technical officials, media, Marketing Partners/suppliers/ licensees, Games-related workforce and other persons, as designated by the IOC, in accordance with the transport terms, conditions and privileges referred to in the Technical Manual on Transport, which forms an integral part of this contract. All aspects of transport shall be subject to the prior written approval of the IOC.

In order to deliver the Olympic transport system, host cities establish an Olympic client pyramid that prioritizes different groups.

The client service planning division develops and approves transport service levels for each of these Games' client groups and sees that they meet IOC approved timelines. In addition, they manage all Games client information deliverables – communications, publications and Games-time transport information desks. One major transport task for the host city is transporting the millions of local residents who have to go about their daily lives during the Olympics. One striking feature is that transport services for all aforementioned client groups are free of charge. Table 12.2 summarizes these transport privileges afforded to the current IOC accreditation transport codes.

Transport for athletes and for essential personnel like judges (TA and TF) is extremely time-sensitive and consequently highly vulnerable. The goal of the IOC is to provide them with safe, reliable and secure systems that minimize their inconvenience. Therefore, multiple restrictions and demands exist that have been met by hosts with different responses. For example, athletes should have free

Table 12.2. IOC transport codes and associated transport privileges.

Transport Code	Description	Transport Privileges
T1	Allocated Vehicle and Driver	Allocated Vehicle and Driver, Games Client Transport System, Free Public Transport Systems
T2	Allocated Vehicles and Drivers	Allocated Vehicle and Driver, Games Client Transport System, Free Public Transport Systems
T3	Games Client Transport System	Games Client Transport System Free Public Transport Systems
TA	Athletes / NOC Transport System	Athletes / NOC Transport System Free Public Transport Systems
TF	Technical Officials / International Federations Transport system	Technical Officials / International Federations Transport System Free Public Transport Systems
TM	Media Transport system	Media Transport System Free Public Transport Systems
TP	Public Transport Systems	Free Public Transport Systems

Note: T1–T2 transport is reserved for heads of state, VIPs and selected IOC and NOC officials (Bovy and Liaudat, 2003).
Source: IOC, 2013c, p. 98_471.

flow traffic condition between the Olympic Village and their non-competition, competition, and training sites. As a response, the primary Olympic bus network has evolved and now has become a standard feature of Olympic bids. Arrival and departure of athletes in the host city is also of crucial importance, as many other procedures, such as accreditation, have to take place upon arrival. Consequently airports have invested heavily in routing procedures. Athens 2004, for example, developed an Express Facility at the airport, which was essentially a terminal exclusively used by Olympic Family Members (Odoni et al., 2009).

The media (TM) has to be treated as a distinct transport group. Just like judges, their timely arrival is crucial, so is their experience of the local transport system, because they report to the world about the Games. If they broadcast a poor image, the global city picture is severely tainted.

Visitors and volunteers (TP) frequently face language barriers and are unfamiliar with the local transport system. Given that there can frequently be more than two million visitors, the IOC recommends that host cities should rely on 100 per cent use of public transport to cater for their needs. Consequently, it has become common practice to link the entrance ticket to an event as a free pass on all public transport modes. To handle the demands of all the client groups mentioned above, the host city usually combines the transport passes with a ticket and invents a sophisticated multi-model transport operations plan using road, rail, bus, and active transportation measures.

Managing Olympic Transport

The management of Olympic transport is essential to staging successful Games. After at least 7 years of planning, the city's transport system has to handle millions of additional travellers for three weeks. The key to succeeding in efficiently handling such an increase is the modification of travel behaviour through new infrastructure, different operational procedures, incentives and penalties. To handle Olympic client groups that require road transport, several traffic management techniques including travel demand management help create efficient traffic flows. Hensher and Brewer (2002) identified five transport pressure points: trains, buses, taxis, airport and roads and parking. Based on these pressure points, Currie and Shalaby (2012) suggested several transport demand management measures grouped into six categories: travel capacity creation measures, travel behaviour change/marketing measures, traffic efficiency measures, traffic bans, and public transport emphasis (for further information, see Currie and Delbosc, 2011; Currie and Shalaby, 2012).

The goal of transport demand management is to achieve a base load reduction on transport systems, as in the case of Utah Department of Transportation which aimed to reduce the background traffic by 20 per cent (Njord, 2002). There are three main measures to achieve such reductions. The first is trip elimination, such as vacation, telecommuting or the temporary relocation of inner-city workers to other branches. The second involves shifting peak demand, which includes measures such as the imposition of driving restrictions for downtown travel during rush hours or requiring trucks and freight deliveries to stores located in the inner city to take place during the night. The third is to encourage modal shift, whereby residents are persuaded to commute via public transport instead of private vehicles (Kassens-Noor, 2010b). Intelligent Transportation Systems have become key to achieving the necessary alterations in travel behaviour. They are used to provide information to residents and local businesses, organize parking policies and enforce driving restrictions. In particular, the Games in the new millennium have relied on decision-support systems to manage transport networks, as in the case of Athens (Karlaftis et al., 2004) or London, which offered the most sophisticated real-time traffic and transport monitoring system to date.

The IOC requires that transport information is communicated via 'one message–one voice' and that only one agency should be in charge of Olympic Transport services. Consequently, host cities have established temporary centres that lead, coordinate and manage transport services through top-down structure. Frequently mentioned by Olympic transport agencies is the challenge to train and manage out-of-towners, who are temporarily employed to support Olympic transport operations. Essential personnel, for example bus drivers, must adhere to the rigid Olympic schedule despite not being familiar with the local transport system. In the worst cases, they lose their way and athletes are delayed for their competitions. As a solution, Hensher and Brewer (2002) propose that local personnel mentor out-of-towners.

Besides travel demand management, Olympic hosts have to invest in infrastructure and implement mode-specific management techniques to make their transport systems Olympic-ready. Due to specific Olympic transport demands and experience with the Olympic Transport System, multiple best practices for different travel means have evolved.

Rail systems have become the primary means of moving Olympic ticket holders to their events. London's Stratford station achieved peak supply capacity of up to 500,000 passengers per hour during the London Games. Ever since Sydney 2000, each Olympic city either already had or has constructed a new rail line to the main Olympic sites. Even Rio de Janeiro, where the transport network will rely primarily on high-capacity Bus Rapid Transit, is constructing an underground system linking Ipanema to Barra de Tijuca. This public transport option can significantly increase capacity in travel volume and time (Currie and Shalaby, 2012).

Two bus systems, called the primary and secondary Olympic network, are operated on road networks. The primary Olympic bus network is meant only for Olympic client groups and has buses using exclusive lanes on designated road space. Similarly, the secondary Olympic bus network connects venues for Olympic ticket holders. The Olympic bus fleet service, which is responsible for planning, designing, procuring, testing, operating, and delivering the OCOG Fleet vehicles and services according to IOC requirements, includes services planning, fleet and driver procurement, and fleet facilities management (IOC, 2013b). Measures for managing transit operations include free public transport with Olympic entrance ticket, park and ride facilities, shuttle services from rail to stadia, shuttle services from the park and ride, encouraging day charter bus trips, encouraging walking and biking, 24/7 operation of trains and buses (Kassens-Noor, 2010b). In order to handle additional travellers, enhancements to the existing services need to be tested well ahead of the Games.

Road systems undergo upgrades in the run up to the Olympics such as line expansions (Vancouver 2010), ITS infrastructures (Atlanta 1996), or new roads and highways (Barcelona 1992). New or significantly overhauled traffic management centres, new intelligent transportation systems, surveillance cameras, and variable message signs are implemented routinely to reorient routine traffic, to impose new driving and parking restrictions around venues, in the inner city, and the Olympic ring; they also signal road closures and line restrictions (Kassens-Noor, 2010b). These traffic-efficiency measures improve traffic flow and reduce delays. They are accompanied by prolonged public campaigns that encourage the perception that driving is illegal or extremely expensive (Currie and Shalaby, 2012). In Games before 2000, cars were crucial for moving people across the city. In later Games, their importance decreased. For example, in contrast to expectations, tourists and spectators rarely used taxis and rental cars during the Sydney Games. In contrast, IOC delegates continued to rely heavily on cars: 'the shuttle buses around the main Homebush precinct catering solely for IOC delegates were not well utilized at all. Game officials are much more accustomed to chauffeur driven VIP cars' (Hensher and Brewer, 2002, p. 385).

Active transport has come to play a major role in cycle-friendly and walkable cities, especially within highly clustered Olympic venue sites like Homebush Bay in Sydney or London's Olympic Park. While the priority provisions for cyclists and pedestrians have largely encompassed locations close to venues (Kassens-Noor, 2010b), its importance seems to be increasing as Boston and Hamburg, two early contenders for the 2024 Olympics developed highly clustered Games concepts in which 90 per cent of all venues were within a 10 kilometre circle.

The management of Paralympic transport presents one of the greatest challenges for an Organizing Committee. Not only have access options to people with disabilities traditionally lagged behind in cities, but also knowledge on how to provide safe access and accommodate needs of people with special needs is not well-established in Olympic planning (Darcy, 2003). Darcy (2001), for instance, listed twelve issues which evolved through test events for the Sydney Olympic Games that needed solutions within the twelve months leading up to the Opening Ceremony. Consequently, people with disabilities must be an integral part of the key planning process rather than mere consultants, in order to rely on their understanding of how space is being used and to point out the suite of problems in existing and planned transportation networks.

Best practices on how to manage Olympic transport will evolve as new cities host the Games with different and innovative concepts tailored to their unique challenges. These new concepts become demands and standards as the Games move from one city to the next. For example, Beijing's air pollution problem demanded the creation of emission reduction plans. Those standards carried over to London as the low carbon Games (Tian and Brimblecombe, 2008) and evolved into new ideas, including the zero-carbon and zero-waste promises of Tokyo 2020 (TOCOPG, 2012). These ideas set new demands on transportation and require innovative solutions for managing transport. Consequently, testing in new environments and under certain conditions becomes extremely important because transport planners must evaluate these measures to best suit their Olympic transport network and foster the city's urban plans (Kassens-Noor, 2013a). Likewise, emergency procedures and the role transport needs to play have become crucially important (Minis and Tsamboulas, 2008).

Leveraging Olympic Transport Legacies

Planning Olympic transport has evolved from purely managing the Games to leveraging the legacies these events could bring. Legacy can be physical transport infrastructure such as new or upgraded airports, roads (motorways, expressways, arterial roads, BRT routes), rail (metro, subway, national, regional and suburban rail, tramway, light rail), marine (ferries), cable transport systems, new or improved transport areas outside venues (parking, loading zones, holding and staging areas) and approaches to roadways and loading areas as well as transport facilities including transport hubs, terminals and depots. Legacy can also be behavioural, such as an increase in public transport usage post-Games or the experiences gained from handling Olympic transport being applied to other major events staged in the host city. Since the IOC introduced the concept of sustainability, transport assessment and legacy considerations have largely integrated benefits for the populace. Health, in particular, can benefit from mode shifts from car usage to active transport options (McCarthy et al., 2010). Legacy can also be environmental, such as emission reductions or emission increases due to modified infrastructures and operational transport procedures post-Games.

While many transport legacies are place-specific, Kassens-Noor (2013b) identified six common legacies created through an Olympic Games across five hosts despite the different transport systems in place. These were: new or improved connections between airports and city centres; airport improvements; creation and revitalization of parks with high-capacity transport access; new high-capacity transport modes; additional road capacity; and advanced Intelligent Transport Systems. The author argued that similar features of the Olympic Transport System produced similar legacies, hypothesizing that this pattern will evolve as new demands are placed on Olympic Transport Systems. To prompt potential cities on thinking how to leverage the must-haves for an Olympic Games, the IOC required bidders to link the managing and the legacy of the Games in the bid. To prompt potential cities on thinking how to leverage the must-haves for an

Olympic Games, the IOC required bidders to link the managing and the legacy of the Games in the bid, with specific requests that bidders justify their investment in terms of the host's long-term development. Transport has become an integral part for such justifications (IOC, 2001–2013).

Transport legacy is initiated through the Games, yet long-term benefits need to be adopted willingly and accepted by the populace (Ieromonachou et al., 2010). The pre-conditions for such acceptance are prevalent: the Olympic Games now come with a promise that transportation systems will undergo significant upgrades because they need to function flawlessly for a much larger population group. All around, residents view the Games as an opportunity to improve accessibility and mobility (see for example Bovy, 2001; Darcy, 2003; ECMT, 2003; Misener et al., 2013). Translating this promise into permanence requires public input and strategic long-term planning. For example, London 2012, now hailed as the most sustainable Olympics, had invested 10 years in planning transport for the Olympics in an effort to stage a successful Games and reap the benefits that they could bring (Hendy, 2012). One particular legacy that hosts have increasingly used as a leveraging strategy to improve transport flows is Intelligent Transportation Systems. Compared to new infrastructures, Intelligent Transportation Systems are cheaper to install while increasing efficiency, safety, and reliability.

Leveraging legacies is an art and a science. Therefore, much thought has to be given to which and in what ways temporary measures can be turned into permanent ones to improve travel conditions in the host city. For example, Mexico City 1968 introduced a temporary measure to allow access to the city centre based on odd and even license plate numbers: every other day, odd ones were allowed, then even ones the next day. Making this a permanent measure failed, because households kept two plates per car, and were able to drive into the city with the same car. In contrast, measures implemented for the Beijing Olympic Games resulted in a permanent reduction of air pollutants (Liu et al., 2008). While we can learn which legacies to foster and which to avoid from Olympic history, legacy always lies in the eye of the beholder and can be seen as positive or negative by different stakeholders.

Conclusion

For host cities it is vital to integrate strategically the planning, managing and leveraging of Olympic transport. In regards to urban development, the Barcelona model has frequently been used to highlight how such strategic integration can be achieved. For transport, London 2012 has set new benchmarks on how to advance transport agendas, integrate them strategically into a long-term transport plan (including connecting the city to continental Europe), and leverage many Olympic transport legacies for the benefit of the residents. To be fair, not only did London have a metropolitan planning agency in place but also had a well-functioning transport system to leverage the public and active transport driven strategies for Games time. Many other hosts, like Rio de Janeiro 2016, face very different pre-Games conditions that require rethinking of transport strategies for the Games and beyond.

The IOC practiced science of Transfer of Knowledge, by which host cities observe each other, by which experts consult on strategies and plans, and by which IOC members advise on better strategies, has grown tremendously, covering thousands of pages in technical manuals, an extranet with collated data including reports, data and best practices from previous Games. The standards are increasing by which higher costs frequently correlate with better transport services. With the new Agenda 2020 in place, hosts must devise cost-efficient and sustainable ways to adhere to both.

Part III

City Portraits

Chapter 13

Berlin 1936

Monika Meyer

The sports venues of the 1936 Olympic Games left Berlin a significant but difficult legacy. The grounds of the former Reichssportfeld, especially the Olympic Stadium, are important reminders of the history of the City of Berlin and the German state. They show us that sport cannot be non-political. In a staged spectacle the image of a tolerant and open regime was played to the world, but behind the illusion Jews and political dissidents were persecuted systematically and preparations were made for World War II, which had devastating effects on Europe and beyond.

This chapter analyses the construction history of the Berlin Olympic Stadium and its surroundings up to the present. Observations on aspects of National Socialism (Nazism), with which the 1936 Olympic Games are always associated, are touched upon and presented only to the extent that they are significant to the topic. Nevertheless, the focus would be too narrow if the history of the Olympic facilities concentrated only on the period around 1936. The history of the sports facilities began at the start of the twentieth century during the formation of the German Olympic Movement. The various phases of stadia and sports field development were closely tied to Germany's efforts to host the Olympic Games, with the movement first becoming successful during Germany's Weimar Republic. Since 1946 the stadium and other former Olympic facilities have repeatedly been the setting for great national and international events. Especially noteworthy are the games of the 1974 FIFA World Cup that presented the opportunity for the first fundamental renovations. Berlin's renewed bid for the 2000 Olympic Games was controversial both in the city and nationwide, and provoked a lengthy discussion about the future of the stadium: should it be torn down on the basis of cost or kept as a historical building complex? The final decision favoured the Olympic Stadium, which was adapted for contemporary sport in preparation for the 2006 FIFA World Cup.

Becoming an Olympic City

Since the founding of the IOC in 1894, German sports officials had argued seriously about whether holding an international sports competition would comply with the

Olympic tradition of ancient Greece and whether German participation would be sensible. This discussion remained active in Germany into the Nazi period. Between 1896 and 1904, independent committees were formed for Germany's participation in the Olympic Games, and each time they had to discuss this issue with the public, sports associations and government authorities. In 1904 the first successful German national committee for the Olympic Games was formed out of the committee for the Games in St. Louis: the *Deutscher Reichsausschuss für die Olympische Spiele* (DRAfOS). The goals of DRAfOS were to organize national games, to have German teams participate in international games, and to bring German sports clubs together in a unified association for physical fitness.

Efforts to bring the Games to Berlin in 1908 and 1912 failed because there was no suitable stadium available. After financing had been secured in 1911 and the start of stadium construction had been set for September 1912, the IOC at their meeting in Stockholm in July of 1912 decided to grant Berlin the Games for 1916. In 1913 Carl Diem[1] became the General Secretary of the Organizing Committee for the Berlin Games. The Deutsches Stadion (German Stadium) was inaugurated later that same year.

Due to the outbreak of the First World War in 1914, the 1916 Olympic Games were cancelled without an official declaration by Germany, the city or the IOC.[2] In the period following the First World War, sports officials, notably from France, pressed for the exclusion of German athletes from the international arena. This prevented German participation at Antwerp 1920 or the 1924 Games in Chamonix and Paris, with the IOC no longer including German members in its lists.[3] However, Pierre de Coubertin and Carl Diem made efforts to find ways to lead Germany back into the Olympic Movement. In 1924, German members were again appointed, and Germany received an invitation to Amsterdam 1928.

The thought of a renewed candidacy of Berlin seemed logical and so, at their meeting on 29 January 1927, the DOA (German Olympic Committee – *Deutscher Olympischer Ausschuss*)[4] decided that Berlin should bid for the 1936 Games. The official bid was announced at the 29th IOC Session held in Berlin in May 1930. A year later Berlin was chosen at the 1931 Session in Barcelona. On 24 January 1933, the Organizing Committee held their founding meeting. Theodor Lewald,[5] who was voted President, presented the Committee's goals: conversion of the Deutsches Stadion, the composition of an Olympic anthem, the organization of an art exhibit and the presentation of an Olympic festival. Six days later on 30 January 1933, Adolf Hitler was appointed *Reichskanzler* and the National-Socialist dictatorship began in Germany.

Sport during the Third Reich

The position of the *Nationalsozialistische Deutsche Arbeiterpartei* (NSDAP) was strengthened again in March by the elections for parliament (the Reichstag). The streamlining of sport by the regime began when the Interior Minister appointed

SA-Gruppenführer Hans von Tschammer und Osten as *Reichssportkommisar and Reichssportführer*. The National Socialists quickly liquidated the *Deutscher Reichsausschuss für Leibesübung* (DRAfL).[6] The guidelines passed on 24 May 1933 for creating the *Deutscher Reichsbund für Leibesübungen* established a sports organization according to the *Führerprinzip*. The *Reichssportführer* was also the head of the DOA and a member of the leadership of the Organizing Committee of the Olympic Games.

For a long time the Nazis had mounted anti-Olympic campaigns. During the period of the Weimar Republic, these efforts were generally unsuccessful but, after Hitler became *Reichskanzler*, many in the NSDAP saw a chance to prevent the Olympic Games from being an international event and to hold Germanic or German combat games instead. The *Kampfring gegen die Olympischen Spiele*, an organization of National-Socialist student groups, demanded on 6 February 1933 that 'the 1936 Olympic Games must not be held in Germany' (Schmidt, 1992, p. 219). Just six days after winning the Reichstag election, however, Hitler received Lewald, with Joseph Goebbels[7] also present, and declared that he would support the Games (*Ibid.*, p. 220).

Hitler and Goebbels had recognized very early on the opportunities for Nazi propaganda in hosting the Olympic Games in Germany with its international presentation and the appropriation of the classical Olympic ideal. On 15 January 1934, Goebbels founded a propaganda committee within the Organizing Committee and thereby created an instrument to manipulate the Games to his liking (see Hoffmann, 1993, pp. 12ff).

After Hitler's appointment as *Reichskanzler*, the world, and especially the United States, raised concerns that the Games could be misused by the new German rulers. On 3 May 1933, IOC President Count Henri de Baillet-Latour wrote to the German IOC members, saying that 'they must bring proof to the upcoming session in Vienna that the government of the Reich does not oppose the Olympic rules' (quoted in Schmidt, 1992, p. 12). The misgivings continued and there were repeated attempts during the preparation period of the Games to create an international boycott (Hoffmann, 1993, p. 12). These efforts increased further as the Nazi system was consolidated and the persecution of Jews became more and more obvious from actions such as the 'Nuremberg Laws' of 1935. In June 1936, after many failed attempts to come to an international decision, the Congress of the 'International Committee for the Defence of Olympic Ideals' in Paris called for a boycott of the Games. The same congress proclaimed an 'Olympiad of the People' in Barcelona for 19–26 July 1936. However, due to Franco's coup which started on 17 July 1936, these games could not begin and the boycott did not occur.

Olympic Facilities

The Olympic Stadium and the sports facilities are located in a hilly and wooded area in the western part of the city. This area had been used for military purposes

since the early nineteenth century and was accessed from an army road leading
west. At the beginning of the twentieth century the Kaiser indicated his intention
to turn this site over to the public for recreation and leisure. In 1906 the Prussian
Federation of Horse-Breeding and Horseracing Sports was able to lease a plot of
land to build a horse racecourse and for general sporting purposes. Between 1907
and 1909, Rennbahn Grunewald was built here to the plans designed by Otto
March[8] and Albert Brodersen while taking the utmost care to preserve the existing
Grunewald pines on site. The racecourse was torn down in March 1934 for the
new construction of the Reichssportfeld. The area itself was peripheral to the city,
but always had well-developed access to transport. Two roads, two commuter train
lines (S-Bahn) built at the beginning of the twentieth century, and an underground
train (U-Bahn) line connected the sports grounds with the centre of Berlin.

After the unsuccessful bid in Rome to host the 1908 Olympic Games, the
DRAfOS and committed athletes attempted to secure financing for an Olympic
stadium from 1906 to 1911. In February 1906 the first stadium proposal by Otto
March was published in the press, and commentaries even then were printed with
regard to future Olympic Games. As the discussions on the financing were drawn
out, the stadium was not opened until 1913 after nine months of construction:

> The stadium [was] in a dug-out hollow in the interior space of the horse racecourse in
> Grunewald. In order to not block the view of the back straight, only low stands [could] be
> built [50,000 spectators]. In the otherwise large interior space there [was] a 600 m-long
> track and a 666 2/3 m-long bicycle course… The spectator seating across from the stand
> side [was] left out as space for a 100 m-long swimming pool. Under the swimming pool
> stands there [were] rooms for a stadium laboratory. (Borges *et al.*, 1995, p. 122)

At the prompting of Carl Diem, further expansion took place after the
founding of the Deutsche Hochschule für Leibesübungen in 1919. As a result,
the Deutsches Stadion was expanded according to the plans of architect Johannes
Seiffert. The Hochschule opened on 15 May 1920 and Diem commissioned
Seiffert in 1924 to propose sites for its enlargement. Seiffert chose a 20 hectare
area north of the racecourse, where the Deutsches Sportforum was built in three
phases between 1926 and 1936. It was designed by Seiffert as well as by Werner
and Walter March, with the Nazis beginning to influence matters in 1933. Up to
then, Werner March had designed open, interconnected spaces and had pursued
a modest but prominent effect. Instead, the map of the area in 1936 revealed a
monumental site – 300 metres long and 220 metres wide – with an interior field
of honour referring to an oversized hall of pillars. The college became an academy,
the Reichsakademie für Leibesübung.

Meanwhile, plans for changes to the stadium were under way. In 1925 the
DRAfL began considering a modernization of the stadium and commissioned
Werner March[9] to create a draft proposal, which he produced in 1927. The stadium
was to be adapted to the latest hygienic standards and expanded for an audience

of 80,000. The design proposed by March was presented to the IOC at its 1930 Berlin Session. It called for deepening the stadium and expanding the stands to hold 70,000 spectators. The swimming pool would also be relocated to the narrow eastern end of the stadium where it would be accessed from a prominent plaza. At the Deutsche Bauausstellung 1931, March displayed a model for the conversion of the stadium. A few months later, he presented his proposals to the DOA. When the approval was given for hosting the 1936 Olympic Games, March was commissioned to plan the stadium.

On the day the Olympic Organizing Committee was founded, one week before Hitler was appointed *Reichskanzler*, the committee decided to avoid costly new construction and to expand the existing stadium instead. That strategy, however, did not meet with the approval of the National Socialists. Their influence led to a complete alteration of the plans in favour of a new stadium. In the spring of 1934 the Deutsches Stadion was torn down to make way for the construction of the Olympic Stadium.

From earliest conceptions, the Deutsches Stadion was intended to be the central sports venue of the Olympic Games. Until October 1933, considerations were centred on the modernization of the stadium, but Hitler then decided that the core of the events would be the Reichssportfeld,[10] with an Olympic stadium built on the site of the Deutsches Stadion itself.[11] A tour of the construction site by Hitler on 5 October 1933 accompanied by Frick, the Interior Minister, and Lewald marked the beginning of a phase in which Werner March's construction and urban planning design were broadly overhauled in line with the Nazis' demand for symbolic presence. Hitler ordered the demolition of the horse racecourse and the generous expansion of the sports sites. He wanted the 'largest stadium, the largest assembly field, the largest open-air theatre' (Schmidt, 1992, p. 30). He also intended to relocate the traditional May festival from the field in Tempelhof to the Reichssportfeld.

In the newspaper *Vossische Zeitung* for 6 October 1933, Hitler explained, 'German sport needs something gigantic' (Schäche, 1991, 2001). After DRAfL was disbanded and the racecourse was acquired, the German Reich was the sole owner of the land and developer of the sports facilities. By 9 October 1933, Werner March[12] had revised his designs, but they did not yet contain the large assembly field that Hitler wanted. Therefore, the meeting on 10 October 1933 at Hitler's offices with Frick and Goebbels as well as Lewald and Diem did not lead to the desired approval but instead to further planning decisions by Hitler on the construction and layout of the stadium. He demanded an assembly field for 500,000 people (Maifeld) and an open-air theatre for 200,000 spectators (called the Dietrich-Eckart-Bühne).

By December 1933, March had created three variants that differed particularly in their layout and size of the assembly grounds. All designs assumed that the racecourse would be abandoned, but the existing buildings and the surrounding park-like facilities would remain intact. Furthermore, March maintained the development of the Sportforum, the Graditzer Allee, the Schwarzbergallee (as the main entrance to the grounds), and the S-Bahn train line as the southern boundary of the grounds in all his alternative designs. Invariably, the assembly field was west of the stadium and the open-air theatre was in the Murellen ravine (Murellenschlucht).

At another meeting with Hitler on 14 December 1933, Werner March presented a solution using modified plans and a scale-model. They showed the double–axis plan that was finally implemented: an east–west axis which emerged from the Schwarzbergallee containing the sequence of Olympic Plaza (Olympischer Platz), the stadium, the Maifeld and the Fuehrer Tower (Führerturm); and a north-south axis that integrated the street Rennbahnstrasse and led to the central stadium (figure 13.1). This proposal had an assembly field of 107,000 square metres and was estimated to hold 150,000 people.[13] Werner March received approval to start construction according to this solution. The estimated costs had since increased from 2.6 million Reichsmarks to more than 36 million.[14]

The Reichssportfeld was opened on 23 and 24 May 1936 with the central complex of the Olympic Stadium, Maifeld (figure 13.2) and swimming stadium (figure 13.3), as well as the riding arena, the hockey stadium, the Sportforum with a number of sports and training areas, the open-air theatre, a tennis stadium with various tennis courts, a dance space, a firing range, residence halls, parking lots and areas for small businesses. With the Reichssportfeld, March had effectively designed the first Olympic park complex in history (Wimmer, 1976, p. 192).[15] He included the spatial design and the landscaping considerations of earlier

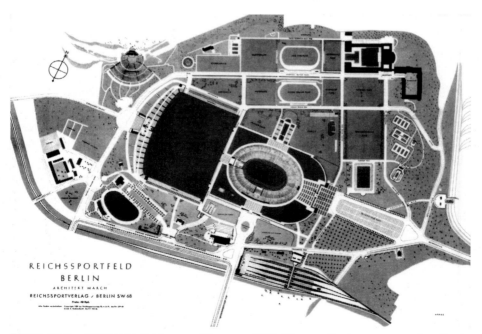

Figure 13.1. Reichssportfeld, map of the area, 1937. (*Source*: Contemporary postcard)

Figure 13.2.   Maifeld, 1936. (*Source*: Umminger, 1976, S. 208)

Figure 13.3.   Swimming pool, 2005. (*Photo*: Monika Meyer)

developments, the existing usable facilities, optimal transport access for the entire facility and for individual sports venues, and the 'construction plan elevated to a gigantic level by the developer' (Eckert and Schäche, 1992). Moreover:

> March's overall design presents a clear arrangement of space and a dominant east–
> west axis that the broad spaces and expansiveness of the facilities are arranged along.
> The grounds are differentiated by the staggered height contours of the accompanying

sports facilities that are adapted to the available situation on site. The integration of the *Reichssportfeld* into the landscape is accomplished on one hand with the natural effects of plants on the scarce areas available between the sports sites and on the other hand with the expansion of the green belt leading around the grounds to achieve the desired bridging affect into the adjacent wooded areas. (*Ibid.*)

Instructed to abandon the planned renovation of the German Stadium in favour of building a new Olympic stadium, Werner March looked for inspiration to the historical models of Antiquity, such as the Coliseum in Rome, and to contemporary stadium structures, such as the Olympic stadium in Amsterdam. In addition, the basis for his design was also formed by considerations of view and of organizing how to empty the stadium.[16] March proposed an oval stadium, the longitudinal axis of which would run along an east–west line. As in the Deutsches Stadion, the interior space would be a sunken area. This made it possible to place the middle level of the stadium at the level of the surrounding terrain, which significantly improved the development of the stadium. The tiers of seating towards the west were non-continuous so that the marathon gate opened to a view of the bell tower on the Maifeld and created a monumental entry into the stadium.

Though the stadium's shape was obviously a matter for debate, there were serious arguments about the exterior between Hitler and Speer[17] on one side and Werner March on the other. After Hitler toured the stadium grounds and viewed a test section of the façade on 31 October 1934, he expressed his irritation about the thin abutments and the missing stone coverings. The contrasts between March's contemporary architectural perception and Speer's powerful and forceful views could no longer be bridged, and so in February 1935 March was relieved of his decision-making responsibilities for the styling of the stadium.[18] Despite this interference into his designs, Werner March received the gold medal for the Reichssportfeld and the silver medal for the stadium in architectural competitions in 1936; the 'Grand Prix' of the Paris World Exhibition in 1937; as well as other honours and medals abroad.

The Maifeld was west of the Olympic Stadium and was laid out as an assembly field, measuring 395 metres by 295 metres, which would accommodate 180,000 people. A set of stairs separated the lower-lying field from the level of the stadium. Four towers and four large sculptures emphasized the spatial differentiation. Banks of earth form the boundaries on the north and south sides of the field. On the west side, the monumental east–west axis of the Reichssportfeld reached its end point at the stands with the Führer and speaker stand and the bell tower. In the middle of the stands, the bell tower rose over the three-storey structure that gave access to the field and the tower as well as the Langemarckhalle on the middle storey. Construction of this 50 metres by 10 metres hall of honour for athletes who died in the First World War is attributed to Carl Diem who himself participated in the battle at Langemarck as a soldier and brought soil from the German soldiers' cemetery back to Berlin.

The open-air Dietrich-Eckart-Bühne theatre,[19] which Goebbels demanded, represented an 'important instrument for fulfilling cultural duties of the people and mental and political promotion to the nation' (Schmidt, 1992, p. 60). He wanted 'to fill the German people … with a national will in the sense of National Socialism' (*Ibid.*). As in many other locations in Germany, a large theatre was to be created here for Germanic festivals of song and dedication and other political events. Goebbels wanted the theatre to hold 500,000 to 1,000,000 people. However, March never proposed a structure that even approached such numbers. His first proposal was for an arena for 35,000 spectators; in the end, it was built for 20,000 people. In the 30 metre-deep natural basin of the Murellenschlucht, March created an open-air theatre in the image of the Theatre of Epidauros from Antiquity.

In the final designs, the swimming stadium was along the cross axis on the north side of the stadium. Two grandstands, facing one another with a total crowd capacity of 17,000, were fitted with two watchtower-like staircases and framed the pool for swimming and diving. In contrast to the Olympic stadium, the swimming stadium remained largely free from interference from Hitler and Speer.[20] Noticeably, there was no Führer or speaker podium in this stadium. Elsewhere, Werner also integrated a hockey stadium for 18,000 spectators into the sports sites of the Sportforum.

A number of the other sports venues in Berlin are also worth mentioning. The Deutschlandhalle (Germany Hall) on the Berlin trade fair grounds (Messegelände), near the Eichkamp S-Bahn station, was built for 20,000 spectators and was the first hall ever built for Olympic Games. For the rowing competitions, the existing facility on the Langer See in Berlin-Grünau was expanded and a stage was added. At the Avus automobile racecourse, the Münster architect Clemens Schürmann built a velodrome.

The Olympic Village

During the first discussions of the spatial organization of the Olympics, Werner March had intended that the military grounds in Döberitz, about 15 kilometres west of the Olympic Stadium, should become the site of the Olympic Village. This huge area was located between Spandau and Wustermark, Falkensee and Potsdam. There were large barracks on the avenue Hamburger Chaussee and a parade ground further south. On 28 March 1933, the Organizing Committee asked Reichsminister General Field Marshal von Blomberg to make the Döberitz Barracks available for use as the Olympic Village. There were 280 rooms available in the officers' barracks. However, the head of the Wehrmacht Office, General von Reichenau, who was himself interested in sport and the Olympic Games, made the further suggestion to use part of the training area north of the Hamburger Chaussee to build a separate Olympic Village. This suggestion was accepted at the site tour that took place on 7 November 1933.

On 26 April 1934, the Organizing Committee gave the *Reichswehr* the public memorandum entitled 'Olympic Village' with the request to begin the necessary measures. From that point, the Reichswehr acted as the developer of the Olympic Village. It commissioned Werner March to propose a draft scheme for building the facility. He then founded a consortium of architects including Dr Georg Steinmetz, who was responsible for the residential buildings, Walter March, in charge of the shared facilities, and Heinrich Wiepking-Jürgensmann, responsible for landscaping. The implemented design had an organic urban quality (figure 13.4). There was an entry plaza along the Hamburger Chaussee that enabled traffic to flow freely underneath the freeway. The reception halls that formed almost a quarter-circle bordered the area on the northwest. The Village extended from this entry area along streets that followed the edges of a valley floor. The individual residential buildings followed the natural contour lines and enclosed green 'village commons'. At the end of the valley, the businesses and dining halls were housed in the Haus der Nationen (House of Nations). The grounds were marked by the existing trees, as well as a hilly topography, brooks and a small lake. In addition, the Village had a swimming hall and a sports hall, as well as a Finnish

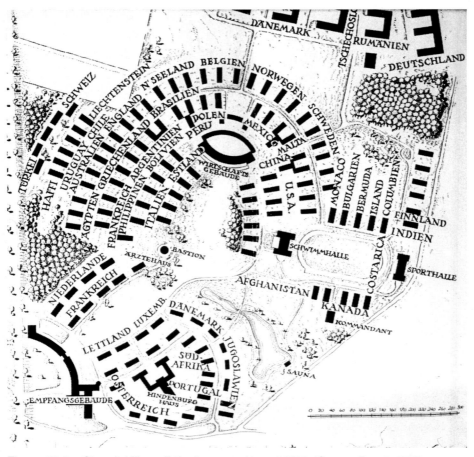

Figure 13.4. Olympic Village, Döberitz, general layout 1936. (*Source*: Troost, 1938)

sauna at the lake. The scattered settlement of one-storey bungalows in an almost idyllic and attractively set landscape met with general approval.[21] In February 1936 the Village had to be expanded to the neighbouring Flak barracks in order to house the surprisingly high number of registered athletes. The completed Village was handed over on 10 April 1936 (see also Chapter 8 above).

Ceremonial Aspects

The Berlin Olympic Games were characterized by an unprecedented level of ritualization. This change originated not only with the Nazi rulers but also with the German sports officials who were in contact and agreement with the IOC during their preparations. In this spirit, Carl Diem had the idea in 1931 of a torch relay from ancient Olympia to each location of the Games – a ritual that has been a permanent part of the Opening Ceremony of the Olympics since Berlin 1936. In 1932 there was a competition for an Olympic anthem. On 31 July 1933, Pierre de Coubertin met Carl Diem and determined that Beethoven's chorus on Schiller's ode 'An die Freude' would be an element of the opening ceremony. The performance of the 'Olympic Youth' festival written by Carl Diem was planned. On 20 October 1934, Richard Strauss finished composing his Olympic anthem with lyrics by Robert Lubahn. This was presented to Hitler on 29 March 1935.

The opening day of the Games was designed as a day-long stage production about Adolf Hitler, Nazi Germany and the Olympic Games. The day began with a reveille concert for the IOC in front of the Hotel Adlon, on the avenue Unter den Linden. After a celebration by the National-Socialist Youth in the Lustgarten, the arrival of the Olympic flame was celebrated by 28,000 members of the Hitler Youth, participants of the international youth camp and a group of student athletes. At the same time, there were school sports events at seventy playgrounds and sports facilities throughout Berlin. Hitler held a reception for the IOC in the Reichskanzler-Palais and rode from there with members of the IOC, the Organizing Committee and representatives of the government and the NSDAP party to the Reichssportfeld. In an unprecedented ceremony, this group entered the Olympic Stadium through the marathon staircase, processed together and took their place in the honorary boxes to the sounds of Richard Wagner's *Huldigungsmarsch*. As noted in the *Deutsche Olympiade Kalender*: 'In this way Hitler held the attention of the spectators for several minutes. He also benefited from the form of entry into the stadium for officials and honoured guests that was already used at previous Games' (quoted in Borges *et al.*, 1995, p. 273).

Subsequent Usage

The fate of the Olympic complex at Berlin makes a fascinating story in the light of current interest in legacy, with its destiny inextricably interwoven with the advent and aftermath of war, the partition of the city and its eventual reunification. In the plans for 'Berlin, the City of Colleges', the Reichssportfeld represented the central assembly and sports grounds. The urban area on both sides of the Heerstrasse was to have a complete re-configuration with large ring roads and spokes, but these plans were never implemented (see also Matzerath, 1984, pp. 308–311). In 1938, parts of the tunnel system were converted to bunkers and a manufacturing facility for anti-aircraft weapon fuses. In the period before and during the war, various large athletic and political events were held on the grounds and in the Olympic Stadium. The International Olympic Institute under the direction of Carl Diem moved into the buildings of the Deutsches Sportforum. Most of its activities ended after it was severely damaged by bombing in 1943.

On 26 June 1945, Diem composed a public memorandum in Berlin for the continued use of the Reichssportfeld. He described it as a 'People's park, symbolic German sports site, central German place of learning, practice grounds for greater Berlin and a central seat of administration of sport'. Essentially, it should continue to be used as it had been previously, but the administrative area was reduced and the settlement of the Friedrich-Wilhelm-Universität was suggested (Schmidt, 1992, p. 331). In June 1945, the stadium was again being used for practical purposes, with the swimming stadium in operation and available to the general public. This short phase of opening the grounds ended in July 1945 when the British Army requisitioned the Reichssportfeld. Henceforth, the facility was made accessible to the public only partially and in phases, transferring the Olympic Stadium, the swimming stadium with the Frauenplatz, the riding grounds and the hockey area to the Magistrat (city council) of Greater Berlin on 22 June 1949. From 1963 onwards, the stadia came under the administration of the Land (region) of Berlin.

The main facilities of the Reichssportfeld have been registered landmarks since 1966, but there have been numerous changes to meet changing needs. The Olympic Stadium has undergone a series of renovations and conversions since 1949; the most extensive being its partial covering, to a design by the architect Friedrich Wilhelm Krahe, for the 1974 FIFA World Cup. The swimming stadium also underwent a series of modernizations and structural changes. The most comprehensive were the measures for the 1978 World Swimming Championships when more pools were built in the surrounding green spaces. The theatre, known today as the Waldbühne, saw the installation of an open-air movie theatre in 1951, with the war-destroyed stage area rebuilt in 1961. In 1982 a tent roof structure designed by Wolfgang Noack was constructed over the stage, making it a venue for large concerts. Public access to the Maifeld, as well as the eastern entry zone of the stadium, was only granted for specific events. Initially after 1945 the shrine to the fallen soldiers and the bell tower lay in ruins, with the remains of the bell tower blown up for safety reasons in 1947. Both were rebuilt between 1960 and 1962, again under the direction of Werner March, although a lively debate broke out about the use of the Langemarckhalle. From 1988 to 1990, a sports centre (Horst-

Korber-Sportzentrum) was built along the Glockenturmstrasse according to plans devised by the architectural firm of Langhof, Hänni and Meerstein. It contains a regional performance centre for various types of sport such as handball, hockey and volleyball.

The British Forces installed their Berlin headquarters in all other areas, covering the entire Sportforum and the tennis stadium. These areas were inaccessible to the public and lay outside the authority of any German planning body. In 1956, the Haus des Deutschen Sports, the Friesenhaus and the gymnastics hall were rebuilt. The rebuilding preserved the outward appearance, but adapted the buildings' interiors to meet the needs of the British administration. Various buildings of the British Army, unconnected with sports, were also erected on the grounds.

Further Bids

In 1990, the treaty among the Allies, the reunification of the two German republics and the reuniting of the two halves of Berlin, provided the opportunity for a comprehensive use of the former Reichssportfeld. In Berlin, support quickly grew among the public for the idea of celebrating the beginning of a new epoch in world history by hosting the 2000 Olympic Games. They also recognized the opportunity of renovating the stadium with the financial means that would no doubt be made available for hosting the Games.

For the Olympic bid, the FPB (*Freie Planungsgruppe*), was commissioned to draft a spatial design. By October 1990, the Berlin Senate had defined the basic principles of the plan. These included the idea that the Reichssportfeld and the Olympic Stadium would be the location for the Opening and Closing Ceremonies and the competitions in track and field, football, baseball, hockey, modern pentathlon and water polo. The Olympic Village would be built in a neighbouring wooded area in Ruhleben. The unique feature of these plans was their inclusion of other existing sports facilities in the western and eastern parts of the city. In its bid, the FPB linked its proposed expansion of the northern line of the S-Bahn ring into an Olympic Express with its scheme for modernizing the sports venues near the northern line for the Olympic Games. This scheme would have been the first time in the history of the Olympics that a decentralized layout for the Games would be tied effectively to the building of a public transport system usable after the Games. These plans, however, were shelved in 1993 when the IOC awarded the 2000 Olympic Games to Sydney (see also Alberts, 2009). In 2014 a further attempt at an Olympic bid was initiated; this time for the 2024 Games. The concept was based on reusing existing sports venues and buildings. However, the DOSB (Deutscher Olympischer Sportbund) favoured Hamburg (Grohmann, 2015), although lack of public support in the referendum of November 2015 led to the withdrawal of Hamburg's candidature.

The failure to gain the 2000 nomination had completely changed the outlook facing both the Land of Berlin, which held the rights of use of the Reichssportfeld, and for the German state, the landowner. By losing the bid for the Games, they also lost the opportunity to finance at least part of the significant renovation tasks with a profitable event. After the British forces left Berlin according to the Treaty of 1994, Berlin had the additional burden of having the Haus des Deutschen Sports and the Sportforum again available for other uses.

The essential aspect of all thinking about using the Reichssportfeld and the stadia was the restoration and conversion costs as well as the historical significance of the facilities. The costs of renovating the Reichssportfeld were estimated at about €5 billion, but the financial situation of the City of Berlin and the German state was extremely strained. From that perspective, restoration without financing from revenues was hardly imaginable. Possible plans for public facilities included a recreational area, a historical park or a sports facility, but none of these could be financed. Officials and politicians then considered how commercial uses might improve returns. Basic uses under consideration, such as an amusement park, hotel, shopping centre, residential area or office space, would increase the visitor numbers, but additional music events were complicated by the noise problems. As almost all the buildings and a large part of the open spaces were registered landmarks, it would be more difficult to promote the grounds to private investors.

The Olympic Stadium posed particular problems. Complaints from international sports associations about its shabby and insufficient facilities and its structural condition meant that its long-term use could no longer be guaranteed. However, the award in 1998 of a different mega-event, the 2006 FIFA World Cup, to the German national football association provided an opportunity for a full review given that the Olympic Stadium in Berlin would be its most important venue. On the basis of various appraisals and an architectural competition, Berlin and the German Federal government decided to renovate the Olympic Stadium according to the plans of the Hamburg-based practice gmp (Architekten von Gerkan, Marg und Partner). Construction work was completed in 2004 at a cost of €242 million, of which Berlin funded €46 million (figure 13.5).

With regard to other major installations, the Deutsches Sportforum was again placed under the administration of the Federal government in September 1994, and was open on a limited basis for sports clubs. Today, the fields and facilities of the Sportforum are used for professional and amateur sports alike, and the diverse activities of a wide variety of clubs define the grounds. For its part, the Olympic Village was shaped by its long association with military purposes. As originally intended, the Wehrmacht used the Olympic Village after the Olympic Games. The Soviet Red Army requisitioned the facilities from 1945 to 1991 and used them to house Soviet soldiers and their families. Very few of the athletes' residences remained. Instead, a large number of concrete tower blocks of up to five storeys were built, although integration into the landscape remained largely intact. The community building, the Hindenburghaus, the sports and swimming halls and the original buildings intended for athletes from Switzerland, Turkey and the USA were all still maintained and used. When the Russian troops left in 1991,

Figure 13.5. Olympic stadium, view from Olympischer Platz, 2005. (*Source*: gmp, Marcus Bredt, Berlin)

the Village was empty and succumbed to disrepair, looting and vandalism. The swimming hall was destroyed by arson in 1993.

Since 1994, the regional development society of the Land Brandenburg has attempted to develop the entire 120-hectares barracks area into a residential neighbourhood, albeit with little success. There was discussion of using the Haus der Nationen as a hotel or office space, but no definite use is in sight for the Hindenburghaus, which was the cultural centre of the Olympic Village. The lake also has been mostly filled in, although plans exist for its recreation if circumstances allow.

Conclusion

The facilities in Berlin are some of the most impressive structures of the Olympic Games of the modern era, although the area had only a limited effect on the development of the city.[22] The choice of location for the Games was determined by personal relationships and financial problems, not urban design or overall considerations of city interests. The chosen site, however, was satisfactory in many ways for implementing a sufficient area, quality of development and a uniquely designed sports venue for the politically symbolic intentions of the time. The Reichssportfeld was designed as a venue for mass events in such a way that different events could be held separately and simultaneously at different points on the grounds.

Werner March's designs had significant urban and landscaping qualities. It is an urban planning accomplishment still recognized today that he integrated a facility capable of holding almost 400,000 people at a time into the pastoral landscape of Grunewald between the Havel and Spree rivers while overcoming issues concerning travel by large numbers of people to and from the site. The extension of the plans into monumental proportions had its basis in Hitler's intention to create the prototype of a venue for National Socialist assemblies. Such abuse of the Games, the athletes, the spectators and the Olympic ideal for the propagandistic goals of the Nazi government was indissolubly linked to this kind of forceful architecture.

The Olympic Village is also unique in the history of the Olympic Games, as it was built by the military and was intended for military purposes after the Games. The layout and use of the Village are contradictory. The almost idyllic setting is still recognizable today, with the Haus der Nationen strongly resembling the organic architecture of Alvar Aalto. This is in direct contrast to the monumental architecture of the Olympic grounds and the intentional use of the Village after the Games as barracks. It is distressing in retrospect to see the similarities when comparing the Village entrance and the Olympians' housing with the barracks at Dachau, Auschwitz and Majdanek. Just as unsettling is the knowledge that the peaceful co-existence of nations took place in such barracks.

The thought of again holding the Olympic Games for 2000 at the former Reichssportfeld seemed logical but still provoked widespread protest. Issues of dealing with and re-using the architectural legacy of Nazism proved to be a significant problem for the public. There was also the concern that the necessary investment for both parts of Berlin to grow together again would instead be used for symbolic building projects. Cost remained a source of public disquiet in the face of proposals for the 2014 Games. However, part of the 2000 bid's designs was completed. The northern line of the S-Bahn ring was made operational again which significantly improved the infrastructure and traffic connections for the northern part of Berlin. Individual sports facilities were modernized or rebuilt and the planned Olympic Village on the inlet in Rummelsburg (Rummelsburger Bucht) was partially completed as a waterfront housing development with a mixture of residences and services.

Notes

1. Carl Diem (1882–1962) was organizer and patron of German athletics from 1903 onwards. He was the General Secretary for the 1916 Olympic Games; a co-founder of the German College of Physical Education (Deutsche Hochschule für Leibesübungen) in 1929; the General Secretary of the Organizing Committee for the 1936 Olympic Games from 1933 to 1937; the Director of the Reichssportfeld in 1936; Director of the International Olympic Institute in Berlin from 1938 to 1945; founder of the German College of Physical Education (Deutsche Hochschule für Leibesübungen) in Cologne in 1947; and secretary of the newly founded German National Olympic Committee from 1950 to 1952. From 1906 onwards, Diem composed reports and wrote books about the Olympic Games. At the end of July 1912 Carl Diem's book *Die Olympischen Spiele 1912* was published as the first Olympic book in German (Diem, 1912). Three decades later, in 1942, he published his three-volume work *Olympische Flamme* (Diem, 1942).

2. A winter sports festival which had been planned for February 1916 in the Black Forest and Berlin was not held. As a substitute for these games, there were national Olympic Games in Amsterdam from 24 June to 3 September 1916, and an international sports festival was staged in Stockholm on 8 July 1916 for Scandinavian athletes.

3.   During this time the idea of holding national Olympic Games was formed. Such games were held in Berlin in 1922, in Cologne in 1926, in Breslau in 1930, in Nuremberg in 1934, and in Breslau again in 1938. The Breslau games in 1938 were also the first German gymnastics and sports festival (*Deutsches Turn- und Sportfest*).

4.   The German Olympic Committee (DOA) was constituted in February 1926 as a sub-committee of the national committee for physical fitness (DRAfL – *Deutscher Reichsausschuss für Leibesübungen*), which originated in the DRAfOS.

5.   Theodor Lewald (1860–1947) was the Secretary of State in the Interior Ministry and was the acting National Commissioner (*Reichskommissar*) in 1903 for the World's Fair of 1904 in St Louis. Starting in 1919, he was the President of the DRAfL and by 1933 he was the President of the Organizing Committee for the 1936 Olympic Games. In 1924 Lewald was appointed to the IOC at the behest of Coubertin and, in 1925, he was appointed to the Executive Board of the IOC. In 1938 he resigned from the IOC. Lewald was publicly reviled by the Nazis as a 'half-Jew' and was forced in 1933 to give up the headship of the DRAfL.

6.   The National Committee for Physical Fitness (DRAfL) originated in the DRAfOS in 1917 (see also note 4 above).

7.   Director of the newly created Ministry for 'People's Enlightenment and Propaganda' (*Reichsministerium für Volksaufklärung und Propaganda*).

8.   Otto March (1845–1913) lived and worked in Berlin. After his studies at the Berlin Academy for Construction (Berliner Bauakademie), he began a career as an independent architect in addition to his job in the public sector. His proposals influenced his contemporaries and later architects such as Ernst May, Walter Hegemann and his son, Werner March.

9.   Werner March (1894–1976), son of architect Otto March, became well known due to his proposals for the Reichssportfeld in Berlin for the 1936 Olympic Games. After his studies in architecture in Dresden and Berlin, he worked as an independent architect starting in 1925. In 1936 March became director of the Technical Institute for the Construction of Practice Venues (Technisches Institut für Übungsstättenbau) at the National Academy for Physical Fitness (Reichsakademie für Leibesübungen). In Germany, he performed various tasks of urban planning and construction of large structures until he volunteered for military service in 1940. In 1946, March worked as a planner for urban history in Minden. In 1953, March became Ordinarius of the Professorship for Urban Planning and Housing at the Technische Universität Berlin. In the 1950s and 1960s he received international contracts for the construction of stadia in countries such as Egypt and Greece.

10.   March's plans for the Reichssportfeld and especially the influence of Hitler, Goebbels and Speer are described comprehensively in Schmidt (1992). Wolfgang Schäche (1991) holds a significantly different opinion regarding the disagreements between Hitler and Speer on one side and March on the other. 'To that extent, the almost bizarre thesis of interpreting the Olympic Stadium with its architectural contradictions as documentation of rivalling ideologies (contemporary architect versus regressive position of Hitler and Speer) is therefore to be approached with extreme scepticism'.

11.   Other sites for the Olympic events were dispersed throughout the city, with the sailing competitions held in Kiel.

12.   As the architect, he was responsible for the urban planning and the architecture of the grounds; Heinrich Wiepking-Jürgensmann was responsible for the landscape architecture.

13.   It is worth noting that despite the enormous pressure placed on him, March knew how to create the dimensions of the Reichssportfeld facilities so that they still maintained a human scale.

14.   On 15 December 1933, Hitler was quoted in the newspaper *Völkischer Beobachter* as saying: 'On this day I have given my final approval for the start and the completion of the structures on the stadium grounds. Germany will thereby have a sports venue unequalled by any other in the world' (cited in Hoffmann, 1993, p. 17).

15.   Eckert and Schäche (1992) on this topic wrote: 'The Reichssportfeld facility in this design presents a sports complex designed by function and purpose that already was developed in the 1920s. In this context, note the following path-breaking facilities: the Müngersdorf sports complex in Cologne by Fritz Encke (1920–1923), the Zentralsportpark in Frankfurt am Main by Max Bromme (1921–1925), the Volkspark with the "Rote Erde" stadium in Dortmund by city planning commissioner (Stadtbaurat) Strobel (1925–1927) or the Sportpark Tempelhof by Ottokar Wagler in Berlin'.

16.   See also the text by Werner March as published in Schmidt (1992, pp. 42 ff and 64 ff).

17.   Architect Albert Speer (1905–1981) was one of Hitler's closest confidants which placed him in an exceptional position. The dictator appreciated Speer's unconditional loyalty and the ability with which he created large construction projects in short amounts of time. Hitler saw Speer as the artist and visionary that he himself would like to have been. Beginning in 1932 Speer received construction contracts from the Nazis and in 1934 became the most influential architect in the Third Reich. In 1938 he was appointed as the general building inspector (*Generalbausinspekteur*) for the capital city of the Reich, Berlin. Among his most important projects are the monumental structures and productions for the Reich party conventions in Nuremberg, the chancellery (*Reichskanzlei*), the German pavilion for the Paris World Exposition in 1937 and the plans for the conversion of Berlin into 'Germania', capital city of the world, with numerous monumental structures. In 1942 Hitler appointed him to be the Minister for Weapons and Ammunition (*Reichsminister für Bewaffnung und Munition*), and in 1943 he became the Minister for Armament and War Production (*Reichsminister für Rüstung und Kriegsproduktion*). Speer's organizing of the war economy was based on using forced labour and prisoners from concentration camps. In the Nuremberg Trials in 1946 he was sentenced for war crimes and crimes against humanity. After his release he published his memoirs (Speer, 1969), in which he attempted to portray himself as a 'respectable Nazi' and 'misled citizen'. However, more recent publications reveal his role as one of the most brutal leaders of the regime.

18.   Schmidt (1992, p. 46) continued: 'The overall contemporary architectural design for the Olympic Stadium is no longer recognizable today. The stylistic adjustments made by architect Albert Speer during the realization planning continued to alter the outward appearance of the stadium. Almost all of March's intended construction elements and wall surfaces made of nidged concrete were covered with shell limestone. The natural stone material was intended to express the values of simplicity, durability, hardiness, being down-to-earth, greatness and power that were propagated by the National Socialists'.

19.   Naming the theatre after the founder of the anti-Semitic newspaper *Auf gut deutsch* and the first editor of the *Völkischer Beobachter* was an indication of the Nazi orientation of the theatre. See also Schmidt (1992, p. 60).

20.   Hitler admitted in 1935 that: 'He was certainly not satisfied with everything happening at the Reichssportfeld, but he did not have enough time that year to attend to such matters' (quoted in Schmidt, 1992, p. 62).

21.   From today's perspective, the history of the Village's origins and its intended use after the Olympic Games as a military facility are irreconcilable with the Olympic message of peace. The entrance buildings of the facilities and athletes' barracks are macabre, as they appear in an only slightly adapted form of the Nazi concentration camps.

22.   A comparative evaluation of the urban planning effects of large events on the locations where they are held is explored by the author in her work *Der planbare Nutzen: Stadtentwicklung durch Weltausstellungen und Olympische Spiele* (Meyer-Künzel, 2002). The urban planning for events is documented and evaluated in the context of each political, social and cultural situation. The work therefore compiles a cross section of the planning goals of large events, their realization and their long-term use after the Games and explains them with extensive pictures and planning materials.

Chapter 14

Mexico City 1968

Michael Barke

The torch for the 1968 Games was lit at Olympia in mid-August 1968. It then began a journey that moved from Greece and circulated to European sites with Olympic and Mexican connections. These included Genoa (Italy), the birthplace of Christopher Columbus, Palos (Spain), where Columbus's expedition started in 1492, and Barcelona, a major seat of the Spanish empire. From Europe the torch was conveyed by sea to San Salvador, the site of Columbus's first landing in the Americas, then on to Vera Cruz where four additional torches were lit. The five torches, echoing the five Olympic rings, then made their way to Mexico City by different routes. On 11 October, they arrived at the pyramid of the Moon at Teotihuacán to the north of Mexico City, where the Aztec ritual of New Fire – celebrating the resurgence of life and the triumph of light over darkness – was re-enacted. On the evening of 12 October, Norma Enriqueta Basilio, a 20 year old runner from Baja California, lit the Olympic flame; the first woman in Olympic history to be given the honour.

Representations of Mexico's history featured strongly in the ceremonies leading up to the Games, but the intention to engage fully with the present was symbolized in the choice of a young female to light the flame. She 'represented a new kind of Mexican, tall, thin and beautiful, contrasting the older generation that she called short and fat' (quoted in Witherspoon, 2003, p. 113). Although Mexico's rich cultural history was not ignored during the Nineteenth Olympiad, it was reinterpreted in a variety of ways, emphasizing national unity. More than anything, from the Mexican perspective, the project was about modernity. The President of the Organizing Committee, the distinguished architect, Pedro Ramirez Vázquez, later commented 'of least importance was the Olympic competition; the records fade away, but the image of a country does not' (quoted in Rivas and Sarhandi, 2005). Despite the efforts of the political elite from the late nineteenth century onwards (Tenorio-Trillo, 1996), the organizers of the Mexican Olympics – both sporting and cultural – were well aware that much of the rest of the world saw the country in Third World terms and their response was driven by the need to counter such stereotypes at almost every turn. Thus, issues of international prestige were never very far from the minds of the chief protagonists (Brewster and Brewster, 2009).

Mexico City 1968 remains one of the most memorable meetings of modern times – and perhaps more because of non-sporting events than some undeniably spectacular sporting achievements. However, along with Berlin 1936 and Moscow 1980, the Mexico City Games demonstrated overtly the political context of the modern Olympics. Whereas the politicization of the Berlin games could easily be dismissed as an aberration of Nazi Germany, Mexico City was more significant in that no single ideology could be held responsible for events and the manifestations of politicization were apparent in many different ways, some obvious, others more subtle. Some were internal to the host country; many others were products of issues and pressures external to Mexico. After 1968, it became impossible to deny the inextricable linkage between sport and politics.

The Mexico City Games were also highly significant in terms of the development of the relationship between the Olympics and television (Wenn, 1993, 1995). From this juncture, the way that the Games were 'packaged' and 'sold' would be as important as the actual Games events themselves. Indeed, it has been claimed that Mexico City 1968 'sticks in the mind because the originality and cogency of its system of communication converted it into a paradigm of modern graphic and event design' (Rivas and Sarhandi, 2005). Yet with regard to the role of television, the selective framing of events was foreshadowed at the Opening Ceremony, when the cameras studiously avoided the massed ranks of heavily armed security forces surrounding the stadium.

Another notable feature of the 1968 Games was that they were the first held within Latin America or, more significantly, in a 'developing' country. This was a remarkable choice that requires explanation. How did Mexico manage to win the contest to stage the 1968 Olympics? Having done so, how did a relatively poor developing country set about staging the Games in infrastructural terms? This process, itself inevitably immensely complicated and expensive to accomplish, has deterred many cities and countries from entering the competition to host the Games. How then did Mexico and its capital city accomplish this feat and at what cost? The answers raise further questions about how the Games were promoted, not least to the Mexican people and citizens of Mexico City. Questions of how the country and city presented themselves to the outside world are fundamental here. Finally, with the benefit of hindsight and nearly five decades of reflection we can ask what the 1968 Olympics really meant in their wider context, that is, beyond the sports fields and arenas. This series of issues is still debated in the historiography of modern Mexico (Brewster and Brewster, 2009), but it is perhaps insufficiently recognized that the answers may be very different from an 'internal' perspective than from an 'external' one.

Winning the Games

Answers to these questions begin by noting that the Mexican elite had, from the late nineteenth century, sought to portray their country in modern terms and to engage with international cosmopolitanism (Tenorio-Trillo, 1996). Participation in World's Fairs, in the Olympic Games and, eventually, presenting a bid to host those Games represented a natural progression in nation building and representation. Adolfo López Mateos, President of Mexico from 1959 to 1964, took the decision to compete for the Olympic Games of 1968. He continued to be involved after retiring as President, serving on the Committee that organized the Games. Remarkably, López Mateos managed the feat of staying on good terms with the United States while refusing to break ties with Cuba's new revolutionary government. He was also the first Mexican president to travel widely abroad (Riding, 1987) in a determined attempt to establish Mexico's international prestige. Mateos saw hosting the Olympic Games as a major step forward in establishing Mexico as a modern nation on the international stage (Krauze, 1997). Although a very different President and with considerably less charisma, Gustavo Díaz Ordaz, his successor from 1964 to 1970, eventually became no less determined that Mexico should host the Games and in a way that would enhance Mexico's international prestige. His inherent authoritarianism and inflexible perspective led him to interpret the student movement of 1968 as a communist-inspired plot to disrupt the Olympics; an interpretation that was almost certainly inaccurate (Zolov, 1999). Nevertheless, it is clear that, in competing to host the 1968 Olympics, national boosterism was placed on the agenda very early in the process.

There were three important components to this strategy. The first was to establish international legitimacy for what was still a single party state. The second was to generate a stronger sense of nationalism while, third, demonstrating the modernity of Mexico. We shall return to these issues later, but what must concern us first is the international scale and the factors operative at this level that led to the first successful Olympic bid made by a developing nation.

Ostensibly, there were considerable objections to Mexico, with doubts being expressed about the country's ability to organize the Olympic Games (Arbena, 1996; C. Brewster, 2010) and, especially, about the altitude issue. Mexico went to great lengths to counter both these objections, having sponsored numerous scientific studies on the effects of altitude, offering to defray the expenses of athletes whilst acclimatizing to conditions in Mexico City and hosting a 'mini-Olympics' in 1967 (Wrynn, 2004). Support on the altitude issue eventually came from a somewhat unexpected quarter in the form of Avery Brundage, President of the IOC who observed: 'The Olympic Games belong to all the world, not the part of it at sea level' (quoted in Guttmann, 1984, p. 123).

Ultimately, the competition to hold the Games, although initially seeming to be formidable, turned out to be not particularly strong. Three other cities competed to host the 1968 Olympics – Detroit, Buenos Aires and Lyon. Detroit had also attempted to host the Games in 1952, 1956, 1960, and 1964 and was to try again – unsuccessfully – in 1972. Despite its long involvement in the bidding process, Detroit's bid in 1968 was lacklustre and revealed weaknesses in the accommodation available, failure to mobilize significant local enthusiasm, and shortcomings in financial arrangements (Zimmerman, 1963). Detroit's bid was not helped by the fact that Los Angeles, only six months before the final vote, had challenged Detroit's bid to represent the United States at the IOC decision-making meeting in Baden-Baden in October 1963 (Anon., 1963). The rival campaigns of Los Angeles and Detroit undoubtedly harmed Detroit's ultimate bid in the eyes of the IOC adjudicators, particularly through Los Angeles pointing out previous Detroit failures and publicly airing its continuing weaknesses (Witherspoon, 2003). The bid from Buenos Aires was widely recognized as weak, lacking in detail or any real sense of enthusiasm and, in the event, only received two votes. Lyon probably represented a greater threat with advantages of governmental support, France's record in hosting previous Olympics, the city's accessibility from Africa and the Middle East, and promises to enlarge the airport and expand an existing stadium from a capacity of 60,000 to 95,000 (Daley, 1963). Lyon's bid was partially undermined by core-periphery rivalries with Paris (Terret, 2004) but also by its 'European' focus. The promotional media campaign was entitled '*Lyon, grande ville européenne*'. Thus, despite Lyon's claims that competing cities used dubious ploys (Michela, 1963) its bid was actually flawed. The Mexican strategy was skilful, determined and enthusiastic and struck many of the right notes with the voting panel, including dealing effectively with the altitude issue (Wrynn, 2004).

Whether by fortune or from subtle appreciation of the international mood, the Mexican bid caught the imagination of the times, presenting a distinctive and appealing image, albeit one with a specific national agenda. Thus, in their presentations (quoted in Witherspoon, 2003, p. 41), Senator Carillo presented the Mexican people as:

> simple, humble, hard-working and honest. They were a determined people who had transformed their nation after the Mexican Revolution, and the Olympics would symbolize the success of that transformation.

and Dr. Eduardo Hay, concluded with:

> We seek the Games not for us, not for our business, but for our youth. That is why we are asking for this. Not to have another title. You can be sure that the Mexican public will be with you with the best of them.

In contrast to Lyon's strategy, the Mexican delegation also exploited Cold War political allegiances to the full with intensive lobbying of the Soviet and related members of the IOC and, of course, its natural allies in the Third World representatives. Through this means, Mexico won support from Latin American, African and Soviet-bloc representatives in order to defeat the main opponents from North America and Europe. An effective bid from a developing country that could demonstrate its capacity to put on the Games was therefore always going to appeal to a large number of the voters in this new international environment. López

Mateos and the Mexican delegation understood this very well. Avery Brundage himself (who had voted for Detroit) commented:

> What helped Mexico was that it is one of the smaller-scale countries, and some members felt they could do more for the Olympic movement by giving encouragement to such a country. (Quoted in Witherspoon, 2003, p. 44)

Hence, its campaign was highly effective and skilfully managed, and in the final analysis Mexico City won the right to stage the 1968 Games because of geopolitical alignments and the prevalent international atmosphere of the 1960s. This atmosphere worked in favour of Mexico in a manner not previously seen and, with the ending of the Cold War, probably unlikely to be repeated.

Yet there was more to Mexico City's bid than politics. Unlike Detroit, Lyon and Buenos Aires, Mexico City could draw on the country's impressive record of accomplishment in hosting major international events, with the capacity to meet most of their accompanying demands. Mexico had staged the 1926 and 1954 Central American and Caribbean Games, the 1955 Pan-American Games when over 2,000 athletes from twenty-two countries attended, the Modern World Pentathlon Championships of 1962 and the National Children and Junior Sports Games of 1961 and 1962. Mexico City itself had numerous and impressive sports facilities and arenas, many of them built recently and publicly funded (Arbena, 1991; Brewster, 2005), a large number of hotels and other visitor facilities, and an apparently dynamic growth-oriented philosophy, albeit one that had yet to engage with contemporary ideas of city-regional planning (Campbell and Wilk, 1986).

The development of these facilities reflected the profound belief of the protagonists of the Mexican Revolution that in the process of nation-building sport could be one of the main instruments through which this could be achieved (McGehee, 1993; Brewster and Brewster, 2010). The Mexican government gradually came to understand the wider significance of sport and participation in international events, especially after the Central American Games of 1926 when 'Mexicans had held what they considered to be their own Olympics' (*Ibid.*, p. 326). Symbolic events, most notably associated with November 20, 'Revolution Day', celebrating Francisco Madero's call to arms in 1910 against the 34-year rule of Porfirio Díaz, were celebrated with parades at which athletes took a prominent place (over 50,000 in 1934) and 'sports that were perceived as modern and western led the way' (Lorey, 1997, p. 51). 'Gradually Mexican cities and towns began to create a nation by acting it out in countless local and regional exhibitions, parades and gatherings' (Tenorio-Trillo, 1996, p. 245). From 1930 the annual 'Revolutionary Games' were inaugurated. Sport, and especially international sport, became not only an opportunity to promote the image of the country abroad but also to provide a unifying focus around which different regions, peoples, and sections of society could rally (Brewster, 2005). 'By the late 1920s regional integration became one of the featured themes of sports displays on November 20' (Lorey, 1997, p. 55) and the subservience of the regions to the centre was symbolized by the ritual relay race from Puebla to Mexico City.[1]

The first major physical manifestation of this desire to use sport as a means of national unification after the chaos of the Mexican Revolution of 1910–1919 was the construction of a National Stadium in May 1924 (McGehee, 1993). In the same year Mexico sent its first group of athletes to the Paris Olympics, although they were privately funded. This participation led directly to Mexico hosting the 1926 Central American Games which, although modest, stimulated an interest in sport more generally. However, it was not until 1932 that a national sport confederation was established with the specific objective of creating 'an integrated nation [composed] of healthy, virile and dynamic men' (quoted in Arbena, 1991, p. 355).

Interest in sport grew rapidly from the 1930s and especially in the post-war years, although an emergent issue at this time was the extent to which Mexico was importing and imitating developed, Western, and especially US sporting activities rather than recognizing its indigenous sporting culture. Inevitably, the former was the preserve – at least initially – of the mainly white middle classes and the meaning of such activities for the *mestizo* and Indian populations was highly contested.

A major boost was provided by the 1955 Pan-American Games, in support of which the government built an Athletes' Village, numerous sporting facilities and distributed over 1.5 million free tickets to the public. Avery Brundage had observed 'the second Pan-American Games will be held in Mexico City in 1955 and new facilities of Olympic calibre are already under construction'. The event was a great success in terms of the facilities and organization and produced a generation of athletics fans in Mexico. The combination of popular support and government ideology, which 'interpreted participation in the Games as an opportunity to express national identification' (Espy, 1979, p. viii), provided a dual impetus for bids to host the world's major sporting events.

Producing the Games

The process of bidding for, and winning, the right to stage the 1968 Olympic Games was integral to a much larger project on the part of the Mexican Government. It was part of a campaign to establish international recognition, to create a stronger sense of nationhood and also to modernize the nation. The Olympic bid and that for the 1970 FIFA World Cup only make sense within this wider context and it is no coincidence that this agenda was driven forward by one of Mexico's most outward looking Presidents. Yet, despite the representation of Mexico as a united, confident, modernizing nation, K. Brewster (2010) has argued that preparations to host the Games demonstrated fundamental insecurities, particularly relating to the way the elite viewed their compatriots. In the view of the former, a public education campaign became necessary before Mexico could become 'fit for foreign consumption' (*Ibid.*, p. 51). This included spending 24 million pesos on renovating squares, the prohibition of street trading in certain parts of the city, 200,000 leaflets distributed on how to be 'a good host', 700 radio and 144 television broadcasts on the same theme, several with the participation of the hugely popular Mexican comic film actor Cantinflas (Mario Moreno). A Chaplinesque figure, Cantinflas had specialized in roles where the 'little man' challenged and exposed the absurdities of officialdom and bureaucracy, but in these Olympic broadcasts he now promoted conformist, 'establishment' views on norms of behaviour.

The production of the Games also had important spatial consequences. Major investments were made in transport and tourism, but these served to reinforce the position of Mexico City as the centralized hub of the country (Nolan and Nolan, 1988; Clancy, 1999). Indeed, despite various attempts to achieve the opposite (Barkin and King, 1970), with some recent checking of urban population growth rates (P.M. Ward, 1998) most political, social and economic processes since the mid twentieth century have served to highlight the concentration of economic and political power in Mexico City.

All the sporting events were held within the city apart from sailing which took place at the Acapulco yacht club (Arbena, 1996). In winning the bid, the Mexican delegation had made much of the fact that, in contrast to their competitor cities, considerable infrastructure was already in place. Nevertheless, there was much more that needed to be done. The basic budget amounted to $84 million of federal spending and $75 million from private sources for projects directly related to the Games, especially the building of the Olympic Village with twenty-nine structures varying from six to ten storeys (Witherspoon, 2003, p. 108). However, this excluded other infrastructure such as a new six-lane motorway linking the main facilities, improved water supply and sewage disposal systems and, controversially, the new subway system. Although promoted as a key modernization project linked to the 1968 Olympics, work on the subway system did not start until 1967 and was only partially opened by 1969.

Ward (1990, p. 217) has argued that in Mexico City, 'the purpose of monuments constructed since the 1960s appears to be one of reinforcement: of the modern, of the abstract, and of the international'. This process was boosted by the Olympic Games and laid Mexico City's cultural environment firmly open to international scrutiny. An important component of the ideological background to Mexico City 1968 was to demonstrate Mexico's engagement with modernity and this was best demonstrated in the 'audacious plan for decentralized facilities that turned the whole city into a temporary festival ground' (Gordon, 1983, p. 99). Facilities were deliberately spread around the city in a conscious attempt to integrate the Olympics more widely and encourage participation after the Games. The relationship between the sporting events and urban structure disdained the recent convention of using the former as a regeneration tool. The overall philosophy was expansionist. Emphasis was placed on large-scale transport planning, on freeway building and catering for motor vehicles; trends that inevitably privileged an advance to the periphery rather than a focus on the core. New peripheral motorways were built and the city's public transport system was increased by an additional 1,500 special vehicles to provide access to the new and existing facilities, scattered widely over Mexico City, in an 'unprecedented dispersion' (Muñoz, 1997, p. 35), some being over 30 kilometres apart. In an attempt to resolve the problems of dispersal, Mexico City introduced the then innovative *Olympic Identity Programme* where Olympic routes were colour coded and marked by streamers whilst enormous balloons or fibre glass figures indicated the sites themselves (Liao and Pitts, 2006).

The main focus was in the south of the city at the Miguel Hidalgo Olympic Village, containing 5,000 units in several tower blocks – 'more than previous Olympic villages, it was a city' (Gordon, 1983, p. 101). A second Olympic village, the Narciso Mendoza Village, also known as Villa Coapa, was built for the Cultural Olympics with 686 houses and flats, the latter in four-storey blocks (Muñoz, 1997). Both Villages were inspired by the features of mass social housing prevalent in Europe in the 1960s and reflected the *grandes ensembles* tradition (*Ibid.*). The new 25,000-seat Sports Palace for indoor sports, costing $8 million was 9 miles (more than 14 kilometres) to the north-east of the Olympic Village at the Magdalena Mixhuca Sports Park where the velodrome was also located, whilst the new Olympic Pool and Gymnasium was built in the smart southern suburb of Coyoacan. The rowing basin was located still further south at Xochimilco. Although not built with Olympic funds, the Aztec stadium (designed by Pedro Ramírez Vázquez in 1966) was used for Olympic football in 1968 and later for the FIFA World Cup Finals in 1970 and 1986. Among the other renovated buildings was the 12,800 capacity National Auditorium at Chapultepec, used mainly for gymnastics. Athletic events were located at the renovated University City Stadium built in 1953 but expanded to a capacity of 80,000. Inevitably, there was much scepticism from the 'First World' about whether these sites would be ready in time (see Giniger, 1968a, 1968b).

The main axis for the games was the Route of Friendship in the southern periphery of the city, a newly built motorway connecting most of the main Olympic locations. This route became famous for one of the most high-profile cultural events associated with the Olympics, with Pedro Ramírez Vázquez and the architect and sculptor Mathias Goeritz promoting its iconic status (Goeritz, 1970).[2] In 1966, Goeritz proposed that the Olympics should be marked with an invitation to sculptors from around the world to create a sequence of abstract sculptures in concrete, which would be sited along the Route of Friendship. Goeritz's ideology was clear in his speech of welcome to the international sculptors, where he asserted his belief that:

An art integrated from the very inception of the urban plan is of fundamental importance in our age. This means that artistic work will have to leave its environment of art for art's sake and establish contact with the masses by means of total planning. (Quoted in Wendl, 1998, p. 115)

In the event, eighteen sculptures were executed along a 17-kilometre stretch of the motorway with the Olympic Village at its centre. The sculptures were initially well signed and illuminated at night and the critical reception was generally favourable but, for a long time, the subsequent fate of the sculptures was less fortunate.

The design of the logo also reflected contemporary modernity, incorporating psychedelic imagery but also reflecting the Pacific Coast Huichol Indian designs that used stark black and white lines. The number '68' was generated from the geometry of the five Olympic rings with MEXICO set in the middle of a series of concentric swirls and the whole logo was claimed to be a fusion of Mexican indigenous culture with the Op Art movement then spreading over the globe (Brewster, 2005).[3]

The infrastructure of the 1968 Olympics was clearly intended to demonstrate to the world Mexico's advance as a modern nation. This message was also reinforced in other ways. The new buildings did not celebrate Mexico's rich pre-Columbian cultural heritage but rather 'reflect[ed] a technology of rapidly rising sophistication in an economy where labour was still cheap ... they were designed by architects and engineers of international outlook – citizens of architecture's world state' (Gordon, 1983, p. 107), and the cultural festival accompanying the Olympics similarly played down indigenous cultural forms and sought to celebrate internationalism. The chief protagonists were emphatic in their desire to break away from the value laden stereotype of Mexico as 'the land of *mañana*' (Zolov, 2004, p. 168). This intention was clear to two foreign artists involved in designing the Olympic logo, Peter Murdoch from Britain and Lance Wyman from the United States, whose only instruction was that 'the sleeping man with the sombrero did not properly represent Mexico' (*Ibid.*, p. 173).

After the excesses of Tokyo 1964, the Mexico City Olympics were perceived as comparatively low cost, but in the context of a developing country this is, of course, a relative concept. The total cost of building and organization was $175.8 million, of which $53.6 million (30 per cent) was spent on new or remodelled sports facilities, $16.5 million on municipal improvements, $16 million on the Olympic Village and $12.7million on the Cultural Village. The remaining $77 million was spent on direct outlays by the Organizing Committee, the vast majority of which was spent in Mexico City. Nevertheless, there were numerous other, Olympics-related expenditures which never entered the official calculations, not least the wages of the security forces massed outside the key locations. $20 million income came from ticket sales, television rights, and profits from Olympic souvenirs. In total, the 'official' Mexican government subsidy was about $56.8 million (Gordon, 1983, p. 108). At the peak of the Games, 14,000 people were employed directly, but the majority only on a temporary basis. Hardly surprisingly, 1968 was a good year for economic growth in Mexico – net tourism receipts increased by 15.5 per cent to $510 million and GNP increased by 7.1 per cent (Hofstadter, 1974).

For the first time, the sporting Olympics were accompanied by a Cultural Festival continuing throughout the Olympic year with the participation of ninety-seven countries (Arbena, 1996). International figures were invited, including Robert Graves, Arthur Miller, Eugene Ionesco, Martha Graham, Evgeny Evtushenko, John Cage, Dave Brubeck, Duke Ellington, and Alexander Calder (who designed the 80 foot high sculpture *El Sol Rojo* outside the re-opened Aztec stadium). Many of the cultural events took place in the Olympic Village and in the extensive Chapultepec Park on the western side of the city, although museums and auditoria all over the city were also used. Overall, there were 1,500 events throughout the Olympic year of which 550 were dispersed through the country (Zolov, 2004).

The Cultural Festival was conceived as an integral part of the whole Olympic experience and was organized by Pedro Ramírez Vázquez as Chairman of the Mexican Olympic Committee. It has been argued that the main driving force for this was to 're-energize Mexican domestic support for the Olympics following nearly three years of divisions and doubts' (Zolov, 2004, p. 168). Yet, there was no obvious attempt to appeal to a broad spectrum of Mexican society. Although Mexican folk culture (especially dance) played some part in the Cultural Olympics, each participating nation was asked to bring 'jointly with their athletic delegations two works of art: one representative of any of its brilliant cultural stages of the past; the other the best of its contemporary art' (*Ibid.*, p. 175). The celebration was clearly international and it seems difficult to imagine how inviting numerous foreigners to come and display their folk heritage could actually enthuse a population as large, diverse and geographically distinctive as that of Mexico. Indeed, an alternative explanation of the significance of the Cultural Festival has been offered, namely that it reflected Mexico's desire to be the 'champion' of the Third World and this explains '… the use of the cultural aspects of the Olympiad as a platform for Third World cultures' (Brewster and Brewster, 2009, p. 719).

Assessing the Games

While the efficiency of organization for Mexico City 1968 took many international observers by surprise it was not an opportunity for unqualified self-congratulation. Rodríguez Kuri (2003) argued that the background to the organization of the Cultural Olympics in particular demonstrated a 'matured modernity' within Mexico. Yet the preceding discussion has demonstrated that the main driver of the Mexican Olympic project of 1968 was the need to convince the world outside of its capabilities and, as part of that project, no opposition could be tolerated.

The official announcement that Mexico City had been awarded the 1968 Olympic Games was met with almost universal joy within Mexico. For example, as a Mexican student (quoted in Calvert, 1973, p. 316) argued in 1968:

> the very fact that this country has been chosen as the theatre for the Olympic games signifies that it has reached a high degree of development and equipment. One can see other signs in the intensity of foreign investment and the level of productivity we have attained here.

This optimistic view, however, was soon challenged. The government had certainly hoped that the excitement of preparing for the Olympics would generate an atmosphere of popular support. Although sport was demonstrably being used as an instrument of unity, it has been claimed that Mexicans evidenced an ability to resist such cultural impositions (Brewster, 2005). In this context, the events immediately preceding the Olympics in the summer of 1968 are often cited. For example, Essex and Chalkley (1998, p. 192) observed:

> the costs of the Games were such that many ordinary Mexicans questioned whether the money might not have been better spent on dealing with poverty and alleviating the city's severe social problems. This opposition resulted in violent protests which police and army units quelled with force.

However, this is to recycle a common misunderstanding about the student movement of 1968. Many Mexicans did question the cost of the Games but most informed views now agree that this was not the primary basis of the civil unrest of 1968 (Shi, 2014) (figures 14.1 and 14.2). Although the savage repression and massacre at the Tlatelolco rally on 2 October was undoubtedly exacerbated by the fact that Mexico was about to stage the Opening Ceremony (Preston and Dillon, 2004), the student movement was intent on reminding the world that Mexico was a one-party state with a history of corruption and police repression (Zolov, 1999). The Olympics provided the opportunity for higher profile protest but it was not the object of the protest.

Figure 14.1. Security forces facing demonstration in Mexico City, October 1968.

Figure 14.2. Detainees being strip-searched, Mexico City, 1968.

Any sympathy and good feeling that the Mexican government may have won through its difficulties in the summer of 1968 was quickly eroded by its subsequent behaviour. According to official statistics the death toll at Tlatelolco was forty-nine. Foreign journalists estimated the figure at well over 200, later adjusted upwards to 260 deaths and over 1,200 injured (Toohey and Veal, 2000). An Italian journalist, Oriana Fallaci, had attended the rally and was wounded. Instead of receiving help from the state security guards, her watch was stolen from her wrist (Preston and Dillon, 2004). Injured students were indiscriminately tortured in an attempt to uncover the names of organizers and ringleaders of their movement (Witherspoon, 2003). The government quickly took steps to lay the blame firmly at the door of the usual suspects – communists and other foreign agitators – whilst sentencing over 100 'ringleaders' to heavy terms in jail, some for 25 years. The Olympic Games continued but the image of Mexico, so carefully prepared and massaged in the years leading up to October 1968, was now something much darker than the planned official representation. Whatever the roots of the student protest of 1968, most of the benefits of hosting the Olympics – the modern image, the enhanced presence on the international stage and the attempt to create the sense of one nation – were eroded by the repression and the evident lack of political harmony, despite all the effort to present such an image (Zolov, 2004).

Turning from the political repercussions of the events surrounding the Games, one of the main alleged benefits for hosting the Olympic Games is the prospect of an enhanced city. However, increased awareness is not the same as enhanced image and in the case of Mexico City the latter proved to be problematic. The Games themselves went off remarkably well and the organization and staging were generally judged to be good. Yet the dominant and lasting images were of the 'Black Power' demonstration by the American sprinters Tommy Smith and John Carlos during the 200 metres medal ceremony, the police repression of Tlatelolco, and the fact that the Games were on the point of cancellation at least twice – once through the potential boycott of countries objecting to the invitation to participate sent to South Africa (Hill, 1996), and once through the security fears following the 12 October massacre.

The Games also served to highlight Mexico City's problems of urban infrastructure, especially those to do with transport. The concept of a decentralized Games proved to have many practical difficulties, with some of the transport infrastructure not completed on time. Contemporary accounts also pointed to the cosmetic nature of some of the alleged urban improvements – 'many of the construction projects taking place within Mexico City were carried out with little or no consultation with the Mayor of Mexico City' (Brewster and Brewster, 2009, p. 795). The gaudiness and liberal use of colour in street decoration could not wipe out the reality, for example on the walls of neighbouring slums, which were painted in shocking pink, purple and yellow, temporarily hiding the deprivation within (Salázar, 1968).

Although seen as an integral part of the modern image of the 1968 Olympics, the sculptures on the Route of Friendship were quickly usurped from their original purpose, adorned with graffiti and used to convey entirely different messages. The Australian Clement Meadmore's sculpture was illegally enclosed by a private school which then used it as their logo. Most of these damaged, overgrown structures were either ignored or forgotten for over 20 years (Fernández Contreras, 2008) until a partial renovation programme in the 1990s (Reyes, 2009). More recently (2012) the Ruta de Amistad has been included in the World Monuments Watch in an attempt to increase awareness of their relative neglect but a proposed plan intends to relocate the most threatened sculptures in two parks, completely undermining the initial concept. Other elements of the Olympic iconography were also usurped and used as part of the 1968 protest campaign. For example, the symbolic white doves of peace used widely in the graphic arts programme in association with the official motto for the Olympics, '*Todo es possible en la paz*': Everything is possible in Peace, were ironically spattered with red paint after the October massacre.

Initially, the Olympic Village also had a different fate from that originally intended, which had been to sell the 904 four-room apartments in the private market. Two years after the Games, however, the Village was still half empty with no one on the waiting list (Schmitt, 1971). The city centre is 9 miles (15 kilometres) to the north, there are no shops or supermarkets and no significant places of employment adjacent to the site, so a car is essential. A major deterrent to early rapid sales was that the apartments were severely vandalized by the athletes themselves (*Ibid.*, p. 261). Subsequently, the two Olympic villages have ended up as 'gated' dormitory commuter areas entirely dependent on private transport (Muñoz, 1997).

A final epitaph on the 1968 Olympics relates to the historiography of Mexico City. In the main English language monograph on Mexico City (Ward, 1990), the Olympic Games warrant only a brief mention (*Ibid.*, p. 217) and in its equivalent by two French authors they received none at all (Bataillon and Rivière d'Arc, 1979). In the context of the evolution of the modern urban structure of Mexico City, the Olympic Games of 1968 are little more than a footnote. Consequently it is difficult to argue a case for any underlying change in city structure emanating from the Olympics. A more sustained phenomenon is the annual student demonstration held each October in memory of the Tlatelolco massacre. Indeed, the fortieth anniversary of the Games was marked solely with a celebration of the graphic design component of the event but, somewhat ironically given the forward looking ideology that was so prominent in Mexico's winning and presentation of the Games, this exhibition was almost entirely retrospective, celebrating the 1960s (MacMasters, 2008). Nevertheless, in the broader context of the city, its relationship to Mexican governance and the perception of the nation on the global stage, the events of 1968 are of fundamental significance, albeit profoundly different from those originally intended.

Notes

1. Although Spanish is, of course, the official language of Mexico, there are at least ninety indigenous languages, mostly with a regional ethnic basis.

2. Ramírez Vázquez designed the National Museum of Anthropology and the Aztec Stadium in Mexico City and went on to design the administrative buildings of the IOC and the Olympic Museum in Lausanne, Switzerland. Mathias Goeritz had designed a group of high-rise concrete towers in Mexico City called the Torres de Satelite in the suburb of Ciudad Satelite, planned in direct relationship to a super-highway.

3. However, note the exchange between Terrazas and Trueblood and Daoud Sarhandi in *Eye*, No 59, Spring 2006 (available at http://www.eyemagazine.com/opinion/article/letters-eye-59-this-is-not-mexico), on the provenance of the Olympic symbol.

Chapter 15

Munich 1972

Monika Meyer

The stimulus for Munich's application to host the Olympic Summer Games came in October 1965 from a proposal from the President of the National Olympic Committee (NOC) of the Federal Republic, Willi Daume. The initial reaction of the Lord Mayor, Hans-Jochen Vogel, to the proposal was lukewarm. In view of Germany's recent history, he envisaged a low chance of success for the city's candidacy. Yet he quickly recognized the great opportunities that an event of this size presented for the city, especially in terms of replanning and redevelopment. This chapter considers the place of the 1972 Games in the post-war planning of Munich, the plan for the Olympic Park, Olympic legacy and its management and finally the attempts to repeat the experience through bidding for the Winter Games.[1]

Urban Development in Munich after 1945

No less than 39 per cent of the urban fabric and 70 per cent of Munich's historic central Altstadt were destroyed in the Second World War.[2] The reconstruction effort got off to a slow start and the last areas of rubble were only removed in 1956. The main aim of reconstruction was to relieve the housing shortage. After the War and right up to the 1960s, Germany's cities expanded considerably, largely due to waves of refugees and displaced persons. From 1945 to 1955 Munich had its highest rate of population growth at around 20,000 new residents per annum. By 1957 the population had reached one million. This expansion drove demand for housing, public buildings and services, transportation and business premises.

It was the aim of the planning authorities to preserve and reconstruct urban structures on the basis of the historic city outlines, thereby reviving Munich's pre-war look and feel. Much effort was thus spent on reconstructing and developing the inner city. Entire blocks were removed in order to create more open space and also to improve public hygiene. By retaining the former street layout, it was possible to use the still intact utility and waste disposal pipe networks. The historic Altstadt crossroads at the Marienplatz remained the hub of public as well as private transport. This redevelopment concept laid the groundwork for later problems, as the mediaeval tangle of narrow streets proved unable to cope with the huge rise in pedestrian and motorized traffic. The option of laying down new roads through abandoned areas was scarcely explored. Instead, the transport network underwent only piecemeal expansion.

Munich was one of the first cities in Germany[3] to begin drawing up a land-use plan in order to channel uncontrolled growth, as well as a general transportation plan for the Bavarian capital and its surroundings. These plans were completed in 1963, and formed the basis for the green space plan of 1969, which also incorporated planning for sporting areas and facilities. The city's existing green areas along the rivers Isar and Würm as well as the historic parks Englischer Garten, Nymphenburger Schlosspark, Hofgarten and Maximiliansanlagen were complemented with new parks near the large new suburbs to the east, north and north-west. A network of green corridors functioned as the city's lungs, supplying fresh air while also providing areas for leisure pursuits. The land-use plans also designated undeveloped sites as green spaces. From 1950 this concept led to the creation of such green sites as the southern Isar meadows, the Sendlinger Wald, the enlargement of the Hirschgarten and eventually the Olympiapark in 1972.

Alongside the designation of residential and commercial areas, a further aim of urban planning was to redesign the city's transportation system. The continuation of the only partially completed Altstadtring (an inner-city ring road) and the creation of a middle and outer ring road were intended to divert through-traffic away from the city centre. These measures enabled the historic crossroads to be transformed into Germany's first pedestrian zone. However, the growth in commercial traffic as well as holiday traffic heading south quickly stretched the capacity of the inner-city road network to breaking point. In 1971 construction began on Munich's autobahns.

The main public transport axes continued to follow a radial design. Now the goal was to integrate the Deutsche Bundesbahn (national railway) with the local rail network. From the 1950s the discussion turned once again to an underground tramway or a local transit railway of the Deutsche Bundesbahn. The centrally located Marienplatz became a hub linking the Deutsche Bundesbahn transport system to the S-Bahn (commuter train lines) and other transport services of the City of Munich. In February 1965 work began on the first stretch of U-Bahn (underground railway). The Marienplatz station was constructed in the years 1967–1971 with four underground floors to accommodate the platforms of the U-Bahn and S-Bahn. Up to this time only a rough plan existed for the design of these networks. Concepts for the creation of an integrated urban transport network, with links to other forms of mass transport as well as the operation and use of the S-Bahn and U-Bahn systems were precipitated by the application to host the Olympic Games.

The Bid

The Munich Olympic Games are regarded as one of the first examples of an international event being exploited for local interests. Most other cities had previously striven to host such an event for the prestige it would bring, in order to boost tourism or to secure additional funding. However, in the case of Munich the original motivation for the bid came from outside the city – namely from the National Olympic Committee (NOC) – who wanted to bring the Games to Germany by selecting a city capable of gaining a favourable response from the IOC. Careful diplomacy leading up to the bid convinced Willi Daume that the international community and the IOC would be open to a bid from the Federal Republic of Germany (Organizing Committee, 1972, I, p. 23).

In Munich itself, as noted above, one of the first people to grasp the opportunity presented by the Olympic Games was the Lord Mayor, Dr Vogel, who used it as a focus and catalyst to revitalize the urban development plan that had lost momentum, as well as expediting projects which were pending. The idea soon gained the support of the national government as well as the Free State of Bavaria, both of whom released extraordinary funding. This money ensured that planning for the expansion of the transport network, other urban development projects and the creation of the urgently required sporting facilities could be stepped up and quickly implemented.[4] Munich's bid was submitted to the IOC in December 1965. The application focused on the fun-filled character of the Games in order to present a clear contrast to the Fascist Games of Berlin 1936 and this was a decisive factor in the bid's success at the IOC meeting in Rome the following April. Here Munich led the voting from the start against Detroit, Madrid and Montreal, winning the Games outright in the second round (Organizing Committee, 1972, I, pp, 1, 25).

Planning and Construction of the Olympic Buildings

The centrepiece of the Olympic facilities was to be the sports park on the Oberwiesenfeld featuring a new stadium, a swimming hall and a large sports hall (figure 15.1). To the north would be the Olympic Village and the Press Centre and Press Complex, to the south the velodrome, a multipurpose sports hall and a training field. Existing venues in the city could be adapted to host other Olympic events (including shooting, archery, fencing, wrestling and dressage). The canoe slalom events were to be held in Augsburg, while sailing was to be hosted in Kiel.

Detailed planning for the Olympic venues began with an urban design competition in 1967. First prize was awarded to the Stuttgart architectural practice of Behnisch and Partners[5] for a sports park that would integrate an artificial landscape of hills and dales in which the key sports venues nestled with a spectacular tent roof hovering above. Based on the existing Schuttberg, the landscape was remodelled and the Nymphenburger Kanal dammed to create a new lake (the Olympiasee). An artificial chain of hills divided the Oberwiesenfeld into three zones. To the north of the Olympic Stadium this created two hollows – one which housed the Central University Sports Facility (ZHS – Zentraler Hochschulsport) and the other the new Olympic Village. The surrounding

Parc olympique
The Olympic Park

Figure 15.1. The Olympic Park. (*Source*: Olympia in München. Offizielles Sonderheft 1972 der Olympiastadt München. München, 1972)

topography was closely integrated with the built structures so that greenery penetrated deep into the residential areas. Dividing this area from the southern parkland a roadway (the Mittlere Ring) bisected the park east–west with raised walkways above the road linking all buildings and separating pedestrians from moving and parked traffic. Other new buildings were added to the south of the Park – the velodrome, located in a depression at the south-west edge of the park, a multipurpose sports hall (the ice arena) used to host the judo and boxing competitions, and a training field to be constructed at the park's southern end.

The New Buildings for the Olympic Games

The foundation stone for the Olympic buildings was laid on 14 July 1969. The Olympic stadium (figure 15.2) was partially sunk into the landscape, thereby concealing much of the building and avoiding an overly monumental impression. Only the west grandstand, under which were situated auxiliary rooms and athletes' facilities, was designed as a tall reinforced-concrete structure. Entirely covered by the tent roof, the grandstand offered seating for 47,000 and standing room for another 33,000.

The grandstands in the sports and swimming halls (figure 15.2) were also

Figure 15.2. The Olympic Stadium, 1994. (*Photo*: Monika Meyer).

Figure 15.3. Swimming Stadium and Theatron, 1994. (*Photo*: Monika Meyer)

designed to match the surrounding landscape, allowing the entrances to be placed at near ground level. Both halls were enclosed with glass façades, which proved difficult to connect to the roofing. The swimming stadium was built into the slope of the hill in such a way as to ensure that the water in the pools and that of the lake were practically touching, and the seating of the Theatron (a Greek-style open-air theatre seen in figure 15.3) led smoothly onto the terraced seating of the swimming hall grandstand. Between the Swimming Hall, Sports Hall and Stadium, a central square (Coubertin Platz) was created on to which spectators spilled out on the way to and from events.

The buildings and sports facilities were not isolated structures but formed a large contiguous landscape unified by the tent roof which formed a continuous structure above the stadium, the sports hall and the swimming hall, extending over the Mittlere Ring to the edge of the Central University Sports Facility. The intention was for the roof to be a single structure to protect spectators from the wind and weather. For the designer, the tent construction created a mental association with the circus as a symbol for a joyful and musical Games.

The competition design proposed constructing a real tent. Like the German Pavilion at the 1967 EXPO in Montreal, the cover was to be made of a polyester fabric that could be taken down after the Games and replaced by solid roofing above the grandstands. Initially, the idea of a temporary textile roof met with the approval of the city authorities and the *Olympiagesellschaft*. This would be a spectacular and inexpensive solution, as well as showcasing Germany's innovative engineering sector. However, the government wanted a more permanent solution that could make a real architectural statement. The engineering practice of Frei Otto (Stuttgart) suggested constructing a pre-stressed network of steel cables to support acrylic glass canopies. In the realized solution, a 78,000 square metre weather-proof membrane of acrylic glass panels was supported by a series of masts and cables. An additional underlying transparent membrane was installed to provide better insulation for the interiors of the venues. This complex and previously untested construction cemented the idea of the 'umbrella' or 'tent', a design concept which went on to become one of the most spectacular technical innovations of recent architectural and civil engineering history.

Even before the application to host the Olympic Games, the State of Bavaria had planned to construct a university sports facility at Oberwiesenfeld. After Munich won the bid, this project was incorporated into the general development plan for the Games. The sports halls, training rooms and lecture halls of the ZHS were used during the Games to accommodate the studios, screening rooms, editing suites and other office spaces of the Media Centre, being reconfigured after the Games for university use. The outdoor sports areas were used by athletes as training and warm-up areas.

The Olympic Village

From the very beginning the planners had a long-term view of the Olympic Village as forming the heart of a new residential district, with only a temporary use as athletes' accommodation. Underlying the development concept was the notion of 'hills of buildings' (figure 15.4). Three chains of seven to fourteen storey, steeply terraced apartment blocks stretched from the central area to the north and west. In front of these high-rise residential blocks lay five-storey flat terraced houses,

Figure 15.4. Olympic Village, 1984. (*Photo*: Monika Meyer)

in front of which were located semi-detached housing of one to three storeys. Most of the apartments featured balconies and outdoor seating towards the south, looking over the Olympic sports venues and the Schuttberg.

Men were housed in the high-rises. One-room apartments, penthouses, multi-room apartments, row houses and bungalows of various types were available for approximately 10,000 athletes and functionaries who were attending. The Olympic women's village for 1,800 female athletes and auxiliary staff was designed as a settlement of closely packed small housing units and an apartment building with shared facilities.[6] Eight hundred houses, constructed from prefabricated concrete slabs with standard furnishings, were laid out to create a dense 'patchwork' estate. The cubic shape of the two-storey 24 square metre apartments with roof gardens as well as the surrounding arrangement of small lanes and squares, gave the settlement the feel of a Moorish village. The exceptional effort and money invested in the concept of the bungalow village can be attributed to the booming economy and the general mood of hope and excitement surrounding the Olympic Games in the 1960s.

The heart of the village was formed by the communal facilities, a shopping centre and the U-Bahn station at the main entrance on Lerchenauer Strasse. All open spaces and paths in the settlement were reserved for pedestrians. Access roads and car parks were located in an underground level below the village, with the main roadway entrance on Lerchenauer Strasse. The artistic design for the village's open spaces was decided by international competition. The winning concept by Hans Hollein proposed a network of coloured 'median guidelines' which criss-crossed the centre and the pathways (figure 15.5). These lengths of tubing supplied

Figure 15.5. Olympic Village public zone with median guidelines, 1984. (*Photo*: Monika Meyer)

the private and public zones with heat, cold air, light and sound. To improve orientation they were coloured to match the separate areas or residential sites to which they led, and were also furnished with signs, bulletin boards, or display panels (Organizing Committee, 1972, I, p. 109).

The intention was to sell off the approximately 5,000 apartments in the men's Village after the conclusion of the Games. The architectural practice of Heinle and Wischer developed floor plans with light, movable partition walls that could be adapted to meet the different requirements of the owners. However, due to the high costs, this innovative design was not implemented in the final construction, and instead the apartments were given fixed floor plans.

Press Complex

The project to develop a press complex can be compared to the Olympic Village in regard to its huge impact on the redevelopment of northern Munich. Here a new city district was erected with high-rise blocks and a shopping centre[7] to provide accommodation for some 4,000 journalists (TV, radio, and press), and which in layout, size and furnishings were comparable to the athletes' lodgings. Located west of the ZHS, at the hub of all Olympic activities, the press complex was accessible on foot from the Olympic park by crossing an S-Bahn overpass and the Kusoczinski-Damm. Otherwise the centre could be reached by autobahn via the Mittlere Ring or by the S-Bahn. On its southern edge, the press centre provided work spaces for 2,800 of the press corps with facilities ranging from photo laboratories, teletype, telephoto, a central telephone hub, news agency, meeting spaces, and club (Organizing Committee, 1972, II, p. 168). After the Games this building was converted into a secondary school for 2,000 pupils and the Press Complex converted to 1,600 apartments of varying sizes (*Ibid,* p. 170). The German Olympic Centre in the ZHS provided facilities for German radio and television services (*Ibid*, p. 190).

Landscape Design

The green space of the Olympiapark was designed to reflect the gentle foothills of the Alps. The dominant elements were the Schuttberg forming the highest elevation and the lake drawn from the waters of the Nymphenberger Kanal. 1.5 million cubic metres of earth from subway excavations and the sites of the sports venues were used to create embankments and hills up to 25 metres in height. The landscape elements and species of plants were varied in such a way as to lend a unique character to different areas of the Olympiapark.

Care was taken to integrate the main sports venues into the landscape, thereby concealing their enormous dimensions. The areas around the Schuttberg and the lake gave the impression of being entirely natural landscapes. The lake became the focal point of the landscape. A concrete Theatron was constructed on its banks in front of the swimming hall. This was used for artistic performances as well as for relaxation.

The strict separation of pedestrian walkways and vehicular traffic was essential to preserving the rural character of the grounds. The slogan for Munich's bid had been an 'Olympic Games in Green Surroundings and with Short Paths'. The landscape design fulfilled this promise of a compact site with short direct routes. Pedestrians were led from the railway stations and other access points via twenty-three (in some cases temporary) bridges to the different sports venues without having to cross any roads or railways. Motorized traffic within the sports park for the delivery of goods or to transport athletes, VIPs or journalists, as well as emergency services, was kept hidden from the spectators.

One problem in designing the Olympiapark was how to cope with the expected mass of visitors. At peak times an influx of 80,000 spectators per hour was predicted. To this end, a network of diverse pathways was laid down to link all parts of the grounds. Wide, tarmacked streets ran from park entrances to the most important competition venues. Spectators in less of a hurry were encouraged to use relaxing 'diversions' and alternative routes to the crowded main axes in the form of cobblestone paths and country trails. These paths were carefully spread out to preserve the scenic character of the green spaces. The desire for a carefree and 'democratic' park extended to notices inviting visitors to walk on the grass and even pick the flowers. The fluid design and naturalistic landscape was intended to contrast with the more formal and regimented landscape of the Berlin Maifeld of 1936 (Schiller and Young, 2010, p. 109).

Urban Measures: Transportation

Administrative structures created at the urban and regional levels for the hosting of the Games proved crucial for the long-term development of the city. The establishment of an Investment Planning and Olympic Agency laid the foundation for the city's Urban Development Unit (*Stadtentwicklungsreferat*). In regard to transport policy, existing differences between the Social Democratic city council and the Christian Socialist municipal authorities could be overcome. Through close cooperation between the city authorities, the local municipalities and the government of the State of Bavaria, it proved possible to realize the integrated MVV (Münchener Verkehrs- und Tarifverbund) transport network of urban railway and tram lines, Bundesbahn railways and regional transport networks that had been envisaged since the 1960s, linking the city to distant parts of the region. At the same time Erdinger Moos was chosen as the location for Munich's international Franz-Josef-Strauss airport, which opened in 1992.

The question of transport, however, overshadowed all other issues in the City Council's deliberations on the application for the 1972 games. The expansion of the transportation network, an endeavour considerably accelerated by the hosting of the Olympic Games, can be considered one of the most far-reaching developments. Munich's *Stadtrat* (City Council) viewed the execution of the Olympic Games as: 'a unique opportunity … to completely transform in a short space of time the transport infrastructure of the city and entire region to accommodate the new demands. Priority has been placed on work to develop an efficient rapid transit rail network' (quoted in Jäger, 1994). The years between the positive decision of the IOC and the actual hosting of the Olympic Games were a period of intensive planning and construction in Munich. As streets were dug up and tunnels excavated, the city resembled one enormous building site.

The new Marienplatz station in the city centre became one of the most important hubs for passengers on the S-Bahn and U-Bahn networks. The S-Bahn station Olympiastadion (Stadium) and the U-Bahn station at the Olympic Village provided rail access to the Olympic site. During the Games the S-Bahn ran on a double-track normally used for freight to provide connections to the stations. The platforms at the Olympiastadion stop were also designed to handle long-distance and local express trains.

In May 1972 the 4 kilometre stretch of the U-Bahn was opened to connect the city centre and the Olympic Village. This section, which was not included in the initial network design and was exclusively built for the Olympic Games, had wide repercussions: the planned four main axes of the U-Bahn and S-Bahn were reduced to three. Through the energizing effect of the Olympic Games and the financial support of the *Olympiabaugesellschaft*, construction work on roads and bridges as laid out in the main transportation plan could be completed much earlier than scheduled. In particular, the sections of the middle ring road around the Olympic site were contracted and paid for by the *Olympiabaugesellschaft*. The expansion of public transport networks and the associated reduction in private traffic created the preconditions for closure of the city centre to all vehicles. The pedestrian zones between Karlstor and Altes Rathaus could thus be laid out in the years 1967 to 1972.

The estimated costs just for transport infrastructure were DM105.5 million. The energizing effect of the Games meant that these projects could be quickly executed. The decision to incorporate the development of the radial transport system (which had been established at the beginning of the 1960s) into the planning for the Olympic Games was certainly the correct one, at least from the perspective of the time. Today the preference would be for a network-like transport system.

After the Games: Managing and Marketing the Olympiapark

In 1970, before the Games took place, the *Münchner Olympiapark GmbH* was set up with an initial capital of DM10 million and charged with the administration and organization of the Olympic sports venues. During the construction phase, it monitored and supervised the building measures in order to safeguard a sensible and efficient use of all the facilities over the longer term. The company's tasks included the management and marketing of the Olympic facilities, the acquisition of sponsors as well as the maintenance of all buildings and open spaces. A budget of DM10 to 15 million was required for these activities. After the Games the company became the sole leaseholder of the Olympic site.

In 1972 the German government made a one-off payment of DM130 million to *Münchner Olympiapark GmbH*, thereby discharging itself of any financial obligations in connection with the continued use of the Olympic facilities (as was specified by the consortium contract of 1967). Through astute investments and healthy interest income, this sum of capital continued to grow up to the end of the twentieth century, so that the City of Munich did not have to pay any maintenance costs for the site up to that time.

The company has regular earnings through renting out the sports venues and ancillary buildings for large events such as matches of the German football league, presentations of fun sports activities, concerts and exhibitions as well as tourist activities such as guided tours through the stadium and trips up the TV tower. In particular, the company sees the hosting of diverse major sporting and cultural events as a real success. Nevertheless, the loss of league football matches hit the company's income considerably. In addition, the Olympic buildings are showing their age. In the 1990s there was already discussion on how best to protect and secure the venues, and indeed whether the Olympic site should be placed under a preservation order. In particular, the acrylic glass panels and concrete structural elements were in need of extensive repair. The interiors of the sports and swimming halls also required work.

The question of modernizing the Olympic stadium arose during Germany's application to host the World Cup of 2006, as the building no longer met FIFA's criteria. At first FC Bayern München supported the idea. The club had in fact wanted to convert the structure into a dedicated football stadium for some time. However, the conversion plans were abandoned after many years of heated debate, and particularly when architect Günther Behnisch voiced his opposition. In collaboration with the city's second club, TSV 1869 München, plans were drawn up for a new football stadium on the city outskirts. Subsequently, the Allianz-Arena opened in 2005 and the Olympic Stadium lost its anchor tenant.

The ensemble of Olympic sports facilities was eventually placed under a protection order, thereby avoiding demolition, a step that had been seriously discussed. Today the stadium could perhaps be described as a 'luxurious ruin', located in a charming park with outstanding transport connections (Brandt and Heller, 2014). After losing the profitable football league games, the *Olympiaparkgesellschaft* has attempted to secure revenue by encouraging diverse and, at times, unorthodox usage of the stadium and facilities of the sport park. In some cases such inappropriate use of the stadium has damaged the structure. For example, to better accommodate motorsport events, the grass surface has now been replaced by concrete (*Ibid.*, 12).

Taken overall, the Olympiapark is one of Munich's most important recreational areas, accommodating a wide range of leisure pursuits such as jogging, kite flying and skiing. The sports venues are used both for amateur sports activities and for cultural events and top sporting events. Up to 2014 Olympiapark Munich had been the venue for thirty-three world championships, twelve European championships and 100 national championships.[8] Yet it should be pointed out that some events, particularly winter events such as the Audi FIS Ski World Cup 2013 on the Olympiaberg (Olympic Mountain) have severely disturbed the local flora through the spraying of artificial snow as well as through technical installations.

The Olympic site and sporting venues have become a tourist attraction for Munich. The park is an important recreational area for the city's north-west. Since 1972 around 111.6 million paying visitors have visited the buildings, while an estimated 198.6 million locals and holidaymakers have made use of the green areas and the park's freely accessible facilities.[9] Tours of the Olympic Stadium offer roof-top walks, abseiling and zip line packages; the Olympic tower (a 291 metre tall telecommunications tower) boasts a revolving restaurant and, since 2004, the Rock Museum Munich of music memorabilia. In 2006 Merlin entertainments opened Sea Life München next to the Olympic Tower.

The Olympiapark is one of two urban green spaces in Munich financed by major events, the other being the Westpark, constructed for the International Garden Expo 1983, which is also intended to have as significant an impact on the city as the seventeenth-century Nymphenburg Park to the west and the eighteenth-century Englischer Garten to the east. Thus the concept of the 'Olympic Games in Green Surroundings' has indeed provided a lasting recreational legacy for the city, with unrestricted use as well as low construction and maintenance costs. Moreover the idea of the 'carefree Games' was meant to infuse post-Games use (Organizing Committee, 1972, II, p. 33).

The Wider City

In retrospect, one of the most obvious effects of the Games was the structural and spatial enhancement of areas in the north of Munich that had traditionally been amongst the city's most neglected. Previously the image here had been largely conditioned by military usage and heavy industry. The fact that this area was used for rubble disposal in the post-war years underscores the impression of it firmly belonging to the city outskirts. The idea for a sports park in this location – a project originally unrelated to the bid to host the Olympic Games – was inspired by the attempts of other German cities to deal with their large rubble dumps. Hanover, for example, developed its Volks- und Sportpark while Berlin created a sports park at the Teufelsseechaussee. The execution of the Olympic Games accelerated plans for the park. Instead of the scheduled 15 years, the project was completed in only six. It can be said with some certainty that the Olympic Games served to raise the quality of the urban development and landscape design measures as well as ensuring architectural excellence and the Olympiapark has done much to revitalize the area.

Ten years after the Games, a large-scale spatial plan was adopted for northern Munich, which is still in place today. However, in view of the polluting industries and often unattractive sites that serve to create a poor image, this district is still regarded as a problem zone. Efforts have been made to satisfy the high demand in Munich for housing by constructing new estates of multi-storey apartment blocks. To ensure proximity to the city centre and sufficient green space, these have been located on undeveloped sites south of the Olympiapark and especially in areas formerly used by the military. Simultaneously, the city authorities have attempted to remedy structural and transport deficiencies. Roads have been modernized and commercial hubs have been created at public transport stops.

For the city of Munich as a whole, the developments associated with the Games ushered in a new era. This period saw the birth of the world famous 'City with a Heart' as well as Germany's leading research and economic powerhouse. The city's positive image, as well as the long-term rise in population and industrial strength, was mutually reinforcing. Today Munich is not just one of the world's top business locations; it also one of the best ranked places for quality of life and is one of the most attractive German cities for tourists, and not just around the time of the *Oktoberfest*. Population growth is expected to continue, with current forecasts indicating around 200,000 additional residents and 100,000 extra jobs by 2030, even though the city is already facing a shortage of land for new housing and infrastructure.

As the outstanding event of Munich's post-war years, the 1972 Olympic Games kick-started a range of developments that have permanently altered the face of the city, particularly in the areas of transport and housing. After the Games, the success of the Olympic site continued for a comparatively long period. The Press Complex and Olympic Village were turned into residential areas. After some initial difficulties in marketing the Olympic Village, it has gone on to become one of Munich's most popular neighbourhoods. Residents particularly enjoy its atmosphere, the communal public spaces, good local services, great transport connections and proximity to green space.

The Games took place at a boom time for Germany, when a heady optimism was in the air. This euphoric mood was reflected in the use of modern technologies and means of transport. During this period, the City of Munich initiated the comprehensive and large-scale planning of its spatial development. At the time the development measures were seen as positive and sensible, whereas over time the decisions taken must be viewed more critically (see Geipel *et al.*, 1993).

Subsequent Applications to Host the Games in 2018 and 2022

In view of the boost the Olympic Summer Games 1972 gave to the city's development, the idea of repeating the process was attractive. Important actors such as the Lord Mayor, the City Parliament as well as business and media representatives were all certain that Munich needed fresh impetus, and that this could be gained through a bid for the 2018 Winter Olympic Games. Supported by a feasibility study confirming the suitability of the city as a host, Munich made an application at national level in 2005. In 2007 the *Deutsche Olympische Sportbund* (DOSB) unanimously agreed to support the city's application, which was then submitted to the IOC at international level in 2009.

The concept was based on two main sites: the snow competitions were to take place in Garmisch-Partenkirchen and the ice competitions in Munich, primarily at the Olympic Sport Park. The city intended to underline its ecological profile by exploiting and converting existing buildings as well as through its climate-neutral concept. It was intended to redesign the Olympic hall, the Olympic swimming hall and the Olympic stadium for use as winter sports venues as well as to host the opening and closing ceremonies. Furthermore, new halls were to be erected at the ZHS site and the site of the demolished velodrome, as well as a new multi-functional hall in the Olympiapark. The Olympic Mountain with the filled in Olympic Lake should be the location for ski and snowboard competitions. New buildings needed for the Olympic Village and the Media Village were to be sited on the outskirts of the Olympia Park. However, in July 2011 the members of the IOC voted by large majority in favour of Pyeongchang in South Korea as the location for the Olympic Winter Games.

The widespread support for the application to host the 2018 Games, with major resistance only coming from Garmisch-Partenkirchen, encouraged those responsible to follow the rejection with an immediate application to host the 2022 Winter Games using basically the same concept. Yet this time there was much greater public hostility than with the first application. In a referendum held in November 2013, all four host municipalities (Munich, Garmisch-Partenkirchen, Traunstein and Berchtesgadener Land) voted roundly to reject the Olympic project with a no vote of 52 per cent in Munich and nearly 60 per cent in Traunstein (Grohmann, 2013).

What were the reasons? At only 16 days, the Games are a relatively short event. This is in stark contrast to the high development and construction costs for sports facilities and transport infrastructure as well as for the accommodation for athletes, media representatives, spectators and the Olympic family. Since the 1980s the Games have continually grown in size and in levels of commercialization. While in Vancouver 2010 the number of separate competitions was eighty-six, the plan for the Munich Winter Games was to hold 100 events. As pointed out by the Bavarian network of anti-Olympic campaigners NOlympia, the Host City Contract that host cities are obliged to sign, awards practically all rights to the IOC. The Committee then has the authority to change competitions unilaterally and without compensation, to make increased demands on sports facilities or indeed to cancel the hosting of the Games entirely. Under the contract, the host municipalities have to meet the IOC specifications unconditionally, and bear all risks for their execution. Furthermore, the IOC is the sole distributor of all income from the Games. According to NOlympia, the IOC is, in fact, the only real winner. From the perspective of the local authorities, a renewed boost to Munich's development would almost be counterproductive: as already mentioned, today the city is already facing a housing shortage, the municipal land reserves are practically depleted, while the rents and general living costs, which are already amongst the highest in Germany, are continually rising. Yet it was especially the fear of skyrocketing costs and environmental damage that motivated citizens to vote against the Winter Games.

This rejection by the Bavarian populace reflects a general mood throughout Europe. Initiatives to host the Olympic Games often founder long before the applications are submitted to the IOC. In Switzerland the bid to host the Winter Games 2022 was defeated by referendum, while in Stockholm the application initiative was abruptly cancelled so as not to offer an easy avenue for political attack in an election year (see Chapter 1). It seems as if large international events are now viewed with suspicion by traditional host nations. Yet it would be unfortunate if the Olympic Games were abolished simply because of the IOC's questionable selection procedures or the problems faced by host cities in finding acceptable post-Olympic uses for venues and facilities. The Games are hugely important for society, not least as top athletic performances serve to foster mass sports at the amateur level, thereby improving individual fitness and well being.

Therefore, the international organizations that manage and award such major international events must radically change direction. Also the hosting cities and nations should reconsider their intentions when submitting applications. An alternative perspective is urgently needed regarding the enormous size of the

Olympic Games, and in particular its impact on host cities. One improvement to the application phase would be for the IOC to consider more intensely how venues and infrastructure could be profitably used over the long term. In particular, the sustainability concept, which is often presented in vague and flowery terms, should be pursued more vigorously. It is hoped that the cities and the IOC will have the courage to favour temporary and multi-functional buildings.

Notes

1. This chapter focuses on the site and infrastructural preparations for Munich 1972 and their context within the broader planning for the city. Coverage of the terrorist atrocity that overshadowed the Games can be found in Chapter 9.

2. For information about Munich's history and urban development see BAI (1912).

3. A new planning and building code was introduced in Germany in 1960. The Federal Building Code of 23 June 1960 obliged all municipalities to establish land-use plans and building plans.

4. cf. Letter of the Press and Information Agency of the City of Munich from 29 November 1965 (Munich City Archives, Olympische Spiele 1972, Nr. 67).

5. Günter Behnisch (1922–2010) studied architecture in Stuttgart. He founded his own practice in 1952. His designs for the Olympic Games brought international acclaim.

6. Planning: Werner Wirsing; architecture: G. Eckert.

7. Architecture: Practice of Fred Angerer in cooperation with Alexander von Branca (both from Munich).

8. Figures from www.olympiapark.de.

9. Figures from www.olympiapark.de.

Chapter 16

Sydney 2000

Robert Freestone and Simon Gunasekara

The Games of the XXVII Olympiad were staged in Sydney between 15 September and 1 October 2000. In total, 10,651 athletes from nearly 200 countries competed in 300 events across twenty-eight sports. Sydney 2000 marked only the second time an Australian city had hosted the Summer Olympics, and the second time the Games had been held in the southern hemisphere. It also celebrated 100 years of women's participation in the modern Olympic Games, as well as the debut of two new sports, taekwondo and the triathlon. The total cost of staging the Games has been estimated at A$6.6 billion (Davidson and McNeill, 2012), of which approximately two-thirds were paid for by the public sector, representing 0.6 per cent of the country's GDP in 1990–2000 (Cashman, 2006).

Sydney was awarded the right to host the Games on 23 September 1993. The bid process was managed by the Sydney Olympic Organising Committee (SOCOG) with support from the New South Wales (NSW) state government which made three crucial commitments: to provide venues and facilities; to ensure key support services such as health, security and transport; and to underwrite the costs of staging (OCA, 1998). The Sydney Olympic Park precinct, approximately 9 miles (14 kilometres) west of central Sydney, was developed as the major venue with nine permanent facilities constructed including the Olympic Stadium now known as ANZ Stadium. The events held there included athletics, tennis, swimming, field hockey, table tennis, taekwondo, basketball, and gymnastics. Other suburbs had world class sporting facilities constructed for the Games and these also continue to serve the community for sporting events year round, including the Duncan Gay Velodrome at Bankstown and the Whitewater Stadium and International Regatta Centre in Penrith.

This chapter focuses on the physical planning and transformation of the main site at Homebush Bay.[1] It draws on and acknowledges a growing body of research on the planning processes surrounding the Sydney Olympics (see for example: Preuss, 2007; Toohey, 2008; Cashman, 2011; Dickson *et al.*, 2011; Kassens-Noor, 2012; Leopkey and Parent, 2012; Cox, 2012; Searle, 2012; Davidson, 2013; Mulley and Moutou, 2015). It also makes use of information gained by conducting a series of interviews with key stakeholders involved in the planning and development of Sydney Olympic Park today.[2]

Games organizers claimed to have learned from the worst and best examples of earlier legacy development (Cashman and Hughes, 1999), leading to the tag as 'the best Games ever'. The concept of legacy within the Olympic Games movement had gained popularity in the 1980s, but it was not until the beginning of the millennium that legacy was officially recognized a necessary component for an Olympic bid. The study of legacy is increasingly important as issues of return on investment and securing sustainable and equitable long-term benefits become paramount (Leopkey and Parent, 2012). Our chapter is framed around this notion of legacy and planning for it. We expand on the concept briefly in the next section before identifying a chronology of thinking which frames our narrative around four main stages to characterize the Sydney experience. We conclude with some reflections on the broader implications of this episode in Olympic and planning history.

Legacy

Legacy has a long history in mega-event planning and delivery with mixed results (Chalkley and Essex, 1999; see also Chapter 1), but as a fundamental consideration for Games preparation is especially evident from Barcelona 1992. A key value of mega-events is their potential to be a positive driver for urban development, particularly in infrastructure improvements, urban regeneration and even broader city branding (Johnson, 2008). However, it was not until 2002 that the International Olympic Committee (IOC) made a formal acknowledgement of the importance of legacy. In 2003, legacy was included in the charters of both the International Olympic Committee and the International Paralympic Committee (de Moragas *et al.*, 2003; Andranovich and Burbank, 2011; Leopkey and Parent, 2012).

Discussion of legacy can be fraught, because the construction of legacy is contestable in the eyes of different stakeholders, cumulative impacts colour expectations, and the time elapsed before coming to fruition is not always agreed (Toohey, 2008). A reasonable time has now elapsed since the 2000 Games to gain a better overall appreciation but this still remains a live story. From the start, planning in Sydney paid particular if not explicit attention to legacy, notably by emphasizing sustainability as a dominant theme (Cashman, 2011; Dickson *et al.*, 2011; Kassens-Noor, 2012). This was largely aspirational at the beginning, but then gradually attained greater form and substance. However, aspirations of a wide and deep legacy were overtaken by the demands of event planning, resource constraints, intractable stakeholder positions that demanded pragmatic compromise, and time itself.

There have been claims and counter-claims regarding the legacy of the Sydney Olympics. Notwithstanding conspicuous successes, such as the introduction of sophisticated environmental management systems and the development of regional parklands, the legacy is tinged by significant lost opportunities (Cox, 2012; Kassens-Noor, 2012). Most forward thinking has come post-Games and ironically has had to address the spatial and functional constraints within the Sydney Olympic Park precinct.

The appreciation and development of legacy for Sydney 2000 can be interpreted historically through four stages that correspond with the bid development, detailed facilities planning, initial post-Games legacy development and metropolitan integration (table 16.1). Stage one, dubbed *Reactive Engagement*, refers to *ad hoc*

Table 16.1. Planning for the legacy of the Sydney 2000 Games.

Stage 1 (pre-bid) *Reactive Engagement*	Stage 2 (post-bid) *Articulated Development*	Stage 3 (post-games) *Consequential Legacy Planning*	Stage 4 (new horizon) *Metropolitan integration*
site selection (population growth, transport, environmental effect, cost); scoping site remediation (brownfield)	site remediation and environmental management measures; venue and facility development; transport infrastructure development; creation of the parklands	finding a viable future through encouraging new development; testing market interest	upscaling residential and commercial development; competitive development; role in regional context; governance

Source: Compiled by authors.

legacy gestures in response to immediate infrastructure requirements or to community pressure through the processes of site selection and scoping of site remediation works prior to the official bid. The focus was on short-term financial event success. Conflicting goals between the short and longer term were ignored or managed out. Stage two, *Articulated Development* (the post-bid phase), saw more attention devoted to legacy, although still largely within a site-specific, short-term and reactive framework. The range of planning activities increased significantly, with a strong 'green games' theme, but with infrastructural investment remaining geared to event planning. Stage three, *Consequential Legacy Planning*, coming immediately after the Games, saw a more explicit future focus centred on economic development, in particular the attention to large-scale residential and commercial development, but informed by a strong environmental ethic. Stage four, *Metropolitan Integration*, overlaps but extends this process into the present-day with commercial, residential and infrastructural investment prioritized, albeit framed more explicitly within a metropolitan rather than local planning context and with broader governance issues rising to the surface.

Pre-Bid: Imagining an Olympic Standard Sporting Precinct

The first stage of legacy planning covers the period from 1973 to 1992. The Homebush Bay area had been the subject of planning investigation since the 1970s.

With a view to attracting the 1988 Olympics to Sydney, leading planner-architect Walter Bunning was engaged by the state government to consider the siting and development of a major new sports complex and evaluated twenty possible sites across the metropolitan area in terms of four main criteria: location in relation to both the city's recreational needs and possible international requirements; accessibility to public and private transport; effect on the environment visually and in terms of noise pollution; and cost factors. Bunning's 1973 report advocated development of surplus government-owned land at Homebush Bay. This pleased community groups campaigning against projected redevelopment of Centennial Park in Sydney's eastern suburbs. Heavy industry including abattoirs and armaments was deserting Homebush, creating brownfield opportunities but leaving the area seriously polluted, degraded and contaminated (figure 16.1). The Bay site boasted a number of positive opportunities including its location near the geographic centre of the metropolitan area, ideally positioned to address Sydney's growing westward population; its ability to connect to existing transport networks; and delivery of environmental benefits. This recommendation was never seriously considered, but initiated a debate on urban regeneration subsequently played out through a succession of competing development plans produced by various state agencies.

Figure 16.1. Homebush Bay from the air, looking east down the Parramatta River to central Sydney, late 1960s. The locality is dominated by the state abattoirs and saleyard complex. The government brickworks are identified by the chimney stacks and large quarry beyond nearer the head of the bay. (*Source*: State Library of New South Wales, Government Printing Office 2-45332)

Prior land occupation helped shape future planning and development decision-making and similarly a series of locational decisions made in the early to mid-1980s: the NSW State Sports centre opened in 1984 followed by the development of the Australia Centre business park on long-term leasehold land (Cashman, 2011). Later came the opening of Bicentennial Park in 1988. In December 1990 the federal government announced that it would release 84 hectares of land at Homebush Bay in what would become the core Olympic site.

In the lead up to the bid, Olympic responsibilities at the state level were shared by several agencies, leading to a lack of clarity about the direction of the project and degree of private sector involvement (Cashman, 2011). This led to the establishment in 1992 of the Homebush Bay Development Corporation (HBDC), an archetypal project-specific delivery agency, to promote, coordinate, manage and secure the orderly and economic development of the 'growth centre' at Homebush in anticipation of a successful Games bid. Its first master plan in 1992 retained flexibility to proceed with development even if the bid was not successful, and alongside the sporting facilities was the prospect of more hi-tech business capturing the rise of the knowledge economy. The master plan established an urban core surrounded by extensive parklands. The orthogonal grid of the former abattoir pens was inscribed on the site transected by a major new north–south boulevard (Johnson, 1999).

It was initially intended that Homebush Bay would serve two immediate purposes: not only a world class sporting hub but also a new permanent home for the Royal Easter Show (an annual town-country fair) relocated from the inner city to make way for a controversial Fox movie studios development (Williams, 1997). Most attention was given to conceptualize the site as a facility for the Games. Writing at the time, Myer (1996, p. 2) commented: 'the primary motivation for most of the current activity at Homebush Bay is meeting the requirements of the 2000 Olympics – and longer term planning issues generally appear to receive a lower priority'.

However, the 'green promise' was emerging as a hallmark of Sydney's bid for the Games (McGeoch and Korporaal, 1994). The bid coincided with the move by the IOC to recognize the environment as a core principle of Olympism (see Chapter 2). With the environment formally confirmed as the third dimension of Olympism, after sport and culture, in 1995, Sydney's green programme engaged with two major agendas. These were: emergent global concerns surrounding depletion of resources and the adverse impacts of non-renewable energy sources; and an array of site-specific remediation challenges far beyond what Bunning had comprehended. Homebush Bay was beset by a range of environmental constraints. There were significant areas of low lying flood-prone land, poor geotechnical conditions, and extensive landfill that had been inadequately supervised and included dioxin, asbestos and other hazardous materials.

Homebush Bay was envisioned as a unique location combining sports and environmental legacies with commercial development. The design of venues and accompanying facilities would facilitate future use through flexible seating structures, relocation and greater public use post-Games. However, the bid for the Games was not explicitly linked to a wider urban regeneration planning framework. This helps explains why the connections to existing regional planning frameworks were weak from the outset.

Post Bid: Articulating Development between 1993 and 2000

This second stage covers the period from the successful bid to the actual staging of the Games. Despite good intentions to balance short- and longer-term planning agendas, the pressing demands of Games preparation dominated the agenda. Cashman and Hughes (1999) highlighted the pressure to focus on short-term imperatives coming from the top echelons of the NSW government to ensure that there was minimal risk that the Games would fail, be delayed or run significantly over-budget. This occupied much of the time and energy of planning and design teams, and marginalized forward thinking.

In September 1993 the HBDC was given Olympic responsibilities. Key elements in that respect were: environmental management and renewal; provision of transport and infrastructure; master planning and urban design; asset management and facilities maintenance. Importantly, it had to deliver most of the Olympic facilities including the stadium; the tennis, baseball and archery centres; and the athlete and media villages. There was still concern that Olympic responsibilities were fragmented across government and with the design and construction programme falling behind schedule a new Olympic Co-ordination Authority (OCA) came into being with fresh leadership to drive development (Davidson and McNeill, 2012). Creation of the OCA publicly signalled that high-level coordination was a major priority of the state government (Cashman, 2011). A new ministerial portfolio was created to help rationalize governance and bring the costs associated with Games investment into one structure. The appointment of a Minister for the Olympics, Michael Knight, who was also the president of the board of SOCOG, was a crucial and beneficial decision.

While legacy took a back seat, it was not forgotten altogether and was injected through four main elements: (1) site remediation and environmental management measures; (2) venue development; (3) transport infrastructure; and (4) creation of perimeter parklands. We briefly look at each of these in turn.

Addressing the 'green' promises that were part of the successful bid, extensive funding was invested in site remediation and development of sophisticated environmental management measures: for example, through treatment and containment of waste to reduce the exposure to contamination; stormwater capture and water recycling to re-use and conserve resources; cultivation of new wetlands to reduce flood levels, provide habitat, irrigation, aesthetics and restore creek catchment function; and the development of green building guidelines that considered the entire lifecycle of materials, waste management and the use of energy (Cashman, 2011). Particular attention was paid to energy conservation, use of renewable energy, passive solar buildings, appropriate material selection, density of development, and appliance and equipment selections. The Water Reclamation and Management Scheme (WRAMS), one of the world's largest wastewater recycling systems, was installed. Design of facilities was intended to maximize opportunities for energy conservation and recycling of resources. While Sydney's credentials as the 'Green Games' were assisted by a partnership with Greenpeace Australia, the realities of delivering on bid claims proved more challenging than first recognized (Lenskyj, 2002) and the outcomes were mixed. Thus, although the green utopianism of the original Athlete's Village was sacrificed for more pragmatic commercial considerations (Thalis and Cantrill, 1994), it still supported one of the largest solar powered installations in the world.

The OCA developed a revised and final master plan in 1996, dividing the site into four main areas: an urban core (sporting, entertainment, commercial facilities, plus the new Showground); the Newington residential district based on the Athletes' Village; a major metropolitan park; and a waterfront development. George Hargreaves, a renowned American landscape architect, further shaped the public domain through creating more space between venues, paving, mature trees, and water features. A design review panel was set up to consider major public works. In retrospect, the late 1990s emerges as a remarkably fertile and innovative period, which helped establish sustainability and design excellence as touchstones for new architectural and urban design standards in Sydney (Weirick, 1999). The Olympic enterprise employed a Who's Who of Sydney's most eminent architects, landscape architects and urban designers (Bingham Hall, 1999). A consortium headed by Multiplex and Hambros Australia was chosen to design, construct and operate the flagship $463m stadium with a games capacity of 110,000 and post-games of 80,000 (figure 16.2). It was always intended that the venues and facilities would be developed for multi-purpose use that would outlast the Games event itself.

Figure 16.2. The Olympic Stadium under construction, 1998. Designed by Bligh Voller Nield in association with Lobb Architects, the stadium officially opened in June 1999 more than a year in advance of the Games. (*Photo*: Robert Freestone)

During this stage in development a critical decision was made regarding transport infrastructure with profound downstream implications (Kassens-Noor, 2012). Several options were considered for transport connections, including exclusive bus transport, light and heavy rail. The government's preferred option was to construct a rail loop off the main western railway line into a new station, along with a ferry wharf and extensive internal road network accompanied by cycling and walking paths. The rail loop was the critical decision. While it served Games needs well, it has enshrined Sydney Olympic Park as a dead-end network destination (Owen, 2001; García, 2011). Further, the additional roads constructed to support access alongside the creation of 10,000 car parking spaces have promoted car-dependency. Establishment of the Olympic Roads and Transport Authority (ORTA) was a positive action, whereby all statutory decisions regarding Games transport were made by a powerful single agency (Owen, 2002; Mulley and Moutou, 2015). However, even this underscores an approach dominated almost exclusively by the event itself with its completely immovable deadline (Kassens-Noor, 2012).

The creation of one of the largest metropolitan parklands in Australia providing 1,064 acres (430 hectares) of ecologically significant wetlands, woodlands and remediated lands and a network of over 25 miles (40 kilometres) of pedestrian and cycle paths is one of the enduring legacies of the Sydney Games. The Parklands, extending Bicentennial Park, have a very clear set of management principles, enshrined in various pieces of legislation, including a statutory plan of management (2003). There are seventeen management precincts, each with a detailed, legislatively regulated set of characteristics with regard to planting, ecosystems and human use (Davidson and McNeill, 2012). Ironically, construction of the Parklands still met heavy resistance in the 1990s and required determination by the OCA to proceed.

While Sydney Olympic Park was taking shape through the 1990s as a major outcome of public enterprise, it was difficult to attract the interest of private investors with an eye to the future because the site was seen as too far away from the central business district and carrying too many commercial risks. Two Accor hotels were opened in 2000, initially to house essential personnel, but the early resistance in the market only increased the pressure on the government to ensure that the short-term imperative of staging a successful Games event was achieved.

Post Games: Legacy Planning 2000–2010

The third stage of more explicit legacy planning dawned in late October 2000, immediately after the end of the Sydney Olympic and Paralympic Games. Here the realities of adapting a low-density complex of elite sporting venues into a more sustainable urban precinct were inescapably confronted. Balancing an Olympic Games-standard capacity to accommodate periodic major sporting, leisure, and exhibition events with more quotidian living-employment opportunities to deliver an ongoing return on major public and private investment has been central. Planning rhetoric has consistently revolved around creation of a vibrant mixed-use precinct with strong urban design and environmental management practices. The Sydney Olympic Park Authority (SOPA), created in 2001, was a new agency vested with the responsibility to develop and manage Sydney Olympic Park as a special place for sporting, recreational, educational and business activities for the benefit of the community (Cashman, 2011).

There was media criticism during 2001 and 2002 regarding the lack of activity and seeming absence of long-range planning for future development. There was unease regarding the fate of a site that attracted such significant public investment. Elizabeth Farrelly (2012) wrote that 'you don't often find places quite as lonesome as Sydney Olympic Park'. This sentiment was expressed differently by others: 'ghost town' and 'white elephant'. There was a need for a switch in thinking from the operation of an event to strategic land development to ensure the return on investment with the main focus on residential and commercial development, but there was still uncertainty as to what the precinct could best become – an office zone, a new urban village, an educational centre, or a leisure and culture complex.

Nevertheless, much was going on behind the scenes even if not all that visible to the general public. In the first decade from 2000 a series of formal planning documents was prepared to guide development, notably the *Sydney Olympic Park Vision for Beyond 2000* (2001), *Draft Master Plan* (2001), *Master Plan* (2001), and *Vision 2025* (2004) leading to the *Master Plan 2030* (2010). SOPA inherited three key ingredients from OCA's post-Games vision: new development to attract more people on a daily basis; building on the carnival and festival atmosphere as a premier venue for major sporting and entertainment attractions; and cultivating a green oasis through progressive development of the Parklands. Five main precincts were envisaged: the town centre (transport hub, commercial and tourism); the core sporting and recreation precinct; south-west (campus development and IT); east (commercial and residential); and a relict brick pit (ecological significance).

The *Sydney Olympic Park Vision for Beyond 2000* and the *2001 Draft Master Plan* both employed this precinct-based development model. The Draft Master Plan nominated key development sites that in some form were carried through into subsequent plans. In 2005, a major collaborative design initiative was undertaken by international and local multidisciplinary experts in the areas of planning, urban design, development, environmental sustainability, and transport planning, with the findings reported in *Vision 2025* (Lochhead, 2005). This document was an important step towards looking at the potential of what Sydney Olympic Park could be with regard to land use, layout and the way in which it integrates with the surrounding area. The visioning document provided details down to the height of buildings within different precincts and transition to a more intimate scale supporting a variety of uses. *Vision 2025* also gave SOPA the structure for what is now *Master Plan 2030* (Cashman, 2011). *Master Plan 2030* finalized in 2010 is the current long-term planning document for Sydney Olympic Park (figure 16.3). It

Figure 16.3. Master Plan 2030 illustration prepared by Tim Throsby (2006). The large block sections reflect the ten precincts described in the plan ranging from sporting, residential, commercial, educational and stadia uses. (*Source*: Tim Throsby & Associates)

aimed to make Sydney Olympic Park more liveable through higher density, fine grain, mixed-use precincts with greater permeability (Cashman, 2011). Critics highlighted a tension between the sustainability legacy and a pro-development neo-liberal ideology (Davidson, 2013).

Commercial development was an early developmental priority, and provided some continuity to the Australia Centre business park from the 1980s. A total of eleven major commercial office buildings have been developed since 2000, with more in various stages of planning and construction (SOPA, 2015). A key player in this development has been a private developer, General Property Trust (GPT), which acquired long-term leases from the NSW government in the 1980s. GPT developed and tenanted progressively the Quad Business Park in four stages between 2001 and 2008. Queensland-based developer Watpac completed the Fujitsu building in 2010 at a cost of A\$32.5 million. The major employer is now the Commonwealth Bank which opened two buildings housing 3,500 staff engaged primarily in 'back office' functions. The main locational attractions were reduced office rents compared to the city and availability of parking. The Bank worked alongside SOPA in creating social and cultural programmes for employees and other workers in the town centre. With employment rising, additional shops and food outlets were opened to diversify the range of local businesses. One indicator of the economic momentum set in train was the opening of additional accommodation. Due to the success of the first of the two hotels, Accor announced in 2005 that it would build a five-star hotel adjacent to the existing hotels. This was opened in 2008 at the same time as the two-star Ibis budget hotel was unveiled. Sydney Olympic Park is now home to six different hotels catering for a broad spectrum of visitors from business conference attendees to families visiting for major events.

In all, more than 150 developments worth A$1.1 billion have been approved since the Olympic Games. The town centre attracts a growing daily workforce of 9,500 and business visitor numbers to the Park are also on the rise. The precinct is now an economic hub and home to more than 200 organizations. The Park falls within an area that has been ranked as the seventh largest economy in New South Wales and the twentieth largest local economy in Australia (Kimmorley, 2014; Wade, 2014, 2015).

Housing development also accelerated through the 2000s at a scale not originally forecast. This was fuelled by the state government's urban consolidation (compact city) policies and the growing community acceptance of high-rise living underpinned by changing demographic and lifestyle trends. After the Games, the Athletes' Village was integrated into the new residential suburb of Newington which has grown to a population of over 6,000 and has detached to become the responsibility of a neighbouring local authority. In Sydney Olympic Park proper, the turn has been to vertical living. In 2007, the Planning Minister announced the first stage of a A$320 million residential project to construct 685 apartments, with the first residents to call Sydney Olympic Park home arriving in January 2012. The precinct now houses 1,000 residents and their number is set to increase dramatically in the next few years with five new residential developments on the way projected to add a further 1,755 dwellings. This same trend is evident in the immediate environs outside Sydney Olympic Park. A stone's throw away from the town centre in different directions are Wentworth Point, an evolving dense waterfront high-rise precinct, and the Carter Street Priority Precinct, a high-density regeneration of older industrial sites being steered by UrbanGrowth NSW, the state government's main redevelopment agency.

Sydney Olympic Park has continued to be recognized as a premier destination for sporting and entertainment events. Over 10 million people visit the Park each year, more than double the visit numbers in 2000 (SOPA, 2015). Over 5,000 events are held each year ranging from local and international sporting events through music concerts, conferences, to exhibitions and even motor racing. The venues at Sydney Olympic Park continue to be named amongst the best in the world, with Allphones Arena (formerly the Sydney Superdome used for basketball at the Games) being ranked the sixth highest grossing venue in the world, playing host to some of the world's biggest music names. The strength of Sydney Olympic Park contributes significantly to the economic productivity of NSW (Wade, 2014, 2015).

Integrating Sydney Olympic Park in the Metropolitan Region

In the fourth stage, Sydney Olympic Park is transitioning from a standalone centre to playing an active and connected role in a regional context. Figure 16.4 provides an aerial view of the Park as it looks in 2015 (cf. figure 16.1). A neoliberal policy agenda is evident in moves to make the site self-sustaining and to promote

Figure 16.4. Sydney Olympic Park from the air today with the Sydney CBD in the background nearer the coastline. Large sporting venues dominate with new high-rise residential towers bordering the parkland near the town centre. In the foreground is a pre-Olympic liquid waste facility and industrial buildings in the Carter Street Precinct designated for redevelopment into a 'vibrant community'. (*Source*: Courtesy of Sydney Olympic Park Authority, MG7911)

commercial development, while continuing to exploit the sustainability narrative (Davidson, 2013). This stage highlights the struggle faced by governments, who typically bankroll mega-events well ahead of realized benefits, to recover their costs through value-uplifting private infill and redevelopment. The town centre has been framed by a significant number of hotels, commercial offices including banks and residential towers. The 2030 Master Plan for the site is predicated on continued strong growth. However, issues regarding transport and access, the precinct's place in an increasingly competitive market, and questions about continued governance need to be addressed.

The ongoing work of SOPA as an anchor point for integrative planning has been a useful mechanism. The *Master Plan 2030* is currently undergoing its first 5-year interim review, a condition that was written into the document to ensure it remained relevant and evolved as regional demand and economic demands change. Anomalies will be corrected, obsolete development standards will be revised, and future demand for land use re-examined. An underperforming sports and education precinct will be revisited to accommodate a more flexible range of functions. Overall, the intention of the review is to ensure a revised but not radically different plan is evolving in line with market conditions.

The post-Games planning horizon has seen a trial-and-error dynamic in attempts to integrate retrospectively development within broader metropolitan planning agendas (Davidson and McNeill, 2012). *Vision 2025* was used by SOPA to convince the state government to recognize the area for the first time as a specialized centre within the metropolitan planning framework. A 2013 Draft Metropolitan Strategy for Sydney to 2031 made mention for the first time of an 'urban activation precinct', but it was unclear what its scope and scale would be. The current 2014 metropolitan strategy *A Plan for Growing Sydney* prepared by the NSW Department of Planning and Environment identifies Sydney Olympic Park as a strategic centre in Sydney, positioned within the so-called Global Economic Corridor arching from the airport, through the downtown to the western regional centre of Parramatta. Recognition within the metropolitan planning framework provides continued momentum for the site to play a bigger role in the growth of the region.

In this context, transport and accessibility have become major planning issues. Access into Sydney Olympic Park has always been a point of contention, and up until now has been managed successfully, but involves considerable forward planning and management especially when crowd-pulling multiple events are staged. With an ever increasing daily population in the Park and surrounding areas such as Wentworth Point and the Carter Street precinct, more needs to be done to improve access and egress. Planning has been challenged through embarrassing administrative complexities with the major roundabout entry into Sydney Olympic Park being governed by no less than four different authorities. The WestConnex project is a major motorway development in the vicinity that is set to enhance access into and out of the precinct. Problems remain with conventional rail services to and from the Park. During major events direct services are provided, however during weekdays this is not the case. As the daily population increases, the demand for improved services to ensure the economic viability of the Park will continue. The complaint is still heard about the lack of long-term planning for public transport investment and the continued inability for factoring improvements into future planning (Kassens-Noor, 2012). However, in December 2015 the NSW state government confirmed its commitment to a new Light Rail connection providing some relief to connect Sydney Olympic Park with Parramatta (Deloitte Australia, 2015; O'Sullivan 2015).

The role of SOPA into the future is unknown. There is a high cost associated with maintaining the parklands and facilities, yet the allocation of funds from the state government is progressively diminishing. The level of government subsidy for the recurrent budget for the site declined from A\$40.9 million in 2003 to A\$33.3 million in 2011. While SOPA has played a powerful executive role in day-to-day governance under the auspices of the Minister for Planning, its role in recent years has gradually been reduced, with a reduction in staff numbers and an increasing attempt to maximize revenues from leasing and events. Sydney Olympic Park is no longer the relatively isolated enclave it was, with contiguous development pressures in Wentworth Point and Carter Street, Homebush. The interaction of SOPA with the surrounding local authority, other state agencies, and with event-specific bodies such as the Homebush Motor Racing Authority and the Sydney Showgrounds (a quasi-autonomous body within the park) is not completely seamless and has led to gaps, overlaps and conflicts in accountability and governance. A newly established Greater Sydney Commission may well scrutinize strategic and statutory planning responsibilities for the wider locality.

The strength of the current Master Plan in attracting high-value corporate and residential tenants within the town centre has been questioned (Davidson and McNeill, 2012; Yamakawi and Duarte, 2014). With increased growth in both the Sydney and Parramatta central business districts and in other outer and inner suburban business nodes, the commercial market is becoming increasingly competitive. The decision by the Commonwealth Bank in late 2015 to relocate its entire Sydney Olympic Park staff to the Australian Technology Park in inner Sydney caused considerable controversy (Mckenny *et al.*, 2015). At the same time, new commitments are being made to the precinct with NRMA, one of Australia's largest home and car insurance providers, soon to occupy a new headquarters building in the town centre. The competitive environment extends to the core sporting business operations of the Park. The NSW state government has announced plans to invest A\$1.6 billion in the redevelopment and creation of a number of large sporting stadia across Sydney (Lehmann, 2015; Saulwick, 2015). Moreover, there is great rivalry between the current private owners of ANZ Stadium and the long-standing Sydney Cricket and Sports Ground Trust controlling venues near the Sydney CBD to attract peak events such as top football matches.

Conclusion

The experience of the Sydney 2000 Games with respect to 'what happens next' points to several conclusions. First, the conceptualization of legacy in this case was emergent, even organic. There was no firm formula as to what it represented in the larger scheme of things. Only as planning for the Games itself took shape did focused thought about legacy emerge, and even then it was largely subsumed by immediate priorities, timelines and resource constraints. Efforts directed towards integrated regional planning involving the Sydney 2000 sites occurred well after the Games when time and money and interest coincided. It is only recently that Sydney Olympic Park's role in the regeneration of the wider area is becoming clearer.

Secondly, the most outstanding elements of legacy lay in site remediation and environmental planning, although inevitably there is unfinished business (Hawken, 2014). While now regarded as commonplace, at the time the so-called 'green promise' was clearly aspirational, even contestable, and ahead of a firm position taken by the SOGC. It was aspirational because of the scope and scale of environmental measures that were undertaken; contestable because of the cost incurred and the range of stakeholders whose interests needed to be aligned, notably, local authorities, Commonwealth and state governments, developers and other private investors, and the people of NSW who were silent partners in the project.

Thirdly, there was the issue of the political nature of urban design. Funding and transport planning are two areas where the urgent and the possible seemed to overtake the strategic and the long term. Sydney 2000 was by no means alone in this respect and frankly it is doubtful whether a much sharper focus on legacy earlier in the planning process would have made a great deal of difference to legacy development.

Fourthly, there are no practice runs to polish and refine the development of legacy from Olympic Games. At best, a city might have one or two opportunities to host the Games; and even in the latter case, the gap in time is so great that it may be almost impossible to apply learning from one Games to the next. At best, a city can learn from the experience of other cities, even though the contexts and planning trajectories may be very different. In simple terms, in regard to legacy, once the die is cast early in the pre-bid/post-win stage, it is too difficult to adapt and reshape the course of legacy development in real time alongside the hyperbole and sheer momentum of immediate Games planning and delivery. In other words, there is a critical path dependency arising from the implications of early choices that constrain the scope of future legacy planning. In the experience of Sydney 2000, early choices were made about the site, the goals of the Games bid, the focus on delivering the Games on time, and managing risk that, arguably, locked in a course of legacy planning that constrained the options for enhancing legacy planning in the future.

Fifthly, the impacts of the Games were uneven and, as Searle (2012) reported, the lack of growth in tourism after 2000 contributed to a decline in Sydney's overall growth in the post-Olympic period. Its population increase of 13 per cent between 1991 and 2001 was reduced to 10.8 per cent between 2001 and 2010. Moreover, contrary to expectations, Sydney's non-residential construction dropped significantly in 1999–2000 and 2000–2001 as pre-Olympic construction was completed. The Olympic Games failed to generate post-2000 economic development to offset this situation. This slowed the progress of post-Games legacy planning. Searle (*Ibid.*) claimed that the Games actually generated a loss in Australian real private and public consumption of $2.1 billion.

There is no denying that the Sydney Olympic Games were successful as an event, and that its footprint will remain evident for years to come. The creation of a development authority to guide post-games development from 2001 was in itself a major step forward. London 2012 saw an admission that organizers had 'shamelessly used' Sydney Olympic Park as a reference point for post-games planning (Kimmorley, 2014). The challenge facing post-Games organizations like SOPA is not simply to wind down the Olympic infrastructure and to avoid ongoing costs, but to access new investment opportunities (Cashman, 2006). This has been achieved in Sydney and more than a decade on continues to be the case. Legacy as a product of the Olympic Games is enduring and evolving and this knowledge will continue to be perfected and translated in future Games. For Sydney, a new and protracted era has arrived where the former Olympic precinct has to survive in a far more competitive business environment, a very different socio-demographic situation with new work and living demands, and a shifting sub-regional setting demanding new types of connections and calling forth new forms of governance.

Notes

1.   This chapter differs from focus of the earlier 'Sydney 2000' chapter authored by Beatriz García (2011) which essentially interpreted Sydney's cultural discourse through the Olympic experience.

2.   D. Van Der Breggen, Executive Manager, Development and Planning, Sydney Olympic Park Authority, 22 June 2015; C. Bagley, Executive Manager, Major Projects, Sydney Olympic Park Authority, 9 October 2015; K. Grega, CEO, Sydney Olympic Park Business Association, 9 October 2015. Interviews conducted in 2013 are also drawn upon: C. Johnson, CEO, Urban Taskforce, 27 September 2013; D. Richmond, former CEO, Olympic Co-ordination Authority, 4 October 2013; M. Knight, former NSW Government Minister for the Olympics, current Chairman of Sydney Olympic Park Authority Board, 21 October 2013. We thank all our respondents for valuable insights but take responsibility for the findings reported.

Chapter 17

Athens 2004

Margaret M. Gold

In 2004 the Olympics will return to the place where they were born, where they were revived and where they will be renewed. The ATHENS 2004 Olympic Games are more than an opportunity to participate in the greatest celebration of humanity. They are an opportunity to be part of a story as old as history itself. And when it comes to making history, there is really no place like home.

ATHOC (2004, p. 31)

The relationship between Greece and the Olympic Games is like no other. The slogan 'There's no Place like Home', used in all the advertising for the 2004 Games, resonated with Greek identity, collective memory and historical experience. As home to the classical Olympics, the Games go to the very heart of Greek culture. Indeed, from the point at which Greece regained its independence in 1830, the possibility of reviving the Games, along with the drive to rebuild Athens as a worthy successor of the grand city of Antiquity, became key themes for those seeking to restore Greek values and identity. While not inseparable, there would always be a close link between staging the Olympics and the regeneration of Athens – the most likely host city whenever the Games returned to Greece.

This chapter looks at the 2004 Summer Olympic Games against this background. Its early sections chart the growth of the Olympic movement in Athens alongside attempts to regenerate the city, a period that culminated in the first Olympiad of 1896 and the 1906 Intercalated Games. The subsequent sections analyse the decision to bid for the centenary 1996 Games and its failure, the successful bid made in 1997 to stage the 2004 Games, and the urban planning strategy associated with that event. Finally, there is an assessment of the urban legacy bequeathed by Athens 2004.

An Immature Metropolis

Athens at the start of the nineteenth century was far from the grand city of classical imagining, as 'filtered through European scholarship and imagination' (Waterfield, 2004, p. 29). The handful of more adventurous visitors that made their way to this corner of the Ottoman Empire were confronted by a small provincial centre with a population of around 10,000. The upper town on the Acropolis contained the Turkish garrison with barracks, housing, shops and a mosque intermingled with the remains of the Parthenon and other classical structures. A lower town on the northern and eastern slopes of the Acropolis housed the Greek, Albanian and Turkish civilian populations. The city itself fared badly in the fight for independence (1821–1830). Although Greece gained its independence after the signing of the London Protocol in February 1830, the Turkish garrison did not leave finally until 1833. By this time the population had fallen to 6,000 and the city was described by the traveller Christopher Wordsworth in 1832 as: 'lying in ruins. The streets are almost deserted: nearly all the houses are without roofs. The churches are reduced to bare walls and heaps of stones and mortar. There is but one church in which the service is performed' (cited in Bastéa, 2000, p. 10). At this time, it was not even the Greek capital, with Nauplion, a strategic Venetian fortress on the east coast of the Peloponnesus, serving that function until 1833.

Understandably, thinking soon turned to finding readily recognizable symbolic strategies through which to reassert a sense of nationhood, of which the two that most readily came to the fore were the reconstruction of Athens and the revival of the Olympics. Two German-trained architects Stamatios Kleanthes and Eduard Schaubert, for example, had visited Athens in 1830–1831 and produced a plan for a city of 35–40,000 people. It featured a baroque-inspired layout based on radial axes (meeting at present day Omonia Square) where the Royal Palace, Parliament and Senate would be placed, and a series of grids creating nodal points for other key buildings (Travlos, 1981, pp. 393–394). The opposition to the necessary demolitions to implement the plan, the lack of resources to carry it through and the immediate pressure of population influx as the functions of government were established in Athens and exiles returned, meant that the plan needed almost immediate amendment. Instead, the new Athens developed gradually rather than by radical reconstruction, with an approach that sought to respect the classical archaeology, while creating a new neo-classical townscape.

The idea for the revival of the Olympic Games developed around the same time as the initial schemes for replanning Athens, although not without fierce debate between those that believed their restoration was essential for reviving Greek culture, values and identity and those who saw the Games as a cultural irrelevance and practical impossibility. The Greek poet Panagiotos Soutsos, for instance, launched a campaign in 1835 based around a series of poems that featured figures from the past calling on present-day Greeks to reinstate the Olympic Games. As early as January 1837, a Royal Decree established a 'national gathering' with competitions in agriculture, industry and athletics, with the specified athletic events being those associated with the ancient Games: discus, javelin, long jump, foot races, wrestling, and chariot racing (Young, 1987, p. 273; 2004, p. 141). The ancient Panathenian Stadium formed a natural focus for such activity and was restored to serve as the setting for two of the three Zappas Games (1870 and 1875; see Chapter 2).[1] Various attempts were made to revive that series, notably in 1892, but they were thwarted by financial difficulties. The initiative of the Coubertin-led IOC in reviving the Olympics and choosing Athens as the site for the 1896 Games, therefore, served the interests of both Greece and the Olympic movement. Athens gained a new Olympic Games with international recognition and participation, whereas the revived Games benefited from the imprimatur of being held on Greek soil. However, the IOC's preference for an ambulatory festival and fierce resistance to giving the Games a permanent home in Greece meant that, apart from the Intercalated Games of 1906, Athens would not receive another Olympic festival until the twenty-first century.

Bidding

By 1990, when the city next formally sought the Games, Athens was a byword for the problems characteristic of many Mediterranean cities (Wynn, 1984; Leontidou, 1990). A plethora of further plans commissioned from foreign architects and planners had come and gone in the face of military conflict and political and economic problems, with none adopted (Sonne, 2003, p. 146). Athens experienced rapid growth in the 1960s and 1970s, driven by industrial investment, rural–urban migration, a building boom and spontaneous development at the urban fringe – much of it illegal and unplanned. Public transport was poor and the city suffered severe environmental pollution and congestion. Although a capital city, Athens was not competitive with other major centres in Europe (Leontidou, 1990, p. 263) and was unable to offer inducements to counteract its relatively isolated position. Certainly, the idea of seeking the modern Olympic Games, with its inevitable financial burden, appeared implausible before Los Angeles 1984 established the new financial model.

Athens's first, and unsuccessful, bid campaign for the return of the Games between 1987 and 1990 should be seen against this background. The city's reasons for bidding reflected a mixture of the general and specific. Like most potential host cities, there was a broad place promotional message that sought to offset negative features (such as stereotypes about the Greek economy and culture) with positive images of a 'new face for Greece, outward looking and ready to take-up the challenges of globalization'.[2] The city looked to the mega-event to make Athens ready to compete in a world market for jobs and investment, while simultaneously enhancing Greek sporting infrastructure and helping to solve urban problems. As Vissilis Harissis, Director of the Organization for Athens, the body responsible for coordinating the Athens city plan, noted forcefully: 'Getting the Olympics is the best chance we'll ever have to save Athens. It'll be like fighting a war: there will be money and an incentive' (Hope, 1990).

Yet behind these broader objectives lay another set of ambitions that emanated from Greece's special relationship with the Olympics. The Greeks looked to the Olympics to help the nation recapture its soul; linking the ancient and modern in a meaningful and contemporary way for the twenty-first century. At the same time the Greeks wanted to reassert traditional values, especially as a reaction to the politicized and commercialized Games of the 1970s and 1980s when calls periodically surfaced that the Games might be able to regain their core values by returning to their geographical roots (Pound, 2004, p. 4). There was a strong sense that Greece wanted to 'correct the course' of the Modern Olympic Movement (ATHOC, 2005, I, p. 63). While talk of a permanent home for the Games had subsided, there seemed an incontestable logic in a Greek bid to host the Twenty-Sixth Olympiad in 1996 to celebrate the centenary of the revival.

The bid achieved Parliamentary approval in April 1986, with the Bid Committee presenting Athens's candidacy to the IOC in 1988 and the final Bid File in March 1990 for the IOC meeting in Tokyo the following September. The case was put that 70 per cent of the sports facilities were already in place or would be completed for the planned Eleventh Mediterranean Games in 1991. The documentation trumpeted Athens's experience in organizing international sporting competitions, listing twelve events hosted between the European Athletics Championships of 1982 and the Men's World and European Weightlifting Championships in 1989. Three of these, it was noted, had won awards from the International Press Association for the best organized press facilities. However, its publicity tactically overlooked the twin disasters of 1982 – the IAAF Golden Marathon when police failed to close the last 5 kilometres of the course to traffic, with runners encountering rush hour traffic, or the fact that the track in the new Olympic Stadium had not been laid by the time athletes were arriving for the European Athletics Championships (Payne, 2006, p. 258).

The strategic plan sought to concentrate the sports facilities in two centres. The first, the Athens Olympic Sports Complex (AOSC), would be at Maroussi, a suburban municipality 9 kilometres north-east of central Athens. This would build on existing facilities, most notably the stadium constructed between 1980 and 1982 for the European Athletic Championships, which was always seen as providing Greece with a facility of international standing that would allow Athens to compete for international events. AOSC would feature the stadium, velodrome, swimming complex, multi-purpose sports hall, an indoor hall and tennis centre, the Press Village, Main Press Centre and International Broadcasting Centre. The second complex, on the coast south of Athens at Faliro Bay and the nearby Karaiskaki Stadium,[3] would make use of the existing Stadio Erinis end Filias (Peace and Friendship Stadium) and new facilities to accommodate basketball, wrestling, judo, boxing, handball, baseball and yachting. Existing facilities in Athens would be used for sports such as archery and shooting, while the city centre would be the focus of the cultural festivities, making use of the classical legacy such as the Panathenian Stadium and Herodeion. The centre would house IOC members, the Olympic Family and official guests, with the Olympic Village scheduled for construction on the northern fringes of the Athens Metropolitan Area on the slopes of Mount Parnitha. The Olympic Ring promised travel times of only 12 minutes between the Olympic Village and stadium and 18 minutes to Faliro Bay. Road projects, new metro lines, a new tramline, improvements to the existing Helleniki International Airport on the coast east of Faliro Bay and a new international airport at Sparta were also planned.[4]

The eventual decision to award the centenary Games to Atlanta came as a shock. Melina Mercouri, the Greek Culture Minister, protested that 'Coca Cola won over the Parthenon' and the Prime Minister, Andreas Papandreou, called it 'an injustice against Greece' committed by the international community (Senn, 1999, p. 250). Rather later, the official Report from Athens 2004 (ATHOC, 2005, I, p. 65) placed part of the blame for the bid's failure on the perception of political instability that was created by the three general elections in eight months leading up to the IOC decision – a factor noted in the IOC Evaluation Commission's report. The Athens team was also accused of taking an arrogant approach towards endorsement, but the real stumbling block was the size of the task needed to provide the required infrastructure and setting for the Games. Even the Mayor of Athens had recognized in 1987 that a radical transformation was required to deal with the city's atmospheric pollution, traffic congestion, noise, lack of parking, shortage of open space and new sports facilities, outmoded media facilities and deficiencies in the public transport network. Such was the scale of the problems that although he supported the government's plan to host the Games, he stated that 'if we are in danger of looking ridiculous, I will not go along with it, and I will stand up and tell the public the truth' (quoted in Anon, 1987).

Greece's wish to stage the Games quickly resurfaced after the disappointment of the award to Atlanta. In 1995, the government toyed with the idea of seeking the 2008 Games outside the customary bidding procedure by requesting 'a direct award' of the Games as 'an honour' recognizing the special status of Athens. This was pursued for a while but the impracticality of obtaining the support of two-thirds of the IOC for the necessary change in the IOC Charter led the Hellenic Olympic Committee, in December 1995, to canvass vigorously for a conventional bid for the 2004 Games. Athens's candidature was submitted on 6 January 1996, five days before the official deadline, joining a group of cities already well ahead with their preparations. These comprised Rome, regarded as the favourite, along with Buenos Aires, Cape Town, Istanbul, Lille, Rio de Janeiro, St Petersburg, San Juan (Puerto Rico), Seville and Stockholm (ATHOC, 2005, I, pp. 67–68).

Not wholly surprisingly, Athens's final bid document for the 1997 IOC decision bore similarities to the failed 1990 bid, but with a less strident tone in the presentation (AOBC, 1997). The accompanying statements from politicians and officials now stressed the profound economic changes in Greece and Athens, particularly in the context of membership of the European Union. The Mayor, Dimitris Avramopoulos, wrote about the need to:

> give renewed impetus to the Olympic Ideal and to help the Olympic Movement start afresh at the beginning of a new century. Athens is ready, and we Athenians – all of us – are sensible of the responsibility that stems from the supreme and noble honour that, we hope, awaits us.

The Minister of Sport, Andreas Fouras, assured the IOC that the:

> long-term programme of construction and installation of equipment which will ensure that
> long before 2000 – and regardless of whether Athens is awarded the Games – the city will
> have made good the few shortcomings it still displays in the facilities necessary for all the
> Olympic sports.

The Master Plan sought to concentrate the Games in a small number of locations while making use of existing sports infrastructure. Indeed, the bid claimed that 75 per cent of the competition venues and 92 per cent of the training venues were already in place. The backbone of the strategy remained to use the locations identified in the earlier bid – the Olympic Village on the slopes of Mount Parnitha; AOSC at Maroussi to host seven events (athletics, basketball, cycling, football, gymnastics, swimming and tennis); central Athens (Cultural Olympiad and accommodation for Official Visitors); and the Faliro Coastal Zone, designated as a major regeneration project for Athens's 'Riviera', which would house baseball, boxing, fencing, handball, hockey, judo, wrestling, softball, taekwondo and volleyball.

The plan envisaged four further sites within the Athens conurbation – the Nikaia indoor hall for weightlifting and the Peristeri indoor hall for badminton (both in the west); in the north the Galatsi gymnasium for table tennis; and in the east, Goudi for the modern pentathlon. Beyond the conurbation, the equestrian and archery events were located at Tatoi in the north on Mount Parnitha; rowing, canoeing and kayaking at Schinas on the coast north-east of Athens near the ancient battlefield of Marathon; shooting at Markopoulo south-east of Athens; and sailing and the triathlon along the coast at, respectively, Kosmas and Glyfada. The Olympic Ring project remained as before to link the conurbation sporting venues. Investment in roads and in metro, tramlines and suburban railways would improve movement throughout the metropolis and provide access to the other venues. A new international airport at Sparta had become a central part of the planning strategy, although for the period up to and including the Games it would work in conjunction with the existing airport at Helliniki. The latter was proposed for closure in late 2004 (AOBC, 1997). A 4-year Cultural Olympiad was planned, with events taking place in Greece and abroad to 'restore the Olympic Ideal' in the opening years of the new Millennium. The estimated budget was $1.607 billion with the principal sources of income being television rights, sponsorship, licensing, official suppliers, donations, ticket sales and lotteries (*Ibid.*, p. 162). The non-OCOG budget, however, was $7.35 billion, which included expenditure on roads, airport construction and landscaping.

Planning Athens 2004

The IOC's decision in September 1997 to award the 2004 Games to Athens reflected the quality of the campaign run by the Greek bidding team led by

Gianna Angelopoulos-Daskalaki. Despite assurances that the same team would lead the planning and organization of the Games, they were replaced on return to Athens (Payne, 2006, p. 259). Moreover, instead of immediate implementation of the master plan, the government instigated a review in early 1998 'to eliminate potential problems that might arise during the implementation phase due to the existing zoning and town planning legislation' (ATHOC, 2005, I, p. 143). These considerations, coupled with community views on site decisions and rethinking about the logistics of the festival, led to considerable and time-consuming changes to the original strategy.

The final scheme that emerged retained the AOSC complex at its heart, but the government decided to concentrate less activity in the Faliro area while retaining it as a 'pole' of the Games and maintaining the goal of urban regeneration for the area. After exploring the idea of moving some events to Aspropyrgos, west of the Athens conurbation – which proved unacceptable to both the IOC and the International Federations (*Ibid.*, p. 144) – it was decided to use the site of the much criticized Athens International Airport at Helleniki.[5] Faliro was now to stage only four rather than eleven sports (volleyball, beach volleyball, handball and taekwando), Helleniki would handle baseball, fencing, hockey, softball, basketball, some of the handball matches from Faliro and, after a court case (see below), the canoe and kayak slalom centre (*Ibid.*). Boxing and badminton were moved to, respectively, Peristeri and the Goudi complex. Two sports were moved to sites with classical connotations to assert the sense of Greek ownership of the Games: archery to the Panathenian Stadium and the shot put to Olympia. The decision on Olympia was controversial. The first suggestion was to stage the javelin or discus there because these were events that featured in the Ancient Games. This encountered opposition from the archaeologists due to potential damage to the site (see Chapter 2). The shot put was finally selected as likely to create fewer problems, but the Archaeological Service insisted that no electronic equipment could be used, the throwing circle was to be portable, and that 15,000 free tickets could be issued for spectators to sit on the grass, obviating the need to build a temporary grandstand.[6]

These changes to the original strategy set back the timetable. Some locations needed planning from scratch, with the transport strategy requiring revision to take into consideration the new sites and relocated sports. The process of rethinking, with associated debates, contributed to the now infamous delays in the completion of venues and infrastructure that Payne (2006, p. 261) called the 'three lost years'. Although it was claimed that 75 per cent of the venues already existed, the renovation work envisaged for some was ambitious; for example, amounting to demolition and rebuilding of the swimming complex and tennis centre at AOSC. Additional problems arose from the presence of multiple and often conflicting agencies (Beriatos and Gospodini, 2004, p. 193), the difficulties of gaining cooperation from officials from different political parties, the bureaucratic planning system, and from archaeological discoveries made during construction that required excavation and recording before work could continue. In some instances plans had to be adjusted in order to preserve structures, such as the re-siting of the Olympic Village site to avoid archaeological remains (see below). Matters were not helped by the increased security concerns that inflated costs and caused a review of the layout of sports facilities.

The resulting delays in finalizing venues or in sites becoming available for development caused alarm at the IOC, with Samaranch warning Greece in April 2000 that they might lose the Games if action was not forthcoming. The sense of crisis was fanned by the press, although some observers (e.g. Waterfield, 2004, p. 372) felt that there was insufficient recognition of the complexities of operating in an ancient city such as Athens. The government reacted by bringing Gianna Angelopoulos-Daskalaki back to the development team (Payne, 2006, pp. 261–262), making available emergency funds and introducing new legislation and mechanisms to speed up the development process (Pyrgiotis, 2003, p. 417). This all added substantially to the cost of the Games, with 'speed bonuses' offered by government as an incentive to improve completion, coupled with threats of loss of licences to contactors that failed to complete on time.

This final plan for the Games was described by Beriatos and Gospodini (2004, p. 197) as a 'scattered model' suggestive of a strategy for promoting 'multi-nucleus urban regeneration and development' (Ibid., p. 192), in contrast to cities like Barcelona which focused investment on a few key locations. The plan diluted the original logic of concentrating development in major nodes by spreading the benefits of Olympic investment geographically to include poorer neighbourhoods lacking leisure facilities. However, there was no proper strategic planning for the period after 2004, and the plan contained apparent contradictions. Despite espousing the desire to protect and create open space, development focused primarily on greenfield sites and overlooked possible brownfield locations. Emphasis was placed on gaining spectacular buildings and monuments to create a sense of place and to signify the 2004 Games, yet these structures are outside the main tourist areas.

Broadly speaking, the plan proposed three approaches to preparing the city for the Games. The first concerned the permanent structures: the sports venues, transport infrastructure, city renovation, and arts infrastructure that were designed to be a physical legacy for the city. The second involved a series of temporary interventions designed to house additional sports capacity, visitor accommodation and traffic movements. These also included measures to shape the 'look' of the city in order to provide it with a festive atmosphere that clearly identified it with the Olympics. The third comprised attempts to encourage volunteering and change the behaviour of the population by tackling issues such as litter and smoking.

Olympic Facilities

AOSC was the spectacular centrepiece of the Olympics, eventually developing into a focus that went far beyond simple renovation of the complex created for the 1982 European Athletic Championships. Having decided that it wanted an 'architectural landmark of international recognition', the Ministry of Culture approached the Spanish architect Santiago Calatrava in March 2001 to submit a master plan. The result was a series of projects, including equipping the Olympic stadium with an innovative two leaf, laminated glass roof to protect spectators from the fierce sunlight, roofing the velodrome, bringing about the aesthetic unification of the various structures and plazas of the site by means of landscaping and an installation – the sinuous 'Wall of Nations' – that could also double as a giant video screen (Tzonis, 2005). The stadium roof in particular was a complex design and was only moved into position on the day that the IOC set as a deadline for the project to be either in place or abandoned (Payne, 2006, p. 269). Even so, shortage of time meant that only 9,000 of the projected 17,000 trees were planted around the stadium.

In the original plan, Faliro Bay was recognized as a prime candidate for regeneration. This area had developed in the 1870s as an elegant resort serving the Athenian middle class but a century later, cut off from adjacent residential districts by the coastal highway, it had declined into a virtual no man's land, degraded, polluted, and an illegal dumping ground. The nearby low-lying housing districts of Moschato and Kallithea were also subject to flooding. The Olympics provided a unique occasion for upgrading this area, again opening Athens to the sea and supplying much needed public open space. The downgrading of Faliro from the second most important Games complex to one staging just four events, none of which had any great importance within Greek sporting culture, meant there would be no legacy of specialized sports facilities here. Most construction work involved renovation of the two existing stadia – the Peace and Friendship Stadium for volleyball and the Karaiskaki for part of the football competition.

Having said this, the area did receive a moderate amount of remodelling. The race course at the east end of the site was moved and the land cleared. The Illissos River was canalized as part of the flood protection works, a marina was constructed in the east of the site and the area landscaped. An 800-metre-long esplanade was built from the old race track over the coastal highway to the new indoor sports hall and marinas. This connected the residential area with the renovated coastal zone, with walkways radiating westwards towards the beach volleyball arena. Improvements to roads and a new tram network linked the site to the centre of Athens and to the other Olympic venues. This was to be a prelude to planned post-Games projects intended to continue the anti-flooding work and move the coastal highway into a cutting allowing new bridges to the park beyond.

Of the two new buildings constructed for the Olympics, the beach volleyball centre was intended to become an open-air theatre and the indoor sports hall for handball and taekwando was to be converted into a Metropolitan Convention Centre taking advantage of its proximity to major hotels, the city centre and the coast (Romanos et al., 2005, p. 6). Landscaping the area to the west of the theatre would create a 'green zone', with an environmental centre and communal sports facilities.

The old race track would become open space with water sports at the end of the esplanade. More tentative plans foresaw an Opera House on the race course site, an archaeological park to display classical structures from the regeneration project (*Ibid.*, pp. 4–6) and a heritage park including the Military Museum in the Syngrou villa, the Naval Museum and a new contemporary art museum (Sykianaki, 2003, p. 21). In total, the Coastal Leisure Park would provide 100 hectares of accessible open space (Sykianaki and Psihogias, 2006, p. 12).

The principle of coastal revitalization was continued further south with the redevelopment of the airport site at Helleniki. This entailed conversion of hangars to create indoor halls for fencing and basketball as well as provision of facilities for softball, baseball, hockey, canoeing and kayaking (ATHOC, 2005, p. 144). Not surprisingly, conversion of this site tended to produce a sports centre with a ground plan dominated by the exiting geometry of the airport. Suggestions for post-Games usage hazily envisaged the conversion of the East Airport Terminal, designed by Eero Saarinen in 1960, into a Conference and Exhibition Centre and luxury hotel, with the surrounding area touted as the largest metropolitan park in Europe. The question of how many Convention Centres Athens actually required scarcely entered the equation.

The retreat from the original concentrated approach led to a scattering of other centres throughout the region. These included sailing at Aghios Kosmas, the modern pentathlon at the Goudi Olympic Complex at the foot of Mount Ymittos, weightlifting at Nikea, and the equestrian centre at Markopoulo (a significant archaeological site). Perhaps the most difficult location was the Schinas Rowing Centre, which attracted international controversy. Originally a wetland area, this coastal site had been partly drained for agriculture in the 1920s and had been used for civil and military aviation since the 1950s. The official viewpoint was that this was a degraded wetland in need of protection and the removal of existing installations. The 2.25 kilometre rowing course would be on the line of the old runway, along with practice facilities, an adjacent 400-metre slalom course for canoes and kayaks, grandstands for 10,000 spectators with space for 40,000 more along the course, associated start and finish towers, car parks, boathouses and visitor facilities. By contrast, environmentalists saw it as a rare ecological habitat with a delicate freshwater wetland used by 176 bird species, and with a rare stone pine forest on the coastal dunes. Archaeologists and historians saw it as the site of the battle of Marathon and an important cultural landscape. The Greek government was criticized for removing the area from a list of sites to be submitted for Natura 2000 status – the European Union's initiative to guarantee the maintenance, or re-establishment, of important habitats (Metera *et al.*, 2005, p. 7).

When the Greek government ignored the European Commission's request for it to be reinstated, four environmental groups took the government to court.[7] Archaeological and heritage groups joined the protest, arguing that the Battle of Marathon had raged though the area and the development was akin to building a sports complex on the battlefield at Gettysburg. The government countered by saying that the area was previously under the sea and that there was no evidence of archaeological importance. The outcome did not prevent use of the site for the Olympics, but did produce concessions. The area received National Park status, the facilities were moved to the western end of the site, provision of visitor facilities were curtailed, and the slalom course was re-sited at Helleniki (see above). There was also a commitment to restore the wetlands and create an environmental zone and archaeological park.

The site of the Olympic Village was chosen partly because the government already owned half of the land thereby reducing the need for compulsory purchase, and partly because the development, with its associated services, would 'upgrade the neglected area of the north-west section of the Greater Athens area' (AOBC, 1997, p. 26). The bid document had claimed the housing would be built to the highest environmental standards using solar energy, water management systems, planting of indigenous species and landscaping to create an ecological park. It was designed to accommodate 17,428 participants, with the maximum occupation level during the Olympics being 14,243 and 7,166 during the Paralympics (ATHOC, 2005, II, p. 49). In addition, the Village development was intended to be self-financing, with the accommodation sold after the Games to middle-income families (*Ibid.*, p. 26).

From the outset, the authorities were criticized for lack of progress, although discovery of the remains of Hadrian's aqueduct on the site caused delay for excavation and redesign to protect the archaeology. Rather more criticism came from environmentalists, initially because the development encroached into an environmentally sensitive area and later due to the failure to implement the environmental elements as originally planned. The World Wildlife Fund, for example, criticized the lack of inbuilt water-saving measures, the irrigation of planting in the surrounding areas from tap water, the lack of photovoltaic cells or solar heating systems in the design, and the failure to use environmentally friendly materials such as certified timber or ozone friendly cooling systems (WWF, 2004, pp. 8, 9).

Infrastructure

The Olympics provided an opportunity to take a fresh and comprehensive look at transport within Greater Athens, with its attendant problems of congestion, parking, slow travel times, pollution and the unpopularity of the public transport system (comprising bus, trolley bus, metro and suburban railway networks). The metro consisted of a single line dating back to the 1860s which by 1957 ran from Piraeus to Kifissia. By this time, however, the city had long since expanded into Attica, with large swathes reliant on trams (until 1961), trolleybuses (from 1949), diesel buses and the private car. Investment in improving public transport and creating an integrated transport system for the first time, therefore, was paramount.

A proportion of the investment was scheduled before gaining the Games; for example, contracts for two new metro lines were signed in 1991. Nevertheless, early progress was extremely slow due to bureaucratic problems, geological difficulties and delays for archaeological excavations ahead of station construction. Lack of progress on line 3, which connected with the airport, particularly concerned the IOC, with one observer commenting in 2002 that 'there are plans to extend this line all the way to the airport, but work has yet to start on this' (Dubin *et al.*, 2004). It remained incomplete at the time of the Games but, in reaching Doukaissia Plakentias by July 2004, it was possible to run services to the airport using a suburban rail line. Concerns over pollution led to replacement of the aged bus fleet, with environmentally-friendly vehicles that also offered greater accessibility for the disabled. Developments specifically for the Games included a new tram network that connected central Athens with the coastal Olympic venues – with one branch serving the Faliro Coastal Zone and the other heading south to Helleniki, Agios Kosmas and ending at Glyfada. The route was not a rapid mode of transport however, given that traffic lights, frequent stops and vehicles obstructing the lines caused it to be 'strangely sluggish' (Sales, 2005, p. 29). The road network received investment to improve connections between Athens and other major centres and to create an outer ring road interlinking the Olympic venues, the international airport and the city. AOSC gained a ring road that operated during the Games as a clockwise one-way system reserved for Olympic traffic (ATHOC, 2005, p. 173). Elsewhere, a new Traffic Management System meant that traffic flows could be managed to prioritize Olympic traffic, with appropriate signage and dedicated lanes. In the final event, the free-moving traffic was a public relations coup for a city where congestion and traffic jams were regarded as endemic.

Cultural infrastructure also benefited from the Olympics. Major Athenian museums such as the National Archaeological Museum, Byzantine Museum and the National Gallery were renovated for the Games, although in the case of the National Archaeological Museum the task was made more challenging by damage from the 1999 earthquake (it was not fully opened until 2005). The Olympics were also a vehicle for developing contemporary art. This led to the foundation of two complexes, both housed in former industrial premises: Technopolis, an arts and performance space that also houses a small Maria Callas Museum; and the Athinais, a restored silk factory that contains a theatre, cinema, music space, museum space, restaurants, bars and cafés, and conference facilities. These have acted as exemplars for further developments, most notably the National Museum of Contemporary Art, which opened in 2005 in a converted brewery and the proposed new City of Athens Art Gallery, in a converted silk factory in Metaxourgio.

Beautification

As was seen with the examples of Mexico City 1968 (Chapter 14) and Atlanta 1996 (Chapter 2), beautification of a city is a contentious issue, prioritizing impressing visitors over the interests of the poor, whether through redistribution of resources or displacement of previous residents. These issues arose in the case of Athens, but in the context of the longstanding desire to remake it as a city in keeping with the splendours of its august past. The return of the Games in 2004 witnessed a flurry of activity to beautify the city centre – the focus of the festivities and cultural activities that accompanied the Games, as well as the venue for the cycling road race and the finish of the marathon at the Panathenian Stadium (Sykianaki, 2003, p. 11). Perhaps the most important of the measures taken in relation to the Games was the unification of archaeological sites – a project that dated back to the 1832 plan which suggested that, when cleared and planted, the 'whole would be a museum of ancient building-art second to none in the world' (quoted in Bastéa, 2000, p. 219). The idea of a unified cultural-historic area had resurfaced periodically over the next century and a half, but financial and practical problems hindered progress (Papageorgiou-Ventas, 1994, p. 28). In 1993, a formal scheme to link the key classical sites by landscaped pedestrian routes and green open spaces received European Union funding. Its rationale rested in part on romantic nationalism, partly on a wish to marry together the old and the new into a functional whole, and partly on creating a unique tourist amenity that could compete with the great European tourist cities (*Ibid.*, p. 398).

The city's planners considered it imperative to complete a major part of this project in time both to receive Olympic visitors and accommodate the road race which was planned to use the newly-pedestrianized streets around the Acropolis. By the Games, for instance, it was possible to walk from the Panathenian Stadium to the ancient cemetery at Kerameikos, via the Olympieion, the south side of the Acropolis, the Theatre of Dionysus and the ancient agora (see figure 17.1). By contrast, other projects such as the restoration of the Parthenon and the

Figure 17.1. Pedestrianized street beneath the Acropolis; part of the project unifying the archaeological sites (June 2009). (*Photo*: Margaret Gold)

development of the new Acropolis Museum proved impossible to complete before the Games, due particularly to archaeological and conservation issues.

The programme for improving central Athens also encompassed improvements to street lighting, the refurbishment of city squares, restoration of façades, floodlighting monuments and key buildings, planting and landscaping, renewal of street furniture, repaving roads and improving pavements. Work was also carried out to upgrade the waste management systems of the city. The staging of the Paralympic Games had an important impact in improving access for the disabled, with installation of more than 7,000 wheelchair ramps (Bokoyannis, 2006, p. 6), modifications to public transport, and encouragement from ATHOC for businesses to cater for the needs of the disabled (see Chapter 5).

Besides the regeneration schemes and other projects that made a permanent contribution to the quality of life of residents and visitors, there were also the temporary measures that announced that the city was *en fête*. The notion of giving the city a distinctive 'look' during the Olympic festival, a recurrent theme since Tokyo 1964 (see Chapter 2), was again observed at Athens. Like its predecessors, this involved the careful selection of colours, logos, decorations and artwork, with the creation of a Kit of Parts that could be applied to all the venues and arranged so that athletes, visitors and television audiences could see the legend 'ATHENS 2004' and the Olympic Rings at all venues and along significant routes. This creation of 'visual identity' (ATHOC, 2005, I, p. 331) involved specification of a twenty-colour palette, centring on blue (sky and sea), yellow and oranges (summertime), red and fuchsia (flowers), green (landscape) and grey (stone) (*Ibid.*, p. 319). Construction sites and ugly buildings disappeared behind large building wraps, with images of ancient Olympia and photographs by Greek artists. Conscious of the over-commercialism of Atlanta 1996 – about which the Greeks had made considerable reference when bidding for the Games – attempts were made to control advertising displays throughout the city. By the summer of 2004, 5,000 billboards had been removed and official sites given over to sponsors and used for messages promoting the Olympic ideal. In the process, the Organizing Committee effectively enhanced the value of the investment made by sponsors in offering them 'a whole new level of protection against ambush marketing', comprising 'the most tightly controlled' marketplace to date (Payne, 2006, pp. 262–263, 266).

Legacy

Ensuring that Olympic sports facilities have viable alternative uses is a challenge with which many cities have struggled once the Games are over, and Athens certainly made much of the idea that it was creating permanent facilities that would have post-Olympic use (Kissoudi, 2008). Over the 7-year preparation period, official statements constantly speculated on the post-Games legacy, with the city clearly looking for a multifaceted outcome (ATHOC, 2005, II, p. 525). Leisure, cultural, sporting and conference uses were typically mentioned, but unless there is state involvement (as in the case of a government ministry using premises for offices) or end-users are directly identified and involved in construction (e.g. the Press Villages were funded by the universities for halls of residence), it is not so easy to dictate use.

In terms of immediate effect, there was the reality of a city which, with little margin for error, completed the facilities in time for the Games despite the scepticism of journalists who, only weeks earlier, described the rubble on building sites and listed the work still outstanding. There was spectacular television footage of the Opening Ceremony and the striking backdrop of the city. All this confirmed that the 'smoggy Aegean backwater' had indeed been 'transformed' (the most common adjective used) into a city of beautiful boulevards, clear and azure skies, a growing number of art centres, a vibrant and cutting edge spirit and the finest metro in Europe (Correspondent, 2004). Sadly for the organizers, the drug scandal involving Greek athletes on the eve of the Opening Ceremony was a public relations disaster both in the context of Athens promising a return to the core values of the Olympics and in diverting attention away from the city.[8] By the end of the Games, however, attention had re-focused on the Games, with consensus being that the Games had been run well, with praise for the scheduling, transport and the athletes' facilities.

The longer term impact of the Games remains contentious. The Official Report (ATHOC, 2005, II, p. 525) outlined their legacy in terms of transport improvements, reduced pollution, land reclamation, sports facilities, beautification of the city, a culture of cooperation, civic spirit and job training, concluding:

> The Games were a 17-day advertisement for our competence and sophistication, potential investors discovered that Greece has the talent, attitude and infrastructure – and the EU membership – to compete internationally. Finally we Greeks proved to ourselves that we can do whatever we set ourselves to doing, under extraordinary pressure, with a global audience. After the Olympic Games, we know we can compete with anybody.

The Director for the Organization for the Planning and Environmental Protection of Athens, Catherine Sykianaki and her colleague Sakis Psihogias (2006, p. 11) maintained that the physical legacy of the Games in terms of 'renewal and regeneration' represented a 'catching up process after some decades of inertia had eroded the competitiveness and quality of life of Athens'. The city now had an infrastructure conducive to economic growth. IOC marketing specialist Michael Payne (2006, p. 271) believed that the Games helped 're-brand Greece as a country' and that they had successfully managed to combine the mythological and traditional images with modern, dynamic designs. The Athens communication team even talked of 'just in time delivery' as if 'it was something that had been planned all the time so that the country could showcase its efficiency and ingenuity at the last minute' (*Ibid.*, p. 269) to counteract the press view that it was in fact a 'last minute approach' (Smith, 2003). However, notwithstanding such promotional gloss, there is no doubt that corners were cut, plans cancelled and tasks left incomplete; issues which impacted on post-Games planning.

Popular tourist literature applauds the changes made in connection with the Games that transformed Athens into a more attractive tourist destination:

> Major urban renewal has breathed new life into Athens' historic centre, spectacularly reconciling its ancient and modern faces with charming car-free streets that wind along well-trodden ancient paths, making it feel like you're walking through a giant archaeological park... The city's radical pre-Olympics makeover went well beyond new infrastructure. There's a newfound confidence and creative energy, particularly in emerging arts, dining and entertainment hotspots in newly hip, urban neighbourhoods. (Kyriakopoulos, 2009, p. 7)

By contrast, and despite the frequency with which images of the iconic Olympic complex are reproduced as symbols of the new Athens, their peripheral locations are far removed from the normal tourist circuit and, although easily reached by public transport, do not yet provide the animated public spaces that many assumed they would become.

The Games were praised for placing disability on the agenda, although some warn that the city lags behind other capitals and more needs to be done.[9] Vozikis (2009, p. 496), for example, notes that greater vigilance is required if the gains made in creating a more accessible physical environment for those with mobility problems are to remain effective. She notes that too often lifts remain out of order, disabled toilets are used for storage and illegal parking is tolerated in disabled spaces.

Environmentalists, as mentioned previously, were particularly critical that the rules laid down in the tender for the Olympic Village were largely ignored when reducing construction costs became the priority. In more measured tones, commentators from the United Nations Environment Programme noted that while there had been undoubted achievements in the areas of transport, coastal rehabilitation and improvements in public awareness of environmental issues, in the matter of energy consumption and the building of eco-friendly facilities standards had fallen 'below expectations'. They regretted that there had not been more consultation at the preparation stages with 'key stakeholders, particularly environmental NGOs'.[10] For its part, the environmental assessment of the Games by the World Wildlife Fund (WWF) in July 2004 evaluated eighteen environmental performance indicators with a score from 0 (very disappointing) to 4 (very positive). As table 17.1 shows, Athens's average was just 0.77, scoring zero on no less than eleven of the criteria, including protection of natural habitats, protection of open spaces, siting of Olympic venues, use of green technologies, green energy, water saving, integrated waste management and recycling, and respect for environmental legislation. The highest scores were for public awareness (4), improvement of the built environment (3) and public transport (3). The WWF's assessment was that there had been no effort to integrate the environment into the planning of the Games and that opportunities were missed to improve environmental management

Table 17.1. Olympic environmental assessment, Athens 2004.

Issue	Score	Highlighted Examples
Overall Planning		
Environmental planning	0	Principles of the Environmental Policy of ATHOC published 2001 – more a communications tool than an environmental strategy
Environmental assessment	0	Absence of concrete and measurable environmental commitments
Natural Environment		
Protection of natural habitats	0	Schinas Rowing and canoeing centre. Fragile environmental areas trapped by the expansion of the urban web
Urban Environment		
Protection of open spaces	0	Use of open space for venues: Galatsi, Maroussi Press facilities, Olympic Village; failure to complete the ecological park at Faliro
Increase of urban green	0	Failure to plant Mediterranean species; planting out of season and requiring irrigation
Improvement of the built environment	3	Façades, removal of billboards, pedestrian network, unification of archaeological sites, street cleaning
Transport		
Public transport	3	Metro, gas powered buses, urban rail and tram network, public awareness campaign to reduce car usage. No cycle facilities
Constructions		
Siting of Olympic venues	0	Lack of public consultation over sites
Use of existing infrastructure	1	Olympic Stadium and Peace and Friendship Stadium used
Use of green technologies	0	Failed to include environmental obligations in the contracts for the Olympic Village: use of solar power, water saving systems, ozone-friendly cooling systems, certified timber. Debris abandoned at constructions sites
Energy		
Green energy	0	Solar and wind energy options not considered for the Olympic sites
Water		
Water saving scheme	0	Tap water used for irrigation of Olympic Village site; 16 km pipeline supplies tap water to Schinais competition reservoirs in dry periods
Waste		
Integrated waste management and recycling	0	No integrated waste management strategy. Recycling bins provided at Olympic venues
Public Participation		
Social consultation	1	No stakeholder consultation. Opposition to the sites for Schinas Rowing Centre, Galatsi, Olympic Village, Press Centre
Transparency	1	Poor information; NGOs with an international base had more success in obtaining information than other groups
Public information	1	Website used as a promotional rather than an information tool. Central role therefore played by the press in highlighting issues
General Issues		
Respect for environmental legislation	0	Existing legislation bypassed, for example in the case of the Press Village Maroussi
Public awareness	4	Good environmental education and awareness to reduce car usage and water consumption
Total Score	0.77	

(4 = very positive; 3 = positive; 2 = fair; 1 = disappointing; 0 = very disappointing)
Source: Compiled from World Wildlife Fund Greece (2004) *Environmental Assessment of the Athens 2004 Olympic Games*, July 2004.

in areas where Athens is vulnerable, such as water supply, energy provision and waste disposal. Indeed, nothing was done to promote renewable energy or water conservation or to tackle waste management other than to purchase a new fleet of dust carts.

Finding worthwhile uses for Games facilities once the Games are over is another canon of sustainable Olympic development. This question is the one that has come to bedevil the final reputation of the Games with press coverage that has been relentlessly negative. The summer of 2008 saw a spate of articles as the Beijing Games loomed, looking back to Athens as an example of how not to plan an Olympics. The same stories were repeated 6 years later to mark the tenth anniversary of the Games. Picking just three headlines gives the flavour of the coverage: from the *Daily Telegraph* in 2008 came 'Athens' deserted Games sites a warning to London Olympics' (Moore, 2008); the *Chicago Tribune* reported 'Testament to progress atrophies after Games – Athens Olympic venues suffer from lack of long-range planning. Chicago should take note' (Hersh, 2008); and the *Daily Mail* (Evans, 2014) 'The new ruins of Athens: rusting and decaying 10 years on, how Greece's Olympics turned into a £7 billion white elephant'. Whichever decade the coverage came from it repeated the same trope: photographs of dirty, graffiti-covered, seemingly abandoned facilities in a sea of derelict open space, locked away behind high fences or, in the case of the coastal facilities at Faliro, surrounded by gypsy encampments.[11] The former Olympic Village did not escape press censure with descriptions of abandoned and deteriorating homes, failing businesses and unusable leisure facilities (Anon, 2011).

Legacy had already become a political issue in Greece, with the two major national political parties accusing one another over which bore more blame for the lack of post-Games strategy. The New Democracy Party, in power since March 2004, claimed that PASOK, their Socialist predecessors, had no proper business plans for the Olympic sites. PASOK countered that facilities were being allowed to deteriorate.[12] The New Democracy government established a state-owned holding company, Hellenic Olympic Properties (HOP), to which it transferred twenty-two venues. These included all the Athens sports facilities, the Media Press Centre and the International Broadcasting Centre but not the AOSC complex, the Olympic Village or Press Villages. AOSC remains an international sports complex and the Villages had post-Games plans in place. HOP's brief was to achieve 'sustainable commercial development' in areas of activity compatible with government strategy, with a general framework of permitted uses laid down in legislation passed in 2005–2006 (HOP, 2006). HOP was to manage the remaining sites until lease-holders could be found in the form of foreign or domestic investors or public-private partnerships, thus helping to recoup building costs, avoid the expense of maintaining the venues (estimated at $100 million per annum) and benefit local communities in terms of cultural amenity and jobs.

Understandably, HOP faced the problem that the locations of the venues reflected political, landownership and pragmatic considerations rather than planning for post-Games commercial use. A stated aim for the free-standing venues was to improve the infrastructure of the unplanned suburbs, but the municipalities could not afford to maintain them (MSNBC, 2004). The Faliro and Helleniki complexes were meant to generate critical mass since they contain a number of attractions but it was estimated back in 2005, for example, that the cost of running Faliro was €5–7 million as against an income from the Marina and Indoor Hall of €2–4 million (Romanos et al., 2005, p. 6).

Therefore, progress towards realizing a new life for the venues has been patchy (see Kissoudi, 2008). Tenders were invited for the Badminton Hall at Goudi, the International Broadcasting Centre, the canoe-kayak slalom course at Helleniki, the sailing centre at Agio Kosmas, and the Galatsi Olympic Indoor Hall in 2005. In March 2006, further tenders were invited for the beach volleyball centre at Faliro. At the time of writing, only two of these projects are operational. In May 2006, a consortium signed a 25-year lease on the Badminton Hall for €12.5 million.[13] The Badminton Theatre opened in 2007 as a 2,500-seater auditorium – the largest in Greece – and capable of staging large-scale productions of opera, ballet, theatre and popular concerts from 'Evita' to Matthew Bourne's 'Swan Lake'. Conference facilities were added in 2012 to allow it to host events.

At the International Broadcasting Centre (IBC) site, the Golden Hall, a luxury shopping mall, opened in November 2008. With 131 shops and 1,400 parking spaces, it was advertised as being the 'ultimate fashion destination for the northern suburbs of Athens'. It was expected to attract between 7 and 9 million visits in its first full year of operation (Michaelidou, 2009, p. 58). Two museums were planned for the remaining part of the IBC building which abuts the Olympic Stadium. One is a national project, the Museum of the Greek Olympic Games, and the other an International Museum of Athletics and an associated Hall of Fame. An agreement relating to the latter was signed with the International Association of Athletics Federations in 2005 (IAAF, 2005). Neither museum has yet materialized, although the Olympic Museum is still part of Lamda Development's plans for the expansion of the Golden Hall following their purchase in 2013 of a 90-year lease for the whole site (Lamda Development, 2016). The neighbouring Main Press Centre was taken over by the Ministry of Health in 2007.

The table tennis and rhythmic gymnastics venue at Galatsi was to have been the second Olympic site to host a shopping mall. This demand from the retail sector reflects the fact that Greece reportedly had the lowest ratio of shopping centre space per 1,000 inhabitants in the EU in 2007 at 50 square metres per 1,000 inhabitants compared to the EU average of 150, with Athens not getting its first mall until 2005 (Bouras, 2007). The Galatsi project, unveiled in 2006 was to provide 35,000 square metres of retail space while retaining the table tennis and rhythmic gymnastics venue for sport. It was originally due for completion in 2008, but was rescheduled for 2009. Subsequent delays in obtaining permits meant the project was then hit by the economic downturn and construction still had not begun by March 2010 (Boston, 2010).

Further projects stalled. The canoe-kayak slalom centre was intended to become a water park, but was never completed. The Beach Volleyball arena on the coast at Faliro was to have become an open-air theatre opening in 2008, but permits were delayed and plans changed so it remains semi-abandoned. A private–public partnership was approved for the work required to adapt the Faliro Pavilion (Taekwondo Arena) for use as an International Conference Centre and to maintain and manage it for a 25-year period, but little materialized save for hosting the occasional trade fair or concert. It was announced in March 2010 that it had been decided to renegotiate the agreement over the building (Correspondent, 2010).

In contrast to this picture of failed legacy, it should be noted that plans for the site next to the Taekwondo Stadium are moving apace. The Stavros Niarchios Foundation Cultural Centre is being built on the site of the old Athens race course, which was cleared for parking spaces during the Olympics. This development takes advantage of the public works along the coast particularly the promenade across the motorway which links the site with the coast and adjacent Olympic venues (see figure 17.2). The project houses two national institutions: the National Library of Greece, and Greek National Opera surrounded by 42 acres (17 hectares) of landscaped parkland. The project has cost over $800m (over €580m) and after

Figure17.2. Pedestrian promenade over the coastal motorway built for Athens 2004, linking the Taekwando Arena with the site for the Stavros Niarchios Foundation Centre, which will house the National Library and National Opera in a landscaped park (June 2009). (*Photo:* Margaret Gold)

a delay of 2 years, construction started in 2012 with a view to opening in 2016 (SNF, 2009, 2016).[14] On completion, it will be transferred to the state with the aim of creating a coastal cultural quarter capable of serving the local community, the Athenian public, Greek nationals and tourists.

Most of the other sites in the HOP portfolio have acquired public uses. Three are being used by sports federations: the Faliro Marina to the National Sailing Federation to become a National Sailing Centre, the Markopolou Equestrian Centre to the Hellenic Equestrian Federation and Schinias Rowing Centre to the Greek Rowing Association for a National and International Rowing Centre. The Markopolou Shooting Centre has become a police shooting academy and headquarters of Police Special Forces, the Nikea weightlifting arena has been given to the University of Piraeus as its second campus, and the Ano Liosia arena used in the wrestling and judo is to be an arts academy.

AOSC raises a familiar problem for Olympic cities, namely, the future of a very large stadium that is scarcely used on any regular basis. The aim is to retain the facilities for sporting use. As elsewhere, there has been usage for football, with the ground initially shared by Panathinaikos and AEK Athens, but stadia essentially built for athletics rarely provide ideal conditions for football. Panathinaikos has the long-term aim of developing its own stadium complex, a plan backed by the Athens Municipality which sees this development as spearheading the regeneration of the Votanikos/Alexandros Avenue area to provide open space, cultural, sporting and commercial facilities in a part of Athens lacking good infrastructure (Bokoyannis, 2006, p. 18). The club's financial difficulties, the economic crisis and local opposition have put this plan on hold and in the meantime the old stadium (Apostolos Nikolaidis) has been refurbished and the team have moved back there (Ioannou, 2014). AEK Athens, which moved to the Olympic stadium in 2003 when their Nikos Goumas Stadium was demolished, has average gates of only

Figure 17.3. The Athens Olympic Sports complex, Maroussi, Athens (June 2009). (*Photo:* Margaret Gold)

27,500 and plan to start building a new stadium 'Agia Sophia' in Nea Filadelfeia their original home in 2016 (AEK, 2016). A familiar pattern can be seen here of football teams keen to vacate Olympic stadia for purpose-built football stadia (see chapter 15). The Olympic stadium is used for rock concerts (about 15–20 a year), but between fixtures the site is bleak (figure 17.3). The Olympic Park covers a large area that easily absorbs the trickle of visitors that come to see the iconic architecture. There are no visitor facilities or stadium tours, but persistent reports of the site being locked are untrue.

Economic Crisis

The worsening economic crisis has had a two-fold effect on the Olympic legacy. In the first place the lack of strategic planning from the outset meant that the opportunities to capitalize on the possibilities created by the Games were largely wasted (Ziakas and Boukas, 2012, p. 301). It would have been difficult to rectify the situation in the best of times, but with the financial crisis, any appropriate conditions 'for the effective management of the Olympic legacy' were lost (Boukas *et al.*, 2013, p. 220). The result has been that the notion of legacy evaporated in the face of a trope of 'burden' (Papanikolaou, 2013, p. 4).

The second issue related to the conditions imposed on Greece by the international bailouts of 2010, 2012, and 2015. Greece was expected to generate income by asset sales. In 2011, Hellenic Olympic Properties along with the Hellenic Tourist Properties and the Hellenic Public Real-Estate Corporation combined to form a new body, the Public Properties Company. This now had a portfolio of over 70,000 properties from ports, airports, banks, utilities, and hotels and the remaining twelve Olympic properties (PPC, 2015). Its role is to manage the development and sales of assets. The body charged with the actual sale of land, properties, businesses and leases is the Hellenic Republic Asset Development Fund (HRADF) also established in 2011 as part of the privatization strategy intended to re-establish credibility as a 'prerequisite for Greece to return to global capital markets' (HRADF, 2016). This process is intended to raise cash for the state to offset negotiated bailout loans and attract direct investment into undercapitalized assets and encourage the development of unexploited assets with the view ultimately of promoting economic growth (*Ibid.*).

The Hellinikon airport site is one of the properties transferred to HRADF. This 1,530-acre (620-hectare) site had proved a challenge with its concentration of arenas for sports not popular in Greece. The baseball ground was leased to Ethnikos Football SA and occasional trade shows have been held in the old fencing hall. The old arrivals, departure and charter buildings became the Hellenikon Exhibition Centre, but the envisaged Hellenikon Metropolitan Park had not materialized. The original 2005 plans for a Metropolitan Park, which would have provided much needed public open space and recreation facilities including museums, were superseded by ambitious plans for a new urban quarter that would be a 'landmark of national importance and international visibility' and reposition Athens as a destination city (Hellenikon SA, 2016, p. 2). This 'new vibrant city within Athens' would provide 11,000 homes for a residential population of between 33,000 and 44,000 people, leisure and recreation including museums, sports, recreational facilities and entertainment, a marina, a business park, convention centre, hotel, shopping mall, education research and innovation clusters and a major hospital (Pollalis *et al.*, 2013, pp. 2, 13–14). The site was initially put up for tender in 2011 and finally a deal worth €915m was agreed in 2014 for a 99-year lease with a consortium led by the Lamda Development (from Greece), with Fosun (China) and Al Maabar (Abu Dhabi) (Tagaris, 2014). Opposition groups by contrast have described this as 'the most valuable real estate asset in Europe' being offered at 'an unacceptably low price'. They want a development closer to the 2005 vision, which prioritized public access, recreation space, and sustainability, believing that the proposed development will not benefit surrounding communities. Public incursions on to the site to remove fencing, plant trees or the 2011 Festival of Resistance and Creativity have been ways in which local communities have indicated their frustration with current proposals (City of Hellinikon-Argyroupoli, 2013). Given the bureaucratic, legal and political challenges that lie ahead, the likelihood of any development starting on the site in the near future is remote.

Meanwhile Greece has been enmeshed in the humanitarian crisis facing Europe in 2015 as migrants try to reach Europe by sea – principally from Turkey. In the first 11 months of 2015, 758,596 reached Greece by sea compared to 43,518 in the whole of 2014. Empty Olympic venues have been pressed into service in response to the crisis with temporary reception centres established in the Hockey facility in Hellinikon and the Taekwondo stadium at Faliro (HRGSMC, 2015). In October 2015 migrants were moved from public squares in the centre of Athens to Galatsi Hall (Taylor, 2015). The refusal of Macedonia to admit migrants from counties other than Syria, Afghanistan and Iraq led to the transport of a further 1,000 migrants camped out at the border crossing back to the Faliro Pavilion at the end of December (Strickland, 2015).

Conclusion

For Greece, Athens 2004 was about more than acquiring a set of Olympic venues; the Games were also seen as a means of achieving place promotional goals and the 'soft legacy' of support services, training, employment, attitudinal changes, and organizational knowledge that comes from the successful planning and management of a hallmark event (METREX, 2006, p. 6). In the case of Athens, this included the 'positive climate of opinion within which continued progress could be made' (*Ibid.*, p. 7). Greek politicians quickly latched on to these ideas. Prime Minister Costas Karamanlis, for example, stated at the start of the Games that 'Greece will be a more experienced, a more optimistic and self-confident country' (Beard, 2004). In attempting to learn what such assertions meant in practice, Sykianaki and Psihogias (2006, p. 13) identified four important areas in which Athens 2004 created new working practices that might profoundly affect the city's future development. The first was in pioneering private–public partnerships as a new way of generating development funds. The government introduced legislation in 2005 to provide a framework for such partnerships, then new to Greek practice. This was seen as central to economic policy, something that would support entrepreneurship and make the Greek economy internationally oriented and competitive.[15] Secondly, it was argued that the Games had highlighted the problems of bureaucracy and encouraged a more flexible approach to problem solving. Thirdly, the Games were seen as a vehicle that showed how the city could use major events to lever investment, modernize the built environment and expand Athens's international role. Finally, the Olympics were felt to have mobilized citizens in the affairs of the city. Any such improvements however, have been put under strain by the economic crisis.

Calculating the costs and benefits of an Olympic Games is a daunting task given the powerful indirect, as well as direct, effects of staging the Games for the domestic economy and society. They also depend on political viewpoint. Radical critics on the Left argued that, quite apart from impact on civil liberties, the long-term consequences of staging the Games included reinforcement of trends towards the militarization of urban space, environmental damage and destruction of heritage. Each could have costs for society beyond those that can be imputed in economic terms. Moreover, assessments of costs also depend on the accounting procedures adopted, particularly judgments as to whether or not investment was purely related to the Games or would have happened anyway (e.g. transport improvements and urban beautification). At the end of 2004, for example, the Economy and Finance Minister George Alogoskoufis assessed the cost of the Games as €8.954 million but consciously omitted costs of the airport and metro, even though their development was expedited for the Games, and the continuing costs of maintaining venues until occupiers can be found.[16]

When looked at in narrow economic terms, ATHOC balanced its books and is eventually expected to declare a profit thanks to larger-than-expected contributions from IOC broadcast and sponsorship revenues. Games spending helped the sluggish Greek economy to record a 4 per cent annual increase (Payne, 2006, p. 271), but most of the revenue benefited the Athens region. Regional politicians argue that Athens sucked in investment at the expense of other regions, reinforcing the city's primacy and undoing 'past tendencies for decentralisation' (Coccossis *et al.*, 2003, p. 3). There is, however, consensus that the Games were expensive and over-budget, with infrastructural projects costing 37 per cent more than in the original plan. Greece was the smallest nation to host the Games since Finland in 1952, and there is no doubt that the scale of expenditure expected by the start of the twenty-first century was a strain for a small economy. In Greece's case, European Union membership and access to its funds were of central importance – in particular the Cohesion Fund (for which Greece was one of the major beneficiaries) and the access to loans from the European Investment Bank. European ties, however, also impose costs. The conditions attached to membership of the European Economic and Monetary Union (EEMU) meant that steps were needed to lower Greece's deficit, which, at 6.1 per cent of Gross Domestic Product in 2004, was more than double the limit set by the terms of the EEMU. This resulted in Greece requiring increased taxes, cuts in public spending and wage restraint measures to realign its economy.[17]

The economic crisis that engulfed Greece by 2008 has further added to the cost of the Games by making the legacy goals of the government more difficult to attain. Yet notwithstanding the cost calculations, Athens 2004 is popularly remembered within Greece as a success that confounded journalist critics and came as a relief to those with any measure of responsibility for staging the Games. After the negative publicity surrounding the delays and descriptions of building sites that were relayed to television viewers and newspaper readers in the weeks leading up to the Olympics, the hurried completion of the sites (even if the landscaping and planting was incomplete), the new public transport, and the spectacular Opening Ceremony created the aura of success. The city gained a tangible legacy of infrastructure that can provide the basis for the hoped-for cultural, convention and business tourism trade. The centre of Athens is pedestrian-friendly and guidebooks wax lyrical on the transformation of the city, although few short-break visitors will see the Olympic venues themselves. The cultural sector has benefited from new performance spaces, exhibition spaces and renovated museums. Certainly tourist numbers to Greece increased in the years following the Games (Cartalis, 2015, p. 195) and despite the recession tourism has started to grow again prompting headlines such as 'Greek tourism bounces back' (Kotogiannis and Hope, 2014). The Games undoubtedly accelerated urban renewal and brought investment in transport and telecommunications. In turn, as Sykianaki and Psihogias (2006, p. 11) argued, these developments produced a more 'conducive environment for economic growth', which would be consolidated in a new Structural Plan for the Athens Metropolitan Area. Whatever costs have been incurred, it is scarcely plausible that the range of changes experienced would have occurred without being driven by the approach of an Olympic Opening Ceremony. Certainly most Greek politicians would have settled for this outcome if they had been offered it before the event.

Notes

1.   The first Zappas Games of 1859 were held in Loudovikou Square (Plateia Eleftheris).

2.   Yannis Pyrgiotis, Executive Director of the Organizing Committee for the Olympic Games (Pyrgiotis, 2003, p. 414).

3.   It was built on the site of the velodrome constructed for the 1896 Games.

4.   Information from a poster entitled 'Athens 96: Return to the Future', produced by the Executive Committee for the Candidacy of Athens for the 1996 Olympic Games.

5.   In the bid document this airport was to be replaced by the new Elefthenos Venizelos

International Airport near Sparta, and Helliniki was to continue in operation until the Games were over. Under the new plan it was closed in 2001.

6. Even so the site manager Xenia Arapogianni was quoted as saying 'We still have misgivings about the sanctuary being used in this way. Ancient Olympia isn't a film or television set', but the local mayor hoped that the television coverage would spur tourist development (Special Correspondent, 2004). Olympia also benefited from renovation and three new museums.

7. These were the World Wildlife Fund Hellas; Greek Society for the Protection of the Environment and Cultural Heritage; Hellenic Society for the Protection of Nature; Hellenic Ornithological Society.

8. Two of Greece's athletic stars, Kostas Kenteris and Ekaterini Thanou, failed to report for a drugs test on the eve of the Opening Ceremony and ended up in an Athens hospital under somewhat confused circumstances.

9. Information compiled from Dubin *et al.* (2004), Facaros and Theodorou (2005) and Sales (2005).

10. UNEP Press Release 2004/37, August. Available at: http://www.unep.org.

11. Alexandridis (2007, p. 13), in his study of the housing impact of the 2004 Games, estimated that 2,700 Roma were affected by the Games either through evictions or the abandonment of relocation projects.

12. Hellenic Republic Embassy of Greece, press releases, 12 October and 13 November 2004.

13. Three companies were involved Adam Productions (event organizers), Half Note Jazz Club (club owners and event organizers) and Allou Fun Park (Greece's largest Amusement park). Information from Hellenic Republic Embassy of Greece, press release, 16 May 2006.

14. The site plan, unveiled in October 2009, is by the Italian architect Renzo Piano.

15. Information from Ministry of Economics, press release, 4 August 2006.

16. Information from Hellenic Republic Embassy of Greece, press release, 14 November 2004.

17. The aim was to get it down to 3 per cent by the end of 2006 (Church, 2005).

Chapter 18

Beijing 2008

Ian G. Cook and Steven Miles

It would be difficult indeed not to be impressed with the scale and majesty of the Beijing Olympics in 2008. From the spectacular Opening Ceremony up until the almost as impressive Closing Ceremony, the Games were run effectively and efficiently. There were some hitches and glitches, but as a modern mega-event the Beijing Olympics set a high bar for the subsequent London Olympics and later successors to live up to, not least because of the economic recession that has gripped the globe since 2008–2009. As Lord Sebastian Coe, Chair and CEO of the London 2012 Games stated to the delight of Xinhua, the Chinese State-Run News Agency, in July 2009 at an African Olympic meeting in Abuja, Nigeria:

> Beijing was fantastic, the venues were superb, the planning was superb, the athletes were well looked after, and they performed well because they were well looked after.[1]

Although Coe suggested that he was excited rather than challenged by the success of Beijing, this was exactly what the Chinese authorities wanted to hear. After all the concerns expressed beforehand concerning human rights, social costs, atmospheric pollution and other issues, the People's Republic of China (PRC) had achieved their objectives, to impress such a respected Olympian as Lord Coe, and to develop a model for future Olympics. As social scientists, however, it behoves the authors to take a more critical perspective, to note the successes that did occur, but also the problems that arose, and to consider both the pluses and minuses of Beijing's legacy and the longer-term implications of the Olympics for the reinvention of China as a participant in the global economy.

Beijing itself is a city that has undergone significant transformation in recent decades, and anyone who has travelled to Beijing since the early 1990s will have witnessed enormous changes, with the city rapidly metamorphosing into an 'internationalized metropolis' (Cook, 2006). This period has seen Beijing make not one, but two, bids to host the Summer Olympics. The first bid was submitted in 1992–1993 and was eventually rejected, with Sydney winning the race to host the 2000 Olympics. 'Human rights' were cited as a major reason for the rejection of this bid, unsurprising given that Tiananmen was fresh in the memory, with the tanks being sent in to clear the square on 4 June 1989. Environmental issues, however, were also a major factor. Beijing had already hosted the Asian Games by that date, and so the city had already spent a considerable sum on stadia, a Games Village, and on transport infrastructure. Foreign observers noted how most schoolchildren in Beijing in 1992 seemed to sport the bright yellow baseball cap bearing the Asian Games logo. There was an air of expectancy that China would be awarded the 2000 Summer Olympic Games. The disappointment at rejection was palpable.

In contrast, the announcement in June 2001 that Beijing would host the Olympics in 2008 was greeted by mass rejoicing. Even Shanghai, often cast as a rival of Beijing, witnessed warm celebrations when the result was announced, not least because Shanghai was due to co-host the soccer tournament (figure 18.1). The announcement provided a sense of vindication of China's improved standing in the world. When the PRC was founded on 1 October 1949, Mao Zedong said in his address to the new nation that China had stood up and would never be humiliated again. After many years of effort, of marked successes and notable failures, the opportunity to host the 2008 Olympics was proof that China had not only stood up, but also that it was no longer a pariah state and was ready to take its rightful place as one of the leading countries on earth. To analyse the Beijing Olympics, therefore, is not only to analyse the specific urban dimension of this Olympic City, but also to contextualize Beijing's successful bid within the rise of the New China, a China that is proud of its past and increasingly proud of its present.

Figure 18.1. Shanghai joins in the celebrations: Sofitel Hotel, central Shanghai after the announcement of the successful bid.

This wider contextualization highlights negatives as well as positives concerning the Beijing Olympics. This chapter, therefore, first examines China's uneven transformation, before considering Beijing's development path. The ensuing sections consider the bidding process, the relationship between the Olympics and urban regeneration and the controversies that beset the pre-Olympic period, including the environment, resettlement, human rights, corruption, and obesity. The Games themselves are then examined in terms of their impact and how they were organized, before the legacy is considered in terms of international prestige, environmental impact within Beijing, the social and cultural dimension within the city and beyond, and how the massive Olympic site is to be funded in future.

China's Uneven Transformation

The dramatic changes in China that took place in the second half of the twentieth century are well known (Cannon, 2000; Cook and Murray, 2001). The establishment of the PRC as a communist state led by the Chinese Communist Party (CCP) gave rise to three alternative models of development: first the Soviet model in which centralization and heavy industry were key features; then the Maoist model in which the decentralized commune was a major element; and finally the Dengist model of market socialism, or 'socialism with Chinese characteristics'. The Dengist model took China, probably irrevocably, down the capitalist road – albeit under strong direction from the Chinese state. It was based on an Open Door for foreign direct investment (FDI), with the objective of modernizing China's agriculture, industry, defence, science and technology. Under the market reforms unleashed by Deng and his successors, China's 'Gold Coast' has been opened up to global connections and China is now in rapid transition from being a closed, poverty-stricken rural society towards being open, wealthy and, for many, urban. In brief, the Chinese state sets the preconditions for investment to enter, the local state (at province, city or town level) provides the infrastructure, and foreign companies provide the necessary investment through which China's resources of land and labour can be fully exploited. The scale and pace of change are phenomenal, especially in China's emerging cities, where the processes of globalization and urbanization interlock so dramatically (Wu, 2006, 2007). The emergence of China as an economic superpower has been built on the apparently limitless potential of cheap labour and an aspirational population that in the aftermath of Tiananmen were happy to accept a social contract in which they were given the freedoms associated with a consumer society in exchange for the maintenance of the political and human rights *status quo*.

China has twenty-nine Provinces, plus four cities run directly via central government (Beijing, Shanghai, Tianjin and Chongqing). Initially, most FDI flowed via Hong Kong into the neighbouring Guangdong Province. In 1997, Guangdong experienced $12.6 billion of actually utilized FDI. Although the annual total dropped slightly in 1998–1999 due to the combined effects of the

Asian financial crisis plus a degree of investment saturation in the Pearl River delta, by 2003 FDI in Guangdong was still high at $7.8 billion (National Bureau of Statistics, 1999, 2006). Shanghai and neighbouring provinces in the 'arrowhead' of the Yangtze River delta are fast developing as an alternative attraction for FDI, with the corresponding figures for actually utilized FDI in Shanghai in 1997 and 2003 being $4.2 billion and $5.5 billion respectively. As for Beijing itself, the corresponding data show that by 1997 $1.6 billion FDI was utilized, rising to $2.2 billion in 2003. Part of the 'China miracle', this type of investment is ploughed into export-oriented manufacturing, the property market, the retail sector and other activities, fuelling the dramatic transformation noted above. Multinational and transnational companies such as Volkswagen, Audi, McDonalds, KFC, Samsung, Apple, Microsoft, BP, B&Q and many more are engaged in this continuing struggle to enter the lucrative China market.

This investment, however, is spatially uneven. It is clear that the cycle of circular and cumulative causation, to use the old terminology associated with Gunnar Myrdal (e.g.1968), is very much oriented towards the coast. Chai (1996, p. 57), for instance, in his analysis of east–west income differentials from 1978–1991, found that regional income disparity had increased significantly. The trend of concentration of investment resources along the Eastern seaboard was reinforced by the export-led growth and FDI policies adopted during this period. The eastern seaboard had ports facilitating the imports of raw materials and exports of manufacturing. Consequently, most of the export processing facilities tended to concentrate in the coastal areas. Furthermore its proximity to the potential foreign investors as well as the special investment incentives created by the central government had attracted most of China's foreign investments into these areas.

Many other studies have similarly indicated the deeply embedded nature of these spatial contrasts (see Cook and Murray, 2001). They are also found with regards to urban–rural differentials and can also vary, as would be expected, at the local scale within provinces, perhaps reflecting upland–lowland contrasts, for example. In recent years the Chinese leadership has seemed particularly concerned to tackle such disparities, emphasizing the importance of investment in the western provinces, and of tackling rural deprivation. The huge stimulus package of 4 trillion yuan announced early in 2009 has a significant rural dimension, designed not only to support rural growth *in situ*, but also to slow down the exodus to China's cities and thus reduce spatial imbalances. Whether government can effectively redress these imbalances remains to be seen, however, in the light of the massive attraction of development in the eastern seaboard (Zhang, 2014). China's Gini Coefficent, a measure of inequality, now outstrips the USA and has increased by one-third in the last 35 years (Garst, 2015). Investment in the Beijing Olympics, of course, adds still further to this uneven development, and thus to the imbalance at the national scale.

Beijing's Development Path

Despite a long and distinguished history, under communism Beijing became an austere, drab producer city, full of steel mills and petrochemical works (Cook, 2006). It was heavily influenced by the Soviet style of planning with wide thoroughfares, mid-rise flats on a large scale, occasional grand buildings, and the expansion of Tiananmen Square to become the new heart of the city. The population of 1.2 million in 1949 within the old boundaries, by the early 1980s was probably 4.14 million within its expanded boundaries, including 1.76 million specifically classified as 'urban' (Dong, 1985). In the western outskirts, the Shihjingshan Iron and Steel Works (also known as Shougang, or the Capital Iron and Steel Works) became one of China's largest. The city was worthy but dull, and by the 1970s an increasing proportion of its population was beginning to complain of the endless diet of revolutionary dramas and operas. The average family would aspire to own a radio, watch and bicycle and there was little in the way of luxury available to the mass of the population. As for externalities, Zhou (1992, p. 30) observed that:

> over a rather long period, Beijing put undue emphasis on heavy industry at the expense of light industry, which was underdeveloped. The excessive heavy industry created a shortage of water, electricity and transport capacity, and worsened environmental pollution. Little attention was paid to housing and public facilities… The urban population expanded while the commercial service network decreased.

Today, Beijing is worlds apart from this brief sketch. The reform period has ushered in a period of massive urban change, with new hotels, banks, high-rise residences, ring roads, new subway lines, the largest shopping mall in Asia (Oriental Plaza) and the whole paraphernalia of a city that is seeking to internationalize and have a presence at the global scale (Cook, 2006; Gu and Cook, 2011). The total population was officially estimated at 14.93 million in 2004, which includes the *liudong renkou*, or 'floating population', who do not have resident status. These are the migrants who are usually tolerated by the authorities, if not by the long-term residents themselves who see the newcomers as 'new urban outcasts' (Solinger, 1995), and supply, for instance, the cheap labour on which the rapid pace of construction is based, work which is '3D' – difficult, demanding and dangerous (Shen, 2002). Urban migrants or 'floaters' are often either exploited by their employers or self-exploited insofar as they work exceptionally long hours, more so given the intensity of the building programme and the tight deadlines associated with the Olympics, often below the minimum wage and often not receiving pay until weeks after it's due. As Friedman (2005) puts it, the urban migrants are the cannon fodder of China's industrial revolution.

Contemporary Beijing often seems to resemble a giant building site. All around, huge new buildings are in various stages of construction, often cloaked in huge nets to prevent tools falling on passers-by. The streets are hazardous due to the trenches which have been dug for pipes and cables, the pavements which are being laid, the trees that have been knocked down or are being replanted, and the trucks and workers' buses which cut across the flows of pedestrians and bicycles into the corrugated iron fortresses which surround the sites. By early 1999, with the advent of the fiftieth anniversary of the PRC, there were an estimated 5,000 building sites in the city (Cook, 2000).

Adoption of the trappings of modern consumer society accompanied this transformation of the built environment. Supermarkets carry Western-style red wines and beer, bread and cakes. The streets have American fast food chains (e.g. McDonalds, Kentucky Fried Chicken and Dunkin' Donut). Chinese tastes now extend to Western motor vehicles (BMW, Cherokee Jeep, Audi, Volkswagen, Mercedes and even Ferrari), clothing (Zara and Gap), perfumes (Calvin Klein or Chanel), electrical goods (Sony, Phillips and Panasonic), and housing, with executive-style estates of detached houses complete with nearby golf courses and private schools, perhaps within the complex itself. For the growing middle class, material goods are in full supply, although these are often more expensive than in Western countries. For the working class, too, the department stores are rapidly expanding their size and product range. A night out is increasingly to a Hard Rock Cafe, pub or disco, usually featuring Western music, and a holiday is often taken overseas in such cities as London, Paris, New York or Tokyo. It is in the light of such changes that Beijing made its bids for the Olympics.

The Bidding Process

As in other Communist societies, sport became an important element in promoting the nation and patriotism. The annual *China Statistical Yearbook* on 'Culture, Sports and Public Health' routinely tabulates such outputs as 'Visits between Chinese and Foreign Sports Delegations', 'Activities of Mass Sports', 'World Records Chalked up by Chinese Athletes by Events' and 'World Championships won by Chinese Athletes'. Dong (2005, p. 533) showed that 'Chinese political and sports officials openly acknowledged that they viewed sport as an instrument for the promotion of national pride and identity... Contemporary competitive sport in China is motivated by nationalism and in turn contributes to the enhancement of patriotism'. From the mid-1980s, a strategy was developed to maximize gold medals, with an interesting feature being the success of female athletes, and the high proportion of females relative to males in the Chinese team. This has not always been unproblematic. There have been well publicized defections of top athletes plus question marks over the training methods and unprecedented success of 'Ma's Barmy Army' (after their trainer) of female marathon runners as well as the Chinese swimming team, with questions raised as to whether such athletes were 'chemically enhanced'. Dong showed that the first time the question as to when China could actually host the Olympics was raised as far back as 1908 in the *Tianjin Youth Magazine*, but it was at the end of the successful Asian Games in 1990 that a huge banner was unfurled, stating 'With the success of the Asiad, we look forward to hosting the Olympic Games' (cited by Dong, 2005, p. 538).

As noted above, Beijing failed on this occasion, losing to Sydney by only two votes for the right to host the Millennial Olympics in 2000. There were suggestions (e.g. GamesBids.com, 2006) that there was a vote scandal at this time, but there was also strong opposition from Human Rights groups and the 'Free Tibet' movement, which were vehemently opposed to a successful bid from China. Although the Asian Games had been successful, the shadow of Tiananmen still loomed large as far as many Western governments were concerned (see Broudehoux, 2004), and Beijing was still a severely polluted city at that time, with a relatively poor infrastructure. It was certainly no surprise to most observers that the 1990s bid was unsuccessful.

By 2001, however, much had changed. China had decided to bid once more, primarily as part of the drive to modernize and internationalize Beijing. The city, one of five shortlisted, prepared for the final visit of the bidding panel in February 2001 with great care. *Inter alia*, the short- and longer-term measures taken included investment in awareness of the 2008 bid, for example, illuminations in Olympic colours, billboards, magazines in taxis, the Millennium Museum showing Olympic films and displays, street signs in English, investment in infrastructure (notably the fourth and fifth ring roads), development of new hotels; painting of older buildings to improve appearances; spraying the grass green; establishment of parks, green and silver bins to increase awareness of environment (i.e. waste recycling), removal of older cars from the city to reduce air pollution, banning people burning coal in the city, and the closure of the Shougang steel plant.

The bid adopted the overarching slogan of 'New Beijing: Great Olympics', with subsidiary themes of delivering a 'high-tech Olympics', a 'green Olympics' and a 'people's Olympics'. It featured a plan to construct an Olympic Park and strategies to address the serious environmental issues faced by the Chinese capital. The commitments included:

◆ An Olympic Park covering an area of 1,215 hectares. It would include an 80,000 seat stadium, fourteen gymnasia, an Athletes' Village and an international exhibition centre, surrounded by a 760-hectare forest and greenbelt.

◆ During the tenth Five-Year Plan period (2001–2005) Beijing would build three green ecological belts, aiming to raise its green coverage to 48 per cent. By 2005, 'the city will realize the complete and safe disposal of treated waste and 96 per cent waste waster will also be treated' (Gao, 2001).

◆ If Beijing gained the nomination 'there will be 5,750 sports venues by 2008 with twenty-three major stadiums to hold events. And last year a new airport was opened that can move three million passengers a month. Beijing will have 72,000 rooms in 241 quality hotels and there are plans to build a $500 million national theatre on the edge of Tiananmen Square, to hold cultural events during the Games' (*Ibid.*)

◆ 'The government plans to spend the equivalent of $15 billion on anti-pollution efforts through 2008, roughly nine times what China's Olympic committee organizers estimate the Games would cost' (GameBids.com, 2006).

Beijing's long-term plan for environmental protection to 2010 had its time-scale reduced to ensure readiness for the 2008 games. From 1998 to 2007, the plan envisaged such features as:

◆ total expenditure of $12.2 billion on protection and enhancement of the ecological environment;
◆ fourteen new wastewater treatment plants to be built to improve the sewage treatment rates to 90 per cent from 42 per cent;
◆ 240 square kilometres of trees and grass to be planted around Beijing to create a 'green coverage' area of more than 50 per cent;
◆ 200 industrial enterprises to change production or be shifted out of the downtown area altogether to reduce pollution levels;
◆ completion of the fourth and fifth ring roads, five new subway lines, 90 per cent of buses and 70 per cent of taxis to use natural gas.[2]

In all, it was forecast at the time that 280 billion yuan ($33.8 billion) of investment would be made in the period to 2008, mainly in stadia and gymnasia, increasing China's annual GNP growth by 0.3–0.4 per cent and Beijing's by 2.5 per cent (Xin, 2001). With these and other activities, the potential impact of the Olympics would be enormous, adding further to China's growing power and prestige on the international stage, and contributing significantly to Beijing's urban development. The city would move away from being a producer city towards being a city of consumption, of knowledge-based activities, and a city with an enhanced international profile.

For their part, the visiting panel were impressed by these and other evidence not just of the commitment of Beijing's residents to the Olympic ideal but also that of the nation as a whole. By May 2001 the Olympic Evaluation Commission Report was summarized as:

This is a government-driven bid with considerable assistance of the NOC (National Olympic Committee). The combination of a good sports concept with complete Government support results in a high quality bid.

The Commission notes the process and pace of change taking place in China and Beijing and the possible challenges caused by population and economic growth in the period leading up to 2008 but is confident that these challenges can be met.

There is an environmental challenge but the strong government actions and investment in this area should resolve this and improve the city.

It is the Commission's belief that a Beijing Games would leave a unique legacy to China and to sport and the Commission is confident that Beijing could organize an excellent Games. (www.GamesBids.com/archives/2008/Beijing.htm)

Beijing's success soon afterwards (13 July 2001) was the climax of a series of celebrations, beginning with the return of Hong Kong in 1997, Macao in 1999, the fiftieth Anniversary of the PRC in 1999 and the eightieth Anniversary of the founding of the CCP in July 2001. Later, China unsuccessfully bid for the 2010 FIFA World Cup and successfully for a World Exposition in Shanghai in the same year. It is difficult to underestimate the symbolic nature of these successes for China's people, the CCP and the leadership of the nation. It is indeed fair to say that the Olympics in particular and the city marketing that they imply serve a strong ideological purpose, not least insofar as it uses the city and its consumption as a focal point for the naturalization of power (Broudehoux, 2004).

Urban Regeneration

In the years following the bid's success, Beijing saw considerable work and investment towards realizing the Olympic dream. In many respects, the Olympics were a national rather than just a city-based event. Key elements of the Games were staged away from Beijing, notably, sailing (Qingdao, Shandong Province), equestrian (Hong Kong), and football (Tianjin, Shanghai, Shenyang and Qinhuangdao). In the case of Qingdao, Shanghai and Hong Kong these cities are located 800 km, 1,070 km and 1,970 km, respectively from Beijing. Most of the effort and investment, however, was expended in Beijing itself. In 2003, work was begun on four Olympic venues, with a further eleven begun in 2004. By mid-2006, forty-four major projects were underway. The Olympic Village lies due north of the central city on the main north–south axis, and the now famous main stadium is in the shape of a 'bird's nest' lattice-work structure (figure 18.2); in the environs, for several years were the inevitable sheets of corrugated iron surrounding related construction activities. Beijing International Airport was considerably modernized and expanded through the building of an enormous Terminal 3. Many new subway lines were built for the Olympics (figure 18.3), while a new loop line was opened to the north of the city in 2002.

The Beijing Organising Committee for the Games of the XXIX Olympiad (BOCOG) held its first plenary session in January 2004 at which it was announced that the first phase of development was complete (Cook, 2006). The second phase would run from 2004 to 2006, leaving the time from 2007 until the Games' Opening Ceremony for test events and fine-tuning. Construction of new hotels, road infrastructure and other essential facilities continued apace, including parks

Figure 18.2. The Bird's Nest – the National Stadium, August 2008.

Figure 18.3. New underground station, Beijing 2008.

and water recycling centres. The new Opera House (Beijing National Theatre) behind the Great Hall of the People was also completed, notwithstanding the controversies over its huge cost and 'jelly-fish' or 'blob' architectural design (see Broudehoux, 2004). On the symbolic side, the new Beijing Olympic logo – 'Chinese Seal, Dancing Beijing' – was unveiled in August 2003, combining 'elements of engraving, calligraphy, painting and poetry' and bringing together elements of the ancient and the modern (www.GamesBids.com/archives/2008/Beijing.htm).

BOCOG 'is requiring all proprietors ... to follow "green" environmental guidelines in the construction of Olympic venues' (Lei, 2004). Sustainable development was a key element with the main tasks identified by the executive vice-president of BOCOG as 'controlling air pollution, especially reducing the coal and industrial pollution and vehicle discharges, effective disposal of municipal sewage and municipal refuse, raising the green land acreage to 50 per cent' (*Ibid.*). As an indication of success in these endeavours, in March 2006 Chaoyang District became the first urban area in Beijing to be named a 'model ecological zone', following three suburban districts of Yanqing, Pinggu and Miyun (Li, 2006). Over 60 square kilometres of green zones were created 2004–2008, and according to the municipal authorities: 'Greenbelts cover 43.5 per cent of the district, and green public space has reached an average of 15 square meters per person. Meanwhile, air and water quality has improved' (*Ibid*). The Capital Iron and Steel Works were gradually relocated to a coastal location some distance from the capital in Shandong Province. In the early 2000s it seemed that Beijing's environmental quality was becoming better than it was, with more blue sky days (one of the set targets), more tree planting, more green spaces, increased use of LPG in buses, and greater restrictions on pollution via industry or vehicles. Nevertheless, there were still many concerns before the Games as to the pollution impact on Olympic athletes, while a number of other concerns also raised disquiet in some quarters.

Pre-Games Controversies

Despite the environmental focus of the Olympic plans and the improvements noted above, data from the European Satellite Agency in October 2005 stressed that Beijing remained the most polluted city in the world, while it and neighbouring provinces had the world's worst levels of nitrogen dioxide (Watts, 2005). Despite the huge volume of tree planting in recent years, China's plans were disrupted by a huge sandstorm that hit the city on 16 April 2006. Around 330,000 tons of dust was estimated to have fallen on Beijing that day, while the next saw most of north and northwest China enveloped in sandstorms. This was chastening for the authorities, given that it coincided with the Sixth National Conference on Environmental Protection. Addressing the conference, then Premier Wen Jiabao commented: 'Repeated sandstorms should send a warning to us all, we should feel heavy loads on our shoulders while meeting here to discuss environmental problems' (www.GamesBids.com/archives/2008/Beijing.htm). Yet while the government claims to take environmental issues seriously, the pace of social and economic change often outstrips the ability to regulate and control environmental pollution. For example, in 2003 the level of car ownership in Beijing reached the anticipated level for 2010. Much higher taxation rates were announced for large vehicles with rates on small-engine cars being reduced, but in a society with such a fast rate of wealth creation and where social status is increasingly a product of conspicuous consumption, it is probable that most people will not be deterred from buying larger vehicles unless punitive measures are taken. The authorities promised to respond by severely restricting vehicle use while the Olympics were taking place which could mean, since Beijing is a city the size of Los Angeles, that the impact of any restrictions would be considerable.

Another controversial aspect of the Olympics schedule was demolition to make way for the new structures associated with the Games. The set target was 9 million square metres of 'dilapidated housing', replaced by new houses that would supply a living area of 18 square metres per capita (Xin, 2001). This is part of an ongoing process of demolition across the whole city, which particularly threatens the old *hutong* and *siheyuan* areas (Cook, 2000, 2006; Cook and Murray, 2001). In brief, these old, often dilapidated, single-storey houses arranged along narrow lanes, originally with access to the 'Hong Tong' or water well, are in areas that ill befit the dreams of planners and developers concerned with creating the grand structures of an internationalized Olympic metropolis. From 1991 to 2003, 1.5 million people were relocated from such areas out to the high-rise residential blocks in the suburbs. The previous Mayor admitted that the difficult problem of resettlement of families affected by this demolition process 'remains to be solved'; the new Mayor, Wang Qishan, while admitting that some of these relocation projects violated the law, stated that older parts of the city would still continue to be demolished to make way for the Olympics projects (cited in Cook, 2006). Some estimates suggest that approximately 300,000 people were evicted specifically because of the Olympics, although the PRC government denied this (Acharya, 2005). Certainly, the main Olympic site is far from the city centre, and in the early 1990s when Cook visited the Geographical Institute of the Chinese Academy of Sciences in that area much of the journey was past fields rather than housing so it is hard to see that much of the total urban displacement was due to the Olympics *per se*. Further, some were displaced temporarily while the Olympic area was under construction, with local roads considerably widened at the expense of pre-existing apartment blocks, rebuilt beside narrowed roads after the Olympics took place.

Nevertheless, the question of population displacement is a reminder that the issue of human rights refuses to disappear. Organizations such as Amnesty International or Human Rights Watch Asia continue to deplore human rights violations by the Chinese authorities. These crystallize around a number of broad themes, such as the overall lack of democracy, use of the death penalty, the occupation of Tibet, Uighur (Muslim) insurgency in Xinjiang Province and the treatment of the Falun Gong (a Buddhist sect). Security in China, including internet security is tight, so the likelihood of violence marring the Olympics in 2008 was low, but there remained the possibility of public protests concerning these and other potential issues. Indeed, as in other countries previously, the upheaval created by the Games could actually *contribute* to protest and dissent. For their part, the Chinese authorities retaliated by defending their human rights record by pointing to the lack of basic rights in countries such as the United States and maintained that the ongoing war on terrorism and the involvement of the US and UK in Iraq at that time, complete with examples of human rights abuse by US and British soldiers, shows the operation of double standards. In fact, these points made by Cook (2007) proved to be prescient, for the Olympic Torch was beset by protests from Free Tibet activists in many countries and cities, particularly Paris, London, San Francisco and Athens. This in turn led to counter-protests from PRC supporters in Hong Kong and China itself. Meanwhile, the Chinese government continues to condemn Western critiques of China's human rights record on the basis that they amount to an imposition of Western cultural values and constitute a fundamental misunderstanding of Chinese culture and not least the fact that cultural change occurs in China not overnight but over the course of development of a civilization.

Corruption constituted another thorny issue for the Chinese authorities. As shown above, vast sums of foreign investment have entered the country in recent years. Perhaps inevitably, corruption has become a problem for the Chinese government, and some would point to the lack of democratic controls as rendering it very difficult to root out corruption among officials and CCP members. Current President Xi Jinping is leading the internal struggle against corruption in high places. Reports of the first Beijing Olympic official to be sacked over corruption surfaced 2 years before the Games (Watts, 2006a, 2006b). According to these reports, Liu Zhihua, a vice-mayor of Beijing responsible for overseeing construction of sporting venues for the Olympics, was removed by the Standing Committee of the Beijing Municipal People's Congress for 'corruption and dissoluteness'. He was liable to face the death penalty for financial crimes if found guilty of taking an alleged 10 million yuan as a bribe from developers. The huge amount of money that had been budgeted for the various events and venues means that this may well not be the last such case to come to light. Reporting on the case was suppressed before the Olympics to avoid tarnishing China's image but after the Games in October 2008 Liu did in fact receive a death sentence, suspended for 2 years to allow his potential 'good behaviour' to commute the sentence to imprisonment (*The Telegraph*, 2008).

A final pre-Games concern was the contradictions that apply to the Beijing Olympics in particular (Dickson and Schofield, 2005). The main sponsors for the event include 'calorie-dense beverages (Coca-Cola) and food (McDonalds) as well as motorized transportation (Volkswagen)' (*Ibid.*, p. 170). Such sponsorship ran the risk of exacerbating China's growing obesity problem. Other sponsors such as Samsung or Panasonic produce goods that further contribute to a sedentary lifestyle. They argue that 'the world's most populous nation is at the beginning of an explosion in lifestyle-related disease' (*Ibid.*, p. 177), a point supported by Cook and Dummer (2004) who observed that 'the first "fat camp" was opened in Beijing in 1994. This, they argued, reflected 'a growing problem of obesity as Western "junk food" becomes increasingly popular in the cities … obesity in young children increasing by over 50 per cent from 1989 to 1997' (*Ibid.*, p. 338). Although the Olympics would help to encourage a proportion of China's population to take more exercise, as has happened in previous Olympic cities, Dickson and Schofield (2005, p. 177) maintained that this would be insufficient to offset 'the opportunities for massive multinational globalization and ultimately, globesity'. This would surely be the ultimate irony that the Beijing Olympics might contribute to the couch potato syndrome in China and the rest of the globe.

The Games Themselves

There are perhaps two abiding images of the 2008 Beijing Olympics: the awe-inspiring scale and richness of the Games' Opening Ceremony and the vision of Usain Bolt smashing the world record whilst de-accelerating long before the finish of the men's 100 metres. The Opening Ceremony offered a spectacular vision of a city steeped in its own history and yet one that was ready for the challenges facing a nation ready to declare itself a major player in the global economy. Directed by the high-profile film director Zhang Yimou the ceremony featured over 15,000 performers and cost around $100 million to produce. Perhaps most memorable were the mass participation set pieces that offered a timely symbolic reminder of the sheer power of the communist ideal. The sense of co-operation and united endeavour was undoubtedly reflective of broader social norms in China and also represented a statement of global intent on the part of the Chinese Communist Party. The ceremony was in part a physical manifestation of the Games' slogan 'One World, One Dream', of a world united by the Olympic ideal of peace and harmony. Equally however, such a notion reaffirmed China's membership of a world united by the possibilities of consumer capitalism, and by the promise that China is now a fully paid up member of the global economy.

In many respects then the Opening Ceremony was more than just a ceremony in constituting a carefully choreographed (in more ways than one) statement of intent and of an arrival on the world stage that mixed communist images of the obedient masses with the technological wizardry of advanced capitalism. The Opening Ceremony and indeed the Games as a whole served to present to the rest of the world the Chinese way and indeed the inherent belief amongst the Chinese people that the Chinese way is the best. This was queried subsequently, however, when it was revealed that a young girl singer was replaced by another who lip-synched on behalf of her prettier colleague behind the scenes. Similarly, the ubiquitously youthful Olympic volunteers fed into the vision of a youthful newly emerging country and one that was blessed by the riches of hundreds of years of unsurpassed civilization, providing 'an almost picture-perfect blend of idealized chinoiserie and ultra-modern convenience' (Setzekorn, 2008). Even here, however, 'real progress in terms of language fluency and cross-cultural understanding was slight due to the controlled and directed nature of foreigner and volunteer interaction (www.GamesBids.com/archives/2008/Beijing.htm).

Although for the rest of the world the efforts of Usain Bolt will perhaps stay longest in the memory, the Chinese people were no doubt most affected by Lou Xiang's Olympic experience. Lou Xiang was and is the icon and poster boy of the Chinese people. Reported to have made £12 million in one year alone from endorsements by Nike and other sponsors, the city of Beijing was awash with images of the only male Chinese competitor who had a serious chance of gold on the athletics track. In his hands lay the hopes of a nation. Yet there would be no happy ending. Although Lou Xiang made it on to his starting blocks he did not make it over the hurdles in front of him and as such the dreams of a billion Chinese people were left in tatters. Lou Xiang was literally the face of the Olympics and the fact he was forced to pull out through injury was a devastating blow not only to the people of China but to the CCP itself who were no doubt more than happy to promote Lou Xiang as a symbol of an internationally competitive China and less than happy at his demise. As it happened China topped the Olympic Games medal table achieving fifty gold medals in a total of 100 medals in all; this justified the massive investment on the part of the Communist Party to ensure that China was seen to succeed not only as a host, but, at least for now, as the greatest sporting nation on earth.

The Environmental Impact

It would seem that the Beijing Olympics have, despite the negative environmental impact of the construction process, left a positive environmental legacy in a number of ways, although there are also some controversies concerning the exact nature of this legacy. On the positive side, new green areas have been created, including the 'Olympic Green' as a resource for Beijing's citizens, while Watts (2009) reported that restrictions on car use proved to be so successful in reducing air pollution that these restrictions were extended by a further 12 months. This means that, according to the Beijing Traffic Management Bureau, one-fifth of the city's 3.6 million private vehicles and a third of official cars continue to be barred from the roads every weekday, thus reducing emissions by 10 per cent, while plans to widen a ban on high-polluting cars and trucks from the centre to cover the whole city will save a similar amount.[3] Such claims were supported by a report by the United Nations Environment Programme (UNEP), published in February 2009 (Xinhua News Agency, 2009). The report stated that Beijing had 'raised the environmental bar and the Games left a lasting legacy for the city'. Positive elements included increased awareness of environmental issues across China but especially in Beijing, among residents and businesses alike, the introduction of Euro IV emission standards for cars instead of the Euro II, creation of '8,800 hectares of green space … using more than 30 million trees and rose bushes', and a rise in blue sky days from 'less than 180 in 2000 to 274 days in 2008'. Lesser improvements were also recorded in waste disposal and recycling.

This 'big tick' (UNEP, 2009) for the Olympic environmental improvements was not, however, supported by an analysis of particulate matter in an eight-week period around the Games. The analysis, involving US and Chinese environmental scientists, caused some controversy in China, and led to the Chinese author backtracking on the article's conclusions (AP, 2009*b*). The study, by scientists from Oregon State University and Peking University, funded by the National Science Foundations of the United States and China, found that the level of particulate pollution in Beijing was twice as bad as in Athens, Greece; three times as bad as in Atlanta, Georgia; and 3.5 times as bad as in Sydney, Australia. The authors suggested that some pollution was due to the movement of the regional air mass from polluted regions beyond the city, but also that good weather on other occasions was responsible for reduction in air pollution to a greater extent than anti-pollution policies. Wang *et al.* (2010) found similarly that weather conditions in the wider Beijing area were also important, with variation in pollution being partly dependent on whether the airflow came from dirtier or cleaner regions and how much rainfall there was to dampen down air pollution, but that policies also had a significant influence. Cook has conducted regular field courses in Beijing over a 20-year period from 1992 to 2012 and can bear witness to the fact that Beijing air quality improved around the time of the Olympics. By 2010, however, the problem of dust storms had reappeared, and by the time of a research visit to Tsinghua University in Beijing in 2013 air pollution in the city had once again reached crisis proportions, especially in the downtown area. This is not least due to the expansion in car ownership in the city, with 800,000 being sold in 2010 alone (Zhang, 2014, p. 155).

The Bird's Nest as White Elephant

As for the longer-term legacy of Beijing 2008, the physical impact of the Games is clear in terms of the massive programme of building work and infrastructural improvements and, most notably perhaps, the new Olympic subway line reflecting what Li *et al.* (2008, p. 261) describe as the emergence of a 'hybrid global megacity'. Yet the smog soon returned to the city and the key sporting venues have largely stood unused. A key area of concern regarding the legacy of the Beijing Olympics is one that is also found elsewhere with other Olympics, namely who will pay for and use the new Olympic facilities, in particular the spectacular Bird's Nest. During field work in Beijing in March 2009, Cook first became aware that, at least for some, there were concerns that the Bird's Nest might transmogrify into a White Elephant with very high upkeep. Although Beijing's success in gaining the 2022 Winter Games supplies a further use for the stadium at a mega-event which, at the time of writing, is more than 6 years hence, the high costs of retaining the stadium on a month-to-month basis remain. Its construction cost has been reported as 3.5 billion RMB (approximately $427 million) and the maintenance cost 170 million RMB. There are also loan costs to pay, as well as maintenance. One suggested solution was that the biggest football (soccer) team in Beijing, Beijing Guo An, would take over the stadium, but although football is increasingly popular in China it is highly unlikely that support for this team would be sufficient to maintain such a huge stadium, while there are also high costs involved in preparing the pitch for each match. Sponsorship for the stadium by the likes of Adidas was also considered, but rejected due to the national importance of the venue. Instead, it would seem at the time of writing that a combination of visitor numbers (thousands pay 50 RMB to enter the stadium) and cultural events including a 'Charm of China' summer concert series, involving such celebrities as Plácido Domingo and Jackie Chan, will be used to raise the funds required to keep this enormous stadium going (*People's Daily*, 2009). At least, perhaps, the award of the 2022 Winter Games puts other options aside for the foreseeable future such as conversion of the stadium into a shopping and entertainment complex.

The Bird's Nest, of course, does not exist in glorious iconic isolation. It sits beside the Beijing National Aquatic Centre 'The Water Cube', which is equally architecturally striking. The upkeep of such buildings is excessively expensive while the long-term use of such facilities is questionable. For example, there appears to be limited need for a public swimming facility of this kind and it is more likely to be used in the long term as a venue for elite aquatic sports. Some of the other facilities available on Olympic Park will no doubt in time inevitably be demolished. What remains is most likely to offer some kind of a private haven: a space of elite consumption founded upon the memories of three weeks in the summer of 2008. This reflects a broader concern that the primary long-term impact of the Olympic Games is to redefine Beijing as a space for consumption so that the Olympic Green area in particular becomes a glitzy space for privatized public pleasures. As Marvin (2008, p. 249) puts it:

The official version of post-Olympic commercial, exhibition, sports, and entertainment spaces on the Green and elsewhere paints a civic picture of obedient consumers attuned more to immediate gratification than politics. In Lefebvrian terms the Green is a wholly new conceived space, a cagey gamble by a new generation of rulers who are betting that stripping national space of overt political content will diffuse its potential for 'lived' protest. They are likely to be encouraged by nearly two decades of public response to commercial malls and nighttime strips.

The concern here is that the Olympics have transformed the city of Beijing but have done so at considerable cost by adopting a model that is all about developing leisure enclaves for the rich that have simply served to impoverish the public life of the city. Of course, the primary role of the Olympics, as we suggested above, is a symbolic one that is concerned with portraying confident harmonious China but the problem is that China is more harmonious for some than it is for others, with the *fu-erdai* or scions of the rich being seen as a problem today (Garst, 2015). Indeed, the costs of the Olympics inevitably falls on those who least benefit from them. In quoting the pertinent figures, the Beijing municipal government, for example, spent over $10 billion on transport and infrastructure. Broudehoux (2004) argued that such investment blindly disregards local needs, there being no hard evidence that the local population actually benefits from the anticipated economic boom that would result. For Broudehoux (*Ibid.*) the winners in such a scenario are always the multinational businesses involved in sport through sports tourism and property while the locals are left to deal with increased taxation, soaring rents and restricted civil liberties.

Branding

In part this discussion concerns the different levels of branding to which different institutions and actors at different levels are exposed. At the national level, the People's Republic of China has to a great extent overcome many negative external perceptions of China as a rather severe, autocratic, dictatorial society in which dissent is not tolerated, giving an impression of 'a peaceful China, a civilized China, and a progressive China' according to Te (2009, p. 84). The IOC agrees with this view, insisting that 'lasting legacies' were produced for Beijing and its people, and that as regards criticisms of human rights, 'the games have elevated international dialogue on such issues' as the leader of the IOC evaluation commission put it (AP, 2009*a*). Others may be less sanguine, including those who welcomed the alternative Tibetan Freedom Torch that was carried through more than fifty cities before completing its journey near the Tibet border in Ladakh, India (International Tibet Network, 2008), or the 149 people who applied for permission to protest at the officially designated three protest zones – all seventy-seven applications were withdrawn or rejected (Watts, 2008), 'and in one case two elderly women who had applied to protest were initially sentenced to re-education by labour, though this sentence was later cancelled' (Fahey, 2009, p. 384). The Chinese citizens, nonetheless, 'displayed new standards of national quality development', of 'civilization', 'passion' and 'smile' (Te, 2009, pp. 88–89).

Such contrasting perspectives are also shown in the survey conducted by Zhang and Zhao (2009) in different locations in Beijing, Tiananmen, Sanlitun and Houhai, with 100 respondents. There were high ratings of Beijing's position and power in international affairs and of the cultural significance of the city. 'In ranking, the respondents considered the tangible, eye-catching indigenous liberal arts and ancient architectures as the foremost representative cultural symbols of Beijing' (*Ibid.*, p. 250). In contrast were low scores on 'liveability', with low ratings for 'ecological conditions, the provision of public amenities, the standard of public services, and urban governance' (*Ibid.*). The sustainability of environmental improvements via the Games was questioned, while there were also concerns about rising property prices, notwithstanding the global recession. Despite successes during the Games:

> the respondents were sceptical about the introduction of a new quality of life and the
> common good by the Beijing Olympics. While official branding tried to sell the friendly,

smiling and comfortable city, people generally thought that a one-time event could not help to satisfy material needs of the economically and socially marginalized groups (including the city's laid-off workers and rural low-skilled migrants working in the city). (*Ibid.*, pp. 251–252)

Conclusion

There is no doubt that in many ways the Beijing Olympics were an enormous success and that they succeeded in portraying a new confident China to the global audience. China expanded its 'soft power' overseas (Gu and Cook, 2011, p. 124). The human rights issue never went away, images of protestors interrupting the Olympic torch procession were undoubtedly damaging to the CCP, but ultimately the image of a revitalized China appears to have generally won through, not least as a result of the awe-inspiring Opening Ceremony. Certainly in comparison, London's contribution to the Beijing Closing Ceremony was modest to say the least; a modesty that became an economic necessity given the global recession.

For Brownell (2008) the greatest bequest of the Beijing Games will be its human and cultural legacy and in particular the way in which the Games provided an opportunity to train Chinese people for a globalizing world. As far as the future of China is concerned the Games have, of course, played an important part in ensuring the nation's role as a key player on the world stage: its unrelenting enthusiasm and commitment to the Games reflecting its commitment not only to being a full member of the global community but as a leading player in the drive towards the construction of a global society (Close *et al.*, 2007). A key concern in this respect is the degree to which the China that emerges from the 2008 Olympics reflects and reinforces a particular set of values broadly described as those associated with global consumer capitalism; a set of values that are more attainable in theory than in practice for many social groups, including the migrant population discussed above. The concern here is that the 'One World, One Dream' to which the Games so vocally referred turns out to be a world in which only some components of Chinese society can actually partake.

Notes

1.   www.chinaview.cn/index.htm/7-7-2009.

2.   www.beijing-olympic.org.cn/xbxa/ztzt/gree/gree-index.shtm.

3.   According to *China Daily*, Beijing Municipal Transportation Commission is considering further vehicle restrictions in 2016, see http://www.chinadaily.com.cn/china/2016-01-22/content_23207104.htm.

Chapter 19

London 2012

Graeme Evans and Özlem Edizel

The London 2012 Summer Olympics were born out of failure. First came the failure of preceding English cities, Birmingham (1992) and Manchester (1996 and 2000), to bid successfully for this mega-event. The accumulating support for London was therefore fuelled by the realization that only the capital had the capacity, capability and cachet to compete on a world stage. Secondly, a more domestic failure also stalked London 2012; the ill-fated Millennium Festival centred on the Millennium Dome in London's Greenwich peninsula, which was perceived to be a failure in terms of confused purpose and content, high cost, lower-than-predicted visitor numbers, and critically, the legacy of the iconic building itself (Evans, 1996a). Could London do it better this time – in spectator numbers, experience, media opinion, cost and legacy uses? On Wednesday 6 July 2005, the International Olympic Committee's meeting in Singapore voted to award the 2012 Summer Olympics to London. The decision represented a combination of Eurovision-style partisanship, tactical voting, global schmoozing, and notably the failure of its direct competitors and the long-term favourites.[1] London's *coup de theatre* was a multicultural-faced group of excited East End children in contrast to the sombre-suited Parisian messieurs. These failures have therefore informed the strategy for the London 2012 Games and shaped the narratives which accompanied it across changing political regimes.

However, as celebrations began the next day in Stratford, the heart of the prospective Olympic Park, four suicide bombers killed fifty-six people including themselves in attacks on underground trains and a bus in central London. The 2012 award celebration party was cut short and thinking inevitably started to focus on the size of the task ahead, with all its attendant problems. These began with the security concerns, the need to face the renewed terror threat, and the woefully underestimated capital budget used in the successful bid. This not only excluded the extra security costs, but also VAT and other taxes on construction that together added £1.5 billion to the original £4 billion bid estimate. By March 2007 the publicly-funded Olympic infrastructure budget stood at £9.375bn, excluding the costs of staging the event, land acquisition and wider regeneration and transport investment, including the legacy conversion of Olympic facilities themselves.

This chapter provides a critique of the London 2012 Olympic project from the bid period to the post-award development, delivery and 'post-event' legacy phase. Earlier editions of this chapter on London 2012 (Evans, 2007, 2010) focused in particular on the bidding, build up and aspirations of the 2012 Games, while we have also written in depth elsewhere on how London 'Dressed Up' for the Games (Edizel *et al.*, 2013) and the design and master planning process (Evans, 2015). London 2012 has also spawned a healthy attention to evaluation, including official meta-evaluation studies (see Chapter 2), and a wide range of academic perspectives which provide a rich source of material, including many doctoral theses. This chapter will therefore not attempt to synthesize or select but will offer a particular reflection on the event process, its legacy and future planning of the Olympic site, including perspectives from resident surveys.

Regeneration Games

In discussing the rationale for the hosting of hallmark events – whether site, area or sub-regional in scale – Hall (1992, p. 29) developed a chronology which identified the period from the early 1960s as one characterized by the 'city of renewal'. Over 50 years on, it is surprising to note that a review of literature on the Olympics found only nine out of over 2,000 entries specifically on 'regeneration' or 'renewal' (Veal and Tooney, 2012). Articles and reports, and a growing number of edited collections, are dominated by 'impacts' – economic, physical, political (urban regimes and globalization) and tourism – and themes of marketing, image and place-making. By contrast, analyses of long-term regeneration effects were notable by their absence, despite Barcelona's status as 'exemplar' in this respect. However, London 2012 marked a turning point (preceded perhaps by the urban Beijing Olympics), with regeneration and legacy dominating the Olympic rationale and literature, although Olympic effects tend to be subsumed into wider redevelopment and competitive city narratives. This makes it problematic to measure the true impact and cost of the Games (and similar large-scale, event-based regeneration projects).

In the case of London, this event phase also represents the 'unfinished business' of, first, the precursor London Docklands Development Corporation which had presided over the development of Canary Wharf and other inner docklands areas between 1979 and 1993, and, secondly, the London Thames Gateway Development Corporation that had taken over planning powers from incumbent local authorities in 2005 until it was wound up in 2012 in the spirit of 'localism'. In the decade before London's Olympics bid, successive schemes of area-based regeneration had continued in this area while strategically the Lower Lea Valley, within which the Olympic site is situated, had been designated as a key sub-regional regeneration area in successive London Plans crossing borough boundaries. The Mayor's new Olympic legacy authority, the London Legacy Development Corporation (LLDC) – also with extended land-use planning powers – now operates within these designated areas of the London Boroughs (LBs) of Hackney, Newham, Tower Hamlets and Waltham Forest (figure 19.1).

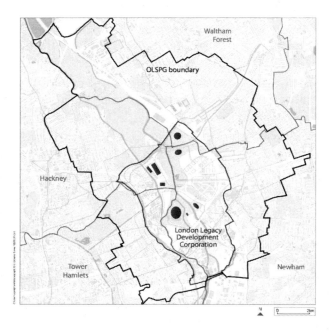

Figure 19.1. LLDC Area Map: Olympic Legacy Supplementary Planning Guidance (OLSPG) and LLDC boundaries (*Source*: GLA, 2012)

In London's bid the greatest emphasis was placed on the legacy and after-effects of the Olympic leverage opportunity, rather than the event, its content and purpose. As Allen (2006, p. 3) indicated early on: 'Talk of the "Olympic Legacy" is so common that it has started to sound like a tautology; shorthand for the perceived wisdom that the Olympics has everything to do with urban regeneration and only a passing concern with patriotism, athletics or public spectacle'. This presents a fundamental problem to the national Olympic and city regeneration delivery agencies. The financial, land ownership and usage, construction, and related infrastructural and promotional efforts are of necessity dominated by the event delivery objectives and cost pressures and targets. National performance in the competition itself, i.e. in the final medal league table, is the test of sporting success.[2] It is here that compromises in community benefits (social, local economy and procurement), design quality and after-use, are most likely to be made:

> it's now becoming clear that the idea is something of a smokescreen. In practice, it's becoming apparent that this legacy involves putting the narrowly technical demands of the (27) days of the games above everything else, and then trying to adapt the site for long-term use afterwards. (Sudjic, 2006)

The visionary master plans, artists' impressions and promises at the bidding and consultation stage are just that – promises. Barcelona's Olympic Village housing, for example, was privately sold but not 'affordably' as promised (Nel-lo, 1997), as was also the case in London. The final form and function of the Olympic site is therefore dictated by budget and contractual realities, political stamina and consensus, as it was in other regenerating Olympic cities.

Following the host city award in 2005, the Olympic Delivery Authority (ODA) and the Mayor's London Development Agency (LDA) hastily took over compulsory land purchase and strategic planning powers in place of the locally-elected authorities. The LDA's initial responsibility for land acquisition and preparation was only a transitory role, however, since another unelected body, the Olympic Park Legacy Company (OPLC) was formed in 2009 by the Mayor with national government Communities (DCLG) and Olympics (DCMS) ministers, to further develop and dispose of land and facilities post-event. This new body was itself wound up to be replaced by a Mayoral development corporation, the London Legacy Development Corporation (LLDC) in April 2012 under the central government's 2011 Localism Act. This also transferred land-use planning powers previously held by the London Thames Gateway Development Corporation and ODA to the LLDC, including local authority land within the Olympic zone (figure 19.1).

This fragmented and temporal governance structure contrasts with inner-city regeneration organizations in other countries where a long-term agency is established to see through phased redevelopment, such as in La Défense (EPAD) Paris, *Euromediteranee* Marseilles, German IBAs (*Internationaler Bauausstellungen*) e.g. Emscher Park (Ruhr) and Bilbao's waterfront. This international experience and the lessons from London Docklands in terms of governance, distributive effects and gentrification (Butler, 2007) do not appear to feature in London2012 Olympic planning, organizational structures and evaluation efforts. Rather, the current approach can be seen to mirror this earlier regeneration trajectory to which London 2012 is in many senses an extension both spatially and chronologically, with the Olympic opportunity the new *force majeure* required to remove the barriers to the exceptional levels of public sector investment and top-down land-use development. Historically this also represents the goal of readdressing convergence strategies to tackle the imbalance between west and east London through successive waves of regeneration and the creation of a new 'destination'. This has echoes of earlier London Olympics and World's Fairs centred on White City in west London (e.g. 1908) where the promotion of electrified railway and underground routes gave access to and from the newly developed outer London suburbs. The reassertion of London via Olympic branding and massive public regeneration investment – inevitably diverting funding from the regions and regional cities – was enabled, again, by an erstwhile national event.

Olympic Visions

The preceding 'national' public project with sub-regional regeneration goals was the Millennium Dome across the river from Canary Wharf on the Greenwich peninsula. The Greenwich site had been selected as the location for the national Millennium celebration, first conceived in 1995, from a shortlist of four sites. These included two other British Gas-owned derelict sites in Newham and in the

Table 19.1 London 2012 Olympic and legacy visions.

London 2012 Olympic Objectives (2005) and Legacy (DCMS, 2007a)	London 2012 Olympic Legacy Programmes (LDA, 2009)	UK Government Legacy Commitments (DCMS, 2010)	London Mayor Olympic Legacy Commitments	London 2012 Host Borough Legacy Framework	London Legacy Development Corporation 10 Year Plan (LLDC, 2014)
'Green', sustainable games, Lower Lea Valley regeneration. *Making the Olympic Park a blueprint for sustainable living*	Olympic Park & Land delivery	Sustainable communities: Promoting community engagement and achieving participation across all groups in society through the Games	Delivering a sustainable Games and developing sustainable communities	Nexus with physical regeneration	A successful and accessible Park with world-class sporting venues, leisure space for local people
Cultural Legacy, Olympic Festivals, Creative Hub. *Demonstrating that the UK is a creative, inclusive and welcoming place to live in, visit and for business*	Culture; Tourism and Business	Tourism and Business opportunities: Exploiting to the full the opportunities for economic growth offered by hosting the Games	Showcasing London as a diverse, inclusive, creative and welcoming city	Visitor economy	A new heart for East London securing investment, nurturing talent to create, design and make world-beating 21st century goods and services
Participation in Sport and Culture. *Making the UK a world leading sporting nation; inspiring a generation of young people to take part in volunteering, cultural and physical activity*	Sports participation (including Healthy & Active Workplace)	Harnessing the UK's passion for sport to increase grass roots participation, particularly by young people	Increasing opportunities for Londoners to become involved in sport	Sporting legacy; Culture	Park offering leisure space for local people, arenas for thrilling sport, enticing visitor entertainment and a busy programme of sporting, cultural and community events to attract visitors
Park, environmental and transport improvements, Olympic Institute and Media Centre. *Transforming the heart of East London* (LEST)	Tourism & Business; London Employment & Skills Taskforce	Ensuring that the Olympic Park can be developed after the Games as one of the principal drivers of regeneration in East London	Ensuring Londoners benefit from new jobs, business and volunteering opportunities; transforming the heart of East London	Nexus with physical regeneration	Opportunities and transformational change for local people, opening up access to education and jobs, connecting communities and bridging the gap between east London and the rest of the capital

Source: Evans, 2010 and 2015.

Midlands, namely, Derby, and the Birmingham International Exhibition Centre. Like the Olympic Park the site required toxic waste and poisoned soil to be removed prior to construction[3] and formed part of a £4 billion regeneration of the wider Greenwich peninsula. Conceived as the centre of the nation's celebration of the new Millennium in 2000, its vague purpose and escalating capital cost cast a cloud over such public *grands projets* in Britain. The four themes for the Millennium Exhibition award: *The Environment*; *Art, Culture*; *Community Activity*; and *Improved access to the natural and technological world*, intended to deliver 'the best event of its kind in the world',[4] are, however, echoed in the Olympic visions and delivery programmes promoted by both national and London City governments, as well as host boroughs (table 19.1), and with the current strategic priorities articulated in the Mayor's most recent 10 year plan.

Financing London 2012

The design and development of the London 2012 Olympic project took place during an extreme cycle of economic boom and bust. The bid and cost estimates were produced in an unprecedented period of consumption and construction growth globally, and in the UK particularly in residential development. This boom had been fuelled by further liberalization and availability of credit following the dot.com crash (2000–2001). Low borrowing rates leading to speculation and what became known in the USA as 'sub-prime' lending, led to the beginning of the downfall of several financial institutions in the USA (e.g. Lehmans), the UK (e.g. Northern Rock) and elsewhere. London's capital bid estimates were quickly exposed, as the award made the project a reality. Construction costs rose rapidly as decisions over venue design looked to existing developers and star architects to produce the required Olympic effect – at a price. History confirms that architects of ambitious schemes – from Corbusier and Koolhaus to Hadid – seldom come in anywhere near their original budget, while global demand for materials and consultants made this a suppliers' market. By the time the global credit crunch and ensuing economic crisis took effect in the UK during 2007–2008, the Olympic budget overruns were established and not recoverable. To make things worse, the recession and the drying up of credit limited commercial sponsorship interest in Olympic projects. In the case of the Olympic Village reluctance by commercial developers to invest, necessitated further public funding and increases in the core budget.

Not surprisingly capital and running cost overruns, along with planning for exceptional security and terrorism risks, were the main concerns in the development phase. Like the Millennium Dome, the Olympics were also reliant upon National Lottery ticket sales – £2.175 billion, up from £1.5 billion in the original budget, via a special Olympic lottery, and ticket revenue of £300 million. A total of 9.6 million tickets were to be made available, with 8 million for the Olympics and 1.6 million for the Paralympics. Seventy-five per cent were priced at £48, but there were considerable variations, for example, the prices for the Opening Ceremony varied between two symbolic low and high figures – £20.12 and £2,012 respectively. The diversion of National Lottery funds to the Olympics was controversial in terms of the negative impact on other UK regions and the established beneficiaries of the UK state lottery (including the arts, heritage, sports, community, charity, education, science and technology). However, this was also expedient as it comprised a 'soft' source of 'off-balance sheet' funding for the government: technically not public funding or spending. The Lottery had been established by the previous Conservative government in 1994 to provide funding for good causes which were to be 'additional' to government's own spending on public services and provision (Evans, 1996a). It was not designed to meet either a shortfall in public sector spending projects or programmes, or to be directed by government, but to respond to applicants based on need. Lottery funded projects are also required to meet a public accessibility test. It is doubtful, however, if either additionality or public benefit tests were adhered to in the Lottery contributions to the Olympics development costs or whether any of the contribution will be repaid from subsequent post-event asset sales, given the ongoing capital spend on the Olympic Park.

The British public, of course, had a choice whether to buy lottery tickets or to attend the Olympics. By contrast, London rate payers had no choice. A £20 per annum extra tax was levied on each household to raise a further £625 million towards the Games. The then Labour London Mayor, Ken Livingstone, pledged that Londoners would pay no more than £240 each towards the Games, despite the rising costs. Overspend by the Mayor's development agency (LDA) on land acquisition and other unfunded commitments inevitably had to be recovered via Londoners – whether through direct tax receipts, or reductions in London services (for instance on culture, transport and regeneration). So it is no surprise that in a 2006 BBC London poll of the public's attitude towards the London Olympics, nearly 80 per cent believed that the Games would end up costing Londoners more than this levy.

With the history of cost overruns and unrealistic and unrealized budget and visitor forecasts, the modern Olympics have a major credibility problem. The firm of consultants used to prepare the visitor forecasts and impact assessment for the Millennium Dome 10 years earlier (Price Waterhouse, 1994) was again used for London 2012 in both impact (PriceWaterhouseCoopers, 2005) and evaluation exercises (PriceWaterhouseCoopers, 2009). Distancing and distinguishing the project from its precursors also allows the promoters to ignore warnings and claim immunity when history repeats itself. The *post hoc* reviews that governments tend to commission are more about attributing blame and non-compliance than implementing a real change in organizational behaviour and assessment regimes. Experience with the Dome, major public facilities such as the Scottish Parliament building (Sudjic, 2005), the Jubilee Line Extension, and recent sporting stadia – for example, the rebuilt Wembley Stadium[5] – suggests that the cost of publicly procured mega-event facilities are very hard to control and almost guaranteed to degenerate into contractual disputes and political controversy. Ironically the UK had been undergoing a massive public facility building programme under the New Labour administration (1997–2010), notably in transport, public health care (the largest hospital rebuilding programme in the world), and education ('Building Schools for the Future'). This investment was substantially funded outside the public spending balance sheet, under the government's private finance initiative (PFI). The PFI, however, was not used to finance Olympic capital projects. This is an indication of the poor viability of such facilities, since PFI contractors earn their considerable returns on facility management and leaseback to the public sector, in return for risk capital investment in the development phase.

Only one bidder emerged for the main London 2012 stadium development and the ODA had difficulty in generating competitive bids for the other venues, as a lack of free market competition drove up prices and placed contractors in an unhealthily strong position (Raco, 2014). When combined with major transport and regeneration projects, the capital risk multiplies. In the case of the Olympics, this risk ultimately is underwritten by the state and municipal authorities, with the most direct and acute impacts falling on local communities and businesses.

Attempting to apply a cost-benefit analysis to an Olympic Games impact assessment initially requires estimating capital and revenue costs, but, like the bidding and national campaigning processes, this aspect is also confused and fluid. Short (2008, p. 332) also noted that: 'objective cost-benefit analysis of hosting the Games remains at a rudimentary stage, with few accurate or comprehensive studies and few comparative data'. In the first place, the income and costs of the event from bidding to staging, are distributed between international, national and city-regional organizations and sponsors, and budgeting is not transparent.[6] Whether state-led or privately sponsored, much investment and expenditure is 'off-balance sheet', understating the true resource cost and impacts. Secondly, there is the challenge of attributing expenditure to the Olympic event itself. Strictly, commitments made prior to the decision to bid for the Games for, say, transport and other environmental improvements, as well as in sporting, hospitality and media facilities and any benefits arising, such as jobs, should be discounted. Stratford, the main transport and retail hub for the development, was already the subject of town centre and urban design schemes, including new housing. The Westfield shopping centre (figure 19.2), a £2 billion commercial development, received planning approval in 2002, 3 years prior to the Olympic bid. In addition, over £80 million had been invested in public-realm projects around the fringes of the Park prior to the 2012 Games with more than £300 million in regeneration funding being received by the London Borough of Newham between 1996 and 2004. Governments, however, often anticipate bidding for future mega-events as part of place-making and regeneration strategies, and investment is also planned, but not necessarily implemented, as part of the competitive bidding process, as putative hosts talk up their capacity to host the future Games.

Figure 19.2. Map of the Olympic Park at 'Games time' (*Source*: LOCOG, 2011).

Comparing and attributing Olympic Games and related regeneration expenditure, therefore, is as much of an art as a science (see Chapter 6; also Preuss, 2004*b*). When major transport improvements, site clearance and security considerations are taken into account, total investment rises substantially. In the case of Beijing, the estimated costs were $40 billion to get the Chinese capital's infrastructure ready for 2008, with $23 billion for the Games themselves (BBC Sport, 2006). The spectre of the Athens 2004 Games also hovered over London. This eventually required expenditure of $12 billion, more than double the budget, with security costs (post-9/11) and poor ticket sales adding to the deficit. This was in addition to $16 billion in transport and other infrastructure development. Before that, Sydney 2000 cost over $2.8 billion against an initial budget of $1 billion (Cashman, 2006) and Rio's bid budget for the 2016 Summer Games is estimated at $14 billion. London 2012 is no exception to this credibility gap between bid estimates, promises and naïve assumptions, and the realities of the land acquisition, construction and delivery package. The line between Olympics and regeneration and renewal becomes impossible to detect. The twenty-first century capital city Olympic Games have proved to be the most expensive to date. Ironically this was the reason in the previous century (after Tokyo 1964) that these cities became wary of hosting the event, but their interest has returned despite this trend.

London's £4 billion capital budget and £1.5 billion operating budget included in the Candidate File submitted to the IOC in 2005 (LOCOG, 2004) was supplemented by the additional financing of site infrastructure (£800 million), and investment in sport at community and elite levels (£900 million). Post-award, the messy process of procurement and the vagaries of construction and materials costs (e.g. steel) driven up by a global building boom, not least in China (including the Beijing Olympics) had been fuelled by 'oversights' in costing, which included (as already mentioned) omitting Value Added Tax on construction and not allowing for adequate inflation. London was also spending £7 billion on rail infrastructure including the Channel Tunnel Rail Link (CTRL) and East London line, as well as £1.5 billion on regeneration programmes in the Lower Lea Valley. These were largely over and above the Olympic budget: '75 percent of every pound we spend is for long-term regeneration' according to an ODA spokesman (BBC Sport, 2008).

The Olympic budget quickly increased from the bid stage, with the £1.5 billion operating budget re-estimated at £2 billion; compulsory land purchases and compensation rising from £478 million to over £1 billion; and with construction inflation that was running at 7 per cent (versus 3 per cent in the original budget). The £2.375 billion capital cost of the sports venues alone was forecast by late-2006 to have risen by £900 million to £3.3 billion. In March 2007 the government announced its revised budget of £9.235 billion for the construction and security costs – £5.3bn higher than at the bid stage – which excludes the event staging costs (LOCOG), land acquisition (LDA) and other government Olympic-related programmes (sports and culture programmes) and wider transport and infrastructure investment in and around the Olympic catchment area (Gold and Gold, 2009). The cost of individual facility budgets such as the main stadium increased by 20 per cent; the aquatics centre originally budgeted at £75 million was forecast to cost £244 million, even after design changes (e.g. roof span) imposed early on to reduce costs; while the Athletes' Village increased in cost by over 60 per cent, and with private sector financing unable to be delivered by Lend Lease as the credit crunch hit, government also had to put in an additional £324m of public funding (Evans, 2010).

Frustratingly, a line by line comparison between the budget estimates is difficult to undertake for London 2012, as the UK government's Public Accounts Committee observed: 'despite the £5.9 billion increase in the public funding for the Games, the Department has not specified what will be delivered in return for this expenditure and the current budget cannot be reconciled to the commitments in the original bid' (HCCPA, 2008, p. 5). This opaque reporting of public spending continues with the 'final' outturn figures, grouping expenditure in different headings from those used in the bid and revised capital budgets (Grant Thornton et al., 2013) making variance analysis impossible. So that while claims of the Olympics being 'delivered on time and on budget' are made by lead contractors and government, this is only based on a 'final' budget which had already been increased by over 100 per cent, and included substantial contingency in order that this higher budget would not be breached. Even so, venues, operations, the media centre, Athletes' Village and ODA programmes were all overspent.

An 82 per cent ticket yield was forecast but in reality in total 11 million tickets (97 per cent) were sold out of a total 11.3 million available. Of these, 8.21 million were Olympic Games tickets and 2.78 million were for the Paralympics. A total of £659 million was raised for LOCOG's operating budget to stage the Games. 319,000 tickets (263,000 Olympic and 55,000 Paralympic) were unsold, the majority of these being early rounds for Olympic Football. However, empty seats were a feature of several events, with a significant proportion of tickets allocated to members of the so-called 'Olympic family' and sponsors, who did not take up their seats. On the sailing finals day, of 851 tickets only one was available to the public, the rest went to sponsors whilst for Danny Boyle's iconic Opening Ceremony – one of the most in-demand tickets of the fortnight – only 44 per cent of the tickets were available to the public while 66 per cent went to the 'Olympic family'. On the day in the velodrome when Sir Chris Hoy, Jason Kenny, Phillip Hindes won the men's sprint final, only 43 per cent of tickets were available to the public.

In addition to sports related events, the IOC-designated Cultural Olympiad,[7] an ambitious 4-year national cultural programme was held (García, 2013b). This included the World Shakespeare Festival, a museums project 'Stories of the World', 'Unlimited' a festival of deaf and disabled artists, and Artists Taking the Lead which commissioned regional projects. In the case of London, this included 'Bus Tops' – video screens on the top of bus shelters on which artists and the public could create messages and images to be viewed by passengers on the top of double-decker buses. The culmination of the Cultural Olympiad was the London 2012 Festival held from 21 June to 9 September, with a curated programme of 'high quality artistic animations, events, installations and interventions across live performance, film and visual arts' (LOCOG, 2013a). It took place in town centres, squares and parks across the thirty-three London boroughs and throughout the UK. The London 2012 Festival series of branded events engaged more than 25,000 artists creating 33,631 different cultural activities. There were 11.3 million public attendances at free events and 4.8 million at events which charged (García, 2013b, pp. 17, 68).

Legacy Costs

Public investment does not cease at the event stage. Capital and revenue spending continues in the legacy phase with an estimated spend of over £500 million for the planning, development and post-Games transformation of the Olympic Park between 2012 and 2016. Most of this was to fall in the 3 years 2014–2017 after the reopening of the Park, with spending on LLDC Park Operations and Corporate services totalling £80 million (LLDC, 2014). A large element in this ongoing capital spend is the conversion of the main stadium to a football ground for West Ham Football Club, costing an additional £272 million, which was not foreseen when the stadium was first designed and built. This 54,000 seat stadium will eventually have cost over £700 million, far more than if it had been designed for this purpose in the first place. Despite the largesse available to a premier league football club, West Ham FC will pay only £15 million of these conversion costs and remarkably only £2.5 million p.a. to lease the stadium for 99 years (this sum is reduced if the club is relegated from the Premier League). Further retrofitting has also been carried out at the AccelorMittal Orbit tower with a giant slide to be installed in an attempt to make this attraction more popular; reportedly it lost £540,000 in 2014–2015 from 120,000 visitors against a business plan forecast of £1.2 million profit from 350,000 visitors. Finally, the lack of a legacy plan for the Aquatic Centre has meant that its internal design and operation is less than ideal (and no substitute for traditional municipal pools, several of which have closed in Newham and other host boroughs). User access to this centre – best viewed from a distance – is also awkward and illegible. A blue-coloured film has had to be retrofitted to the exterior windows in order to reduce the glare which meant that lifeguards could not see swimmers underwater (Evans, 2015).

Local Impacts

London and, more so, the outside world never expected the city to win the 2012 bid. Land acquisition and relocations had, not surprisingly, been taken less than seriously. The planning, IOC review visit and press support built up a momentum in the last few months, as credibility and confidence grew – but second place was regarded as the 'best' outcome. The regeneration legacy was not reliant on the Olympics; this would be the icing on the cake and provide the international cachet, even for an established world city and cultural capital. London's bid therefore rested pragmatically on both broader regeneration and legacy plans, including explicit 'with' and 'without' games scenarios. This formed the consultation roadshow that was rolled out to the East London communities who would be most affected by the regeneration games. The master-planning team, led by the US firm of AECOM (formerly EDAW), with stadium architects Populous (formerly HOK) and urban designers Allies and Morrison, also employed a firm of community architects, Fluid, to undertake the community consultation on the Olympic and Legacy plans (Fluid, 2003). Community engagement included over thirty public events, the distribution of 400,000 public information leaflets to incumbent households and the requisite (temporary) website.

LOCOG also organized several community meetings and drop-in sessions in the London 2012 host boroughs. Parking restrictions, security issues and additional signage that were to be in place during the Games were introduced during these meetings. An estimated 5,000 people participated in the event programme held in various community venues in the five Olympic boroughs. Local businesses (around 300 firms) and 'hard to reach' groups were also targeted to ensure their voice was at least heard. The firm undertaking the consultation also worked with the Lea Valley Matrix Group, but this group had been established and led by the London Development Agency itself, comprising businesses, boroughs and local regeneration partnerships. It was not a representative or independent community organization (Harskamp, 2006). Closer to the Games, the DCMS undertook a Host Borough Survey – a one-off, area-specific survey – that covered the six Olympic host boroughs of Barking and Dagenham, Greenwich, Hackney, Newham, Tower Hamlets and Waltham Forest, in addition to the annual DCMS *Taking Part* Survey[8] which covered the whole of England. We have also incorporated survey data based on focus group meetings held by the authors with local residents living in the four Host Boroughs immediately bordering the Olympic Park – Hackney, Newham, Tower Hamlets and Waltham Forest (Edizel, 2014).

Although the importance of local engagement in decision-making through government initiatives had been highlighted (ODPM, 2004) – in order to have strong, empowered and active communities – locals complained that the meetings organized by the Olympic organizations and local authorities were more informative than participative and felt that they were not involved in the decision-making. More than half of the respondents of the Host Borough Survey said that they were not informed about any action or meeting regarding community consultation and the ones that *were* engaged with these meetings mentioned that the plans were already set and the officials were not genuinely asking for the residents' ideas. During a Tower Hamlets focus group, a resident observed: 'they have been holding meetings, but whether the meetings are effective is a different thing … they are holding meetings to tick the boxes, obviously; I don't think they actually impart any information to us', whilst a Hackney resident said: 'having a meeting is one thing, having people actively participating in the decisions being made is something totally different. I mean, anybody can hold a meeting, but are they really involving groups locally?'.

There were two main reasons for locating the Olympic Park in this area of East London. The first, which needs little emphasis, was the availability of so-called brownfield, or previously developed, land and existing transport extensions to rail and underground systems, including Eurostar and the Jubilee Line Extension (Evans and Shaw, 2001). Given that the Olympic zone, located in the Lower Lee Valley, had been the site for industry, waterways, marsh and farm land for several centuries, this ignored the reality that much of the land developed for the Olympics was open and green space, albeit with neglected canals and a legacy of polluted land and water. While the 'new' park is promoted as the key additional amenity for this part of London, in fact the Olympic development has produced much new hardscape, but reduced the amount of open and green space (figure 19.3).

The other rationale for this location was the disadvantaged profile of incumbent communities in Newham and the adjoining riparian 'Olympic' boroughs. Relative 'deprivation' is measured in England by a number of economic, environmental and social (including education) factors, weighted by government towards

Figure 19.3. Olympic development area, 2003 aerial view and 2030 plan (*Source*: LLDC in Evans, 2015)

employment and economic participation, as opposed to factors such as housing, crime and safety. These include individual domains such as income, education and skills, health, and housing and environment together producing a composite standard by which local areas are ranked in a national 'Index of Multiple Deprivation' (IMD). This provides a national league table which is used as the prime criteria for regional and other publicly-funded regeneration assistance programmes. Comparing the Olympic zone neighbourhoods with Olympic sub-regions, and with London and England as a whole, this showed that 83 per cent of the Olympic communities (and 39 per cent of the five boroughs) were ranked in the top ten most income-deprived areas in England, and 47 per cent in the worst five (figure 19.4). This income ranking had worsened for the Olympic area since the bid was submitted (ODPM, 2004) and represents the baseline against which

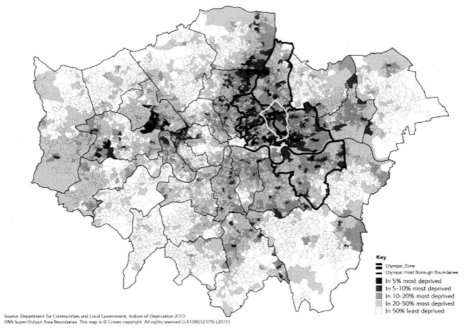

Source: Department for Communities and Local Government, Indices of Deprivation 2010
ONS Super Output Area Boundaries. This map is © Crown copyright. All rights reserved (LA100032379) (2011)

Key
- Olympic Zone
- Olympic Host Borough Boundaries
- In 5% most deprived
- In 5-10% most deprived
- In 10-20% most deprived
- In 20-50% most deprived
- In 50% least deprived

Figure 19.4. Index of Multiple Deprivation in London showing the five Olympic Boroughs and the Olympic Zone.

progress and improvement is measured. Therefore the changes in deprivation may well start to reflect displacement, as well as the failure of regeneration, at least in the short term, to reach those on lower incomes. However, as higher income residents move in, this ranking may well change. The literature often claims that hosting mega-events can increase community cohesion and a tendency to engage in voluntary work (Smith, 2012; Misener and Mason, 2006). Similarly, tackling deprivation and increasing community cohesion through the Games were of great importance to the London 2012 host boroughs. One of the visions of the Olympic host boroughs has therefore been to tackle deprivation through preventing the cycle of gentrification whereby residents who prosper and move out of the area are replaced by higher income newcomers, but this is hampered by the housing market and lack of social housing within the legacy developments themselves.

Housing

Housing development was already under way in Stratford and in a number of canalside developments prior to the Games, so the Athletes' Village (now renamed East Village) represents the first non-sports legacy, providing 2,818 new homes, including 1,379 affordable residences, for sale and rent, along with an academy school and polyclinic. However, the catchment for these new community facilities was much wider than the local area. Cost and timing has meant that compromises to the original master plan had to be made from the planned four- to eight-storey blocks to standardized blocks of six to twelve storeys and finally to eight to ten. Housing affordability is a serious misnomer in this case, since for property purchase, the value of a one-bed apartment would require borrowing of five times the average earnings of a Newham resident, while affordable rent can represent 80 per cent of market rates under current government guidelines. Legacy and plan promises of 35 per cent affordable housing in Olympic legacy housing was made up of affordable rent, shared ownership and social rent. This target has already been reduced in the case of Chobham Manor due to open in 2016 and to 30 per cent (from 40 per cent target) in the new canalside urban villages (1,500 dwellings) of East Wick and Sweetwater (figure 19.5). Even here, the affordable housing is funded by the public sector via the LLDC, and in Bernstock's (2014, p. 135) view: 'another development that is likely to make a relatively negligible impact on the urgent need for genuinely affordable housing in the area'.

A further 1,000 planned homes, however, have already been cut from the revised Legacy plan (now 7,000 versus the original estimate of 9,000 to 10,000) to accommodate a new 'cultural hub' which includes outposts of the Victoria and Albert Museum, London College of Fashion, Sadler's Wells Theatre, University College London and Loughborough University, with headline claims of 10,000 jobs and an economic impact of billions. In the words of Mayor Boris Johnson:

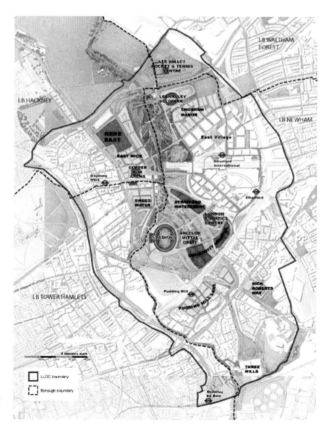

Figure 19.5. Olympic Park Special Planning Guidance area and housing/development zones. (*Source*: LLDC)

'The idea behind Olympicopolis is simple and draws on the extraordinary foresight of our Victorian ancestors. We want to use Queen Elizabeth Olympic Park as a catalyst for the industries and technologies in which London now leads the world in order to create thousands of new jobs' (LLDC, 2013). Johnson's rationale for this is also that it would lead to more homes being built in the future in the surrounding area.

The attraction of the Olympic zone served by new transport links to central London, Canary Wharf and the suburbs had already seen the borough of Newham produce the highest increases in average house prices in the UK between 1999 and 2009; up 190 per cent compared with the national average of 117 per cent. At the same time there have been above average rises in the neighbouring Olympic host boroughs of Hackney (143 per cent) and Tower Hamlets (146 per cent). This has occurred despite the house price and credit crunch since the banking crisis first hit during 2007. Gentrification was already underway in this area prior to any Olympic effects and was even identified in annual government surveys of legacy impacts as a perceived benefit of London 2012. While improved transport and sports venues were seen as the long-term benefits with most potential by those surveyed nationally, regeneration of the area scored highest amongst Londoners – particularly amongst higher socio-economic groups who were twice as likely to mention this factor than lower groups (DCMS, 2008, p. 31).

The Olympics therefore has provided an investment leverage opportunity to accelerate development, with 25 per cent of London's entire housing growth predicated on developments within the Olympic zone. Those respondents who lived in Newham generally agreed that the Games has increased numbers of people moving (63 per cent), while a Hackney resident noted the new accommodation in the Park, saying: 'if they're gonna regenerate the flats into super-duper flats, we're not gonna get the same sort of atmosphere that we have if they're ordinary people living in them. They're gonna send us away since normal people won't be able to afford them'. As a result of improvements in facilities and infrastructure, the area has become more attractive for middle- and high-income groups, and social division remains a challenge. As experienced in other Olympic cities, residents, environmentalists, businesses, creatives and others were anxious about the negative impacts, spiralling costs, and displacement arising from the development. The re-opening of the Park, arrival of new communities and new housing developments in the Park and new schools were not surprisingly expected to impact property prices significantly.

Community Cohesion

Of those host borough residents surveyed, 72 per cent believed that they belong to their local area and 41 per cent that people from different backgrounds get on well in their neighbourhood. However, the views differed when questioned about the effect of the Games on feelings of belonging and community cohesion. It is fair to say that residents did not believe that hosting the Games contributed to community spirit. As a Hackney resident noted: 'I can't see any community spirit generated from hosting the Olympic Games'. Against that, a respondent from Tower Hamlets believed that the Games would strengthen community spirit: 'I think the Olympics have brought the positive side to the East End of London, because it's a once in a lifetime event that is happening in the East End of London. So I don't want to knock the Olympics down in that sense, and I think yes, it will encourage community spirit'.

One of the most significant findings of the Host Borough Survey was that Newham respondents were more supportive and positive about the Games compared with Tower Hamlets, Hackney and Waltham Forest residents. Almost half the Newham respondents (42 per cent) felt that the regeneration resulting from the Games was 'important' in their decision to move into the area and more than half of them mentioned that their area has been regenerated positively through the Games. Moreover, Newham residents tended to agree that the Olympics increased the job opportunities for locals. In addition, more Newham residents had seen the plans compared to other host boroughs. This may be because Newham owns a significant part of the Olympic Park and some important facilities such as the Stadium, Aquatic Centre, with Stratford International Train Station and Westfield Shopping Centre are also located in the borough. Being close to all these facilities and potential opportunities has obviously made these Newham residents more supportive of the Games and legacy. The main weakness however was that the majority of the participants had not seen the plans to improve the Olympic Park area. Housing plans had the lowest degree of satisfaction, while increases in housing prices were a big concern and locals thought that the new houses were not for them. Those who lived in Newham generally agreed that the Games had increased pressures on housing in the local area. In terms of positive expectations from the Games, over half of the respondents believed that the long-term impacts of the 2012 Games would improve the image of the local area; improve sports facilities; and improve local retail and shopping facilities.

Opposition to the Olympics was evident locally, particularly from local housing interests, business and artist groups in the face of displacement (Powell and Marrero-Guillamon, 2012). Ideological resistance was also apparent (Cohen, 2013), but the Olympic good news story and the outsider status of the London bid lessened the negative press. Most observers did not expect the city to win and so opposition was not coordinated. Following the award in July 2005, organized resistance focused on monitoring the development process and legacy promises[9] and on campaigning against land and premises relocation as the pace of issuing compulsory purchase orders intensified. Three years after the 2004 bid feasibility plan the Olympic Park Masterplan was approved by central and local government. With construction commencing, an infamous and impervious blue wall was erected around the Olympic site cutting off access to and through the area for local people, which intensified local dissatisfaction and exclusion. Despite the Olympic

Park development and new access routes, bridges and pathways, the east–west divide (Stratford, Newham–Hackney Wick) which was master planned to be 'stitched together' still persists and communities are still largely territorial in their horizons (Evans, 2015).

Employment

When designated, the area presented a wholly different picture on the ground. Criss-crossed by a maze of river channels and canals, the area contained a mosaic of undeveloped flood plain and industrial land. Some of the latter was long derelict, but other sites involved manufacturing facilities and other employment activity which needed to be relocated. Within months of the award to London, Compulsory Purchase Orders were sent to nearly 300 businesses within the Olympic Park zone. These employed over 5,000 in the Marshgate Lane industrial area and several hundred in other sites. Compensation offered to firms who had benefited from cheap and scarce industrial premises in proximity to central London and national transport access was reported to be 20 to 30 per cent less than the original prices paid by owners: 'the Marshgate Lane Business Group argued that the LDA had allocated £450 million to relocate all the businesses when professional advisers to the businesses estimated that the real cost will be more than £1.5 billion' (COHRE, 2007b, p. 14). The LDA spent £1.3 billion on this exercise, leaving an excess debt of £500 million after intermediate land sales. Over the course of the land acquisition and clearance of the Lower Lea Valley area, businesses employing nearly 15,000 workers were reportedly forced to move with some firms offered alternative locations over 50 miles (80 km) away. Reluctantly most firms settled or had their appeals turned down at Inquiry. There has been surprisingly little follow up or monitoring of the impact of the enforced relocation of businesses by the LDA or other local authorities, and the direct and indirect loss of employment arising is again not reflected in the headline employment figures predicted for the new leisure-retail economy.

The loss of firms through relocation or cessation obviously has an impact on local employment and multiplier effects on the local economy, but the nature of production also suffers. This included artists and designer-makers located in Acme Studios on Carpenters Road, premises housing 140 studios that are now demolished. New studios have been incorporated in mixed-use developments in Stratford, but these have only replaced a fraction of this provision and the studio community will never be replaced at the previous scale and concentration. It is estimated that over 25 per cent of the UK's total artist studio provision (6,000 artists in 135 buildings) were located in the Olympic host boroughs, occupying genuinely affordable and supportive studio premises. This cultural asset has therefore been under threat, and the gentrification effect continues in the years following the Games with the further development of the Hackney Wick and Fish Island industrial buildings for housing. As Millington (2009) observed: 'The irony is that, while London's vibrant, diverse and influential culture has been promoted as a significant aspect of London 2012, the very studio complexes that have contributed to that vitality, along with other supporting businesses such as materials suppliers are under threat and some have disappeared altogether'.

Conclusion

The Olympic Park and associated environmental improvements are thus the main physical features of the Olympic legacy, with new and converted housing literally populating what was a low-density group of urban neighbourhoods. However, it is the economic regeneration and consequent social benefits – given the association of poor housing, health, education and crime with poverty and lack of work – that have been used to justify the sustainability of London 2012, and ultimately the longer term benefits to offset the explicitly stated and indeterminate direct and indirect costs.

How the Olympics are assessed now and in the future will itself form part of the narratives and history surrounding this latest episode in mega-event regeneration. In narrower evaluation and appraisal terms required by public bodies dispersing taxpayers' money, official impact studies seek to measure change and cause-and-effect attributable to Olympic and other investment programmes. The Olympic Games Impact Study (OGIS) is now a requirement for all host cities, with London undertaking this exercise based on a collection of indicators. A disconnected range of impact studies are also being commissioned by government departments – Culture (DCMS), Communities (DCLG) and Business (BERR), including a meta-evaluation study by the DCMS seeking to synthesize all the studies. These are driven by government evaluation frameworks and imperatives and are unlikely to reflect the full experience of, or impact on communities, stakeholders, or longer-term distributive effects. The government's official Pre-Games OGIS report (UEL/TGIS, 2010, p. 25) using some sixty indicator sets, however, had found 'below average performance for the environmental outcomes indicators', as well as social outcomes indicators, with gains yet to be measured from Olympic facility lifecycle and energy consumption analysis. As Bernstock (2014, p. 202) concluded: 'the real risk is that the area will be regenerated, but with very little benefit to those existing communities'. From the survey of host borough residents carried out just prior to the Games, only a minority thought that preparations had a positive impact on improved housing (28 per cent), education, health and community facilities (26 per cent), with more agreeing that parks and green spaces (39 per cent) and the image of area (49 per cent) had improved. Respondents also thought that crime, pollution, pressures on local amenities, as well as 'churn' would *increase* over the longer term – hardly an endorsement of the legacy of a 'sustainable community' that the project had promised (see table 19.1).

The counterfactual – what would have happened without the Olympics in terms of regeneration and what were the opportunity costs from the public investment – can never be fully answered. Yet these are the most important questions underlying the Olympic regeneration's rationale, on which the London bid rested. As Hall (1992, p. 83) suggested:

> it should be recognised that social impact evaluation will ask the difficult question of who benefits? A question which goes to the very heart of why cities host hallmark events in order to improve or rejuvenate their image and attract tourism and investment.

Getz (2009, p. 76) optimistically argued that in answering this question: 'the effect would be to ensure that the usual claims of economic benefits are not accepted at face value, and that social, cultural and environmental measures of value would be equal to the economic'. In reality the inability, politically, to embrace the full impacts and decision-making rationales honestly and transparently, is in part a reflection of the fragmented governance and delivery structure; the stop-go regeneration regimes imposed over a 30 to 50 year period; and also the limitations of political and budget horizons as agencies are unable to commit to programmes beyond their likely shelf lives. In some respects this is likely to let the Olympic machine 'off the hook' in terms of full blown evaluation and attribution, but this is not a reason for failing to try to capture as full an analysis and assessment of 'impact' and 'legacy' as is possible – particularly with the benefit of renewed academic and public interest in the phenomenon, and a wider range of available data and tools to analyse this than has previously been the case.

Notes

1. A misplaced vote might have helped London win the 2012 Olympics. Moscow and New York were eliminated in the first two rounds. An IOC committee member (President of the Greek Olympic Committee) had then mistakenly voted for Paris rather than Madrid in the third round. Paris received 33 votes to Madrid's 31 in that round, eliminating the Spanish capital. Had Madrid received the vote rather than Paris, the cities would have tied with 32 each, seven fewer than London, and entered a tiebreaker. London beat Paris 54–50 in the final round. In the run up to the IOC vote in Singapore, London was still ranked third after Paris, the clear favourite, and Madrid. No city had hosted the Games more than twice (London and Paris) and London had never won by competition, only hosting by default in 1908 and 1948.

2. According to the Chief Executive of the British Olympic Association, Simon Clegg: 'The sole measurement of the Games won't be on how efficient the organizing committee is, or how beautifully architectured the design of the stadiums are – it'll be decided on how many British athletes stand on the podium and collect medals' (http://ukolympics.org.uk). The official target was to improve the place in the Olympic medal table from tenth in 2004 to fourth in 2012 and the results went beyond expectations. Great Britain moved to third place in the Summer Olympics Medal Table 2012 (http://www.olympic.org/).

3. The Olympic site located in this part of East London had traditionally been the dumping ground for toxic waste, including mustard gas stored during World War I, as well as engineering and manufacturing that produced pollutants resulting in poisoned soil and water.

4. The main criticisms of the Millennium project were the escalating cost and unclear purpose and content, as well as the problem of promoting the event as a national celebration in a non-central London location (Evans, 1996b, 1999). Despite this, the experience of visitors was

generally positive with 88 per cent saying that they had a 'fun day' (BBC 'Vote on the Dome'). The final cost of the Dome was £790 million, of which £600 million was funded by the National Lottery and the balance from ticket sales. This was £200 million or 50 per cent over the original budget estimate, due to a shortfall in visitor numbers – around 6.5 million people came, compared with 12–18 million in the original business plan (Price Waterhouse, 1994; Evans, 1996a). The situation was exacerbated by the failure to secure its after-use and disposal. By 2005 the costs of annual insurance and security costs for the vacant facility were put at £1 million. The site had been sold following the year-long 'Millennium Experience' exhibition in December 2001 to Meridian Delta Ltd., a subsidiary of Quintain Estates & Development and Lend Lease (backed by Philip Anschutz, American billionaire oil, rail, sport and telecoms entrepreneur) with plans for a 20,000 seat sports and entertainment venue, and a housing and office development on the surrounding 150 acres (60.7 ha). Lend Lease, an Australian property development company, was also the developer of the Olympic Village, housing athletes and providing a mix of social and private housing after the 2012 games. The Chief Executive (CEO) of the Olympic Delivery Authority (ODA) David Higgins was also CEO of the Lend Lease Group from 1995. In May 2005 Anschutz sold the rights to the Dome to O2, a mobile phone company. The refurbished Dome rebranded the O2, was reopened to the public on 24 June 2007. A bid for the O2 to host the UK's first 'super casino' failed in 2007 when the government awarded this licence to Manchester. For the 2012 Olympics, the Dome and adjoining temporary arenas were designated for use as a venue for the artistic gymnastics, trampolining and basketball finals. Due to IOC sponsorship regulations, however, it was to be officially known as 'North Greenwich Arena' during the Games.

5.   Massively over-budget and failing to complete to agreed timetables, Wembley Stadium left the Australian Multiplex developer near bankruptcy.

6.   Government claims for 'transparency' in decision-making and financing of the Olympics are able to be side stepped under the mask of 'commercial confidentiality' in the procurement process and in special adviser contracts.

7.   The Cultural Olympiad is an IOC 'branded' event, encompassing the opening, medal and closing ceremonies, torch relay and a national event programme delivered for London 2012 regionally by the Arts Council, the BBC and Royal Philharmonic Orchestra with local events promoted by the Greater London Authority, local and regional authorities. The Olympic Park Legacy Corporation is also responsible for public art, installations and related events as well as other cultural aspects of the Park design and heritage.

8.   *Taking Part* is a survey undertaken by DCMS which collects data on many aspects of leisure, culture and sport participation in England, as well as an in-depth range of socio-demographic information on respondents. The Host Borough Survey was a one-off, area-specific survey commissioned to inform the Meta-Evaluation of London 2012 Olympics (DCMS) and gathered information on the views, behaviours and attitudes of the residents in the six Olympic host boroughs. The raw data from Host Borough Survey has been analysed together with the focus group meetings with local residents to have more realistic and in-depth results on what people thought about London 2012 related regeneration and their involvement in the decision-making process. These two data sets were collected around the same time periods and targeted to understand similar issues; therefore they were easily integrated in this analysis, using a mixed method to gain an understanding of the community approach (Edizel, 2014).

9.   Games Monitor: debunking the Olympic myths (www.gamesmonitor.org/uk) and see Blowe (2004).

Chapter 20

Rio de Janeiro 2016

Gabriel Silvestre

As one enters the viewing platform of the Olympic Park at Barra da Tijuca, a bold statement is displayed on the wall above the balcony: 'The Games must serve the city'. The statement is credited to former Barcelona Mayor Pasqual Maragall whose quote Eduardo Paes, Mayor of Rio de Janeiro borrowed, eager to equate the urban interventions for the 2016 Games with the wide-ranging transformation witnessed in the Catalan capital more than two decades ago. It is claimed that Rio is undergoing a watershed moment with mega-events propelling it to global city status (Paes, 2015). Expectations are at such a level that when Paes was confronted by a recent study showing marginal benefits for cities hosting mega-events the answer was bold: 'We will leave Barcelona in the dust' (Fernandes, 2015).

Comparisons aside, it is useful to hold on to the mayor's promise to ask: how are the Games serving the city? What kinds of transformations are being induced by the mega-event? For that, it is important to examine how the Olympic moment translates into changes and continuities in the developmental trajectory of Rio de Janeiro. The complexity of Rio's geography is often understood in binary terms: the hills and the 'asphalt'; the formal and the informal; the North and the South Ends. How does the preparation for the 2016 Games relate to these dichotomies?

This chapter offers an overview of Rio de Janeiro's past, current processes of change, and a preliminary discussion of the legacies that will be left by the event. The first part charts the history of urban change including events and mega-projects that have shaped the development of the city. The second examines the different Olympic bids the city has prepared in the last two decades followed by an analysis of the preparations and their impacts 6 years after the Olympic nomination. Finally, the conclusion attempts to answer the questions posed as the start of the Olympics approaches.

From the Belle Époque to the Era of Mega-Events

Francisco Pereira Passos is another political figure with whom Eduardo Paes is keen to be associated.[1] Mayor of Rio de Janeiro between 1902 and 1906, he is credited with the wholesale transformation of Rio's central area, a feat likened to that of

Baron Haussmann's transformation of Paris that served as its model (Benchimol, 1990). The city's densely populated *Centro* experienced a frenetic and profound programme of works with the ultimate goal of 'civilizing' and 'embellishing' the capital of the 'new Brazil', by then a young republic and the world's largest coffee producer, with the material and cultural traits of a modern and cosmopolitan city (Abreu, 2008). That meant overcoming the colonial character of the city, which with its narrow humid, dank roads, conferred the aspect of a large Portuguese village. Therefore, the programme of works envisaged: the modernization of the city port (actually undertaken by the federal government), vital for the country's economy and to keep up with regional competition from Buenos Aires and Montevideo; the opening up of new thoroughfares to regulate the traffic flow; and the upgrading of the utilities infrastructure. Culturally, it oversaw the construction of a host of institutional buildings of eclectic European architecture, plazas and promenades, while repressing 'uncivilized customs' such as carnival celebrations, street hawking and stray dogs (Needell, 1987). Crowning such transformation was the construction of *Avenida Central* (now Avenida Rio Branco) a Paris-inspired boulevard with cafés and tea houses, an opera house, national library and other civic institutions. Coupled with a hygienist justification, Passos's bulldozing efforts saw the demolition of hundreds of tenement houses, home to many urban poor composed of freed slaves, migrants and immigrants, attracted by the proximity to labour opportunities. A consequence of this action was the displacement of

Figure 20.1. Avenida Central with its influence from mid-nineeteenth century Paris epitomized the urban interventions that marked Rio de Janeiro's belle époque. (*Source*: Acervo AGCRJ)

thousands of poor residents to more distant neighbourhoods served by the railway or to precarious self-built homes on the hills near the city centre. The increasing formation of so-called *favelas* by 1916 was such that a local magazine called for a 'rigorous censorship' of the 'parasitic neighbourhoods of the hills' that were 'wrecking with their sordid existence the efforts made to dot the capital of Brazil with the magnificent aspects of a great metropolis' (*Revista da Semana*, cited in Abreu, 2008, p. 89).

In the first quarter of the twentieth century two corridors of urban development that socially and spatially stratified the city had matured (Abreu, 2008). One followed the coastline south of the centre led by the opening of tramways to the wealthy neighbourhoods of Glória and Botafogo, where the elite built their airy and large mansions, and across the hills into Copacabana, Ipanema and Leblon, where urban Rio found its beach identity (O'Donnell, 2013). The other vector followed north from Centro, along the rail lines departing from Central do Brasil station towards industrial and rural districts such as Engenho de Dentro and Deodoro, and into the Baixada Fluminense region. Rio was quickly evolving into a teeming metropolis reaching a population of more than a million in 1920 and more than doubling that figure after the Second World War (Abreu, 2008).

The federal capital continued to be selectively transformed by grand projects. The levelling of Castelo Hill in 1922 was justified on the grounds of improving air circulation and hygiene while also opening a prime piece of land in the city centre by dislodging 'undesirables' (Kessel, 2001). Its urgency was due to the hosting of the International Exposition celebrating Brazil's centenary as an independent state with temporary pavilions erected on the cleared grounds. The earth removed was used as landfill to extend the seashore thus creating the neighbourhood of Urca and shrinking the size of Rodrigo de Freitas lagoon. By the mid-twentieth century Rio had become an exotic international destination with visits from Hollywood stars and serving as a movie set for the shooting of musicals (O'Donnell, 2013).

The increasing complexity of metropolitan Rio during the dictatorship period (1962–1984) was expressed as 'highway fever' (Abreu, 2008) that excused the construction of new roads, tunnels and flyovers such as the Perimetral elevated expressway over the port area; the Aterro do Flamengo expressway facilitating the traffic flow between Centro and the South End; and the cross bay Rio-Niteroi bridge. However, these works were testimony to the beginning of the slow political and economic decline of the city with the construction of Brasilia as the new federal capital, which meant not only a loss of status but also the departure of important elements of the city economy. Amidst the global economic crisis, Brazil reached the 1980s with an unsustainable level of external debt and reduced growth. Structural adjustment programmes conditioned by the loans from multilateral institutions further increased levels of poverty and unemployment. Crime levels soared in Rio while organized armed groups started to take control of the *favelas* as bases for their illicit activities.

The Rio de Janeiro of the 'lost decades' of the 1980s and 1990s still attracted worldwide attention. This time, rather than the scenes of international celebrities frolicking on the sands of Copacabana, it was the execution of homeless children at Candelária and unarmed civilians at Vigário Geral that captured international headlines. Some of the business elite left the city afraid of the wave of kidnappings while companies transferred their activities to other cities. The urban space became increasingly fortified with walls and surveillance cameras to secure residences, offices and commerce. The booming area of Barra da Tijuca, the new urban frontier for Rio's upper and middle classes, epitomized the increasing spatial segregation of the city with exclusive enclaves of gated communities, shopping malls and expressways. In retrospect, it is difficult to imagine that an Olympic candidature could emerge in such adverse conditions. However, it was precisely the seductive idea of an urban turnaround promoted by a former host city that would motivate the Rio Olympic project.

Serial Bidding

From the mid-1990s Rio de Janeiro bid three times to host the Olympic Games and went to great lengths to host the 2007 Pan American Games as a way to boost its hosting credentials. The bidding for the mega-event took place as urban politics were being redefined. It was an outcome of international policy exchange, desired for its strategic use in leveraging urban development and refining the city image. The process of Olympic bidding was thus influenced by two movements. One has its place in the City Hall in the redefinition of urban and planning policies where contact with the experience of Barcelona motivated the 2004 bid. The other has its place in the Brazilian Olympic Committee (BOC) where the ascendancy of a new chairman was intimately linked to the quest to bring the Olympics to Rio.

The 2004 Olympic Bid and the Barcelona Connection

The origin of Rio de Janeiro's Olympic project lies in the policy exchange that took place between the municipality and Barcelona during the 1990s (Silvestre, 2012). Fresh from hosting the 1992 Games that helped to 'put the city on the map', Barcelona's planners and urban managers undertook a series of initiatives to take advantage of the city's strengthened international profile (Borja, 1996). Among these was the offer of consultancy services in public management targeting Latin America as a key market (Associació Pla Estratègic Barcelona 2000, 1994). Promoted by the municipal department of international relations, Catalan policy-makers and companies were soon advising local governments in areas such as traffic engineering, waste collection and water management. However, it would be in the assistance for the elaboration of strategic plans that a greater market was found and in Rio de Janeiro it was their most challenging project.

The 1992 municipal elections in Rio saw the victory of Cesar Maia, a former left-wing federal deputy who found space in the more conservative spectrum running for the Brazilian Democratic Movement Party (PMDB). Maia was keen to develop his image as conciliator between the technocrat and the politician, forming a cabinet of specialists and looking for new methods to bring efficiency to public management (Novais, 2010). Interested in the concept of strategic planning, he was advised by his secretary of urbanism Luiz Paulo Conde, an architectural scholar with professional links to Barcelona, to listen to the proposal of the Catalan policy-makers who were subsequently hired. According to the consultancy brief, the goal of the strategic plan was to:

> set a vision for Rio de Janeiro – a competitive city integrated to international life – where it is assured for its population the full exercise of their citizenship. This vision will include a range of macro-economic, social, urban, cultural and environmental infrastructure projects that will define the development of the city in the next decade. The strategic plan will define a frame able to integrate all these macro-projects in a coherent manner. (PCRJ, 1993, p. 4)

Elaborated between 1993 and 1995 the plan set a central objective[2] underpinned by strategies, objectives and activities to be implemented by policies and projects. A key element of the strategic plan was the bid to host the 2004 Olympic Games by virtue of establishing 'projects with fixed deadlines and effects on its image at home and abroad, to become a centre of regional, national and international attraction' (PCRJ, 1996, p. 25). The idea was born out of the exchange between Rio's political leaders and the Catalan consultants, who extolled the experience of the 1992 Games in leveraging funding for development projects and in city marketing. A new team of consultants was formed bringing the expertise of the planners of the 1992 Games headed by architect Lluis Millet, responsible for the master plan and infrastructural projects of the Barcelona Olympics. Working frantically during the second half of 1995, Millet proposed to adapt the underlying principle of territorial balance that informed his plan for the Barcelona Games by distributing Olympic clusters in the four quadrants of the city: North, South, West and Barra. The urban interventions in each cluster were expected to stimulate trickle-down effects in the surrounding areas and thus encompass most of the city's urban space (RBC, 1996). The centrepiece of his proposal was the Olympic Park cluster in the Fundão Island, located in the city's North End, home to the Federal University of Rio de Janeiro. The university campus offered the advantages of being located next to the international airport and important expressways, while facilitating security and having abundant vacant land for the construction of Olympic facilities. It was proposed to change the isolated character of the island into an 'area of new centrality' by 'opening' it up to the city with the construction of a science park, private housing, convention centre and a new linear park on over 5 kilometres of seafront (Rio 2004 Bid Committee, 1996, p. 24).

Millet's proposal divided opinion among the members of the bidding committee. On one side was Conde and representatives of the federal government, who were supportive of the plan. On the other was Maia and Carlos Nuzman, president of BOC, advocating the use of Barra as main stage for the Games. In the end, Millet's proposal prevailed and the bid book was submitted to the IOC. The official candidature of Rio captured public imagination attracting a million people to Copacabana beach in support of the bid on the eve of IOC's announcement of the cities shortlisted to the second and final phase (Montenegro and Bahiense, 1997). Their hopes ended prematurely as Rio was left out of the final round of voting that included Athens, Buenos Aires, Cape Town, Rome and Stockholm.

The 2012 Olympic Bid and the Hosting of the 2007 Pan-American Games

In the aftermath of the IOC shortlist decision newspapers searched for the reasons for the failure of the 2004 bid. Blame fell on the inexperience of the bid committee; the weak promotional strategy; the feasibility of the cleaning programme for the Guanabara Bay that surrounded Fundão Island; the undeveloped transport and telecommunications infrastructure of the city; and the strong political character of the bid (Anon, 1997; Ventura and Araújo, 1997). Political motivation was understood to have jeopardized the governance of the bid and the nature of the proposed urban interventions. Federal government actors had taken control of the candidature and sidelined the mayor and the BOC's president. The absence of the mayor during the visit of the IOC Evaluation Commission and the marginal role of BOC did not help to boost Rio's chances. Nuzman expressed complaints about BOC being 'underused' arguing that '[t]here is a great rejection when the [national Olympic] committee is not the one leading the way, when there is a political emphasis in the candidature' (Varsano and Bittencourt, 1997). Finally, the discourse of using the event to improve the material conditions of deprived areas around Fundão Olympic Park was seen as more politically motivated than realistic to the city's chances of convincing IOC members. For Maia:

> submitting a city for the Olympics means taking the best features of the municipality and offering them to the International Olympic Committee ... Rio decided to insist on the idea of an Olympics for the city, hoping that the Games would serve to promote urban and social reforms. It is an appealing strategy but also very risky. (Ventura and Araújo, 1997, p. 26)

A subsequent bid for the 2008 Games was contemplated but never progressed. Instead Nuzman and Maia assumed responsibility for the Olympic project and completely re-designed the general proposals. According to Nuzman '[the] Rio 2004 debacle served to define a new strategy' (Anon, 2002) centred on two key foundations. First was to move the centre of the Olympic master plan to booming Barra da Tijuca:

> The choice of Barra is very important. During the Olympic candidature for 2004, Mayor Cesar Maia and I were against the choice of Fundão. The preference for Barra is due to the

more available space… At Barra it is possible to build 70% to 80% of the Olympic facilities. The mayor Cesar Maia had the vision in thinking of Barra and in areas such as the racetrack near Riocentro. There is space to build a permanent sports park. I believe the racetrack is underused. The Formula 1 is now in São Paulo. Brazil has other important racetracks in Paraná, Goiás and Brasília. So, Brazil does not have enough auto and motorcycle racing competitions to justify this. This racetrack could give way to a great Olympic city. I have already explained this to the mayor. It rests on the city to decide. (Nuzman, 2002)

The decision for Barra was also pragmatically defended by Maia:

Barra represents the idea of one single signature. All it takes is one signature from the mayor to define everything. In Fundão decisions depend on the president, the education minister, the chancellor, the dean, the mayor… (Ventura and Araújo, 1997, p. 26)

Secondly, it was understood that the city had to prove itself in organizing other events before preparing another Olympic bid. Following the advice of IOC president Juan Antonio Samaranch, attention focused on the regional Pan-American Games, to which a bid was launched and awarded in 2002 (Anon, 2000). As championed by Nuzman, the new sports venues were to be located at the Jacarepaguá racetrack where a nearby gated development project would serve as accommodation for athletes. Soon after the *Pan-American Sports Organization* (PASO) awarded the Pan-American Games to Rio, the city announced a new Olympic bid for the 2012 Games. The Pan-American Games would thus serve as a two-step strategy with the planned venues reappraised to conform to the IOC requirements. The construction of an Olympic stadium was announced on rail yards in the northern neighbourhood of Engenho de Dentro along with rescaled projects for an aquatics centre, velodrome and sports arena at Barra.

At this stage Luis Inácio Lula da Silva, from the opposition Workers' Party (PT), was elected president of Brazil. A dedicated Ministry of Sports was established and the president fully endorsed the new bid. However, Rio's Olympic ambitions were cut short once again in the application phase as the candidature did not achieve a sufficient score in the technical evaluation, particularly in the items of transport, accommodation, safety and security (IOC, 2004*b*). Despite the setback, the federal government was confident that, with the 2007 Pan-American Games, 'Rio would demonstrate unequivocal proof of its ability to organize a great international event' (Souza, 2002). Indeed support from the federal government proved to be more than a symbolic gesture as the soaring costs of the preparation for the Pan-American Games were compromising the municipality's budget. Plans to improve and extend the public transport network were discarded and the project became essentially venue-oriented. Running out of time, the project was rescued by federal aid and the preparations were completed just in time for the start of the event. The general public responded well, with good attendance at the competitions while being praised by the IOC. The retooled Olympic strategy started to bear fruits, giving confidence to its promoters to move to their next objective.

Winning the 2016 Olympic Bid

A few weeks after hosting the 2007 Pan-American Games, an official bid application was submitted to the IOC. The planning concept considered the master plan of the Pan-American Games as a base line to further develop the Jacarepaguá racetrack with new facilities that would in effect bring the motorsport activities to an end. A compact Games with all competitions held in the city and with most venues located at Barra was one of the strongest selling points of the candidature.

Parallel to these initial steps, city hall was going through the decennial review discussions of its statutory master plan, the *Plano Diretor*. A significant outcome of this process was the definition of macro zones to inform urban development policies. Accordingly, Rio's territory was divided into four such zones that roughly matched the city's informal categorical areas: the South End where development should be controlled due to the compactness and maturity of its built-up area; the West End where there was a growth of deprived neighbourhoods which should be assisted; the North End which was longer established and yet had great levels of deprivation and where development should be encouraged; and finally the Barra region whose real estate speculation should be conditioned by public and private investments in infrastructure (PCRJ, 2011).

When juxtaposed, the Olympic master plan and the city statutory master plan were in conflict. Barra was the preferential destination of investments in infrastructure while the Deodoro region in the West End would be the secondary Olympic cluster, with the use of existing stadia in the North End. Initial animosity between the city planning department and the technical team of the bid committee was reconciled by revising the location of some venues, albeit these were rather modest, such as the use of the Sambadrome for the archery competition or the sponsors' village at the port area. Nevertheless, the Olympic bid offered a window of opportunity for pending works and projects developed by the municipality's planning and transport staff, such as rainwater reservoirs for flood control and the implementation of a network of Bus Rapid Transit (BRT) corridors. The final Olympic master plan proposed in the bid book was not as compact and less reliant on large-scale works as its promoters would have liked, but rather than compromising the city's chances, the foreign consultants advising the candidature saw the mediation between the needs of the mega-events and public policies as an appealing sales pitch.

The role of external consultants during the candidature was an important one (see Oliveira, 2015). Since the Pan-American Games, experts involved with the Sydney 2000 Games had been advising on the planning and organization of the sports events. In these years, the gap between candidate cities to satisfy standard requirements for the Olympic Games became narrower while marketing and communications played an increasing role (Payne, 2009). The Rio de Janeiro candidature spared no expense in hiring some of the most sought-after marketing and public relations consultants of the mega-event industry. Consultants fresh from the winning London 2012 bid, such as communications director Mike Lee, and former IOC insiders such as former secretary general Francoise Zweifel and previous marketing director Michael Payne, crafted the bid with a 'clear vision for the Olympic Movement' (*Ibid.*).

Finally, the Rio bid was set against a favourable political and economic context in contrast to the 2004 candidature. The bid was fully supported by the three levels of government and the international presence and reputation of President Lula contributed to the promotion of the bid. In the second half of the 2000s the Brazilian economy was experiencing high rates of growth and the discovery of a large oil basin off Rio de Janeiro's coast further boosted confidence in the candidature. Brazil was already selected as host of the FIFA 2014 World Cup but this did not seem to affect Rio's chances as international bookmakers pointed to Rio as a likely contender on the eve of IOC's meeting in Denmark. The momentum was highly favourable and press coverage positive, as argued by strategic adviser Michael Payne (2009), noting that 'by the time the IOC was turning to Copenhagen, the world's press were running headlines 'The Rise and Rise of Brazil: Faster, Stronger, Higher'. The hosting rights awarded to Rio on 2 October 2009 opened a 7-year period of preparatory works which would intensely impact upon the lives of the *cariocas* (as residents of Rio are known).

Producing the Olympic City

The preparations for Rio de Janeiro 2016 overlap and intersect with other unfolding processes. As noted earlier, the context to the award was one of economic growth which, in combination with fiscal and distribution policies, stimulated employment and consumption levels. Locally, the growth of the oil and gas industry impacted on Rio, with the installation of new national and foreign companies. It is also important to note the security policy implemented by the state of Rio, which has ended the presence of armed groups at some *favelas*. Finally, the city also played a key role in the hosting of the 2014 World Cup with seven matches including the final played at Maracanã stadium. Altogether these processes help to explain the sudden rise in local prices, especially in real estate where house prices increased by 227 per cent between January 2010 and May 2015, making Rio the most expensive city in the country (FIPE ZAP, 2015). In the sections below, analysis focuses on those items more directly attributed to the 2016 event and where urban, social and environmental impacts have been most noticeable.

Master Plan and Olympic Venues

The Olympic master plan presents the organization of competitions in four cluster areas around the city (figure 20.2) which suggests a balanced distribution between the North, South, West and Barra regions. However, the concentration of competitions and the extent of urban interventions vary considerably among them.

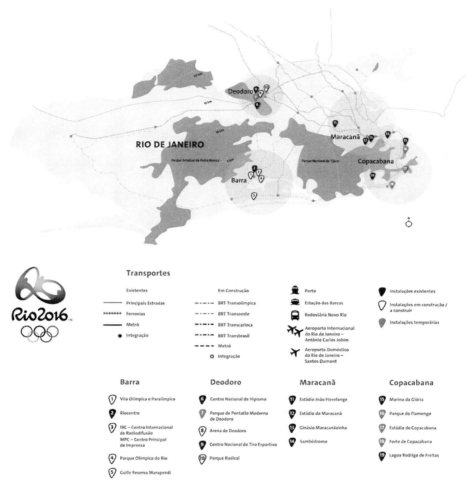

Figure 20.2. The Olympic clusters of the Rio 2016 Games. (*Source*: Rio de Janeiro City Council)

In the Copacabana zone, where the main tourist district is located, interventions will have a minimal impact. The outdoor competitions of rowing, beach volleyball and triathlon will use existing and temporary facilities having the city's famed beaches and mountains as a backdrop. Another zone encompasses the stadia of Maracanã, recently revamped for the 2014 FIFA World Cup, and the Olympic Stadium at Engenho de Dentro, built for the 2007 Pan-American Games. A novel feature in the history of the Olympics will be the organization of the Opening and Closing ceremonies at a different stadium than that to be used for the athletics track and field competitions. In reality, it is in the zones of Deodoro and Barra that substantial processes of urban change have been triggered.

Deodoro, in the city's West End, presents the case of an isolated site where interventions are essentially *ad hoc*. In fact, the Olympic facilities will be located within *Vila Militar*, a planned community of the Brazilian Army. Military facilities will be used for the shooting and equestrian competitions while training grounds will give way to the hockey and rugby arenas. These facilities are mostly existing and temporary and will not produce major changes in the area. In contrast, land belonging to the Brazilian Army will be transformed into the X-Park, where new parkland dedicated to the practice of extreme sports is planned. The site will make use of the BMX tracks and the canoe slalom facility built for the Games. It has been forecast to become the city's second largest park and will help to 'reinforce local youngsters' prospects for social and sporting development' (PCRJ, 2015, p. 44). New transport links will improve access to other parts of the city although it is yet to be known what impact will be caused by the new flyovers and expressways running through the neighbouring area of Magalhães Bastos (Davies, 2014).

On the other hand, the Barra zone will be the centrepiece of the Games where sixteen competitions will be held. As argued earlier, it is an area of strong real estate speculation and where post-event plans have been most clearly defined. The Olympic Park is being developed on the former site of a Formula 1 circuit on a peninsula on the Jacarepaguá lagoon. It will house nine sports arenas which will stage the competitions of gymnastics, swimming, cycling, tennis, basketball, handball, fencing, wrestling and taekwondo, in addition to housing the broadcasting and media centres. The avoidance of expensive and unused venues has been a constant presence in the public discourse and provisions have been accommodated to guarantee the post-event use of the arenas. The most interesting cases are those of the handball arena and the aquatics centre, both temporary facilities developed with consideration for their after use. The venues will be dismantled after the event and reassembled for use in public schools and as public swimming pools.

The Olympic Park is being developed via a public–private partnership where a consortium of developers is responsible for the delivery of part of the venues and related infrastructure. After the event 75 per cent of the land of the Olympic Park will be transferred to developers to give way to private housing, office towers, hotels and shopping malls. The remaining 25 per cent is where the permanent facilities will be located, to be transformed after the Games into an Olympic Training Centre run by the BOC for the use of elite athletes (figure 20.3). It is still unclear how the centre will be funded and managed and concerns are justified given the underuse and poor maintenance of the venues built for the 2007 Pan-American Games (Guerra, 2015).

The Olympic Village is being developed next to the Olympic Park, a task given to the private sector with an 'attractive financing package' provided by the state Federal Savings Bank (Rio 2016 Bid Committee, 2009a, p. 205). The project envisions the construction of thirty-one towers of seventeen storeys each totalling 3,604 units to accommodate 18,000 athletes and team members. After the Games the site will become a complex of gated communities, with *Ilha Pura* currently promoted as a new 'neighbourhood committed to good taste, luxury and sophistication' (Ilha Pura, 2015). Athletes will also make use of training grounds at the adjacent Athletes' Park and a private beach at a cordoned-off area on Reserva beach.

The confidence in the market to repeat the feat of the Pan-American Village as

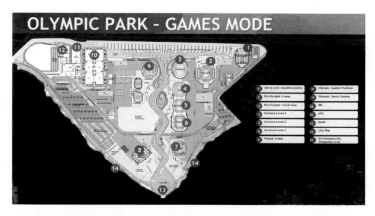

Figure 20.3. Master plans of the Olympic Park for the Games and for the post-event phase. (*Source*: Rio de Janeiro City Council)

expressed in the bid book has floundered so far. Whereas all the accommodation units of the 2007 event were sold within 10 hours of their release, demand has been slow for the initial sales of the Olympic Village, mirroring the slowdown in demand for real estate and of the Brazilian economy since 2014 (Anon, 2015*b*).

As a result of being the main Olympic cluster, Barra is the focus of much of the public policies and private investment. Revised planning restrictions have allowed the construction of taller Olympic-related housing and hotels. In the post-event scenario access to the region will be significantly improved with extended metro lines, duplicated highways and the new BRT corridors linking Barra to the city centre and the international airport.

Governance and Budget

The bidding campaign emphasized the alliance and full support of the three levels of government and the sizeable funding earmarked for the delivery of the Games. The election of Eduardo Paes as mayor in 2008 reproduced at the local scale the political alliance between his party, the PMDB, and PT found at the federal and state government levels. This was portrayed as an unprecedented alignment capable of overcoming the usual personal and party feuds and bureaucratic barriers. While indeed it seemed to facilitate the speeding up of projects such as the waterfront regeneration (discussed below), the definition of the governance structure for the delivery of the Games was contested and slow to be resolved.

Initially it was proposed to create a body along the lines of the Olympic Delivery Authority responsible for the London 2012 Games. The Olympic Public Authority (APO) would be a public consortium formed by the federal, state and municipal governments with centralized powers to deliver the infrastructure and services necessary for the organization of the event (the non-OCOG attributes). However, institutional conflict over responsibilities and legal obstacles to ensure complete powers weakened the remit of APO. While the approval of the institution at the federal level was delayed, the municipality decided to create its own delivery authority, the Municipal Olympic Company (EOM). In this dual institutional arrangement both bodies are nominally credited with delivering the Games. In practice, EOM operates as the main delivery body, especially after projects under the responsibility of the federal and the state governments were devolved to the municipality, such as the Olympic Park and the Deodoro sports complex. In the end Mayor Paes's efforts to be the poster child of the event prevailed, while APO has the role of reporting on the federal government activities and the consolidated budget.

Rio's candidature for the Games anticipated in 2008 that it would cost a total of $14.42 billion split between the OCOG's budget for staging the Games ($2.82 billion) and the non-OCOG budget for delivering the related infrastructure and services ($11.6 billion) (Rio 2016 Bid Committee, 2009b). This was the highest budget of all candidate cities but promotional material stressed Brazil's positioning during the global financial crisis as a 'small island in an ocean of negative economic results' (Ministério do Esporte, 2009, p. 100). Strong emphasis was put on the earmarked national infrastructural budget of $240 billion from which the Games would draw (Rio 2016 Bid Committee, 2009a, p. 35).

The total costs updated one year prior to the start of the event amounted to an increase of 34 per cent on the original budget, excluding service expenditures such as security, educational programmes and fan zones (APO, 2015a, 2015b). Mayor Paes explained that the total costs could in fact only be known after the staging of the event (Dolzan, 2015). It was decided to further split the non-OCOG budget in two categories. The Responsibility Matrix lists all the structural projects directly related to the Games under the remit of each government level. This includes the construction and reform of venues, temporary installations, infrastructure and equipment. The second category is the Public Policies Plan, also referred to as the Legacy Plan, which includes expenditure on mobility, urban regeneration and environmental programmes understood to have been fast tracked as a result of hosting of the event. This separate category is aimed at giving more evidence of projects to be considered as event legacies (table 20.1).

Table 20.1. Rio 2016 budget estimates (BRL million).

Expenditure	Estimates 2015	Source of Funding
OCOG budget	*7,400*	Self-financed
Responsibility Matrix	*6,608*	
Olympic Village	2,909.5	Private
Olympic Park (ppp)	1,678.0	PPP
Olympic Park (public)	730.1	Federal and municipal
Deodoro sports complex	832.4	Federal
Sambodromo	65.0	Private and Municipal
Golf course	60.0	PPP
Marina da Gloria	60.0	Private
Olympic stadium	52.3	Municipal
Athlete's park	40.3	Municipal
Power/Electricity Infrastructure	180.4	Federal
Legacy Plan	*24,106*	
Metro Line 4	8,791	State
Porto Maravilha	8,200	PPP
BRT	2,373	Municipal
Environmental programmes	1,628	State, municipal and private
Light railway	1,189	Federal and private
Roads	974	Municipal
Urban renewal	695	Federal and municipal
Guanabara Bay cleaning programme	114	State
Doping control laboratory	110	Federal
Social programmes	31	Federal
Total	*38,114*	

Note: The announced budget has yet to confirm expenditure on security and other services while some projects in the responsibility matrix and legacy plan – such as the reform of train stations, the Maracanazinho arena and the rowing stadium – are awaiting definition.
Source: APO, 2015*a*, 2015*b*.

Figure 20.4. Aerial view of the Olympic Park as of May 2015. Vila Autódromo can be seen in the bottom right. (*Source*: Renato Sette Camara/Rio de Janeiro City Council)

Promoters refute criticism of the Olympic budget by citing statistics for the participation of the private sector. Accordingly, some 60 per cent of the costs are covered by private funding (APO, 2015a, 2015b). These are largely represented by the construction of the Olympic Village, the new golf course and the public–private partnerships behind the construction of the Olympic Park and the regeneration programme of the port area. Despite being touted as enterprises 'where there is not a single cent from the public purse' (Brito, 2014), interest from developers was only possible with the alteration of planning restrictions and the transfer of land ownership. In all cases floor-area ratios were changed to allow taller buildings to be erected. At the Olympic Park where land ownership of the previous racetrack belonged to the municipality, 78 per cent will be transferred to the private partner to explore commercial activities including private housing, hotels and shopping malls. The compensation and relocation of the evicted families living next to the Park in Vila Autódromo and the construction of a new racetrack at a protected green field site in Deodoro are both actually existing costs resulting from the destruction of the Jacarepaguá racetrack. However, they are not included in the Olympic budget and stand as reminders of the need for close scrutiny and inclusion of the social and environmental costs.

Security and Safety

IOC evaluations of Rio's Olympic candidatures all noted security and safety as being problematic and the city consistently achieved low scores in relation to other bidding cities (IOC, 1997b, 2004b, 2008b). Responses have invariably made reference to the absence of terrorist activities in the country and to the fact that the hosting of the UN Earth Summit in 1992 occurred with no incidents (Rio 2016 Bid Committee, 2009a) – when a tight security operation was carried out epitomized by the presence of tanks on the streets of Rio. More recently, an extensive security programme has been introduced, which despite not being designed in response to the hosting of mega-events has become closely implicated with it.

Starting in December 2008 the Pacifying Police Unit (UPP) programme has sought to take back territorial control of *favelas* from organized criminal groups by the installation of police stations and implementing community policing and providing public infrastructure (Freeman, 2014). Prior announcement of an intervention seeks to influence drug gangs to leave the area thus avoiding armed conflicts with the arrival of the elite police forces. By the summer of 2015 some forty *favelas* had been targeted and a significant reduction of violent crimes occurred in the first 4 years of the programme (Cano *et al.*, 2012).

However, as Cano *et al.* (*Ibid*) have noted, the selection of *favelas* was not supported by indicators such as crime statistics. Rather, it was highly suggestive of forming a 'security belt' around the Maracanã stadium and near other Olympic and tourist sites, thus 'ignoring the most violent areas of the metropolitan region, which are the Baixada Fluminense and the North End of Rio (*Ibid*, p. 194). Police have also confirmed in interviews that the hosting of the World Cup and the Olympics were determinants in guiding decisions over the expansion of UPP operations (Vigna, 2013; Negreiros, 2014). Recent escalating violence and police abuse at some of the 'pacified *favelas*' have made residents doubtful of the longevity of the programme after the Games (Puff, 2013, 2014).

Responsibility for security during the Olympics will be shared between the Organizing Committee, the federal Extraordinary Secretariat of *Security* for Major Events, and the Ministry of Defence. While the former two will coordinate operations at the venues and in the city supplemented by private security personnel (Werneck and Maltchik, 2015), the latter is responsible for equipping the territory against potential threats. The defence strategy includes the hiring of fighter aircraft from the Swedish government and missile systems from Russia (Batista, 2015; Anon, 2015*a*).

Mobility

Rio's growth has always been dictated by overcoming its challenging landscape and the expansion of the transport network played a vital part in pushing the city limits. As noted earlier, just as electric tramways opened the seafront of the South End for the *carioca* elite, working-class neighbourhoods were established along the railways cutting through the North End and the Baixada Fluminense region. In the 1970s the marshlands of Barra da Tijuca represented a new frontier after the gradual development of Copacabana, Ipanema, Leblon and São Conrado. Consistent with the planning rationale developed for Brasilia, planner Lucio Costa devised the organization of new neighbourhoods along expressways resulting in the primacy of the individual motor vehicle.

Between 1991 and 2010 the population residing in the Barra region grew from 526,302 to 909,955 (IPP, 2011). Encircled by mountain chains, access to the rest of the city was possible via the coastline and through the valley north of Jacarepaguá, but by the 1990s traffic flow was already saturated. Having Barra as the main stage of the Games suggested that improved access to the area and transportation was another theme in which the city trailed behind other bids. The 2016 bid promised the creation of a 'High Performance Transport Ring' and introduced the concept of the BRT system as a feasible way to connect the four Olympic clusters and deliver a new transport network in time for the event (Rio 2016 OCOG, 2009).

Barra acts as the nodal point of the three segregated bus corridors tied to the Olympic deadline. Totalling 117 kilometres, they consist of the Transoeste corridor linking Barra to the West End and a new metro terminal; the Transcarioca line, which cuts through the North End towards the international airport; and the Transolimpica, linking the Olympic Park with Deodoro.

Proponents of the BRT system (figure 20.5), such as former Bogotá mayor Enrique Peñalosa who became a global advocate of the policy, argued that it represents the only viable transport solution in terms of scale and cost for large

Figure 20.5. The new BRT system of segregated bus lanes was devised to connect the Olympic clusters and the international airport and stand as the transport legacy of the 2016 Games. (*Source*: Renato Sette Camara/Rio de Janeiro City Council)

cities in the Global South (Peñalosa, 2013). It is presented as a compromise between the lower costs of surface systems and the operation and comfort of underground. Critics on the other hand, point to the marginalization of metro and rail expansion and that the system presents only temporary results as it can saturate quickly. The experience of the Transoeste and Transcarioca corridors already in operation seem to corroborate the latter argument. Press coverage of the systems inaugurated in 2012 and 2014 respectively document overcrowding and safety worries as routine occurrences (Victor and Ribeiro, 2015; França, 2015).

The Olympic Transport Ring also envisioned expanded metro lines and upgraded rail services. The construction of the metro line 4 is the most expensive project associated with the Games consuming 23 per cent of the total budget at a 2015 updated cost of BRL 8.8 billion (APO, 2015a). It will extend the service running along the South End coastline for 10 miles (16 km) with six new stations reaching Barra da Tijuca at its eastern point – a substitute for the previously planned BRT corridor (Rio 2016 OCOG, 2009). Finally, it was also emphasized that the rail system would be completely renovated in order to deliver a 'world-class' service to the densely populated areas in the North and West regions (Rio 2016 Olympic Bidding Committee, 2009). After reaching a peak of one million daily passengers at the beginning of the 1980s, the service currently carries around 620,000 passengers every day with frequent problems of disrupted services and overcrowding (Supervia, 2015; Souza, 2014). Olympic-related investments promised to 'drastically focus on changing both the image and the effectiveness of the railway, upgrading stations, fully modernizing the rolling stock, upgrading infrastructure and systems, and improving maintenance works' (Rio 2016 OCOG, 2009, p. 26).

However, only the refurbishment of six rail stations serving Olympic venues were included in the 'Legacy Plan' with the remainder of the upgrading works the responsibility of the private operator. A recent change in the terms of the contract transferred the refurbishment of the stations to the private operator and was followed by a reduction in the number of carriages to be purchased (Nogueira, 2015). The revised agreement shows the marginalization of improvements in the areas of highest demand for public transport. The new BRT corridors and the expanded metro network will significantly improve transport connections in the region of Barra, but substantially improved services for the commuters based in the North and Baixada Fluminense areas – the latter responsible for a flow of two million passengers daily to Rio (Observatório Sebrae, 2013) – will have to wait for the time being.

Environment

The greatest gamble of Rio's Olympic-dependent programme of interventions was the cleaning up of the waters of Guanabara Bay in order to offer optimal conditions for the sailing competitions. Water pollution has grown exponentially since the 1960s due to industrial activity and the discharge of raw sewage from the sixteen municipalities of the Rio de Janeiro Metropolitan Region on the shores of the bay. The Olympic bid set out the objective to treat 80 per cent of the sewage by 2016 but recent figures suggest a more modest outcome.

A state-led sanitation plan has been in place since 1995 but it has been marred by the lack of coordination among stakeholders and funding discontinuities, and by 2007 it achieved the treatment of only 12 per cent of the sewage (Werneck, 2012; Rio 2016 OCOG, 2014; Neves, 2015). Thus the hosting of the Games presented the opportunity to leverage funding and efforts to accelerate the sanitation policy and improve environmental conditions for the population of 8.5 million. Despite showing progress leading to the treatment of 50 per cent of sewage in 2013 (Rio 2016 OCOG, 2014), the selection of public policies for the 'Legacy Plan' included a modest set of programmes totalling BRL124.67 million – 0.3 per cent of the total budget (Konchinski, 2014b). They related to sewerage works in the central Rio area, river barriers and collecting barges. The latter two are mitigation efforts to avoid floating garbage near the competition areas while post-event targets remain uncertain.

Revised targets also compromised the reforestation pledge to compensate for carbon emission resulting from works for the Games. After expanding the original plan of planting 24 million trees by a further 10 million, a readjusted figure of a mere 8.1 million was announced (Konchinski, 2015). The figure contrasts with the deforestation of 104 square miles (270 square kilometres) of Atlantic rainforest for the construction of the Transolímpica corridor and the duplication of the Joá elevated express way (Konchinski, 2014a).

Finally, the construction of the Olympic golf course has also been responsible for the loss of natural environment. The sport, alongside rugby, was included in the Games by the IOC after candidate cities had concluded their final proposals. The Rio de Janeiro Olympic golf course will be located on the shores of the Marapendi Lagoon in Barra in an area previously protected as a natural site. Alleging financial and logistical reasons for not using the two existing private golf clubs, the municipality partnered with the private developer owning land north of the preservation area to build a course from scratch (PCRJ, 2015). According to the terms of the PPP the developer is responsible for the construction and maintenance costs of the venue. In return the municipality revised planning restrictions to allow taller luxury buildings to be constructed on the private land. After the event the venue will be operated as a public golf course for a period of 20 years before returning to the private owner (*Ibid.*).

Urban Regeneration

The largest regeneration project linked with the Olympics is located 18 miles (30 kilometres) away from the Olympic Park at the port area next to the city centre. The *Porto Maravilha* programme aims to regenerate five million square metres of docklands, rail yards and warehouses into a new mixed-use neighbourhood. Signature buildings by some of the stars of the architecture world such as Santiago Calatrava and Norman Foster are profoundly changing the waterfront landscape with office towers, residential condominiums, museums, an aquarium and a renewed public space. Despite not featuring any prominent Olympic facility, the programme is being heralded as the main legacy of the Games.

The inadequacies of the port to adapt to the new container technology since the 1960s and the construction of the new Port of Itaguaí in 1982 led to the decline of activities and to the dereliction of buildings. Plans for urban renewal have come in succession but were overturned by conflicting public interests, institutional resistance on the part of the port authority, and insufficient demand from private investors. The announcement of the programme in a press conference with Rio's mayor, the governor and the Brazilian president came shortly before the award of the Games in Copenhagen. It signalled that joint intergovernmental efforts would finally make the policy happen.

Whereas previous plans failed to progress from the study phase or produced only minor interventions, the announcement of *Porto Maravilha* took place in very favourable circumstances.[3] First, political alignments facilitated negotiations and in this case the release of land belonging to the three levels of government. Secondly, the strong growth of the Brazilian economy in the latter half of the 2000s, and of Rio in particular, created a strong demand for office space. The growth of the oil and gas industry with the discovery of new deep-sea basins was an important factor pushing corporate demand for new office space in Rio. Thirdly, new planning instruments introduced in 2001 enabled the implementation of self-financed regeneration schemes. The Urban Operations Instrument foresees public capture of planning gain by selling additional building rights to erect taller buildings to developers and the money re-invested in the regeneration of the area. Fourthly, there was the interest and lobbying of four of the largest Brazilian construction companies which produced the feasibility plan for the regeneration programme and won the bid for engineering works and provision of services. Finally, there was the momentum given by the hosting of the incoming mega-events, which further enhanced Rio's visibility and pushed for the fast-track approval of by-laws and planning permissions.

Despite presenting plans to be developed independently of the Olympic project, the association with the Games is strategic in a number of ways. In aligning the project with the Olympic deadline, it reassures investors about the completion of infrastructural works. Since the launch it has resulted in the demolition of an elevated expressway and its substitution by an underground tunnel, the upgrading of electricity, sanitation and telecommunications structures, new roads and renewed pavements and urban furniture. It also enabled the municipality to leverage federal funding to implement a new light railway system. Finally, the scale of the project, the confidence in the market demands and the private financial resources of the PPP supported the discourse of profound urban change. Its inclusion in the Legacy Plan considerably boosts the legacy itself and the share of private funding.

This programme has the potential to contribute positively to the regeneration of a central and historic area, opening up new public spaces and cultural facilities while attracting new businesses. However, there is the danger of it becoming a corporate ghetto and encouraging the gentrification of nearby neighbourhoods, some of the few low-income areas close enough to the *Centro* job market. So far most of the proposed developments consist of office towers and corporate hotels. The valorisation of land is a consequence of regeneration schemes, and more so in property-led projects such as *Porto Maravilha*. Social impacts can be mitigated by public policies and there is an attempt to moderate such outcomes in the City Statute by requesting local government to address the economic and social needs of residents directly impacted by Urban Operations. In this sense there was an expectation of new social housing to be included in the programme, especially because all the building rights were bought by the Federal Savings Bank, a state institution that is also responsible for financing social housing in the country. However, only a limited number of restored houses have been converted into social housing. Residential development for the middle class has also been slow to materialize, raising doubts about the ability to avoid empty streets in the Rio's central business district in the evenings and weekends.

Social Impacts

The history of urban change in Rio has invariably imposed substantial costs on the city's poor. As seen earlier during the Pereira Passos reforms, tenement houses were targeted by the urban interventions leading to the displacement of residents to nearby hills and substandard housing along the railway. Another period of intense displacement took place in the 1960s during Carlos Lacerda's term of office. His pledge for re-ordering the urban space also resulted in the wholesale removal of *favelas* in the South End with families relocated to social housing projects such as *Cidade de Deus* in the then distant region of Barra (Silva, 2004). During the military dictatorship, the Negrão de Lima slum clearance programme affected more than 70,500 people (Valladares quoted in Brum, 2012). This troublesome historical legacy is once again repeated with the hosting of the 2016 Games contributing to the displacement of residents of *favelas* and low-income neighbourhoods.

Social impacts associated with the hosting of major events are extensive and well documented (Brent Ritchie and Hall, 1999; Lenskyj, 2002; 2008; Silvestre, 2008; Hayes and Horne, 2011; Minnaert, 2012) with the displacement of residents representing the most dramatic impact (Olds, 1998; COHRE, 2007a; Porter *et al.*, 2009; Rolnik, 2009). The preparations for Rio de Janeiro 2016 have accumulated a problematic track record in this respect as parts of, or entire, *favelas* are removed to give way to the works associated with the event (figure 20.6). Faulhaber and Azevedo (2015) examined all the removal and expropriation decrees during the Paes government between 2009 and 2012, reaching a figure of 20,229 affected households and an estimate of more than 65,000 people. The reasons for displacement included works for the Olympic Park; the BRT corridors; works carried out by the secretariat of housing and other secretariats; and those considered at risk. The figure places Eduardo Paes's regime among the worst offenders in terms of evictions, second only to the aforementioned Negrão de Lima.

The case of removal is even more dramatic when the experience of those affected is exposed. Silvestre and Oliveira (2012) documented the initial cases of displacement caused by works for Transoeste along Americas Avenue in Barra region, which became standard practice for other removals. After an area is declared for 'public utility' and a list of properties is published, city officials promptly visit a *favela* to inform residents of their eviction and to earmark houses for demolition. Residents are given the option either to accept financial compensation, which only takes the built structure into account, or to be relocated to the housing projects of *Minha Casa MInha* mostly situated in the city's western edge (figure 20.7), otherwise they risk being left empty-handed. Compensation is often insufficient to acquire a similar dwelling, even in local favelas, and the move to distant social housing brings financial and social hardship due to added commuting costs and the abrupt rupture of the social fabric. Those who accept the municipality's offers have their houses immediately cleared leaving the remaining residents to live among rubble and litter. Delay to compensate or relocate has left families vulnerable, having to live with family and friends or be rendered homeless (*Ibid.*).

Official discourse claims that the removal of the *favela* of Vila Autódromo is the only case directly linked with the Games (Anon, 2012; Rio 2016 OCOG, 2014). It is argued that infrastructure-induced displacement, such as the BRT corridors, are the result of policies that would be carried out regardless of hosting the event

Figure 20.6. The favela of Vila do Recreio II was cleared to give way to a BRT corridor. The houses in the background belong to the few residents still resisting eviction in May 2011. (*Source*: Nelma Gusmão de Oliveira)

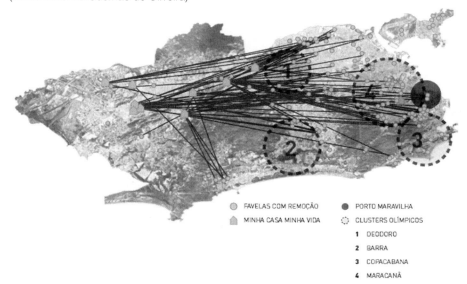

FAVELAS COM REMOÇÃO   PORTO MARAVILHA

MINHA CASA MINHA VIDA   CLUSTERS OLÍMPICOS

1 DEODORO

2 BARRA

3 COPACABANA

4 MARACANÃ

Figure 20.7. The map presents the location of favelas expropriated between 2009 and 2013 (in circles) and the destination of those accepting relocation to the Minha Casa Minha Vida social housing programme, largely concentrated in the West End. (*Source*: Lucas Faulhaber)

(Rio 2016 OCOG, 2014). Vila Autódromo is located on the edge of the former Jacarepaguá circuit initially settled by fishermen in the 1960s and expanded with the arrival of the workforce employed for the construction of the same circuit and the nearby Riocentro convention centre in the following decade. Since the early 1990s the *favela* has been subject to continuous threats of removal despite those living there having their right to stay recognized in the 1990s by the state of Rio (the landowner of the circuit). Ownership was transferred to the municipality in 1998 and since then the threats intensified first with the hosting of the Pan-

American Games and finally with the Olympic award. Their singular case among other *favelas* prompted the assistance of local architecture and planning schools to help the resident's association develop a bottom-up alternative proposal (AMPVA, 2012).

In demonstrating that the upgrading of the *favela* did not compromise the works for the Olympic Park and that it would cost less than the compensation and relocation to another site, the plan won the Deutsche Bank Urban Age Award in 2013 (Tanaka, 2014). However, the municipality was adamant that clearing the site was necessary and was now included in the PPP contract for the development of the Olympic Park. Different reasons ranging from exposure to natural hazards (Bastos and Schmidt, 2010); environmental damage (Magalhães, 2011); event security (AMPVA, 2012, p. 9); the construction of the MPC (Anon, 2012); the BRT corridor (Tanaka, 2014); and the duplication of access roads (Mendonça and Puff, 2015), were alleged at different times without fully disclosing details and plans despite public requests. In contrast to the options given in other cases, relocation was to a housing project 1.5 kilometres away. The 6-year intimidation process and psychological stress common in other *favelas* described above led most residents to accept negotiation, leaving a small group to challenge the municipality's plan. However, violent clashes with the police in June 2015 gained worldwide attention as the remaining residents fought for their right to stay (Watts, 2015).

Conclusion

This chapter has offered a critical analysis of the preparations for Rio de Janeiro 2016. The spatial implications of the event were contextualized against a historical background of urban interventions and its rationale was traced through the consecutive Olympic bids produced since the 1990s. This concluding section revisits the opening vignette in an attempt to answer the questions posed.

In taking the experience of Barcelona 1992 as a reference point, it was expected that the hosting of the Olympic Games could offer a step change for the city, especially in terms of its urban infrastructure. However, the analysis of Rio's bids for the Games demonstrates the lack of coordination between the Olympic project and city planning policies in order to, as in the case of its Mediterranean counterpart, fast-track urgent projects for the city. Resulting from the enthusiasm of the first strategic plan, the 2004 bid was prepared by foreign experts with *carte blanche* to propose a plan that could promote effects similar to those seen in the Catalan capital. For all its unrealistic ambitions, the project was true to its intention to distribute benefits more widely. In centring the event in the Fundão Island it was expected that the preparation timeframe would have boosted the programmes for cleaning the waters of Guanabara Bay and the upgrading adjacent slums while leaving a legacy of a recovered waterfront and new and renewed facilities for a public university. The reading of the causes of failure in this first attempt served to steer the Olympic project in another direction, by choosing Barra da Tijuca as the centrepiece of future bids and to move away from the premise of hosting mega-events to promote urban change. The Olympic project became a pragmatic plan centralized in the mayor's and BOC decisions to build the credibility of Rio's candidature and win the hosting rights of the Games. The construction of sport venues in a peninsula isolated from its surroundings for the 2007 Pan-American Games produced negligible improvements to the city.

Once Barra was firmly established in the master plan of the Olympic project it served to legitimize public policies to an already developed and privileged part of the city despite conflicting with the general guidance of the city's statutory master plan. Improvements to road access, environmental programmes and the extension of the metro network came under the Olympic banner while other programmes with the potential of promoting wider territorial benefits, such as the upgrading of the rail service and of the treatment of raw sewage discharged in Guanabara Bay were deemed low priorities and their targets postponed. The new BRT network, though centred on Barra, takes advantage of previous studies and can potentially improve the transport system in the West and North End. However, the initial experience has confirmed criticism of rapid saturation and overcrowding.

Contrasting the current preparations to other rounds of great urban change, the revanchist nature of some policies reinforces the history of great social burden. For most of the thousands of households evicted since 2009 stability and material improvement meant being displaced to the city's edge far from the job markets and in areas lacking developed infrastructure. It can be argued that it is unrealistic to expect that the hosting of a mega-event can serve to resolve deeply embedded social and urban injustices. But equally it can serve to exacerbate those injustices, and in the projects carried out under its name downplay social and environmental costs.

Notes

1.   The efforts of Eduardo Paes to measure himself against Pereira Passos are not only rhetoric. Allegedly he intended to inaugurate the first phase of works for the regeneration of the port area dressed up in historical clothes alluding to Passos. Dissuaded by his staff, an actor posed at his side on the balcony of the Jardins do Valongo instead (Tabak, 2012).

2.   As is common practice in this kind of consultancy exercise, stated goals are aspirational and vague, making obligatory references to city image, competition for investments and quality of life. The objective set for Rio was to 'Make Rio de Janeiro a metropolis with a better quality of life, socially integrated, respecting citizenship and confirming its vocation for culture and joie-de-vivre. An enterprising competitive metropolis, with capacity to be a centre of knowledge and business generation for Brazil, and its privileged connection with other countries' (PCRJ, 1996, p. 23).

3.   The following observations are based on current research undertaken by the author on the making and delivery of the Porto Maravilha regeneration project.

Chapter 21

Tokyo 2020

Yasushi Aoyama

On 7 September 2013 the International Olympic Committee voted at a general meeting in Buenos Aires to hold the 2020 Summer Olympics in Tokyo, Japan. The main reason for Tokyo's selection was its ability to provide an optimal setting in which Olympic athletes can gather and compete. Tokyo towered over the other candidates in evaluations with respect to safety, efficiency, and operational reliability. Tokyo's effective presentation to the IOC general meeting was an added point in its favour. Paralympic long jumper Masumi Sato left a particularly deep impression with her account of the vital role athletics had played in helping her overcome disability and disaster – 'saved by sport' was how she put it.

Tokyo needed a potent theme, and the theme of disaster recovery would not have convinced the IOC on its own – after all, people all over the world are suffering from the ravages of war, terrorism, civil strife, poverty, and natural disasters. Masumi Sato's speech showed what a meaningful role sport, and the Olympics in particular, can play in society and human life. Finally, Prime Minister Shinzo Abe helped seal the deal by dispelling concerns over leakage of radioactive water from the disabled nuclear power plant in Fukushima.

Once Tokyo had prevailed, the question was: what should it do to prepare for 2020? To begin with, the goal should not be the passive one of hosting the Games without mishap. We need to approach the 2020 Olympics as an opportunity to refashion Tokyo into a twenty-first century city, and Japanese society into a twenty-first century society. Preparations for the 1964 Games transformed Tokyo into a city of continuously grade-separated highways, beginning with the Shuto (Tokyo Metropolitan) Expressway Inner Circular Route and Ring Road 7, and Tokyo was linked to Osaka via the high-speed Shinkansen 'bullet train'. These projects created an urban structure of unparalleled efficiency that was to contribute immeasurably to Japan's rapid economic growth in the ensuing years. Furthermore, neither continuous grade separation nor the Shinkansen were ideas borrowed from the West; they were Japanese innovations, born of determination to spearhead modern engineering for the new era. As a result, Tokyo 1964 is credited with contributing more to urban progress than almost any other Olympic Games.

Turning Tokyo into a Cultural Mecca

In like fashion, the 2020 Olympics should be approached as an opportunity to present the world with a new urban model for the twenty-first century. The focus this time should be on sport, culture, urban parks, and waterside amenities; all vital components of a twenty-first century city serving a mature society. Without overlooking the need to build more high-quality office and apartment buildings over the next 7 years, we should place even higher priority on the goal of showcasing Tokyo as a model of urban comfort and liveability by expanding the city's athletic and cultural facilities, fostering an urban lifestyle that values those resources, and creating urban spaces rich in greenery and water.

Twentieth-century urban design pursued efficiency above all else. In the twenty-first century, the key goals are liveability and quality of life. Just as Tokyo took advantage of the 1964 Olympics to transform itself into a model of urban efficiency, it should approach the 2020 Olympics as an opportunity to turn itself into an exemplar of urban comfort and liveability. Tokyo has already set to work on a variety of infrastructure projects in preparation for the 2020 Olympics. Indeed, it faces a plethora of challenges on this front, including road and rail improvements, opening services on the new maglev (magnetic levitation) Shinkansen line, and all the issues surrounding Haneda Airport – not to mention the nuts and bolts of building and operating new athletic facilities to host the Olympic competition. While this process is unlikely to proceed without controversy or disagreement, we know that Japanese society has the capacity to meet these challenges satisfactorily.

In this chapter, I would like to give some thought to the larger purpose of such improvements – what vision they are serving and how we expect them to transform Tokyo and Japanese society as a whole. In the run-up to the 1964 Olympics, the aims were clear: to host the Games in a manner that showcased Japanese technology and the fruits of industrialization, and laid the foundation for further economic growth, reflecting the nation's determination to catch up with and overtake the industrial West. The situation is very different going into the 2020 Olympics. We have left behind the industrial age and have entered the advanced information age as a mature society. Tokyo must demonstrate that it has transformed itself accordingly. On the economic and demographic level, a mature society is characterized by an aging demographic structure and a low rate of economic growth. In terms of lifestyle and outlook, a truly mature society is one that welcomes people, customs, and beliefs of all kinds and spares no effort to improve the quality of life. This translates into an urban culture in which people can enjoy sports, the arts, and entertainment to the fullest.

When it comes to efficiency and safety, Tokyo ranks very high among the accepted global cities. If we compare Tokyo, New York, and London, for example, Tokyo is unquestionably the safest, cleanest, and most orderly of the three. Its subways and trains are the most convenient. Even traffic congestion is less severe than in New York or London. Nonetheless, Tokyo lacks those qualities that draw millions of people to New York and London from all over the world. New York and London offer countless and endlessly varied cultural and entertainment opportunities, from sports to fashion, from art and music to industry events. Most of these programmes and resources are commercially sustainable because so many residents take advantage of them. In the years ahead, Tokyo's value and appeal as a city will hinge more and more on such cultural facilities as sports arenas, museums, and event halls. This is why Tokyo cannot afford to limit its pre-Olympic development plans to sleek office buildings and high-rise apartments.

The Olympics are first and foremost a celebration of athletic competition, but in recent years, the opening and closing ceremonies have turned them into an important cultural, artistic, and fashion statement as well. It is not unrealistic to hope that the 2020 Olympics will spur the development of a new culture of *joie de vivre* among the Japanese people. If, in the future, Tokyo can look back on the 2020 Olympics as the turning point in the city's evolution into a mecca for culture-loving, event-loving tourists, that alone will assure its importance in Olympic history.

The Venue Master Plan for Tokyo 2020 is shown in figure 21.1. The Olympic Village (figure 21.2) would be built on the site of the old Harumi International Convention Centre. In this Village about 6,000 apartments will be built for the athletes and after the games they will be repurposed as housing. This area will be a model community leading up to the 'hydrogen society' of the future (see Nagata, 2014). Harumi island is a pleasant and clean environment surrounded

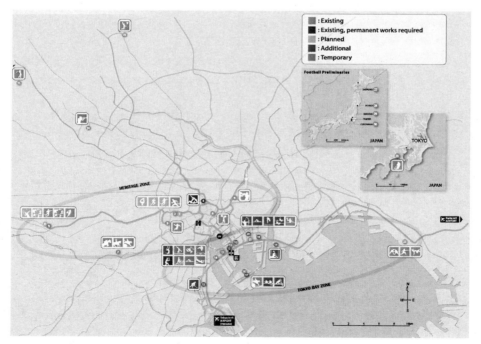

Figure 21.1. Venue Master Plan, Tokyo 2020 Summer Olympics and Paralympic Games as of September 2015.

Figure 21.2. The Olympic Village Site, Old Harumi International Convention Centre, May 2010.

Figure 21.3. The redevelopment of the former Gaien District as depicted in a 1:1000 scale model by Mori Building Company (June 2015). The features from left to right are the National Stadium (demolished in 2015), the Second Baseball Stadium, the Jingu Baseball Stadium, and the Rugby stadium.

on all sides by Tokyo Bay. At first Tokyo planned that most competition venues must be within 5 miles (8 kilometres) of the Olympic and Paralympic Village.[1] In June 2015, however, the IOC announced that several indoor tournaments will take place at the Makuhari Messe conference centre in Chiba Prefecture, the badminton venue at Chofu in western Tokyo, and sailing events at Enoshima Yacht Harbour in Kanagawa Prefecture. The switch is being made to reduce costs, but does not essentially change the compact Games concept because it is only a small change of the competition venues. It will increase collaboration between Tokyo and the surrounding area. Finally, in addition to the project to rebuild the

National Stadium as the new Olympic Stadium (see also Chapter 1), the Tokyo metropolitan government unveiled a plan of the redeveloped Gaien district. It includes plans to rebuild the baseball and rugby stadiums. It will provide access routes to each facility from nearby subway stations.

The Paralympics and Social Inclusion

Another challenge for Tokyo as it prepares for the 2020 Olympics is how to transform itself into a socially more inclusive city. In recent years, the Paralympics have emerged as a focal point of the Olympic hosting experience. A key issue in this context is the degree to which a city makes itself barrier-free by meeting standards for universal access. Tokyo has worked actively to stay abreast of this global trend, installing barrier-free sidewalk ramps, elevators at subway stations, and, more recently, signage for the visually impaired. In fact, one gets the impression that Tokyo is ahead of most of the world's major cities in this regard, but it still has much left to do. We should strive to make Tokyo an even more liveable city for the disabled – a city that is accessible to all, not only by virtue of its barrier-free construction but also because of the welcoming and helpful attitude of its citizens.

Access is not just a physical issue. One of our key goals should be to make Tokyo friendly and accessible to people of all ethnicities, faiths, and lifestyles as they gather for the Olympic Games, to ensure that athletes and spectators can travel smoothly and comfortably even beyond the confines of the Olympic Village. To take just one example, Tokyo at present has very few restaurants that observe Islamic dietary laws. Many of my graduate students are international and a substantial number of them are Muslims. Unfortunately, I have to advise these students to bring their own meals when they go into the city for fieldwork, since there are so few halal restaurants. Of course, many inns and shops will accommodate the needs of Muslims if someone explains these in advance, but even so, day-to-day life can be very complicated for Muslim visitors and residents. This state of affairs reflects the insularity of a society that remains largely unwilling to accept immigrants and refugees.

Those who arrive in Japan for the Olympics are sure to find a warmer welcome, even from people who look askance at immigrants and refugees. It will be a brief period of interaction (less than a month), but still an important opportunity for the Japanese to broaden their perspective and learn from people whose customs and values differ from their own. May the Olympics hasten Japan's evolution into a truly inclusive society, where people of all ethnicities, religions, cultures, and customs can feel at home.

London 2012 offered important lessons in inclusiveness. On that occasion the city's redevelopment projects focused on the East End, known for its concentrations of ethnic communities and low-income households. These redevelopment efforts were designed to make a permanent difference to the lives of the residents by improving education, employment, and housing. This shows more social inclusiveness. For Pierre de Coubertin, father of the modern Olympic Games, the goal of the Olympic movement was to contribute to world peace and harmony through sport 'practiced without discrimination of any kind' (IOC, 2004b, p. 9). In this regard, I am hopeful that the experience of hosting the 2020 Olympics will prove an important learning experience for Japanese society as a whole.

The True Legacy of the 1964 Olympics

Urban Tokyo was reduced to ashes again by the fire-bombings of 1945. In 1947, two years after the war's end, the Tokyo metropolitan government adopted a war reconstruction plan focused on road construction, but the plan failed to win the approval of the GHQ, the administrative headquarters of the US Occupation, and it was shelved. The road network envisioned would have included the 40-metre-wide Ring Road No. 7. This would have provided an important foundation for economic growth had it been implemented, but GHQ ordered that priority be placed on the construction of National Route 16, linking various US military bases to the south and west of Tokyo, such as Iruma, Yokota, and Atsugi.

The decisive turning point came when Tokyo was selected to host the 1964 Olympics. At that point construction began in earnest, not only on the long-delayed Ring Road No. 7 but also on the innovative Shuto Expressway, which circled Tokyo's central wards. The Shuto Expressway featured total grade separation by means of an overpass or tunnel at every crossing, a feature unusual among the world's urban roadways. Ring Road No. 7 and the Shuto Expressway were to play a key role supporting Japan's economic growth in the succeeding years, and the 1964 Tokyo Olympics were notable for their contribution to urban development.

Initial plans for the 1964 Tokyo Olympics called for construction of the Olympic Village in Asaka in Saitama Prefecture. Operating on this premise, the Tokyo metropolitan government planned two major highways connecting Tokyo and Saitama: the Shuto Expressway Route 5, a long highway running northwest between the city centre and Saitaima, and Ring Road No. 7, a circumferential highway that would link Saitama and Komazawa Olympic Park. When the United States unexpectedly announced that it was giving up its military housing complex in Washington Heights, the site of the Olympic Village shifted to Yoyogi. At that point, some people in the Japanese government began arguing that construction of Shuto Expressway Route 5 and Ring Road No. 7 could wait. The Tokyo metropolitan government prevailed, however, arguing that both highways were indispensable to Tokyo, Olympics or no Olympics. Later on, the existence of Route 5 figured in the decision to build Saitama New Urban Centre, a modern business district in downtown Saitama city. The impetus for Ring Road No. 7 actually goes back much further. This road was originally part of a plan drawn up in 1927 to cope with Tokyo's rapid outward expansion following the Great Kanto Earthquake of 1923. However, the Second World War and the US occupation intervened, with the road failing to materialize until the Olympics provided a fresh

Figure 21.4. Grade-separated crossing at Akasaka Mitsuke, the heart of Tokyo.

impetus. As the ring road crossed the various radial arteries running between the city centre and the periphery, such as the Koshu Kaido and Ome Kaido, it was built on a succession of overpasses to create grade-separated crossings (figure 21.4). The Tokyo Metropolitan Expressway is essentially a continuously grade-separated road network.

To elaborate, for a major world city, Tokyo has a low road-area ratio and its streets are relatively narrow. Yet traffic congestion is less severe than in New York or London. For this we can thank the unique grade-separated urban highway network established in preparation for the 1964 Olympics. Ever since the Meiji Restoration of 1868, urban development in Japan had followed the lead of other nations as the nation strove to catch up with the industrial West. Tokyo's continuously grade-separated road system, however, was a uniquely Japanese concept with no Western equivalent. One senses an unshakable resolve on the part of the city administrators of that time, not merely to celebrate the coming of the Olympics but to make the most of the opportunity and build what Tokyo needed to function effectively going forward, solving issues that had concerned the city's planners for years.

If asked to identify the legacy of the 1964 Olympics, some might point to the athletic facilities built at that time, many of which remain in use today. Certainly these contributed to Tokyo's development. But the most important legacy of the 1964 Games was Tokyo's unique highway system, with its continuous grade separation, and the Shinkansen high-speed train network. The Shuto Expressway Central Circular Route was completed in March 2015 (figure 21.5). It will do

Figure 21.5. The Shuto Expressway Central Circular Route during construction (photograph taken in November 2014; the road was completed in March 2015).

much to relieve traffic congestion in central Tokyo. Now the drive from Shinjyuku to Haneda Airport takes only about 20 minutes. It will also seal the legacy of former Governor Shintaro Ishihara as the man who kept the funds flowing for this highway over a period of 13 years. It is only thanks to Ishihara's great popularity and overwhelming mandate that he managed to secure budget allocations for a costly undertaking that probably never earned anyone a single vote.

With regard to the railways, the opening of the high-speed train service on the new Tokaido Shinkansen just 10 days before the start of the Olympics was a theatrical triumph. Yet perhaps even more impressive was the way Japan continued to expand the Shinkansen network and upgrade its trains at a time when railway progress had ground to a halt in many advanced industrial countries. Here, too, Japan led the way with its own advanced technology. The urban transportation system was enhanced by improvements in the commuter rail system. One important development was the advent of an interline through service between the Tokyo subway system and the national and private commuter rail lines linking Tokyo with the suburbs. This allowed a passenger to embark at a station near his or her suburban home and ride straight into the heart of the city without transferring.

As Japan's rapid economic growth continued, Tokyo's monopoly on central political and economic command functions emerged as an issue of national concern. There was much talk of transferring certain functions of the capital outside of Tokyo, and a few government agencies were actually relocated. The momentum for dispersal has dwindled considerably, however, as Japanese society has matured and the focus began to shift from purely economic indicators of prosperity to quality-of-life issues. Increasingly, people have come to see that living standards cannot be measured purely in monetary terms and that proximity to the centre of political and economic power is by no means an unmixed blessing in terms of quality of life. According to the most recent statistics[2] available as of April 2012, the Greater Tokyo Area, encompassing Tokyo Metropolis and the three adjacent prefectures,[3] has a gross domestic product of about $1.65 trillion and a population of about 35 million, making it the world's largest metropolitan area. By way of comparison, the New York metropolitan area[4] has a GDP of $1.21 trillion and a population of 18.9 million, while the Greater London metropolitan area[5] has a GDP of $377 billion and a population of 15 million.

The Rise to a Global Knowledge Centre

Today, in response to the rise of an advanced information society, office buildings are being transformed from places for the performance of routine administrative tasks to bases for the transmission and reception of information and centres for the kind of knowledge-intensive activity that generates wealth. While it might have been supposed that the internet would reduce the movement of people, since we can send and receive information to or from anywhere without leaving the room, the opposite has happened. In the information age, people are moving about more than ever. In Tokyo, the New Marunouchi Building was completed in 2002. In 2003 Roppongi Hills opened, and that year the number of passengers travelling from the suburbs into central Tokyo on privately operated commuter lines rose for the first time in about a decade. The surge came not from commuters but from people visiting the exciting new buildings in the heart of the city. That was more than 10 years ago. Since then office buildings have continued to spring up in central Tokyo and the adjoining areas, most of which go far beyond traditional office-building functions with the inclusion of hotels, restaurants, stores, personal services, educational facilities, and more. This is because, in the advanced information age, the core function of the office building has evolved from the mass processing of paperwork and clerical tasks to the creation and exchange of knowledge. Today machines take care of the routine clerical work, leaving human beings to devote themselves to activities involving higher-order thinking. Today, this is the way wealth is generated.

Cultures and civilizations flourish and advance through interchange. People are stimulated and inspired to further intellectual growth through contact with experts in other disciplines. That is why people keep moving as they strive to improve their own knowledge and understanding. So a city is the centre for interaction. If we define the basic features of a city in terms of:

◆ clustered living
◆ urban infrastructure
◆ centricity with respect to the surrounding areas

it then seems reasonable to trace Tokyo's urban origins back to the construction of Edo Castle in 1457. The job of urban policy-makers is to respond to this evolution with the appropriate public policies. Yet in an era in which the market holds sway, urban policy must not unnecessarily restrict or distort the behaviour of the private sector. Urban policy, which pertains not only to city planning but to such diverse fields as economics, social welfare, labour, and education, is an important component of any effective response to the evolution of the city. It is also the framework within which Olympic-related developments must fit.

Understanding this, the Tokyo metropolitan government, in an effort to keep pace with the times, outlined a major change of course in its 1995 Tokyo Plan, defying conventional wisdom with a programme focused on the upgrading of city-centre functions, the construction of ring roads, and the transformation of Haneda Airport into an international hub. In many ways the new policy signified a shift from quantity to quality in urban planning, an awareness of the need to focus less on creating new urban centres and more on upgrading the functions of existing centres while improving the quality of amenities and urban space for those living and working in the city. This policy shares a fundamental orientation with the concept of the compact (high-density) city, which has been gaining momentum worldwide in recent years.

Tokyo Metropolis stretches out some 100 kilometres from east to west, but from north to south it is barely 20 kilometres at its narrowest point. Tokyo's urban functions cannot be contained within the boundaries of this unnaturally long and narrow administrative unit. The range of Tokyo's big-city functions and activities roughly corresponds to an area 100 kilometres in diameter circumscribed by the planned Ken-O (or Metropolitan Inter-City) Expressway. This basically defines the range of daily economic and social activity in the Tokyo metropolitan area. Tokyo's strength and appeal as a city lie in the way the entire megalopolis has come to function as one vast centre of intellectual activity. Knowledge, culture, technology, industry, manpower, services, and businesses of all kinds are concentrated here. Of the three widely acknowledged 'world cities' – Tokyo, New York, and London – Tokyo reigns supreme in size (with a metropolitan area population of 30 million), if not in diversity. Whether we like it or not, we cannot make sense of Tokyo without keeping sight of this megalopolis as a whole. The London Plan (GLA, 2004) cites New York, London, and Tokyo as three 'successful world cities' and keeps their development in mind when mapping out a strategy for London's long-term growth. Such comparisons among the world's great cities are inevitable, and we can hardly ignore them when discussing urban planning in relation to Tokyo. The proposed extension of the Urban Renaissance Special Measures Law should not merely delay the expiration of existing measures but expand them with the goal of integrating tax policies, financial policies, and every type of regulation into the Tokyo plan and designing a mechanism for the creation of new functions in the city centre, including measures to enhance the operation of the newly internationalized Haneda Airport.

City planning policy today is predicated on land-use zones, and when an area is zoned for land use, such regulations as floor-area ratio, building-to-land ratio, and maximum building height proceed almost automatically. Instead of arguing the merits of dividing land-use zones among the twenty-three wards, we should be debating an even more fundamental problem, namely, whether we should continue operating under a City Planning Law predicated on separation of uses. The creation of separate residential, commercial, and industrial zones in urban planning was necessary in the period of rapid industrialization, but in a complex, multi-functional city like today's Tokyo, the entire system has become obsolete. After all, the concentration of multiple functions is a basic assumption of the compact-city concept that the government itself has sanctioned.

In Japan disputes over new construction projects are not uncommon, but they rarely if ever centre on floor-area ratio. Most frequently the issue is height. The frequency of these disputes points to a gap between the means by which city planners control development and the values of ordinary people. For years I have advocated a shift to urban development regulations focused on the criteria of building height, form, colour, facing material, and harmony with the surroundings. Generally speaking, zoning regulations should permit construction of super-high-rise buildings in the city centre and nearby business districts, but forbid high-rise buildings in the outer neighbourhoods.

Tokyo has worked hard to build an extensive and user-friendly subway system. This is one of the busiest in the world, with an annual ridership of more than 3 billion – far more than either the New York Subway (about 1.6 billion) or the London Underground (about 1 billion). But the Tokyo subway has numerous issues that need to be addressed, including excessive crowding at stations like Shinjuku-sanchome, Kamiyacho, and Toranomon; and such improvements as installation of safety barriers and upgrades to protect against natural disasters. In central Tokyo and the areas immediately adjacent, where the Olympic venues will be concentrated, we will need to move forward on a number of fronts to address longstanding public transportation issues and implement needed improvements. Among the subway-related projects demanding attention are the 'Yurakucho Line–Hanzomon Line connector'[6] and the 'Haneda Airport Access Line'.[7] In addition to these projects, the city will be expected to make substantial progress on disaster preparedness in the form of structural renovation of ageing apartment buildings and the widening of streets to provide emergency access in densely built areas. By a strange coincidence, the Tokyo metropolitan government adopted a new ordinance regarding the earthquake-proofing of buildings along emergency access roadways on 11 March 2011, the very day of the Great East Japan Earthquake. The new system adopts a more aggressive approach to promoting renovation in order to quake-proof commercial and apartment buildings, subsidizing up to five-sixths of the cost of renovation. Unfortunately, the system covers only streets facing main thoroughfares. It promises little if any progress for the countless substandard buildings along the side streets running between those major roads. As long as we rely on the market mechanism to solve things, the rebuilding and renovation of ageing condominiums will not proceed at an acceptable pace. Structural renovation is often financially unfeasible without government assistance, particularly in the densely inhabited areas where substandard buildings pose the biggest public threat in the event of a disaster. If the market mechanism cannot solve the problem, then public housing policy must step in. For Tokyo, the development of effective policies to promote timely renovation of aging, substandard buildings is an urgent priority.

Another urgent problem from the standpoint of disaster management is the large number of narrow streets in Tokyo's densely built neighbourhoods. There are vast residential tracts – including those bordering Ring Road No. 7 – whose streets are too narrow for emergency vehicles to pass, and these need to be rebuilt before a major earthquake hits. Many of these neighbourhoods are also packed with condominium and apartment buildings constructed during the era of rapid economic growth. These buildings are now rapidly deteriorating. The day is fast approaching when the need to rebuild or remove these structures will become a major issue. There was a time when any land left vacant by demolition was automatically slated for construction of multi-unit housing, office buildings, or some other commercial use. Henceforth, we should focus on using such land for public recreational uses such as parkland, waterfront development, athletic centres or cultural facilities. Just as the athletic facilities built for the 1964 Olympics have aged and deteriorated, so has the city as a whole, since so much of what we see in Tokyo today was built for that occasion. Even if Tokyo had not been selected to host the Games in 2020, it would still be our duty to confront Tokyo's weaknesses head-on, tackle these difficult challenges, and present the world with a new model of urban planning.

Conclusion

I think that there must be a difference between the 1964 Tokyo Olympics' legacy and the 2020 Tokyo Olympics' legacy (figure 21.6). We have left behind the industrial age and have entered the advanced information age as a mature society. A mature society is one that welcomes peoples, customs, and beliefs of all kinds and spares no effort to improve the quality of life. This translates into an urban culture in which people can enjoy sports, the arts, and entertainment to the fullest. We need to approach the 2020 Olympics as an opportunity to refashion Tokyo into a twenty-first-century city.

The Legacy of the Olympics is not only about athletic facilities. The legacy includes related facilities, urban development and social evolution. These are very important legacies of the Olympics. If asked to identify the legacy of the 1964 Olympics, some might point to the athletic facilities built at that time, many of which, as said above, remain in use today. Certainly these contributed to Tokyo's development. In 1964, the success of the women's volleyball team fuelled a huge

Legacy

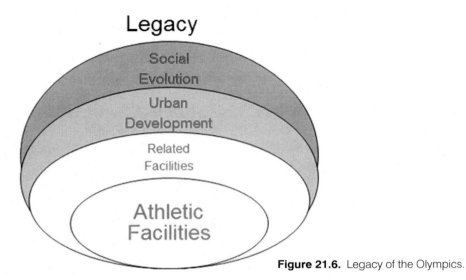

Figure 21.6. Legacy of the Olympics.

surge in the popularity of women's social volleyball leagues, or *Mama-san barē*. That phenomenon helped create a new social climate in which the idea that 'a woman's place is in the home' gave way to a broad acceptance of women's active participation in society at every level. In that sense, the 1964 Olympics provided an important impetus for social change in Japan.

The focus this time should be on sports, culture, urban parks, and waterside amenities – all vital components of a twenty-first century city serving a mature society. In Japan, people now speak less of urban planning and more about community development. In Europe, the preferred term has shifted from 'land-use planning' to 'spatial planning'. In the United States, the buzzword is 'smart growth', rather than 'growth management' of the past. In China, the theme of Expo 2010 in Shanghai was 'Best City, Best Life'. All of these developments suggest that people are pursuing a more holistic approach to urban planning that integrates concerns about welfare, education, economy, and the environment.

As the situation stands now, local merchants' associations, neighbourhood associations, and other community groups have to get permission from multiple agencies – the Tokyo metropolitan government, the municipal government, police and fire officials, and so forth – in order to hold an event in a local street or park. The system needs to be streamlined so that these community organizations can complete the process through a single office. Our leaders in the central government are always talking about revitalizing the economy through deregulation and decentralization. The Tokyo metropolitan government should apply these principles locally, relaxing its land-use regulations and promoting the devolution of power to community self-government organizations in the interests of community revitalization. The 2020 Olympics offer the perfect opportunity for Tokyo to shift to such policies and present itself to the world as an exemplar of the mature city of tomorrow.

The Tokyo metropolitan government formulated 'The Tokyo Plan' in 1995 and 'The New City Planning Vision for Tokyo' in 2001. In this context, the government aimed to build 'The Ringed Megalopolis Structure'. Thanks to this policy, the Shuto (Tokyo Metropolitan) Expressway Inner Circular Route[8] was completed in 2015, the fourth runway at Haneda airport was constructed and the airport was internationalized in 2010, and the heart of Tokyo was renewed. But Tokyo as a whole still needs a comprehensive grand design.

The Tokyo metropolitan government decided to formulate a new urban grand design[9] for Tokyo by the 2040s. Tokyo 2020 is a milestone, but only the beginning. For Tokyo the post-Games era is vitally important.

Notes

1. Tokyo 2020 Candidate City file was published by the Tokyo 2020 Bid Committee in December 2012 (see TOCOPG, 2012).

2. Statistics taken from Tokyo toshi hakusho [Tokyo Urban White Paper] 2013.

3. Tokyo Metropolis and the three adjacent prefectures are roughly 13,000 square kilometres; about 200 kilometres in diameter.

4. The New York metropolitan area is Metropolitan Statistical Area; a 17,000 square kilometres area, about 300 kilometres in diameter, encompassing ten counties in New York State, twelve in New Jersey, and one in Pennsylvania.

5. The greater London metropolitan area measures 15,000 square kilometres (160 kilometres in diameter comprising Greater London and environs), has a GDP of $377 billion and a population of 15 million.

6. Yurakucho Line–Hanzomon Line connector (additions to No. 8 and No. 11 Tokyo Metro lines): connecting line starting at Toyosu on the Yurakucho Line, passing through Toyocho on the Tozai Line, then following the existing Hanzomon Line north as far as Oshiage, and extending on to Kameyu on the Joban Line; line connecting Yotsugi and Matsudo stations.

7. The Haneda Airport Access Line Plan by Japanese Railways East Company proposes to convert the freight line into a passenger line to connect Tokyo Station and Haneda Airport in 18 minutes. It also connects Shinjyuku Station, Shinkiba Station and Haneda Airport.

8. By the Shuto (Tokyo Metropolitan) Expressway Inner Circular Route, the drive from Shinjyuku to Haneda Airport takes about only 20 minutes.

9. Governer Masuzoe declared in June 2015 his administration's intention to formulate a new urban grand design in the Assembly.

References

The references listed in this bibliography include both the primary and secondary sources used in writing this book. Full publication details are not always given for the small number of sources listed here that were published before 1900, since some were privately published and bear only the names of their printers.

2010 Legacies Now (2008) *Collaborate, Participate, Celebrate: Annual Review 2007–08*. Vancouver: 2010 Legacies Now.

2010 Legacies Now (2009) *About Us*. Available at: http://www.2010legaciesnow.com/about_us/.

Abend, L. (2014) Why nobody wants to host the 2022 Winter Olympics. *Time*, 3 October. Available at: http://time.com/3462070/olympics-winter-2022/.

Abreu, M.A. (2008) *A Evolução Urbana do Rio de Janeiro*, 4th ed. Rio de Janeiro: IPP/PCRJ.

Acharya, S.K. (2005) Urban development in post-reform China: insights from Beijing. *Norsk Geografisk Tidsskrift*, **59**, pp. 229–236.

ACOG (Atlanta Committee for the Olympic Games) (1990) *Welcome to a Brave and Beautiful City*. Atlanta: ACOG.

ACOG (1998) *Official Report of the XXVI Olympic Games*. Atlanta: ACOG.

AEK (2016) Agia Sophia – Centre of sports, culture and memory. Available at: http://www.aekfc.gr/stp/agia-sofia-42938.htm?lang=en&path=-23324611.

Agamben, G. (2005) *State of Exception*. Chicago, IL: University of Chicago Press.

Alaska Dispatch (2012) Anti-terrorism tool at forefront of 2012 London Olympic security, 4 May. Available at: http://www.alaskadispatch.com/article/anti-terrorism-tools-forefront-2012-london-olympics-security.

Alberts, H.C. (2009) Berlin's failed bid to host the 2000 Summer Olympic Games: urban development and the improvement of sports facilities. *International Journal of Urban and Regional Research*, **33**(2), pp. 502–516.

Alekseyeva, A. (2014) Sochi 2014 and the rhetoric of a new Russia: image construction through mega-events. *East European Politics*, **30**(2), pp. 158–174.

Alexandridis, T. (2007) *The Housing Impact of the 2004 Olympic Games in Athens. Background Paper*. Geneva: Centre on Housing Rights and Evictions.

Allen, I. (2006) Should regeneration be based on a fleeting and extraordinary event? *Architects' Journal*, **224**, 30 November, p. 3.

Allen, J. and Cochrane, A. (2014) The urban unbound: London's politics and the 2012 Olympic Games. *International Journal of Urban and Regional Research*, **38**(5), pp. 1609–1624.

Alpha Bank (2004) *The Impact of the Olympic Games on the Greek Economy*. Athens: Alpha Bank.

Amateur Photographer (2012) Fish photographer caught in Olympics terror alert, 23 May. Available at: http://www.amateurphotographer.co.uk/photo-news/538771/fish-photographer-caught-in-olympics-terror-alert.

AMPVA (Associação de Moradores e Pescadores da Vila Autódromo) (2012) *Plano Popular da Vila Autódromo: Plano de Desenvolvimento Urbano, Econômico, Social e Cultural*. Rio de Janeiro: AMPVA.

Andranovich, G. and Burbank, M.J. (2011) Contextualizing Olympic legacies. *Urban Geography*, **32**(6), pp. 823–844.

Andranovich, G., Burbank, M.J. and Heying, C.H. (2001) Olympic Cities: lessons learned from mega-event politics. *Journal of Urban Affairs*, **23**, pp.113–131.

Anon (1904) *Universal Exposition, Saint Louis 1904: Preliminary Programme of Physical Culture, Olympic Games and World's Championship Contests*. St. Louis, MO: Organizing Committee.

Anon (1907) The Olympic Games. *The Times*, 30 March, p. 10.

Anon (1910) Dover, Robert. *Encyclopaedia Britannica*, 11th ed., vol. 8. Cambridge: Cambridge University Press, p. 453.

Anon (1963) Two cities battle to host the Olympics. *Business Week*, 23 February, p. 36.

Anon (1987) The future of Athens: a city in transition. *Financial Times*, 6 May.

Anon (1997) Os erros que derrubaram o Rio. *Jornal do Brasil*, 8 March, p. 19.

Anon (2000) Um elogio Olímpico. *Jornal do Brasil*, 24 May, p. 24

Anon (2002) Rio-2004 serviu como lição. *Jornal do Brasil*, 26 August, p. C6.

Anon (2011) Greece's Olympic dream has turned into a nightmare for Village residents. *Daily Telegraph*, 23 June. Available at: http://www.telegraph.co.uk/finance/financialcrisis/8595360/Greeces-Olympic-dream-has-turned-into-a-nightmare-for-Village-residents.html.

Anon (2012) 'Estamos tirando pessoas de áreas de risco', diz Paes sobre remoção na Vila Autódromo. *O Dia*, 20 November. Available at: http://odia.ig.com.br/portal/rio/estamos-tirando-pessoas-de-%C3%A1reas-de-risco-diz-paes-sobre-remo%C3%A7%C3%A3o-na-vila-aut%C3%B3dromo-1.517206.

Anon (2013) Boris Johnson: The Olympic Park will be the Albertopolis of the east. *Evening Standard*, 4 December 2013. Available at: http://www.standard.co.uk/comment/comment/boris-johnson-the-olympic-park-will-be-the-albertopolis-of-the-east-8982871.html.

Anon (2015a) Brasil pretende alugar sistemas de defesa para as Olimpíadas. *Exame*, 15 April. Available at: http://exame.abril.com.br/brasil/noticias/brasil-pretende-alugar-sistemas-de-defesa-para-as-olimpiadas.

Anon (2015b) Vila Olímpica: desaquecimento imobiliário não é problema. *Terra*, 18 April. Available at: http://esportes.terra.com.br/jogos-olimpicos/2016/vila-olimpica-desaquecimento-imobiliario-nao-e-problema-para-construtoras,e411a0dbe0dcc410VgnCLD200000b1bf46d0RCRD.html.

Anon (2015c) 'Pre-legacy' of Rio 2016 Games begins as Olympic venue is opened to underprivileged communities. *Rio2016*, 23 December. Available at: http://www.rio2016.com/en/news/pre-legacy-of-rio-2016-games-begins-as-olympic-venue-is-opened-to-underprivileged-communities.

AOBC (Athens 2004 Olympic Bid Committee) (1997) *Athens Candidate City*. Athens: AOBC.

AP (Associated Press) (2009a) IOC congratulates itself for Beijing Olympics. *CBS News*, 7 October. Available at: http://www.cbsnews.com/news/ioc-congratulates-itself-for-beijing-olympics/.

AP (2009b) Study: Beijing's air worse than at past Olympics. 21 June. Available at: http://www.usnews.com/science/articles/2009/06/21/study-beijings-air-worse-than-at-past-olympics.

AP (2014) IOC struggling to find cities to host Olympics. *Huffington Post*, 31 May. Available at: http://www.huffingtonpost.com/2014/05/31/ioc-olympics-host-cities_n_5425341.html.

AP (2015) Boston's referendum on 2024 Olympics raises doubts among IOC members. *The Guardian*, 2 April. Available at: http://www.theguardian.com/sport/2015/apr/02/bostons-referendum-on-2024-olympics-raises-doubts-among-ioc-members.

APO (Autoridade Pública Olímpica) (2015a) *Plano de Políticas Públicas – Legado 1ª atualização*. Available at: http://www.apo.gov.br/wp-content/downloads/abril/PlanodePoliticasPublicasV2.pdf.

APO (2015b) *Matriz de Responsbilidades 2ª atualização*. Available at: http://www.apo.gov.br/wp-content/uploads/2015/01/Matriz_V3_28_01_2015.pdf.

Arbaci, S. and Tapada-Berteli, T. (2012) Social inequality and urban regeneration in Barcelona city centre: reconsidering success. *European Urban and Regional Studies*, **19**(3), pp. 287–311.

Arbena, J.L. (1991) Sport, development, and Mexican nationalism, 1920–1970. *Journal of Sport History*, **18**, pp. 350–364.

Arbena, J.L. (1996) Mexico City 1968: the Games of the XIXth Olympiad, in Findling, J.E. and Pelle, K.D. (eds.) *Historical Dictionary of the Modern Olympic Movement*. Westport, CN: Greenwood Press, pp. 139–147.

Arnold, B. (1992) The past as propaganda. *Archaeology*, **45**(July/August), pp. 30–37.

Arnold, R. and Foxall, A. (2014) Lord of the (Five) Rings. *Problems of Post-Communism*, **61**(1), pp. 3–12.

Arsenault, M. and Ryan, A. (2015) Walsh pushes back against USOC pressure. *Boston Globe*, 27 July. Available at: https://www.bostonglobe.com/2015/07/27/walsh-olympic-panel-don-rush-bid/uTux J0Foc9xsLJXQ3IGjdK/story.html.

Associació Pla Estratègic Barcelona 2000 (1994) *II Plan Estratégico Económico y Social Barcelona 2000*. Barcelona: Associació Pla Estratègic Barcelona 2000.

ATC (Australian Tourist Commission) (1998) *1996 Olympic Games Atlanta Report*. September. Sydney: ATC.

ATC (2000) *The Sydney Olympic Games*. ATC research update. April. Sydney: ATC.

ATC (2001) *Olympic Games Tourism Strategy: Overview*. Sydney: Australia Tourist Commission.

Athens Indymedia (2005) CCTV cameras all around us (but some destroyed). Available at: http://athens.indymedia.org/features.php3?id=394.

ATHOC (Athens Organizing Committee for the Olympic Games) (2004) Archery in the shadow of the Acropolis (advertisement), in Konstandaras, K. (ed.) *Greece: The Ideal Destination*. Athens: Hellenic Sun Editions.

ATHOC (2005) *Official Report of the XXVIII Olympiad*, 2 vols. Athens: Liberis Publications Group.

Audit Office (1999) *Performance audit report, the Sydney 2000 Olympic and Paralympic Games. Review of Estimates*. Sydney: Audit Office.

Baade, R.A., Baumann, R. and Matheson, V.A. (2008) *Slippery Slope? Assessing the Economic Impact of the 2002 Winter Olympic Games in Salt Lake City, Utah*. Department of Economics Faculty Research Series, Paper 08-15. Worcester, MA: College of the Holy Cross.

Baade, R.A. and Matheson, V. (2002) Bidding for the Olympics: fool's gold, in Baros, C.P., Ibrahimo, M. and Szymanski, S. (eds.) *Transatlantic Sport: The Comparative Economics of North America and European Sports*. Cheltenham: Edward Elgar, pp. 127–151.

BAB (British Assessment Bureau) (2010) ISO 14001:2004 (ISO 14000) Certification. Available at: http://www.british-assessment.co.uk/ISO-14001-certification-services.htm.

Bachrach, S.D. (2001) *The Nazi Olympics Berlin 1936*. St. Louis, MO: Turtleback Books.

BAI (Bayerischer Architekten und Ingenieurverein e.V.) (eds.) (1912) *München und seine Bauten*. Munich: F. Bruckmann.

Bailey, S. (2008) *Athlete First: A History of the Paralympic Movement*. Oxford: Wiley-Blackwell.

Baker, R.E. and Esherick, C. (2013) *Fundamentals of Sport Management*. Champaign, IL: Human Kinetics.

BALASA (British Amputee and Les Autres Sports Association) (2007) Les Autres Athletes. Available at: http://www.patient.co.uk/showdoc/26739787/.

Barkham, P. (2005a) Chirac's reheated food jokes bring Blair to the boil. *The Guardian*, 5 July. Available at: http://www.theguardian.com/politics/2005/jul/05/g8.france.

Barkham, P. (2005b) Spielberg (ET, Jaws) and Besson (Nikita, Léon). The winner: Goodrich (Travelex ads). *The Guardian,* 7 July. Available at: http://www.theguardian.com/uk/2005/jul/07/Olympics2012.film.

Barkin, D. and King, T. (1970) *Regional Economic Development: The River Basin Approach in Mexico*. Cambridge: Cambridge University Press.

Barnett, C.R. (1996) St. Louis 1904: the Games of the 3rd Olympiad, in Findling, J.E. and Pelle, K.D. (eds.) *Historical Dictionary of the Modern Olympic Movement*. Westport, CN: Greenwood Press, pp. 18–25.

Barney, R.K., Wenn, S.R. and Martyn, S.G. (2004) *Selling the Five Rings: The International Olympic Committee and the Rise of Olympic Commercialism*, revised ed. Salt Lake City. UT: University of Utah Press.

Bastéa, E. (2000) *The Creation of Modern Athens: Planning the Myth*. Cambridge: Cambridge University Press.

Bastos, I. and Schmidt, S. (2010) Prefeitura removerá 119 favelas até o fim de 2012. *O Globo*, 7 January. Available at: http://oglobo.globo.com/rio/prefeitura-removera-119-favelas-ate-fim-de-20123072053#ixzz3czRcpKS3.

Bataillon, C. and Rivière d'Arc, H. (1979) *La Ciudad de México*. Mexico City: Sep Diana.

Batista, H.G. (2015) Ministro da Defesa pede empréstimo de dez caças para segurança das Olimpíadas de 2016. *O Globo*, 6 May. Available at: http://oglobo.globo.com/rio/rio-2016/

ministro-da-defesa-pede-emprestimo-de-dez-cacas-para-seguranca-das-olimpiadas-de-2016-15883339#ixzz3c8L0bsev.

Bauman, Z. (2000) *Liquid Modernity*. Cambridge: Polity Press.

BBC (British Broadcasting Corporation) (2005) Games a £2bn UK tourism boost, 6 July. Available at: http://news.bbc.co.uk/1/hi/uk/4656771.stm.

BBC (2012) In pictures: Beijing's Olympic venue legacy. Available at: http://www.bbc.co.uk/news/in-pictures-18780003.

BBC News (2012*a*) London 2012: major Olympic security test unveiled, 30 April. Available at: http://www.bbc.co.uk/news/uk-17891223.

BBC News (2012*b*) Typhoon jets arrive in London to test Olympic security, 2 May. Available at: http://www.bbc.co.uk/news/uk-17922490.

BBC News (2012*c*) Missiles may be placed at residential flats, 29 April. Available at: http://www.bbc.co.uk/news/uk-17884897.

BBC News (2013) Rio favela has 'more CCTV cameras than London', 11 January. Available at: http://www.bbc.co.uk/news/world-latin-america-20992062.

BBC News (2015) Beijing beats Almaty to host 2022 Winter Olympics. Available at: http://www.bbc.co.uk/news/world-asia-33729708.

BBC News 24 (2006) London's Olympic victory. Broadcast 1 January.

BBC News London (2012) Sonic device deployed in London during Olympics, 12 May. Available at: http://www.bbc.co.uk/news/uk-england-london-18042528.

BBC Sport (2006) Beijing eyes Games profit in 2008. Available at: www.news.bbc.co.uk/go/pr/fr/-/sport1/hi/other_sports/4559728stm.

BBC Sport (2008) Olympic stadium 'hits £525m mark'. BBC News, 18 June. Available at: http:/news.bbc.co.uk/1/hi/England/London/7460188.

Bea, F.X. (1997) Shareholder value. *Wirtschaftswissenschaftliches Studium*, **29**(10), pp. 541–543.

Beard, M. (2004) The Greek heroes, a missed drugs test and a 'motorbike accident' that upset the Games. *The Independent*, 14 August.

BEGOC (Baku European Games Operating Committee) (2015) *Athletics: Games-Time Guide*. Available at: http://www.european-athletics.org/mm/Document/EventsMeetings/General/01/27/62/14/AthleticsGames-timeGuide-FINAL_Neutral.pdf.

Benchimol, J. L. (1990) *Pereira Passos: um Haussmann tropical: a renovação urbana da cidade do Rio de Janeiro no início do século XX*. Rio de Janeiro: PCRJ, Secretaria Municipal de Cultura, Turismo e Esportes, Departamento Geral de Documentação e Informação Cultural.

Beriatos, E. and Gospodini, A. (2004) 'Glocalising' urban landscapes: Athens and the 2004 Olympics. *Cities*, **21**(3), pp. 187–202.

Berlin, P. (2003) What did the Olympics bring Sydney? *New York Times*, 24 December. Available at: http://www.nytimes.com/2003/12/24/news/24iht-t1_2.html.

Bernstock, P. (2014) *Olympic Housing: A Critical Review of London 2012's Legacy*. Aldershot: Ashgate.

Bianchini, F., Dawson, J. and Evans, R. (1992) Flagship projects in urban regeneration, in Healey, P., Davoudi, S., Tavsanoglu, S., O'Toole, M. and Usher, D. (eds.) *Rebuilding the City: Property-Led Urban Regeneration*. London: E. and F.N. Spon, pp. 245–255.

Bianchini, F. and Parkinson, M. (eds.) (1993) *Cultural Policy and Urban Regeneration: The West European Experience*. Manchester: Manchester University Press.

Bingham Hall, P. (1999) *Olympic Architecture: Building Sydney 2000*. Sydney: Watermark Press.

Binyon, M. (1980) The way the Games were won. *The Times*, 4 August.

Blake, A. (2005) *The Economic Impact of the London 2012 Olympics*. Nottingham: Christel DeHaan Tourism and Travel Research Institute.

Blowe, K. (2004) London's Olympics myths. *Radical Activist Network Newsletter*. Available at: www.radicalactivist.net.

BOBICO (Beijing 2008 Olympic Bid Committee) (2001) *Beijing Candidature File*, vol. 1. Available at: http://en.beijing2008.com.

BOCOG (Beijing Organizing Committee for the Games of the XXIX Olympiad) (2003) *Beijing Olympic Action Plan*. Beijing: BOCOG.

BOCOG (2010) *Official Report of the Games of the XXIX Olympiad in Beijing in 2008*. Beijing: BOCOG.

BOGVWCG (Beijing Olympic Games Volunteer Work Coordination Group) (2008) *Manual for being Olympic Volunteers*. Beijing: China Renmin University Press.

Bokoyannis, D. (2006) Athens: The Making of a Contemporary and Friendlier City. Speech, 9 February, Athens Concert Hall. Available at: http://www.cityofathens.gr/files/pdf/highlights/apologismos_omilia_en.pdf.

Bondonio, P. and Campaniello, N. (2006) Torino 2006: What kind of Olympic Winter Games were they? A preliminary account from an organizational and economic perspective. *Olympika: The International Journal of Olympic Studies*, **15**, pp. 355–380.

Bondonio, P. and Guala, C. (2011) Gran Torino? The 2006 Olympic Winter Games and the tourism revival of an ancient city. *Journal of Sport and Tourism*, **16**(4), pp. 303–321.

Booth, D. (1999) Gifts of corruption? Ambiguities of obligation in the Olympic movement. *Olympika*, **8**, pp. 43–68.

Borden, S. (2015) Beijing defeats Almaty in bid to host 2022 Winter Olympics. *New York Times*, 31 July. Available at: http://www.nytimes.com/2015/08/01/sports/olympics/beijing-selected-as-host-of-2022-winter-olympics.html?_r=0.

Borges, W., Lennartz, K., Quanz, D.R. and Teutenberg, W. (1995) *Deutsche Olympiade Kalender. Daten zur Olympischen Bewegung in Deutschland, Teil 1: I. bis XIII. Olympiade (1896–1945) mit Interludium (393–1889) und Praeludium (1889–1996)*. Kassel: Agon Sportverlag.

Borja, F. (1992) *The Winter Olympic Games. Albertville 1992: A Case Study*. Paris: American University of Paris.

Borja, J. (ed.) (1995) *Barcelona: A Model of Urban Transformation 1980–1995*. Quito: Urban Management Series (PGU-LAC).

Borja, J. (1996) The international promotion of Barcelona, in Borja, J. (ed.) *Barcelona: An Urban Transformation Model 1980–1995*. Quito: UNCHS/PNUD/World Bank/GTZ, pp. 276–282.

Boston, W (2010) Global recession and nation's financial crisis force property companies to rethink projects and look abroad. Available at: http://online.wsj.com/articles/SB10001424052748703798904575069423368502324.htm.

Bottero, M., Sacerdotti, S.L. and Mauro, S. (2012) Turin 2006 Olympic Winter Games: impacts and legacies from a tourism perspective. *Journal of Tourism and Cultural Change*, **10**(2), pp. 202–217.

Boukas, N., Ziakas, V. and Boustras, G. (2013) Olympic legacy and cultural tourism: exploring the facets of Athens' Olympic heritage. *International Journal of Heritage Studies*, **19**, pp. 203–228.

Bouras, S. (2007) Greek mall boom challenges tradition. Available at: http://www.nytimes.com/2007/06/11/business/worldbusiness/11iht-regreece.1.6096546.html.

Bovy, P. (2001) Exceptional Mobility Management for Large Events: Transport Issues for the Sydney 2000 Olympics. Union Internationale des transports publics. International Association of Public Transport, 54th World Congress. London.

Bovy, P. (2006) Solving outstanding mega-event transport challenges: the Olympic experience. *Public Transport International*, **6**, pp. 32–34.

Bovy, P. and Liaudat, C. (2003) *Trafic de support logistique de grandes manifestations*. Lausanne: L'Ecole Polytechnique Federale de Lausanne (EPFL).

Boykoff, J. (2014) *Celebration, Capitalism and the Olympic Games*. New York: Routledge.

Boykoff, J. and Fussey, P. (2013) London's shadow legacies: security and activism at the 2012 Olympics. *Contemporary Social Science*, **9**(2), pp. 253–270.

Boyle, P. and Haggerty, K.D. (2009) Spectacular security: mega-events and the security complex. *International Political Sociology*, **3**(3), pp. 257–274.

Boyle, P. and Haggerty, K.D. (2011) Civil cities and urban governance: regulating disorder for the Vancouver Winter Olympics. *Urban Studies*, **48**(15), pp. 3185–3201.

Boyle, P. and Haggerty, K. (2012) Planning for the worst: risk, uncertainty, and the Olympic Games. *British Journal of Sociology*, **63**(2), pp. 241–259.

BPA (British Paralympic Association) (2007) *Sydney 2000*. Available at: http://www.paralympics.org.uk/paralympic_games.asp?section=000100010003&games_code=00010003000300010003.

BPA (2015) *National Paralympic Day 2015*. Available at: http://paralympics.org.uk/npd2015.

Bracewell, D. (2009) Host City Olympic Transportation Plan (HCOTP) for the 2010 Winter Games. Annual Conference of the Transportation Association of Canada, Vancouver.

Brandt, D. and Heller, G. (2014) Olympische Winterspiele München 2022. Großevents und nachhaltige Stadtentwicklung im Widerspruch. *Planerin*, **2**(14), pp. 11–14.

Brent Ritchie, J.R. and Hall, M. (1999) Mega events and human rights, in Taylor, T. (ed.) *How you Play the Game, Papers from the First International Conference on Sports and Human Rights*. Sydney, Australia, pp. 102–115.

Brent Ritchie, J.R. and Smith, B.H. (1991) The impact of a mega-event on host region awareness: a longitudinal study. *Journal of Travel Research*, **30**(1), pp. 3–10.

Brewster, C. (2010) Changing impressions of Mexico for the 1968 Games, in Brewster, K. (ed.) *Reflections on Mexico '68*. Chichester: John Wiley, pp. 23–45.

Brewster, C. and Brewster, K. (2010) Sport and society in post-revolutionary Mexico, in Brewster, C. and Brewster, K. (eds.) *Representing the Nation: Sport and Spectacle in Post-Revolutionary Mexico*. New York: Routledge, pp. 13–37.

Brewster, K. (2005) Patriotic pastimes: the role of sport in post-revolutionary Mexico. *International Journal of the History of Sport*, **22**, pp. 139–157.

Brewster, K. (2010) Teaching Mexicans how to behave: public education on the eve of the Olympics, in Brewster, K. (ed.), *Reflections on Mexico '68*. Chichester: John Wiley, pp. 46–62.

Brewster, K. and Brewster, C. (2009) The Mexico City Olympics. *International Journal of the History of Sport*, **26**(6), pp. 711–880.

Brichford, M. (1996) Munich 1972: the Games of the 20th Olympiad, in Findling, J.E. and Pelle, K.D. (eds.) *Historical Dictionary of the Modern Olympic Movement*. Westport, CT: Greenwood Press, pp. 148–152.

Brito, G. (2014) Paes nega suspeita do TCU de gastos adicionais nas olimpíadas do Rio. *G1*, 19 December. Available at: http://g1.globo.com/rio-de-janeiro/noticia/2014/12/paes-nega-suspeita-do-tcu-de-gastos-adicionais-nas-olimpiadas-do-rio.html.

Brittain, I. (2008) The evolution of the Paralympic Games, in Cashman, R. and Darcy, S. (eds.) *Benchmark Games: The Sydney 2000 Paralympic Games*. Sydney: Walla Walla Press, pp. 19–34.

Brittain, I. (2010) *The Paralympic Games Explained*. London: Routledge.

Broudehoux, A.-M. (2004) *The Making and Selling of Post-Mao Beijing*. London: Routledge.

Brown, G. (2001) Sydney 2000: an invitation to the world. *Olympic Review*, **37**, pp. 15–20.

Brownell, S. (2008) *Beijing's Games: What the Olympics mean to China*. Lanham, MD: Rowman and Littlefield.

Browning, M. (2000) Olympics under the gun. *The Guardian*, 8 March. Available at: http://www.cpa.org.au/gachive2/991games.html.

Brum, M.S. (2012) Ditadura civil-militar e favelas: estigma e restrições ao debate sobre a cidade (1969–1973). *Caderno Metrópole*, **14**(18), pp. 357–379.

Brunet, F. (1993) *Economy of the 1992 Barcelona Olympic Games*. Lausanne: IOC.

Brunet, F. (1995) An economic analysis of the Barcelona '92 Olympic Games: resources, financing and impact, in Moragas, M. de and Botella, M. (eds.) *The Keys of Success: The Social, Sporting, Economic and Communications Impact of Barcelona '92*. Barcelona: Bellaterra, pp. 203–37.

Brunet, F. (2009) The economy of the Barcelona Olympic Games, in Poynter, G. and MacRury, I. (eds.) *Olympic Cities: 2012 and the Remaking of London*, Farnham: Ashgate, pp. 97–119.

Brunet, F. and Xinwen, Z. (2009) The economy of the Beijing Olympic Games: an analysis of prospects and first impacts, in Poynter, G. and MacRury, I. (eds.) *Olympic Cities: 2012 and the Remaking of London*. Farnham: Ashgate, pp. 163–80.

Buchanan, I. and Mallon, B. (2001) *Historical Dictionary of the Olympic Movement*. Lanham, MD: Scarecrow Press.

Buchanan, P. (1992) Barcelona: a city regenerated. *Architectural Review* **191**(August), pp. 11–14.

Bunning, W. (1973) *Report and Review of Moore Park and Alternative Sites in Sydney for a Major Sports Complex* [The Bunning Report]. Sydney.

Burbank, M.J., Andronovich, G.D. and Heying, C.H. (2001) *Olympic Dreams: The Impact of Mega-Events on Local Politics*. Boulder, CO: Lynne Rienner.

Burnosky, R.L. (1994) The History of the Arts in the Olympic Games. Master's Thesis, The American University, Washington DC.

Burns, J. (2005) Written Statement to the US Senate Subcommittee on Trade, Tourism and Economic Development. *Field Hearing on The Economic Impact of the 2010 Vancouver, Canada, Winter Olympics on Oregon and the Pacific Northwest*. Washington: US Government Printing Office.

Burroughs, A. (1999) Winning the bid, in Cashman, R. and Hughes, A. (eds.) *Staging the Olympics: The Event and Its Impact*. Sydney: University of New South Wales Press, pp. 35–45.

Business File (2004) *Going for Gold? A Survey on the Economics of the 2004 Olympic Games*. Athens: Greek Special Survey Series.

Butler, T. (2007) Re-urbanizing London's Docklands: gentrification, suburbanization or new urbanism? *International Journal of Urban and Regional Research*, **31**(4), pp. 759–781.

Butterfield, H. (1931) *The Whig Interpretation of History*. London: George Bell and Sons.

Calavita, N. and Ferrer, A. (2000) Behind Barcelona's success story: citizens movements and planners' power. *Journal of Urban History* **26**, pp. 793–807.

California Olympic Commission (1960) *VIII Olympic Winter Games Squaw Valley, California, Final Report*. Squaw Valley, CA: Organizing Committee.

Calvert, P. (1973) *Mexico: Nation of the Modern World*. London: Ernest Benn.

Campbell, D. (2005) The day Coe won gold. *The Observer*, 10 July.

Campbell, T. and Wilk, D. (1986) Plans and plan-making in the valley of Mexico. *Third World Planning Review*, **8**, pp. 287–313.

Cannon, T. (2000) *China's Economic Growth: The Impact on Regions, Migration and the Environment*. London: Macmillan.

Cano, I., Borges, D. and Ribeiro, E. (2012) *Os Donos do Morro: uma avaliação exploratória do impacto das Unidades de Polícia Pacificadora (UPPs) no Rio de Janeiro*. Rio de Janeiro: FBSP/LAV/UERJ.

Cantelon, H. and Letters, M. (2000) The making of the IOC environmental policy as the third dimension of the Olympic movement. *International Review for the Sociology of Sport*, **35**(3), pp. 294–308.

Capel, H. (2005) *El modelo Barcelona: un exámen crítico*. Barcelona: Edicions del Serbal.

Carisbroke, Lord, Porritt, A., Webb-Johnson, Lord, Heyworth, Lord, Templer, E.M., London, H., Summers, S., Bannister, R., Faure, J.C.A. and Guttmann, L. (1956) Games for the paralysed. *The Times*, 20 March, p. 11.

Carl Diem Institute (1966) *Pierre de Coubertin, The Olympic Idea: Discourses and Essays*. Lausanne: Editions Internationales Olympia.

Cartalis, C. (2015) Sport mega-events as catalysts for sustainable urban development: the case of Athens 2004, in Viegoff, V. and Poynter, G. (eds) *Mega-Event Cities: Urban Legacies of Global Sports Events*. Farnham: Ashgate.

Casciato, M. (2015) Sport and leisure in Rome from the Fascist years to the Olympic Games. *ICOMOS: Hefte des Deutschen Nationalkomitees*, **38**, pp. 29–36.

Cashman, R. (2006) *The Bitter-Sweet Awakening: The Legacy of the Sydney 2000 Olympic Games*. Sydney: Walla Walla Press.

Cashman, R. (2008) The Sydney Olympic Park model: its evolution and realisation, in Hay, A. and Cashman, R. (eds.) *Connecting Mega Events Cities: A Publication for the 9th World Congress of Metropolis*. Sydney: Sydney Olympic Park Authority, pp. 21–39.

Cashman, R. (2009) Regenerating Sydney's West: framing and adapting an Olympic vision, in Poynter, G. and MacRury, I. (eds.) *Olympic Cities: 2012 and the Remaking of London*. Farnham: Ashgate, pp. 133–43.

Cashman, R. (2011) *Sydney Olympic Park 2000 to 2010: History and Legacy*. Sydney: Walla Walla Press.

Cashman, R. and Darcy, S. (2008) (eds.) *Benchmark Games. The Sydney 2000 Paralympic Games*. Sydney: Walla Walla Press, pp. 19–34.

Cashman, R. and Hughes, A. (eds.) (1999) *Staging the Olympics: The Event and Its Impact*. Sydney: University of New South Wales Press.

CEC (Commission of the European Communities) (1992) *Urbanisation and the Function of Cities in the European Community*. Regional Development Studies. Brussels: CEC.

Chai, J.C.H. (1996) Divergent development and regional income gap in China. *Journal of Contemporary Asia*, **26**, pp. 46–58.

Chalip, L. (2004) Beyond impact: a general model for sport event leverage, in Ritchie, B.W. and Adair, D. (eds.) *Sport Tourism: Interrelationships, Impacts and Issues*. Clevedon: Channel View Publications, pp. 226–252.

Chalip, L. and Leyns, A. (2002) Local business leveraging of a sport event: managing an event for economic benefit. *Journal of Sport Management*, **16**(2), pp. 132–158.

Chalkley, B. and Essex, S. (1999) Urban development through hosting international events: a history of the Olympic Games. *Planning Perspectives*, **14**(4), pp. 369–394.

Chandler, R. (1776) *Travels in Greece; Or, an Account of a Tour made at the Expense of the Society of Dilettanti*. Dublin.

Channel 4 (2012) The London 2014 Paralympic Games brought to you by Channel 4. Available at: http://www.channel4.com/media/documents/press/news/Paralympic%20Booklet.pdf.

Chappelet, J.-L. (1997) From Chamonix to Salt Lake City: evolution of the Olympic Village concept at the Winter Games, in Moragas, M. de, Llines, M. and Kidd, B. (eds.) *Olympic Villages: A Hundred Years of Urban Planning and Shared Experiences*. International Symposium on Olympic Villages. Lausanne: Documents of the IOC Museum, pp. 81–88.

Chappelet, J.-L. (2002a) *A Short Overview of the Olympic Winter Games*. Barcelona: Centre d'Estudis Olimpics I de l'Esport, Universitat Autònoma de Barcelona.

Chappelet, J.-L. (2002b) From Lake Placid to Salt Lake City: the challenging growth of the Olympic Winter Games since 1980. *European Journal of Sport Science*, **2**(3), pp. 1–21.

Chappelet, J.-L. (2008) Olympic environmental concerns as a legacy of the Winter Games. *International Journal of the History of Sport*, **25**(14), pp. 1884–1902.

Charmetant, R. (1997) Albertville: Olympism and architecture, in Moragas, M. de, Llines, M. and Kidd, B. (eds.) *Olympic Villages: A Hundred Years of Urban Planning and Shared Experiences*. International Symposium on Olympic Villages. Lausanne: Documents of the IOC Museum, pp. 109–115.

Christensen, P. and Kyle, D.G. (2014) General introduction, in Christensen, P. and Kyle, D.G. (eds.) *A Companion to Sport and Spectacle in Greek and Roman Antiquity*. Chichester: Wiley Blackwell, pp. 1–15.

Church, B. (2005) Forgotten games. *Houston Chronicle*, 13 August.

CIIC (China Internet Information Centre) (2004) Beijing subways improve access for handicapped. *China Daily* (English language edition), 17 August. Available at: http://www.china.org.cn/english/2004/Aug/104219.htm.

City of Hellinikon-Argyroupoli (2013) Hellinikon: development for whom? Available at: http://www.elliniko-argyroupoli.gr/article.php?id=2569.

Clancy, M.J. (1999) Tourism and development: evidence from Mexico. *Annals of Tourism Research*, **26**, pp. 1–20.

Close, P., Askew, D. and Xu Xin (2007) *The Beijing Olympiad: The Political Economy of a Sporting Mega-Event*. London: Routledge.

Coaffee, J. (2009) *Terrorism, Risk and the Global City: Towards Urban Resilience*. Farnham: Ashgate.

Coaffee, J., Fussey, P., and Moore, C. (2011) Laminating security for London 2012: Enhancing security infrastructures to defend mega sporting events. *Urban Studies*, **48**(15), pp. 3311–3328.

Coaffee, J. and Johnston, L. (2007) Accommodating the spectacle, in Gold, J.R. and Gold, M.M. (eds.) *Olympic Cities: Urban Planning, City Agendas and the World's Games, 1896–2012*. London: Routledge, pp. 138–149.

Coaffee, J., Murakami Wood, D. and Rogers, P. (2008) *The Everyday Resilience of the City: How Cities Respond to Terrorism and Disaster*. Basingstoke: Palgrave Macmillan.

Coaffee, J. and Wood, D. (2006) Security is coming home: rethinking scale and constructing resilience in the global urban response to terrorist risk. *International Relations*, **20**, pp. 503–517.

Coates, D. and Wicker, P. (2015) Why were voters against the 2022 Munich Winter Olympics in a referendum? *International Journal of Sport Finance*, **10**(3), pp. 267–283.

Coccossis, H., Deffner, A. and Economou, D. (2003) Urban/regional Co-operation in Greece: Athens, a Capital City under the Shadow of the State. Paper presented to 43rd European Congress of the Regional Science Association (ERSA), University of Jyväskylä. Available at: http://www.jyu.fi/ersa2003/cdrom/papers/358.pdf.

Cohen, P. (2013) *On the Wrong Side of the Track? East London and the Post Olympics*. London: Lawrence and Wishart.

Cohen, S. (1996) *The Games of '36: A Pictorial History of the 1936 Olympic Games in Germany*. Missoula, MT: Pictorial Histories Publishing Company.

COHRE (Centre on Housing Rights and Evictions) (2007a) *Fair Play for Housing Rights: Mega-Events, Olympic Games and Housing Rights*. Geneva: COHRE.

COHRE (2007b) *Hosting the 2012 Olympic Games: London's Olympic Preparations and Housing Rights Concerns*. Geneva: COHRE. Available at: http://www.cohre.org/store/attachments/London_background_paper.pdf.

COJO (Comité d'Organisation des Jeux Olympiques de 1924 à Paris) (1924) *Les Jeux de la VIIIe Olympiade Paris 1924: Rapport Officiel*. Paris : Librarie de France.

COJO (Comité d'Organisation des Xemes Jeux Olympiques d'hiver) (1968) *Official Report Xth Winter Olympic Games*. Grenoble: Organizing Committee.

Colvin, S. (1878) Greek Athletics, Greek Religion and Greek Art at Olympia: An Account of Ancient Usages and Modern Discoveries. Paper given to the Liverpool Art Club, 4 February.

Commission of Inquiry (1977) *Report of the Commission of Inquiry into the Cost of the 21st Olympiad*, 3 vols. Quebec: Éditeur Officiel du Québec.

CONI (Comitato Olimpico Nazionale Italiano) (1956) *VII Giochi Olimpici Inversnali, Cortina D'Ampezzo, Rapporto ufficiale*. Rome: Comitato Olimpico Nazionale Italiano.

CONI (1963) *The Games of the XVII Olympiad, Rome 1960: The Official Report of the Organizing Committee*. Rome: CONI.

COOB (Barcelona Olympic Organizing Committee) (1992) *Official Report of the Games of the XXV Olympiad*, 3 vols. Barcelona: COOB.

Cook, I.G. (2000) Pressures of development on China's cities and regions, in Cannon, T. (ed.) *China's Economic Growth: The Impact on Regions, Migration and the Environment*. London: Macmillan, pp. 33–55.

Cook, I.G. (2006) Beijing as an 'internationalized metropolis', in Wu, F. (ed.) *Globalisation and China's Cities*. London: Routledge.

Cook, I.G. (2007) Beijing 2008, in Gold, J.R. and Gold, M.M. (eds.) *Olympic Cities: City Agendas, Planning and the World's Games, 1896–2012*. London: Routledge, pp. 286–297.

Cook, I.G. and Dummer, T.J.B. (2004) Changing health in China: re-evaluating the epidemiological transition model. *Health Policy*, **67**, pp. 329–343.

Cook, I.G. and Murray, G. (2001) *China's Third Revolution: Tensions in the Transition to Post-Communism*. London: Curzon.

Cook, I.R. and Ward, K. (2011) Trans-urban networks of learning, mega events and policy tourism: the case of Manchester's Commonwealth and Olympic Games Projects. *Urban Studies*, **48**(12), pp. 2519–2535.

Correspondent (2004) Going for gold: the Olympics can pay off, but only if you have a city to sell. *Financial Times*, 14/15 August.

Correspondent (2010) Olympics sites to get new life. Available at: http://www.ekathimerini.com/4dcgi/_w_articles_politics_2_19/03/2010_115743.

Coubertin, P. de (1913) La question d'argent. *Revue Olympique*, **13**(12), pp. 183–185.

COWGOC (Calgary Olympic Winter Games Organizing Committee/Calgary Olympic Development Association) (1988) *XV Olympic Winter Games: Official Report*. Calgary: Organizing Committee.

Cox, G. (2012) Sustaining a legacy: From Sydney 2000's environmental guidelines to the Commission for a Sustainable London 2012. *Australian Planner*, **49**(3), pp. 203–214.

Cox, G., Darcy, M. and Bounds, M. (1994) *The Olympics and Housing, a Study of Six International Events and Analysis of Potential Impacts of the Sydney 2000 Olympics*. Paper prepared for the Shelter NSW and Housing and Urban Studies Research Group. Sydney: University of Western Sydney-Macarthur.

Coy, M. (2006) Gated communities and urban fragmentation in Latin America: the Brazilian experience. *GeoJournal*, **66**(1/2), pp. 121–32.

Craven, P. (2014) The Paralympic Movement takes off, LSE Public Lecture, 14 October. Available at: http://www.lse.ac.uk/assets/richmedia/channels/publicLecturesAndEvents/slides/20131014_1830_paralympicMovement_sl.pdf.

Crawford, D. (2012) Olympic setting transport records. *Traffic Engineering and Control*, **55**, pp. 168–170.

Crouch, D. and Blitz, R. (2014) IOC hits out as Norway withdraws Winter Olympic bid. *Financial Times*, 2 October. Available at: http://www.ft.com/cms/s/0/d8938ffc-4a04-11e4-8de3-00144feab7de.html#axzz3voho47oJ.

Crowther, N.B. (2003) Elis and Olympia: city, sanctuary and politics, in Phillips, D.J. and Pritchard, D. (eds.) *Sport and Festival in the Ancient Greek World*. Swansea: Classical Press of Wales, pp. 75–100.

Crowther-Dowey, C. and Fussey, P. (2010) *Researching Crime: Approaches, Method and Application*. Basingstoke: Palgrave Macmillan.

Culf, A. (2007) Capital will need 9,000 officers a day to police the Olympics, *The Guardian*, 17 March.

Currie, G., and Delbosc, A. (2011) Assessing travel demand management for the Summer Olympic Games. *Transportation Research Record: Journal of the Transportation Research Board*, No. 2245, pp. 36–48.

Currie, G. and Shalaby, A. (2012) Synthesis of transport planning approaches for the world's largest events. *Transport Reviews*, **32**, pp. 113–136.

Daily Mirror (2012) Armoured cars drafted in as security tightens ahead of the Olympic Games, 8 May. Available at: http://www.mirror.co.uk/sport/other-sports/london-2012-armoured-cars-drafted-824089.

Daily Telegraph (2012) London 2012 Olympics: Metropolitan Police double officers around torch as crowds bigger than predicted, 29 May. Available at: http://www.telegraph.co.uk/sport/olympics/torch-relay/9280127/London-2012-Olympics-Metropolitan-Police-double-officers-around-torch-as-crowds-bigger-than-predicted.html.

Daley, R. (1963) Lyons makes a lavish pitch to be site for 1968 Olympics. *New York Times*, 17 October, p. 47.

Dansero, E., Segre, A. and Mela, A. (2003) Spatial and environmental transformations towards Torino 2006: planning the legacy of the future, in De Moragas, M., Kennett, C. and Puig, N. (eds.) *The Legacy of the Olympic Games 1984–2000, Documents of the Museum*. Lausanne: International Olympic Committee, pp. 83–93.

Darcy, S. (2001) The Games for everyone? Planning for disability and access at the Sydney 2000 Paralympic and Olympic Games. *Disability Studies Quarterly*, **21**, pp. 70–84.

Darcy, S. (2003) The politics of disability and access: the Sydney 2000 Games experience. *Disability and Society*, **18**, pp. 737–757.

Darcy, S., Dickson, T.J. and Benson, A.M. (2014) London 2012 Olympic and Paralympic Games: including volunteers with disabilities – a podium performance? *Event Management*, **18**, pp. 431–446.

Daume, W. (1976) Organising the Games, in Lord Killanin and Rodda, J. (eds.) *The Olympic Games. 80 Years of People, Events and Records*, first edition. London: Barrie and Jenkins, pp. 153–156.

Davenport, J. (1996) Athens 1896: the Games of the 1st Olympiad, in Findling, J.E. and Pelle, K.D. (eds.) *Historical Dictionary of the Modern Olympic Movement*. Westport, CN: Greenwood Press, pp. 3–11.

Davidson, M. (2013) The sustainable and entrepreneurial park? Contradictions and persistent antagonisms at Sydney's Olympic Park. *Urban Geography*, **34**(5), pp. 657–676.

Davidson, M. and McNeill, D. (2012) The redevelopment of Olympic sites: examining the legacy of Sydney Olympic Park. *Urban Studies*, **49**(8), pp. 1625–1641.

Davies, F.A. (2014) Produzindo a 'região olímpica de Deodoro', in Rial, C. and Schwade, E. (eds.) *Anais da 29ª Reunião Brasileira de Antropologia*. Brasília: Kiron.

Davis, J. (2014) A promised future and the open city: issues of anticipation in Olympic legacy designs. *Architectural Research Quarterly*, **18**, pp. 324–341.

DCMS (Department for Culture, Media and Sport) (2004) *Tomorrow's Tourism Today*. London: DCMS.

DCMS (2006) *Welcome>Legacy*. London: DCMS.

DCMS (2007a) *Our Promise for 2012: How the UK will benefit from the Olympic Games and Paralympics Games*. Available at: http://www.culture.gov.uk/reference_library/publications/3660.aspx/.

DCMS (2007b) *Before, During and After: Making the Most of the London 2012 Games*. Available at: http://www.culture.gov.uk/images/publications/2012LegacyActionPlan.pdf.

DCMS (2008) *London 2012: Lessons from Beijing*. Available at: http://www.publications.parliament.uk/pa/cm200809/cmselect/cmcumeds/25/8100703.htm.

DCMS (2010) *London 2012: A Legacy for Disabled People*. London: Office for Disability Issues, DCMS.

DCMS (2012) *Beyond 2012: The London 2012 Legacy Story*. London: DCMS.

Degen, M., and García, M. (2012) The transformation of the 'Barcelona model': an analysis of culture, urban regeneration and governance. *International Journal of Urban and Regional Research*, **36**(5), pp. 1022–1038.

Deloitte Australia (2015) *Restarting Sydney's Heart: Light Rail the Engine of Change*. Sydney: Deloitte Touche Tohmatsu.

de Moragas, M. and Botella, M. (1995) *The Keys to Success*. Barcelona: Centre d'Estudis Olímpics i de l'Esport.

de Moragas, M., Kennett, C. and Puig, N. (eds.) (2003) *The Legacy of the Olympic Games 1984–2000*. Lausanne: International Olympic Committee.

de Moragas Spà, M., Llinés, M. and Kidd, B. (eds.) (1997) *Olympic Villages: A Hundred Years of Urban Planning and Shared Experiences*. Lausanne: International Olympic Committee.

de Pauw, K.P. and Gavron, S.J. (2005) *Disability Sport*, 2nd ed. Champaign, IL: Human Kinetics.

Dickson, G. and Schofield, G. (2005) Globalisation and globesity: the impact of the 2008 Beijing Olympics on China. *International Journal of Sport Management and Marketing*, **1**, pp. 169–179.

Dickson, T.J., Benson, A.M. and Blackman, D.A. (2011) Developing a framework for evaluating Olympic and Paralympic legacies. *Journal of Sport and Tourism*, **16**(4), pp. 285–302.

Diem, C. (1912) *Die Olympischen Spiele 1912*. Berlin: Ausgabe.

Diem, C. (1942) *Olympische Flamme: Das Buch vom Sport*. Berlin: Deutscher Archiv.

Dinnie, K. (2011) *City Branding: Theory and Cases*. Basingstoke: Palgrave.

Dolzan, M. (2015) Apesar de matriz incompleta, prazo será cumprido, diz Paes. *Exame*, 28 January. Available at: http://exame.abril.com.br/brasil/noticias/apesar-de-matriz-incompleta-prazo-sera-cumprido-diz-paes.

Dong, J. (2005) Women, nationalism and the Beijing Olympics: preparing for glory. *International Journal of the History of Sport*, **22**, pp. 530–544.

Dong, L. (1985) Beijing: the development of a socialist capital, in Sit, V.F.S. (ed.) *Chinese Cities*. Oxford: Oxford University Press, pp. 67–93.

Dost, S. (2003) *Das Olympische Dorf 1936 im Wandel der Zeit*. Berlin: Neddermeyer Verlag.

Drees, L. (1968) *Olympia: Gods, Artists, Athletes* (trans. G. Onn). London: Pall Mall Press.

Dubi, C. (2014) IOC statement from Christophe Dubi, IOC Executive Director of the Olympic Games. *Press Release*, 1 October. Lausanne: International Olympic Committee.

Dubi, C. and Felli, G. (2006) Measuring global impact. *Olympic Review*, June. Available at: http://www.olympic.org/Documents/Reports/EN/en_report_1077.pdf,

Dubin, M.S., Ellingham, M., Fisher, J. and Jansz, N. (2004) *The Rough Guide to Greece*. London: Rough Guides.

Duran, P. (2005) The impact of the Olympic Games on tourism. Barcelona: the legacy of the Games 1992–2002, in Urdangarin, I. and Torres, D. (eds.) *New Views on Sport Tourism*. Mallorca: Calliope Publishing, pp. 77–91.

Eckert, R. and Schäche, W. (1992) *Zu Geschichte und Bestand des ehemaligen Reichssportfeldes in Berlin-Charlottenburg: Expertise im Auftrag der Senatsverwaltung für Stadtentwicklung und Umweltschutz*. Berlin.

ECMT (2003) *Transport and Exceptional Public Events* (Roundtable 122). Paris: OECD Publications Service.

Edizel, O. (2014) Governance of Sustainable Event-led Regeneration: The Case of London 2012 Olympics. Unpublished PhD thesis, Brunel University, London.

Edizel, O., Evans, G. and Dong, H. (2013) Dressing up London, in Girginov, V. (ed.) *Handbook of the London2012 Olympic and Paralympic Games*, Vol. 2. London: Routledge, pp. 19–35.

Engel, S. (2012) Abandoned Olympic Cathedrals sit rotting in Beijing. Available at: http://www.bloomberg.com/news/videos/b/4b8bdf6c-52c0-4cf8-a334-46429da2413c.

Endter-Wada, J., Kurtzman, J., Butkus, M., Blahna, D., Klien, C., Burr, S.W., Gibbons, D. and Reiter, D. (2003). Long-range transportation planning in Utah: summary of research results from interviews and focus groups, in *Final Report from Phase II of the 2003 Utah Department of Transportation (UDOT) Benchmark Study*. Salt Lake City: Utah Department of Transportation.

Esparza, L.E. and Price, R. (2015) Convergence repertoires: anti-capitalist protest at the 2010 Vancouver Winter Olympics. *Contemporary Justice Review: Issues in Criminal, Social and Restorative Justice*, **18**(1), pp. 22–41.

Espy, R. (1979) *The Politics of the Olympic Games*. Berkeley, CA: University of California Press.

Essex, S. and Chalkley, B. (1998) Olympic Games: catalyst of urban change. *Leisure Studies*, **17**(3), pp. 187–206.

Essex, S. and Chalkley, B. (2002) Il ruolo dei Giochi Olimpici nella trasformazione urbana, in Bobbio, L. and Guala, C. (eds.) *Olimpiadi e Grandi Eventi*. Rome: Carocci, pp. 57–76.

Essex, S. and Chalkley, B. (2004) Mega-sporting events in urban and regional policy: a history of the winter Olympics. *Planning Perspectives*, **19**, pp. 201–232.

Esteban, J. (1999) *El Projecte Urbanístic: valorar la perifèria i recuperar el centre*. Barcelona: Aula Barcelona.

Evans, G.L. (1996a) Planning for the British Millennium Festival: establishing the visitor baseline and a framework for forecasting. *Journal of Festival Management and Event Tourism*, **3**, pp. 183–196.

Evans, G.L (1996b) The Millennium Festival and urban regeneration: planning, politics and the party, in Robinson, M. and Evans, N. (eds.) *Managing Cultural Resources*. Newcastle: Business Education Publishers, pp. 79–98.

Evans, G.L. (1999) Last chance lottery and the Millennium City, in Whannel, G. and Foley, M. (eds.) *Leisure, Culture and Commerce: Consumption and Participation*, Publication 64. Eastbourne: Leisure Studies Association, pp. 3–22.

Evans, G. (2007) London 2012, in Gold, J.R. and Gold, M.M. (eds.) *Olympic Cities: City Agendas, Planning and the World's Games 1896–2012*, 2nd ed. London: Routledge, pp. 298–317.

Evans, G. (2010) London 2012, in Gold, J.R. and Gold, M.M. (eds.) *Olympic Cities: City Agendas, Planning and the World's Games 1896–2016*, 2nd ed. London: Routledge, pp. 359–389.

Evans, G.L. (2015) Designing legacy and the legacy of design: London 2012 and the regeneration games. *Architectural Review Quarterly*, **18**(4), pp. 353–366.

Evans, G.L. and Shaw, S. (2001) Urban leisure and transport: regeneration effects. *Journal of Leisure Property*, **1**(4), pp. 350–372.

Evans S.J. (2014) The new ruins of Athens: rusting and decaying 10 years on, how Greece's Olympics turned into a £7 billion white elephant. *Daily Mail*, 13 August. Available at: http://www.dailymail.co.uk/news/article-2723515/Athens-Olympics-leave-mixed-legacy-10-years-later.html.

Facaros, D. and Theodorou, L. (2005) *Athens and Southern Greece*, Cadogan Guides 84. Guildford: Globe Pequot Press.

Fahey, M.R. (2009) China, world affairs China, in *Britannica Book of the Year: Events of 2008*. Chicago, IL: Encyclopaedia Britannica, pp. 383–386.

Falk, N. (2003) Urban renaissance: lessons from Turin. *Town and Country Planning*, **72**(7), pp. 213–215.

Farrelly, E. (2012) Putting the home into Homebush. *Sydney Morning Herald*, 5 February, p. 5.

Faulhaber, L. and Azevedo, L. (2015) *SMH2015: Remoções no Rio de Janeiro Olímpico*. Rio de Janeiro: Mórula.

FAZ (Frankfurter Allgemaine Zeitung) (2011) *NBC buys a Vierer–Paket*. Available at: http://www.faz.net/frankfurter-allgemeine-zeitung/sport/nbc-kauft-ein-vierer-paket-1651654.html.

FCO (Foreign and Commonwealth Office) (2011) *Brazil: Rio 2016 Olympics – Sport Security*. Rio de Janeiro: British Consulate General.

Fellmann, B. (1973) The history of excavations at Olympia. *Olympic Review*, 64/65, pp. 109–118, 162. Available at: http://library.la84.org/OlympicInformationCenter/OlympicReview/1973/ore64/ore64f.pdf.

Fernandes, A. (2015) Paes diz que 'vai deixar Barcelona-1992 no chinelo'. *Estadão*, 26 May. Available at: http://esportes.estadao.com.br/noticias/geral,paes-diz-que-rio-2016-vai-deixar-barcelona-1992-no-chinelo,1694328.

Fernández Contreras, R.A. (2008) The route of friendship: a testimony to Mexico City's aesthetic modernity. *Voices of Mexico*, **82**, pp. 34–43.

Finn, P. (2008) Putin directs organisers of 2014 Winter Olympics to protect wilderness. *The Washington Post*, 3 July. Available at: http://www.washingtonpost.com/wp-dyn/content/article/2008/07/03/AR2008070301912.html.

FIPE ZAP (2015) *Índice FIPE ZAP de Preços de Imóveis Anunciados*. Available at: http://www.zap.com.br/imoveis/fipe-zap-b/.

Fluid (2003) *London's Bid for the 2012 Olympic Games. Have Your Say*. London: Fluid/Lower Lea Valley Team.

Flyvbjerg, B., Bruzelius, N. and Rothengatter, W. (2003) *Megaprojects and Risk: An Anatomy of Ambition*. Cambridge: Cambridge University Press.

Flyvbjerg, B. and Stewart, A. (2012) *Olympic Proportions: Cost and Cost Overrun at the Olympics 1960–2012*. Working Papers 3.3, Said Business School, University of Oxford.

França, R. (2015) Transcarioca completa 1 ano com altos e baixos, transportando 230 mil passageiros por dia. *O Globo*, 24 May. Available at: http://oglobo.globo.com/rio/transcarioca-completa-1-ano-com-altos-baixos-transportando-230-mil-passageiros-por-dia-16247236.

Freeman, J. (2012) Neoliberal accumulation strategies and the visible hand of police pacification in Rio de Janeiro. *Revista de Estudos Universitários*, **38**(1), pp. 95–126.

Freeman, J. (2014) Raising the flag over Rio de Janeiro's favelas: citizenship and social control in the Olympic city. *Journal of Latin American Geography*, **13**(1), pp. 7–38.

Freeman, R.E. and McVea, J. (2001) A stakeholder approach to strategic management, in Hitt, M.A., Freeman, R.E. and Harrison, J.S. (eds.) *The Blackwell Handbook of Strategic Management*. Oxford: Blackwell, pp. 189–207.

French, S.P. and Disher, M.E. (1997) Atlanta and the Olympics, a one-year retrospective. *Journal of the American Planning Association*, **63**(3), pp. 379–392.

Friedman, J. (2005) *China's Urban Transition*. Minneapolis, MN: University of Minnesota Press.

Fujimaki, N. (1997) Introducing the ITS project for Nagano Olympic Winter Games in Japan. *Mobility for Everyone*. 4th World Congress on Intelligent Transport Systems, Berlin, pp. 1–8.

Fulcher, M. (2012) Japan's national stadium shortlist announced. *Architects' Journal*, **236**(16), pp. 16–17.

Fussey, P., Coaffee, J., Armstrong, G. and Hobbs, R. (2011) *Sustaining and Securing the Olympic City: Reconfiguring London for 2012 and Beyond*. Farnham: Ashgate.

Gaffney, C. (2010) Mega-events and socio-spatial dynamics in Rio de Janeiro, 1919–2016. *Journal of Latin American Geography*, **9**(1), pp. 7–29.

GameBids (2006) Review of Olympic Bid news and information. Available at: http://www.gamesbids.com/english/index.shtml.

GameBids (2009) Supreme Court rejects environmentalists appeal of Sochi 2014, 21 March, 2007. Available at: www.gamesbid.com/eng/other_news/1174503225.html.

Gao, X. (2001) All about the Olympic Park. *China Internet Information Centre*, 15 April. Available at: www.china.org.cn/english/11125.htm.

García, B. (2000) Comparative analysis of the Olympic cultural program, design and management of Barcelona'92 and Sydney 2000, in Wamsley, K.B., Martyn, S.G., MacDonald, G.H. and Barney, R.K. (eds.) *5th International Symposium for Olympic Research*. London, Ontario: International Centre for Olympic Studies, University of Western Ontario, pp. 153–158.

García, B. (2001) Enhancing sports marketing through cultural and arts programmes: lessons from the Sydney 2000 Olympic Arts Festivals. *Sport Management Review*, **4**, pp. 193–220.

García, B. (2004) Urban regeneration, arts programming and major events: Glasgow 1990, Sydney 2000 and Barcelona 2004. *International Journal of Cultural Policy*, **10**, pp. 103–118.

García, B. (2011) Sydney 2000, in Gold, J.R. and Gold, M.M. (eds.) *Olympic Cities: City Agendas, Planning and the World Games, 1896–2016*. London: Routledge, pp. 287–314.

García, B. (2012) *The Olympic Games and Cultural Policy*. London: Routledge.

García, B. (2013a) The London 2012 Cultural Olympiad and torch relay, in Girginov, V. (ed.) *Handbook of the London 2012 Olympic and Paralympic Games. Vol 1: Making the Games*. London: Routledge, pp. 199–214.

García, B. (2013b) *London 2012 Cultural Olympiad Evaluation*. Liverpool: The Institute of Cultural Capital, the University of Liverpool and Liverpool John Moores University.

García, B. (2015) Placing culture at the heart of the Games: achievements and challenges within the London 2012 Cultural Olympiad, in Poynter, G., Viehoff, V. and Li, Y. (eds.) *The London Olympics and Urban Development: The Mega-Event City*. London: Routledge, pp. 255–270.

García, B. and Cox, T. (2013) *London 2012 Cultural Olympiad Evaluation*. London: Arts Council England.

García, B., Cox, T., Allam, M., Campbell, P., Cogliandro, G., Crone, S., Langen, F., O'Brien, D. and Ortega Nuere, C. (2013) *European Capitals of Culture: success strategies and long-term effects*. Strasbourg: European Parliament.

García, B. and Miah, A. (2007) Ever decreasing circles? The profile of culture at the Olympics. *Culture @ the Olympics*, **9**(2), pp. 10–13.

Garcia, P. (1993) Barcelona and the Olympic Games, in Häussermann, H. and Birklhuber, D. (eds.) *Festivalisation of Urban Policies. Urban Development through Large-Scale Projects*. Opladen: Westdeutscher Verlag, pp. 251–277.

Garst, W.D. (2015) Encourage super-rich to be more charitable. *China Daily*, 23 June. Available at: http://usachinadaily.com.cn/opinion/2015-06/23/content_21075607.htm.

Gartner, W.C. and Shen, J. (1992) The impact of Tiananmen Square on China's tourism image. *Journal of Travel Research*, **30**(4), pp.47–52.

Geipel, R., Helbrecht, I. and Pohl, J. (1993) Die Münchener Olympischen Spiele von 1972 als Instrument der Stadtentwicklungspolitik (The Munich Olympic Games in 1972 as an instrument of urban policy), in Häussermann, H. and. Siebel, W. (eds.) *Die Politik der Festivalisierung und die Festivalisierung der Politik: Große Ereignisse in der Stadtpolitik*. Wiesbaden: Verlag für Sozialwissenschaften, pp. 278–304.

Georgiardis, K. (2000) *Die ideengeschichtliche Grundlage der Erneuerung der Olympischen Spiele im 19. Jahrhundert in Griechenland und ihre Umsetzung 1896 in Athen* (The Intellectual-Historical Foundations of the Revival of the Olympic Games in the Nineteenth Century in Greece and their 1896 Transplantation into Athens). PhD Dissertation. Kassel: Agon-Sportverlag.

Getz, D. (2009) Policy for sustainable and responsible festivals and events: institutionalization of a new paradigm. *Journal of Policy Research in Tourism, Leisure and Events*, **1**(1), pp. 61–78.

Gibson, O. (2009*a*) Tearful Pele and weeping Lula greet historic win for Rio. *The Guardian*, 3 October, pp. 2–3.

Gibson, O. (2009*b*) London's tenacious campaigner Lee makes it back-to-back triumphs in the complexities of bidding, *The Guardian*, Sport section, 3 October, pp. 8–9.

Gibson, O. (2013*a*) Japanese bid's passion earns Tokyo the 2020 Olympic Games. *The Guardian*, 7 September. Available at: http://www.theguardian.com/sport/2013/sep/07/tokyo-2020-olympic-games.

Gibson, O. (2013*b*) Race to host 2020 Olympics intensifies for Tokyo, Madrid and Istanbul, *The Guardian*, 7 January. Available at: http://www.theguardian.com/sport/2013/jan/07/2020-olympics-tokyo-madrid-istanbul.

Gibson, O. (2013*c*) Tokyo wins race to host 2020 Olympic Games. *Observer*, 7 September. Available at: http://www.theguardian.com/sport/2013/sep/07/tokyo-host-2020-olympic-games.

Gilbert, K. and Schantz, O.J. (eds.) (2009) *The Paralympic Games: Empowerment or Side Show?* Aachen: Meyer and Meyer.

Gilbert, K. and Schantz, O.J. (2015) Paralympic legacy: what legacy? in Holt, R. and Ruta, D. (eds.) *The Routledge Handbook of Sport and Legacy: Meeting the Challenge of Major Sports Events*. London: Routledge, pp. 161–75.

Giniger, H. (1968*a*) Mexicans rushing Olympics' complex. *New York Times*, 21 July, V, p. 5.

Giniger, H. (1968*b*) Olympic building is behind schedule. *New York Times*, 8 September, V, p. 10.

GLA (Greater London Authority) (2004) *The London Plan: Spatial Development Strategy for Greater London*. London: GLA. Available at: https://www.london.gov.uk/sites/default/files/the_london_plan_2004.pdf.

GLA (2012) *Olympic Legacy Supplementary Planning Guidance*. London: GLA.

Gleeson, B. (2001) Disability and the open city. *Urban Studies*, **38**, pp. 251–265.

Goeritz, M. (1970) 'The Route of Friendship': Sculpture. *Leonardo*, **3**(4), pp. 397–407.

Gold, J.R. (2012) A SPUR to action: the Society for the Promotion of Urban Renewal, 'anti-scatter' and the crisis of reconstruction. *Planning Perspectives*, **27**(2), pp. 199–223.

Gold, J.R. and Gold, M.M. (2005) *Cities of Culture: Staging International Festivals and the Urban Agenda, 1851–2000*. Aldershot: Ashgate.

Gold, J.R. and Gold, M.M. (2007) Access for all: the rise of the Paralympics within the Olympic movement. *Journal of the Royal Society for the Promotion of Health*, **127**(3), pp. 133–141.

Gold, J.R. and Gold, M.M. (2008) Olympic cities: regeneration, city rebranding and changing urban agendas. *Geography Compass*, **2**, pp. 300–318.

Gold, J.R. and Gold, M.M. (2009) Future indefinite? London 2012, the spectre of retrenchment and the challenge of Olympic sports legacy. *London Journal*, **34**, pp.180–197.

Gold, J.R. and Gold, M.M. (2010) *Olympic Cities: City Agendas, Planning and the World's Games, 1896–2016*, 2nd ed. London: Routledge, pp. 1–13.

Gold, J.R. and Gold, M.M. (2011) The history of events: ideology and historiography, in Page, S. and Connell, J. (eds.) *Routledge Handbook of Event Studies*. London: Routledge, pp. 119–28.

Gold, J.R. and Gold, M.M. (eds.) (2012) *The Making of Olympic Cities*, 4 vols. London: Routledge.

Gold, J.R. and Gold, M.M. (2013) 'Bring it under the legacy umbrella': Olympic host cities and the changing fortunes of the sustainability agenda. *Sustainability*, **5**(8), pp. 3526–3542.

Gold, J.R. and Gold, M.M. (2014) Legacy, sustainability and Olympism: crafting urban outcomes at London 2012. *Revue Internationale des Sciences du Sport et de L'Éducation*, **37**(105), pp. 23–35.

Gold, J.R. and Gold, M.M. (2015) Framing the future: sustainability, legacy and the 2012 London Games, in Holt, R. and Ruta, D. (eds.) *The Routledge Handbook of Sport and Legacy: Meeting the Challenge of Major Sports Events*. London: Routledge, pp. 142–158.

Gold, J.R. and Gold, M.M. (2016) Beyond the event: World's Fairs, the Olympic Games and spaces of urban transformation, in Hein, C. (ed.) *Handbook on Planning History*. London: Routledge (in press).

Gold, J.R. and Gold, M.M. (2017) Olympic futures and urban imaginings: from Albertopolis to Olympicopolis, in Hannigan, J. and Richards, G. (eds.) *The Handbook of New Urban Studies*. London: Sage (in press).

Gold, J.R. and Revill, G. (2003) Exploring landscapes of fear: marginality, spectacle and surveillance. *Capital and Class*, **80**, pp. 27–50.

Gold, J.R. and Revill, G.E. (2006) Gathering the voices of the people? Cecil Sharp, cultural hybridity and the folk music of Appalachia. *GeoJournal*, **63**, pp. 55–66.

Gold, M. and Revill, G. (2007) The Cultural Olympiads: reviving the panegyris, in Gold, J.R. and Gold, M.M. (eds.) *Olympic Cities: City Agendas, Planning and the World's Games, 1896–2012*. London: Routledge, pp. 59–83.

Goldstein, E.S. (1996) Amsterdam: the Games of the 9th Olympiad, in Findling, J.E and Pelle, K.D. (eds.) *Historical Dictionary of the Modern Olympic Movement*. Westport, CN: Greenwood Press, pp. 68–83.

González, M.J. and González, A.L. (2015) Strategic planning and change management. Examples of Barcelona, Seville and Saragossa (Spain). *Bulletin of Geography: Socio-economic Series*, **29**(29), pp. 47–64.

Good, D. (1998) *The Olympic Games' Cultural Olympiad: Identity and Management*. Washington DC: Faculty of the College of Arts and Sciences, American University.

Goodman, S. (1986) *Spirit of Stoke Mandeville: The Story of Sir Ludwig Guttmann*. London: Collins.

Gordon, B.F. (1983) *Olympic Architecture: Building for the Summer Games*. New York: John Wiley.

Gordon, H. (2003) *The Time Of Our Lives: Inside the Sydney Olympics*. Brisbane: University of Queensland Press.

Graham, J., Gilbert, B., Minton, A., Perryman, M., Poynter, G. and Westall, C. (2013) Revisiting the Olympic legacy. *Soundings*, **53**, pp. 82–92.

Graham, S. (2010) *Cities Under Siege: The New Military Urbanism*. London: Verso.

Grant Thornton, Ecorys, Loughborough University, Oxford Economics and Future Inclusion (2013) *Report 5: Post-Games Evaluation, Meta-Evaluation of the Impacts and Legacy of the London 2012 Olympic Games and Paralympic Games*. East London Evidence Base. London: DCMS.

Grey-Thompson, T. (2006) The Olympic Generation: How the 2012 Olympics and Paralympics can create the Difference. Inaugural Lecture, Staffordshire University, 26 October. Available at: http://www.staffs.ac.uk/news/article/dame_tanni.php.

Grohmann, K. (2013) Munich 2022 Games bid ruled out by referendum loss. Reuters, 10 November. Available at: http://www.reuters.com/article/us-olympics-munich-idUSBRE9A90FH20131110.

Grohmann, K. (2015) Hamburg beats Berlin to become Germany's 2024 Games bid. Available at: http://www.reuters.com/article/us-olympics-2024-germany-idUSKBN0MC23E20150316.

Gruneau, R. and Horne, J. (eds.) (2016) *Mega-Events and Globalization: Capital and Spectacle in a Changing World Order*. London: Routledge.

Gu, C. and Cook, I.G. (2011) Beijing: socialist capital and new world city, in Hamnett, S. and Forbes, D. (eds.) *Planning Asian Cities: Risks and Resilience*. London: Routledge, pp. 90–130.

Guerra, M. (2015) A 14 meses para o Rio 2016, principal legado esportivo tem futuro incerto. *Globo Esporte*, 26 May. Available at: http://globoesporte.globo.com/olimpiadas/noticia/2015/05/14-meses-par-ao-rio-2016-principal-legado-esportivo-tem-futuro-incerto.html.

Guoqi, X. (2008) *Olympic Dreams: China and Sports, 1895–2008*. Cambridge, MA: Harvard University Press.

Guttmann, A. (1984) *The Games Must Go On*. New York: Columbia University Press.

Guttmann, A. (2002) *The Olympics: A History of the Modern Games*, 2nd ed. Urbana, IL: University of Illinois Press.

Guttmann, L. (1976) *Textbook of Sport for the Disabled*. Aylesbury: H.M. & M. Publishers.

Halifax plc (2004) Houses go for Gold in Olympic Host Cities. Press Release, 18 October.

Hall, C.M. (1992) *Hallmark Tourist Events: Impacts, Management and Planning*. London: Belhaven.

Hall, P. (1980) *Great Planning Disasters*. London: Weidenfeld and Nicolson.

Hall, T. and Hubbard, P. (eds.) (1998) *The Entrepreneurial City: Geographies of Politics, Regime and Representation*. Chichester: John Wiley.

Hamilos, P. (2013) 2020 Olympics: Madrid disappointed for third time. *The Guardian*, 8 September. Available at: http://www.theguardian.com/sport/2013/sep/08/madrid-2020-olympics-disappointment.

Hampton, J. (2008) *The Austerity Olympics*. London: Aurum Press.

Hanna, M. (1999) *Reconciliation in Olympism: The Sydney 2000 Olympic Games and Australia's Indigenous People*. Sydney: Walla Walla Press.

Hargreaves, J. (2000) *Freedom for Catalonia? Catalan Nationalism, Spanish Identity and the Barcelona Olympic Games*. Cambridge: Cambridge University Press.

Harlan, H.V. (1931) *History of Olympic Games: Ancient and Modern*. Topanga, CA: Athletic Research Bureau.

Harskamp, M. van (2006) Lost in translation. *Rising East*, No. 3, January. Available at: www.uel.ac.uk/risingeast/currentissue/essays/vanharkskamp.htm.

Hart Davis, D. (1986) *Hitler's Games: The 1936 Olympics*. London: Century.

Hawken, S. (2014) Sydney Olympic Park 2030: the city in a park. *Landscape Architecture Australia*, **141**, pp. 21–22.

Hawthorne, F.H. and Price, R. (2001) *The Soulless Stadium: A Memoir of London's White City*. Upminster: 3–2 Books.

Hayes, G. and Horne, J. (2011) Sustainable development, shock and awe? London 2012 and civil society. *Sociology*, **45**(5), pp. 749–764.

Haynes, J. (2001) *Socio-Economic Impact of the Sydney 2000 Olympic Games*. Lucerne: Olympic Studies Centre/Universitat Autònoma de Barcelona.

HCCPA (House of Commons Committee of Public Accounts) (2008) *The Budget for the London 2012 Olympic and Paralympic Games*. London: Stationery Office.

He, G. (ed.) (2008) *Olympic Architecture: Beijing 2008*. Basle: Birkhäuser.

Heck, S. (2014) William Penny Brookes – the founding father of the modern pentathlon? *Sport in History*, **34**(1), pp. 75–89.

Hellenikon, S.A. (2016) *The Company Vision*. Available at: http://www.hellinikon.com/en/the-company/vision.

Hemphill, L., McGreal, S. and Berry, J. (2004) An indicator-based approach to measuring sustainable urban regeneration performance: part 2, empirical evaluation and case-study analysis. *Urban Studies*, **41**(4), pp. 757–772.

Hendy, P. (2012) Transport planning for an Olympic Games. *Journal of Urban Regeneration and Renewal*, **5**, 330–345.

Hensher, D. and Brewer, A. (2002) Going for gold at the Sydney Olympics: how did transport perform? *Transport Reviews*, **22**, pp. 381–399.

Hersh, P. (2008) Testament to progress atrophies after Games. Athens Olympic venues suffer from lack of long-range planning. Chicago should take note. *Chicago Tribune*, 5 August. Available at: http://articles.chicagotribune.com/2008-08-05/news/0808050075_1_athens-olympic-velodrome-oaka/2.

Higgins, D. (2009) What the Victorians did for Us – Invention, Industrialisation and the Here and Now on the Olympic Park. Paper presented to the New London Architecture Conference 'London 2012: Raising the Bar for London's Future Development'.

Hill, C.R. (1992, 1996) *Olympics Politics: Athens to Atlanta, 1896–1996*. Manchester: Manchester University Press.

Hillenbrand, L. (2014) *Unbroken: A World War II Story of Survival, Resilience, and Redemption*. London: Random House.

Hiller, H.H. (1990) The urban transformation of a landmark event: the 1988 Calgary Winter Olympics. *Urban Affairs Quarterly*, **26**, pp. 118–137.

Hiller, H. and Moylan, D. (1999) Mega-events and community obsolescence: redevelopment versus rehabilitation in Victoria Park East. *Canadian Journal of Urban Research*, **8**, pp. 47–81.

HM Government (Her Majesty's Government/Mayor of London) (2011) *CONTEST: The United Kingdom Strategy for Countering Terrorism*. London: The Stationery Office. Available at: http://www.homeoffice.gov.uk/counter-terrorism/.

HMG/ML (Her Majesty's Government/Mayor of London) (2013) *Inspired by 2012: The Legacy from the Olympic and Paralympic Games*. London: Cabinet Office.

HMG/ML (2015) *Inspired by 2012: The Legacy from the Olympic and Paralympic Games. Third Annual Report – Summer 2015*. London: Cabinet Office.

Hoberman, J. (1986) *The Olympic Crisis, Sport, Politics and the Moral Order*. New Rochelle, NY: Caratzas Publishing.

Hobhouse, H. (2002) *The Crystal Palace and the Great Exhibition, Art, Science and Productive Industry: A History of the Royal Commission for the Exhibition of 1851*. London: Athlone Press.

Hoffmann, H. (1993) *Mythos Olympia: Autonomie und Unterwerfung von Sport und Kultur*. Berlin: Aufbau-Verlag.

Hofstadter, D. (ed.) (1974) *Mexico 1946–73*. New York: Facts on File.

Holden, M., MacKenzie, J. and VanWynsberghe, R. (2008) Vancouver's promise of the world's first sustainable Olympic Games. *Environment and Planning C*, **26**(5), pp. 882–905.

Holt, R. and Mason, T. (2000) *Sport in Britain, 1945–2000*. Oxford: Blackwell.

Home Office (2011) *London 2012: Olympic and Paralympic Safety and Security Strategy*. London: The Stationery Office. Available at: http://www.london2012.com/documents/oda-industry-days/oda-security-industry-day-presentation.pdf.

HOOWI (Herausgegeben vom Organisationskomitee der IX Olympischen Winterspiele in Innsbruck) (1967) *Offizieller Bericht der IX Olympischen Winterspiele Innsbruck 1964*. Vienna: Österreichischer Bundesverlag für Unterricht, Wissenschaft und Kunst.

HOP (Hellenic Olympic Properties SA) (2006) Hellenic Olympic Properties: Public Real Estate & Sustainable Commercial Development. Available at: http://www.olympicproperties.gr/.

Hope, K. (1990) A chance to save Athens. *Financial Times*, 27 February.

Hornbuckle, A.R. (1996) Helsinki 1952: the Games of the 15th Olympiad, in Findling, J.E. and Pelle, K.D. (eds.) *Historical Dictionary of the Modern Olympic Movement*. Westport, CN: Greenwood Press, pp. 109–118.

Host Boroughs (2011) *Convergence Framework and Action Plan 2011–2015*. London: Host Boroughs.

Howe, P.D. (2008) *The Cultural Politics of the Paralympic Movement through an Anthropological Lens*. London: Routledge.

Howell, R.A. and Howell, M.L. (1996) Paris 1900: the Games of the 2nd Olympiad, in Findling, J.E. and Pelle, K.D. (eds.) *Historical Dictionary of the Modern Olympic Movement*. Wesport, CT: Greenwood Press, pp. 157–162.

HRADF (Hellenic Republic Asset Development Fund) (2016) *The Fund*. Available at: http://www.hradf.com/en/the-fund/mission.

HRGSMC (Hellenic Republic General Secretariat for Media and Communications) (2015) Greece: dealing with the refugee crisis. Available at: http://www.mfa.gr/missionsabroad/images/stories/missions/geneva-pm/docs/factsheet.pdf.

Hughes, R. (1996) *Barcelona*. New York: Alfred A. Knopf.

Huntington, S.P. (1996) *Kampf der Kulturen. Die Neugestaltung der Weltpolitik im 21. Jahrhundert*. Munich: Europa Verlag.

IAAF (International Association of Athletics Federations) (2005) The International Museum of Athletics is born. Press Release, 23 June. Available at: http://www.iaaf.org/news/kind=101/newsid=29896.html.

Ieromonachou, P., Warren, J. and Potter, S. (2010) The Olympic transport legacy. *Town and Country Planning*, **79**(7), pp. 331–336.

Ilha Pura (1997) *Report of the IOC Evaluation Commission for the Games of the XXVIII Olympiad in 2004*. Lausanne: IOC.

Ilha Pura (2004) *Games of the XXX Olympiad in 2012 – Report by the IOC Candidature Acceptance Working Group to the IOC Executive Board*. Lausanne: IOC.

Ilha Pura (2015) *Meu lugar*. Available at: http://ilhapura.com.br/meu-lugar/.

Imrie, R. (1996) *Disability and the City: International Perspectives*. London: Sage.

Inside the Games (2012) Rio 2016 Olympics will leave legacy of safety and security says city police chief, 15 March. Available at: http://www.insidethegames.biz/olympics/summer-olympics/2016/16233-rio-2016-olympics-will-leave-legacy-of-safety-and-security-says-city-police-chief.

International Business Times (2012) London Olympics 2012: brand police on patrol to enforce sponsors' exclusive rights. 16 July. Available at: http://www.ibtimes.co.uk/london-2012-olympics-banned-words-advertising-gold-363429.

International Tibet Network (2008) The Tibet freedom torch. Available at: http://tibetnetwork.org/beijing-olympics/.

Invictus Foundation (2016) *The Invictus Games Foundation*. Available at: https://invictusgamesfoundation.org/foundation.

Ioannou, T. (2014) Panathinaikos Stadium to be upgraded. *The Times of Change*, 29 April. Available at: http://www.thetoc.gr/eng/news/article/panathinaikos-stadium-upgraded.

IOC (International Olympic Committee) (1949) *44th IOC Session, Rome*. Lausanne: IOC.

IOC (1978) *Agreement between IOC and the City of Los Angeles*. Typescript, 27 October.

IOC (1997a) *Memorias Olimpicas, por Pierre de Coubertin*. Lausanne: IOC.

IOC (1997b) *Report of the IOC Evaluation Commission for the Games of the XXVIII Olympiad in 2004*. Lausanne: IOC.

IOC (1999a) Final Recommendations for IOC Reform Published. Press release, 24 November. Lausanne: IOC.

IOC (1999b) *IOC Crisis and Reform Chronology*. Lausanne: IOC.

IOC (2000) IOC and IPC Sign Cooperation Agreement. Press release, 20 October, Lausanne: IOC.

IOC (2001) IOC and IPC Sign Agreement on the Organisation of the Paralympic Games. Press release, 10 June. Lausanne: IOC.

IOC (2001–2013) *Host City Election Documents*. Lausanne: IOC.

IOC (2003a) *Host City contract for the XXI Olympic Winter Games in the Year 2010*. Lausanne: IOC.

IOC (2003b) *Olympic Games Study Commission: Report to the 115th IOC Session, Prague, July, 2003*. Lausanne: IOC.

IOC (2003c) *The Legacy of the Olympic Games 1984–2000: Conclusions and Recommendations*. Available at: http://multimedia.olympic.org/pdf/en_report_635pdf.

IOC (2004a) *2012 Candidature Procedure and Questionnaire: Games of the XXX Olympiad in 2012*. Lausanne: IOC.

IOC (2004b) *Games of the XXX Olympiad in 2012 – Report by the IOC Candidature Acceptance Working Group to the IOC Executive Board*. Lausanne: IOC.

IOC (2004c) *The Olympic Charter*. Lausanne: IOC.

IOC (2005) *Technical Manual on Olympic Village*. Available at: http://www.gamesmonitor.org.uk/files/Technical_Manual_on_Olympic_Village.pdf.

IOC (2006) *Olympic Movement's Agenda 21: Sport for Sustainable Development*. Lausanne: IOC. Available at: http://www.olympic.org/Documents/Reports/EN/en_report_300.pdf.

IOC (2007) *IOC 2014 Evaluation Committee Report for XXII Olympic Winter Games in 2014*. Lausanne: IOC.

IOC (2008a) *2016 Candidature Procedure and Questionnaire: Games of the XXXI Olympiad*. Lausanne: IOC.

IOC (2008b) *Games of the XXXI Olympiad 2016 Working Group Report*. Lausanne: IOC.

IOC (2009) *The Olympic Movement in Society. IOC Final Report 2005–2008*. Lausanne: IOC.

IOC (2011) *The Olympic Charter*. Lausanne: IOC.

IOC (2012) *Olympic Marketing Fact File*. Available at: http://www.olympic.org/Documents/IOC_Marketing/OLYMPIC-MARKETING-FACT-FILE-2012.pdf.

IOC (2013) Factsheet. London 2012 Facts and Figures. Update – July 2013. Lausanne: IOC.

IOC (2013a) *Candidature Acceptance Procedure: XXIV Olympic Winter Games*. Lausanne: IOC.

IOC (2013b) *Olympic Legacy 2013*. Lausanne: IOC.

IOC (2013c) *Technical Manual on Transport*. 6th update cycle – post London 2012 Olympic Games. Lausanne: IOC.

IOC (2014a) *Olympic Agenda 2020: 20+20 Recommendations*. Lausanne: IOC.

IOC (2014b) *Olympic Agenda 2020: Context and Background*. Lausanne: IOC.

IOC (2015a) Bidding for success: by invitation, *Olympic Review*, April–May–June, Number 95. Lausanne: IOC, pp. 31–33.

IOC (2015b) *Candidate process Olympic Games 2024*. Lausanne: IOC.

IOC (2015c) *Host City Contract Operational Requirements*. Lausanne: IOC.

IOC (2015d) *The Olympic Charter*. Lausanne: IOC.

IOC (2015e) *Olympic Winter Games*. Available at: http://www.olympic.org/uk/games/index_uk.asp.

IOC (2015f) *Report of the 2022 Evaluation Commission*. Lausanne: IOC.

IOC Olympic Studies Centre (various) *Archives: Documentation files*. Lausanne: IOC OSC.

IPC (International Paralympic Committee) (2005) *Annual Report 2004*. Bonn: IPC.

IPC (2006a) *About the IPC*. Bonn: IPC. Available at: http://www.paralympic.org/release/Main_Sections_Menu/IPC/About_the_IPC.

IPC (2006b) *Annual Report 2005*. Bonn: IPC.

IPC (2006c) *IPC Strategic Plan 2006–2009*. Bonn: IPC.

IPC (2008) New Russian law upholds Paralympic standards. Available at: http://www.paralympic.org/Media_Centre/News/General_News/2008_11_07_a.html.

IPC (2009) *Annual Report 2008*. Bonn: International Paralympic Committee. Available at: http://www.paralympic.org/export/sites/default/IPC/Reference_Documents/2009_05_Annual_Report_2008_web.pdf.

IPC (2012) IOC and IPC Extend Co-operation Agreement Until 2020, Media Centre 9 May. Available at: http://www.paralympic.org/news/ioc-and-ipc-extend-co-operation-agreement-until-2020.

IPC (2013) *Accessibility Guide: An Inclusive Approach to the Olympic and Paralympic Games*. Bonn: IPC.

IPC (2014) Media Centre NBC TV deal monumental for Paralympic Movement. IPC Media Centre. Available at: http://www.paralympic.org/video/nbc-tv-deal-monumental-paralympic-movement-tatyana-mcfadden-alana-nichols-angela-ruggiero.

IPC (2015a) *International Paralympic Committee Annual Report 2014*. Bonn: IPC.

IPC (2015b) New law hailed as a landmark in Brazil, Media Centre, 8 July 2015. Available at: http://www.paralympic.org/news/new-law-hailed-landmark-brazil.

IPC (2016) About Us. Available at: http://www.paralympic.org/the-ipc/about-us.

IPP (Instituto Pereira Passos) (2011) *População residente e estimada – Brasil, Estado do Rio de Janeiro e Regiões Administrativas do Município do Rio de Janeiro – 2000/2010/2013–2016/2020 (Tabela Nº 3261)*. Available at: http://portalgeo.rio.rj.gov.br/indice/flanali.asp?codpal=11&pal=DEMOGRAFIA.

IVC (Inter Vistas Consulting) (2002) *The Economic Impact of the 2010 Winter Olympic and Paralympic Games: An Update*. Vancouver: State Government of British Columbia.

Jäger, U. (1994) The Olympic Games in Munich 1972. Paper presented at the International Congress on Hosting the Olympic Games: The Physical Impacts – Environment, Urban Planning, Architecture and Technology, Paris.

Jefferys, K. (2014) *The British Olympic Association: A History*. Basingstoke: Palgrave Macmillan.

Jenkins, R. (2008) *The First London Olympics 1908*. London: Aurum Books.

Jennings, A. and Sambrook, C. (2000) *The Great Olympic Swindle: When the World wanted Its Games back*. London: Simon and Schuster.

Johnson, C. (1999) Planning the Olympic Site, in Bingham-Hall, P. (ed.) *Olympic Architecture: Building Sydney 2000*. Sydney: Watermark Press, pp. 36–45.

Johnson, C. (2005) Olympic ad director speaks of delight. *The Guardian*, 7 July.

Johnson, C. (2008) Introduction: new event horizon, in Hay, A. and Cashman, R. (eds.) *Connecting Cities: Mega Event Cities*. Sydney: Sydney Olympic Park Authority for Metropolis Congress.

Judge, L.W., Petersen, J. and Lydum, M. (2009) The best kept secret in sports: the 2010 Youth Olympic Games. *International Review for the Sociology of Sport*, **44**(2/3), pp. 173–191.

Karlaftis, M.G., Kepaptsoglou, K., Stathopoulos, A. and Starra, A. (2004) Planning Public Transport Networks for the 2004 Summer Olympics with Decision Support System. *Transportation Research Record*, No. 1887, pp. 71–82.

Kasimati, E. (2003) Economic aspects and the Summer Olympics: a review of related research. *International Journal of Tourism Research*, **5**(6), pp. 433–444.

Kassens-Noor, E. (2010*a*) Planning for Peak Demands in Transport Systems – An Agenda for Research, in *Selected Proceedings of the 12th World Conference on Transport Research*. Lisbon: World Conference on Transport Research Society.

Kassens-Noor, E. (2010*b*) Sustaining the momentum – the Olympics as potential catalysts for enhancing urban transport. *Transportation Research Record*, No. 2187, pp. 106–113.

Kassens-Noor, E. (2012) *Planning Olympic Legacies: Transport Dreams and Urban Realities*. London: Routledge.

Kassens-Noor, E. (2013*a*) Managing transport during the Olympic Games., in Frawley, S. and Adair, D. (eds.) *Managing the Olympics*. Sydney: Palgrave Macmillan.

Kassens-Noor, E. (2013*b*) The transport legacy of the Olympic Games, 1992–2012. *Journal of Urban Affairs* **35**, pp. 393–416.

Kearins, K. and Pavlovich, K. (2002) The role of stakeholders in Sydney's Green Games. *Corporate Social Responsibility and Environmental Management*, **9**, pp. 157–69.

Keogh, L. (2009) *London 2012 Olympic Legacies: Conceptualising Legacy, the Role of Communities and Local Government and the Regeneration of East London*. London: Department of Communities and Local Government.

Kerr, S. and Howe, P.D. (2015) What do we mean by Paralympic legacy? in Poynter, G., Viehoff, V. and Li, Y. (eds.) *The London Olympics and Urban Development: The Mega-Event City*. London: Routledge, pp. 193–204.

Kessel, C. (2001) *A vitrine e o espelho: o Rio de Janeiro de Carlos Sampaio*. Rio de Janeiro: PCRJ, Secretaria das Culturas, Departamento Geral de Documentação e Informação Cultural, Arquivo Geral da Cidade do Rio de Janeiro.

Kettle, M. (1999) Corruption probe spares Samaranch. *Guardian*, 2 March.

Kidd, B. (1996) Montreal 1976: the Games of the 21st Olympiad, in Findling, J.E. and Pelle, K.D. (eds.) *Historical Dictionary of the Modern Olympic Movement*. Westport, CN: Greenwood Press, pp. 153–160.

Killanin, Lord (1983) *My Olympic Years*. London: Secker and Warburg.

Kim, J. and Choe, S.-C. (1997) *Seoul: The Making of a Metropolis*. Chichester: John Wiley.

Kim, J.G., Rhee, S.W., Yu, J.C., Koo, K.M. and Hong, J.C. (1989) *Impact of the Seoul Olympic Games on National Development*. Seoul: Korea Development Institute.

Kimmorley, S. (2014) Sydney Olympic Park props up the NSW Economy 14 years after the Olympics. *Business Insider Australia*, 31 May.

Kissoudi, P. (2008) The Athens Olympics: optimistic legacies: post-Olympic assets and the struggle for their realization. *International Journal of the History of Sport*, **25**(14), pp. 1972–1990.

Klassen, L. (2012) Participatory art at the Vancouver 2010 Cultural Olympiad. *Public*, **23**(45), pp. 212–223.

Konchinski, V. (2014*a*) Obra de avenida olímpica derrubará 200 mil m² de Mata Atlântica no Rio. *UOL*, 15 April. Available at: http://esporte.uol.com.br/rio-2016/ultimas-noticias/2014/04/29/rj-corta-96-da-verba-olimpica-para-limpeza-da-baia-de-guanabara.htm.

Konchinski, V. (2014*b*) RJ corta 95% da verba olímpica para limpeza da Baía de Guanabara. *UOL*, 29 April. Available at: http://esporte.uol.com.br/rio-2016/ultimas-noticias/2014/04/29/rj-corta-96-da-verba-olimpica-para-limpeza-da-baia-de-guanabara.htm.

Konchinski, V. (2015) RJ prometeu 34 milhões de árvores para Rio-2016. Deve plantar 8 milhões. *UOL*, 22 May. Available at: http://olimpiadas.uol.com.br/noticias/2015/05/22/rj-prometeu-plantar-34-mi-de-arvores-para-rio-2016-deve-plantar-8-mi.htm.

Kotogiannis, D. and Hope, K. (2014) Greece's tourism bounces back – now for a move upmarket. *Financial Times*, 5 July. Available at: http://www.ft.com/cms/s/0/cda98386-fd41-11e3-bc93-00144feab7de.html#axzz3xVByLYL7.

Krauze, E. (1997) *Biography of Power: A History of Modern Mexico 1810–1996*. New York: Harper Collins.

Kurji, N. and Miska, E. (2011) Vancouver 2010 Olympic and Paralympic Winter Games: BC MoT Traffic Management. Conference and Exhibition of the Transportation Association of Canada, *Transportation Successes: Let's Build on Them*. Ottawa.

Kyriakopoulos, V. (2009) *Athens Encounter*. London: Lonely Planet.

Kyrieleis, H. (2003) The German excavations at Olympia: an introduction, in Phillips, D.J. and Pritchard, D. (eds.) *Sport and Festival in the Ancient Greek World*. Swansea: Classical Press of Wales, pp. 41–60.

Lamda Development (2016) Golden Hall – Shopping Centre Expansion, Athens. Available at: http://www.lamdadev.com/en/investment-portfolio/future-developments/golden-hall-shopping-center-expansion,-athens.html.

Landry, F. and Yerles, M. (1996) *The International Olympic Committee One Hundred Years, the Idea, the Presidents, the Achievements*. Lausanne: IOC.

Lane, P. (2006) The Paralympics 2012. Unpublished lecture, symposium on 'Profiling London', London Metropolitan University, 26 April.

LAOOC (Los Angeles Olympic Organizing Committee) (1985) *Official Report of the Games of the XXIInd Olympiad Los Angeles, 1984*. Los Angeles, CA: Los Angeles Olympic Organizing Committee.

Lappo, G., Chikishev, A. and Bekker, A. (1976) *Moscow, Capital of the Soviet Union: A Short Geographical Survey*. Moscow: Progress Publishers.

Larson, R. and Staley, T. (1998) Atlanta Olympics: the big story, in Thompson, P., Tolloczko, J.J.A. and Clarke, J.N. (eds.) *Stadia, Arenas and Grandstands: Design, Construction and Operation*. London: Spon, pp. 276–283.

Lauermann, J. (2015) Boston's Olympic bid and the evolving urban politics of event-led development. *Urban Geography*, published online 6 August. http://dx.doi.org/10.1080/02723638.2015.1072339.

Law, C.M. (1994) Manchester's bid for the Millennium Olympic Games. *Geography*, **79**, pp. 222–231.

LDA (London Development Agency) (2004) *Statement of Participation: Introduction – Context Document for the Lower Lea Valley Olympic and Legacy Planning Application*. London: London Development Agency.

LDA (2009) *2012 Games Legacy Impact Evaluation Study: Invitation to Tender*. London: Development Agency.

Leake, W.M. (1830) *Travels in the Morea*, 3 vols. London: John Murray.

Leary, M.E. and McCarthy, J. (2013) Introduction: urban regeneration, a global phenomenon, in Leary, M.E. and McCarthy, J. (eds.) *The Routledge Companion to Urban Regeneration*. London: Routledge, pp. 1–6.

Lee, C. (1988) From wartime rubble to Olympic host. *Far Eastern Economic Review*, **140**(36), pp. 60–65.

Lee, J.K. (2005) Marketing and promotion of the Olympic Games. *The Sport Journal*, **8**(3). Available at: www.thesportjournal.org/2005Journal/Vol 8-No3/lee-aug1.asp.

Lehmann, J. (2015) Sydney's $1.5 bid for sporting glory: massive overhaul of stadiums set to begin. *The Daily Telegraph*, 4 September.

Lehrer, U. and Laidley, J. (2008) Old mega-projects newly packaged? Waterfront redevelopment in Toronto. *International Journal of Urban and Regional Research*, **32**(4), pp. 786–803.

Lei, L. (2004) Beijing evolves into Olympic 'green'. *China Daily*, 1 March. Available at: www.chinadaily.com.cn.

Lenskyj, H. (1996) When winners are losers, Toronto and Sydney bids for the Summer Olympics. *Journal of Sport*, **20**(4), pp. 392–410.

Lenskyj, H. (1998) Sport and corporate environmentalism: the case of the Sydney 2000 Olympics. *International Review for the Sociology of Sport*, **33**(4), pp. 341–354.

Lenskyj, H. (2000) *Inside the Olympic Industry: Power, Politics and Activism*. Albany, NY: State University of New York Press.

Lenskyj, H. (2002) *The Best Olympics Ever? The Social Impacts of Sydney 2000*. Albany, NY: State University of New York Press.

Lenskyj, H. (2004) Making the world safe for global capital: the Sydney 2000 Olympics and beyond, in Bale, J. and Christensen, M. (eds.) *Post-Olympism? Questioning Sport in the 21st Century*. Oxford: Berg, 231–42.

Lenskyj, H. (2008) *Olympic Industry Resistance: Challenging Olympic Power and Propaganda*. Albany, NY: State University of New York Press.

Lenskyj, H. (2014) *Sexual Diversity and the Sochi 2014 Olympics*. Basingstoke: Palgrave.

Leontidou, L. (1990) *The Mediterranean City in Transition: Social Change and Urban Development*. Cambridge: Cambridge University Press.

Leopkey, B. and Parent, M.M. (2012) Olympic Games legacy: from general benefits to sustainable long-term legacy. *International Journal of the History of Sport*, **29**(6), pp. 924–943.

Lesjø, J.H. (2000) Lillehammer 1994: planning, figurations and the 'green' Winter Games. *International Review for the Sociology of Sport*, **35**(3), pp. 282–293.

Levett, R. (2004) Is green the new gold? A sustainable games for London, in Vigor, A., Mean, M. and

Tims, C. (eds.) *After the Gold Rush: A Sustainable Olympics for London*. London: IPPR/DEMOS, pp. 69–90.

Li, L.M., Dray-Novey, A.J. and Kong, H. (2008) *Beijing: From Imperial City to Olympic City*. Basingstoke: Palgrave Macmillan.

Li, Y. (2006) Green Chaoyang part of Olympic preparations. *Beijing Today*, 24 March.

Li, Y. (2015) Measuring and assessing the impacts of London 2012, in Poynter, G., Viehoff, V. and Li, Y. (eds.) *The London Olympics and Urban Development: The Mega-Event City*. London: Routledge, pp. 35–47.

Liao, H. and Pitts, A. (2006) A brief historical review of Olympic urbanization. *International Journal of the History of Sport*, **23**(7), pp. 1232–1252.

Lin, C. and Sayed, T. (2010) *Host City Olympic Transportation Plan: Survey Data Analysis and Discussion*. South Vermont, Victoria: ARRB Group Limited.

Lin, X. (2004) Economic impact of Beijing Olympic Games 2008, in *Proceedings of the 2004 Pre-Olympic Congress*, 6–11 August, Thessaloniki, Greece, Vol. 1, p. 100.

Littlewood, A.R. (2000) Olympic Games, in Speake, G. (ed.) *Encyclopaedia of Greece and the Hellenic Tradition*, vol. 2. Chicago, IL: Fitzroy Dearborn, pp. 1176–1179.

Liu, M., Mao, B., Huang, Y., Zhang, J. and Chen, S. (2008) Comparison of pre- and post-Olympic traffic: a case study of several roads in Beijing. *Journal of Transportation Systems Engineering and Information Technology*, **8**, pp. 67–72.

LLDC (London Legacy Development Corporation) (2013) Mayor and Chancellor announce commitment to the development of major new education and arts centres. 4 December. Available at: http://queenelizabetholympicpark.co.uk/news/news-articles/2013/12/mayor-and-chancellor-announce-commitment-to-the-development-of-major-new-education-and-arts-centres.

LLDC (2014) *Ten Year Plan Draft V4*, 9 June. London: Greater London Authority.

LLDC (2015a) Chief Executive's Report to the LLDC Board, 27 October. Available at: https://www.london.gov.uk/LLDC/documents/s50946/Item%206%20-%20Chief%20Executives%20report%20-%20October%202015.rtf?CT=2.

LLDC (2015b) Queen Elizabeth Olympic Park and the Surrounding Area: Five Year Strategy: 2015–2020. Available at: https://www.google.co.uk/webhp?sourceid=chrome-instant&ion=1&espv=2&ie=UTF-8#.

Lloyds Banking Group (2012) *The Economic Impact of the London 2012 Olympic and Paralympic Games*. London: Lloyds Banking Group.

Lochhead, H. (2005) A new vision for Sydney Olympic Park. *Urban Design International*, **10**(3/4), pp. 215–222.

LOCOG (London Organizing Committee for the Olympic Games) (2004) *London 2012: Candidate File*. London: LOCOG. Available at: http://www.london2012.com/en/news/publications/Candidatefile/Candidatefile.htm.

LOCOG (2011) *London 2012 Sustainability Report: A Blueprint for Change*. London: LOCOG.

LOCOG (2013a) *London 2012 Festival – 2012 Olympics*. Available at: http://www.london2012.com/join-in/festival.

LOCOG (2013b) *London 2012 Olympic Games Official Report*, 3 vols. London: LOCOG.

London Evening Standard (2012) Former Royal Marines to ferry around super-rich Games spectators. 28 May. Available at: http://www.thisislondon.co.uk/olympics/olympic-news/london-olympics-2012-former-royal-marines-to-ferry-around-superrich-games-spectators-7793520.html.

Lorey, D.E. (1997) The revolutionary festival in Mexico: November 20 celebrations in the 1920s and 1930s. *The Americas*, **54**, pp. 39–82.

Los Angeles Times (2007) Beijing Olympics visitors to come under widespread surveillance. *Los Angeles Times*, 7 August.

Lovett, C. (1997) *Olympic Marathon: A Centennial History of the Games Most Storied Race*. Westport, CN: Praeger.

LPOOC (Lake Placid Olympic Organizing Committee) (1932) *Official Report III Olympic Winter Games, Lake Placid*. New York: III Olympic Winter Games Committee.

LPOOC (1980) *XIII Olympic Winter Games, Lake Placid New York, Final Report*. Lake Placid, NY: Lake Placid Olympic Organizing Committee.

MacAloon, J.J. (1981) *This Great Symbol: Pierre de Coubertin and the Origins of the Modern Olympic Games*. Chicago, IL: University of Chicago Press.

MacAloon, J.J. (1989) Festival, ritual and TV (Los Angeles 1984), in Jackson, R. and McPhail, T. (eds.) *The Olympic Movement and the Mass Media*, part 6. Calgary: Hunford Enterprises, pp. 21–40.

Macko, S. (1996) Security at the Summer Olympic Games is ready. *EmergencyNet NEWS Service*, **2**, p. 191.

MacMasters, M. (2008) Retrieve the artwork from Mexico 68. *La Jornada*, 24 July.

Magalhães, L.E. (2011) Favela Vila Autódromo também tem casas de classe média. *O Globo*, 4 October. Available at: http://oglobo.globo.com/rio/favela-vila-autodromo-tambem-tem-casas-de-classe-media-2744508#ixzz3 csu0U6pW.

Mahtani, K.R., Protheroe, J., Slight, S.P., Marcos, M., Demarzo, P., Blakeman, T., Barton, C.A., Brijnath, B. and Roberts, N. (2013) Can the London 2012 Olympics 'inspire a generation' to do more physical or sporting activities? An overview of systematic reviews. *BMJ Open*, **3**(1). Available at: http://www.ncbi.nlm.nih.gov/pmc/articles/PMC3549211/.

Mallon, B. (1998) *The 1900 Olympic Games: Results for All Competitors in All Events with Commentary. Results from the Early Olympics 2*. Jefferson, NC: McFarland and Company Inc.

Mallon, B. (1999a) *The 1904 Olympic Games: Results for All Competitors in All Events with Commentary. Results from the Early Olympics 3*. Jefferson, NC: McFarland and Company Inc.

Mallon, B. (1999b) *The 1906 Olympic Games: Results for All Competitors in All Events with Commentary. Results from the Early Olympics 4*. Jefferson, NC: McFarland and Company Inc.

Mallon, B. and Buchanan, I. (2000) *The 1908 Olympic Games: Results for All Competitors in All Events with Commentary. Results from the Early Olympics 5*. Jefferson, NC: McFarland and Company Inc.

Mallon, B. and Widland, T. (1998) *The 1896 Olympic Games: Results for All Competitors in All Events with Commentary. Results from the Early Olympics 1*. Jefferson, NC: McFarland and Company Inc.

Maloney, L. (1996) Barcelona 1992: the Games of the 25th Olympiad, in Findling, J.E. and Pelle, K.D. (eds.) *Historical Dictionary of the Modern Olympic Movement*. Westport, CN: Greenwood Press, pp. 185–193.

Mandell, R.D. (1976) *The First Modern Olympics*. London: Souvenir Press.

Manfred, T. (2015) What the snow-less mountain that will host the 2022 Beijing Olympics looks like in the middle of winter. *Business Insider UK*, 31 July. Available at: http://uk.businessinsider.com/beijing-olympic-mountain-venue-has-barely-any-snow-2015-7?r=US&IR=T.

Mangan, J.A. (2008) Prologue: guarantees of global goodwill: post-Olympic legacies – too many limping white elephants, *International Journal of the History of Sport*, **25**(14), pp. 1869–83.

Maraniss, D. (2008) *Rome 1960: The Olympics that Changed the World*. New York: Simon and Schuster.

Marrs, C. (2003) The benefits of believing (London's 2012 Olympic bid and its potential catalyst for regeneration). *Regeneration and Renewal*, 13 June, p. 23.

Marshall, T. (ed.) (2004) *Transforming Barcelona*. London: Routledge.

Marvin, C. (2008) 'All under heaven': megaspace in Beijing, in Price, M.E. and Dayan, D. (eds.) *Owning the Olympics: Narratives of the New China*. Ann Arbor, MI: University of Michigan Press, pp. 229–259.

Masterton, D. W. (1973) The contribution of the fine arts to the Olympic Games. *Proceedings of the International Olympic Academy*, Athens: IOA, pp. 200–213.

Matsumoto, D.R. (1996) *Unmasking Japan: Myths and Realities about the Emotions of the Japanese*. Stanford, CA: Stanford University Press.

Matthis-Lilley, B. (2014) IOC reportedly made some ridiculous demands to help push Oslo out of 2022 Winter Olympics bidding. *National Post* (Canada), 2 October 2014. Available at: http://news.nationalpost.com/sports/olympics/ioc-reportedly-made-some-ridiculous-demands-to-help-push-oslo-out-of-2022-winter-olympics-bidding.

Matzerath, H. (1984) Berlin, 1890–1940, in Sutcliffe, A. (ed.) *Metropolis, 1890–1940*. London: Mansell, pp. 289–318.

May, V. (1995) Environmental implications of the 1992 Winter Olympic Games. *Tourism Management*, **16**, pp. 269–275.

McCann, B. (2005) Complete the street! *Planning*, **71**(5), pp. 18–23.

McCarthy, M., Ravelli, R.J. and Sinclair-Williams, M. (2010) Health impact assessment of the 2012 London Olympic transport plans. *European Journal of Public Health*, **20**, pp. 619–624.

McGehee, R.V. (1993) The origins of Olympianism in Mexico: the Central American games of 1926. *International Journal of the History of Sport*, **10**, pp. 319–323.

McGeoch, R. and Korporaal, G. (1994) *The Bid: How Australia won the 2000 Games*. Melbourne: Heinemann.

McIntosh, M.J. (2003) The Olympic bid process as a starting point of the legacy development, in Moragas, M. de, Kennett, C. and Puig, N. (eds.) *The Legacy of the Olympic Games 1984–2000*. Lausanne: International Olympic Committee, pp. 450–456.

McKenny, L., Kembrey, M. and Saulwick, J. (2015) Anger as $1 billion redevelopment lures Commonwealth Bank away from Western Sydney. *The Sydney Morning Herald*, 12 November.

McNamee, M.J. (2016) Paralympism, Paralympic values and disability sport: a conceptual and ethical critique. *Disability and Rehabilitation*, published on-line, DOI:10.3109/09638288.2015.1095247.

Mendonça, R. and Puff, J. (2015) Riscos, pressão e escombros: A rotina de quem desafia as remoções da Rio-2016. BBC, 9 May. Available at: http://www.bbc.com/portuguese/noticias/2015/03/150305_rio2016_vila_autodromo_rm_jp.

Merkel, U. (2008) The politics of sport diplomacy and reunification in divided Korea. *International Review for the Sociology of Sport*, **43**(3), pp. 289–311.

Merkel, U. and Kim, M. (2011) Third time lucky!? PyeongChang's bid to host the 2018 Winter Olympics – politics, policy and practice. *The International Journal of the History of Sport*, **28**(16), pp. 2365–83.

Metera, D., Pezold, T. and Piwowarski, W. (2005) *Implementation of Natura 2000 in New EU Member States of Central Europe: An Assessment Report*. Warsaw: The World Conservation Union.

METREX (The Network of European Metropolitan Regions and Areas) (2006) *The Legacies from Major Events: Findings and Conclusions*. Symposium on Planning for Major Events, Turin. Glasgow: METREX. Available at: http://www.eurometrex.org/Docs/Expert_Groups/Major_Events/Torino_Report_2003.pdf.

Metropolitan Police Authority (2007) *Metropolitan Police Service Olympic Programme Update*. Available at: http://www.mpa.gov.uk/committees/x-cop/2007/070201/06/.

Meyer-Künzel, M. (2002) *Der planbare Nutzen: Stadtentwicklung durch Weltausstellungen und Olympische Spiele*. Hamburg: Dölling and Galitz.

Miah, A. and García, B. (2008) We are the media: non-accredited media and citizen journalists at the Olympic Games, in Price, M. and Dayan, D (eds.) *Owning the Olympics. Narratives of the New China*. Ann Arbor: University of Michigan Press, pp. 320–345.

Miah, A. and García, B. (2012) *Olympic Games: The Basics*. London: Routledge.

MIC (Melbourne Invitation Committee) (1948) *The Melbourne Invitation Committee extends a most cordial Invitation to the Esteemed International Olympic Committee to celebrate the XVI Olympiad in Melbourne, Australia in 1956*. Melbourne: G.W. Grant and Sons.

Michaelidou, T. (2009) Main stream. *Athens 4U*, Spring, pp. 7–60.

Michela, I. (1963) Les Lyonnais atterrés: le score plus déprimant que la défaite. *Le Progrès de Lyon*, 19 October, pp. 13–14.

Miller, D. (2003) *Athens to Athens: The Official History of the Olympic Games*. Edinburgh: Mainstream.

Miller, S.G. (2003) The organization and functioning of the Olympic Games, in Phillips, D.J. and Pritchard, D. (eds.) *Sport and Festival in the Ancient Greek World*. Swansea: Classical Press of Wales, pp. 1–40.

Millet, L. (1995) The Games of the city, in de Moragas, M. and Botella, M. (eds.) *The Keys to Success*. Barcelona: Centre d'Estudis Olímpics i de l'Esport, pp. 188–202.

Millington, V. (2009) London 2012: what legacy for artist's studios? *Axis webzine*, Autumn. Available at: http://www.axisweb.org/dlForum.aspx?ESSAYID=18066.

Minis, I. and Tsamboulas, D.A. (2008) Contingency planning and war gaming for the transport operations of the Athens 2004 Olympic Games. *Transport Reviews*, **28**, 259–280.

Ministério do Esporte (2007) *Relatório sobre os XV Jogos Pan Americanos e Parapan Americanos 2007 Governo Federal*. Vols. I and II. Brasília: Governo Federal.

Ministério do Esporte (2009) *Brazil – This is the Country*. Brasília: Governo Federal.

Minnaar, A. (2007) The implementation and impact of crime prevention/crime control open street closed-circuit television surveillance in South African central business districts. *Surveillance and Society*, **4**(3), pp. 174–207.

Minnaert, L. (2012) An Olympic legacy for all? The non-infrastructural outcomes of the Olympic Games for socially excluded groups (Atlanta 1996–Beijing 2008). *Tourism Management*, **33**(2), pp. 361–370.

Misener, L., Darcy, S., Legg, D. and Gilbert, K. (2013) Beyond Olympic legacy: understanding Paralympic legacy through a thematic analysis. *Journal of Sport Management*, **27**, pp. 329–334.

Misener, L. and Mason, D.S. (2006) Creating community networks: can sporting events offer meaningful sources of social capital? *Managing Leisure*, **11**, pp. 39–56.

Monclús, F.J. (2000) Barcelona's planning strategies: from 'Paris of the South' to the 'Capital of West Mediterranean'. *GeoJournal*, **51**, pp. 57–63.

Monclús, F.J. (2003) The Barcelona Model: an original formula? From 'reconstruction' to strategic urban projects (1979–2004). *Planning Perspectives*, **18**, pp. 399–421.

Monroe, D. (1996) Cars, delays finally hit downtown. *The Atlanta Journal Constitution*. 29 July.

Montalban, M.V. (1992) *Barcelona*. London: Verso

Montenegro, C. and Bahiense, C. (1997) Aquele abraço. *Jornal do Brasil*, 3 March, p. 14.

Moore, M. (2008) Athens' deserted Games sites a warning to London Olympics. Available at: http://www.telegraph.co.uk/news/worldnews/europe/greece/2062541/Athens-deserted-Games-sites-a-warning-to-London-Olympics.html.

Moore, M. (2015) Boston withdraws bid for 2024 Olympics. *Financial Times*, 27 July. Available at: http://www.ft.com/cms/s/0/88860e4e-349c-11e5-b05b-b01debd57852.html.

Morse, J. (2001) The Sydney 2000 Olympic Games: how the Australian Tourist Commission leveraged the games for tourism. *Journal of Vacation Marketing*, **7**, pp. 101–107.

MSNBC (Microsoft/National Broadcasting Corporation) (2004) No concrete plans for Greek athletics venues. 30 August. Available at: http://www.msnbc.msn.com/.

Müller, M. (2011) State dirigisme in megaprojects: governing the 2014 Winter Olympics in Sochi. *Environment and Planning A*, **43**, pp. 2091–2108.

Müller, M. (2012) Popular perception of urban transformation through megaevents: understanding support for the 2014 Winter Olympics in Sochi. *Environment and Planning C*, **30**, pp. 693–711.

Müller, M. (2013) *Greening Russia? Mobilising Sustainability for the 2014 Olympic Games in Sochi*. Working Paper, April. Available at: www.martin-muller.net.

Müller, M. (2014) Introduction: Winter Olympics Sochi 2014: what is at stake? *East European Politics*, **30**(2), pp. 153–157.

Müller, M. (2015a) After Sochi 2014: costs and impacts of Russia's Olympic Games. *Eurasian Geography and Economics*, **55**(6), pp. 628–655.

Müller, M. (2015b) What makes an event a mega-event? Definitions and sizes. *Leisure Studies*, **34**(6), pp. 627–642.

Müller N. (1994) *One Hundred Years of Olympic Congresses, 1894–1994*. Lausanne: IOC.

Müller, N. (ed.) (2000) *Pierre de Coubertin, 1893–1937: Olympism, Selected Writings*. Lausanne: IOC.

Muller-Stevens, G. and Lechner, C. (2005) *Strategisches Management: Wie strategische Initiativen zum Wandel führenGebundene Ausgabe*, 3rd ed. Stuttgart: Poeschel.

Mulley, C. and Moutou, C.J. (2015) Not too late to learn from the Sydney Olympics experience: opportunities offered by multimodality in current transport policy. *Cities*, **45**, pp. 117–122.

Muñoz, F. (1997) Historic evolution and urban planning typology of the Olympic Village, in Moragas Spà, M. de, Llinés, M. and Kidd, B. (eds.) *Olympic Villages: A Hundred Years of Urban Planning and Shared Experiences*. Lausanne: IOC, pp. 27–51.

Muñoz, F. (2006) Olympic urbanism and Olympic Villages: planning strategies in Olympic host cities, London 1908 to London 2012. *Sociological Review*, **54** (Supplement), pp. 175–187.

Myer, A. (1996) *Millennium Park: Legacy of the Sydney Olympics*. Sydney: Green Games Watch 2000.

Nagata, K. (2014) Japan rises to challenge of becoming 'hydrogen society'. Available at: http://www.japantimes.co.jp/news/2014/10/12/national/japan-rises-challenge-becoming-hydrogen-society/#.VpQkdxV4aUk.

National Bureau of Statistics (1999) *China Statistical Yearbook 1998*. Beijing: China Statistical Publishing House.

National Bureau of Statistics (2006) *China Statistical Yearbook 2005*. Beijing: China Statistical Publishing House.

Needell, J.D. (1987) *A Tropical Belle Époque: Elite Culture and Society in Turn-of-the-Century Rio de Janeiro*. Cambridge: Cambridge University Press.

Negreiros, D. (2014) UPP: os cinco motivos que levaram à falência o maior projeto do governo Cabral. *Revista Fórum*, 12 February. Available at: http://www.revistaforum.com.br/blog/2014/02/upp-os-cinco-motivos-que-levaram-a-falencia-o-maior-projeto-do-governo-cabral/.

Nel-lo, O. (1997) *The Olympic Games as a Tool for Urban Renewal: The Experience of Barcelona'92 Olympic Village*. Barcelona: Centre d'Estudis Olimpics, Universitat Autònoma de Barcelona. Available at: http://olympicstudies.uab.es/pdf/wp090_eng.pdf.

Nessif, B. (2015) Boston gets U.S. bid to host the 2024 Olympics and these people are really happy about it. *E! Online News*, 9 January. Available at: http://www.eonline.com/uk/news/612806/boston-gets-u-s-bid-to-host-the-2024-olympics-and-these-people-are-really-happy-about-it.

Neves, E. (2015) A um ano da Olímpiada, Rio corre para despoluir a Baía de Guanabara. *Veja Rio*, 6 February. Available at: http://vejario.abril.com.br/materia/cidade/a-um-ano-da-olimpiada-rio-corre-para-despoluir-a-baia-de-guanabara.

New York Times (2007) China finds American allies for security. 18 December.

New York Times (2012) Mission Control, built for cities: I.B.M. takes 'smarter cities' concept to Rio de Janeiro. 3 March.

Nichols, G. and Ralston, R. (2015) The legacy costs of delivering the 2012 Olympic and Paralympic Games through regulatory capitalism. *Leisure Studies*, **34**, pp. 389–404.

Njord, J.R. (2002) An Olympic event: handling transportation during the Olympics. *Public Roads*, **65**, pp. 10–16.

Nogueira, I. (2015) Acordo para Olimpíada tira 30 trens de moradores do RJ. *Folha de S. Paulo*, 14 May. Available at: http://www1.folha.uol.com.br/cotidiano/2015/05/1628801-acordo-para-a-olimpiada-tira-30-trens-de-moradores-do-rj.shtml.

Nolan, M.L. and Nolan, S. (1988) The evolution of tourism in twentieth-century Mexico. *Journal of the West*, **27**(4), pp. 14–25.

Noland, M. and Stahler, K. (2015) An Old Boys' Club no more: pluralism in participation and performance at the Olympic Games. *Journal of Sports Economics*. published online, DOI: 1527002515588138.

NOlympia (2013) *Kurzfassung München 2022*, 16 October. Available at: http://www.nolympia.de.

Novais, P. (2010) *Uma Estratégia Chamada 'Planejamento Estratégico': Deslocamentos espaciais e a atribuição de sentidos da teoria do planejamento urbano*. Rio de Janeiro: 7Letras.

NPC (National People's Congress) (2011) *The Twelfth Five-Year Plan for the National Economic and Social Development of Beijing (2011–2015)*. Available at: http://www.bjpc.gov.cn/fzgh_1/guihua/12_5/Picture_12_F_Y_P/201208/P020120809377417514420.pdf.

NSW Government (2001) *Budget Statement 2001–2002, Sydney 2000 Olympic and Paralympic Games*. Sydney: NSW Government.

NYOBL (New York Olympic Bid Ltd) (2008) Olympism and culture, in *Candidature File for the XXX Games*, Vol 3. New York: NYOBL, pp. 180–189.

Nuzman, C. (2002) 'O Rio nunca mais será o mesmo', interview with Pinto, M.B. and Grijó, F. *Jornal do Brasil*, 1 September, p. C5.

O'Bonsawin, C.M. (2010) 'Olympics on stolen native land': contesting Olympic narratives and asserting indigenous rights within the discourse of the 2010 Vancouver Games. *Sport in Society*, **13**(1), pp. 143–156.

Observatório Sebrae RJ (2013) *Mobilidade urbana e mercado de trabalho na região metropolitana do Rio de Janeiro*. Estudo Estratégico n. 06. Rio de Janeiro: Sebrae.

O'Connor, A. (2008) Disabled groups outraged by Beijing snub. Available at: http://www.timesonline.co.uk/tol/sport/olympics/article4009610.ece.

O'Connor, A. (2009) Vancouver struggling to cover cost of Winter Olympics. *The Times*, 12 February.

OCA (Olympic Co-ordination Authority) (1998) *State of Play '98 Update: A Report to the People of New South Wales*. Sydney: Olympic Co-ordination Authority.

ODA (Olympic Delivery Authority) Security Industry Day: call for security tenders. Available at: http://www.london2012.com/documents/oda-industry-days/oda-security-industry-day-presentation.pdf.

ODA (2011) *Jobs Skills Future Brokerage*. London: ODA. Available at: http://learninglegacy.independent.gov.uk/documents/pdfs/equality-inclusion-employment-and-skills/425009-196-jsf-brokerage-aw.pdf.

Odoni, A., Stamatopoulos, M., Kassens, E. and Metsovitis, I. (2009) Preparing an airport for the Olympic Games: Athens. *Journal of Infrastructure Systems*, **15**, pp. 50–59.

O'Donnell, J. (2013) *A invenção de Copacabana, culturas urbanas e estilos de vida no Rio de Janeiro*. Rio de Janeiro: Zahar.

ODPM (Office of the Deputy Prime Minister) (2004) *The English Indices of Deprivation 2004: Summary (revised)*. London: ODPM.

Office for Disability (2009) *New Legacy Promise puts Disabled People at the Heart of London 2012*. Press release. Available at: http://www.officefordisability.gov.uk/docs/wor/new/0912-paralympics.pdf.

Olds, K. (1998) Urban mega-events, evictions and housing rights: the Canadian case. *Current Issues in Tourism*, **1**(1), pp. 2–46.

Oliveira, N. (2015) *O Poder dos Jogos e os Jogos do Poder: o espetáculo esportivo e a produção da cidade*. Rio de Janeiro: Editora UFRJ/ANPur.

Olson, L.L.K. (1974) Power, Public Policy and the Environment: The Defeat of the 1976 Winter Olympics in Colorado. Unpublished PhD thesis, Department of Political Science, University of Colorado.

OPLC (Olympic Park Legacy Company) (2010) *A Walk around Queen Elizabeth Olympic Park*. London: OPLC.

Øresundstid (2003) History and Culture during the Past 1000 Years: The 19th Century. Available at: http://www.oresundstid.dk/dansk/engelsk/oresundstid/1800/index.htm.

Organisasjonskomiteen (1952) *VI Olympiske Vinterleker Oslo 1952*. Oslo: Organisasjonskomiteen.

Organizing Committee (1908) *The Fourth Olympiad: London 1908 Official Report*. London: British Olympic Association.

Organizing Committee (1928) *The Ninth Olympiad, Amsterdam 1928: Official Report*. Amsterdam: R.H. de Bussig.

Organizing Committee (1937) *The Eleventh Olympiad, Berlin 1936*. Berlin: Amtlicher Bericht.

Organizing Committee (1948) *The Official Report of the Organising Committee for the XIV Olympiad: London 1948*. London: British Olympic Association.

Organizing Committee (1952) *The Official Report of the Games of the XV Olympiad*. Helsinki: Organizing Committee.

Organizing Committee (1958) *The Official Report of the Olympic Committee for the Games of the XVI Olympiad Melbourne 1956*. Melbourne: W.M. Houston, Government Printer.

Organizing Committee (1966) *The Official Report of the Olympic Committee for the Games of the XVIII Olympiad*. Tokyo: Olympic Committee.

Organizing Committee (1969) *The Official Report*, 2 vols. Mexico City: Organizing Committee of the Games of the XIX Olympiad, Mexico.

Organizing Committee (1972) *The Official Report of the Olympic Committee for the Games of the XX Olympiad, Munich 1972*, 2 vols. Munich: Pro-Sport Munchen.

Organizing Committee (1976) *Official Report of the Games of the XXI Olympiad*. Ottawa: COJO-76.

Organizing Committee (1980) *Official Report of the Organizing Committee for the Games of the XXII Olympiad*. Moscow: Progress Publishers.

Organizing Committee (1996) *Official Report of the Games of the XXVI Olympiad*. Atlanta, GA: Atlanta Committee for the Olympic Games.

Ortloff, G.C. and Ortloff, S.C. (1976) *Lake Placid: The Olympic Years, 1937–1980*. Lake Placid, NY: Macromedia.

Orttung, R.W. and Zhemukhov, S. (2014) The 2014 Sochi Olympic mega-project and Russia's political economy. *East European Politics*, **30**(2), pp. 175–191.

O'Sullivan, M. (2015) Parramatta light rail line via Sydney Olympic Park gets green light. *The Sydney Morning Herald*, 8 December. Available at: http://www.smh.com.au/nsw/parramatta-light-rail-line-via-sydney-olympic-park-gets-green-light-20151207-glhxhg.html.

Owen, K.A. (2001) *The Local Impacts of the Sydney 2000 Olympic Games: Processes and Politics of Venue Preparation*. Sydney: Centre for Olympic Studies, University of New South Wales.

Owen, K.A. (2002) The Sydney 2000 Olympics and urban entrepreneurialism: local variations in urban governance. *Australian Geographical Studies*, **40**(3), pp. 323–336.

Oxford Economics (2007) *The value of the London 2012 Olympic and Paralympic Games to UK Tourism*. London: VisitBritain/VisitLondon.

Paes, E. (2015) Interview. Um minuto com Eduardo Paes – Prefeito da cidade do Rio de Janeiro. *Rio Negócios*, 1 June. Available at: http://rio-negocios.com/um-minuto-com-eduardo-paes-prefeito-da-cidade-do-rio-de-janeiro/.

Painter, J. (1998) Entrepreneurs are made, not born: learning and urban regimes in the production of entrepreneurial cities, in Hall, T. and Hubbard, P. (eds.) *The Entrepreneurial City: Geographies of Politics, Regime and Representation*. Chichester: John Wiley, pp. 259–273.

Panagiotopoulou, R. (2008) The Cultural Olympiad of the Athens 2004 Olympic Games: a tribute to culture, tradition and heritage, in Müller, N. and Messing, M. (eds.) *Olympism: Heritage and Responsibility*, Kassel: Agon Sportverlag, pp. 315–37.

Papageorgiou-Ventas, A. (1994) *Athens: The Ancient Heritage and Historic Townscape in a Modern Metropolis*, Library Report 140. Athens: The Archaeological Society at Athens.

Papanikolaou, P. (2013) Athens 2004: ten years later the Olympic infrastructure, the Cultural Olympiad and the 'White elephant' syndrome. *Journal of Power, Politics and Governance*, **1**, pp. 1–9.

Parent, M.M., Kristiansen, E., Skille, E.Å. and Hanstad, D.V. (2015) The sustainability of the Youth Olympic Games: stakeholder networks and institutional perspectives. *International Journal of the History of Sport*, **50**(3), pp. 326–348.

Park, S.-J. (1991) *The Seoul Olympics, the Inside Story*. London: Bellew Publishing.

Parry, J. (2012) The Youth Olympic Games: some ethical issues. *Sport, Ethics and Philosophy*, **6**(2), pp. 138–154.

Pavoni, A. (2015) Resistant legacies. *Annals of Leisure Research*, **18**(4), pp. 470–490.

Payne, M. (2006) *Olympic Turnaround: How the Olympic Games stepped back from the Brink of Extinction to become the World's Best Known Brand*. Westport, CT: Praeger.

Payne, M. (2009) How Rio won the 2016 Olympic Games. *SportsPro*, November. Available at: http://www.michaelr payne.com/how_rio_won.html.

PCRJ (Prefeitura da Cidade do Rio de Janeiro) (1993) *Plano Estratégico para a Cidade do Rio de Janeiro – Conceituação e proposta para execução*. Rio de Janeiro: ACRJ/FIRJAN/PCRJ.

PCRJ (1996) *Strategic Plan for the City of Rio de Janeiro, Rio forever Rio*. Rio de Janeiro: PCRJ.

PCRJ (2011) *Lei Complementar n.111. Dispõe sobre a política urbana e ambiental do município, instiui o plano diretor de desenvolvimento urbano sustentável do município do Rio de Janeiro e dá outras providências.* Rio de Janeiro: PCRJ.

PCRJ (2015) *Explaining the Olympic Golf Course*. Rio de Janeiro: PCRJ. Available at: https://docs.google.com/file/d/0BwMjq4G-w-9eMEo1cHF6TFhwREE/edit.

Peek, L. (2004) How I strolled into the heart of the Games. *The Times*, 14 May, p. 4.

Peñalosa, E. (2013) Buses: not sexy but the only solution, in LSE Cities (ed.) *City Transformations, Urban Age Conference Rio de Janeiro 24–25 October 2013*. London: London School of Economics and Political Science, pp. 19–20.

Peng, J. and Yu, Y. (2008) Beijing Olympics Security Plan. Paper presented at Security and Surveillance at Mega Sport Events: From Beijing 2008 to London 2012 Conference, Durham University.

People's Daily (2009) Post-Olympic road of the Bird's Nest. 1 July. Available at: http://english.peopledaily.com.cn/90001/90782/90873/6690945.html.

Perrottet, T. (2004) *The Naked Olympics: The True Story of the Olympic Games*. New York: Random House.

Perry, K-M. E. and Kang, H.H. (2012) When symbols clash: legitimacy, legality and the 2010 Winter Olympics. *Mass Communication and Society*, **15**(4), pp. 578–597.

Persson, C. (2000) The Olympic Host Selection Process. Unpublished PhD thesis, Luleå University of Technology.

Petrakos, G. and Economou, D. (1999) Internationalisation and structural changes in the European urban system, in Economou, D. and Petrakos, G. (eds.) *The Development of Greek Cities*. Athens: Gutenberg and University of Thessaly Publications.

Petrova, Y. (2014) Posle olimpiady chislo turistov v sochi vyrastet na 30%, no gostinitsy ne budut zapolneny (After the Olympics the number of tourists will grow by 30%, but the hotels won't be full). *Vedomosti*, February 24.

Phillips, E. (2015) *The Olympic Century*. Vol. 7. *VII Olympiad: Antwerp 1920, Chamonix 1924*. Leamington Spa: Warwick Press.

Phillips, T. (2009) Twelve dead and helicopter downed as Rio de Janeiro drug gangs go to war. Available at: www.guardian.co.uk/world/2009/oct/17/rio-favela-violence-helicopter.

Pinson, G. (2002) Political government and governance: strategic planning and the reshaping of political capacity in Turin. *International Journal of Urban and Regional Research*, **26**(3), pp. 477–493.

Pitts, A. and Liao, H. (2009) *Sustainable Olympic Design and Urban Development*. London: Routledge.

Plaza, B. (2006) The return on Investment of the Guggenheim Museum Bilbao. *International Journal of Urban and Regional Research*, **30**(32), pp. 452–467.

PMSU (Prime Minister's Strategy Unit) (2005) *Improving the Life Chances of Disabled People. Final Report Joint Report with Department of Work and Pensions; Department of Health; Department for Education and Skills; Office of the Deputy Prime Minister*. London: PMSU.

Poast, P.D. (2007) Winning the bid: analyzing the International Olympic Committee's host city selections. *International Interactions*, **33**, pp. 75–95.

Pollalis S., Kyriakopoulos V., Papagianni A., Papapetrou, N., Sagia V. and Tritaki, N. (2013) The Urban Development of the Former Athens Airport. Paper presented to AESOP–ACSP Joint Congress, Dublin.

Polley, M. (2011) *The British Olympics: Britain's Olympic Heritage 1612–2012*. London: English Heritage.

POPWGBC (PyeongChang Olympic and Paralympic Winter Games Bid Committee) (2011) *PyeongChang 2018 New Horizons*, Vol. 2. PyeongChang, South Korea: POPWGBC.

Porter, L., Jaconelli, M., Cheyne, J., Eby, D. and Wagenaar, H. (2009) Planning displacement: the real legacy of major sporting events; 'Just a person in a wee flat': being displaced by the Commonwealth Games in Glasgow's East End; Olympian masterplanning in London closing ceremonies; how law, policy and the Winter Olympics are displacing an inconveniently located low-income community in Vancouver Commentary; recovering public ethos: critical analysis for policy and planning. *Planning Theory and Practice*, **10**(3), pp. 395–418.

Poulios, P.C. (2006) The 2004 Athens Olympics: a cost-benefit analysis. *Entertainment and Sports Lawyer*, **24**(1), pp. 1, 18–31.

Pound, R.W. (2004) *Inside the Olympics: A Behind-the-Scenes look at the Politics, the Scandals, and the Glory of the Games*. Toronto: John Wiley and Sons Canada.

Powell, H. and Marrero-Guillamon, I. (eds.) (2012) *The Art of Dissent*. London: Marshgate Press.

Poynter, G. and Roberts, F. (2009) Atlanta 1996: the Centennial Games, in Poynter, G. and MacRury, I. (eds.) *Olympic Cities: 2012 and the Remaking of London*. Farnham: Ashgate, pp.121–31.

PPC (Public Properties Company SA) (2015) In a nutshell. Available at: http://www.etasa.gr/versions/eng/page.aspx.

Preston, J. and Dillon, S. (2004) *Opening Mexico: The Making of a Democracy*. New York: Farrar, Straus and Giroux.

Preuss, H. (1999) *Ökonomische Implikationen der Ausrichtung Olympischer Spiele von München 1972 bis Atlanta 1996*, (*Economic Implications of the Orientation to Atlanta Olympic Games of 1972 Munich to Atlanta 1996*). Kassel: Argon Sportverlag.

Preuss, H. (2000) Electing to Olympic host city a multidimensional decision, in Wamsley, K.B., Martyn, S.G., Macdonald, G.H. and Barney, R.K. (eds.) *Bridging three centuries: intellectual crossroads and the modern Olympic Movement*. Fifth International Symposium for Olympic Research. London, Ontario: International Centre for Olympic Studies, University of Western Ontario, pp. 89–104.

Preuss, H. (2001) Financing Source Development of Mega Sports Events, in *Proceedings of the Sixth Annual Congress of the European College of Sport Science*. Cologne: ECSS.

Preuss, H. (2004a) 2012 Olympische Spiele 2012 in Deutschland. Der stärkste Bewerbungswettbewerb in der olympischen Geschichte, in Horch, H.D., Heydel, J. and Sierau, A. (eds.) *Events im*

Sport, Marketing, Management, Finanzierung. Cologne: Institute of Sport Economics and Sport Management, pp. 225–238.

Preuss, H. (2004*b*) *The Economics of Staging the Olympics: A Comparison of the Games, 1972–2008*. Cheltenham: Edward Elgar.

Preuss, H. (2005) The economic impact of visitors at major multi-sport events. *European Sport Management Quarterly*, **5**(3), pp. 283–305.

Preuss, H. (2007) The conceptualisation and measurement of mega sport event legacies. *Journal of Sport and Tourism*, **12**(3/4), pp. 207–228.

Preuss, H. (2009) Opportunity costs and efficiency of investments in mega sports events. *Journal of Policy Research in Tourism, Leisure and Events*, **1**(2), pp. 131–140.

Preuss, H. (2011) *Kosten und Nutzen Olympischer Winterspiele in Deutschland, Eine Analyse von München 2018*. Wiesbaden: Gabler Verlag.

Preuss, H. (2015) A framework for identifying the legacies of a mega sport event. *Leisure Studies*, **34**(6), pp. 643–664.

Preuss, H. and Alfs, C. (2011) Signalling through the 2008 Beijing Olympics: using mega sport events to change the perception and image of the host. *European Sport Management Quarterly*, **11**(1), pp. 55–71.

Preuss, H. and Solberg, H.A. (2006) Attracting major sporting events: the role of local residents. *European Sport Management Quarterly*, **6**(4), pp. 391–411.

Price Waterhouse (1994) *Britain's Millennium Festival Project at Greenwich*. London: Price Waterhouse.

PriceWaterhouseCoopers (2005) *Olympic Games Impact Study: Final Report*. London: Department for Culture Media and Sport.

PriceWaterhouseCoopers (2009) *London Development Agency 2012 Games Legacy Impact Evaluation Study: Feasibility Study Report*. London: PriceWaterhouseCoopers.

Promyslov, V. (1980) *Moscow: Past and Present*. Moscow: Progress Publishers.

Puff, J. (2013) Em 5 anos, UPPs trazem segurança, mas moradores pedem mais serviços. *BBC Brasil*, 19 December. Available at: http://www.bbc.co.uk/portuguese/noticias/2013/12/131219_upps_abre_vale_jp.shtml.

Puff, J. (2014) Qual o futuro das UPPs no novo governo Pezão? *BBC Brasil*, 29 October. Available at: http://www.bbc.co.uk/portuguese/noticias/2014/10/141026_eleicoes2014_governo_rio_upp_jp_rm.shtml.

Puls, S.L., Sonda, R., de la Rosa, M., Urbina, A.O. and Post, N.T. (2013) Analysis of the room supply in the hotel zone of Cancun, Mexico: EMU 9. *Journal of Tourism Research and Hospitality*, **2**, pp. 1–8.

Putin, V. (2007) Speech at the 119th International Olympic Committee Session, Guatemala, 4 July. Available at: http://archive.kremlin.ru/eng/text/speeches/2007/07/04/2103_type82912 type84779 type127286_136956.shtml.

PyeongChang2018, (2016) *Actualising the Dream Project* (ADP). Available at: http://www.pyeongchang2018.com/horizon/eng/Paralympic_Games/ADP.asp.

Pyrgiotis, Y.N. (2001) The Games in the XXIst century, in IOC (eds.) *Olympic Games and Architecture. The Future for Host Cities*. Lausanne: IOC, pp. 25–29.

Pyrgiotis, Y. (2003) Athens 2004: planning and organising Olympic legacy, in Moragas, M. de, Kennett, C. and Puig, N. (eds.) *The Legacy of the Olympic Games, 1984–2000*. Lausanne: IOC, pp. 414–418.

Raco, M. (2014) Delivering flagship projects in an era of regulatory capitalism: state led privatization and the London Olympics 2012. *International Journal of Urban and Regional Research*, **38**(1), pp. 176–197.

Raco, M. and Tunney, E. (2010) Visibilities and invisibilities in urban development: small business communities and the London Olympics 2012. *Urban Studies*, **47**(10), pp. 2069–2091.

RBC (Rio Barcelona Consultores) (1996) *Rio 2004 Anteprojeto de candidatura Jogos Olímpicos 2004 Rio de Janeiro*. 3 Vols. Rio de Janeiro: RBC.

Redmond, G. (1988) Toward modern revival of the Olympic Games: the various pseudo-Olympics of the nineteenth century, in Seagrave, J.O. and Chu, D. (eds.) *The Olympic Games in Transition*. Champaign, IL: Human Kinetics, pp. 7–21.

Reeve, S. (2001) *One Day in September: The Full Story of the 1972 Munich Olympic Massacre and Israeli Revenge Operation 'Wrath of God'*. New York: Arcade.

Reich, K. (1986) *Making It Happen, Peter Ueberroth and the 1984 Olympics*. Santa Barbara, CA: Capra Press.

Renson, R. (1996) Antwerp 1920: the Games of the 7th Olympiad, in Findling, J.E. and Pelle, K.D. (eds.) *Historical Dictionary of the Modern Olympic Movement*. Westport, CN: Greenwood Press, pp. 54–60.

Reyes, R. (2009) Personal communication with M. Barke, 5 October.

Riding, A. (1987) *Mexico: Inside the Volcano*. London: Hodder and Stoughton.

Riley, D. (2005) Written Statement to the US Senate Subcommittee on Trade, Tourism and Economic Development. *Field Hearing on The Economic Impact of the 2010 Vancouver, Canada, Winter Olympics on Oregon and the Pacific Northwest*. Washington DC: US Government Printing Office.

Rio 2004 Bid Committee (1996) *Rio de Janeiro Candidate to Host the XXVIII Olympic Games in 2004*, Vol. II. Rio de Janeiro: Rio 2004 Bid Committee.

Rio 2016 Bid Committee (2009a) *Candidature File for Rio de Janeiro to Host the 2016 Olympic and Paralympic Games*, 3 Vols. Rio de Janeiro: Rio 2016 Bid Committee.

Rio 2016 Bid Committee (2009b) OCOG and Non-OCOG Budget. *Documentos Candidatura Rio 2016*. https://i3gov. Available at: planejamento.gov.br/balanco/2%2020CIDADANIA%20E%20 INCLUSAO%20SOCIAL/7%20%20Esporte/1%20-%20Documentos/Candidatura%20Rio2016/ BGF%20-%20Candidatura%20Rio2016%20%20Dossi%ea %20de%20Candidatura/.

Rio 2016 OCOG (Rio 2016 Organizing Committee for the Olympic Games) (2009) *Transport Strategic Plan for the Rio 2016 Olympic and Paralympic Games*. Rio de Janeiro: Rio 2016 OCOG.

Rio 2016 OCOG (2014) *Embracing Change. Rio 2016 Sustainability Report*. Rio de Janeiro: Rio 2016 OCOG.

Ritchard, K. (2004) The hotel industry is pinning its hope on gold at Beijing in 2008: but is it a sure winner? *Hotel Asia Pacific*, December.

Rivas, C. and Sarhandi, D. (2005) This is 1968… This is Mexico. *Eye*, No. 56. Available at: http:// www.eyemagazine.com/feature/article/this-is-1968-this-is-mexico.

Roaf, V., van Deventer, K. and Houston, C. (1996) *The Olympics and Development: Lessons and Suggestions*. Observatory, South Africa: Development Action Group.

Roberts, P. (2000) The evolution, definition and purpose of urban regeneration, in Roberts, P. and Sykes, H. (eds.) *Urban Regeneration: A Handbook*. London: Sage, pp. 9–36.

Roche, M. (2000) *Mega-Events and Modernity: Olympics and Expos in the Growth of Global Culture*. London: Routledge.

ROCOG (Rio di Janeiro Organising Committee for the Olympic Games) (2009) *Candidature File for Rio de Janeiro to Host the 2016 Olympic and Paralympic Games*, 3 vols. Rio di Janeiro: ROCOG.

Rodríguez Kuri, A. (2003) Hacia México 68: Pedro Ramírez Vázquez y el proyecto olímpico. *Secuencia*, **56**, pp. 37–73.

Rogan, M. and Rogan, M. (2010) *Britain and the Olympic Games: Past, Present, Legacy*. London: Matador.

Rognoni, G. (1996) The ideas and creativity of the Barcelona '92 Paralympic Ceremonies, in Moragas, M. de, MacAloon, J.J. and Llinos, M. (eds.) *Olympic Ceremonies: Historical Continuity and Cultural Exchange*. Lausanne: IOC, pp. 263–268.

Rolnik, R. (2009) *Report of the Special Rapporteur on Adequate Housing as a Component of the Right to an Adequate Standard of Living, and on the Right to Non-Discrimination in this Context*. New York: United Nations Human Rights Council.

Romanos, A., Vellissaraton, J. and Liveris, K. (2005) Re-shaping Urban Environment through Major Events: The Athens Olympic Games. Paper presented to the 41st ISOCARP Congress. Available at: http://www.isocarp.net/Data/case_studies/665.pdf.

Rosso, E. (2004) Torino: Policies and Actions at a Metropolitan Level. Paper presented at the La Gouvernance Metropolitaine Conference, Montreal.

Rowe, P.G. (2006) *Building Barcelona: A Second Renaixenca*. Barcelona: Actar.

Rürup, R. (ed.) (1996) *1936: Die Olympischen Spiele und der Nationalsozialismus: eine Dokumentation*. Berlin: Argon.

Rustin, M. (2009) Sport, spectacle and society: understanding the Olympics, in Poynter, G. and MacRury, I. (eds.) *Olympic Cities: 2012 and the Remaking of London*, Farnham: Ashgate, pp. 3–21.

Ryall, J. (2013) British-designed stadium to be centre piece of Tokyo 2020 Olympic Games. *The Telegraph*, 8 September. Available at: http://www.telegraph.co.uk/news/worldnews/asia/ japan/10294036/British-designed-stadium-to-be-centre-piece-of-Tokyo-2020-Olympic-Games. html.

Ryan, M. (2009) *For the Glory: Two Olympics, Two Wars, Two Heroes*. London: JR Books.

Ryzhkov, V. (2014) Controlling Russians through travel bans. *The Moscow Times*, 26 May.

Salázar, R. (1968) Wonderland of colour welcomes Olympics. *Los Angeles Times*, 13 October, p. 8.

Sales, E. (ed.) (2005) *Time Out: Athens*, 2nd ed. London: Ebury.

Samaranch, J.A. (1992) Message from the IOC President, in IOC (eds.) *Olympic Solidarity Itinerant School: Marketing Manual*. Lausanne: IOC, p. 2.

Samatas, M. (2004) *Surveillance in Greece: From Anticommunist to Consumer Surveillance*. New York: Pella Publishing.

Samatas, M. (2007) Security and surveillance in the Athens 2004 Olympics: some lessons from a troubled story. *International Criminal Justice Review*, **17**(3), pp. 220–238.

Sanahuja, R. (2002) Olympic City – The City Strategy 10 Years after the Olympic Games in 1992. Paper to the International Conference on Sports Events and Economic Impact, Copenhagen, Denmark.

Sanan, G. (1996) Olympic security operations 1972–94, in Thompson, A. (ed.) *Terrorism and the 2000 Olympics*. Sydney: Australian Defence Force Academy, pp. 33–42.

Sandomir, R. (1999) Olympics: inquiry cites Olympic 'culture' of impropriety. *The New York Times*, 2 March.

Saulwick, K. (2015) Bairds Plan: Sydney will fill the new stadiums, if not the old. *Sydney Morning Herald*, 4 September.

SCCOG (2015) The Southern California Committee for the Olympic Games congratulates Los Angeles. Available at: http://www.sccog.org/.

Schaap, J. (2008) *Triumph: The Untold Story of Jesse Owens and Hitler's Olympics*. Bel Air, CA: Mariner Books.

Schäche, W. (1991) *Architektur und Städtebau in Berlin zwischen 1933 und 1945: Planen und Bauen unter der Ägide der Stadtverwaltung*. Berlin: Mann-Verlag.

Schäche, W. (2001) *Das Reichssportfeld: Architektur im Spannungsfeld von Sport und Macht*. Berlin: Bebra.

Scharr, K., Steinicke, E. and Borsdorf, A. (2011) Sochi/Сочи 2014: Olympic Winter Games between high mountains and seaside. *Revue de Géographie Alpine*, **100**, pp. 1–35.

Scherer, J. (2011) Olympic villages and large-scale urban development: crises of capitalism, deficits of democracy? *Sociology*, **45**, pp. 782–797.

Scherer, K.A. (1995) *100 Jahre Olympische Spiele Idee, Analyse und Bilanz*. Dortmund: Schlossberg.

Schiller, K. and Young, C. (2010) *Munich Olympics and the Making of Modern Germany*. Berkeley, CA: University of California Press.

Schmidt, T. (1992) *Werner March: Architekt des Olympiastadions, 1894–1976*. Basel: Birkhauser Verlag.

Schmitt, H.F. (1971) The Olympic Villages. *Olympic Review*, **44**, pp. 258–261.

Schollmeier, P. (2001) *Bewerbungen um Olympische Spiele. Von Athen 1896 bis Athen 2004*. Germany: Books on Demand.

Scruton, J. (1998) *Stoke Mandeville: Road to the Paralympics: Fifty Years of History*. Aylesbury: Peterhouse.

Searle, G. (2002) Uncertain legacy: Sydney's Olympic stadiums. *European Planning Studies*, **10**, pp. 845–860.

Searle, G. (2012) The long-term urban impacts of the Sydney Olympic Games. *Australian Planner*, **49**(3), pp. 195–202.

Segrave, J.O. (2005) Pietro Metastasio's L'Olimpiade and the survival of the Olympic idea in eighteenth century Europe. *Olimpika*, **14**, pp. 1–28.

Séguillon, D. (2002) The origins and consequences of the first World Games for the Deaf: Paris, 1924. *International Journal of the History of Sport*, **19**, pp. 119–136.

Senn, A.E. (1999) *Power, Politics and the Olympic Games*. Champaign, IL: Human Kinetics.

Setzekorn, E. (2008) An Olympic evaluation. *The China Beat*, 3 September. Available at: http://thechinabeat.blogspot.co.uk/2008/09/olympic-evaluation.html.

Sheil, P. (1998) *Olympic Babylon*. Sydney: Pan Macmillan.

Shen, J. (2002) A study of the temporary population in Chinese cities. *Habitat International*, **26**, pp. 363–377.

Shi, M. (2014) Unstable ground: the 1968 Mexico City student protests. *Yale Review of International Studies*, **3**(2), pp. 63–72.

Shipway, R. (2007) Sustainable legacies for the 2012 Olympic Games. *Journal of the Royal Society for the Promotion of Health*, **127**, pp. 119–124.

Short, J.R. (2008) Globalization, cities and the Summer Olympics. *City,* **12**(3), pp. 321–340.

Siebel, W. (1994) *Was macht eine Stadt urban?, Zur Stadtkultur und Stadtentwicklung.* Oldenburg: Universitätsreden 61, University of Olderburg.

Silva, M.L.P. (2004) A permanência das favelas cariocas e o Plano Doxiadis num contexto de mudanças (1960–1965). *Anais do 8 Seminário de História da Cidade e do Urbanismo.* Niterói: ARQ/URB/UFF.

Silvestre, G. (2008) The social impacts of mega-events: towards a framework. *Esporte e Sociedade,* **4**(10), pp. 1–26.

Silvestre, G. (2012) *An Olympic City in the Making: Rio de Janeiro Mega-Event Strategy 1993–2016.* Lausanne: Olympic Studies Centre, International Olympic Committee.

Silvestre, G., and Oliveira, N.G. (2012) The revanchist logic of mega-events: community displacement in Rio de Janeiro's West End. *Visual Studies,* **27**(2), pp. 204–210.

Simson, V. and Jennings, A. (1992) *The Lord of the Rings: Power, Money and Drugs in the Modern Olympics.* Toronto: Stoddart.

SLOC (Salt Lake Organizing Committee) (2002) *Salt Lake 2002: Official Report of the XIX Olympic Winter Games.* Salt Lake City, UT: Salt Lake Organising Committee.

Smith, A. (n.d.) The Impact of Sports Events on City Images. London: University of Westminster, unpublished paper (*c.* 2003).

Smith, A. (2012) *Events and Urban Regeneration. The Strategic Use of Events to Revitalise Cities.* London: Routledge.

Smith, A. (2014) 'De-risking' East London: Olympic regeneration planning 2000–2012. *European Planning Studies,* **22**(9), pp. 1919–39.

Smith, H. (2003) Athens prays to Zorba to rescue its 'shambolic' Olympic Games. *The Observer,* 13 July.

Smith, H. (2004) Athens shows doubters it will hit games deadline. *The Guardian Online.* Available at: http://sport.guardian.co.uk/olympics/story/0,1278221,00.html.

Smyth, H. (1994) *Marketing the City: The Role of Flagship Development in Urban Regeneration.* London: E. and F.N. Spon.

SNF (Stavros Niarchos Foundation) (2009) Recent News: The Stavros Niarchos Foundation Cultural Centre. Available at: http://www.snf.org/snfcc/EN.index.php?ID=the_park_EN.

SNF (2016) Stavros Niarchos Foundation: FAQs. Available at: http://www.snf.org/en/about/faqs/.

Snyder, C.R., Lassegard, M.A. and Ford, C.E. (1986) Distancing after group success and failure: basking in reflected glory and cutting off reflected failure. *Journal of Personality and Social Psychology,* **51**(2), pp. 382–388.

SOC (Stockholm Organizing Committee) (1913) *The Fifth Olympiad; The Official Report of the Olympic Games of Stockholm, 1912: Issued by the Swedish Olympic Committee,* ed. E. Bergvall and trans. E. Adams-Ray. Stockholm: Wahlstrom and Widstrand.

SOCOG (Sydney Organising Committee for the Olympic Games) (2000) *Official Report of the XXVII Olympiad.* Available at: http://www.gamesinfo.com.au/postgames.

SOCOG (2001) *Official Report of the XXVII Olympiad,* 3 vols. Sydney: SOCOG.

Solinger, D.J. (1995) The floating population in the cities: chances for assimilation? in Davis, D.S. Kraus, R., Naughton, B. and Perry, E.J. (eds.) *Urban Spaces in Contemporary China: The Potential for Autonomy and Community in Post-Mao China.* Cambridge: Cambridge University Press, pp. 113–139.

Sonne, W. (2003) *Representing the State: Capital City Planning in the Early Twentieth Century.* Munich: Prestel.

SOOC (Sochi Olympic Organising Committee) (2009) Games 2014 will double Sochi power supply. Available at: http://sochi2014.com/87868.

SOOC (2014) *Sochi 2014: Legacy Report.* Moscow: Organizing Committee of XXII Olympic Winter Games and XI Paralympic Winter Games of 2014.

SOPA (Sydney Olympic Park Authority) (2009) *Master Plan 2030: A New Master Plan for Sydney's Newest Suburb.* Sydney: Sydney Olympic Park Authority.

SOPA (2014) *Master Plan 2030,* revised version. Available at: http://www.sopa.nsw.gov.au/planning_and_development/master_plan_2030.

SOPA (2015) *Olympic Legacy: A Success Story.* Sydney: Sydney Olympic Park Authority.

Souza, R. (2002) Lula lamenta exclusão do Rio. *Jornal do Brasil,* 19 May, p. C5.

Souza, B. (2014) Quando o Rio de Janeiro terá trens decentes? *Exame*, 10 March. Available at: http://exame.abril. com.br/brasil/noticias/quando-o-rio-de-janeiro-tera-trens-decentes.

Special Correspondent (1948) Games for paralysed archery tournament at Ministry Hospital. *The Times*, 30 July, p. 7.

Special Correspondent (2004) Olympia shot put aims to revive stadium of ancient Games. *Financial Times*, 18 August.

Speer, A. (1969) *Erinnerungen*. Berlin: Propylaen Verlag.

Spencer, R. (2008) Beijing Olympic 2008 opening ceremony giant firework footprints 'faked'. Available at: http://www.telegraph.co.uk/sport/othersports/olympics/2534499/Beijing-Olympic-2008-opening-ceremony-giant-firework-footprints-faked.html.

Spilling, O. (1998) Beyond intermezzo? On the long-term industrial impacts of mega-events: the case of Lillehammer 1994. *Festival Management and Event Tourism*, **5**, pp. 101–122.

Sport England (2016) *The National Picture: Ethnicity and Disability*. Available at: http://www.sportengland.org/research/who-plays-sport/national-picture/.

Stanhope, J.S. (1824) *Olympia: Or Topography Illustrative of the Actual State of the Plain of Olympia, and of the Ruins of the City of Elis*. London.

Stanton, R. (2000) *The Forgotten Olympic Art Competitions: The Story of the Olympic Art Competitions of the Twentieth Century*. Victoria, BC: Trafford.

Sterken, E. (2007) Growth impact of major sporting events, in Preuss, H. (ed.) *The Impact and Evaluation of Major Sporting Events*. London: Routledge, pp. 63–78.

Stone, C.M. (1989) *Regime Politics: Governing Atlanta 1946–1988*. Lawrence, KS: University of Kansas Press.

Strickland, P. (2015) Anger in Greek refugee camp after Idomeni eviction. *Aljazeera*, 12 December. Available at: http://www.aljazeera.com/news/2015/12/anger-greek-refugee-camp-idomeni-eviction-151211143308010.html.

Stump, A.J. (1988) The Games that almost weren't, in Segrave, J.O. and Chu, D. (eds.) *The Olympic Games in Transition*. Champaign, IL: Human Kinetics, pp. 191–199.

Sudjic, D. (2005) *The Edifice Complex*. London: Allen Lane.

Sudjic, D. (2006) Where are the Olympic building plans heading? *The Observer*, 28 May.

Supervia (2015) *Quem Somos*. Available at: http://www.supervia.com.br/quemsomos.php.

Swart, K. and Bob, U. (2004) The seductive discourse of development: the Cape Town 2004 Olympic bid. *Third World Quarterly*, **25**, pp.1311–1324.

Swyngedouw, E., Moulaert, F. and Rodriguez, A. (2002) Neoliberal urbanization in Europe: large-scale urban development projects and the new urban policy. *Antipode*, **34**(3), pp. 542–577.

Sykianaki, C. (2003) Case Study: Athens and Olympic Games 2004. Paper given to symposium on The Legacies from Major Events, Turin. Available at: http://www.eurometrex.org/Docs/Expert_Groups/Major_Events/Torino_Report_2003.pdf.

Sykianaki, C. and Psihogias, S. (2006) Athens Case Study. Paper given to symposium on Planning for Major Events, Turin. Glasgow: METREX. Available at: http://www.eurometrex.org.

Szymanski, S. (2002) The economic impact of the World Cup. *World Economics*, **3**(1), pp. 1–9.

Tabak, F. (2012) Em campanha, Paes tenta vincular sua imagem às transformações feitas por Pereira Passos. *O Globo*, 9 July. Available at: http://oglobo.globo.com/rio/em-campanha-paes-tenta-vincular-sua-imagem-as-transformacoes-feitas-por-pereira-passos-5433676.

Tagaris, K. (2014) Big dreams and angry protests swirl at abandoned Athens airport. Reuters, 26 June. Available at: http://uk.reuters.com/article/2014/06/26/us-greece-airport-idUKKBN0F10YI20 140626.

Tanaka, G. (2014) Vila Autódromo: símbolo de resistência na Cidade Olímpica. *Heinrich-Böll-Stiftung Brasil*, 15 May. Available at: http://br.boell.org/pt-br/2014/05/15/vila-autodromo-simbolo-de-resistencia-na-cidade-olimpica.

Tanaka, Y. (1997) ITS Traffic Management for Nagano Olympic Winter Games in Japan. *Mobility for Everyone*. 4th World Congress on Intelligent Transport Systems, Berlin, pp. 1–5.

Taylor, A. (2015) Greece's abandoned Olympic stadiums get a second life: housing refugees. *Washington Post*, 1 October. Available at: https://www.washingtonpost.com/news/worldviews/wp/2015/10/01/greeces-abandoned-olympic-stadiums-get-a-second-life-housing-refugees/.

Taylor, P. and Gratton, C. (1988) The Olympic Games: an economic analysis. *Leisure Management*, **8**(3), pp. 32–34

Te, B. (2009) Beijing Olympics: a new brand of China. *Asian Social Science*, **5**(3), 84–90.

Telegraph Sport (2012) Doha and Baku out of the running to host 2020 Summer Olympic Games. *Daily Telegraph*, 24 May. Available at: http://www.telegraph.co.uk/sport/olympics/9286809/Doha-and-Baku-out-of-the-running-to-host-2020-Summer-Olympic-Games.html.

Telesca, G. (2014) Dealing with the past and planning the future: the urban renewal of Rome and Barcelona through the Olympic Games. *European Review of History*, **21**(1), pp. 19–36.

Tenorio-Trillo, M. (1996) *Mexico at the World's Fairs: Crafting a Modern Nation*. Berkeley, CA: University of California Press.

Terret, T. (2004) Lyon, the city which never hosted the Olympic Games, in Okubo, I. (ed.) *Sport and Local Identity: Historical Study of Integration and Differentiation*. Sankt Agustin: Academia Verlag, pp. 238–244.

Terret, T. (2008) The Albertville Winter Olympics: unexpected legacies – failed expectations for regional economic development. *International Journal of the History of Sport*, **25**(14), pp. 1903–1921.

Thalis, P. and Cantrill, P.J. (1994) Reinventing the Australian suburb: the Olympic Village competition. *Polis*, **1**, pp. 44–45.

The Guardian (2012a) Metropolitan police plastic bullets stockpile up to 10,000 after UK riots. *The Guardian*, 3 May. Available at: http://www.guardian.co.uk/uk/2012/may/03/metropolitan-police-plastic-bullets-stockpile-riots.

The Guardian (2012b) Olympics welcome does not extend to all in London as police flex muscles. *The Guardian*, 4 May. Available at: http://www.guardian.co.uk/uk/2012/may/04/olympics-welcome-london-police.

The Nation (2012) Protest is coming to the 2012 Olympics. *The Nation*, 21 May. Available at: http://www.thenation.com/blog/167979/protest-coming-london-olympics.

The Telegraph (2008) Corrupt Beijing vice-mayor 'gets death sentence'. *The Telegraph*, 19 October. Available at: http://www.telegraph.co.uk/news/worldnews/asia/china/3227533/Corrupt-Beijing-vice-mayor-gets-death-sentence.html.

Thompson, A. (1999) Security, in Cashman, R. and Hughes, A. (eds.) *Staging the Olympics: The Event and Its Impact*. Sydney: University of New South Wales Press, pp. 106–120.

Thompson, C., Lewis, D., Greenhalgh, T., Taylor, S. and Cummins, S. (2013) A health and social legacy for East London: narratives of 'problem' and 'solution' around London 2012. *Sociological Research Online*, **18**(2).

Thornley, A. (2012) The London 2012 Olympics: what legacy? *Journal of Policy Research in Tourism, Leisure and Events*, **4**(2), pp. 206–210.

Tian, Q.W. and Brimblecombe, P. (2008) Managing air in Olympic cities. *American Journal of Environmental Sciences*, **4**, pp. 439–444.

TOC (Tenth Olympic Committee of the Games of Los Angeles) (1933) *Tenth Olympiad: Los Angeles 1932 Official Report*. Los Angeles, CA: TOC.

TOCOPG (Tokyo Organizing Committee for the Olympic and Paralympic Games) (2012) *Discover Tomorrow Tokyo 2020*, 3 vols. Tokyo: TOCOPG.

Tomlinson, A. (1999) *The Game's Up: Essays in the Cultural Analysis of Sport, Leisure and Popular Culture*. Aldershot: Ashgate.

Tomlinson, A. (2014) Olympic legacies: recurrent rhetoric and harsh realities. *Contemporary Social Science*, **9** pp. 137–158.

Toohey, K. (2008) The Sydney Olympics: striving for legacies – overcoming short-term disappointments and long-term deficiencies. *International Journal of the History of Sport*, **25**(14), pp. 1953–1971.

Toohey, K. and Veal, A.J. (2000, 2007) *The Olympic Games: A Social Science Perspective*. Wallingford: CAB International.

TOROC (Organizing Committee of the XX Turin 2006 Olympic Winter Games) (2005) *Italyart Cultural Olympiad Turin*. Turin: TOROC.

Travel Utah (2002) *Beyond the Games: Assessing the Impact of the 2002 Olympic Winter Games and the Future of Utah Tourism*. Salt Lake City: Utah Division of Travel Development.

Travlos, J. (1981) Athens after the Liberation: planning the new city and exploring the old. *Hesperia*, **50**, pp. 391–407.

Troost, G. (ed.) (1938) *Das Bauen im Neuen Reich*. Bayreuth: Gauverlag Bayerische Ostmark.

Trubina, E. (2015) Mega-events in the context of capitalist modernity: the case of 2014 Sochi Winter Olympics. *Eurasian Geography and Economics*, DOI:10.1080/15387216.2015.1037780.

Tuppen, J. (2000) The restructuring of winter sports resorts in the French Alps: problems, processes and policies. *International Journal of Tourism Research*, **2**, pp. 327–344.

Turismo Torino (2004) *Olympic Games and Tourism: Turin's Tourist Strategy for the 2006 Winter Olympics*. Turin: Turismo Torino.

Turismo Torino (2006) *Torino 2006: One Year On*. Turin: Turismo Torino.

Tzonis, A. (2005) *Santiago Calatrava: The Athens Olympics*. New York: Rizzoli.

Ueberroth, P. with Levin, R. and Quinn, A. (1985) *Made in America: His Own Story*. New York: Morrow.

UEL (University of East London) (2015) *Olympic Games Impact Study – London 2012 Post-Games Report: December 2015*. London: University of East London.

UEL/TGIS (University of East London and the Thames Gateway Institute for Sustainability) (2010) *Olympic Games Impact Study – London 2012 Pre-Games Report: Final October 2010*. London: University of East London and the Thames Gateway Institute for Sustainability.

Umminger, W. (1976) *Die Olympischen Spiele der Neuzeit. Eine illustrierte Kulturgeschichte der Olympischen Spiele von Athen bis München*. Dortmund: Offizielles Standartwerk des Nationalen Olympischen Kommitees für Deutschland.

UNEP (United Nations Environment Programme) (2009) *Beijing Olympics Gets Big Green Tick*. Nairobi: UNEP. Available at: http://www.unep.org/Documents.Multilingual/Default.asp?DocumentID=562&ArticleID=6086&l=en.

USA Today (2006) Host city hopes Games recast its image: Torino officials think new look will boost business, tourism. *USA Today*, 17 February.

Vanolo, A. (2015) The image of the creative city, eight years later: Turin, urban branding and the economic crisis taboo. *Cities*, **46**, pp. 1–7.

Van Rheenen, D. (2014) A skunk at the garden party: the Sochi Olympics, state-sponsored homophobia and prospects for human rights through mega sporting events. *Journal of Sport and Tourism*, **19**(2), pp. 127–144.

Van Wynsberghe, R., Surborg, B. and Wyly, E. (2013) When the Games come to town: neoliberalism, mega-events and social inclusion in the Vancouver 2010 Winter Olympic Games. *International Journal of Urban and Regional Research*, **37**(6), pp. 2074–2093.

Varley, A. (1992) Barcelona's Olympic facelift. *Geographical Magazine*, **64**(7), pp. 20–24.

Varsano, F. and Bittencourt, M. (1997) Nuzman reclama do isolamento do COB. *Jornal do Brasil*, 9 March, p. 28.

Veal, A. J. and Toohey, K. (2012) *The Olympic Games: A Bibliography*. Sydney: School of Leisure, Sport and Tourism, University of Technology. Available at: www.business.uts.edu.au/lst/research.index.

Ventura, M. and Araújo, F. (1997) Muito além de uma correção de rota. *Jornal do Brasil*, 9 March, p. 26.

Victor, M. and Ribeiro, G. (2015) No BRT Transoeste, O DIA flagra superlotação e passageiro desmaiando. *O Dia*, 9 April. Available at: http://odia.ig.com.br/noticia/rio-de-janeiro/2015-04-09/no-brt-transoeste-o-dia-flagra-superlotacao-e-passageiro-desmaiando.html.

Vigna, A. (2013) UPP: o poder simplesmente mudou de mãos? *Le Monde Diplomatique Brasil*, 7 January. Available at: http://www.diplomatique.org.br/artigo.php?id=1328.

Vigor, A., Mean, M. and Tims, C. (eds.) (2004) *After the Gold Rush: A Sustainable Olympics for London*. London: IPPR/DEMOS.

VisitBritain (2010) *Britain Marketing and 2012 Games Global Strategy*. London: Visit Britain.

Voeltz, R.A. (1996) London 1948: the Games of the 14th Olympiad, in Findling, J.E. and Pelle, K.D. (eds.) *Historical Dictionary of the Modern Olympic Movement*. Westport, CN: Greenwood Press, pp. 103–108.

Vozikis, K. (2009) Are there accessible environments in Athens, Greece today? *WSEAS Transactions on Environment and Development*, **5**(7), pp. 488–497.

Vugts, J.F.T. (1992) *Olympiade: Geschidenis van de Olympische Spelen vanaf het begin tot 1992*. Utrecht: SNS Bank.

V&A (Victoria and Albert Museum) (2015) The 2015 Henry Cole Lecture: Delivered by Boris Johnson, 29 January. Available at: http://www.vam.ac.uk/content/articles/t/sackler-lectures/.

Wade, M. (2014) Sydney Olympic Park: how the west was won. *The Sydney Morning Herald*, 31 May.

Wade, M (2015) Sydney is Australia's most valuable location, but public transport is its weakness. *The Sydney Morning Herald*, 4 April.

Wall Street Journal (2004) Securing the Olympic Games. *Wall Street Journal*, 22 August.

Wang, T., Nie, W., Gao, J., Xue, L.K., Gao, X.M., Wang, X.F., Qiu, J., Poon, C.N., Meinardi, S., Blake, D., Wang, S.L., Ding, A.J., Chai, F.H., Zhang, Q.Z. and Wang, W.X. (2010) Air quality during the 2008 Beijing Olympics: secondary pollutants and regional impact. *Atmospheric Chemistry and Physics*, **10**, 7603–7615.

Ward, P.M. (1990) *Mexico City: The Production and Reproduction of an Urban Environment*. London: Belhaven Press.

Ward, P.M. (1998) Future livelihoods in Mexico City: a glimpse into the new millennium. *Cities*, **15**, pp. 63–74.

Ward, S.V. (1998) *Selling Places*. London: E. and F.N. Spon.

Warren, R. (2002) Situating the city and September 11th: military urban doctrine, 'pop-up' armies and spatial chess. *International Journal of Urban and Regional Research*, **26**(3), pp. 614–619.

Waterfield, R. (2004) *Athens: A History from Ancient Ideal to Modern City*. London: Macmillan.

Watts, A. (2008) Beijing: A protest free zone? *Sky News*, 20 August. Available at: http://news.sky.com/story/627418/beijing-a-protest-free-zone.

Watts, J. (2005) Satellite data reveals Beijing as air pollution capital of world. *The Guardian*, 31 October.

Watts, J. (2006a) Beijing to ban drivers for blue sky Olympics. *The Guardian*, 7 April.

Watts, J. (2006b) Beijing Olympic official sacked over corruption. *The Guardian*, 13 June.

Watts, J. (2009) Beijing keeps Olympic restrictions on cars after air quality improves. *The Guardian*, 6 April.

Watts, J. (2015) Forced evictions in Rio favela for 2016 Olympics trigger violent clashes. *The Guardian*, 3 June. Available at: http://www.theguardian.com/world/2015/jun/03/forced-evictions-vila-auto dromo-rio-olympics-protests.

Weaver, C. (2014) Russia's Sochi loses tourism lustre to Crimea. *Financial Times*, 9 September.

Weed, M. (2008) *Olympic Tourism*. Oxford: Elsevier.

Weed, M. (2012) What's Worth Leveraging? A Meta-Analysis of the Volume and Value of Olympic Tourism Flows. Paper to the ESRC Seminar, Going for Gold: Leveraging the Olympic Tourism Legacy beyond 2012. Bournemouth.

Weed, M. and Bull, C. (2009) *Sports Tourism: Participants, Policy and Providers*, 2nd ed. Oxford: Elsevier.

Weed, M., Stephens, J. and Bull, C. (2011) An exogenous shock to the system? The London 2012 Olympic and Paralympic Games and British tourism policy. *Journal of Sport and Tourism*, **16**(4), pp. 345–377.

Wei, Y.H.D. and Yu, D.L. (2006) State policy and the globalisation of Beijing: emerging themes. *Habitat International*, **30**, pp. 377–395.

Weirick, J. (1999) Urban design, in Cashman, R. and Hughes, A. (eds.) *Staging the Olympics: The Event and Its Impact*. Sydney: University of New South Wales Press, pp. 70–82.

Welch, P.D. (1996) Paris 1924: the Games of the 8th Olympiad, in Findling, J.E. and Pelle, K.D. (eds.) *Historical Dictionary of the Modern Olympic Movement*. Westport, CN: Greenwood Press, pp. 61–67.

Wendl, K. (1998) The route of friendship: a cultural/artistic event of the Games of the XIX Olympiad in Mexico City, 1968. *Olympika*, **7**, pp. 113–134.

Wenn, S.R. (1993) Lights! Camera! Little action: television, Avery Brundage, and the Melbourne Olympics. *Sporting Traditions*, **1**, pp. 38–53.

Wenn, S.R. (1995) Growing pains: the Olympic movement and television, 1966–1972. *Olympika*, **4**, pp. 1–22.

Werneck, F. (2012) Em 20 anos, despoluição da Baía de Guanabara vira esgoto. *O Estado de S.Paulo*, 21 March. Available at: http://www.estadao.com.br/noticias/geral,em-20-anos-despoluicao-da-baia-de-guanabara-vira-csgoto-imp-,851258.

Werneck, A. and Matchik, R. (2015) Força Nacional atuará com 13 mil homens na segurança de instalações olímpicas. *O Globo*, 6 May. Available at: http://oglobo.globo.com/rio/forca-nacional-atuara-com-13-mil-homens-na-seguranca-de-instalacoes-olimpicas-16074696#ixzz3c8Kbu16e.

Whitelegg, D. (2000) Going for gold: Atlanta's bid for fame. *International Journal of Urban and Regional Research*, **24**, pp. 801–817.

Williams, P. (1997) Out-foxing the people? Recent state involvement in the planning system. *Urban Policy Research*, **15**(2), pp. 129–136.

Wilson, H. (1996) What is an Olympic City? Visions of Sydney 2000. *Media, Culture and Society*, **18**, pp. 603–618.

Wilson, S. (2014) Bach: 'I am still assured' of security in Sochi. *Associated Press*, 3 February. Available at: http://bigstory.ap.org/article/bach-i-am-still-assured-security-sochi.

Wimmer, M. (1976) *Olympic Buildings*. Leipzig: Edition Leipzig.

Wingfield-Hayes, R. (2015) Japan scraps 2020 Olympic stadium design. *BBC News*, 17 July. Available at: www.bbc.co.uk/news/world-asia-33563243.

Winkler, A. (2007) *Torino: City Report*. London: London School of Economics, Centre for Analysis of Social Exclusion.

Witherspoon, K.B. (2003) Protest at the Pyramid: The 1968 Mexico City Olympics and the Politicization of the Olympic Games. Unpublished PhD thesis, Florida State University.

WOS (Wenlock Olympian Society) (2006) Wenlock Olympian Society. Available at: http://www.wenlock-olympian-society.org.uk/.

Wrynn, A. (2004) The human factor: science, medicine and the International Olympic Committee, 1900–70. *Sport in Society*, **7**, pp. 211–231.

Wu, F. (ed.) (2006) *Globalisation and China's Cities*. London: Routledge.

Wu, F. (ed.) (2007) *China's Emerging Cities*. London: Routledge.

WWF (World Wildlife Fund) (2004) *Environmental Assessment of the Athens 2004 Olympic Games*. Athens: WWF Greece.

Wynn, M. (ed.) (1984) *Planning and Urban Growth in Southern Europe*. London: Mansell.

Xin, Y. (2001) Olympic economy: a huge temptation. Available at: www.bjreview.com.cn/bjreview/EN/2001/200134/Nationalissues-200134(A).htm.

Xinhua News Agency (2009) Beijing Olympics met environmental pledges. 19 February. Available at: http://china.org.cn/environment/report_review/2009-02/19/content_17300306.htm.

Yamawaki, Y. and Duarte, F. (2014) Olympic and urban legacy in Sydney: urban transformations and real estate a decade after the Games. *Journal of Urban Design*, **19**(4), pp. 511–540.

Yannopoulos, D. (2003) Entrepreneurs set eyes on post-Olympic windfall. *Athens News*, 26 August.

Yew, W. (1996) *The Olympic Image: The First 100 years*. Edmonton, Alberta: Quon Editions.

Yoon, H. (2009) The legacy of the 1988 Seoul Olympic Games, in Poynter, G. and MacRury, I. (eds.) *Olympic Cities: 2012 and the Remaking of London*. Farnham: Ashgate, pp.121–31.

Young, D.C. (1987) The origins of the modern Olympics: a new version. *International Journal of the History of Sport*, **4**, pp. 271–300.

Young, D.C. (1996) *The Modern Olympics: A Struggle for Revival*. Baltimore, MD: Johns Hopkins University Press.

Young, D.C. (1998) Further thoughts on some issues of early Olympic history. *Journal of Olympic History*, **6**(3), pp. 29–41.

Young, D.C. (2004) *A Brief History of the Olympic Games*. Oxford: Blackwell.

Zhang, F. (2014) *China's Urbanization and the World Economy*. Cheltenham: Edward Elgar.

Zhang, J. and Wu, F. (2008) Mega-event marketing and urban growth coalitions: a case study of Nanjing Olympic New Town. *Town Planning Review*, **79**(2/3), pp. 209–226.

Zhang, L. and Zhao, S.X. (2009) City branding and the Olympic effect: a case study of Beijing. *Cities*, **26**, pp. 245–254.

Zhou, S. (1992) *China: Provincial Geography*. Beijing: Foreign Languages Press.

Ziakos, V. and Boukas, N. (2012) A neglected legacy: examining the challenges and potential for sport and tourism development in post-Olympic Athens. *International Journal of Event and Festival Management*, **3**, pp. 292–316.

Zimmerman, P. (1963) Financial nightmare ruins Detroit's Olympic Dream. *Los Angeles Times*, 10 March, D, p. 2.

Zolov, E. (1999) *Refried Elvis: The Rise of the Mexican Counterculture*. Berkeley, CA: University of California Press.

Zolov, E. (2004) Showcasing the 'land of tomorrow': Mexico and the 1968 Olympics. *The Americas*, **61**, pp. 159–188.

Index